THESPIS

Vernon Blackwood

D0744924

THESPIS

RITUAL, MYTH, AND DRAMA IN THE ANCIENT NEAR EAST

THEODOR H. GASTER

Foreword by Gilbert Murray

HARPER TORCHBOOKS ♦ The Academy Library

Harper & Row, Publishers, New York

TO

LOTTA

הנני זכרתי לך . . .

Jeremiah 2:2

THESPIS

Copyright © 1950, 1961 by Theodor H. Gaster.

Printed in the United States of America.

This book was originally published in 1950 by Henry Schuman, Inc.; a new, revised edition was issued by Doubleday & Company, Inc. in 1961. It is here reprinted by arrangement.

First HARPER TORCHBOOK edition published 1966 by
Harper & Row, Publishers, Incorporated
49 East 33rd Street
New York, N.Y. 10016.

Library of Congress Catalog Card Number: 61-7650.

This book is sold subject to the condition that it shall not, by way of trade, be lent, re-sold, hired out, or otherwise disposed of without the publisher's consent, in any form of binding or cover other than that in which it is published.

THE COVER DESIGN
Reproduced from an archaic Greek *patera* in the British Museum. It depicts the rude, rustic celebration out of which drama evolved. Some of the participants are being conveyed to the festivities in a primitive mulecart which recalls that traditionally associated with Thespis.

CONTENTS

FOREWORD

It is hardly an exaggeration to say that when we look back to the beginnings of European literature we find everywhere drama, and always drama derived from a religious ritual designed to ensure the rebirth of the dead world. Under ancient conditions, it was anxious work for every human group, when the harvest was over, to face the winter, when all life seemed gone, followed by the spring when, as Alcman puts it, "it blooms but there is not enough to eat." Men could live only in the hope that a living and fruitful world would eventually be reborn. If there was no rebirth, there was famine. We scarcely realize today how close primitive communities stood to that recurring danger.

Greek tradition explicitly testifies to a close connection of drama with Dionysus, and the meaning of this becomes clear as soon as we recognize in Dionysus the spirit of the Renouveau. In an Excursus to the late Jane Harrison's *Themis* (Cambridge, 1912), I pointed out the recurrence in several Greek tragedies of a regular Dionysiac ritual, closely similar, as Herodotus says (ii, 42), to that of the Egyptian Osiris. It comprises a CONFLICT between the god and his enemy; a DEATH OR DISASTER, which often takes the form of a *Sparagmos* or Tearing-in-Pieces; a NARRATIVE by a MESSENGER; a LAMENTATION, and finally an ANAGNORISIS OR DISCOVERY, and a THEOPHANY bringing comfort. This closely resembles the ritual of Osiris as a wheat god; his fight with his enemy Set; the *sparagmos* of the wheat sheaf; the lamentation; the discovery of the new shoots of wheat growing, and the birth of a new god. Moreover, similar rites obtained elsewhere in connection with Linos (the flax), Attis (the pine), Dionysus (the vine or fruit tree), Tammuz and other vegetation gods.

But this was by no means the only form of the rebirth ritual. Most often, perhaps, it was not the same god who was reborn, but a Son of the god, who took his throne and his place. There is, for example, the sequence, in Hesiod, of Ouranos, Kronos, and Zeus, to be followed in turn by the unknown Son of Zeus, greater than his father. There is likewise Dionysus, the "New Zeus," whom, according to the Orphic formula, "his father seats upon the royal throne, arms with the sceptre, and makes king of the cosmic gods" (Lobeck, C. A., *Aglaophamus* [Königsberg, 1829], 552). Indeed, the very name Dionysus is believed to mean "Zeus-young" or "Zeus-son" (cf. Cook, A. B., *Zeus* ii [Cambridge, 1925], 271 ff.).

Yet another form of the pattern may be recognized in the plot of several ancient Greek tragedies: a god loves a mortal woman; their offspring, a son or a pair of twins, is discovered and cast out to die, while the mother is imprisoned and otherwise punished — a true *mater dolorosa* — until eventually the son is rediscovered, found to be of divine birth, and established as king. The symbolism is clear: the sun- or sky-god descends to fructify the frozen earth in rain and lightning; there is a long period of waiting; then the Young God is discovered in the first bloom of spring. This form was reproduced in almost sardonic fashion in the *Ion* of Euripides, but it lived on, reduced from divine to human terms, in the New Comedy. Moreover, there can be little doubt that its central idea, that of the Son of God redeeming a dead or dying world and introducing a new kingdom free from the stains of the past, has survived even to the present day and has exercised a lasting influence on the formulae of Christian worship in modern Greece. One recalls the anxious old woman whom J. C. Lawson met during Holy Week in Euboea. "Of course I am anxious," said she, "for if Christ does not rise tomorrow, we shall have no corn this year" (*Modern Greek Folklore and Ancient Greek Religion* [Cambridge, 1910], 573).

For Greek tragedy, then, the case is clear; and that something very similar holds also for the other great branch of Hellenic drama has been shown by the late Francis Cornford in his work, *The Origins of Attic Comedy* (Cambridge, 1914). Moreover, Cornford has pointed out that the same method may be applied even to the poems of Hesiod and that, if these be regarded as relics of ritual drama, many of the incongruities which now appear in them at once become intelligible.

Nor is it only in ancient Greek literature that the influence of the Seasonal Pattern may be detected. In her fine study,

The Elder Edda and Ancient Scandinavian Drama (Cambridge, 1920), Bertha S. Phillpotts has demonstrated how much of earliest and greatest Norse poetry, which has come down to us in the form of narrative or song, must in its original form have been ritual drama dealing with the seasonal death and rebirth of the fruitful world.

In the present volume, Dr. Gaster has turned his vast learning to demonstrating, in fields far beyond my reach, the existence of a similar pattern, based on the same seasonal drama, in the extant remains of Canaanite, Hittite, Egyptian, and Hebrew literature. He has shown that here too the same variety of forms obtains, and he has traced the essential structure backwards to purely functional procedures and forwards to residual survivals in hymns, psalms, and other forms of liturgical composition. The result is to my mind very impressive.

The instinctive fundamental desire of the human group to ensure that it shall survive and not die is a great thing in itself, and passes in almost all this primeval literature into something more: a consciousness that man, though he desperately needs bread, does not live by bread alone, but longs for a new life, a new age, with young gods, not stained by the deaths and impurities of the past.

GILBERT MURRAY

AUTHOR'S PREFACE

It has long been suggested by students of such diverse compositions as the Indic Rig Veda, Greek tragedy and comedy, the Scandinavian Elder Edda, ancient Chinese folk songs, the Grail romances, and the English mummers' play that there is an intimate connection between certain forms of literature and certain traditional patterns of ritual. The purpose of this book is to explore that theory in yet another area. Its thesis is, in a nutshell, that some of the mythological texts which have come down to us from the ancient Near East likewise reflect, in their themes and structures and in the sequence of their component episodes, a pattern and sequence of ritual acts which, from time immemorial, have characterized major seasonal festivals in most parts of the world.

To demonstrate this thesis, I first discuss (in Part One) the relation between myth and ritual *per se*, and offer a picture of the standard seasonal program, based on ancient and modern evidence. Then (in Part Two) I present and analyze in detail a series of Canaanite, Hittite, and Egyptian mythological texts in which, I claim, the same pattern may be detected in literary form. Finally (in Part Three), I seek to show how the pattern survived, in greatly attenuated and less dramatic form, in the structure of certain Biblical psalms and of other liturgical compositions.

To prevent fundamental misunderstanding, it should be observed at the outset that what is here under discussion is not the origin of each particular composition presented, but that of the genre as a whole. It is not argued that the texts themselves were actually the libretti of liturgical dramas or the spoken accompaniments of ritual acts (though some of them, such as the Hittite *Snaring of the Dragon* and the Canaanite *Poem of the Gracious Gods*, seem certainly to have been so), but only that they are mythic and literary articulations of the same basic Seasonal Pattern. In other words, I am trying to discover what first conditioned the peculiar form and content of that genre, but I fully realize that most of the texts are a long way removed from that primitive origin; indeed, it is an essential part of my thesis that the genre underwent normal artistic evolution (or degeneration) and ended up, as often as not, as a mere literary convention.

Throughout the presentation, considerable use is made of comparative religion and folklore. It is hoped that — quite apart from the correctness or incorrectness of the basic thesis — the material adduced from these sources will be found useful in the interpretation of the texts. Here, however, it may be pointed out and emphasized that in comparing the customs of diverse cultures, I do not assume any *direct* relationship between them. The comparison is on the psychological, not the historical level. I am endeavoring only to show that certain rudimentary reactions to the rhythms of nature and the succession of the seasons characterize virtually all men everywhere and find expression in such similar terms that what appears in any one particular culture may often be elucidated by alignment with parallel phenomena elsewhere. In this respect, the historical unrelatedness of the several cultures, and the fact that each of them also possesses its own peculiar traits and distinctive features, enhances, rather than weakens, the argument. The general soundness of this method of comparison may, in fact, be pertinently illustrated from the analogy of language. It is possible to assemble literally hundreds of parallels between the figurative and metaphorical use of words in the Semitic languages on the one hand and the Indo-European on the other. This shows clearly that both groups share a common stock of natural images. Yet there is no philological relationship between them. If, for instance, one were to compare the use in both of the word for "head" in the sense of "source of a river," the comparison would be psychologically valid and legitimate, regardless of the fact that, philologically, Hebrew *ro'sh* has nothing whatever to do with Greek *kephalê* or Latin *caput!*

It should be observed also in this connection that the extensive use of comparative religion and folklore is not for a moment intended as a substitute for, but rather as a complement to, that sound philological exegesis from which all interpretations of ancient texts must necessarily proceed. I would repudiate unequivocally any suggestion that it implies a contempt for, or derogation of, the patient and invaluable labors of philologists. At the same time, however, the reader may be reminded of the ancient Sanskrit parable which relates that, once upon a time, Mind and Speech came before God and asked Him to decide which of the two was the superior. God decided in favor of Mind, on the ground that Speech but imitated its actions and walked in its footsteps.

A few words about details.

The TRANSLATIONS (except for the Egyptian material) have been made, in all cases, directly from the original texts. Since, however, they are designed for the general reader, and not merely for the initiated, explanatory rubrics and captions have been introduced.

Insofar as the *style* of the renderings is concerned, my object has been to convey to a modern reader the same sort of impression as would have been received by the ancient audience. To this end, proper names have sometimes been translated. Thus, the artisan god of the Canaanites is presented, not as Kthr-w-Khss, but as Sir Adroit-and-Cunning, which is what that name means. Similarly, the god of the netherworld appears as the Lord of Hell, rather than as the meaningless Horon, and the lackey of the goddess Asherat as Sir Holy-and-Blessed, rather than as Qdsh-w-Amrr. These names would originally have conveyed the same sort of impression as Bold Slasher or Little Devil Doubt in the English mummers' plays. Moreover, names which are familiar to English readers from the pages of the Old Testament are presented, with but slight modifications, in their conventional form, regardless of pedantic accuracy. Thus, there seems no point in writing 'Ilu for the deity whom everyone will recognize more readily as El, nor in disguising Baal as Ba'lu. For the same reason, the Canaanite *th* has been reproduced as *sh* (e.g., Asherat, *not* Athrt), except in notes of philological character. It should be observed, however, that the pronunciation of the Canaanite names is often doubtful, the texts employing a purely consonantal script.

The languages in which the texts are written are still in process of elucidation. It is but to be expected, therefore, that further research will improve the rendering of this or that phrase and consequently modify the interpretation of certain passages. The main thesis of the book depends, however, on the over-all sense and sequence, and these may be regarded as reasonably assured.

Asterisks indicate a gap in the original texts; dots, that it is (at least to me) unintelligible.

In transliterating Oriental words and names, I have had, for typographical reasons, to make some compromises with pedantry. In general, *ḥ* appears simply as *h*, and *ḫ* as *kh*. The Semitic *ṣ* is represented by *s* when it occurs in proper names (e.g., A-r-s-aya), and as *ts* in notes of philological character; ʿ does duty for the *ʿayin*-sound, and *gh* for *ghayin;* *t* stands both for *t* (taw) and for *t* (teth); *sh* and *th* are to be read everywhere as single sounds. Scholars will surely recognize their friends even without the finery of diacritical points; laymen will scarcely lose sleep over this. At any rate, it was the best I could do, and I hope the reader will forgive any lapses from consistency which may have escaped me.

Throughout the COMMENTARIES the work of other scholars has been constantly laid under contribution, though as often as not I have taken an independent line. Mere discussion of rival views has, however, been generally avoided on the grounds that, while it might have added piquancy to the volume, it would also have added bulk. For the same reason, and also because this book is addressed to general students of literature and not only to specialists, purely philological matter has been excluded, except where vital to an argument.

This book was originally published in 1950. For the present edition, it has been thoroughly revised and largely rewritten. The translations and commentaries have been overhauled, and both the Hittite texts and the Canaanite *Poem of the Gracious Gods* now appear in an entirely new form. I am indebted to those of my colleagues who, by their critical reviews, have helped me to better understanding and deeper insight.

Most of this book was written in conditions of very considerable difficulty and privation. I am therefore all the more indebted to those good friends who helped to smooth a thorny path, and would here record in grateful and affectionate remembrance the names of the late Ralph Marcus and Robert H. Pfeiffer who, by their ever-ready counsel and suggestion, acted as constant stimulators of the mind and revivers of the drooping spirit. Among the living, I have owed much to the kindly interest of Professor Harry A. Wolfson, and, above all, to the help and encouragement of the Littauer Foundation and of its President, Mr. Harry Starr, whose generosity made the seemingly impossible possible. I am especially sensible also of the ready sympathy and helpfulness of Mr. Pyke Johnson, of Anchor Books, of the openhandedness with which he permitted me to make extensive revisions — and of his unremitting and incredible patience.

In its present form, this book represents the work of twenty-two uneasy years. More has gone into it than writing and research, and that more is the measure of what I owe to the devotion and sacrifice of my wife who, in addition to taking upon herself all the technical and complicated work of reading the proofs, styling the original edition, and seeing this one through the press, has been with it from beginning to end, planning and testing, suggesting and worrying, sharing its joys and alleviating its disappointments. Everything in it except its faults is hers as well as mine.

T. H. G.

New York
October 18, 1959

SYNOPSIS

Seasonal *rituals* are functional in character. Their purpose is periodically to revive the *topocosm,* that is, the entire complex of any given locality conceived as a living organism. But this topocosm possesses both a punctual and a durative aspect, representing, not only the actual and present community, but also that ideal and continuous entity of which the latter is but the current manifestation. Accordingly, seasonal rituals are accompanied by *myths* which are designed to present the purely functional acts in terms of ideal and durative situations. The interpenetration of the myth and ritual creates *drama.*

In most parts of the world, seasonal rituals follow a common pattern. This pattern is based on the conception that life is vouchsafed in a series of leases which have annually to be renewed. The renewal is achieved, however, not through divine providence alone but also through the concerted effort of men; and the rituals are designed primarily to recruit and regiment that effort. They fall into the two clear divisions of *Kenosis,* or Emptying, and *Plerosis,* or Filling, the former representing the evacuation of life, the latter its replenishment. Rites of Kenosis include the observance of fasts, lents, and similar austerities, all designed to indicate that the topocosm is in a state of suspended animation. Rites of Plerosis include mock combats against the forces of drought or evil, mass mating, the performance of rain charms and the like, all designed to effect the reinvigoration of the topocosm.

The rites originally performed by the community as a whole tend in time to be centered in a single representative individual, viz., the king. It is the king who then undergoes the temporary eclipse, who fights against the noxious powers, and who serves as the bridegroom in a "sacred marriage."

What the king does on the punctual plane, the god does on the durative. Accordingly, all the ceremonies performed by the king are transmuted, through the medium of myth, into deeds done by the god. This transmutation in turn gives rise to the idea that the king and the other performers of the seasonal rites are merely impersonating acts originally performed by the gods, and the tendency develops to represent what is really a parallel situation on the durative plane as something that happened primordially — the archetype of what may be periodically repeated with the same effect. Presentation then becomes representation; the ritual turns into drama.

The Seasonal Pattern may be traced in many of the calendar festivals of the Ancient Near East. Representative instances are the Akitu (New Year) Festival of the Babylonians and Assyrians and the New Year–Day of Atonement–Feast of Ingathering complex of the Israelites. It may be recognized also in Egypt and among the Hittites, and — at least vestigially — in the Asianic mysteries of Attis.

In course of time, as new conceptions evolve, the urgency of the primitive seasonal rituals tends to recede. But the Pattern lingers on in increasingly meaningless folk customs and in the conventions of literary style. Recent studies have shown that it may be recognized behind the conventional structure of Greek tragedy and comedy and behind the European mummers' play. Using the same approach, it is here shown that several mythological texts which have come down to us from the Ancient Near East likewise ascend to the Seasonal Pattern, reflecting in their general themes and in the sequence of their episodes the basic motifs and sequence of acts in the primitive ritual. It is fully conceded, however, that most of the texts in question now stand a long way from the primitive form and have been subjected to considerable literary and artistic development. What is at issue is, in fact, the history of the literary genre as a whole, not of the particular compositions.

The mythological texts in which the Pattern is here detected are the following:

The CANAANITE poems of *Baal*, *Aqhat*, and *The Gracious Gods*, from Ras Shamra-Ugarit;

The BABYLONIAN Epic of Creation (*Enuma Elish*);

The HITTITE myths of *Hahhimas* and *Telipinu* and of *The Snaring of the Dragon*. The last-named was, in fact, the cultic myth of the annual Puruli Festival;

The EGYPTIAN "dramatic" texts from Edfu and from the Ramesseum, and the so-called "Memphite Creation Play" inscribed on the celebrated "Shabaka Stone."

The texts revolve around different elements of the primitive Seasonal Pattern, some of them concentrating on the ritual combat, others on the eclipse and renewal of kingship, and others again on the disappearance and restoration of the genius of topocosmic vitality. Moreover, while some (i.e., the Hittite texts) are actually accompanied by ritual directions, and must therefore have been recited at public ceremonies, others appear to be purely literary compositions, and one of them (viz., the Canaanite *Poem of the Gracious Gods*) even verges on the burlesque, in the manner of the English mummers' play and of the modern Carnival dramas of Northern Greece. All of these compositions, except the Babylonian *Epic of Creation* and the Egyptian Edfu drama, are here presented in translation, with running commentaries setting forth their relation to the seasonal ritual and elucidating them in the light of comparative religion and folklore. They are grouped according to their various dominant themes.

The Seasonal Pattern survived not only in formal myths but also — albeit in severely attenuated guise — in the hymns and chants associated with the liturgy. It may be recognized in the structure of several Biblical psalms, while sophisticated literary developments of it may be detected in the same way in the choral odes of the *Bacchae* of Euripides, in the Homeric *Hymn to Demeter,* and even in some of the hymns of the medieval Church.

PART ONE

THE SEASONAL PATTERN

CHAPTER ONE

RITUAL AND MYTH

§1. All over the world, from time immemorial, it has been the custom to usher in years and seasons by means of public ceremonies. These, however, are neither arbitrary nor haphazard, nor are they mere diversions. On the contrary, they follow everywhere a more or less uniform and consistent pattern and serve a distinctly *functional* purpose. They represent the mechanism whereby, at a primitive level, society seeks periodically to renew its vitality and thus ensure its continuance.

From the standpoint of a primitive community, life is not so much a progression from cradle to grave as a series of leases annually or periodically renewed and best exemplified in the revolution of the seasons. The renewal, however, is not effected by grace of superior providence or by any automatic law of nature; for of such the primitive has no conception. Rather has it to be fought for and won by the concerted effort of men. Accordingly, a regular program of activities is established, which, performed periodically under communal sanction, will furnish the necessary replenishment of life and vitality. This program constitutes the pattern of the seasonal ceremonies.

§2. The activities fall into two main divisions which we may call, respectively, rites of Kenosis, or Emptying, and rites of Plerosis, or Filling. The former portray and symbolize the eclipse of life and vitality at the end of each lease, and are exemplified by lenten periods, fasts, austerities, and other expressions of mortification or suspended animation. The latter, on the other hand, portray and symbolize the revitalization which ensues at the beginning of the new lease, and are exemplified by rites of mass mating, ceremonial purgations of evil and noxiousness (both physical and "moral"),[1] and magical procedures designed to promote fertility, produce rain, relume the sun, and so forth.

§3. Basic to the entire procedure is the conception that what is in turn eclipsed and revitalized is not merely the human community of a given area or locality but the total corporate unit of all elements, animate and inanimate alike, which together constitute its distinctive character and "atmosphere." To this wider entity we may assign the name *topocosm,* formed (on the analogy of *microcosm* and *macrocosm*) from Greek *topos,* "place," and *cosmos,* "world, order."[2] The seasonal ceremonies are the economic regimen of this topocosm.

From the outset, however, they are more than mere ritual. The essence of the topocosm is that it possesses a twofold character, at once real and punctual, and ideal and durative, the former aspect being necessarily immerged in the latter, as a moment is immerged in time. If it is bodied forth as a real and concrete organism in the present, it exists also as an ideal, timeless entity, embracing but transcending the here and now in exactly the same way that the ideal America embraces but transcends the present generation of Americans.[3] The successive leases of its life therefore exist not only in the reality of the present but also in a kind of infinite continuum of which the present is but the current phase. Accordingly, the seasonal ceremonies which mark the beginnings and ends of those leases possess at once a punctual and a transcendent aspect. In the former, they serve as effective mechanisms for articulating immediate situations and satisfying immediate needs. In the latter, however, they objectify, in terms of the present, situations which are intrinsically durative and sempiternal. Thus they are, from the start, not only direct experiences but also and at the same time representations—not only rituals but also dramas.

§4. The connecting link between these two aspects is myth. The function of myth (so obstinately misunderstood) is to translate the real into terms of the ideal, the punctual into terms of the durative and transcendental. This it does by projecting the procedures of ritual to the plane of ideal situations, which they are then taken to objectify and reproduce. Myth is therefore an essential ingredient in the pattern of the seasonal ceremonies; and the interpenetration of ritual and myth provides the key to the essential nature of drama.

In this context, myth is not, as Robertson Smith maintained, a mere outgrowth of ritual, an artistic or literary interpretation imposed later upon sacral acts; nor is it merely, as Jane Harrison insisted, the spoken correlative of "things done." Rather, it is the expression of a parallel aspect inherent in them from the beginning; and its function within the scheme of the Seasonal Pattern is to translate the punctual into terms of the durative, the real into those of the ideal.

Moreover, the impulse which inspires myth is no mere flight of literary or artistic fancy, nor can mythology itself be defined in terms of its articulation. To do so is to mistake the form for the essence; it is as if one were to define prayer solely in terms of litany, or music in those of score and scale. Mythology is a function of religio-social behavior, not a department of literature or art; the latter are merely its vehicles or instruments.

NOTES

1. In primitive thought, of course, the two categories are not rigidly distinguished. Morality, or the social code, is identified and validated as the innate structural order of the world – the same order which governs its physical phenomena and which is determined by the gods.

2. That the social unit embraces more than the mere human community was already recognized by Robertson Smith in his classic exposition of the subject in *Religion of the Semites*, 271 ff.; but while he perceived its spatial extension beyond that community, he missed the essential point that it extends in time as well as in space, embracing past, present, and future in one ideal, durative entity.

3. Symbols of the topocosmic concept in modern thought are Alma Mater, La France, etc.

CHAPTER TWO

INGREDIENTS OF THE SEASONAL PATTERN

§1. Compact of hopes and fears, of promise and apprehension, and symbolizing — as previously explained — both the "emptying," or evacuation (*kenosis*), and the "filling," or replenishment (*plerosis*), of corporate vitality, the Seasonal Pattern consists of four major elements.

First come rites of MORTIFICATION, symbolizing the state of suspended animation which ensues at the end of the year, when one lease of life has drawn to a close and the next is not yet assured.

Second come rites of PURGATION, whereby the community seeks to rid itself of all noxiousness and contagion, both physical and moral, and of all evil influences which might impair the prosperity of the coming year and thereby threaten the desired renewal of vitality.

Third come rites of INVIGORATION, whereby the community attempts, by its own concerted and regimented effort, to galvanize its moribund condition and to procure that new lease of life which is imperative for the continuance of the topocosm.

Last come rites of JUBILATION, which bespeak men's sense of relief when the new year has indeed begun and the continuance of their own lives and that of the topocosm is thereby assured.

I

§2. Rites of MORTIFICATION are represented primarily by communal lents, fasts, and similar austerities, all of which symbolize, in greater or lesser degree, a state of suspended animation. The most familiar instances — both going back to "pagan" antecedents — are, of course, the Christian Lent and the Mohammedan Ramadan.[1] But these are by no means unique; the usage is abundantly attested both in ancient civilizations and among primitive peoples of the present day.

§3. To begin with examples drawn from antiquity: the Babylonians recognized the first week, or even the first sixteen days of the New Year month of Teshrit, as a lenten period.[2] Among the Hebrews, the autumnal Feast of Ingathering (Asif) was preceded by a solemn Day of Catharsis (Yom ha-Kippurim), when all work stopped, the entire community fasted, and evil was expelled in the form of a scapegoat.[3] Similarly, in Greece, the Festival of Thesmophoria, in the latter part of October, was characterized by fasting. Indeed, the third day was called specifically "the Fast";[4] and in Cyprus, abstention from food obtained throughout the preceding nine days.[5] So too the Feast of the "Yellow Grain-Mother" (Demeter Chloê) held in Athens in mid-May (sixth day of Thargêlion), when the corn was ripe, was marked by rites of mortification.[6] On the island of Lemnos, fires were extinguished annually for nine days during which sacrifices were offered to the dead and to the powers of the netherworld.[6a] In the Asianic Attis cult, the annual resurrection of that fertility spirit in spring was preceded by a few days of fasting and ceremonial austerities (*hagisteiai, castus*).[7] Last, in Rome, the Festival of Ceres, goddess of crops, held in April, was introduced by a fast, while in October a nine-day fast in honor of that goddess was ceremonially observed.[8] The latter custom seems also to have obtained at the annual festival of Bacchus.[9]

§4. Turning now to evidence derived from primitive peoples of the present day, the following examples may be cited. In Cambodia, the first three days of the year (which begins in mid-March) are a period of solemn abstinence, when sexual relations are forbidden; while during the first seven days, no living thing may be killed, no business concluded, and all litigation and controversy are suspended.[10] Among the Cherokees and Choctaws, the New Year festival, in August, is called *Busk*, or "Fast," and no food is tasted for two nights and one day preceding the eating of the new crops.[11] The same usage and the same name obtain also among the Creeks.[12] The Comanches fast for seven days in connection with the annual festival at which they rekindle their sacred fires.[13] In the Malay Peninsula special taboos are imposed for three days before the reaping of rice: rice, salt, oil, money, etc., may not leave the house; hair must be cut, and perfect quiet observed.[14] Similarly, the Mao of Manipur observe a *genna,* or period of taboo, for four days at the beginning of the harvest;[15] while the Mayans used to inaugurate their Festival of Pacum Chac, held in the latter half of May (when the sun attains its zenith over Yucatan) by imposing a five-day fast upon their local chieftains.[16] The same thing was done also at their Feast of Chickaban, celebrated in late October (or early November) in the town of Mani.[17] In South Massam, fasting takes place before the *Walaga* Festival;[18] among the Natchez of Mississippi, for three days before harvest;[19] in New Guinea, before the yam festival;[20] and in Peru, before the summer-solstice festival of Raymi.[21]

In Morocco, the New Year month of Muharram,[22] and, in the Jewish religion, the three weeks between 17 of Tammuz and 9 of Ab (in midsummer) are observed as a lenten period. The two dates are recognized as fasts, and during the entire three weeks no meat is eaten.[23] Traditionally, this is said to commemorate the siege and fall of Jerusalem both in 586 B.C. and again in 70 A.D., but there is reason to believe that the custom was really borrowed from Babylonia, where this was a crucial period in the seasonal cult of Tammuz, dying and reviving genius of fertility.[24] Similarly, the month of Iyar, which precedes the Palestinian barley harvest, is observed — as was the corresponding month of May among the Romans — as a quasi-lenten period during which no marriages may be solemnized and various other restrictions are imposed.[25] Among the Ossetes of the Caucasus, a feast of the dead (*Komakhsan*) is observed around harvesttime and is followed by a one-month fast designed to induce Tutyr (St. Theodore of Tyre) to restrain his wolves and spare the sheep. The fast begins at the termination of Carnival.[26]

§5. It has been suggested by Robertson Smith and others[27] that preharvest fasts originated in the necessity of preparing the body for the subsequent sacramental meal between the god and the community. Fasting for such purposes is indeed attested in many religions.[28] In the light of the foregoing evidence, however, it is plain that this explanation is altogether too narrow. Such fasts alternate in popular usage with wider forms of abstinence and restraint, and must therefore possess the same general significance. What this significance is comes out very clearly from the fact that fasts and abstinences are likewise characteristic of intercalary (or epagomenal) periods, which, since they stand, as it were, "outside of time," are usually regarded as periods of suspended animation. Thus — to cite but a few representative examples — the five supplementary days which were added at the end of the normal year in the Aztec calendar were known as *nemontemi*, "unfit for work," all religious ceremonies and civil business being then suspended.[29] Similarly, the Mayas of Yucatan, who use the same system, style these days *xma kaba kin*, "days without name," and refrain thereon from onerous work and even from personal ablutions.[30] So, too, in the Central Provinces in India, the intercalary months, which occur triennially and which are called "excreta" (*malmas*), are marked by abstinence;[31] while among the Tigre tribes of Ethiopia similar restrictions are imposed during the five or six epagomenal days preceding the festival of St. John.[32] The usage survives also in the European observance of the Twelve Days between December 25 and January 6.[33] These, as most scholars now agree, were originally intercalary days,[34] and they are characterized in popular usage by various forms of abstinence and restraint and by the ceremonial expulsion of evil. It is evident, then, that the primary purpose of seasonal fasts and lents is to represent the state of suspended animation which ensues at the end of a life lease, or in the "vacant" days of an epagomenal period.

§6. This interpretation is supported by two significant arguments. The first is that in many other cases where fasting occurs as a religious rite, the same basic motive may be recognized. Thus, in many parts of the world it is customary to fast during a period of mourning. To cite but a few instances, this usage obtains in the Andaman Islands,[35] in Fiji,[36] Samoa,[37] China,[38] and Korea,[39] as well as among various African tribes.[40]

Similarly, fasting is a frequent concomitant of marriage ceremonies, as, for example, among the Wa-teita of East Africa,[41] the Macusi of British Guiana,[42] and the Tlingits of Alaska,[43] not to speak of orthodox Jews.[44] Again, fasting usually precedes rites of initiation.[44a] This is attested, for example, among the Algonquins,[45] the Bellacoola tribe of British Columbia,[46] the Guaranis of Southern Brazil,[47] the

Matacos of Gran Chaco,[48] the Ojibwa,[49] the Roro-speaking tribes of New Guinea,[50] and various primitive peoples in Australia,[51] New South Wales,[52] the Torres Strait,[53] and Bank Island.[54] Initiants into the ancient mysteries of Isis, Attis, and Mithra were likewise obliged to fast,[55] and the same practice obtained also among the neophytes in the Greek mysteries at Eleusis.[56] Now, the common factor in all these instances is what may be described as the *occlusion of personality* — a kind of individual kenosis.[57] In the case of mourning, the fasting and abstinence express the fact that the demise of any single constituent member automatically impairs the corporate vitality of the entire group (or rather of the topocosm), so that all are in a state of temporary "death," or suspended animation. Similarly, in the case of marriage, what is thereby expressed is the abandonment by each partner of his or her single individuality and their fusion in a new, joint entity; they "become one flesh." So too in the case of initiation: by means of fasting and abstinence, the candidate evacuates his former selfhood, preparatory to merging in the corporate personality of the group. In each instance, therefore, the fasting and abstinence symbolizes a state of suspended animation; and this strengthens our view that they possess the same significance in the seasonal ceremonies, when, as we have seen, such a state is indeed believed to exist.

§7. The second argument in favor of our interpretation is purely philological: the Hebrew terms for ritual fasting really denote a *constraint of personality* and have no primary reference to mere abstention from food. Thus, in the prescriptions for the annual Day of Catharsis in Leviticus 16:29–31, the term employed (*'innah nefesh*) means literally "to abase the self," implying a general mortification.[58] Similarly, the word (*'a/sarah* or *'a/sereth*) which is used frequently in the Old Testament[59] in connection with the convening of sacred assemblies, especially in times of drought and distress, derives from the root *'-ts-r,* "restrain," and thus denotes a *lent,* or period of taboo.[60]

§8. Closely related to Mortification is the practice of howling and wailing at seasonal ceremonies.[61] This is well attested throughout ancient civilizations.

The Egyptians, says Diodorus, used to shed tears and cry

upon Isis at the first cutting of the corn;[62] and their summer festival was marked, according to Herodotus, by the chanting of a doleful lay called Maneros.[63] The latter, it is believed, is a distortion of the Egyptian words *maa n per.k*, "come to thy house,"[64] which constitute the initial phrase in seasonal lamentations for Osiris which have actually come down to us.[65] The custom is attested also, at a much later date, by Firmicus Maternus, who reproaches the pagan Egyptians for "lamenting over the crops and wailing over the growing seed."[66] The lamentation, say Herodotus and various other Classical writers, was accompanied on the flute;[67] and Moret has pointed out that one of the scenes sculptured on the walls of the Fifth Dynasty Tomb of Tî actually portrays a man standing piping beside reapers![68]

In Mesopotamia the harvest was accompanied by the utterance of a ritual cry known as *alalu*, or ululation.[69] This cry is paralleled in other parts of the ancient world. Thus, in Judges 9:27 it is stated specifically that the inhabitants of Shechem performed the analogous rite of *hillulim* on the occasion of the vintage, and the custom still survives in parts of Palestine;[70] while Plutarch informs us that the traditional cry at the Attic vintage festival of Oschophoria, in midsummer, was *eleleu*.[71] Similarly, according to a writer quoted by Athenaeus, the ritual dirges uttered in the mysteries of Demeter and Kore went under the name of *iouloi* (or *houloi*), i.e., "howls";[72] and it is probably to such a cry that the prophet Micah consciously alludes when he exclaims (7:1): "*Al^elai li* [EV. Woe is me!], for I am become like *the harvestings of summer fruits*, like *the gleanings of the vintage*." Lamentations were likewise a characteristic feature of the Eleusinian Mysteries.[73]

§9. In our extant sources, these traditional howlings and wailings are usually associated with specific deities or spirits of fertility, being regarded as dirges over their annual disappearance from the earth. The lamentations for Osiris in Egypt, Attis in Asia Minor, and Adonis in Syria are well known.[74] Similarly, in the Babylonian *Epic of Gilgamesh* (vi, 46–47)[75] and again in the *Poem of the Descent of Ishtar to the Netherworld* (rev. 56–57),[76] mention is made explicitly of the annual weeping for Tammuz, lord of fertility, and the technical term *elelu* is actually employed. Moreover, an early Babylonian text published by Reisner (SBH, 145, iii

12–15) and another of Arsacid date (ZA 6 [1891], 243:34) define the month of Tammuz, in midsummer, as a period of wailing, ritual lamentation, and weeping;[77] while an Old Assyrian almanac (KAR 178, vi 10) prescribes weeping for its second day.[78] This seasonal ululation, which obtained likewise in the Greek cult of Demeter and Kore,[79] survived, indeed, into the Christian era, for a medieval Arabic antiquary records the performance of it at Harran.[80]

§10. Yet despite these later mythological interpretations, there is reason to suspect that the seasonal howlings and wailings were not originally signs of mourning at all. Two arguments may be adduced. The first is that in several cases the deities or spirits who are thus supposedly lamented bear names which are nothing but artificial personifications of the wailings themselves![81] The Greeks, for example, promptly invented a corn goddess, Ioulô, whom the *iouloi*, or "howls," of the Demeter cult were supposed to invoke.[82] Similarly, out of the *hylagmos* or "ululation" of the seasonal ceremonies they concocted the familiar figure of Hylas,[83] for whom it was then said to be uttered; and out of the *litê ersês*, or seasonal "prayer for rain," they invented the fertility spirit Lityerses.[84] So too Iacchos as a name for Dionysus owes its origin to the ritual cry *iacchos;*[85] while the doleful Phoenician refrain *ai lanû,* "woe unto us," evidently chanted in the seasonal laments, was transformed into a Greek *ai Linou,* "woe for Linos," and gave birth to the Adonis-like figure of that name.[86] By the same process the Sumerians appear to have created a god, Alala, out of the *alala* or ritual wail;[87] and, according to Welcker,[88] the Basque hero Lelo, who is lamented in traditional folk songs, is but a projection of the *lelo,* or dirge.

§11. The second argument in favor of the view that the seasonal weepings and wailings need not have originated as rites of mourning derives from the acute observation of the late Maurice Canney that tears are not necessarily an expression of sorrow, but may be induced equally by any form of violent excitement.[89] Accordingly, although so interpreted in later times, the shedding of tears in ritual need not have originated as an act of mourning; it may have been but the natural concomitant of frenzy and hysteria. Similarly, the loud cries which subsequently developed into exclamations of grief may have been, in the first place, nothing but shrieks and yells of excitement.

There is much to be said in favor of this view. In the first place, it is worth noting that in several cultures, while the shedding of tears at seasonal ceremonies is indeed attested, it is not associated with mourning, being interpreted in quite a different manner. Thus, among the Toradjas, Galelarese, and Javanese of Indonesia,[90] tears are regarded — as are blood, sweat, semen, and urine elsewhere[91] — as effusions of the "soul-substance," so that the shedding of them serves as a means of reinvigorating the earth and even of reviving the dead. Indeed, this power is attributed even to the tears of animals. Thus, at Great Bassam, in Guinea, oxen are slaughtered annually as part of a procedure designed to procure a good harvest, and it is an essential part of the ceremony that they be made to weep. To this end, indeed, women sit in front of them and throw manioc meal and palm wine into their eyes to make them weep, while they chant, "Ox will weep."[92] Again, among the Khonds of Bengal,[93] and likewise in Mexico,[94] the shedding of tears is believed to be an homeopathic method of producing rain; while a similar belief in their magical efficacy may be recognized in the fact that at one stage of the Babylonian New Year (Akitu) ceremonies, the king was ritually slapped and induced to weep, such weeping being deemed propitious.[95] Magical weeping of this kind may also have obtained among the ancient Hebrews; for, according to Canney,[96] a specific allusion to it may be recognized in the familiar words of Psalm 126:5–6:

> They that sow in tears shall reap in joy.
> He that goeth forth weeping,
> bearing the trail of seed,
> shall doubtless return with rejoicing,
> bearing his sheaves.[97]

§12. To these two major arguments may be added a third. In most of the ancient languages, the words for "howl of pain" and "cry of joy" are undifferentiated, or at least akin, both going back to a single onomatopoeic root meaning simply, "yell." Thus, in Greek, the verb *elelizô* is used indiscriminately in both senses, as are also the analogous *ololuzô* and *alalazô*. Similarly, the Hebrew *h-l-l*, "shout for joy," is related to *'a-l-l* and *y-l-l*, "cry woe," just as is the Accadian *elêlu* to the antithetical *alâlu*. Accordingly, when words of this type are used as the technical terms for the seasonal practices, it is possible to infer that their original meaning was simply "yell," and that they did not necessarily imply doleful lamentation.

§13. If these arguments are correct, the practice of howling and wailing at seasonal ceremonies need not be interpreted as acts of mourning, but rather as mere expressions of excitement or as functional procedures designed to promote fertility through the magical properties of tears. In the latter case, they would fall into the category of rites of Invigoration rather than of Mortification. This, of course, is not to deny that a certain element of mourning must always have been present. The languor of the earth in the hot summer, the falling of the leaves and the departure of the songbirds in autumn, and the long sleep and desolation of winter are bound, at all times, to inspire sentiments of sorrow and regret. The only point that is here made is that rites of howling and wailing are not necessarily to be construed as expressions of such sentiments.

II

§14. Seasonal rites of PURGATION are almost universally attested in both the ancient and modern worlds.[98] Thus, among the Romans, the last month of the year was dedicated especially to communal purification and was therefore termed February, from a verb (*februare*) meaning "to purify."[99] Temples and sacred vessels were likewise thoroughly scoured at this season.[100] Similarly, the annual Feast of Sowing (Feriae Sementivae) was characterized by a ceremonial lustration of crops, fields, and peasantry;[101] and the same thing took place also at the rustic Parish Festival (Paganalia).[102]

Among the Hebrews, the autumnal Festival of Ingathering (Asif) was preceded by a solemn Day of Catharsis (Yom ha-Kippurim). The occasion was marked by a fast, a suspension of normal activities, and the expulsion of a scapegoat which was supposed to carry into the wilderness the accumulated burden of communal sin and wrongdoing.[103] So too among the Greeks, the Athenian Festival of Thargêlia, held in May, featured a purgatory expulsion of human scapegoats.[104] Nor is the custom unattested among primitive peoples. Thus — to quote from the examples assembled by Frazer — the Incas of Peru used ceremonially to expel disease at the Festival of Situa, celebrated just before the onset of the rainy season in September.[105] Similarly, in Siam,[106] and likewise too among the Wotyaks of Eastern Russia,[107] the forces of evil are solemnly banished on the last day of the year. Among the Hos of Togoland, West Africa,[108] and of Kiriwina in Southeast New Guinea,[109] evil spirits are exorcised annually before the eating of new yams; and the occasion is preceded, in the former case, by a period of fasting. Among the tribes of Hindu Kush, evil is expelled after the harvest;[110] in Chitral the ceremony is called "devil-driving."[111] In Cambodia, the rite takes place in March;[112] and among the Eskimos of Point Barrow, in Alaska, the evil spirit Tuña is expelled annually at the moment when the sun reappears.[113] At Cape Coast Castle, the demon Abonsam is driven forth annually after a four weeks' period of mortification;[114] and in Tonquin there is a similar expulsion (called *theckydaw*) once a year.[115]

A peculiarly striking instance of this communal purgation is afforded by the Japanese ceremony of *ohoharahi,* or "great purification," performed by the Mikado or a member of the Nakatomi priestly clan twice yearly, on the last days of the sixth and twelfth months. Ministers of state, officials, and people are purified from ceremonial offenses committed during the preceding half-year, special emphasis being placed on mischievous interferences with agricultural operations. Offerings are thrown into the river or sea and are supposed (like the scapegoat) to bear away the sins of the people.[116] Analogous also is the Ashanti Feast of Odwira, or Purgation, held annually in September. The entire nation is thereby purified from defilement, the king is reconsecrated, departed monarchs are propitiated, shrines are cleansed, and there is a feast of the dead.[117]

§15. In most (though not in all) cases the purgation is effected with the aid of fire.[118] This is true, for example, of the instances quoted from the Incas and the Eskimos of Point Barrow. It is likewise in this way that the rite is (or was) performed annually on Twelfth Day in the canton of Labruguière in the South of France, where the evil spirits are (or were) expelled by means of blazing torches.[119] Similarly, it is customary at Fez and among the Berber-speaking tribes of Morocco to light fires on the rooftops on the Festival of ʿAshura, which is the Mohammedan New Year, and for children and unmarried men to leap over them, while they cry, "We have shaken over thee, O bonfire (*taʿashurt*), the fleas and lice and illnesses both spiritual and physical."[120] The same custom obtains also, on the same date, in Tunis.[121] Analogously, too, a Babylonian text which describes the ceremonies of the New Year (Akitu) Festival refers to the custom of tossing firebrands into the air;[122] and a late Jewish source asserts categorically that "he who attaches a firebrand to the wall of a house and cries Avaunt! performs a pagan practice."[123] Bonfires are also a standard feature of Halloween ceremonies in Britain, and they were likewise lit at Midsummer. Of the latter, the antiquary Bourne states categorically that they were kindled in order that "the lustful Dragons might be driven away."[124]

§16. What is done for men has also to be done for gods. Temples too must be purged and cleansed at the beginning of the new lease of life. In Egypt, sacred buildings were ritually aspersed during the annual celebration of the mysteries of Osiris;[125] and the Bremner–Rhind Papyrus I, 2–3 states explicitly that "the entire temple is to be purified [consecrated]" before the recital of the lamentations for that god.[126] Similarly, in Mesopotamia, the sacred emblems in the temple were cleansed and purified during the month of Teshrit — the month of the autumnal New Year;[127] and on the fifth day of the vernal New Year (Akitu) Festival, an elaborate rite of purgation took place in the sanctuary.[128] A similar practice obtained among the Hebrews in the observance of the Day of Purgation or Atonement,[129] while among the Moslems of Morocco water is aspersed on human beings and animals and on the walls and floors of dwellings at the New Year Festival (ʿAshura) on the tenth day of Muharram.[130]

§17. Sometimes the rite of purgation takes the form of ceremonially destroying and then replacing the furniture and vessels of the local temple. Two representative examples may be cited, the one ancient and the other modern. In the Hittite text, KUB XXV 31, 6–7, it is stated that at the spring or summer festival of Puruli it was customary to burn the sacred fleeces and other appurtenances and to replace them with new ones; while the Mayan ceremony of *oc-na,* performed in January, included the rite of breaking the clay idols and censers and of subsequently repairing and repainting the temples.[131]

§18. Analogous also is the custom of removing from the temple, or similar sacred edifice, boughs and twigs imported during the previous year's celebration and of replacing them with new ones. The best example of this is, of course, the common European usage of introducing new Maypoles at seasonal ceremonies in spring;[132] but it is possible also to cite far earlier instances. In the Hittite text just mentioned there is a specific reference to the importation of a new *eyan,* or evergreen tree, into the temple at the Feast of Puruli;[133] while the Romans marked the Old New Year of March 1 by changing the laurels in the houses of the *rex sacrorum* and in the (Old) Chapel of the Wards.[134]

III

§19. Rites of INVIGORATION take various forms, of which the most common and the most important is the Ritual Combat, or mimetic battle between Life and Death, Summer and Winter, Old Year and New.

§20. The combat is abundantly attested in both ancient and modern civilizations and survives prominently in popular custom.[135] "In many places [in Germany]," says Grimm, "two persons, disguised as Summer and Winter, make their appearance, the one clothed with ivy or *singrün,* the other with straw or moss, and they fight one another till Summer wins. The custom . . . belongs chiefly to districts in the middle Rhine, beyond it in the Palatinate, this side of it in the Odenwald betwixt Main and Neckar."[136] Similarly, in Styria,[137] and in the neighboring mountains of Carinthia,[138] it used to be the custom, in March or at St. Mary's Candlemas, for two bands, one with winter clothes and snowballs and the other with green summer headgear, pitchforks, and scythes, to engage in combat; while at Voitzenberg, in the Ukermark district, a fight between Summer and Winter was (or is) staged on Christmas Eve, the antagonists being impersonated, as a rule, by old women.[139] The usage is, indeed, ubiquitous. In Sweden, two companies of mounted troops, the one dressed in furs and the other in fresh leaves and flowers, used to stage a set-to on May Day; the latter, representing the forces of Summer, naturally won.[140] Similarly, fights between Summer and Winter were a regular feature of midsummer ceremonies in the villages of Russia.[141] In the Brahmi Confederacy of Baluchistan, a ritual combat is staged by the women whenever rain is needed;[142] while among the Malayans, a mock combat takes place every three or four years in order to expel demons.[143] Among the Iroquois, the New Year Festival, held in late January or early February, included a mimetic combat between Life-God (Teharonhiawagon) and Winter (Tawiskaron);[144] and among the Yakut, such contests characterize the two great tribal festivals of Aiy-ysyakh (Good Spirits) in spring and of Abassy-ysyakh (Bads Spirits) in autumn.[145] On each occasion, Spring (called *aiy-uola,* "good spirit"), dressed in white and riding a white horse, engages Winter (called *abassy-uola,* "bad spirit"), clothed in red and riding a roan horse. An analogous procedure marks the Basque Carnival masquerade at La Soule in the South of France, where Les Rouges fight Les Noires.[146] Among ancient examples, mention may be made especially of the Greek *ballêtai*[147] and the Sicilian *agôn en skillais,*[148] while Herodotus records the Egyptian practice of staging an annual "fight with clubs" at which "they bash each other's heads and, so I think, may even die of wounds."[149] Such a fight, it may be added, is actually portrayed on a relief in the tomb of Kheryaf at Thebes.[150] So too, in Mexican ritual, the priest of the maize goddess Centeotl engaged in combat with soldiers at the annual festival of that deity.[151]

§21. In course of time, the real significance of the combat tends to be forgotten and it then comes to be explained as the commemoration of some historic encounter. This process, too, is well represented in both ancient and modern sources.[152] A few examples will suffice. In ancient Egypt, the combat staged annually at Memphis during the Festival of Sokar (the twenty-sixth day of Khoiakh) was presented as a contest between rival factions in the city of Buto, the predynastic capital.[153] Similarly, among the Hittites, the Ritual Combat was taken to re-enact some early border clash between themselves and their neighbors, the Masa (Maeonians?);[154] while, according to Ewald, the combat between the warriors of Abner and those of Joab, recounted in II Samuel 2:14–17, is of the same order.[155] Plutarch, in his *Life of Alexander*, describes an analogous mock combat between two teams of the Emperor's followers, headed respectively by an "Alexander" and a "Darius."[156] Scarcely less illuminating is the description of the Macedonian Festival of Xandika given by the Roman historian Livy. Held shortly before the vernal equinox, at the beginning of the season of military campaigns, this festival consisted of a ceremonial lustration or purgation (*lustratio*) and parade (*decursus*) of the troops, followed by a mock combat (*simulacrum ludicrum pugnae*) led by the two royal princes. The proceedings ended with a fast.[157] As Usener has pointed out,[158] this contest, staged at the equinox, is really but a disguised version of the Ritual Combat.

§22. Modern examples of this historicizing process may also be cited. A football game held annually on Fastern's E'en at Jedburgh, in Scotland, is popularly regarded as commemorating a fierce battle between the Scots and the English at Ferniehurst Castle, near Jedwater;[159] while a mimetic battle fought in various parts of England at Hocktide (i.e., on the Tuesday following the second Sunday after Easter) is similarly interpreted as commemorating a fight between the English and the invading Danes.[160] All these instances are regarded by folklorists as historicizations of the Ritual Combat; and this conclusion is confirmed by the fact that, in most cases, they occur on dates characterized elsewhere by the survival of more primitive, unhistoricized examples of the same institution.

§23. Sometimes the historicization assumes a mythological character. Thus, according to the Mahabhasya, or "Great Commentary" on the grammar of Panini (c. 145 B.C.), the traditional Indic story of the death of Kamsa at the hands of Krishna was actually enacted and reproduced in dialogue by minstrels or rhapsodists (*granthika*), the supporters of the former having black faces and those of the latter, red. As A. B. Keith has suggested, and as the analogy of seasonal dramas elsewhere (e.g., the Basque combat between Les Rouges and Les Noires) would seem to confirm, these performances may be regarded as attenuated survivals of the Ritual Combat, which was thus mythologically historicized.[161]

In the same way, the Irish legend that the Tuatha Dé Danann vanquished the Firbolgs on May Day, and the Welsh myth of Gwythur's fight with Gwyn for possession of Creidylad, are recognized by MacCulloch as historicizations of the Ritual Combat;[162] and we shall see later[163] that in several of the Old Testament psalms the traditional myth of the god's victory over the Dragon — itself projected from the Ritual Combat — is historicized as the triumph of Yahweh over the enemies of Israel.

§24. Sometimes, too, the traditional rite is given a *local* setting without being historicized. Thus, at Gambach, in Hessen (Germany), it takes the form of a combat between the inhabitants of that village and those of the neighboring hamlet of Griebel;[164] while at Slitrig, in Scotland, the opposing teams consist of men from the western and eastern banks of the river, respectively.[165] Similarly, the annual fight at Edinburgh, on Shrove Tuesday, is between the "uppies" and "doonies" — that is, between men living above Mercat's Cross, toward Castlehill, and those living below it, toward Townfoot;[166] while at Ludlow, in England, it is the men of the Corn Street Ward and those of the Broad Street Ward who annually contend in a tug-o'-war on the same date.[167]

§25. Finally, there are cases where the combat simply survives as a traditional institution without any rational attempt to explain it, whether by historicization or by localization. At Scone (Scotland), for example, bachelors contend at football against married men on Shrove Tuesday, but nobody knows why or wherefore.[168] Similarly, in "merrie England" it used to be the custom on May Day for one village to contend with another in dancing matches, each side raising the cry, "*Hey for our town!*"[169] And these two examples could be readily multiplied.

§26. Occasionally, the Ritual Combat degenerates into a mere *race*. This development is attested in ancient and modern usage alike.[170] At Babylon, for example, a foot race was a standard feature of the New Year (Akitu) ceremonies;[171] while in Greece at the Eleusinian Mysteries[172] and in Rome at the annual Festival of Robigalia (March 25)[173] such races were likewise run. Among modern peoples, we may cite the buffalo races held during October and

November in the villages of South Kanara (Southern India) as a means of expelling demons[174] before the second crop is sown;[175] and likewise the races that used to be run at Kilmarnock, in Scotland, on Fastern's E'en.[176]

§27. Invigoration is also effected by rites involving *sexual intercourse.* These, as is well known, are a characteristic concomitant of Carnival celebrations. But they are more than a mere expression of animal spirits, the instinct being exploited at the same time for purely functional purposes. Rites of this kind obtained, for instance, at the Roman Festival of Anna Perenna — an ancient New Year festival — on the Ides of March;[177] while evidence of it among primitive peoples of the present day has been collected by Frazer, Margold, and others.[178] Thus, among the Pipiles of Central America, copulation takes place in the fields at the moment when the first seeds are deposited in the earth.[179] Similarly, in parts of the Ukraine, married couples copulate in the fields on St. George's Day (April 23) in order to promote the fertility of the crops and to achieve what we may now define as the revival of the topocosm.[180] In Java, husbands and wives adopt the same practice as a means of stimulating the growth of rice;[181] while in Amboyna men copulate mimetically with trees whenever the harvest is threatened.[182] So, too, among the Hereros of South West Africa[183] and among various Bantu peoples,[184] mass mating and sexual promiscuity are obligatory at specific seasons of the year; while the Garos encourage men and women to sleep together after certain major seasonal festivals.[185]

§28. It is not impossible that the famous story of the rape of the Sabine women[186] is but a legendary reflection of a seasonal rite of sexual promiscuity. The incident, it will be recalled, is said to have taken place in August on the occasion of a festival; and Frazer has made it probable that the festival in question was that of the Consualia, an agricultural celebration held on August 21.[187] A similar explanation may apply also to the Biblical story in Judges 21:19–23, relating how the men of Benjamin carried off the women of Shiloh on the occasion of a seasonal festival.

§29. The institution of sexual promiscuity at seasonal crises survives in European folklore in the attenuated form of compulsory kissing or "lifting" on certain days of the year. "Kissing fairs" and "hocking days" (cf. German *hoch*, "high") are well attested. Thus, in the Arader Komitat of Nagyhalmagy (Hungary), a *markt* is held annually on March 15 at which women may be kissed without risk of rebuff.[188] Similarly, in certain parts of England, girls may be "lifted" with impunity on May 15; and at Hungerford, in Berkshire, the second Thursday after Easter is "hocking day," when the "tuttimen" go about the streets, "lifting" or "hocking" the women and exacting a kiss from each.[189] Analogous, of course, is the religiously observed Yuletide custom of kissing under the mistletoe — a custom which derives, as every folklorist knows, from the cruder primitive usage of compulsory prostitution at seasonal festivals.[190]

§30. Another attenuation of sexual promiscuity at seasonal festivals and topocosmic crises may be seen in popular traditions to the effect that certain crucial days of the year are particularly auspicious for the choosing of husbands or wives.[191] The Talmud tells us, for example, that it was customary in Jerusalem to choose brides on the Day of Atonement and on the fifteenth day of Ab (August), the occasion of an ancient festival;[192] and it will be observed that it was just at this time of year that the rape of the Sabine women is said to have taken place. Similarly, in some parts of England, St. Rock's Day, which falls on August 16, was esteemed especially propitious for the choosing of mates.[193] In the same way, too, it is the custom in Spanish Galicia for girls to repair at harvesttime to a duly selected barn, where their ardent swains attend upon them;[194] and among the Thompson River Indians of British Columbia, husbands and wives are chosen at a seasonal festival held in the springhouse.[195]

§31. Nor are sexual promiscuity and mass mating the only means whereby society seeks to achieve revival at the close of its periodic leases of life. Another method is the formal recruitment of new members into the body of the community. For this reason Initiation is a frequent element of seasonal ceremonies. Indeed, it is a constant and essential ingredient of the ancient "mysteries" which were invariably associated with seasonal crises.[196] Furthermore, it is significant that the Hebrews preceded their spring Festival of

Passover with rites of circumcision, whereby new members were formally admitted to the fold.[197] Similarly, Moslem Arabs observe the custom of performing mass circumcisions in spring, shortly before the harvest festival.[198] Such usages are recorded, for instance, both among the bedouins and in connection with the spring rites at Mecca and the Nebi Musa (Eastertide) celebrations at Jericho.[199] In the same way, the American Indian tribe of the Haida initiate and tattoo children at their annual potlatch festival;[200] and the natives of Swaziland, in British South Africa, at their harvest ceremony of *incwala*.[201]

§32. The connection between Initiation and Invigoration is brought out especially by the fact that the former is frequently identified with *rebirth*.[202] The most obvious illustration of this lies, of course, in the very word "neophyte" (lit., "newly emplanted") by which initiants are commonly known,[203] as well as in the ideas of regeneration (and even immortality) which are invariably associated with admission to the mysteries in ancient cults. Thus, in the mysteries of Attis, the candidate was looked upon as "one about to die"; when he had performed the required rites, he emerged to new life.[204] Similarly, among the natives of the Lower Congo, initiation is termed "resurrection" (*kimbasi*), and the ritual involves a mimetic resuscitation of the neophytes, who fall as if dead at the feet of the sorcerer.[205] Analogous ideas are reported also among other primitive peoples.[206, 207]

IV

§33. Rites of JUBILATION scarcely require documentation or comment. They are a natural and inevitable expression of relief when the harvest has been assured and the new lease of life is thereby inaugurated.[208] The most obvious demonstration of this is the fact that the word "festival," which originally denoted no more than the ritual meal eaten in common at topocosmic crises, came in time to acquire the meaning of an essentially *joyous* celebration and ultimately to serve as the most appropriate designation of the seasonal ceremonies as a whole. It is worth observing also that both in the Romanized Festival of Isis[209] and in that of Attis,[210] the final stage of the celebration, after the preliminary fasting and mourning, was known by the specific name of Hilaria, or Jollification; while among the Hebrews it was expressly enjoined by law (Deuteronomy 16:14) that the seasonal pilgrimages were to be occasions of rejoicing. Indeed, so largely did the element of merriment come to predominate in the popular consciousness, and to such an extent were its earlier connotations subsumed to the modern sense of "festival," that the prophet Amos (8:10) could use the word *hag*, which had originally denoted the seasonal pilgrimage, as the direct antithesis of "mourning" ("I will turn your *hagim* [EV. "feasts"] into mourning, and all your songs into lamentations"). In the same way, the Romans saw nothing incongruous in forbidding expressions of mourning during the Festival of Ceres, although that occasion had been characterized originally as much by mortification and lament as by subsequent joy and hilarity.[211]

V

§34. Apart from the rites of mortification, purgation, invigoration, and jubilation, the topocosmic character of seasonal crises is expressed also by two other constant elements, viz., the *return of the dead* and the *communal meal.*

§35. The belief that the dead return at seasonal festivals is attested throughout the ancient and modern worlds.[212] The underlying idea, as we can now recognize, is that these occasions are of concern not only to the actual and present but equally to the ideal and durative community. Thus, in Babylon, it was believed that the dead "ascended" and ate of the sacrifices offered in connection with the annual weeping for Tammuz, the god of fertility;[213] while a ritual calendar states explicitly that in the month of Ab (August) the "heroes ascend from the courts of the netherworld."[214] Similarly, in Egypt, it was the custom at Siut to light lamps for the dead on the last and first days of the year — a practice which survives in our modern Feast of All Souls.[215]

Among the Persians, the dead were held to return at the Feast of Tirajan.[216] The Mandaeans used to celebrate a feast of the dead in the New Year month of Tishri;[217] while to this day Jews visit the graves of parents between the first (New Year) and tenth (Day of Atonement) of Tishri, and during the whole of the preceding month.[218] According to the lexicographer Hesychius, the Greeks believed that the dead returned at the Festival of Anthesteria, in March;[219] while the Romans included in their spring festivals the Parentalia, or Feast of the Ancestral Dead, and the Lemuria, or Feast of Ghosts.[220] They also held a festival of the dead on January 1,[221] just as in other parts of Europe it is still held on the eve of the old New Year, viz., November 1 (Allhallows Night). In the Trobriand Islands there is an annual feast called Milmala at which the dead are believed to return;[222] while the Tuareg visit ancestral graves on the first day of the lenten period of Ramadan.[223] The Zunī in western New Mexico visit the sacred lake of the dead at the summer solstice, the return therefrom marking the inauguration of the summer dances.[224] The Mordovins hold feasts of the dead both in spring and in autumn.[225] In Tongking a festival of the dead, called Kin-tien, is held annually in December;[226] while at Krasnagorka, in Russia, a similar pagan festival (now largely Christianized) is (or was) held between Easter and Whitsun.[227] The Tepozteclans of Mexico keep an annual Vigil of All Souls, when they offer meats to the dead and await their return.[228] The Siamese hold that the dead return at their New Year feast in April;[229] while the Celtic winter Festival of Samhaim included a feast of the dead.[230] Similarly, Jewish folklore entertains the fancy that the tribal patriarchs of Israel visit their descendants during the autumnal harvest Festival of Booths (Sukkoth) in the capacity of honored guests (*ushpizin;* Latin, *hospes*).[231] In ancient Mexico, the seventeenth of the twenty periods into which the year was divided was called Tititl, or Commemoration of the Dead, and was followed by a feast of increase.[232] Among the Huzul of the Ukraine, dead ancestors are thought to return at Easter and Christmas. Money is provided for them, and the congregation kneels and prays, "O God, let all the dead and lost return and drink with us."[233]

Sometimes, indeed, the laying of ancestral ghosts figures as an essential part of the seasonal ceremonies. Among the Greeks, for example, the last day of the Festival of Anthesteria, held in early spring, was marked by a rite designed to exorcise the *kêres* or spirits who were believed to be roaming the earth at this season;[234] while at the Roman Festival of Lemuria, held in May, the father of each household solemnly banished the ancestral ghosts, exclaiming nine times, "Depart, ancestral spirits (*Manes exite paterni*)."[235, 236]

§36. The communal meal is a standard element of seasonal celebrations. Indeed, the very fact that "feast" and "festival" have come to be virtual synonyms is eloquent testimony to its prevalence. So well known is it, in fact, that it would be superfluous to accumulate examples.[237] The significant point is, however, that these meals are almost invariably believed to involve the presence of gods as well as mortals. So basic, indeed, is this conception that it even leads to a diversity of view as to which is host and which is guest. Thus, among the Babylonians, the New Year (Akitu) Festival was popularly known as the "feast" (*kirêtu*) of the gods,[238] and once a year — probably on that occasion — a collation (*tâkultu*) was offered to them.[239] Similarly, at Delphi, the Greeks used annually to fete the gods in the month of March–April, which was therefore known as Theoxenios, or "month of the regalement of the gods."[240] On the other hand, a scholiast on Pindar speaks specifically of feasts at which the gods periodically entertained departed heroes,[241] and the Hebrew prophets sometimes include such a feast among those other features of the New Year Festival which they project into the picture of the final "day of Yahweh" (cf. Isaiah 25:6; Zephaniah 1:7).[242] In the long run, the divergence of view is not really important except inasmuch as it points to the real nature and significance of the banquets. They are not to be dismissed as mere expressions of jubilation on the part of men; rather are they ceremonies of communion at which, by the medium of commensality, the topocosmic bond is periodically renewed. This renewal naturally takes place at the moment when the topocosm enters a new lease of life, and since all the vicissitudes of that entity possess at once a durative as well as a punctual element (see Chapter One), gods as well as mortals are perforce involved. The point is well brought out in the classic formulation of Robertson Smith:

> Primarily the circle of common religion and of common social duties was identical with that of natural kinship, and the god himself was conceived as a being of the same stock with his worshippers. It was natural, therefore, that the kinsmen and their kindred god should seal and strengthen their fellowship by meeting together from time to time to nourish their common life by a common meal.[243]

VI

§37. Finally, there is one other aspect of the seasonal festivals to which attention must be directed: *they are often made to coincide with the solstice or equinox.* The Asianic mysteries of Attis, for example, culminated in the triumphant re-emergence of that god of fertility on the day of the vernal equinox (March 25).[244] Similarly, in Mesopotamia, the rites of Tammuz were held in the month of the spring solstice;[245] and the prophet Ezekiel, though he seems to have muddled his dates, expressly associates the weeping for that god with a ceremony of adoring the rising sun (Ezekiel 8:14–16). Moreover, an old Assyrian calendar for the month of Tammuz prescribes significantly that the "weeping" for that god, which is to take place on the first day, is to be followed immediately, on the second, by "the presentation of gifts to the sun-god";[246] while a Babylonian hymn belonging to the Tammuz cycle represents the sun-god as assuring the sister of the dead genius of fertility that he himself would restore to her "the verdure which hath been removed" and "the crushed grain which hath been carried away."[247] Significant also is the fact that among the Israelites, both the spring festival (Pentecost) and the autumn Festival of Ingathering fell in the months of the equinoxes, the latter being expressly associated with that event in the ritual calendar of Exodus 34:22.[248] This is especially noteworthy because the same solar association of the great seasonal festivals appears already, at an earlier period, in the Canaanite texts from Ras Shamra-Ugarit. *The Poem of the Gracious Gods,* which can be shown to have been the "book of words" for the spring festival, includes a liturgical invocation in which, in addition to those deities, the sun-goddess (Shapash) also is adored. Similarly, in the *Poem of Baal,* which is really the cult myth of the autumn festival, a particularly important role is assigned to this same sun-goddess. It is she who retrieves Baal, genius of rainfall and fertility, from the netherworld (I AB i, 8–16), and it is she who urges his rival Môt, genius of drought and sterility, to give up the fight against him (I AB vi, 22–29). Indeed, so cardinal a part does she play in behalf of Baal that she is formally commended in words which look uncommonly as though they had been incorporated by the poet from some traditional hymn (ibid., 40–52).[249] Again, it should be observed that in Syria and the eastern portions of the Roman Empire the Festival of the "New Age" was likewise combined with an important solar date, viz., the alleged birthday of the sun on November 18.[250] An inscription first published by Domaszewski and containing the text of an order issued by Licinius to his troops in Salsovia describes the celebration of that day.[251] Similarly, the *Acta Dasii* refer to the observance of an analogous festival of Kronos held at Durostorum (Silistria) on the same date;[252] and it is now established that in Roman times Kronos was identified with the sun-god (Hêlios).[253] The same date, it should be added, was claimed by Clement of Alexandria as the birthday of the Christian Savior.[254] Indeed, so firmly established was the connection between the festivals of new life and the worship of the sun that the Church was obliged to fix Christmas on what had originally been the birthday of the solarized savior Mithra and to associate the date of Christ's resurrection (Easter) with the vernal equinox.[255] Similarly, the Irish celebration of Lammastide, in August, was associated with the worship of Lug, the sun-god.[256]

The reason for this association is not hard to fathom: the re-emergence of the sun, especially in spring, was an obvious date from which to reckon the renewal of the world's vitality; *vere natus orbis est.*[257] Similarly, the decline of the sun was a natural occasion from which to date the eclipse of such vitality.

VII

§38. Up to this point we have been considering the seasonal ceremonies as rites performed collectively by the community as a whole. In course of time, however, the tendency arises to concentrate them in a single individual who is taken to personify and epitomize the entire group or topocosm as it appears in its contemporary aspect. This individual is the king — that is, the representative of the "kin" or social organism (cp. O.E. *kyn-ig,* German, *könig*). He is regarded as at once the vessel and the steward of communal and topocosmic vitality. Consequently, all the things which were previously done by the group as a whole in order to ensure and maintain its existence now tend to be done representatively by the king.[258] Thus, in place of the communal mortification when the lease of life comes to an end, it is the king who now suffers a ritual passion, fasting and abasing himself, and being ultimately "killed," or deposed.[259] Similarly, instead of the whole group's performing acts of sexual promiscuity in order to achieve regeneration, the same end is now served by the king's indulging in a ritual marriage with a specially chosen bride.[260] And instead of the whole group's subsequently greeting its rebirth in rites of jubilation, it is now the king who is ceremonially reinstated, or, if he has been killed, replaced by a successor.[261]

§39. This prominence of the king in seasonal ceremonies is especially well attested in the ancient Near East. The Babylonian New Year (Akitu) festivities, for example, included a ritual abasement and reinstatement of the king.[262] The Egyptian seasonal festival at Memphis (and probably also at Edfu and other centers) was accompanied by a coronation.[263] The Attis mysteries celebrated in March included a sacrifice *pro salute imperatoris.*[264] The Hittite festival of the "day of the year" featured prayers for the king and queen.[265] Nor is the custom by any means confined to the Orient or to ancient times. As Frazer has pointed out,[266] it is this usage which really underlies the European custom of crowning a mock king or queen on the first of May.[267]

NOTES

For complete titles of works cited, see Bibliography.

1. On the pagan antecedents of Lent, cf. GB ix, 347 ff.; on those of Ramadan, cf. Welhausen, *Reste,*[2] 97.

2. KAV, p. 120, II, 22–38; KAR 177, rev. iii. Cf. Labat, *Royauté,* 315.

3. Leviticus 16.

4. Aristophanes, *Birds,* 1519; Plutarch, *De Is. et Os.,* 69. The fast was projected into myth: the Homeric *Hymn to Demeter,* which was probably designed for a "mystery," represents the Mother Goddess as abstaining from food during the search for Persephone (ll. 49–50), and the same detail is preserved also by Callimachus, *Dem.,* 17. See Spanheim, *Callimachus,* 671 f.; Hermann, *Gottesd. Alterthümer,* ed. Stark, §56.18; Roscher, "Die enneadischen Fristen," in ASGW 12 (1903), 14 ff.

5. Diodorus Sic., v. 4; Plato, *Epist.,* 349D; cf. Allen-Sikes-Halliday, *Homeric Hymns,* 135.

6. Farnell, *Cults,* iii. 34.

6a. Philostratus, *Heroica* xx 24; Frazer, *Fasti* iii 23.

7. Julian, *Or.,* v. 173 D ff.; 177 A; Arnobius, v 16; Tertullian, *De jejunio,* xvi; Sallustius, *De diis et mundo* iv; Hepding, *Attis,* 182 ff.

8. Jejunium Cereris (in October), Livy, xxxvi 37; Ovid, *Met.* x 432; *Fasti* iv 535; Arnobius, v 16; Petavius in Jul. *Or,* v, p. 88; Lobeck, *Aglaophamus,* i. 189; Böttiger, *Kunstm.,* i. 132; Wissowa, *Rel. u. Kultus d. Römer,*[1] 246; Marquardt, *Rom. Staatsverwaltung,*[2] iii. 372, n. 3; Wissowa, in PW iii 1780.—CIL i 811 (v 87) mentions a [*C*]*ereres Cast*[*us*].

9. Livy, xxxix 9.

10. Cabaton, ERE iii 161a. Fasting is also observed during the three-to-four-month period of "retreat" which begins in July. It is significant that the word *vosa,* which denotes this retreat, is identical with the Pali *vassa,* "rainy season."

11. Spence, ERE iii 507a, 568b. *Busk* = *pusikta,* "fasting."

12. Adair, *Hist. Amer. Indians,* 96 ff.

13. Palmer, "The Tribes of the 35th Parallel," in *Harper's* magazine 17 (1889), 451.

14. Skeat, ERE viii 358b.

15. Hodson, *Naga Tribes of Manipur,* 167 ff.; *idem,* in JAI 36 (1906), 94 f.

16. Seler, ERE iii 308b.

17. *Ibid.,* 309a.

18. Seligman, *Melanesians of Br. New Guinea,* 590.

19. Chateaubriand, *Voyage en Amérique,* 130 f.

20. Brown, *New Zealand and its Aborigines,* 113.

21. Prescott, *Peru,* 50.

21a. Westermarck, *Pagan Survivals,* 148–49.

22. Friedlaender, *Jewish Religion,* 412; Schauss, *Jewish Festivals,* 101–02.

23. Schauss, *op. cit.;* 96 ff. But there is evidence that the fast really antedated the destruction of the Second Temple, for in TB Ta'anith 12a, Eleazar ben Zadok, who lived before that event, already alludes to it; cf. Bacher, *Agada der Tannaiten,* i 46–47; Weiss, *Dor Dor ve-Doreshav,* ii 120.

24. Langdon, *Menologies,* 119–26.

25. Friedlaender, *op. cit.,* 392. Cf. Ovid, *Fasti* ii 557–58; v 487, and Frazer *in loc.;* Porphyrion on Horace, *Ep.* ii 2, 209 (p. 343 Meyer). In general, cf. Gaidoz, "Le mariage en mai," in *Mélusine* 7 (1894), 105–11.

26. Minns, ERE ix 573b.

27. Robertson Smith, *Rel. Sem.,*[3] 434 f.; Crawley, *Mystic Rose,*[2] i 186.

28. GB viii 73, 75 ff., 83; ix 291 ff.

29. Seler, ERE iii 308a.

30. *Ibid.,* viii 506a.

31. *Census of India,* 1911, vol. x, 144, quoted in Frazer, *Fasti* ii 40.

32. Littmann, *Princeton Exped. to Abyssinia,* ii 245; cf. Frazer, *Fasti, loc. cit.*

33. Frazer, *op. cit.,* ii 45–46, 48; *idem,* GB vi (*Scapegoat*) 313 ff.

34. Cf. Loth, "Les douze jours supplémentaires (*gourdeziou*) des Bretons et les douze jours Germains et Indous," in RC 24 (1903), 311 ff.; MacCulloch, ERE iii 79 ff.; Frazer, *op. cit.,* ii 46 f. It is contended by A. Weber (SBAW 37 [1898], 2 ff.) that the twelve days are mentioned already as a sacred season in Brahmana literature, but this is questioned by Schrader, ERE ii 47b.

34a. S. Friberger, *Das Fasten im Alten Israel* (Agram, 1929); Heinisch, "Die Trauergebraüche bei den Israeliten," in *Biblische Zeitfragen* 13 (1931), 7–8, pp. 70 ff.

35. JAI 12 (1882), 142.

36. Williams-Calvert, *Fiji,* i 169.

37. Turner, *Samoa,* 142.

38. Ki Li, in SBE xxvii 87.

39. Ross, *Corea* 322.

40. ERE v 760b. In South Africa the fasting is restricted to one day: JAI 19 (1890), 280.

41. Thomson, *Through Masai Land,* 57.

42. Im Thurm, *Indians of Guiana,* 222.

43. Bancroft, *Pacific States,* i 111.

44. Cf. Reifmann, in *Kochebê Yizhaq,* 32 (1865), 31.

44a. Crawley, *Mystic Rose,*[2] ii 12, 60–61.

45. Charlevoix, *Nouvelle France,* vi 67.

46. GB, one-vol. ed., 600–01.

47. *Ibid.*

48. *Ibid.*

49. *Ibid.;* Radin, "Some Aspects of Puberty Fasting among the Ojibwa," in *Canad. Geol. Mus.,* 1914.

50. ERE v 761b.

51. Howitt, in JAI 13 (1884), 455; 14 (1885), 316.

52. Palmer, in JAI 13 (1884), 295.

53. Haddon, in JAI 19 (1890), 309.

54. ERE v 761b.

55. Herodotus, ii 40 (Isis); Cumont, *Mithra,* tr. Showerman, 141, 160; *supra,* n. 7 (Attis). The Syrian Christians used likewise to fast before the "holy mysteries": Budge, *Governors,* ii 666; cf. Angus, *Mystery Rel. and Christianity,* 85 ff.

56. Cf. the initiatory formula, *enêsteusa* ("I fasted"), Clem. Alex., *Protrep.* ii 18; Dieterich, *Mithrasliturgie* 21.

57. Gaster, in FL 49 (1938), 367–68.

58. Cf. also Leviticus 23: 27, 32; Numbers 29:7; Psalms 35:13; Isaiah 58:3, 5.

59. II Kings 10:20; Joel 1:14; 2:15; Isaiah 1:13. The word is often used as a parallel to "solemn assembly" (Leviticus 23:36; Numbers 29:35; Deuteronomy 16:8) or to "feast" (Amos 5:21; Nehemiah 8:18; II Chronicles 7:9).

60. Cf. Schwally, *Sem. Kriegsalterthümer*, 60. The word *'aṣereth* is also used for the fiftieth day after Passover (i.e., Pentecost) and Tabernacles (MR Cant. vii 2 §2; PRK §30; Josephus, *Ant.* iii. 10, 6), and in modern Arabic it denotes Easter. Cf. also E. Katsch, in VT 2 (1952), 65 f.

61. Cf. Van Selms, "Weenen als aanvengsrite," NTT 24 (1935), 119–27.

62. Diodorus Sic., i 14.

63. Herodotus, ii 79; Julius Pollux, iv 54; Pausanias, ix 29, 7; Athenaeus, xiv 11, 620 A.

64. Brugsch, *Adonisklage u. Linoslied*, 24; Wiedemann, *Herodotos zweites Buch*, 24–26.

65. Cf. J. de Horrack, *Les lament. d'Isis et Nephthys* (1866); Budge, *Osiris* ii 59–66; Moret, *Mystères égypt.*, 24–26. The text is preserved also, in later literary form, in a Berlin papyrus: Moret, *Rois et dieux*, 89.

66. *De errore prof. relig. ii* 7 (addressed to the Egyptians): *Cur plangitis fruges terrae et crescentia lugetis semina?* Cf. also Diodorus, i 14, 2; Moret, *Mise à mort du dieu en Égypte*, 19 ff.

67. Herod., ii 48, etc. Similarly, at the Festival of Adonis, the lament was accompanied on the flute: Glotz, in RGG 33 (1920), 206.

68. Moret, *Mise à mort* 21 (and fig. 2); Montet, *Scènes de la vie privée de l'ancien empire*, 201–02, Pl. xvi.

69. Oppenheim, in BASOR 103 (1946), 11–14.

70. Dalman, *Arbeit u. Sitte*, i 566.

71. Plutarch, *Thes.* 22 (reading *spendontes*, with Cornford, for the *speudontes* of the mss.).

72. Semus, *apud* Athen., xiv, 618 E; cf. Spanheim, *Callimachus*, 649.

73. Rohde, *Psyche*,[1] 289.

74. GB vii (Corn and Wild), ch. vii. For the laments in the Osiris cult, cf. Moret, "Rituels agraires de l'ancien Orient . . ." in *Annuaire de l'hist. de Phil. et d'hist. orientales* 3 (1935), 311 ff.; for the Attis cult, cf. Hepding, *Attis*, 128, 196; Diod. Sic., iii 59, 7; Plutarch, *Alcibiades* 18; Arrian, *Tactica* 33.4; for the Adonis cult, cf. Sappho, 63, 108 Wharton; Ammianus Marcellinus, xxii 9, 15; xix. 1, 11; Aristophanes, *Lys.*, 365–661; Theocritus, *Idyll.* xv; Bion, *Epitaph. Adonidos* 1, 40. Cf. also Jeremiah 22:18 (omitting *ve-hoi ahoth*, with LXX); 34:5. For the weeping in the Babylonian Akitu ceremonies, cf. VAT 9555. 29.

75. "For Tammuz, the husband of thy youth hast thou instituted weeping [*bitakku*] from year to year."

76. CT XV, Pl. 48.

77. Langdon, *Menologies,* 120 f.
78. Labat, RA 38 (1941), 28.
79. Cf. Proclus in Plato, *Rep.* i 215, Kroll; Marinus, *Vita Procli,* c. 33 Boissonade.
80. Chwolson, *Ssabier,* ii 27.
81. On the derivation of divine names from ritual cries, cf. G. Hoffmann, in ZA 11 (1896), 229.
82. See above, n. 72.
83. Kretschmer, in *Glotta* 14 (1923), 13.
84. Klausen, *Aeneas u. die Penaten,* i. 121, endorsed by Gruppe, *Griech. Mythol.,* 966, n. 6. On the lityerses song, cf. Theocritus, x 41; Athenaeus, 619A, and, especially, Photius, *Bibl.* i 54 and Scholiast on Theocritus, *loc. cit.*
85. Pausanias, iv 31, 4.
86. Brugsch, *op. cit.;* Movers, *Phönizier,* i 246; Mannhardt, WFK ii 281; Stammer, *De Lino* (1855); Eissfeldt, "Linos u. Aliyan," in *Mélanges Dussaud* i, 161 ff.
87. Oppenheim, in BASOR, No. 103.
88. Welcker, *Schriften* i 27 ff. Cf. also Schwenk, *Mythol. d. Slawen,* 227–29.
89. Canney, *Givers of Life,* 54 f., 60 f.; *idem,* "The Magic of Tears," in JMEOS 12 (1926), 47–54.
90. Kruijt, ERE vii 234a. Cf. also P. Ten Kate, "Het endefeest" (on the funeral feast of the Toradjas) in C. Medl. N. Zendel, 1913. (I have not seen this study.)
91. ERE vii 234; xii 127a.
92. Hecquard, *Reise an die Küste und in das Innere von West-Afrika* (1854), 41–43, quoted in GB viii 9.
93. Macpherson, *Mem. Service in India,* 113–31 (GB vii 248, n. 2).
94. Sahagun, ed. Jourdanet-Simon, ii. 86.
95. Cf. A. Krappe, *Balor,* 26; Wensinck, in AcOr I (1923), 183 ff.; Dombart, in JSOR 8 (1924), 115; Furlani, in SMSR 4 (1928), 1–16, 305–07.
96. ET 1925, 44 f.; Hvidberg, "Vom Weinen und Lachen im AT," in ZAW 57 (1939), 150–52.
97. In seeking evidence of magical weeping caution must be exercised, lest this interpretation be imposed wrongly on what are really but meaningless survivals of mourning proper. Thus, when Cherokee priests weep at the four corners of the field after working the first corn (GB, one-vol. ed., 372), or when the inhabitants of Oldenburg, in Germany, perform similar rites (Strackerjan, i 47), there is no reason to conclude that anything more is involved than a mere attenuation of some primitive mourning over the crops. Nevertheless, it is extremely difficult, and often virtually impossible, to decide whether a given practice is a genuine case of magical weeping or a mere survival of ritual mourning.

98. Cf. Frazer, *Fasti* ii 278: "Among peoples of the lower culture the ceremonies of public purification, which take the form of a general expulsion of devils, seem generally to fall at the end of the year in order that the people may make a clean start in the new year, having rid themselves, as they imagine, of all the baneful influences that have troubled them in the past." Such purifications are described in GB vi (*Scapegoat*), 224 ff.

99. Frazer, *Fasti* ii 19. Varro, *De lingua latina* vi 34, says that February is so named *quod tum februatur populus.*

100. Joh. Lydus, *De mensibus* iv 25; p. 84 Wuensch.

101. Tibullus II, i 1–20; cf. Preller, *Griech. Mythol.*,[4] i 419 ff.

102. Ovid, *Fasti* i 669; see Frazer *in loc.*

103. Leviticus 16:8–10.

104. Cf. Harpocration, s.v. *pharmakos;* Helladius, *apud* Photius, *Bibl.*, c. 279, p. 534; Harrison, *Prolegomena*, 95 ff., Murray, *Rise of the Greek Epic*, Appendix A. A similar rite took place at Chaeronea: Plutarch, *Quaest. Symp.*, vi 8.

105. GB, one-vol. ed., 554.

106. *Ibid.*, 559.

107. *Ibid.*

108. *Ibid.*, 555.

109. *Ibid.*, 556.

110. *Ibid.*, 557.

111. *Ibid.*

112. *Ibid.*, 559.

113. *Ibid.*, 551.

114. *Ibid.*, 555.

The periodic expulsion of evil spirits must be sharply distinguished from that of ghosts and ancestral spirits, which often takes place at or about the same time. The two things naturally tend to overlap, and they are all too frequently confused by modern investigators. But they are really quite distinct, the latter being but the natural corollary of the belief that the dead rejoin their erstwhile communities at times of topocosmic crisis. We shall therefore reserve the discussion of it until later.

115. GB, one-vol. ed., 558.

116. Aston, *Shinto* (1921), 71–72.

117. Seligman, *Races of Africa*, 72.

118. On fire in purificatory rites, see Blackman, FL 27 (1916), 352–77; C. C. Ellis, *A History of Fire and Flame* (1932); P. E. Froment, *Essai sur le rôle du feu en religion* (1900); J. Hertel, *Die arische Feuerlehre* (1925–31); H. Khunrath, *De igne magorum philosophorumque* (1608); T. F. Dexter, *Fire-Worship in Britain* (1931); Hull, *Folklore of the British Isles*, 229; GB vii/1, 106 ff.

119. GB, one-vol. ed., 561.

120. Westermarck, *Pagan Survivals*, 148, 169 ff.

121. Cf. Monchicourt, *Revue Tunisienne* 17 (1910), 293 ff.

122. K 3476, obv. 8.

123. Tosefta, Shabbat vi 10–11; Scheftelowitz, *Altpaläst. Bauernglaube,* 69 f.

124. Brand, *Antiquities,* 304; GB, one-vol. ed., 614, 617, 632, 635, 636, 706; Saintyves, *Essais de folklore biblique,* 42 f.

125. Sethe, *Dram. Texte,* 139, n. 2.

126. Faulkner, JEA 22 (1936), 122.

127. KAVI 120 ii 22–38; Langdon, *Menologies,* 105.

128. On these rites, cf. Landsberger, *Kult. Kalender,* 79; Hooke, *Myth and Ritual,* 52–53; Morgenstern, AJSL 55 (1938), 22; Dürr, *Heilandserwartung,* 138. The gods themselves underwent purification: Landsberger, 70, n. 4; Zimmern, in *Nöldeke Festschrift,* 959 ff.; Frank, *Studien z. bab. Rel.,* I–II, 28. This took place at the beginning of the month: CT XXXII 12 iv 3; 17 iv 12.

129. Leviticus 16.

130. Westermarck, *Pagan Survivals,* 147.

131. Seler, ERE iii 308b.

132. GB, one-vol. ed., 122 ff.; ERE viii 501a.

133. KUB XXV 31. 7.

134. Macrobius, *Sat.* 1. 12, 6; Solinus, i. 35. The custom was later transferred to January 1: *Geoponica* ii 2; Libanius, *Kal. Descr. T.I.* 75; Ausonius, *Caes. tempus imperii* xii; Sidonius Apollinaris, *Carm.* ii 8; cf. Frazer, *Fasti* iii 36 f.

135. Nilsson, *Gr. Feste,* 402–08; Mannhardt, WFK,[2] i. 33 f., 48; GB vii 98; ix 173, 180 ff.; Warde Fowler, *Festivals,* 290; Usener, ARW 7 (1905), 297–313; Rose, FL 36 (1936), 322; Blackman, in Hooke's *Myth and Ritual,* 22–24; Lesky, in ARW 28 (1926), 73–82; Ehelolf, SPAW (1925), 267–72; Frazer, *Aftermath,* 375; *idem, Pausanias,* iii 267 f.; Banks, *Calendar Customs,* i 19 ff.; Sartori, *Sitte u. Brauch,* iii 120 f., 133 f.; 165, 179, 195, 271; Calderon, CR 26 (1913), 79 ff.

136. Grimm, *Teutonic Mythology,* ii 764 ff.

137. Sartori, *Neueste Reise durch Oesterreich,* ii 348.

138. Grimm, *op. cit.,* 769.

139. Mannhardt, WFK[2] iii 81, n. 4.

140. GB iv (*Dying God*), 354.

141. Ralston, *Songs of the Russian People,* 241.

142. Bray, in *Census of India,* 1911, iv, pt. i, 65 ff.; Frazer, *Aftermath,* 75–77.

143. Winstedt, *Shama, Saiva and Sufi,* 92.

144. Gray, ERE vii 422b.

145. Czaplicka, ERE xii 829a.

146. Alford, FL 39 (1929), 68; 41 (1931), 266.

147. For ritual combats at the feasts of Daulis in Argos, at the Katagôgia in Ephesus, and for the *lithobolia* at Troezen and the *ballachiadai* at Argos, cf. Nilsson, *Gr. Feste,* 402; Usener, ARW 8 (1910), 297; Mannhardt, i 548 f. Warde Fowler, *Festivals,* 290.

148. Nilsson, 413; cf. *supra,* n. 135.

149. ii 63 (at Papremis). For such a combat at Edfu, cf. Erman,

Handbook of Egyptian Religion, 215 ff.; Brugsch, *Drei Festkalender des Tempels von Apollinopolis Magna,* 12 f.

150. Brugsch, *Thesaurus* v 1190. The relief is reproduced, from a drawing by Erman, in Hooke, *Myth and Ritual,* fig. 4, opp. p. 22. Cf. also Ramesseum Drama, Scene 18.

151. Spence, *Mythologies of Mexico and Peru,* 40.

152. See below, pp. 267 ff.

153. Sethe, *Untersuchungen,* iii 134; Hooke, *Myth and Ritual,* 22.

154. KUB XVII 35 iii 9–17, translated below, pp. 268 ff.

155. Ewald, *History of Israel,*[4] tr. Martineau, iii 14.

156. *Vita Alexandri* xxxi. Curiously enough, folk plays introducing "Alexander of Macedon" are likewise performed, during Christmas week, in parts of Scotland: cf. Banks, *Calendar Customs,* ii 111.

157. Livy, xl 6 ff.

158. ARW 7 (1904), 301.

159. Banks, *op. cit.,* i 16.

160. Hone, *Mysteries,* 476. More precisely, it is asserted that the battle commemorates a great massacre of the Danes in England which took place on St. Brice's Day in 1002, during the reign of Ethelred.

161. CQ 4 (1911), 283; Cornford, *Origins of Attic Comedy,* 67.

162. ERE v 841b.

163. See below, Part Three.

164. Sartori, *Sitte u. Brauch,* iii 156, n. 76.

165. Banks, *op. cit.,* i 19.

166. *Ibid.,* 23.

167. Brand, *Antiquities,* i 92.

168. *Statistical Account,* 18 (1796), 88.

169. Bullen, *Lyrics from the Dramatists of the Elizabethan Age,* 293 (commenting on Francis Beaumont's *Ralph the Maylord,* 55–56: "With scarfs and garters as you please/And 'Hey for our town' cried"). Cf. also *idem, Lyrics from Elizabethan Songbooks,* 68: "Then all at once 'For our town' cries, 'Pipe on, for we will have the prize!' "

170. GB vii (*Corn and Wild*), i, ch. iii.

171. Zimmern, in BSGW 70 (1918), fasc. 5, p. 8.

172. GB viii, 92 ff.

173. Cf. Fries, MVAG 15 (1910), ii. 4.

174. I.e., *raksas.*

175. Thurston, *Omens and Superstitions of S. India,* 299; Frazer, *Aftermath,* 375.

176. *National Statistical Account* 5 (1839), i 544.

177. Ovid, *Fasti* iii 523 f. (with Frazer's note); Fowler, *Festivals* 50–54.

178. GB, one-vol. ed., 136–37.

179. *Ibid.,* 136.

180. *Ibid.*, 137. Analogous is the Portuguese custom of *rebolada*, observed in May, before the reaping of flax, at Arçal near Valença do Minho and at Santo Tirso: couples roll together in the fields; Gallop, *Portugal*, 11.

181. *Ibid.*, 136.

182. GB, 137.

183. Brincker, "Charakter u. Gebräuche spez. der Bantu Deutsch-Südwestafrikas," in *Mitt. d. Seminar f. Orient. Sparchen zu Berlin*, iii (1900), p. 2.

184. Fehlinger, *Sexual Life of Primitive People*, 23.

185. *Ibid.*, 15; Playfair, *Garos* 68.

186. Ovid, *Fasti* iii 195 ff. (cf. ii 139); Livy i 13; Plutarch, *Romulus* 14; Dio Halic. ii 45–46.

187. Frazer, *Fasti* ii 51.

188. Lorenz, ARW 17 (1915), 342.

189. Wolf, *Opet*, 43.

190. But see Spence, *Myth and Ritual in Dance, Games and Rhyme*, 42–43, for a different explanation.

191. Westermarck, *Short History of Marriage*, 28.

192. Mishnah, Ta'anith iv. 8.

193. Hazlitt, *Dict. of Faiths and Folklore*, s.v. Similarly, Chapman asserts in his *Monsieur d'Olive*, f. 4 verso, that St. Luke's Day (October 18) is propitious "for to choose husbands."

194. Howes, FL 40 (1929), 56–57.

195. Spence, ERE iii 67a.

196. Cf. E. O. James, "Initiation Rituals" in Hooke's *Myth and Ritual*; ERE, s.v. *Initiation*. Cf. also Malinowski, *Magic, Science, etc.*, 21: "The ordeal (of initiation) is usually associated with the idea of the death and rebirth of the initiated one, which is sometimes enacted in a mimetic performance." The idea comes out also in the use of the word *teleutan*, "die," in the sense of "to be initiated"; cf. Foucart, *Les mystères d'Eleusis*, 56. The theme is fully discussed by Mircea Eliade in his *Birth and Rebirth* (New York, 1958), 28–29, 31–32, 36–37.

197. Exodus 12:48; Joshua 5:2–9.

198. Barton, *Sketch of Sem. Origins*, 99.

199. Doughty, *Arabia Deserta*, i 340–42; Canaan, JPOS 6 (1925), 117 ff.; Snouck Hurgronje, *Mekka*, ii 141–43.

200. Chamberlain, ERE vi 471b.

201. H. Kuper, *Among the Swazi*. The ceremony was filmed in *Pathé Gazette*, March 5, 1931.

202. *Ibid.*, n. 194.

203. I Timothy 3:6.

204. Firmicus Maternus, *De errore prof. rel.*, xviii 1–2; Hepding, *Attis* 194 f.

205. D'Alviella, ERE vii 318a.

206. GB² ix 225 ff.

207. However, in considering these seasonal rites of initiation

we should not overlook the fact that another idea also comes into play. As observed above, seasonal crises involve not only the immediate generation of the here and now but the entire totality of past, present, and anticipated future, which together make up the durative and infinite continuity of the topocosm. Accordingly, at all such crises the unborn and "uninitiated" have also to be included in the community, and formal initiation provides a means of doing so. Conversely, as we shall see later, the ancestral dead are also believed to attend the ceremonies.

208. See especially, Spence, *op. cit.*, 28.

209. Cal. Philocal., CIL I² 334; Wissowa, *Rel. u. Kultus d. Römer,*² 295. The festival fell on November 3.

210. Hepding, *Attis,* 167 ff.; Marquardt, *Röm. Staatsverwaltung,*² ii 372. The festival ended on March 25.

211. Plautus, *Menaech.*, i, 1; Livy, xii 56. Cf. Spanheim, *Callimachus,* 677.

212. GB iv (*Adonis, Attis, Osiris*), ii 51–83.

213. IV R vi, rev. 56–58.

214. KAVI 218, p. 219, ii 1–16.

215. Erman, ZÄS 19 (1882), 164.

216. Mohammed abu Thaleb of Damascus, *apud* Thompson, *Semitic Magic,* 14.

217. Chwolsohn, *Ssabier,* ii 31.

218. Schaeffer, *Myst. Osiris in Abydos,* 114.

219. Hesychius, s.v. *Anthesteria.*

220. Ovid, *Fasti* ii 33–34, 533, 548; v 486; Joh. Lydus, *De mensibus* iv 29.

221. Schneider, ARW 20 (1918), 375–76.

222. Malinowski, *Myth in Prim. Psychology,* 100–01.

223. Rennel Rodd, *People of the Veil,* 274.

224. Kroeber, ERE, xii 871b.

225. Paasonen, ERE viii 847a.

226. Cabaton, ERE xii 380b.

227. Urlin, *Festivals,* 88.

228. Redfield, *Tepoztlan.*

229. GB vi (*Scapegoat*), 150–51.

230. Hull, *Folklore of the British Isles,* 33.

231. Eisenstein, *Otsar Dinim u-Minhagim,* s.v. *ushpizin;* Schauss, *Jewish Festivals,* 92. According to Morgenstern, UJE ii 530, *lel shimmurim* ("night of watching") in Exodus 12:42 refers to a vigil for the returning dead at the vernal equinox. This, however, is extremely doubtful.

232. Seler, ERE viii 616 a–b.

233. *Rapporteur* at the late Ruth Benedict's seminar on folklore, Columbia University, 1943.

234. Harrison, *Ancient Art and Ritual,* 147 f.

235. Philostratus, *Heroica* xx 24; Frazer, *Fasti* ii 23.

236. The belief that the dead return for the annual or seasonal

festivals must be sharply distinguished from another with which it is apt to be confused and with which it tends, indeed, to overlap — namely, the belief that ghosts, specters, and evil spirits then haunt mankind. In Syria, for example, the epagomenal days at the end of February are regarded as a time when spirits are abroad; and in Jewish superstition the same belief is entertained concerning the month of Adar, immediately preceding the vernal New Year (v. Midrash Konen, in Jellinek's *Beth Ha-Midrash,* ii 37; Wohlstein, ZA 8 [1893], 339, n. 19). A similar notion also obtains in Morocco in respect of the first ten days of the New Year month of Muharram (Westermarck, *Pagan Survivals,* 148), and among the Chinka of the Caucasus (Bleichsteiner, *Realencycl. d. Vorgeschichte,* vi 258b). This idea ties in rather with the conception of the preharvest and pre-New Year period as especially critical, open to the machinations of noxious powers. But, of course, these powers are very easily confused with the ancestral spirits who are likewise abroad at this season, so that ceremonies originally designed to purge the former tend to develop into pious adieus to the latter.

237. Thomsen, ARW 7 (1909), 464 ff.; Sykes, *Sacrifices,* 59 ff.; Robertson Smith, *Rel. Sem.,*[3] 268 ff., 596 f.; Driver, ICC on Exodus 18:12.

238. Landsberger, *Kalender,* 14; *ARAB,* ii §436 (building inscription for *akitu* chapel at Asshur); Pallis, *Akitu,* 173.

239. Labat, *Royauté,* 286–87.

240. Pindar, *Paean* vi, in Diel, *Anthol. Lyrica,* Supplementum, 60 ff.; Philodamus, *ibid.,* ii 252 f.; Pfister, P-W, v/2, 2256–58; Nilsson, *Feste,* 160 ff.

241. On Pindar, *Nem.* vii 168.

242. On the other hand, note that Deuteronomy 12:7 speaks of eating "in the presence of Yahweh"; on this, see S. A. Cook in Robertson Smith, *Rel. Sem.,*[3] 596.

243. Robertson Smith, *op. cit.,* 275.

244. Cf. Arnobius, v 42; Macrobius, *Sat.,* i, 21. 7–11; Hepding, *Attis,* 44, 63.

245. Langdon, *Menologies,* 119 ff.

246. Labat, RA 38 (1941), 28.

247. Langdon, *Tammuz and Ishtar,* 32.

248. Cf. also TJ Sanhedrin 18d.

249. See below, Commentary on *The Poem of Baal,* §LXXII.

250. Rankin, *Hanukkah,* 205 f.

251. *Ibid.,* 201.

252. Boll. ARW 19 (1916–19), 342; Weber, *ibid.,* 315 f.

253. Boll, *op. cit.,* 240; Rankin, 206 f.

254. Cf. Weber, *op. cit.,* 325 f.

255. Rankin, *op. cit.,* 201 f.

256. Hull, *Folklore of the British Isles,* 280.

257. *Pervigilium Veneris* 3.

258. Gaster, RR 9 (1945), 269–71.

259. GB, one-vol. ed., chap. xxiv. The killing is, of course, often purely mimetic.

260. GB ii 129–55; Herodotus, i 181; Johnston, JAOS 18 (1897), 153 ff.; Moret, *Royauté,* 48–73; Plutarch, *Qu. Conv.* viii, 1. 6; Demosthenes, *Contra N.,* 73–78; Aristotle, *Const. Athen.* iii. 5; Preller, *Gr. Mythol.,*[4] i 681 ff. For the sacred marriage in Crete, cf. Diod. Sic., v 73; at Samos, Lactantius, *Inst.* i 17; at Athens, Photius, s.v. *hieros gamos.* See fully Gruppe, *Griech. Mythol.,* 1134, n. 9.

261. Frankfort, *Kingship and the Gods,* 168–69, 183–84, 320.

262. Pallis, *Akitu,* 139 ff., 265 ff.; Labat, *Royauté,* 87 ff.; Thureau Dangin, *Rit, accad.,* 144, lines 415 ff.

263. Frankfort, *op. cit.,* 129–32.

264. Tertullian, *Apologetica,* ch. xxv. The same usage obtains also at New Year in Madagascar: Shaw, JTVI 20 (1887), 167.

265. Otten, in OLZ, 1956, 101 ff.

266. GB, one-vol. ed., 130, 157, 320.

267. In considering the role of the king in these ceremonies, it is important to realize the exact duplication of his functions with acts previously or even contemporaneously performed by the group as a whole. For the essence of the matter is that the king is merely an individual representative of his people and, in fact, of the topocosm in which they live. Failure to note this duplication has led to a gross misconstruction of his role and, indeed, of his entire position in primitive society. It has been assumed that he is simply the representative of the god and as such conveys the gifts of the god to the community of his worshipers, producing rain, and (by his "sacred marriage") insuring fecundity. If he is hedged with divinity, this is explained as due to the fact that he is but the incarnation of a god who imparts it to him; and if he suffers a passion as well as a triumph, this is accounted for by the assumption that he is merely personifying the dying and reviving god of the year — Tammuz, Osiris, Adonis, or the like. The truth is, however, that in playing the role he does, the king is actually doing no more than his people; they too "die" and are "revived," and they too produce rain and insure fecundity by means of sexual intercourse. Moreover, it is quite incorrect to say that the king is an incarnation of the god in the sense that he is a human being arbitrarily invested with divinity by some external and superior godhead. On the contrary, as the representative of the immediate topocosm, he *is* the god in his present, as distinct from his durative, aspect, and such divinity as he possesses is innate rather than conferred. See Gaster, T. H., "Divine Kingship in the Ancient Near East," in RR 9 (1945), 267 ff.

CHAPTER THREE

THE SEASONAL PATTERN IN ANCIENT NEAR EASTERN RITUAL

§1. On the basis of the foregoing evidence, it is now possible to construct the following picture of a typical seasonal ceremony. Such a picture is, of course, synthetic and composite, since all the elements rarely survive together in any single instance. Nevertheless, its typical and representative character is guaranteed by the fact that each of them is indeed widespread and not confined to any one particular culture.

The ceremony takes place on a crucial calendar date, often coincident with solstice or equinox, which marks the beginning of a new season or year.

I. It opens with a series of public rites designed to express the state of suspended animation which besets society and its total environment, i.e., the "topocosm," at the expiration of each annual or seasonal lease of life. These rites take the form of fasts, lents, and similar austerities.

The king, as representative of the topocosmic spirit, is deposed or slain.

II. This initial stage is frequently accompanied or followed by a "vacant period" marking the interval between the expiration of the old lease and the inauguration of the new. This period is regarded as "epagomenal," or outside the normal calendar. The customary order of society is reversed, the customary activities suspended.

A temporary king, or interrex, is appointed.

III. Next, machinery is set in motion to remove all evil influences and noxious powers. This is done by such ceremonies as the expulsion of human or animal scapegoats, the exorcism of demons, the lustration of crops, fields, and people by fire and water, and — in the more advanced cultures — by a ceremonial shriving of sin.

The king is ceremonially purified or performs penitential rites, often including a confession of sins.

IV. The negative side of the ceremony being thus completed, the positive side ensues.

The king engages an antagonist in mock combat.

Efforts are made to introduce new life and vitality. A combat is staged between the forces of the old and the new, Life and Death, Fertility and Blight, the positive, vital force being triumphant and his opponent discomfited and/or banished. (Often the combat comes to be historicized and is then interpreted as the commemoration of an historical event.)

The king undergoes a "sacred marriage."

In addition, magical rites are performed to stimulate vegetation, relume the sun, promote human fecundity, and the like. The last-named take the form of rites of sexual license. (The emphasis here is on the revitalization of the entire topocosm, not of human society alone.)

The king is ceremonially reinstated, or a successor inducted.

V. Finally, the ceremony issues in a joyous celebration of the new-won life. A feast is held as a method of cementing through commensality the social bond of the community. (This tends to degenerate into a common jamboree.)

A frequent concomitant of the seasonal ceremony is a feast of the dead, the spirits of departed ancestors being believed to rejoin the community at moments of topocosmic crisis.

The pattern may be recognized in many of the calendar festivals of the ancient Near East.

§2. Take, first, the New Year (Akitu) Festival of the Babylonians and Assyrians.[1] As observed at Babylon during the first eleven days of the year, this included the following elements:

(a) A preliminary period of *lenten mortification*, regarded as outside the regular calendar.[2]

(b) A *suspension of the normal order of society*, slaves enjoying a short-lived authority over their masters[3] and a *temporary king being appointed.*[4]

(c) A ceremonial *purgation of the temple.*

On the fifth day of the festival the temple was sprinkled with water and fumigated with incense. Then a sheep was beheaded and the walls of the chapel of Nabu were rubbed with its body. This done, the head and body were together thrown into the river, while the officiating priest and slaughterer were sent into the desert or outside the city to observe a quarantine until the end of the festival. The ceremony was called *kuppuru.*[5] Its purpose was to transfer any latent impurity in the temple to the carcass of the sheep and thereby to remove it from the community. It may be compared with that performed by the Hebrews on their own Day of Kippurim (cf. Leviticus 16).

(d) The *dispatch of a human scapegoat* as a means of removing blight and contagion.

On the sixth day of the festival a condemned criminal was paraded along the street and beaten about the head.[6]

(e) A *mimetic combat,* mythologized as the battle of the divine champion against the Dragon or similar monstrous adversary (e.g., Marduk against Tiamat, Ninurta against Zu, etc.).[7]

The festival was also characterized by ceremonial races,[7a] a familiar attenuation of the traditional combat [see Chapter Two, §26].

(f) The formal *deposition and reinstatement of the king,* and his *induction into a special pavilion* (*bit akiti*).[8]

On the fifth day of the festival the king was led into an inner chapel of the temple, where the high priest divested him of his regalia, slapped his face, pulled his ears, and forced him to his knees before the image of the god. In this attitude of abasement he was then obliged to recite a kind of "negative confession," protesting his innocence of potential charges of tyranny and despotism. The recitation ended, he was reinvested and resumed his regal status. Once more, however, the high priest slapped his face, though on this occasion for the express purpose of drawing tears, which were considered a propitious omen (originally, a rain charm?) for the coming year.

The central portion of the Akitu ceremonies took place in a special pavilion called "the Akitu house" (*bit akiti*) on the outskirts of the city. Such an edifice has been excavated at Asshur, the ancient capital of Assyria.[9]

(g) A *sacred marriage,* in which the king played the part of the bridegroom.[10]

The marriage took place in the *bit akiti;* VAT 662; G. Reisner, SBH, No. VIII (p. 145), col. i, 7–8.

(h) A *feast of communion*, which appears to have taken the form of a *theoxenia*, or regalement of the gods.

On a building inscription in the *bit akiti* at Asshur, the festival is described as a "banquet" (*kirêtu*).[11] Further, we know from Assyrian sources that once a year the king invited the gods to a banquet and invoked them to bless city, land, king, and people. This ceremony was called *takultu*, or "collation," but it is not yet absolutely certain that it took place at the Akitu Festival. Parallels from other parts of the world would suggest, however, that New Year was the most appropriate occasion for its performance.[12]

(i) The *return of the dead*.

Funerary offerings were presented at the festival.[13] Moreover, the month of Teshrit, which was the first of the autumnal year and in which the festival was celebrated at Erech, was believed to be characterized by the fact that the dead then ascended from the netherworld.[14]

(k) It should be observed also that the eclipse and renewal of topocosmic life at the New Year Festival was represented at the same time by the performance of a sacred pantomime in which the god was portrayed as having sunk into the netherworld and was ritually bewailed. Subsequently, of course, he returned to earth.[15]

Thus, it is apparent that the program of the Akitu Festival was marked by all the characteristics of the Seasonal Pattern. Moreover, that festival originally took place at or about the time of the *equinox*, being observed alternatively (in the various cities of Babylonia and Assyria) at the vernal or autumnal occurrence of that event.[16]

§3. Take, again, the great autumnal festival (Asif) of the Hebrews. To be sure, the descriptions of it contained in the Old Testament are[17] of relatively late date and represent a stage in its development when it had been: (a) accommodated to a lunar calendar, (b) interpreted, on historicizing lines, as the memorial of a particular event in the career of Israel, and (c) broken down into a series of separate and independent festivals. Nevertheless, when due allowance is made for these developments, it is still possible to recover, at least in broad outline, the original form of the festival and to discern therein the contours of the Seasonal Pattern.

(a) The Festival of Asif, or "Ingathering," fell originally at or about the time of the *autumnal equinox* and comprised the three stages which came later to be distinguished as (a) New Year's Day, (b) the Day of Purgation or Atonement (Kippurim), and (c) the Feast of Booths (Sukkoth). Considered as a single whole, it thus embraced the standard elements of Mortification, Purgation, Invigoration, and Jubilation.

(b) The first two stages came eventually to be concentrated in the Day of Purgation or Atonement, but, in its original form, this was probably but the culmination of a ten-day *lenten period.*[18] It was marked by a *purgation of the temple,* its vessels and personnel; a ritual *purification and "shriving" of the people;* and the *dispatch of a scapegoat* as a means of removing impurity and contagion.[19] Moreover, it was accompanied by the usual *mortification;* the community observed a public *fast and suspension of activity,* the Hebrew expression for which (viz., *'innah nefesh*) properly denotes a *constriction or restraint of the personality.*[20]

(c) The two latter stages — those of Invigoration and Jubilation — were represented by a series of rites which came eventually to be distributed over New Year's Day and the Feast of Booths. Many of these are known to us only in their mythic transmutations; but on the principle that seasonal myths are but the durative counterparts of seasonal rituals (see Chapter One), we must be prepared to recognize in them the reflection of underlying punctual performances. They included: (a) a *mimetic combat* between the god and the Dragon (or some similar adversary); (b) the triumphant procession of the divine victor and his *installation as king in a special pavilion or palace;* (c) the performance of *magical rites to stimulate rainfall and fertility;* and (d) an emphasis upon the *solar* aspects of the occasion.

(d) That the reaffirmation of the god's sovereignty formed a central theme of the festival is indicated expressly in Zechariah 14:16, where the celebration of the Feast of Booths is associated with a pilgrimage to Jerusalem for the purpose of making obeisance before "the King Yahweh Sebaoth [EV. the LORD of Hosts]."[21] Moreover, it is now commonly agreed that many of the Old Testament Psalms were, in fact, designed for this occasion or at least modeled upon hymns then recited; and, as we shall see clearly in Part Three, there is constant reference in those compositions to the battle between the god and the Dragon (or similar adversary) and to the subsequent installation of the former in a special palace or pavilion.[22]

(e) The element of Invigoration was represented also by an elaborate rain-making ceremony which, though not mentioned in the Old Testament, is described in detail in the Mishnah.[23] On the first night of the festival, water was brought into the temple at Jerusalem from the neighboring pool of Siloam and was solemnly poured out upon the ground. Jewish tradition fully understood the purpose of the ceremony, putting into the mouth of God the words: "Offer water before me on the Feast of Booths, so that the rains of the year may be blessed unto you,"[24] and that this explanation is correct is indicated by the exactly parallel practice recorded by Lucian[25] as having been performed twice annually (i.e., at the spring and autumn festivals?) at the Syrian temple in Hierapolis (Membij). Moreover, it should be observed that, according to Zechariah 14:17, the penalty for failing to make the pilgrimage to Yahweh at the Feast of Booths was to be *lack of rainfall.*[26]

(f) Last, there is the *solar* element of the festival. Exodus 34:22 states clearly that it took place at the autumnal equinox (*tequfath ha-shanah*),[27] and its connection with this solar event is also emphasized in the Talmud (T. J. Sanhedrin, 18d). But what is especially significant in this respect is that, according to the scriptural account in I Kings 8:12–13 (= II Chronicles 6:1–2), when Solomon dedicated the First Temple *at the autumn festival* (I Kings 8:2 = II Chronicles 5:3), he recited a poem *which has manifest solar implications.* As preserved in the Masoretic recension, the text of that poem is, to be sure, both incomplete and slightly corrupt, but with the aid of the Greek (Septuagint) Version, it is possible to restore its original form, and it is then seen to contain a specific allusion to the sun's "standing fixed" in heaven.[28] It is apparent that such an allusion would be peculiarly appropriate to a festival celebrated at the autumnal equinox, when the sun is about to descend into the netherworld. What Solomon did (or what the chronicler thought he must have done) was to recite a traditional chant used on that occasion at the ceremony of dedicating the pavilion of the sun-god. That pavilion was regarded as a kind of "sun trap" — an earthly abode by residing in which the god might be saved from the darkling regions below.

That this interpretation is correct is proved by the actual orientation of the temple. Archaeologists have discovered that it was built on an axis not quite due EW, but slightly NE-SW, in such a way that its entrance faced directly toward the summit of the Mount of Olives. Now, it is above that summit that the sun rises at or about the time of the autumnal equinox, so that its rays would then pour down directly upon the altar, as a kind of solar theophany![29]

§4. An excellent, if brief, description of the ceremonies at the Egyptian Festival of Osiris, exhibiting several of the standard traits of the Seasonal Pattern, is given by a certain Ikhernofret who officiated as "mystagogue" at Abydos during the reign of Sesostris (Senusret) III, a king of the Twelfth Dynasty, ca. 1870 B.C. The description is contained in lines 17–24 of a limestone stele originally in the Drovetti Collection but acquired, in 1837–38, by the Königliches Museum in Berlin.[30] It reads as follows:

> 17. I arranged the expedition of Wep-wawet[a] when he went to the aid of his father.
>
> 18. I beat back those who attacked the Bark of Neshmet,[b] and I overthrew the foes of Osiris.
>
> I arranged the Great Procession and escorted the god[c] on his journey.
>
> 19. I launched the god's ship, and . . . Thoth . . . the voyage. I provided a crew for the ship of the Lord of Abydos who is called He-Who-Appears-in-Truth. I decked the ship with gorgeous trappings so that it might sail to the region of Peker.[d]
>
> 20. I conducted the god to his grave in Peker.
>
> 21. I championed Wenen-nefru (Unnefer), on the day of the Great Combat and overthrew all his adversaries[e] beside the waters of Nedit.
>
> I caused him to sail in his ship. It was laden with his beauty.
>
> I caused the hearts of the Easterners to swell with joy, and I brought gladness to the Westerners at the sight of the

[a] The jackal-god, brother of Anubis, evidently represented in the procession by a theriomorphic effigy mounted on a pole (Schaefer).

[b] The sacred bark of Osiris.

[c] I.e., Osiris.

[d] I.e., Osiris, as the rerisen god.

[e] I.e., Umm-el-qa'ab, near Abydos.

Bark of Neshmet. It put in at the port of Abydos; and Osiris, the first of all Westerners, the Lord of Abydos, was conducted to his palace.

§5. Last, the Seasonal Pattern is discernible in the later Asianic mysteries of Attis. To be sure, the ancient *testimonia* (derived mainly from censorious Church Fathers) are concerned more with their mythological than with their ritual aspects, but it is not difficult — particularly on the strength of abundant analogies — to extract from the descriptions of the latter the punctual program of the former. The available evidence has been admirably collected and digested in H. Hepding's well-known monograph *Attis* (Giessen, 1903), so that we may here confine ourselves to a mere tabulation of the relevant elements. Suffice it only to observe, by way of general introduction, that the mysteries celebrated the annual death and resurrection of Attis, spirit of life and fertility, and that they were therefore of the same character as those of the Egyptian Osiris, the Mesopotamian Tammuz, the Hittite Telipinu, the Syrian Baal and Adonis, and the Greek Persephone.

(a) The ceremonies took place at the time of the vernal equinox and lasted from March 21 until March 25.[31]

(b) They commenced with a period of mortification, coupled with purgation. This was exemplified by fasting, austerities, and ululation.[32]

(c) The notion of topsy-turvydom or suspension of normal activities at the end of the life lease was symbolized by a general saturnalian license, characterized, as in other parts of the world, by masquerades and interchange of garments.[33]

(d) A prominent feature of the ceremonies was the reception of new initiants. These were regarded as being "about to die" until formally admitted into the communion.[34]

(e) The sacred marriage of Attis and Cybele-Rhea was celebrated in a subterranean cavern, priests and votaries serving as "bridesmen."[35]

(f) The high point was reached at the moment when, on the day of the equinox, the sun first dawned on the horizon. This was regarded as the triumphant epiphany of Attis, and was preceded by an all-night vigil.[36]

(g) The reinvigoration of the king is indicated by the fact that, in Roman times, the slaughter of the bull was regarded at the same time as a sacrifice for the health and welfare of the emperor (*pro salute imperatoris*).[37]

(h) The ceremonies concluded with a general jubilation, called *Hilaria* by Roman writers.[38]

NOTES

1. Dhorme, *Les relig. de Bab. et d'Ass.*, 242–47 (with bibliography, 255–56); Labat, *Royauté*, 161 ff.; Engnell, *Divine Kingship*, ch. ii; Landsberger, *Kalender*, 12–14; Langdon, *Menologies*, 98–109; Pallis, *Akitu;* Dombart, JSOR 8 (1924), 103–22; Wensinck, AcOr. 1 (1923), 159–99; Zimmern, BSGW, Phil.-hist. Kl. 58 (1906), 126–56; 70 (1918), 1–52. Good popular accounts are: Böhl, *Neujahrsfest*, etc.; Gadd, in Hooke's *Myth and Ritual*, 47–58; Zimmern, AO 25/3.

The Akitu rituals are published in Thureau Dangin, *Rit. accad.*, 86 ff., 127–54. Analogous texts from Erech are edited by the same scholar in RA 19 (1922), 141–48; 20 (1923), 107–12.

On the meaning of the term Akitu, cf. M. Streck, OLZ, 1905. 375 ff.; Landsberger, *loc. cit.*

2. KAVI, p. 120, ii 22–28; KARI 177, r. iii; Labat, *op. cit.*, 315; Langdon, *op. cit.*, 101, n. 2; 105.

3. Haupt, "Purim," in BA 6 (1906), 25; Langdon, JRAS, 1924. 65–72; Zimmern, AO 25/3, 23.

4. The matter is mentioned particularly in the letter of Arad-Ea, priest of Sin, to the king concerning the Akitu Festival at Harran, BM 81–7–27. Many scholars contend, however, that this refers to a special substitution on a single specific occasion, not to a general practice; cf. Güterbock, ZA 42 (1934), 60; Ebeling, *Tod u. Leben*, 62–63; Engnell, *op. cit.*, 103 f.; Meissner, *Bab. u. Ass.*, i 48, 337; ii 99; Pallis, *op. cit.*, 141 f. See further King, *Chronicles*, 12–14; 8–17.

5. KAVI, p. 120 ii 22–38; Landsberger, 79; Langdon, 105; Zimmern, AO 25/3, 10–11. Cf. also Morgenstern, AJSL 55 (1938), 22.

6. VAT 9555, rev. 10–11. Analogous is the parade of a condemned felon at the Greek Festival of Thargelia. Such a practice, I believe, really underlies Isaiah 53.

7. VAT 9555: 23, 69; Smith, JRAS 1928.867, n. 1; ILN, June 2, 1928.

7a. VAT 9555, rev. 7–9; Zimmern, BSGW, Phil.-hist. Kl. 70 (1918), 8.

8. Dombart, *op. cit.*, 115; Furlani, SMSR 4 (1928), 1–16, 305–07; Wensinck, *op. cit.*, 183 ff.; Engnell, 53 ff.; Langdon, *Epic of Creation*, 26; Zimmern, *Christusmyth*, 38.

9. Pallis, *op. cit.*, 110–16.

10. VAT 633, obv. 1–10; KB VI/2, 25 ff.; Gudea Statue E = *ISA,* 120–24; Statue G = *ibid.,* 128–30; Reisner, *Hymnen,* viii, obv. 8. Cf. also: Engnell, 56–57; Labat, *op. cit.,* 162 f., 226 ff.; Pallis, 197 ff.; Zimmern, AO 25/3, 10; Harper, *Letters,* No. 65 (= Pfeiffer, No. 217); VAT 662.

11. MDOG 38 (1908), 19; Pallis, 173.

12. Cf. Frankema, *Takultu.* Two recensions of the ritual are extant, viz., (*a*) II R 66 (duplicate, KAVI 57) of the reign of Sennacherib; and (*b*) KARI 214 (duplicates KAVI 83; KARI 325). The ceremony is mentioned in inscriptions of Adad-nirari I and of Shalmaneser I; cf. Ebeling-Meissner-Weidner, *Altor. Bibliothek,* i, 108.33; 109, n. 10; 110.34; Müller, MVAG 41/3 (1937), 51, n. 2; Labat, *Royauté,* 286–87.

13. Langdon, *Menologies,* 36, 99, 105.

14. KAVI 218, p. 119, ii. 1–16.

15. Langdon, *Epic of Creation,* 34 ff.

16. Note that in the Babylonian liturgy for the festival, the victorious god Marduk was explicitly hymned as *the sun:* KB VI/2, 26 ff.; Zimmern, AO 25/3, 4–5; *idem.,* BSGW, Phil.-hist. Kl. 70 (1918), 34 ff.

17. Exodus 23:16; 34:22; Leviticus 23:33–35; Deuteronomy 16:13–15.

18. In Jewish observance, the ten days between New Year and the Day of Atonement are marked as a lenten and penitential period.

19. Leviticus 16:11–24, 33–34.

20. Leviticus 16:29.

21. This passage is read in the synagogue as the prophetical lesson for the first day of the Feast of Tabernacles.

22. See below, pp. 444.

23. Mishnah, Sukkah iv.9. Cf. Hooke, *op. cit.,* 138; Patai, *Man and Temple,* 24–53; Scheftelowitz, *Altpal. Bauernglaube,* 93–95; Feuchtwang, MGWJ 54 (1910), 535 ff.

24. Tos. Sukkah 3.18, p. 197 f.; PRK 193b, Buber.

25. *De Dea Syria,* 3, 48.

26. See above, n. 21.

27. Lit., "the revolution of the year." For the meaning, cf. Morgenstern, HUCA 1 (1924), 16 f. Properly speaking, of course, the expression can apply to any of the solstices or equinoxes; cf. Snaith, *The Jewish New Year Festival,* 34–36.

28. Burney, *Kings,* 110 f.; Thackeray, *Septuagint in Jewish Worship,* 76 ff.

29. On the solar features of the temple at Jerusalem, cf. Graham-May, *Culture and Conscience,* 237 f. Cf. also (but with caution) Hollis in Hooke's *Myth and Ritual,* 87 ff.

30. The best edition is that of Schaefer, *Die Mysterien des Osiris in Abydos* (1904).

31. Hepding, *Attis,* 44, 49, 54.

32. See above, Chapter Two, n. 55; Hepding, 155 ff.
33. Herodian, *Tēs meta Markon basileias historiai,* I, 10, §§5–7; Gaster, JBL 60 (1941), 302.
34. Firmicus Maternus, *De errore prof. rel.,* xviii, 1–2; Hepding, 49, 194 ff.
35. Nicander, *Alex.,* 7–8, and Schol. *in loc.;* Hesychius, s.v. *Kubela.*
36. Hepding, 165 f. On such vigils in Greek cults, cf. Homer, *Hymn to Demeter,* 292–93 (ed. Allen-Sikes-Halliday,[2] 120 ff.); Herod., iv. 76; Euripides, *Helen,* 1365; AP vii 223; Graillot, *Cybele,* 130 ff.; Roscher, *Nektar u. Ambrosia,* 2, 9.
37. See above, Chapter Two, n. 264.
38. Hepding, 167 ff.

EXCURSUS

An excellent picture of the typical Seasonal Pattern is painted by the biblical prophecies of Joel, dating, it would seem, from the fifth or fourth century B.C. The prophet likens the situation of his people to that which obtains during the annual period of mortification or suspended animation, and advises that relief may be obtained by recourse to the same sort of methods that are then customarily employed. In delivering his message he therefore introduces a sustained series of allusions to the seasonal practices, and his words thus afford a convenient summarization of our theme.

Mortification: ululation

I. 8. Wail [*eli*] like a virgin[1] girt in sackcloth
for the lover[2] of her youth.
9. Cut off is meal offering and libation
from Yahweh's House.[3]
A-mourning are the priests,
Yahweh's ministers.
10. Blighted is the field, dried up is the soil;
yea, blighted is the corn,
spoiled is the must,
the new oil fails.
11. Abashed are husbandmen,
vintners raise their wailing [*helilu*],
for the wheat and for the barley,
for perished is the harvest of the field.

12. Spoiled is the vine,
and the fig tree wilts,
pomegranate, palm, and quince,
all the trees of the field are withered;
spoiled is the joy of all mankind!

All-night vigil for the lost god of fertility

13. Gird yourselves in sackcloth
and beat your breasts;
raise a wailing, ye that minister at the altar!
Come, keep an all-night vigil, O ye priests,
Yahweh's ministers!
For withheld from the House of your God
is meal-offering and libation.

Even the gods are starving

14. Proclaim a sacred fast,
declare a term of restraint;
gather together the elders,
all who dwell in the land,
unto the House of your God,
and to Yahweh cry ye aloud:

Fasting and lenten period

15. "Woe worth the day!
[For nigh is Yahweh's day,
and like doom from the Doomster it comes!]
16. Before our very eyes
food is cut off,
from the House of our God
all gladness and joy.
17. Wizened are the grains
underneath their clods(?);
desolate are the barns,
the granaries are wrecked,[4]
for all the corn is spoiled.

Annual blight rationalized as penalty for sin

18. Ah, how the beasts make moan!
Distraught are the herds of cattle
for pasture have they none.
Why, even the flocks of sheep
now pay the wages of guilt!
19. Yahweh, I call upon thee,
for fire has devoured the pastures of the lea,
flame has consumed all the trees of the field.
20. Likewise the beasts of the field
go a-yearning for thee,

for the watercourses are dry
[and fire has devoured the pastures of the lea]."

. . .

Moral purgation as a means of securing the new lease of life

II. 12. Even now, so Yahweh saith,
turn full-hearted to me,
with fasting and weeping and mourning.
13. And rend your hearts and not your garments,
and return to Yahweh your God,
for gracious and merciful is He,
long-suffering and abounding in kindness,
and He will relent of the evil.
14. Who knows but that once again
He will relent,
and leave behind him a blessing
— meal-offering and libation
for Yahweh your God?

Fasting, lent, and sacred convocation

15. Sound the trumpet in Zion;[5]
Proclaim a sacred fast;
declare a term of restraint:
Gather the people together;
16. Place the folk under sacred taboo;
Assemble the old, gather the babes [and them that suck at the breast],
let the bridegroom come forth from his chamber,
and the bride from her bower.
17. Between the forecourt and altar
let the priests, Yahweh's ministers, weep,
and let them say:
"Yahweh, spare thy people,
and let not thine heritage become a reproach,
that nations may take them for a byword.[6]
Wherefore should they say among the nations:
Where is their god?"

Banishing of the Power of Death and Aridity (here historicized)

18. Then, maybe, Yahweh will be zealous for his land,
and have compassion on his people,
19. and Yahweh will answer and say to his people:[7]
"Behold, I send unto you
corn and must and new oil
and you shall have your fill thereof;
and I will not suffer you more
to be a reproach among the peoples.

20. And I will remove the Northerner from you
and thrust him out to a land desert and waste;
his front to the eastern sea
and his rear to the western sea;
and the stink of him shall rise,
and the stench of him go up,
because he thought to do proudly.

Reinvigoration

21. O land, be not afeared;
be glad and rejoice;
for 'tis Yahweh now
who will do proud things for you!
22. O beasts of the field, be not afeared,
for the pastures of the lea now are green,
for the tree yields its fruit,
fig tree and vine give their substance.

Restoration of rainfall

23. And ye, O sons of Zion,
be glad and rejoice in Yahweh your God,
for he has now given to you
the early rain in due season
and poured down the rain unto you,
even the early rain
and the late rain in the first month.[8]
24. And now the granaries are full of corn,
and the vats run over with must and new oil.

. . .

Eschatological interpretation of annual determination of destinies

IV. 2. I will collect all the peoples
and bring them down to the Valley of Jeho-shaphat
and there will I enter suit [*nishpatti*] with them
on account of my people and my heritage
even Israel whom they scattered 'mid the peoples,
and my land which they took for their portion . . .

. . .

Projection of Ritual Combat

9. Proclaim this among the peoples;
declare a sacred war;
rouse the soldiers to combat,
let all the warriors rally and come up.
10. Beat your plowshares to swords
and your pruning hooks to spears;
let even the weakling say:
I am a mighty man.

. . .

12. Let the nations be roused to combat
and come up to the Valley of Jeho-shaphat
for there will I sit to judge [*lishpôt*] all the peoples
round about.

. . .

Ultimate era of reinvigoration

16. And Yahweh will roar out of Zion
and from Jerusalem give forth his voice;
and heaven and earth will quake.
But Yahweh will be a refuge for his people,
and an asylum for the children of Israel,

. . .

17β. and Jerusalem shall be sacrosanct,
strangers shall pass through it no more.

18. And it shall be on that day:
the mountains shall drip new wine,
and the hillsides flow with milk,[9]
and all the watercourses of Judah
shall flow with water;
and a spring shall emerge from Yahweh's House
And water the Valley of the Acacias . . .

(EXCURSUS) NOTES

1. Hebrew *b^etulah,* which at once suggests *Btlt 'nt,* "the Virgin Anat," who annually wails for Baal.

2. Hebrew *ba'al,* which at once suggests the bewailed Baal.

3. On this as a stock element of the laments in the mysteries, see Chapter Four, §17.

4. For *nehersû mamgurôt* of the received text we read *nehersû-ma mgurôt* (cf. Haggai 2:19), with the archaic enclitic *-ma;* cf. Gaster, JBL 68 (1947), 58, n. 2.

5. This recalls the fact that the trumpet was indeed blown in the analogous Attis mysteries. Ezekiel (7:14) likewise plays on this. Cf. Gaster, JBL 60 (1941), 301.

6. We take the Hebrew words *limshol bam* to mean "to take them for a byword, make proverbs about them," rather than "to rule over them," because the point of the verse lies in the prophet's satirical play upon the ritual cry "Where is Mighty Baal?" (*Baal,* §LIV; I AB iv 26, 39).

7. In the mouth of the prophet, the reference is, of course, to Israel, but in the mysteries – to which he is satirically alluding – the "people" of Baal were his immediate family who feared extinction as the result of his disappearance (Cf. *Baal,* § LV; I AB i

6: "Baal is dead! And what now of the clan [*l'im*] of Baal's line?"). The verbs should be read as imperfects with *waw conjunctivum.*

8. So, with RV, we interpret the Hebrew, *barishon* LXX: *kathôs emprosthen* ("as before"); Vulgate: *sicut in principio* ("as in the beginning"); AJV: "at the first"; Moffatt: "as of old."

9. A cliché in descriptions of the new life; cf. Commentary on *Baal,* §LXIII.

CHAPTER FOUR

THE SEASONAL PATTERN IN ANCIENT NEAR EASTERN MYTH

I

§1. The *function* of myth is, as we have said, to bring out in articulate fashion the inherent durative significance of the ritual program.[1] Its *method* is to construe the punctual order of ceremonies in terms of an ideal situation involving "gods" or similar transcendent and preterpunctual beings. Its *effect* is to turn presentation into *re*presentation, to introduce the element of mimesis and to confer upon the participants the added and parallel role of actors, so that they are at one and the same time both protagonists of a direct experience and impersonators of characters other than their own.[2]

With due allowance for artistic embellishment, the "plot" of the seasonal myth will be basically identical with the pattern of the seasonal ritual. Moreover, just as the latter fall, as a rule, into the two well-defined types of the Combat and the Death-and-Resurrection, so too do the former, and just as the latter is usually epitomized in the activities of a central representative figure, i.e., the king, so too is the former in that of a central "god" (commonly identified with the spirit of vitality and vegetation), who is, of course, nothing but a durative projection of the king.

§2. When, for example, the Ritual Combat is staged in the towns and villages of England, the accompanying myth asserts,[3] that St. George, the patron saint of that country, is fighting the Dragon or (in a more historicized version) his inveterate enemy, the Turkish Knight.[4] Similarly, when the combat was staged in ancient Babylon, the concomitant myth identified the victor with Marduk, god of that city and embodiment of its durative, topocosmic essence;[5] and among the Hittites, the punctual ritual, performed annually at the spring festival of Puruli, was taken to represent a battle royal between a national weather god and the dragon Illuyankas.[6] So too among the Canaanites, it was Baal, lord of the land, who was thought to be subduing the turbulent spirit of the waters (Yam)[7] or the fell genius of aridity (Mot).[8] Among the Egyptians, it was Ra' who was engaging the monster 'Apep,[9] or Horus who was contending with his rival Set and thereby avenging his slain father Osiris.[10] Among the Hebrews, it was Yahweh (Jehovah) doing battle with the "crooked serpent" Leviathan, or with Tannin, "the Dragon," or with Rahab, "the Rager."[11]

In the same way, when the Egyptians formally reinstated their king at the New Year Festival,[12] it was, said the accompanying myth, Horus who was being inducted as the reincarnation of his father Osiris;[13] and when the Babylonians did likewise at their analogous Akitu Festival,[14] it was the triumphant Marduk who was being enthroned in his special pavilion.[15] And when subsequently the reappointed king presided over the constitutional assembly (*pukhru*)[16] to reaffirm the topocosmic regime, it was Marduk who was presiding over the parliament (*pukhru*) of the gods to determine the order of the world and the destinies of mankind.[17]

In like manner, too, when a weeping woman — representative of the seasonal wailers — marched in the annual New Year's parade at Babylon, she was represented in the concomitant myth as the goddess bewailing the vanished lord of fertility;[18] while in Egypt, the two female "keeners" — the two "kites," as they were called[19] — who performed this rite were identified as the goddesses Isis and Nephthys wailing, like some early Mary and Martha, over the corpse of the discomfited Osiris.[20] In Syria, it was Astarte lamenting Adonis, and in Asia Minor it was Cybele crying on Attis. Among the Greeks, the women who observed the statutory fast during the Festival of Thesmophoria were projected by the accompanying myth into the figure of Demeter, the Grain Mother, wandering disconsolately without food or drink in search of the abducted Persephone.[21] Often, indeed, the purely functional ululation was (and still is) developed under the influence of the myth into a formal mimetic funeral of the topocosmic spirit of fertility: in Egypt, it was Osiris who was being buried and bewailed; in Syria, it was Adonis, and in Asia Minor, it was Attis; while in modern Romania, it is *kalojan*, "beautiful John,"[22] and among the Abruzzi, it is *Pietro Pico*, "little Peter."[23]

Finally, when the king performed the ritual act of connubium (the so-called "sacred marriage"), a purely "economic" measure designed to galvanize the vitality of the topocosm, this was translated in the accompanying myth into the nuptials of a god and goddess, e.g., of Marduk and Zarpanitum at Babylon, Nabu and Tashmetu at Borsippa, Osiris and Isis in Egypt, Attis and Cybele in Asia Minor, and Zeus and Hera (or their local equivalents) in Greece.[24] Indeed, in Mesopotamia, a specific reference to such divine espousals was actually introduced into the accompanying "book of words."[24a]

§3. Seasonal myths of this kind may be either implicit or explicit. In the former case, the durative significance of the ritual is simply taken for granted, and it is tacitly assumed, without express dialogue or narrative, that the performers are at the same time acting out an ideal situation and endued with an ideal, preterpunctual character. This we may suppose to have been the primitive stage, and hence the earliest form of drama. It is represented, to a certain extent, in the situation implied by the so-called mystagogical texts discovered at Asshur, the ancient capital of Assyria.[25] These texts provide a running commentary on the ritual of the New Year (Akitu) Festival, in which each detail is related to an incident in the passion and resurrection of a topocosmic god or to his subsequent triumph, as the resurrected savior, over a monstrous dragon-like adversary. Thus, as previously mentioned, when the women of the city wander distraught during the period of topocosmic eclipse, they are taken to portray the distraught goddess wandering in search of the departed god. Similarly, when foot races are run — a characteristic seasonal rite[26] — they are taken to represent the eager dispatch of the savior-god against the Monster;[27] and when an animal is ceremonially milked — a familiar type of dairy charm[28] — this is interpreted as symbolizing the suckling of that god by a divine mother or wet nurse.[29] In all these cases, what is involved is not really impersonation but correspondence; the sacral act and the associated myth are really parallel expressions, on the punctual and durative planes, respectively, of one and the same thing.

§4. In our extant sources, however, the durative aspect is no longer merely implicit but receives, as a rule, definite and explicit articulation. The earliest form is the Mystery,[30] in which ritual and myth enjoy equal status, the former being not yet subsumed in the latter, as ultimately becomes the case. This form is best represented in the so-called Egyptian Coronation Drama inscribed on a papyrus discovered by Quibell, in 1896, in the precincts of the Ramesseum at Thebes. Unrolled and pieced together with phenomenal skill by the famous Berlin papyrologist Hugo Ibscher, it was first published, in 1928, by the late Kurt Sethe, to whom belongs the credit of demonstrating its dramatic character.[31] The papyrus itself was written in the reign of Sesostris [Senusret] I, a king of the Twelfth Dynasty (ca. 1970 B.C.), but according to Sethe, the contents go back a further millennium and a half to the time of the First Dynasty (ca. 3300 B.C.).[32] This would therefore be the earliest literary specimen of drama yet known.

The text gives an account of the traditional ceremonies at the installation of the king, which was celebrated in conjunction with the New Year ceremonies during the month of Khoiakh.[33] Its basic theme is thus the kenosis and plerosis of topocosmic vitality, as symbolized in the passion and revival of the king. Divided into forty-six scenes, it embraces the following standard elements of the Ritual Pattern:

1. The staging of a Ritual Combat [scene 18].
2. The burial of the defeated old king and his subsequent resurrection in the person of his successor (symbolized by the lowering and raising of ceremonial pillars) [scenes 3, 13–15, 26–28, 39–42].
3. The investiture and installation of the new king [scenes 6, 8, 23–25, 27–28, 31, 33, 35].
4. The celebration of a communal feast, to which the governors of the several nomes of Egypt are invited [scenes 21–22, 30, 32, 43–44].
5. The equipment of a royal bark in which the new king tours the principal cities of Egypt in company with his household [scenes 1–2, 7, 10–11, 16].
6. The performance of magical rites designed to promote fertility, e.g., the threshing of grain, milking of animals [scenes 5, 9, 19].
7. The presentation of offerings and performance of certain obscure rites [scenes 3–4, 12, 17, 20, 29, 34(?), 43–44].

Each detail of the ritual program is, however, invested at the same time with a durative significance, and this is brought out explicitly in the form of a mythological "key" attached to every scene.[34] The new king is here identified with the god Horus, and the old king with his slain father Osiris. The Ritual Combat is the battle between Horus and Set. The members of the royal household are the "children of Horus" who aid him in this conflict. The two priestesses who perform the seasonal ululation are the goddesses Isis and Nephthys, bewailing the discomfited Osiris. The official who invests the new king is the god Thoth, who adjudicates the quarrel between Horus and Set. The various articles of the regalia are given a symbolic meaning in terms of the concomitant myth; the beads of carnelian represent the great Eye of Horus, which was suffused with blood when it was wrested from him by his rival Set; the two clubs or maces represent the testicles of Set, which Horus plucks from him in the combat and then engrafts upon himself in order to acquire added vigor; the threshing of the grain represents the thrashing or belaboring of Osiris by Set. In many cases the mythological point is conveyed to the audience by means of grotesque and fantastic puns.[35] Thus, the identification of the maces with the engrafted testicles is pointed up by the fact that the Egyptian word for "mace, club," viz., *'b;*, at once suggests that for "engraft," viz., *i'b;* while the interpretation of the threshing of the grain as representing Set's thrashing of his father Osiris is brought home by the fact that the word for "grain," viz., *it*, is homophonous with that for "father."

Following an initial description of the ritual act and a subsequent explanation of it in mythological terms, each scene contains words of accompanying mythological dialogue, with clear indications of the speaker and the person addressed. Further, there are brief rubrics enumerating the stage properties required and (in most cases) stating the assumed locale of the action. A schematized rendering of Scenes 30 and 31 will make this clear.[36]

SCENE 30

RITUAL ACT: An invitation is extended to the governors of the several nomes of Upper and Lower Egypt.

MYTHOLOGICAL INTERPRETATION: This represents the summons issued to the gods by Thoth, at the behest of Geb, to come and attend upon the presence of Horus.

DIALOGUE: Says Geb to the Children of Horus and the Followers of Set:

"Come, wait upon the presence of Horus.
Thou, Horus, art their lord."

STAGE DIRECTIONS AND PERSONNEL:
(*in mythological terms*): Attendance of the gods. Horus.
(*in ritual terms*): Arrival of the governors of the nomes of Upper and Lower Egypt.

SCENE 31

RITUAL ACT: The chief officiant produces various pigments and cosmetics which are in turn conveyed to the king.

MYTHOLOGICAL INTERPRETATION: This represents Thoth restoring the stolen Eye of Horus and addressing him concerning it.

A. DIALOGUE: Says Thoth to Horus:

"I hereby convey thy bright eye [*W Ḏ ; t*] to thy face!"

STAGE PROPERTIES: A Horus Eye. Green pigment [*W ; Ḏ. w*] for the eyes.

B. DIALOGUE: Says Thoth to Horus:

"May the eye grace [*D M y*] thy face!"

STAGE PROPERTIES: A Horus Eye. Black pigment [*m s D M. t*] for the eyes.

DIALOGUE: Says Thoth to Horus:

"May thine eye nervermore be troubled nor lose its winelike luster!"

STAGE PROPERTIES: A Horus Eye. Wine-red pigment for the eyes.

DIALOGUE: Says Thoth to Horus:

"I hereby convey unto thee the perfume of divinity and the pure Eye which was wrested from thee!"

STAGE PROPERTIES: A Horus Eye. Frankincense.

DIALOGUE: [missing]

STAGE PROPERTIES: Double-plumed crown, to be placed on the king's head by the Wardens of the Great Plumes.

DIALOGUE: Says Thoth to Horus:

"Perfume thy face herewith so that it be thoroughly perfumed!"

STAGE PROPERTIES AND DIRECTIONS: A Horus Eye. Thorough perfuming (sc. of the king).

Here, then, we have an excellent example of that pristine stage of drama in which it still belongs within the realm of religion rather than of literature and in which ritual and myth still go hand in hand as inseparable correlatives in a single complex.

§5. With the growth of urban life, however, new conceptions emerge, and the processes of nature are no longer considered so dependent upon the operations of men. When that happens, the traditional ceremonies lose their urgency and tend to survive not on account of any functional efficacy but solely by reason of their wider mythological significance and of their purely artistic appeal. Ritual then becomes subsumed in myth. The participants are no longer protagonists of a direct experience but mere actors or guisers (*personae*) reproducing an ideal or imaginary situation and impersonating characters other than themselves. Dramatic ritual then becomes drama proper, moving from the domain of rustic Thalia into that of buskined Melpomene.

Yet never can Drama wholly forget the rock whence it was hewn. Beneath all of its subsequent superstructure there remains always the basic foundation of the Ritual Pattern. Reduced to its bare essentials and shorn of its diverse elaborations and embellishments, it revolves always around the central theme of Conflict, Discomfiture, and Restoration. Moreover, the farther back we go, the more likely are we to find such other ingredients of the original design as, for instance, the Sacred Marriage, the Feast of Communion, and the Expulsion of Evil — all of them disguised, of course, and duly woven into the fabric of a more or less sophisticated plot.

§6. Nowhere has this been more clearly demonstrated than in recent studies of classical Greek tragedy and comedy. Thanks to the researches of Gilbert Murray,[37] Jane Harrison,[38] Francis Cornford,[39] and others, it has now become possible to recognize that, even after it had emerged from the embryonic stage and long outgrown its primitive functional purpose, Greek drama nevertheless retained the basic form and structure of its rude prototype.[40] The pattern of the ritual became the plot of the drama, its component rites and ceremonies being translated into successive acts and scenes. Thus, as Murray has shown, the average Euripidean tragedy (e.g., the *Bacchae, Hippolytus,* or *Andromache*) contains as standard and stereotyped elements: (*a*) a Combat (*Agôn*); (*b*) a Passion (*Pathos*); (*c*) a Lamentation (*Thrênos*); and (*d*) a final Epiphany — all of them basic ingredients of the primitive "mystery" or sacred pantomime which revolved around the Combat of the Seasons (or of Life and Death, God and Dragon, etc.) and the Passion, Lamentation for, and eventual Restoration of, the lord of fertility.

Similarly, Cornford has made it clear[41] that the regular divisions of Aristophanic and earlier comedy were determined, in the first instance, by the statutory features of the primitive ritual program and that they embrace, especially in the seemingly inconsequential scenes which follow the Parabasis, such further crucial elements of that program as the Feast of Communion (*Kômos, Theoxenia*) and the Sacred Marriage (*Hieros Gamos*). Indeed, even the antiphonal chorus, with its constant exchange of banter and raillery, is shown to be nothing but a survival of the two opposing teams in the primitive Ritual Combat.

§7. The same method of approach has been applied also, and with equally arresting results, to the European mummers' play. Associated, as was Greek drama, with seasonal festivals or similar important calendar dates, the general structure of the mummers' play is familiar to most people.[42] Two antagonists(usually historicized as "St. George" and "the Turkish Knight," or the like) meet on the field of battle. One taunts and challenges the latter. Then they fall to, and the hero (i.e., "St. George") is slain. Thereupon he is duly lamented. Subsequently, however, he is restored to life through the good offices of a "learned doctor," and inflicts a crushing defeat on his opponent. Then, after a little irrelevant buffoonery, there are a few closing lines in which the actors call down blessing upon the assembled company of spectators and "pass round the hat."

Thanks to the researches of Grimm, Mannhardt, Frazer, Sartori, Chambers, Tiddy,[43] and others, it is now generally recognized that this crude performance (paralleled, in some respects, by the Arabic folk dramas of Hasan and Hosein)[44] is but a survival of the primitive Ritual Pattern, combining the twin elements of (a) the Combat of the Seasons and

(b) the Death-and-Resurrection of the god of fertility. Indeed, in some parts of the world (e.g., in Macedonia) such further elements as the Sacred Marriage and the Birth of the Savior-God are actually introduced.[45]

II

§8. This brings us to our main contention. We propose to show that a number of Ancient Near Eastern myths usually regarded as mere flights of imaginative fancy are really literary articulations of that Seasonal Pattern which has been described in the preceding pages, reflecting in their several episodes the successive elements of a ritual program.

The myths in question formed part of the religious literature of the Canaanites, Hittites, Mesopotamians (Babylonians and Assyrians), and Egyptians, and the majority of them have been recovered only, as the result of archaeological excavations, during the past fifty years. In Part Two of this book we shall offer complete translations and analyses of them. Here, however, for purposes of the general argument, it will be convenient to present a summary survey of their contents, signalizing by SMALL CAPITALS elements derived from the Seasonal Pattern.

§9. The *Canaanite* texts[46] were discovered, in 1930–33, at Ras esh-Shamra ("Fennel Head"), site of the ancient city of Ugarit, on the north coast of Syria. They consist of a series of clay tablets inscribed, in the characters of an hitherto unknown cuneiform alphabet, with lengthy poetic compositions written in what may be termed for convenience a proto-Hebrew dialect. The tablets themselves date approximately from the fourteenth century B.C., but their contents were, no doubt, traditional, and therefore still older. They were preserved as part of the archive of a local temple. In their present state they are neither complete nor consecutive, so that no single composition has come down to us in its entirety. Nevertheless, it is possible to group the extant fragments into certain well-defined cycles and to determine, at least in broad outline, the general tenor of the stories they relate. Those which here concern us are the following:

(a) *The Poem of Baal* [AB]. Consisting at present of six tablets, this presents (with intermediate gaps) the story of the exploits and adventures of a god named Baal or Aliyan Baal (Baal Puissant), genius of rainfall and fertility. The action is concerned mainly with the COMBAT of this god against the dragon Yam (Sir Sea), lord of sea and streams [III AB, A]; his ultimate victory, ACCESSION TO SOVEREIGNTY and INSTALLATION IN A NEWLY BUILT PALACE [II AB]; his subsequent ENCOUNTER WITH MOT, GENIUS OF DROUGHT, and his DISAPPEARANCE INTO THE NETHERWORLD [I*AB]; the TEMPORARY RULE UPON EARTH OF A CERTAIN ATHTAR (ASHTAR) and the eventual RE-EMERGENCE AND TRIUMPH OF THE VANISHED GOD, accompanied by the RE-ESTABLISHMENT OF PEACE AND FERTILITY [I AB; IV–VI AB]. It thus combines the familiar motifs of the combat between the seasons and of the dying and reviving god.

Subsidiary to the six main tablets [I AB–V AB; I* AB] are two others, evidently belonging to variant versions of the story. The one, here designated *The Harrowing of Baal* [BH], describes the DISCOMFITURE OF BAAL DURING THE SEASON OF DROUGHT. While out hunting, he is lured into the pursuit of certain demoniacal creatures who have the appearance and nature of wild beasts (called Raveners [*'qqm*] and Devourers [*aklm*]), and lands in a swamp, where he lies suffering a malarial infection until found and rescued by a caravan of his brethren. Meanwhile, the EARTH LANGUISHES for want of his presence. The other tablet [VI AB] gives an alternative account of the measures taken to achieve his ultimate RESTORATION.

(b) *The Poem of Aqhat* [Aq.].[47] This consists of four tablets containing the remains of ten columns, or about four hundred fifty lines of writing. It tells the story of a youth named Aqhat, son of a chieftain called Daniel, who came into possession of a divine bow destined for the goddess Anat, deity of war and of the chase. By refusing to give it up, he offended the goddess, who was compelled to refer the matter to the supreme god El. The latter ordered the mortal to be punished. Thereupon, the goddess enlisted the services of a certain Yatpan, a hired thug, to assail the youth and knock him unconscious so that the bow might be taken from him. Yatpan, however, bungled the instructions and not only slew Aqhat but also dropped the bow into the waters on the return journey to Anat. The shedding of the youth's blood caused infertility upon earth, and this latter circumstance aroused the suspicions of his sister Paghat ("Maiden"). At first, the body of Aqhat could not be located, nor was it even known that it was he who had been killed. Subsequently, however, a flight of vultures appeared over Daniel's house, and when he ripped open their gizzards he discovered the remains of his son. Thereupon he accorded him honorable burial and summoned wailing women to sing dirges over him. Paghat meanwhile resolved upon vengeance. Hiding a dagger beneath her skirts, she proceeded to the neighboring encampments, under cover of night, in order to hire assistance in this enterprise. By a turn of fate, her steps led her to the tent of Yatpan himself who, in a moment of drunken boasting, betrayed himself as the murderer of Aqhat. At this critical point the text unfortunately breaks off. There is reason to suppose, however, that the SLAIN AQHAT WAS ULTIMATELY REVIVED.[48]

Although this text does not reveal the same ostensibly sacral characteristics as the *Poem of Baal,* and although it has obviously been developed along more purely literary lines, it will be shown in the sequel[49] that it too goes back to the primitive Ritual Pattern and is based upon the familiar seasonal myth of the DYING AND REVIVING GOD whose temporary disappearance brings about the SUMMER DROUGHT.

(c) *The Poem of the Gracious Gods.* This is inscribed on a tablet of seventy-six lines, incomplete at the end. It divides clearly into two parts. The first gives the "book of words" for a seasonal ceremony. The second is purely mythological and describes the SACRED MARRIAGE of the supreme god El to two brides and the subsequent BIRTH of various "gracious and comely gods." One pair of these are the Dioscuric "princes," Dawn and Sunset, and are translated to heaven; the others are distinguished by a gargantuan and insatiable appetite and are left to wander in the Wilderness of Kadesh. The ritual portion refers explicitly to the preliminary trimming of vines. The text was therefore evidently designed for a festival in May–June, when that operation takes place and when the Heavenly Twins are in fact the regnant stars.

The *Hittite* texts emanate from Boghazköy, site of Hattusas, the ancient Hittite capital, about eighty miles west of Ankara, Turkey. They consist of a series of clay tablets inscribed in syllabic cuneiform script and in the so-called Kanesian Hittite language, which is essentially an Indo-European tongue blended with Asianic elements. The tablets themselves date from the fifteenth to the thirteenth centuries B.C., but their contents are clearly of earlier date, representing a survival (and transmutation) of material derived from a remoter Asianic past, before the arrival of the Indo-European invaders. The documents which here concern us are the following:[50]

(a) *The Snaring of the Dragon* (KBo. III 7; KUB XII 66; XVII 5–6). This text, pieced together from four complementary (and sometimes duplicate) documents, presents the cult myth recited or rehearsed on the occasion of an annual festival called Puruli, celebrated in late spring or early summer. The theme of the myth, of which two alternative versions are given, is the COMBAT OF THE WEATHER GOD AGAINST THE DRAGON ILLUYANKAS, AND HIS EVENTUAL VICTORY. Subjoined to the narrative is a ritualistic description of the manner in which the Puruli festival was celebrated at the great cultic center of Nerik. A PROCESSION of the gods and their consorts was arranged, and the TRIUMPHANT WEATHER GOD WAS EVENTUALLY ENTHRONED IN THE TEMPLE AS SUPREME OVERLORD, special estates being assigned to him by the local king.

(b) *The Yuzgat Tablet.* This document, acquired by A. H. Sayce, in 1906, at Yuzgat (Yozgad), near Boghazköy, and probably emanating from the latter site, deals with the PARALYZATION OF THE EARTH BY THE DEMON OF FROST (Hahhimas) and with the efforts made by the gods to locate the absent SUN. All the deities sent to look for him are seized by the demon, until at last — though this portion of the text is missing — the DEMON IS WORSTED, AND LIFE RETURNS. An accompanying ritual prescribes OFFERINGS TO TELIPINU, GOD OF FERTILITY, AND TO THE SUN.

(c) *The Myth of Telipinu* [T] (preserved in several recensions and pieced together from several mutually complementary copies) relates how Telipinu, the GOD OF FERTILITY, DEPARTED FROM THE EARTH in anger and how HE WAS EVENTUALLY BROUGHT BACK AND APPEASED BY MAGICAL MEANS. It it thus, in the main, a version of the familiar seasonal myth of the DEPARTING AND RETURNING GOD, represented elsewhere by the stories of Tammuz, Osiris, Baal, Adonis, Attis, and Persephone.

The Telipinu text represents but one form of a procedure current among the Hittites in times of disaster. The latter was believed to be due to the withdrawal of an offended deity, and the purpose of the procedure was to secure his return. In sister versions virtually the same myth and ritual are associated with a number of other gods and with personal as well as national calamities. Consequently, it cannot be said unequivocally that it refers to the *annual* desiccation of the earth rather than to a single particular occasion. But this possibility cannot be denied out of hand, and it is by no means inconceivable that the elaborate rites of purification which the text describes reflect that familiar SEASONAL PURGATION which we have previously discussed. In that case, the use of the same myth and ritual in other, non-annual contexts would be but a subsequent and secondary development. In itself, the Telipinu myth would be comparable, in a general way, with the Homeric *Hymn to Demeter* (see page 453).

(d) *The Ritual Combat* (KUB XVII 35, iii 9–17). Besides the three main Hittite texts, there is another which may at least claim attention. This is part of a long ritualistic document, and it appears to describe a MOCK COMBAT which formed part of the proceedings. The combat was historicized, in accordance with a familiar process (see Chapter Two, §21) as the commemoration of a whilom encounter between the Hittites (Hatti) and their neighbors, the Masa — probably the classical Maeonians. Such, at least, is the interpretation advanced by Ehelolf, Lesky, Schubart, and others.[51]

The *Babylonian* material consists of (1) the long poem known as *Enuma Elish;* and (2) two mystagogical texts known to Assyriologists as VAT 9555 and K. 3476.

(a) *Enuma Elish,* conventionally known as the *Epic of Creation,* is a composition in six tablets, or "cantos," dealing primarily with the story of how MARDUK, THE GOD OF BABYLON, ENGAGED AND DEFEATED TIAMAT, THE REBEL DRAGON OF THE DEEP, AND HER COTERIE, AND HOW, AFTER HIS VICTORY, HE ACQUIRED SOVEREIGNTY OVER THE GODS, WAS INSTALLED IN A NEWLY BUILT PALACE (ESAGILA) IN BABYLON, ESTABLISHED THE COSMIC ORDER, CREATED MANKIND, AND DETERMINED FATES AND DESTINIES. In its present form, the text was evidently redacted in Babylonia, but there is reason to believe that the story itself goes back to hoary antiquity and probably incorporates a good deal of ancient *Sumerian* material. (Since this text is generally accessible in several excellent editions, it has not been deemed necessary to reproduce it here in full.)[52]

(b) *VAT 9555* and *K. 3476* are fragments of priestly manuals designed to explain the ritual of the Akitu, or New

Year, Festival. Each of the traditional elements of the ritual is related to an incident in the seasonal myth of the "incarceration" and subsequent restoration of Bel-Marduk, the lord of fertility and god of Babylon — e.g., "the magicians who precede the image of Nabu, spelling out an incantation, represent the people of Bel who are raising a dirge for him" (1.27). In this way, the entire gamut of rites and ceremonies is translated into terms of a mythological representation. To be sure, these documents are but learned lucubrations, and the interpretations which they propound can be regarded only as the product of scholarly ingenuity. Nonetheless, they help us to recover details of the ritual and show how, even on this level of academic exegesis, the basic interrelation of rite and myth was clearly apprehended. (These texts, too, are readily accessible in translation, and we have therefore deemed it unnecessary to reproduce them.)[53]

The *Egyptian* material,[53a] the dramatic character of which has already been recognized by Kurt Sethe and Etienne Drioton, consists, apart from the aforementioned *Ramasseum drama* (a) of the following documents:

(b) *The Memphite Drama.* This is inscribed on a slab of black granite now in the British Museum. It was written at the order of Shabaka, a king of the Twenty-fifth or Ethiopian Dynasty, who reigned about 711 B.C. In a preamble, however, that monarch states expressly that it was copied from an older, worn original. The latter is assigned by Sethe to the First Dynasty (ca. 3300 B.C.), but arguments have been advanced by Rusch[54] to show that it should more probably be dated to the Fifth Dynasty, some eight hundred years later (ca. 2500 B.C.). The document has been known to scholars since the middle of the nineteenth century and has been the subject of several translations and commentaries, but the only reliable and virtually definitive edition is that produced by the late Kurt Sethe in 1928, and it is that scholar's rendering and general interpretation that are here followed.

Like its counterpart from the Ramesseum, the Memphite text was evidently designed for an annual ceremony and most probably for that which took place, amid great pomp and splendor, during the last days of the month of Khoiakh. Its theme is the ECLIPSE AND REVIVAL OF THE KING AS THE SYMBOL AND EPITOME OF TOPOCOSMIC VITALITY. The action covers (a) THE DEATH OR DISCOMFITURE OF THE OLD KING; (b) RITUAL LAMENTATION, construed as the recital of dirges over him; (c) A RITUAL COMBAT; and (d) THE INSTALLATION OF THE VICTOR IN THE CITY OF MEMPHIS. As in the Ramesseum drama, the durative aspect of the ceremonies is brought out in an accompanying myth. The king is identified with Horus, and his defunct predecessor with Osiris. The combat is therefore translated into that of Horus and Set, and the subsequent triumphant enthronement of the victor becomes the resurrection and reincarnation of Osiris in the person of his son and his solemn restoration to the cultic center of Memphis. The priestesses who initially utter lamentations are identified with the goddesses Isis and Nephthys wailing for Osiris. Appended to the story is a celebration of the creative powers and glories of Ptah, god of Memphis.

(c) *The Edfu Drama.* Engraven, along with illustrative reliefs, on one of the walls of the temple at Edfu, this presents the text of a sacred drama performed annually at a great festival celebrated on the twenty-first day of the spring month of Mechir. Since it has already been translated, with exhaustive commentary, by Blackman and Fairman, we content ourselves with a mere summary.

The theme of the drama is once again THE REINVIGORATION OF THE KING AS THE SYMBOL AND EPITOME OF TOPOCOSMIC VITALITY; and the action covers (a) A RITUAL COMBAT; (b) THE SUBSEQUENT INSTALLATION OF THE VICTOR AS KING; and (c) THE PERFORMANCE BY HIM OF THE CHARACTERISTIC SEASONAL RITE OF CONNUBIUM. Here too, however, the durative aspect of the ceremonies is brought home by means of an accompanying myth. The king is identified with the local god Horus of Behdet (who tends to be confused with Horus, son of Isis and Osiris, and to be endowed also with the characteristics of the supreme solar deity Ra'). His adversary (called "the Caitiff"[55] and "the Monster")[56] is identified with the fell hippopotamus — a virtual equivalent of the Dragon in sister versions of this seasonal myth. His bride in the ritual connubium is the goddess Hathor of Dendereh.

The text consists of a prologue, three acts (subdivided into scenes), and an epilogue. In its present form it is a Late-Egyptian recension of a more ancient archetype. Editorial manipulation and the exigencies of space have resulted (with but two exceptions) in the complete elimination of such stage directions as occur in the analogous Ramesseum drama; all that now remains is a combination of brief narrative passages and somewhat extended speeches. In one passage there is a statement that "this book is recited by the Precentor (or

Chief Lector)"; and if these words refer to the text as a whole rather than to some particular collection of spells which may have been uttered at a certain stage of the action,[57] they would appear to indicate that the play was performed in dumb show and the accompanying dialogue recited by an attendant official who would have answered, *mutatis mutandis,* to the Sanskrit *sūtradhāra,* the Greek *chorēgos,* the Moslem *mulla* of the Hosein pantomimes, and the medieval European "presenter."[58] This official, however, was evidently assisted by a chorus, for there are certain utterances (e.g., "Hold fast, Horus, hold fast!" — a virtual equivalent of the colloquial American "Attaboy!") which would appear to be exclamations on the part of onlookers. The latter were, in all probability, not the audience as a whole but the company of priests assembled on the stage and identified in the mythological interpretation with the followers of Horus of Behdet.[59]

III

The seasonal pattern is approached, to be sure, from several different angles. Sometimes, as in the Canaanite *Poem of Baal* and the Mesopotamian *Enuma Elish,* it is treated *comprehensively,* and the text embraces in the sequence of its episodes almost all of the successive stages of the ritual program. Sometimes, on the other hand, as in the Hittite *Snaring of the Dragon,* attention is concentrated on a single salient element, such as the seasonal COMBAT AGAINST THE FLOODS OR THE POWERS OF ADVERSITY AND CHAOS; or, as in the *Myth of Telipinu,* on the TEMPORARY ABSENCE OR REMOVAL OF THE STEWARD OF TOPOCOMIC LIFE; or, as in the Egyptian dramas, on his eventual triumphant INSTALLATION OR ENTHRONEMENT. Again, in some cases (e. g., in *The Poem of Baal* and in *Enuma Elish*), the poets hew close to the traditional ritual outline, stolidly and unimaginatively, while in others (e.g., in *Aqhat* and in *The Gracious Gods*), they use it only as scaffolding for a more original and artistic structure, and the Pattern is little more than vestigial, a source of the genre as a whole rather than of the specific composition. It is possible, in fact, to group the texts, according to their dominant themes, into certain well-defined categories (e.g., the Comprehensive Type, the Combat Type, the Disappearing-God Type, the Coronation or *Renouveau* Type, etc.), and, for the clearer demonstration of our central thesis, this arrangement has been adopted in the ensuing translations and analyses.

It is not difficult to recognize in these texts all the characteristic marks of the Seasonal Pattern.[60]

(*a*) All of them feature a COMBAT. — In the *Egyptian* texts, it is the combat of Horus and Set or of Horus and the demonic hippopotamus. — In the *Hittite* texts, it is that of the gods in general against Hahhimas, i.e., Jack Frost (Yuzgat Tablet) or of the weather god against the Dragon Illuyankas (Puruli text). — In the *Babylonian Epic of Creation* it is the fight of Ea against Apsu and Marduk against Tiamat. — In the *Canaanite Poem of Baal*, it is the battle of that god against Yam and, later, against Mot; while in the *Poem of the Gracious Gods* it is watered down into a description of how the spirit of fertility is lacerated and dismembered, *à la* Dionysus, like a trimmed vine.

(*b*) In each case, the issue of the combat is that THE VICTOR ASSUMES SOVEREIGNTY. — In the *Egyptian* texts, Horus becomes king of Upper and Lower Egypt. — In the *Hittite* texts, the weather god is enthroned as king in the cultic center of Nerik, or Telipinu receives royal honors. — In the *Babylonian Epic of Creation*, the triumphant Marduk is installed as king in the newly built temple of Esagila. — In the *Canaanite Poem of Baal*, that god acquires "dominion eternal" by vanquishing Yam.

(*c*) In each case, a prominent feature of the story is the INSTALLATION OF THE TRIUMPHANT GOD IN A SPECIAL PALACE. — In the *Egyptian* Ramesseum and Memphite texts, the action culminates in the installation of Horus (qua Osiris redivivus) within his royal city and palace. — In the *Hittite* myth of *The Snaring of the Dragon*, the victorious weather god is installed in Nerik; while if the *Myth of Telipinu* be read alongside the prayer to that god preserved in KUB XXIV 1–2[61] and of the fragmentary description of the Puruli rites in KUB XXV 31, it will be apparent that its final scenes likewise imply the installation of that god in a new or renovated abode. — In the *Babylonian Epic of Creation*, the triumphant Marduk is installed in a special pavilion [*parakku*] in Esagila.[62] — In the *Canaanite Poem of Baal*, that god, after subduing Yam, is honored by the construction of a special palace.

(*d*) In each case, the action closes with AN ASSEMBLY OF THE GODS, USUALLY ACCOMPANIED BY A BANQUET. — In the

Egyptian Ramesseum text (§§21–22, 30, 32, 34, 43–44), Horus summons the gods to a collation; while in the Memphite text (§61), the gods and their "doubles" [*ku*] repair to that city to hail the new sovereign. — In the *Hittite* myth of *The Snaring of the Dragon,* the gods foregather in Nerik when the weather god is installed as king; and in the *Myth of Telipinu,* they regale themselves at a feast when that god returns to earth. — In the *Babylonian Epic of Creation,* the acknowledgment of Marduk as king is accompanied by a gathering and banquet of the gods. — In the *Canaanite Poem of Baal,* that god invites all the "seventy sons of Asherat" to a banquet when once his palace has been completed; while the *Poem of The Gracious Gods* ends with a scene in which the supreme god El throws open the resources of heaven and earth to his two infant sons and they eat and drink to satiety — clearly, an attenuation of the banquet motif.

(*e*) The element of MORTIFICATION AND ULULATION also appears prominently in these texts. — In the *Egyptian* Ramesseum, Memphite, and Edfu texts, great importance is attached to the *procero* uttered by two priestesses (mythologically identified with the goddesses Isis and Nephthys) who bewail the lifeless Osiris. — The *Hittite Myth of Telipinu* opens with a stereotyped description (closely paralleled in the Babylonian Tammuz liturgies, in the Homeric *Hymn to Demeter,* and in the seasonal litany embedded in the first chapter of the biblical Book of Joel) of the blight caused upon earth by the disappearance of that spirit of fertility. An analogous account of the ravages caused by Hahhimas (Jack Frost) appears in the Yuzgat Tablet; while the Puruli text is introduced by a liturgical formula containing a petition for rain and fertility, i.e., an articulate expression of the seasonal ululation. — In the *Canaanite Poem of Baal,* the ululation is embodied in a speech addressed by El to the sun-goddess Shapash: "Dried up are fields, O Shapash, dried up are the vast fields. Baal is neglecting the furrows of the plowland. Oh, where is Baal Puissant? Where is His Highness, the Lord of the earth?" (I AB iv, 25 f.). Similarly, in a supplementary text (BH ii, 36–45), there is a vivid description of the drying up of the wadies consequent upon the discomfiture and absence from the earth of this same Baal; while in the *Poem of Aqhat,* the slaying of that youth causes infertility of the soil, and he is ceremonially bewailed for seven days.

(*f*) Last, it is possible occasionally to detect traces of the

SACRED MARRIAGE, albeit in severely attenuated form.—The most patent instance of this, as all commentators have recognized, is in the *Canaanite Poem of the Gracious Gods,* where it is to be found in the scene describing the seduction by El of two mortal women and the subsequent birth of the siblings, Dawn and Sunset (Shahar and Shalem).—It may be recognized also, as Oppenheim has observed,[63] in a passage of the *Babylonian Epic of Creation* (I, 77–78) which describes how, after his conquest of Apsu, Ea "erected a holy grove for himself, and Ea and Damkina celebrated (therein) in majesty the sacred marriage."

But it is not only by virtue of such general traits that the texts may be identified as seasonal dramas or, at least, as projections from seasonal rituals. There is also an impressive body of supporting evidence.

(*a*) Most of the texts are explicitly associated with seasonal festivals. Thus, the Hittite myth of *The Snaring of the Dragon* (KBo.III.7) is said expressly to have been recited or rehearsed at the vernal Festival of Puruli; while the Ramesseum and Edfu texts were designed, as most Egyptologists have recognized, for specific festivals in the months of Khoiak and Mechir, respectively, when the new lease of life was thought to commence and when the king was therefore ceremonially reconfirmed. Similarly, the Babylonian *Epic of Creation* was recited before the image of the god on the fourth day of the Akitu or New Year Festival.

(*b*) Moreover, even where such definite indications are lacking, it is sometimes possible to correlate the mythology of one or other text with a specific season of the year. Take, for example, the Canaanite *Poem of the Gracious Gods.* The central theme of this composition is the birth of two siblings who may be identified, as we shall see later, with the Dioscuri or Heavenly Twins; and, in their astral form of Gemini, these happen to be the regnant constellation of the first half of June. A myth concerning their nativity would therefore be peculiarly appropriate to a festival held at that time, and there are thus grounds for an initial presumption that our text may have been designed for just such an occasion.

Similarly, the *Poem of Aqhat* revolves around the tale of a handsome youth who challenges the supremacy in the chase of the goddess Anat, the Syro-Palestinian Artemis, and who is consequently put to death. To be sure, this tale has been blended with the familiar myth of the dying and reviving lord of fertility: the death of Aqhat causes drought and barrenness and, it would appear, he is eventually resurrected. Basically, however, as we shall see later, it is simply a variant of the Classical myth of Orion, and the significant thing about Orion is that in his astral manifestation he disappears from the evening sky from the end of April until the beginning of July, i.e., during the earlier part of that very season in which the earth is rendered infertile by reason of summer drought. There is therefore, once again, an initial presumption that our text is really a seasonal myth designed to explain the cause of that phenomenon and reflecting the ritual procedures associated with it.

Of the same order is the emphasis placed in several of these texts upon the role of the *sun.* Thus, in the Hittite *Yuzgat Tablet,* it is not only for Telipinu, the lord of fertility, but also for the sun-god that a search is instituted (obv. 21–25); and in the ritual portion of that text, sacrifices are prescribed not only for the former but also for the latter (rev. 28, 34–35). Similarly, in the Canaanite *Poem of Baal,* it is the sun-goddess (Shapash) who retrieves the body of that god from the netherworld (I AB, i 8–16), who persuades the rebellious Môt to give up the unequal struggle against him (*ibid.,* vi 22–29), and who is subsequently commended for her solicitude (*ibid.,* vi 42–52); while in the *Poem of the Gracious Gods,* a second exordium (23–27) is addressed not only to those deities but also to "the sun-goddess who makes the vines to burgeon with . . . and grapes."

All of these passages may be construed as further indications that our texts were designed for seasonal festivals; for — as we have seen (Chapter Two, §37) — such festivals usually coincide with *solstice* or *equinox,* when emphasis on the sun would be peculiarly appropriate. Indeed, the Hittite *Yuzgat Tablet* appears to contain an explicit allusion to the imminent re-emergence of the sun on the latter occasion; for when, after due search, the sun-god cannot be located, the supreme deity is made to exclaim:

But my limbs already feel a glow;
he must somehow have lost his way
(obv. 24–25)

i.e., he is lurking close by, though momentarily unseen.

(*c*) Taken by themselves, these mythological combinations might seem, to be sure, to provide but a slender and precarious basis for determining the seasonal occasion of such texts as are not explicitly related to this or that calendar festival. Fortunately, however, the conclusions reached by this line of argument are corroborated — or, at least, very strongly supported — by other indications in the documents themselves. Thus, a rubric in the *Poem of the Gracious Gods* (line 15) prescribes the seething of a kid in milk, and in Exodus 23.19 (E) and 34.26 (J) the "seething of a kid in its mother's milk" is a practice forbidden to the Israelites in connection with the offering of first fruits at the Festival of Pentecost in June! Moreover, as Ginsberg has acutely observed, the very fact that a kid is specified presupposes that the rite took place in spring or summer, since "goats normally yean in the winter in Palestine."[64] Again, one of the constituent elements of that same text is a little song (lines 8–11) properly designed as a chanty to accompany the trimming of vines, and this operation takes place in Palestine during the month of June![65]

Similarly, a prominent feature of the myth of Aqhat is that the remains of the slain youth are recovered in the form of fragments or morsels extracted from the gizzards of vultures which have devoured him (I D, 105–51). Now, strictly speaking, this detail is not essential to the development of the plot; Aqhat could just as well have been recovered in the form of a mangled corpse. When we recall, however, that the *dismemberment* of the god and the subsequent interment of the fragments (or the consumption of them in a rite of omophagy) formed a vital element of the summer "mysteries" associated with such fertility spirits or topocosmic genii as Osiris, Attis, Adonis, Zagreus, and the like, that it reappears in the myth of Baal (I AB, ii 30–37) and that it was likewise incorporated (albeit in disguised and attenuated form) in later Greek tragedy and comedy,[66] it becomes obvious why the poet introduced this seemingly irrelevant detail into his narrative: *it reproduced a traditional rite of the summer festival for which his poem was designed,* and therefore formed part and parcel of a canonical pattern which he was obliged to follow. Had he omitted it, there would have been nothing in his story to explain one of the essential elements of the accompanying ritual procedures; he was accordingly constrained to work it in somehow, albeit in strained and bizarre fashion.

In the same way, the lamentation over Aqhat, which figures so prominently in the poem (I D, 171–88), may be taken to reproduce the characteristic summer rite of Ululation (see Chapter Three, §§8–13) and thus to afford further evidence that the text was indeed designed for a festival celebrated at that season.

Moreover, even where the particular occasions are none so sharply precised, similar subordinate episodes frequently betray the dependence of the texts upon the canonical pattern of seasonal ceremonies. These indications are discussed in detail in our several commentaries. By way of anticipation, however, a few of them may be adduced in this place in order to illustrate the general argument.

(*a*) In the Canaanite *Poem of Baal*, after that god has disappeared from the earth, sovereignty is assumed by a deity named Ashtar (I AB, i 43–65). Later, when Baal is restored, the usurper is ousted (I AB, v 1–6; cf. Gaster, BASOR 101 [Feb. 1946], 23, n. 12). With the wider interpretation of this incident we shall deal later. Here it is sufficient to note that it reproduces the institution of the interrex which is, in fact, one of the most widespread and familiar elements of the Seasonal Pattern.[67]

(*b*) In the same text (II AB, vii 7–12), after the completion of his palace and just before his official occupancy of it, it is said of Baal that

he traveled from [city] to city,
turned from town to town,
assumed possession of sixty-six cities,
of seventy-seven towns,
yea, of eighty . . . . . .,
even of ninety . . . . . .

On the face of it, this episode would seem to have little relevance to the main tenor of the narrative. When it is recalled, however, that among several ancient and primitive peoples the assumption of kingship is usually marked by a tour of the royal territories, and that this procedure was indeed observed at the seasonal festivals of Egypt (where the king toured his provinces by sailing down the Nile in a ceremonial bark) and at the Nuntariyashas Festival of the Hittites, and that it survived in the Roman Festival of Lupercalia and in the "beating of the bounds" which features so prominently in European (especially British) calendar customs,[68] it is not difficult to perceive that the poet was here working into his narrative one of the canonical elements of the seasonal festival for which his composition was designed.

(*c*) In the Hittite *Myth of Telipinu* (KUB XVII 10 iv 27–28), after the restoration to earth of that lord of fertility and after his formal occupancy of his palace, it is said that he "took thought for the king" and that a sacred pole was erected in his house and fleeces of sheep suspended from it. Now, the Hittite text KUB XXV 31, which is a fragmentary account of the rites performed at the annual Festival of Puruli, states expressly that it was the custom on that occasion to present a sacred pole and other appurtenances to Telipinu and to replace last year's soiled fleeces with new ones (lines 5–7). Furthermore, in KUB XXIV 1–2, which is a prayer addressed to Telipinu by the king on each day of a certain festive occasion, there is a particular petition for the life, health, strength, and happiness of the royal family (iii, 1–14; iv, 5–7); while a formal reinvigoration of the king by Telipinu (coupled with the characteristic seasonal rites of building new palaces and expelling evil!) figures as a dominant element of the ritual described in KUB XXIX 1.[69] It is therefore apparent that our mythological text reproduces standard ritual and reflects specific seasonal ceremonies.

Nor is it only by virtue of their *contents* that our texts may be identified as seasonal dramas. Equally cogent is the evidence derived from their *form*.

(*a*) Of the Hittite texts, both the Yuzgat Tablet and *The Snaring of the Dragon* are expressly divided into a mythological and a ritualistic portion; while, conversely, in the Canaanite *Poem of the Gracious Gods* the first part (on the obverse of the tablet) consists of liturgical and ritualistic matter, and the second (on the reverse) of the mythological narrative proper. It is therefore apparent that these texts are more than mere literary compositions, but, in each case, the "book of words" for a religious ceremony.

(*b*) In two instances, the Canaanite poems appear to incorporate the texts of hymns which must originally have enjoyed independent existence as standard and traditional elements of the seasonal "order of service." The first such instance occurs in II AB vii 27 ff. Baal is about to enter the newly built palace. Thereupon, Koshar, the divine architect, bursts forth into the following song of praise:

When Baal opens a rift in the clouds,
When Baal gives forth his holy voice,
When Baal keeps discharging from his lips,
his holy voice convulses the earth,
. . . .
a-quake are the mountains,
a-tremble are the . . . .,
east and west the high places of the earth heave.
The enemies of Baal take to the woods,
the foemen of Hadd to the sides of the mountain!

And Baal replies:

The enemies of Baal — oh, see how they quake!
yes, see how they quake!
They who challenge us are thrown into a panic(?)!
Baal first marks down with his eyes,
then strikes with his hand;
why, even the cedar quakes at the touch of his right hand!

That these lines are taken from a standard hymn to Baal (alias Hadd) as lord of storm and thunder is apparent from the fact that phrases from them are quoted almost verbatim in the Tell Amarna letters (147:14–15) and in sundry poetic passages of the Old Testament (e.g., Psalm 29:5; Nahum 1: 5–6).

The second instance occurs in I AB vi 42 ff. The sun-goddess Shapash has just induced the contumacious Mot to give up the unequal struggle against Baal, and the latter has now occupied the throne of sovereignty. Thereupon he commends the goddess in the following words, assuring her of honor and distinction and promising her that she will be protected on her daily journey by that valiant champion, Koshar-wa-Khasis (Sir Adroit-and-Cunning) who has erewhile distinguished himself by assisting in the conquest of the great Monster of the sea.

Bread of aggrandizement shalt thou eat,
wine of favor shalt thou drink.
O Shapash, o'er the shades (?) shalt thou have dominion,
O Shapash, thou shalt have dominion o'er the upper gods (?);
Lo, gods shall be thy witnesses
and mortals too.
Verily, Koshar shall be thine escort,

Khasis thy companion,
even that Koshar-wa-Khasis who threw into the sea
Monster (?) and Dragon,
even that Koshar-wa-Khasis who hurled them therein!

When we recall that the *Poem of the Gracious Gods* likewise includes an invocation to this goddess (lines 25–26), that a hymn to the sun was similarly recited by Solomon when he dedicated his temple to Yahweh at the autumnal Festival of Ingathering (I Kings, 8:12–13),[70] and that — as pointed out above (Chapter Two, §37) — seasonal festivals usually coincided with solstice or equinox, and when we observe, further, that the several phrases of this speech are paralleled elsewhere in hymns addressed to the solar deity, it becomes evident that the poet has here worked into his narrative one of the standard liturgical compositions of the festival for which his piece was designed.

This device finds a perfect and arresting parallel in the *Bacchae* of Euripides, the choral odes of which are — as most scholars have recognized[71] — nothing but embellished versions of the traditional chants recited in the Bacchic mysteries. Indeed, if the long and beautiful chorus, *Bacchae* 64–169 be compared carefully with the ritual *Paean to Bacchus* discovered at Delphi, it will be found that it reproduces not only the general tenor and sentiment of the latter, but also almost all of its standard clichés and technical terms.[72] Similarly, a choral ode quoted by Porphyry from the lost *Cretans* of Euripides turns out, once again, to be but a poetic elaboration of the canonical Dionysiac chant.[73] Our position is, then, that just as Euripides worked into his literary dramas the standard hymns of the seasonal festivals out of which they evolved, so too did the Canaanite writers.

(*c*) Both the Hittite *Snaring of the Dragon* and the Canaanite *Poem of the Gracious Gods* are introduced by prologues, and each of these prologues may be traced back to a ritual formula customarily recited at seasonal festivals.

In the Hittite text (obv. 5–7), it takes the form of a rhymed petition for rainfall and fertility, the style and language of which are paralleled in similar rogations recited at calendar festivals in many parts of the world. In the Canaanite text (1–7; 23–27), the ritual basis is even more apparent; for the formula is cast in a standard hymnodic pattern, consisting in a solemn invocation of the gods, a recitation of their epithets, and a formula of greeting [*sh-l-m*] extended to the assembled worshipers. It is placed in the mouth of a single speaker, being introduced by the word "*I* will invoke" [*iqra, iqran*].

This, too, possesses an admirable parallel in classical Greek drama; for Greek plays invariably begin with a prologue, and it is now well recognized that this prologue developed out of a more primitive ritual formula (*prorrhēsis*) which served originally, like the Sanskrit *nandi,* not to introduce the characters but to inaugurate the religious ceremonies at which the play was performed. Moreover, the single speaker into whose mouth the prologue is placed in the Canaanite text answers exactly to the Sanskrit *sutradhara* and the Greek *chorêgos,* i.e., the priestly "presenter" of the sacred pantomime.

(*d*) Significant also is the fact that some of the texts presuppose the presence of a chorus. Thus, the Ramesseum Drama (l. 68) speaks explicitly of a "group of conductors" — a term which occurs in other Egyptian texts as designating a branch of the clergy.[74] Similarly, the Edfu text implies a choir of temple singers and musicians who enact the part of the friends and supporters of Horus and who shout encouragements to him in the manner of latter-day "rooters" at a ball game.[75] Furthermore, in the Canaanite *Poem of the Gracious Gods* (line 12), certain *ʿ-r-b-m* are said, at one point, to intone a refrain. The term in question is probably to be identified either with pilgrims in general or else, more specifically, with the Accadian *erib biti* (lit., "one who enters the house") — a generic name for the lesser sacristans or members of a temple staff. Indeed, they are associated in the opening words of greeting (line 7) with persons called *th-n-n-m,* a term which recurs in another Ugaritic text in a list of *sacerdotal officials.*[76]

It is thus once again apparent that our texts were designed for recitation or enactment in connection with temple ceremonies. In other words, they were part of an established order of service rather than mere specimens of literary creativity.

A final point in favor of the view that these texts are the mythic counterpart of seasonal rituals is the fact that they tend to depict the stock situations of the Seasonal Pattern in virtually identical terms. This suggests that they drew upon a stock of phrases and expressions ("clichés") which had become familiar, stereotyped, and — so to speak — canonical, by dint of repetition, year in, year out, in traditional, time-honored ceremonies. The point is best illustrated by a comparison of those passages in the several known myths which describe the failure of rainfall and vegetation consequent upon the withdrawal of the lord of fertility. It will be seen that the same language and the same ideas run through all the versions; and by further comparison with the seasonal litany embedded in the first chapter of the biblical Book of Joel it becomes apparent that this is due to dependence upon a common ritualistic source.

NOTES

1. See above, Chapter One.
2. It is not without significance that ancient speech recognizes no such concept as "myth" in the usually accepted sense of the term. Greek *mythos* means simply "a thing told," and implies only a literary category.
3. See fully R. J. Tiddy, *The Mummers' Play* (1923).
4. Evidently a reminiscence of the Crusades. But note that the adversary is also called "Prussian King" (Cinderford, Gloucestershire), "Black Prince of Darkness" (North Somerset), "Bold Slasher" (Sapperton, Gloucestershire; Overton, Hampshire), "Mince Pie" (Cocking, Sussex), "Little John" (Waterstock, Oxfordshire; Great Wolford, Warwickshire), "Captain Thunderbolt" (Ilmington, Warwickshire), "Bold Striker" (Heptonstall, Yorkshire), "Beelzebub" (Clayworth, Nottinghamshire), and "Arthur Abland" (versus Robin Hood; Kempsford, Gloucestershire).
5. *Enuma Elish, passim.*
6. KBo III 7; see below, pp. 245 ff.
7. Baal, §§XII–XVII.
8. Baal, §§LXIX–LXXI.
9. E.g., Papyrus of Nesi-Amsu; Budge, *Gods* ii 324–28; Roeder, *Urkunden,* 98–115. Cf. also Renouf, TSBA 8 (1883), 215–17 (partially antiquated, but still useful).
10. E.g., in the Ramesseum drama.
11. Isaiah 27:1; 30:7; 51:9–10; Ezekiel 29:2–5; 32:3, etc.
12. Frankfort, *Kingship,* 102 ff.; Moret, *Mystères ég.,* 73–84.
13. This is a prominent theme, for instance, in the Ramesseum drama.
14. Pallis, *Akitu,* 264–65.
15. *Ibid.;* EE VI, 37–48[b].

16. On this term, see Gaster, JQR, N.S. 28 (1947), 289.
17. KAT 515; Pallis, 183 ff.
18. Langdon, *Epic of Creation*, 48–49.
19. Davis-Gardiner, *Tomb of Amenemhet*, 42, with n. 2; Faulkner, JEA 22 (1936), 132.
20. Ram. §XI; Shabaka, Act III.
21. Allen-Sikes-Halliday, *Homeric Hymns*, Introd. to *Hymn to Demeter*.
22. Beza, *Paganism in Roumanian Folklore*, 30.
23. Canziani, FL 39 (1928), 218.
24. See below, Introduction to *The Poem of the Gracious Gods*.
24a. EE I 78; cf. Oppenheim, in *Orientalia* 16 (1947), 214.
25. These are most conveniently presented in Langdon, *op. cit.*, 29–59. See also, Pallis, 208 ff.
26. See above, Chapter Two, §26.
27. VAT 9555. 57–59 (= Langdon, *op. cit.*, 44–47).
28. See Comm. on *Gracious Gods*, §III.
29. VAT 9555.33.
30. It is not without significance that the Egyptian "mystery" was called *sesheta*, "the secret thing," implying that it was regarded – as were all later mysteries – as an esoteric thing reserved to initiants.
31. Sethe, *Dramatische Texte*, i.
32. Sethe's dating is based largely on the mention in this text of a type of priest called *sekhen akh*, "reviver of the spirit," characteristic of the First Dynasty.
33. For a general description of the ceremonies, see Blackman, in Hooke's *Myth and Ritual*, 29–32; Frankfort, *Kingship*, 103–04.
34. The keys list the speakers, the locale, and the stage settings and properties pertinent to each scene. They are reproduced in our rendering.
35. This is a kind of Egyptian forerunner of the later Jewish *midrash*, which makes considerable use of paronomasia in the homiletic exegesis of Scripture.
36. For verse rendering and commentary, see below, pp. 393 ff.
37. In Jane Harrison's *Themis*, 314 ff.
38. *Ancient Art and Ritual* (1913).
39. *The Origin of Attic Comedy* (1934).
40. In the light of the ancient and primitive material presented in this volume, it is apparent that the objections raised by Classicists against the basic contention of the Murray-Harrison-Cornford theory rest on far too narrow a basis. While it may be true that within the Greek field the evolution of drama was not quite as those scholars have supposed, and while many of their particular inferences from later forms may indeed be open to doubt, the ultimate origin of the genre as a whole is now surely beyond question.
41. Cornford, *passim*.

42. Tiddy, *op. cit.*, 73. For a representative mummers' play, see below, pp. 437 ff.

43. See fully, Tiddy, *op. cit.*

44. Cf. Eerdmans, ZA 9 (1894), 280–307.

45. Dawkins, JHS 26 (1906), 191; Wace, ABSA 16 (1909–10), 232; Cornford, 62–65.

46. The standard edition is C. H. Gordon's *Ugaritic Manual.* Useful also is G. R. Driver's *Canaanite Myths and Legends.* Translations by H. L. Ginsberg are included in ANET. Gordon also has published a rendering in his *Ugaritic Literature,* and Driver in the aforementioned work. These versions often differ considerably. The present interpretation is based largely on the writer's independent researches.

47. Originally published as "The Legend of Dan(i)el." But one of the tablets bears the explicit title *lAqht*, i.e., "belonging to (the Poem of) Aqhat."

48. See below, *Aqhat,* Introduction, n. 317.

49. See below, pages 321 ff.

50. For Bibliography, see below, page 111.

51. There is, however, no authority for assuming, as has been done, that there was also a ritual *race;* see Goetze, JCS 1 (1947), 85.

52. The most convenient edition is Langdon's *Epic of Creation,* and the most recent English rendering that of E. A. Speiser in ANET. For some suggestive new interpretations, see Oppenheim, Orientalia 16 (1947), 207–38.

53. See above, n. 25.

53a. For Bibliography, see page 112.

54. OLZ 32 (1929), 145–56.

55. 63. 4, 6.

56. 62.3. He is also called "the Perverse One," 68.2.

57. Blackman-Fairman, JEA 28 (1942), 35–36.

58. Such "reciters" also functioned at Babylonian festivals: Ebeling, *Bruchstücke,* 1; Smith, *Isaiah XL–LV,* 111, n. 138.

59. Blackman-Fairman, *op. cit.*, 35.

60. The distribution of these elements over the several texts is set forth in Table I.

61. Translated by Gurney, AAA 27 (1940), 1 ff.

62. EE VI; Pallis, *Akitu,* 124 f.

63. Orientalia 16 (1947), 214.

64. JRAS 1935. 72.

65. See Comm. in loc.

66. Gilbert Murray, in Jane Harrison's *Themis,* 314 ff.; Cornford, *Origins of Attic Comedy,* 59 ff.

67. Frazer, GB, one-vol. ed., 389 f.; *idem., Fasti,* ii 48 ff. For the mock king at the Persian festival of Sacaea, see Ctesias, ed. Baehr, 449–51. For a temporary "rice-king" in Siam, cf. Cabaton, ERE xi 485a. Winckler, *Altor. Forsch.*, ii 351–58 discovers a ref-

erence to the interrex in a Sabaean inscription (CIS IV 83.3 f), but this interpretation is questionable. See further, Chapter Two, n. 4.

68. II AB vii 5–12; see Comm. on Baal, §XL.

69. Ed. Schwartz, Orientalia 6 (1947), 23–55. For a later translation, see Goetze, ANET, 357–58.

70. Thackeray, *Septuagint in Jewish Worship,* 76 ff.

71. See especially: E. R. Dodds, *Euripides' Bacchae* (1944); Gilbert Murray, *Euripides and his Age*. Cf. also R. P. Winnington-Ingram, *Euripides and Dionysus* (1948).

72. For translations of both texts, see pages 467 ff.

73. Porphyry, *De abstin.,* iv.19, translated by Murray in Jane Harrison's *Prolegomena,* 479.

74. See Comm. on Ram. §XXI.

75. Blackman-Fairman, *op. cit.,* 35.

76. See Comm. in loc.

PART TWO

SEASONAL MYTHS OF THE ANCIENT NEAR EAST

FOREWORD

All folk tales everywhere depend for their point not only on what is stated but also on what is implied. By a hint here and a parenthesis there the narrator will evoke in the minds of his audience a host of familiar ideas and associations necessary to give sense and coherence to the bare sequence of incidents. He will say, for example, that at a given point the witch took her broomstick; and everyone will know at once that she flew through the air. Or he will say that the hero donned his magic boots, and it will be clear to all who hear him that at this juncture miraculous distances were traversed. Similarly, if he introduces a fairy, nobody questions, should the tale require it, but that she possesses the usual magic wand; and if a stepmother enters the cast of characters, it is assumed, on the authority of age-old tradition, that she is a cruel and heartless harridan. These things are part and parcel of a living tradition which all popular narratives take for granted and without which no story can ever be told completely.

In the case, however, of the myths and tales which have come down to us from remote antiquity we are in the awkward predicament that the accompanying tradition has long since died out. All that remains is the bare skeleton of words, and even the most faithful translation of these will often be insufficient to reconstruct the true point and motivation of the narrative as a whole or of this or that particular incident in it. When, for instance, we are told in the Canaanite *Poem of Baal* that in order to reach the abode of Mot, god of the underworld, the divine couriers have to travel to the mountains of Tarhuzizza and Sharumagi, the point is lost to us entirely unless we realize that these names indicate a region to the north of Syria and therefore bespeak an ancient and widespread belief that the underworld lay in the north, close beside the great mountains which were thought to hem in the earth. Similarly, when we read in the Hittite *Myth of Telipinu* that, after the failure of the gods to do so, a bee was sent out to locate that lost divinity, the point is again lost to us unless we bear in mind that in popular superstition beeswax and honey are regarded as instruments of rejuvenation and the sting of the bee as a simple for curing paralysis and similar affections.

Such necessary links in the chain of the narratives can be supplied only by comparative mythology and folklore. If, that is to say, we can succeed in showing that a seeming lack of coherence in a story can be resolved by assuming that the narrator there drew upon a widespread and commonly accepted piece of folklore, we may often clarify what the mere verbal text leaves obscure. That is the method which we have adopted in the following commentaries. We have tried to recognize and point out the presence of motifs familiar in the lore of other peoples — especially other ancient peoples — and to indicate how the assumption of such an element rounds out the narrative and gives it added meaning. We do not claim that the method is without its pitfalls. Above all, the temptation must be avoided of "calling snap" with remote and unique "parallels." Indeed, it may be said with truth that what an Arabic lexicon is in the hands of an undisciplined philologist, that is *The Golden Bough* when used by an undisciplined mythologist. The parallels must be widespread and diverse, and they must in all cases hark back to basic religious or popular notions which indeed find expression in other departments of ancient Near Eastern life. To revert to our examples, nothing would be clarified if it were to be shown only that the belief in an underworld situated in the north obtained exclusively, let us say, among the Papuans. But when we can document this idea for a variety of diverse cultures and also find echoes of it in ancient Near Eastern religious literature and practice, the case is far different. In our detection of motifs we have accordingly kept this essential principle clearly in mind.

This approach to ancient Near Eastern literature is virtually new. Thus far — perhaps by necessity — the material has been studied primarily (and sometimes exclusively) by philologists. Wider interpretations have therefore perforce been neglected; and a tradition has even arisen that the meaning of a text can be regarded as determined when it has been correctly translated. But this ignores the fact that words are, at best, the mere shorthand of thoughts, and that folk tales originate in the mind rather than in the mouth or from the pen. Our task must be to get behind the words to what semanticists call their "referents"; and this is the domain of cultural anthropology and folklore rather than of philology.

In the case of the texts presented in this volume, the basic philological work has very largely been accomplished. Accordingly, we have not thought it necessary to provide a linguistic commentary. We are addressing ourselves primarily to that wider circle of readers who would wish to understand the meaning of these documents as materials of folklore rather than as "texts." Moreover, our purpose in presenting them in the first place is to furnish examples of the development of drama from ritual; they are therefore in the nature of illustrations to our main theme, and as such they are treated. To avoid misunderstanding, however, it may be observed that each document has been studied afresh from the purely philological angle, and that the translations are based upon the writer's independent researches in this field. The only exception is the Egyptian texts, the interpretation of which is original but the rendering of which is taken from the work of Kurt Sethe.

The writer would express the hope that, despite imperfections of performance in the present instance, the method here adopted may enlist the support of Orientalists in the future and contribute to the better understanding of ancient Near Eastern myths and tales.

INDEX OF TEXTS

CANAANITE TEXTS

Only the *editiones principes* by Charles Virolleaud are here listed. The texts have been collected and freshly transliterated by C. H. Gordon in his *Ugaritic Handbook* (Rome, 1947). References to this edition are given in the margin of our renderings. For a bibliography of Ugaritic studies (up to 1945), see de Langhe, R., *Les textes de Ras Shamra-Ugarit et leurs rapports avec le milieu biblique de l'Ancien Testament* (Gembloux, 1945).

1. THE POEM OF BAAL:

III AB, C	SYRIA 24 (1944–45), 1–12
III AB, B	[Gordon 137]
III AB, A	SYRIA 16 (1935), 29–45

II AB *ibid.*, 13 (1932), 113–63
I* AB *ibid.*, 15 (1934), 305–36
I AB *ibid.*, 12 (1931), 193–224; 350–57; 15 (1934), 226–43

Subsidiary Texts:
V AB *La déesse ʿAnat* (Paris, 1938), 1–90
BH (*Harrowing*) SYRIA 16 (1935), 247–66

Unplaced Fragments:
IV AB SYRIA 17 (1936), 150–73
VI AB *La déesse ʿAnat* . . ., 91–102

2. THE POEM OF THE GRACIOUS GODS:
SYRIA 14 (1933), 128–51

3. AQHAT, OR THE STORY OF THE DIVINE BOW:
La légende phénicienne de Danel (Paris, 1936)

HITTITE TEXTS

1. THE PURULI TEXT:
KBo III, 7; KUB XII, 66; KUB XVII, 5–6.
Zimmern, H., in Lehmann-Hass, *Textb. z. Religiongesch* (Leipzig-Erlangen 1922), 339 ff.
idem., "Der Kampf d. Wettergottes mit der Schlange Iluyankas," in *Streitberg Festgabe* (Leipzig, 1924), 430–41.
Sayce, A. H., in JRAS 1922, 177–90; 1927, 90–93.
Friedrich, J., *Hethitisches Elementarbuch,* II (Heidelberg, 1946), 51–53.
Kretschmer, R., "Indra und d. heth. Gott Inaras," in KlF 1 (1929), 309 ff.
Porzig, W., "Iluyankas und Typhon," in KlF 1 (1930), 379–86.
Goetze, A., *ANET*, 125–26.
Furlani, G., *La religione degli Hittiti* (Bologna, 1936), 82–86. [Follows Goetze.]
Seippel, G., *Der Typhonmythus* (= Greifswalder Beitraege z. Literatur u. Stilforschung, 24), Greifswald, 1939.

2. THE YUZGAT TABLET:
Sayce, A. H., and Pinches, T. G., *The Tablet from Yuzgat in the Liverpool Institute of Archaeology* (= Asiatic Scy.

Monographs, vol. xi), London, 1907.
Sayce, A. H., in JRAS 1920, 70–83; 1924, 645–54; 1930, 318–19.
Goetze, A., *Verstreute Boghazköi-Texte* (Marburg, 1930), No. 58.

3. The Myth of Telipinu:
KUB XVII, 10; Scheil, V., in Chantre, E., *Mission en Cappadoce* (Paris, 1898), 58–60; Bo. 2488 (cf. OLZ 36 [1933], 1).
Otten, H., *Die Überlieferungen d. Telipinu-Mythus* (= Mitt. d. Vorderas.-Aeg. Gesellschaft, XLVI, 1), Leipzig, 1942.
Sayce, A. H., in JRAS 1930, 301–19.
Goetze, A., *ANET*, 126–28.
Furlani, G., *La rel. d. hitt.*, 82–86.

4. A Ritual Combat:
KUB XVII, 35 iii 9–17.
Ehelolf, H., in SPAW 21 (1925), 266, 267–72.
Lesky, A., in ARW 24 (1927), 73–82.
Schubart, W., in *Gnomon* 2 (1926), 63.
Goetze, A., *Kleinasien,* 152.
Furlani, G., *La rel. d. hitt.*, 63.
Forrer, E., in *Klio* 30 (1937), 174.
Gaster, T. H., in *'Iraq* 6 (1939), 117–18.

EGYPTIAN TEXTS

1. The Ramesseum Dramatic Papyrus:
Sethe, Kurt, *Dramatische Texte zu altägyptischen Mysterienspiele, II. Der Dramatische Ramesseumpapyrus. Ein Spiel zur Thronbesteigung des Königs* (Leipzig, 1928), 83–264.
Blackman, A. H., in *Myth and Ritual,* ed. S. H. Hooke (London, 1933), 29–32.
Frankfort, H., *Kingship and the Gods* (Chicago, 1948), 123–39; 376–77.

2. The Memphite Drama:
Sethe, Kurt, *Dramatische Texte . . .,* 1–80.
Breasted, J. H., "The Philosophy of a Memphite Priest," in ZÄS 99 (1901), 39–54.
idem., The Dawn of Conscience (New York, 1933), 29–42.
Junker, H., *Die Götterlehre von Memphis* (*Schabaka-*

Inschrift), in *Abh. Preuss. Akad. Wiss.*, Phil.-hist. Kl., No. 23 (Berlin, 1939).

Frenkian, A. M., *L'orient et les origines d'idéalisme subjectif dans la pensée européenne.* Tome I: *La doctrine théologique de Memphis. L'inscription du roi Shabaka* (Paris, 1946).

Holmberg, M. S., *The God Ptah* (Lund-Copenhagen, 1946).

Earlier studies are now virtually useless, because not until the edition of Breasted was it realized that the text is written *boustrophedōn.*

A. THE COMPREHENSIVE TYPE

THE CANAANITE POEM OF BAAL

A. SYNOPSIS

In the gray beginning of years, when their various domains were assigned to the gods, Earth had no lord or master. Two gods especially contended for the position. The one was BAAL, lord of the air and genius of the rain; the other was YAM, master of the sea and of the subterranean waters. Each based his claim on the time-honored Oriental principle that the rightful owner of a piece of land is he who "quickens" it and brings it under cultivation.

III AB, C

The poem opens at the point where the supreme god El accords the sovereignty to Yam, genius of the waters, and orders that a palace be built for him by the divine artisan, Koshar ("Sir Adroit"). Thereupon, however, Ashtar, the spirit of artificial irrigation, interposes a plea for the dignity and privilege accorded to Yam. But his plea is rejected on the grounds that he has no wife, i.e. is still a minor; and the sun-goddess (Shapash) warns him to accept the decision and relinquish his claims.

[II AB, *C]

[There is now a large gap in the text, but the sequence may be supplied from an Egyptian papyrus of the Eighteenth or Nineteenth Dynasty, which appears to represent an adaptation of our tale. This document, formerly in the Amherst Collection and now in the Morgan Library at New York, tells how the sea (*ym*) once gained supremacy over the gods and proceeded to exact exorbitant tribute from them. Thereupon they resorted to the goddess Astarte and besought her intervention. Astarte went down to the shore, "singing and making merry," and so captivated the heart (or excited the lust) of the sea that he offered to accept her in lieu of any further tribute. Seth (i.e., Baal!), however, gave battle in order to defend the honor of his sister and to assert the dignity of the gods.[a]]

II AB, B

Our Canaanite version resumes at the point where the authority of Yam is at last challenged by that genius of rainfall and vegetation. Baal threatens to dethrone him by main force — more specifically, by smiting him with the two divine bludgeons, Aymr and Ygrsh. After an exchange of taunts and threats, Yam sends messengers to El and to the court of the gods, demanding Baal's surrender. El tries to assuage Yam

[a] Attention was first called to the Egyptian papyrus by S. Birch in ÄZ 1871.119. The latest editions of it are those of A. H. Gardiner in *Studies Presented to F. Ll. Griffith* (London, 1932), 74 ff. and in *Late Egyptian Stories* (Brussels, 1932), 76–81. Photographs were published by P. E. Newberry in *The Amherst Papyri* (London, 1899), plates xix–xxii. Other studies are: W. Spiegelberg, in PSBA 24 (1902), 41–50 and A. H. Sayce, in JEA 19 (1933), 56 ff. On the Canaanite background, see fully T. H. Gaster, in BO 9 (1952), 82–85. Other renderings may be found in: A. Erman, *Lit. d. Aegypter* (Leipzig, 1923), 218–20; G. Roeder, *Altaeg. Erzählungen und Märchen* (Jena, 1927), 71–73; G. Lefebvre, *Romans et contes égyptiens de l'époque pharaonique* (Paris, 1949), 106–13; S. Schott, *Altaeg. Liebeslieder* (Zurich, 1950), 212–14.

That this element of the story enjoyed widespread diffusion in the popular lore of the ancient Near East is shown by the fact that it appears also in a Hittite-Hurrian version in the so-called Legend of the Dragon Hedammu (edited by J. Friedrich in AOr. 17 [1949], 230–54). In that version, the all-devouring Hedammu is likewise encountered by "Ishtar," who goes down to the sea with her maid, Kulitta, carrying a *galgaturi* (tamborine?). Hedammu beholds her "naked limbs" and is inflammed with passion. She pretends that she is the ill-treated handmaid of the queen goddess, who has kept her on short rations, and that she has come to the monster to learn from him how to slake an unsatisfied appetite. Eventually, it would appear (cf. Friedrich, pp. 242–43), she overcomes him. The incident is incorporated also into the Hittite-Hurrian story of Ullikummi, the monster made of stone (cf. H. Otten, *Mythen vom Gott Kumarbi: Neue Fragmente* [Berlin, 1950], 21 f.; T. H. Gaster, *The Oldest Stories in the World* [New York, 1952], 119–20). There too, Ishtar goes down to the sea to beguile (or bewitch?) him with music and song. But, being made of stone, he can neither see nor hear, and therefore remains impervious to her charms!

by assuring him that Baal is really friendly and that his ostensible hostility is not to be taken seriously.

Baal decides to give combat. At first, he assumes a braggart air, but subsequently he is warned by his female accomplice that direct encounter with Yam will probably prove fatal.

At this critical juncture, when all seems lost, Koshar comes to the rescue by supplying Baal with the two divine bludgeons, Aymr and Ygrsh, which possess the magical quality of being able to spring from his hand automatically and which therefore furnish a means whereby the Dragon may be felled without danger of direct encounter. In handing over these weapons, Koshar speeds them on their mission by playing on their names. Since that which is called YGRSH at once suggests the Semitic root *g-r-sh*, "expel," it is urged to "*expel* Yam from his throne, Stream from the seat of his dominion." Similarly, that called AYMR suggests a Semitic word, *m-r-y*, meaning "drive." It is therefore urged to "*drive* Yam from his throne, Stream from the seat of his dominion."

The bludgeons dart from the hand of Baal. The first, however, proves ineffective and misses its mark, but the second strikes Yam, who "sinks to the ground." However, just as Baal is on the point of "calling quits," the goddess Ashtart intervenes.

The conclusion of this episode is imperfectly preserved, but it would appear that Yam admits defeat and acknowledges the sovereignty of Baal.

II AB

Baal has now defeated the Dragon and thus acquired title to eternal kingship. But he has no palace on earth, nor even a permanent residence of any kind. Accordingly, he turns to his companion 'Anat and urges her to take up the matter with Asherat, Queen of the Gods, in the hope that the latter will intervene with her husband, El. In support of his plea, he points out that while all the other gods and goddesses have habitations of their own, he and his brides have to be accommodated in those of El and Asherat respectively. In order to obtain the desired residence, he adds, it will be necessary first to get into the good graces of Asherat, for those who enjoy her favor are always treated royally: at her behest, the artisan god immediately fits out gorgeous quarters for them, complete with a mighty dais "weighing twice ten thousand shekels," cast in silver and coated with gold, footstools and couches likewise encrusted with gold, tables filled with all manner of game and venison, tableware made out of precious metals dug out of the very "foundations of the earth," and statues of animals resembling the small cattle of Amurru and the domestic beasts of Yaman, "wherein are wild oxen by the myriads" (Col. I).

While Baal is addressing the goddess, the vanquished Dragon lies prone, but not dead, at their feet. Before attending to her companion's request, 'Anat therefore tries in some way to dispose of the monster. She grasps her spindle — her traditional weapon — and with it keeps thwacking him and driving him further and further back into the sea. To facilitate the operation, she rips off her robe so that she can wade more easily into the waters (II, 1–7).

Next, the goddess takes two sacrificial vessels and boils them over a fire, to offer their contents in propitiation to El. Then she sets forth on the mission of securing the good offices of Asherat. The Queen Mother, seeing her approach, is at first alarmed, since she fears that her intentions are hostile. However, as the young goddess comes near and Asherat beholds the choice presents which she has brought, her apprehensions are allayed and she "rejoices." Then she instructs her servitor, the artisan and fisher god Koshar, to take a large net and imprison the Dragon within it (II, 8–34).

There is now a break in the tablet. Where the text resumes, someone (evidently Asherat) is issuing instructions to prevent the escape of the Dragon, at the same time assuring Baal that his "foundation" will endure "for all generations." Baal, however, replies to this salutation by complaining of the ignominious treatment which he has been receiving in the assembly of the gods. "Why," he insists, "they constantly insult me and spit on me. Rank food is placed on my table, and I am made to drink the cup of shame (or filth)" (III, 2–22).

At length, Baal and 'Anat come into the direct presence of Asherat in order to voice their grievance. The goddess asks why they have come to her rather than to El, and 'Anat replies that they have preferred to approach "the Mother" before carrying their complaint to "the Father." Thereupon Asherat orders entertainment to be provided for them (III, 23–44).

Next (after a slight gap) the goddess commands her lackey, Sir Holy-and-Blessed (Qdsh-w-Amrr), to caparison a colt so that she may journey to El. The lackey does so, and the goddess sets forth, accompanied by Baal and 'Anat. Presently she reaches the abode of El, which is situated "on the height of the North," at the confluence of the upper and lower oceans. The god welcomes her cordially, remarking that her wandering and her "tramping around" must have made her hungry and thirsty. With typical Oriental hospitality, he proffers food and drink and assures her of his benevolent protection. Asherat then lays the petition before him. El, she says, has wisely decreed (for wisdom, like eternal life, is his by nature) that [on defeating the Dragon] Baal is to be king and ruler of the gods. However, he has no palace, and, to remove this reproach, El is now asked to give permission for one to be built for him. The kindhearted, gentle god readily accedes to this request, remarking humorously that *he* can scarcely be expected to do the menial work of construction himself, but that Baal may readily have his house if only the labor be provided for the initial task of collecting and transporting the bricks! (IV)

Asherat thanks him. Once installed, she adds, Baal will be able to fulfill his functions in orderly fashion. "Baal will furnish his rain in due season . . . his gleam will dart earthward as lightning" — an allusion to the electric storms which are thought in the East to presage rain. Then she gives orders that the good news be conveyed to Baal. The caravans are to rally to his "house": the mountains will yield their silver, the hills their choice gold, and a mansion of shining gems and lapis will be upreared. 'Anat (who has been waiting at a distance) speeds hotfoot to Baal with the joyous tidings. The caravans rally to his house; the mountains yield their silver, the hills their choice gold. When the necessary materials have been assembled, the divine artisan, Sir Adroit-and-Cunning (Koshar-wa-Khasis) — the Canaanite Hephaestus — arrives on the scene to supervise the building. He is regaled at a general feast which Baal gives to the gods, and is given the place of honor at the right hand of his host (V, 1–54).

The talk turns to the construction of the house, which Baal urges his guest to accomplish with speed and dispatch. Sir Adroit (Koshar) begins to sketch his plans: the "blueprint" calls for a window and a casement. "No, no," says Baal, "no window and no casement"; and when Sir Adroit protests, he explains that, were window and casement to be installed, his daughters might escape (or be abducted? — the text is defective) and his enemy, the defeated Dragon, would then be able to "have the laugh on him" (V, 55–61). Sir Adroit, however, presses his plans, and elaborates on the sumptuous luxury of the house. Lebanon and Siryon are furnishing the choicest timbers; fires are being kept burning for six days to melt down the gold and silver. Baal's imagination is fired, and he orders the gods to be further regaled on a lavish scale (VI).

There follows a fragmentary and enigmatic passage referring to the treatment of the defeated Dragon, but only the words "on his pate" are intelligible. Evidently, Baal administers a *coup de grâce* (VII, 1–4).

Baal then leaves his guests and proceeds to annex an "empire" by seizing possession of "sixty-six cities, seventy-seven towns, yea, eighty . . ., even ninety. . . ." Then he returns to his house, and informs Sir Adroit that he has changed his mind about the window and casement; they may be installed. Sir Adroit smiles, and points out the advantages of his design: whenever the window and casement are opened, this will be a sign to Baal to open a rift in the clouds and send down his rain (VII, 5–41). He goes on to describe the power of Baal as a storm god. When he utters his voice (thunder), he rocks the earth. The hills quake', the high places of the earth tremble. The foes of Baal hasten helter-skelter to the shade of the forests or the sides of the mountains. "Yes," replies Baal, "how they quake — those foes of Baal. Those who challenge us are stricken with terror. Baal marks them out and strikes them down (lit., "Baal's eyes anticipate his hands"; VII, 42–52). He then proceeds to announce that he will brook no rival to his sovereignty, and serves notice on Môt, the god of death and aridity, that he will tolerate no interference from him. Môt, excluded from the banquet, is ordered to confine himself, while on earth, to the sunscorched, rainless deserts, where "the tall, shaggy ostriches roam," while Baal wields undisputed sway over gods and men, giving them sustenance and "satisfying the families of the earth." The divine messengers, Gpn and Ugr, the genii of vineyard (*gpn*) and field (*ugr*), are commissioned to convey this message to Môt. They are told to go to the farthermost northern climes, to the two mounds which form the outer bourne of the earth, the mountains of Targhuzizza and Sharrumagi — evidently located in Asia Minor, where the deities Tarhu and Sharruma were worshiped — to uproot mountain and forest, and go down to the depths and corruption of the netherworld, to the realm where Môt dwells. They are to take care, however, not to go too near him, lest he place them "like a lamb in his mouth" and they be crushed between his jaws. His power, they are reminded, is formidable: it is at his will that the sun scorches during the torrid summer days, and the skies flash with electric storms. Keeping their distance, they are to tell him, in Baal's name, that the god has now had a house built for himself [and has installed himself as king. He will henceforth brook no usurpation of his dominion] (VIII).

I*AB

Again there is a break in the text. Where the narrative resumes (on another tablet), Gpn and Ugr have duly relayed the message. That message, it would seem, also contained a broad hint of Baal's intention now to take on other potential resisters of his sovereignty, notably the dragon Leviathan.

Môt, anxious to lure him into the netherworld, sends back word that such exploits would merely wear him out and impair his celestial power, even as he (Môt) himself is now as good as dead as the result of venturing on such an unequal encounter. However, he adds, although his fare is mud, he (Môt, i.e. Death) still retains his proverbial appetite, and, if Baal prefers to exclude him from the housewarming in the upper world, he for his part would be only too happy to regale Baal down below! (I)

[Gap of about 50 lines.]

The invitation is conveyed to Baal, who at first shrinks from accepting it. He beholds the earth gaping to receive him and ready to swallow him up "like a canape or a piece of fruit." He therefore sends a message of abject surrender to Môt: "Thy slave am I, and one of thy perpetual servants!" (II, 1–12).

On receipt of the message, Môt rejoices and (apparently) taunts his adversary (II, 13–26).

[Gap of about 36 lines.]

There follow two fragmentary columns, only the left-hand sides of which are preserved. The first opens with an appeal to the earth to "pay heed," and continues with what appears to be a dialogue with Môt, involving mention of large quantities of sheep. The most probable interpretation is that Baal invokes the earth to spare him the perils of descent to the netherworld, and at the same time tries to buy off Môt with lavish gifts (III–IV).

[Gap of about 55 lines.]

The second column refers to a banquet, and apparently repeats Môt's invitation to Baal.

[Gap of about 40 lines.]

There is now no way out, and Baal has perforce to descend to the netherworld. He is bidden by some unnamed speaker ('Anat?) to take with him his winds and his rains, and go down, accompanied by his brides and by his male and female servants. Directions are given to him as to how to reach his destination. He is to steer his course toward the mountains that bound the earth, to lift them upon his hands and go down "into the corruption of the earth, be counted with them that go down into the earth, and experience nothingness like one who has died" (V, 1–17[a]).

Before doing so, however, he is instructed to perform a curious act. He is to copulate with a calf in the pastureland, the idea being — in accordance with a well-known primitive notion — that he may thereby acquire bull-like strength to fortify him for the impending ordeal. Baal complies with these instructions (V, 17[b]–25).

There is now a further gap of about forty lines. Where the text resumes, we find two unnamed persons — probably Gpn and Ugr — reporting to El their discovery that Baal has "fallen into the earth" and died. El at once institutes rites of mourning. He descends from his throne and sits upon the ground; pours dust and ashes on his head; dons funereal raiment; takes a stone and gashes his flesh, "cutting furrows in his chest as 'twere a garden, scoring his back as 'twere a valley." Then he utters a formal lament, and announces his intention of descending to the earth in order to investigate the matter. Moreover, he instructs 'Anat likewise to descend and to speed to the place where Baal disappeared (VI).

I AB

'Anat in turn performs rites of mourning, and then summons the sun-goddess (Shapash), when she next descends into the netherworld, to load the body of Baal upon her ('Anat's) shoulders so that she may carry it up to the "height of the North"—the divine abode—for burial. The sun-goddess complies, and a hecatomb is offered in honor of the dead god (I, 1–31).

'Anat then directs her steps toward El, at the confluence of the heavenly and subterranean oceans. Prostrating herself before him, she announces that Baal is dead, and that "His Highness, the lord of the earth, has perished," adding sardonically that this might perhaps be welcome news to the rest of the gods (I, 32–42).

El's reaction is that another god must now be appointed as king in place of Baal. Accordingly, he invites Asherat to name a candidate. Asherat replies that whoever is appointed must, in any case, be able to match up to Baal. El agrees, and Asherat thereupon proposes 'Ashtar, genius of artificial irrigation. 'Ashtar is then placed upon the throne of Baal, but fails to measure up to its size. He therefore descends to the earth to exercise his dominion there. The gods are invited to celebrate the event at a banquet (I, 43–67).

'Anat, however, is full of sorrow and disquiet; "like the heart of a cow toward its calf, of a ewe toward its lamb, so is the heart of 'Anat toward Baal." She therefore wanders high and low in search of Môt (Death and Aridity), the god responsible for his discomfiture. At length she finds him. Grasping the edge of his robe in supplication, she implores him to restore her brother. But Môt disdainfully rejects her plea. "What do you want?" he asks. "Whenever I walk abroad, the breath of life automatically departs from mankind. If I come to earth's pleasant places, they are turned immediately to a wilderness, and if I come to earth's beautiful places, they are turned at once to parched fields. If I happen to encounter Baal, I instantly swallow him up; he becomes like a lamb in my mouth." "It is at my will," he adds, "that the sun scorches during the torrid summer season, and the skies flash with electric storms" (II, 1–25).

'Anat bides her time. Eventually, she encounters Môt and lays violent hands on him: "with a sword she rips him up; with a winnowing fan she scatters his members; in fire she burns him; in a mill she grinds him; over the fields she strews his remains" (II, 26–37).

[There is now a gap of some 40 lines.]

Môt having thus been routed, the supreme god El has a dream in which he beholds a return of fertility: "the heavens rain down fatness, the wadies flow with honey." He recognizes this as a sign that Baal is not really dead and, in great joy, bids ʿAnat instruct the sun-goddess to keep an eye open for him on her daily travels. The springs, he says, have run dry, and the soil is in need of cultivation; but for this the presence and good offices of Baal are required. ʿAnat conveys the message to the sun-goddess, who agrees to undertake the search[b] (III–IV).

[There is now a further gap, again of about 40 lines.]

Meanwhile, Baal, now completely restored, engages in a fierce combat with all the other gods, "the sons of Asherat," in order once more to assert himself as king. "Mighty as they are, he trounces them roundly; distinguished as they are, he belabors them with a bludgeon; illustrious as they are, he fells them to the ground." The god ʿAshtar, who was appointed as his successor, is driven ignominiously from his throne (V, 1–6).[c]

A period of time elapses. At length, Môt, likewise revived, flings down a challenge. "Would," he says to Baal, "that I might see *you* treated as I have been treated — ripped up by the sword, burned in fire, scattered by a winnowing fan, ground in a mill, and strewn over the field!" Baal's immediate reaction is lost to us, owing to another tantalizing break in the text. Apparently, however, he accepts the challenge, for in the next episode we find him driving Môt from his seat and launching a mass assault upon him (V, 7–VI, 35).

Môt complains that his adversary has turned all the gods against him, but nevertheless engages Baal in single combat. The fight rages fiercely: "they gore like wild bulls, bite like serpents, attack like rushing beasts." Now the one triumphs, now the other. At last, the sun-goddess, looking from heaven upon the scene, intervenes and advises Môt that further resistance is futile. El will not brook his conduct, being clearly on the side of Baal: "He will pluck up the mainstays of your dwelling, overturn the throne of your sovereignty, break the

[b] Apparently, she bids ʿAnat rally Baal's kinsmen to celebrate his impending return, but the meaning of the text (IV, 42–43) is not quite clear.

[c] This passage has been completely misunderstood by previous commentators. As the sequel shows, it is ʿAshtar, not Môt, who is routed.

scepter of your dominion." Thereupon, in abject terror, Môt surrenders, and acknowledges the kingship of Baal.

[There follow 4 fragmentary lines.]

Baal now turns to the sun-goddess and reveals to her the reward which she will receive for her solicitude and aid. She will "eat the bread of aggrandizement, drink the wine of favor." When she sinks daily into the earth, she will be acknowledged also in the realm of the dead and be known as the "sun-goddess of the Shades" [*Shpsh rpim*]. Both the gods and the spirits of the netherworld will be her "witnesses."[d] She will have as her companion and escort Koshar-wa-Khasis (Sir Adroit-and-Cunning), who was so instrumental in helping to defeat the Dragon. (The idea is that she will be protected against the celestial dragon who, according to a common notion of ancient and primitive folklore, daily tries to swallow up the sun and temporarily succeeds at eclipses.) (VI, 40–52.)

Here the text breaks off.

B. INTERPRETATION

§1. On the face of it, the *Poem of Baal* is a simple, exciting story of the quarrels and contentions of various gods and goddesses, and it is as such that it has been generally regarded. To dismiss it as this and no more is, however, to lose sight of its essential significance; in reality, *it is a nature myth and its theme is the alternation of the seasons.*

The key to the correct interpretation lies in the very names and characters of the protagonists.

§2. Baal is the god of the rain. It is said of him explicitly that he "appoints the due seasons of his rains"[1] and that "his gleam (darts) earthward in the form of lightning."[2] He "opens a rift in the clouds" to send forth his voice and discharge his rains.[3] He is "the Rider on the Clouds,"[4] synonymous with Hadd (Hadad),[5] "the Crasher,"[6] lord of the thunder. When he utters his voice, the earth is convulsed, the mountains quake, the high places reel.[7] At the touch of his right hand, even cedars wilt.[8] During the period when he is absent from the earth, rivers run dry and fields lan-

[d] The interpretation of this passage is, however, by no means certain.

guish;[9] conversely, the replenishment of the wadies is a sure sign of his imminent return.[10] One of his brides is Tallaya,[11] nymph of the dew or morning mist (Hebrew *tal*), while another is Arsaya, nymph of the soil (Hebrew *eres*).[12] Furthermore, he has — at least, initially — no dwelling upon earth; he is therefore a god of the upper air.

In Arabic (and vestigially in Accadian and Hebrew) the expression "land of Baal" means *soil watered by rain.*[13]

§3. Yam, on the other hand, is the god of the sea; but of the sea in an extended sense, which includes all lakes, rivers, and other inland expanses of water,[14] such as were considered in ancient thought to be fed by the upsurging of the subterranean ocean.[15] He is described explicitly as "Lord of the Sea" and "Prince of the Stream."[16]

§4. Mot — whose name means "Death" — is the god of all that lacks life and vitality.[17] He is described as wandering forth over hill and dale and automatically turning them to desolation.[17a] When he is abroad, the breath of life forsakes mankind.[18] His natural habitation is the sun-scorched desert[19] or, alternatively, the darkling region of the netherworld.[20] He is the genius of the torrid summer heat; it is at his whim that "the sun scorches and the heavens flash," sc. with electric storms.[21]

In Arabic, the cognate word *mawāt* means *dead soil which remains arid and infertile.*[22]

§5. Each of these gods was recognized as sovereign in his own domain. Both Baal and Yam are expressly characterized as "princes" or "hignesses" (*zbl*);[23] while the latter in turn shares with Môt the common designation "beloved of El/God" (*mdd* or *ydd Il*),[24] a royal title corresponding to that frequently affected by Babylonian and Assyrian kings.[25] Moreover, the fragmentary text III AB,C explicitly relates the appointment of Yam by El;[26] while the netherworld is just as explicitly defined as the "inherited estate" of Môt.[27]

§6. Baal, Yam, and Môt are thus the direct equivalents of

[*] The name is pronounced Artsaya. In our transliteration *s* here does duty for the Semitic *ts*-sound. Similarly, *eres* is pronounced *erets.*

the classical Zeus, Poseidon, and Hades (Pluto) among whom the world was likewise divided and who reigned respectively over the sky, the waters, and the netherworld. Their three-cornered contest for dominion over the earth represents, however, more than a mere conflict of natural forces; what it symbolizes and allegorizes is, specifically, the alternation of the seasons in the Syro-Palestinian year.[28] Baal, as genius of the rainfall, holds sway during the wet season, from late September until early May. But he does so only after curbing and subduing Yam, the rival power of the waters which, at the beginning of that season, threaten to overwhelm the earth with floods and equinoctial gales and thereby to "possess" it.[29] And he is in turn succeeded by Môt, genius of drought and aridity, who enjoys a free hand upon earth during the dry season from early May until late September.

The contest is predicated upon the ancient Oriental principle that title to land is established by "quickening" it.[30] Baal's claim is, by implication, that he does so by sending the rains; Yam's that he does so by feeding the rivers and wadies. Môt, on the other hand, takes a different line. His argument is (again by implication) that a large part of the earth is, in any case, constantly under his domination and the whole of it in fact subject to him for several months of the year.

§7. That our poem is indeed an allegory of the seasons is shown also by the nature and role of its subsidiary characters, viz., 'Ashtar, Shapash, G-p-n and U-g-r, and Baal's brides, Tallaya and Arsaya.

'Ashtar[31] is described as being nominated by Asherath, queen of the gods, to succeed Baal after the latter's removal from the earth.[32] However, he does not quite "make the grade"; for while he certainly goes down to earth and exercises some sort of sway upon it, it is said distinctly that he is found to be too small to occupy the throne of Baal in heaven![33] 'Ashtar is likewise a rival of Yam; for in the fragmentary text III AB,C we find him petulantly laying claim to the dignities which El decides to confer upon the latter.[34] But here again he does not "make the grade," his claim being rejected on the grounds that he has no wife, i.e., is still a minor. It is apparent, therefore, that 'Ashtar is a god of inferior status who aspires to dominion over both the earth and the waters but who is regarded in each case as not fully qualified to wield it.

Now, in Arabic, just as "land of Baal" means rain-watered soil, and just as *mawāt* means arid and infertile soil, so there is a term *'athtarī* — cognate with the name 'Ashtar — which means *soil artificially irrigated,* and there is even a word *'athur* denoting a canal or trench dug for purposes of irrigation.[35] 'Ashtar, therefore, is the genius of artificial irrigation — a role which the cognate deities 'Athtar and Ishtar seem likewise to fill in South Arabian and Mesopotamian religion;[36] and the reason why he is said to exercise his powers on earth during the period when Baal is ousted is that during the dry season the soil of Syria and Palestine is, in fact, dependent for moisture upon artificial irrigation.[37] At the same time, our allegorical poem is careful to bring out the point that this is no full substitute for rain: 'Ashtar's ministrations are significantly confined to the earth; it is said expressly that he cannot fill the place of Baal in heaven!

§8. Shapash is the sun-goddess.[38] It is Shapash whose aid 'Anat enlists in her search for the ousted Baal.[39] It is she too who succeeds in retrieving that god from the netherworld;[40] and it is she who subsequently urges Môt to give up the struggle against him[41] and whose services are therefore commended by the restored lord of the rains.[42]

All this is part and parcel of the standard seasonal myth. In the Hittite version, it is the sun-god who is similarly dispatched to look for Telipinu, the vanished genius of fertility;[43] and in the Greek version, it is to Hêlios, the sun-god, that the disconsolate Demeter addresses herself when in search of the abducted Persephone; and it is Hêlios who first reports the latter's whereabouts.[44] The parallel role of Shapash thus affords further evidence that our poem is indeed a seasonal allegory.

The basis of this role is not far to seek. Ae we have seen [Chapter Two, §37], the beginnings of the seasons were usually correlated in antiquity with solstice and equinox. Accordingly, the sun had perforce to play a prominent part in any myth connected with those occasions.

§9. In the same way, Baal's two couriers G-p-n and U-g-r bear names which show that they are but personifications of agricultural and, more specifically, of seasonal phenomena. G-p-n is a familiar Semitic word for vine. He may therefore be regarded as the genius of the vintage which in fact takes place in Syria and Palestine at the beginning of the rainy season.[45] As for U-G-R, this name is probably connected with the Accadian *ugaru* (from Sumerian *agar*) meaning field.[46] The divine pair thus personify the viticultural and agricultural features of the wet season.

§10. To Baal's two brides, TALLAYA, "Nymph of the Dew," and ARSAYA, "Nymph of the Soil," we have already alluded (above, §2). It should be observed, however, that each possesses a specifically *seasonal* connotation. In the former we may recognize more particularly a personification of the special drop-forming dew (Arabic *sebib*) which is a characteristic precursor of the wet season in Syria and Palestine and which is actually called *tal* in the Old Testament.[47] As for the latter, while the connection of the soil with rain is self-apparent, the applicability of the name Arsaya to a daughter of the rain god is illustrated especially by the fact that in Arabic a denominative verb derived from the cognate word for "earth, soil," means specifically *to collect moisture and become luxuriant.*[48]

§11. In further support of our view that the subsidiary characters of the story, viz., Ashtar, Shapash, G-p-n and U-g-r, and Tallaya and Arsaya, are but personifications of natural phenomena, designed to point up its seasonal character, it may be observed that none of them, with the single exception of Shapash, is in fact mentioned in the purely ritualistic texts from Ras Shamra.[49] This shows that they were figures of myth rather than of formal cult.

§12. But the poem is more than a mere literary allegory of the seasons. Both its structure and its sequence correspond exactly to those of the Ritual Pattern.

THE FIRST TABLET (III AB,B) relates the triumph of Baal over the Dragon of the Sea (Yam). This answers to the ritual battle with the Dragon, personification of evil or — in a more strictly meteorological sense — of the floods and equinoctial gales. As we have seen (Chapter Two, §20), the battle is a cardinal element of seasonal ceremonies in many parts of the world.

THE SECOND TABLET (II AB) deals with the construction of a palace for Baal and with his installation as king of the earth. This is the durative counterpart of the annual installation of the king. As we have seen (Chapter Four, §13), the construction of pavilions for kings and gods is a prominent feature of seasonal celebrations.

Concomitant with this installation is the banishment of Môt, the dread power of death and drought, to the netherworld and the barren wastes. This, of course, is the durative counterpart of the expulsion of Death (or the analogous figure of Old Year, Blight, etc.) in seasonal ceremonies (see Chapter Two, §14).

The Third Tablet (I* AB) introduces the related seasonal motif of the dying and reviving god. Baal is lured into the netherworld and imprisoned therein. This motif — so familiar from the Tammuz-Osiris-Attis-Adonis cycle — symbolizes the punctual eclipse of the topocosm at the end of each life lease and the discomfiture of its personification — the king.

The Fourth Tablet (I AB) describes the wailing for Baal — a projection of the seasonal ululations; the ursurpation of his dominion by the upstart Ashtar — a projection of the interrex; the restoration of Baal through the aid of the sungoddess — a projection of the solar aspects of the seasonal festival; and his final defeat of Môt — a projection of the Ritual Combat. *On both internal and external grounds, therefore, there is every reason for seeing in the Canaanite* Poem of Baal *a seasonal myth based on the traditional ritual drama of the autumn festival.*

NOTES

1. II AB, iv 68.
2. *Ibid.* 71.
3. II AB, vii 27–29.
4. II AB, iii 11, 18; I*AB, ii 7; III AB,A 8, 29, 33; IV AB, i 7; iii 22, 37. For Teutonic parallels (Gothic *Thorsåkan;* Old Norse *reistarslag,* etc.), see Grimm, *Teutonic Mythology,* 166–67. Thor is called *Reidhartyr,* "god of the chariot."
5. II AB, vi 55; I*AB, i 23–24, iv 7–8; IV AB ii 1–2; *Harrowing* i 40. Similarly, in CT XXV, 16.32, *Ba-'- lu* is listed as an equivalent of Adad.
6. Cp. Arabic *h-d-d,* "crash." Analogous are the Old Teutonic names for thunder, viz., OHG *caprëh<prëhhen,* "to break," and MHG *klec, krach<krachen;* cf. Grimm, *op. cit.,* 178.

7. II AB, vii 29–35.

8. *Ibid.* 41.

9. I AB, iii–iv 25–28; *Harrowing* ii 44–45.

10. I AB, iii 6–9.

11. II AB, i 18; I*AB, v 11; V AB,A 24, C 4, E 4, 50.

12. *Ibid.*

13. For the Arabic term *ba'l* or *arḍ ba'l,* cf. Dalman, *Arbeit u. Sitte,* i, 126; A. Musil, *Arabia Petraea,* ii, 2; S. Curtiss, *Ursem. Religion,* 108; A. Lods, *Israel,* 140–41; K. Hitti, *Short History of the Arabs,* 20; Bokhari, 95 Bulac, defines it as "anything watered by fountains or clouds," and from this Robertson Smith, *Rel. Sem.,* 199 (followed by Barton, *Sem. Origins,* 103 f., and agreeing with Welhausen, *Reste,* 146, and Vogelstein, *Landschaft,* 96 f.) concluded that it denoted soil watered by natural means. But, as Dalman points out (*loc. cit.*), land irrigated by subterranean waters is called quite distinctly *saqi.*

In Mishnaic Hebrew, *bet ha-ba'al,* "place/house of Baal," and *s^e deh ha-ba'al,* "field of ba'al," are similarly contrasted with artificially irrigated soil, called *bet ha-shelakhin,* "place of runnels": Sheb. II 19; Sukkah III 3; Ter. X 11; cf. Epstein, ZAW 33 (1913), 82–83. Cf. also Isaiah 62:4, where there is a play on the two meanings of both *'^a zubah* and *b^e 'ulah,* whereby the abandoned and subsequently irrigated soil is compared to a divorced and subsequently remarried woman; cf. Gaster, AOr. 5 (1933), 119.

The usage may be recognized also in Accadian, for note that in Gilgamesh XI, 41, *qaqqar ^d Bêl,* "soil of Bel (Baal)," has this meaning in contrast to *apsu!* (The entire passage 39–45 is instructive.)

14. The word "sea" is used in this extended sense in all the Semitic languages; cp., for example, Dead *Sea, Sea* of Galilee, etc. German uses *See* in the same way.

15. Cf. Wensinck, *Ocean,* 17; Patai, *Man and Temple,* 59 ff. For the same reason, the Greek Poseidon was the god not only of the ocean but also of springs, cf. Gruppe, *Gr. Myth.,* 1147.

16. It would appear that Yam was recognized by the Canaanites as a full-fledged member of the pantheon. In the sacrificial tariff, RS 1.13, he is mentioned beside U-th-kh-r-y, who is the Hurrian goddess Ishkhara, counterpart of the Semitic Ishtar. Similarly, in RS 9.6, he occurs beside Asherat. Bauer (*AKRS,* 1, fn. k) and Nielsen (*RS Mythol.,* 29) equate Y-m in both passages with Hebrew *yom,* "day," regarding him as god of the day. But seeing that Ishkhara, with whom he is associated in 1.13, is specifically described in CT XXVI, 42 i 10; V R 46, 31 b as "Ishkhara of the ocean" (*^d Ish-kha-ra ti-am-at; ^d Ish-kha-ra tam-dim*), and that Asherath, with whom he is associated in 9.6, is regularly styled "Asherath of the sea" in the Ugaritic mythological texts, his marine character would seem to be assured; cf. Gaster, AfO 12 (1938), 148. – A personal name *'bd-Ym,* "servant of Yam," occurs in RS 80:ii 18;

300.18, rev. 15 Gordon. Similar are *Ym-y* in 322:v.12 and *Ym-il,* "Yam is God," in 322:v.4. With this last Virolleaud compares Yemuel in Genesis 46:10. E. Kutsher (*Kedem* 1 [1942], 44) would also recognize Yam in the legend *L^e-ḤYM* on a seal of the eighth century B.C. from Tell Far'ah (Tirzah?). This he interprets as *La-'^{a}hi-Yam,* on the analogy of *Hiram* = *Ahiram.* (We may also compare *HYRQ* = *Ahiyarak* on a docket from Assur; Lidzbarski, *Ephemeris,* 205 and *HYWH* — *Ahiyahū* on an eighth-century B.C. ostracon from Tell Qasîle; Maisler, JNES 10 (1951), 266.)

17. A Babylonian Mu-u-tu, god of death, is mentioned in Ebeling, *Tod und Leben,* 5; cf. von Soden, W., in ZA 43 (1936), 16; Ebeling, ACTAT, ed.2, 127, n. 9; Böhl, F., in AfO 11 (1936), 208 f. Cf. also Harper, *Letters* vi 540, r.3.

It has been assumed by some scholars (e.g., Ginsberg, JBL 57 [1938], 211, and Dussaud, *Decouvertes,* 104) that Mot has nothing to do with Death, but equates rather with Accad. *mutu,* Heb. **mat,* etc., "man, hero," which certainly occurs in Ugaritic (e.g., GG 40). This, however, ignores the patent antithesis between Baal and Mot corresponding to that between Arabic *ard ba'l* and *mawat.* It also fails to account for the fact that the two places specified as the habitat of Mot, viz., the netherworld (II AB, viii 10–14; I*AB, ii 16) and the desert (II AB vii 56 f.) happen to be those known in Semitic parlance as dwellings of *Death* (see below, n. 20).

Cassuto (*Orientalia* 7 [1938], 286) finds a further argument in the fact that in II AB, vi 8–13 the divine architect refuses to install windows in the palace of Baal for fear that Mot might climb through them and abduct his daughters. This, says Cassuto (followed by Albright, *Archaeology and the Religion of Israel* 198, n. 45 and, more cautiously, by Ginsberg, JBL 62 [1943], 113) recalls Jeremiah 9:20, where Death (Hebrew *Mawet*) is said to climb through windows. Unfortunately, however, this argument must be abandoned, for the fact is that Mot is nowhere mentioned in that passage; the adversary whom Baal fears is Yam (see Commentary on §XXXVI).

Another scholar (Vivian Jacobs, HTR 38 [1945], 80 ff.) has advanced the view that Mot, even if literally meaning "Death," denotes rather the spirit of the grain or of vegetation, who is often fused in seasonal folklore with the figure of "the Death." This view rests mainly on the fact that Mot is said to be winnowed, ground, and burned (I AB ii, 31 ff.) — a fate appropriate only to the personification of the corn (cf. John Barley corn). The argument is seductive, but rigid logic must not be expected in the domain of myth. Mot is also described as a power who roams abroad turning all fertile places to desolation (I AB, ii 15–20) — a characterization which is just as certainly *in*appropriate to the spirit of the corn. This shows that the conception of the fell spirit was fluid and elastic and that, in the popular mind, he was so much identified with the "Adversary" that even the reaping of the grain was regarded as symbolic of his passion.

17a. I AB, ii 15–20.

18. *Ibid.*

19. II AB, vii 55–57. Note that in Arabic and Accadian folklore, the desert is the natural habitat of noxious demons and jinns; cf. *Utukke Limnuti* A iv 5 = Thompson, *Devils*, i, 122.

20. II AB, viii 10–14; I*AB ii 16. In Accadian, the netherworld is indeed called *bit muti;* cf. CT XVIII, 30 rev. 28–30, where É.KUR.BAD is equated with (a) *irsitu,* "earth, netherworld"; (b) *bit muti,* 'house of death'; and (c) *naqbaru,* "grave"; cf. Ebeling, *Tod und Leben,* No. 5, rev. 17; Tallquist, *Totenwelt,* 7, n. 1; Haupt, AJSL 20 (1904), 161. Similarly, in Hebrew it is called by metonymy *mawet,* "Death"; Isaiah 28:15; 38:18; Hosea 13:14; Psalms 6:6; 9:14; 18:5(?); 22:16; Job 28:22; 30:23, etc.

21. II AB, ii 24–25.

22. Arabic *ard mawat* denotes "ownerless, discarded, and waterless land." Cp. also *mawatun,* "uncultivated land"; "land with no herbage or pasture," etc.; Lane, *Lex.* 2741–42. Cf. also Qu'ran 29.63; 25.49. The usage may be recognized also in Genesis 47:19–20 and in the LXX reading (incorrect though it may be) of II Samuel 1:21: "Mountains in Gilboa, let there be no dew nor rain upon you, ye mountains of *death* (*s de mawet*)." Cf. also Hosea 2:5: "And I will make her like the desert and render her like a dry land, and *cause her to die* [*wa-hamitha*]," where the word is used in a double sense. The name Hadramaut (Hebrew Hasarmawet) for the arid stretches of South Arabia reflects, of course, the same usage. In Latin, sterile soil is likewise said to "die"; cf. Martial, *Ep.* xiii,12: *suburbanus ne moriatur ager;* Statius, *Theb.* v, 528: *morituroque ad sibila campus;* cf. Gesenius, *Thesaurus,* s.v.

23. Baal is "prince of the earth" (*zbl ars*) in I AB, iii–iv 28, 40; III AB,A 8. Yam is regularly styled "prince of the sea" (*zbl ym*) in III AB,A and C.

24. Yam is called "beloved of El" (*mdd Il*) in II AB, ii 34; vi 12; vii 3–4; V AB,D 35–36. Mot is called "beloved of El" (*ydd Il*) in II AB, vii 46–47; I*AB, i 8, 13; I AB vi 31. In II AB, vii 47–48, *ydd* stands alone, parallel to Mot.

25. I.e., *naram ili* or *migir ili.* For a list of instances, cf. Labat, *Royauté,* 113 f. The style seems also to have been known among the Hebrews, for this would explain why the prophet Nathan gives the name *Yedid-Yah,* "beloved of Yahweh," to the infant Solomon, destined to be king of Israel (II Samuel 12:25).

26. III AB,C 21–22.

27. II AB, viii 13–14; I*AB ii 16.

28. The Syro-Palestinian year consists of two seasons, the dry and the wet; Dalman, *Arbeit und Sitte,* i 34 f.; Smith, *Historical Geography,* 75. They are known in Arabic as *sef* and *shita,* and in

Hebrew as *qais* and *horeph* (Genesis 8:22; Jeremiah 36:22; Psalms 74:17). The Mishnah distinguishes between "days of rain" and "days of the sun" Dalman, *Arbeit und Sitte, loc. cit.;* cf. Ta'an. III) while in Modern Palestine, November inaugurates the wet season and May the dry; lib., ii 36. A similar twofold division of the year obtains among several primitive peoples. Thus, among the Maipuri, there is a wet season called *ca-repo,* "rain," and a dry called *ca-miti,* "glowing splendor of the sun"; while the Wagogo recognize a dry season (*ki-bahu*) and a wet (*ki-fugu*); cf. Claus, *Wagogo,* 38; Nilsson, *Primitive Time-reckoning,* 54–56. For early Teutonic parallels, cf. Grimm, *Teutonic Mythology* 754. So too, in Celtic lore, the year is divided into the two seasons of "summer-half" (*samradh*) and "winter-half" (*geimhredh*); ERE XIII, V, 838a.

29. Dalman, *op. cit.,* I/ii, 307 f.

30. Cf. Nawawi, *Minhaj,* iii 171 Van den Berg; Welhausen, *Reste,* 108; Robertson Smith, *Rel. Sem.,* 95–97 (referring especially to Abu Yusuf Ya'qub, *Kitab al-Kharaj* [Cairo, 1882], 37).

31. For the spelling 'Ashtar, cf. CT XXV, Pl. 18, rev. 16; Clay, *Morgan* iv 25.39; CT XXV 17 ii 7; K.3500, where this is given as the W. Semitic form of the more familiar Ishtar.

32. I AB, i 53–54.

33. *Ib.,* 59–63.

34. *Syria* 24 (1944–45), 1–12.

35. Robertson Smith, *op. cit.,* 98–99; Bokhari, ii 122 Bulac; Welhausen, *Vak.,* 420; Barton, *Sem. Origins,* 105, 127; Plessis, *Istar-Astarte,* 11 f. This sense of the root *'-sh-r* should also be recognized in the Hebrew text of Psalm 65:10, where the virtually antithetical *sh-q-h* denotes the alternative method of supplying moisture from subterranean sources; cp. Arabic *saqi* of land so watered.

36. Cf. CIS IV 41, 43, 47; Glaser, 888.2; Müller, ZDNG 37 (1883), 371–75. Cf. also Höfner, WZKM 40 (1933), 24; Rhodokanakis, *Stud.,* ii. 83; Nielsen, *Ras-Schamra Mythologie,* 54, n. 4; Ryckmans, i. 17. A similar role is played by the Mesopotamian Ishtar; cf. Craig, *Shamash,* I, Pl. 15–17: "Without thee, (O Ishtar,) is no canal opened up, no river dammed"; Barton, *Hebraica* 10 (1894), 73. Langdon, *Sem. Mythol.,* 348, asserts categorically that Tammuz and Ishtar were "at least in Sumer essentially deities of irrigation."

37. Dalman, *loc. cit.*

38. The name is usually regarded as related to Babylonian Shamash, Hebrew *shemesh,* etc., "sun." This, however, is by no means certain. As a common noun, Heb. *shemesh* is sometimes feminine.

39. I AB, iii 22–48.

40. I AB, i 8 ff.

41. I AB, vi 22–29.

42. *Ibid.*, 42–52.
43. Yuzgat Tablet, obv. 31 ff.
44. Homeric *Hymn to Demeter*, 69–87; Ovid, *Fasti*, iv 515–18.
45. Dalman, *op. cit.*, i, 160 ff.
46. Albright, BASOR 84 (1941), 14, n. 2. There is little probability in Cassuto's view (*Tarbiz* 12 1941, 173) that G-p-n means "winged" (from *gp*, "wing") and U-g-r "hireling" (from *'a-g-r*, "hire"), although it is interesting to note that in Slavonic mythology the messenger of the gods is called Algis, which Schwenk, *Die Mythol. d. Slawen*, 107, derived from Lithuanian and Latvian *alga*, "salary," i.e., "hireling"!
47. Dalman, *op. cit.*, i, 94; Smith, *Historical Geography of the Holy Land*, 65.
48. Cf. Lane, *Lex.*, 47c. Cp. also the German expression *Landregen.*
49. In V AB, D 40 Virolleaud restores the name Ar[s]. However, that passage deals with the monsters vanquished by 'Anat and even mentions Leviathan and Yam. What we require, therefore, is the name of such a being, and comparison with I AB, vi 50 shows that it can be nothing other than Ar[sh], which there stands parallel to Tannin, 'Dragon.' – Similarly, in RS 17.1, at the head of a list of deities, Bauer restores [A]rs; but this too is uncertain, and it would seem just as possible to read [*y*]*rs*, 'may they show favor,' with Ginsberg.

This is not to deny, of course, that a deity of the earth was known to the Semitic religions. Indeed, [d]E-ir-si-tu is specifically mentioned in the Asshur text, VAT 10173, ii 24 (= Schröder, ZA 33 [1921], 130); while Julius Lewy (HUCA 19 1945–46, 429, n. 134) sees a relic of such an earth-deity in the name Arqiel (i.e. Earth-god) given to one of the fallen angels in Enoch vi. – On the concept of Mother Earth among the Semites, cf. Dittmar, ZNTW 9 (1908), 341–44; Nöldeke, ARW 8 (1910), 161 ff.; Baudissin, *Adonis u. Esmun*, 20, n. 1; 443 ff.; 505 ff.; Briem, ARW 24 (1926), 179–95; Stein, *Tarbiz* 9 (1938), 257–77.

Widengren, *Psalm 110*, pp. 9 ff., thinks that the word *tal* (EV. "dew") in Ps. 110.3 is a personification, indicating the existence of a dew-god, to whom the king is there likened; but (a) the text is uncertain – LXX omits the word – and (b) see Gaster, JMEOS 21 (1937), 40, for a different interpretation of the verse. Cf. also Dalman, *op. cit.*, i, 94. Engnell, *Divine Kingship*, 82, n. 5, cites the proper names Abi-tal (II Sam. 3:4) and Y[e]hi-tal (APO 22:57) as evidence for a deity Tal, but the interpretation of these names is far from certain.

Virolleaud (RA 37 [1940], 36, n. 1) finds the deity Gpn in the personal name Gupana of the Ugaritic document, RS 11839.18 (= RA 38 [1941], 9). This, however, is doubtful, because *-ana* is a common ending of *Hurrian* names at Ugarit, e.g. Hudiyana, Zukriyana, Hinaqana, Mahizana, etc. (cf. De Langhe, *Textes de Ras Shamra-Ugarit*, ii, 257 ff.).

A. THE AUTUMN CYCLE

The Waters Return

III AB, C   Gordon: 129

YAM IS APPOINTED LORD OF THE EARTH

The text is too fragmentary for connected translation, but it may be summarized as follows:

I

3–10: Someone whose name is missing repairs to the court of El, "at the source of the Two Rivers, hard by the fountains of the Two Deeps." He makes obeisance, and a conversation ensues concerning the building of a palace for Yam, "prince of the sea" and "ruler of the stream(s)." Mention is made in this connection of the divine architect Koshar-wa-Khasis ("Sir Adroit-and-Cunning"), and the language employed is the same as that which is used later (§XXXV; II AB iv–v, 113–16) to describe the erection of a palace for Baal.

According to Virolleaud, the first editor of our fragment, the person who is here described as coming before El is none other than Koshar-wa-Khasis himself, and the passage describes how he received orders to bulid a mansion or palace for Yam. (The relevant verbs, "build" and "uprear," are translated as imperatives.)

We would propose an alternative explanation. The person who comes before El is not Koshar-wa-Khasis, but 'Ashtar, who draws the attention of the supreme god to the fact that the divine architect is currently building a palace for Yam and who seeks to secure this privilege for himself. The verbal forms which have been construed as imperatives may be understood as third person plural of the imperfect tense (active or passive). This construction, as we shall see, gives sequence and coherence to the entire text.

II

11–14: The next few lines are too fragmentary to yield a connected sense, but they are evidently a continuation of the speech which forms the main substance of the preceding passage, since no alternative speaker is introduced and some of the verbs appear to be in the imperative. We recognize mention of "fever" and "fire" and possibly also of "streams of water." There appears also to be an appeal to the person addressed (i.e., El?) to "call a servitor from the fields" and to have him "draw Yam out of the sea." It may be suggested, therefore — though the suggestion is necessarily tentative — that in these lines 'Ashtar entreats El to have Yam removed from the sea and visited with discomfiture, thus paving the way for his own accession to dominion.

III

15–18^b: The sun-goddess (Shapash) is now introduced. In words reminiscent of the warning which she later issues to Mot (I AB vi 26–29), she advises 'Ashtar to "retire from the presence of Prince Sea, [the presence of the Regent of the Strea]m(s)" lest El hear his contumacious words and "uproot the mainstays of thy dwelling, overturn the throne of thy kingship, break the scepter of thine authority."

IV

18^c–21^a: 'Ashtar replies, but the text is largely unintelligible, and it is not clear whether that reply is addressed directly to the sun-goddess or to El himself. From the fact that the supreme deity is referred to as "the Bull, El, my father" and that the subsequent passage (21^b–24^a) begins, "then the Bull his father pronounces(?)," and that this style is regularly employed in petitions, it would seem that the latter may well be the case. In any event, 'Ashtar here complains that he alone has "no house like the gods, nor precinct like the sacred beings." In other words, despite the advice of the sun-goddess, he presses his claim for the privileges which El has accorded to Yam.

V

21^b–24^a: The supreme god himself now issues his fiat, advising the importunate 'Ashtar that he has appointed "Prince Sea" and the Regent of the Stream(s) to be king, and will grant dominion to none else. Moreover, he adds, there is a further reason why the privilege should not be conferred upon 'Ashtar: he has no wife, as have all the other gods, i.e., he is still a minor. This last observation, it should be noted, tallies in general sense with the description of 'Ashtar in I AB i 56–65:

So 'Ashtar the formidable went up
to the heights of the North,
took his seat on the throne of Baal Puissant;
(But) his feet did not reach the footstool,
his head did not reach the top.
So 'Ashtar the formidable said:
"I can not reign as king in the heights of the North!"
And down went 'Ashtar the formidable,
down from the throne of Baal Puissant,
and proceeded to reign o'er the whole wide earth.

That passage implies that when that god aspired to usurp the throne of Baal in heaven, he was likewise found too small for the job.

The Defeat of the Dragon

BAAL DISCOMFITS YAM

For the proper appreciation of what follows, the formal translation must be preceded by a discussion of the theme as a whole.

The fight of god and dragon — a counterpart of that enacted in ritual in order to bring in the new lease of life — is a constant theme of seasonal myths throughout the world. Moreover, as the concept of time develops from the cyclic to the progressive, this fight comes to be projected both *backward* into cosmogony and *forward* into eschatology; for that which was regarded in more primitive thought as the necessary preliminary to each successive lease of life comes now to be regarded as the necessary preliminary to the entire series and likewise to the establishment of the new dispensation at the end of the present order. In the familiar language of Judeo-Christian cosmogony and apocalypse, the God who engaged and vanquished Leviathan at the beginning of days will perforce do so again at the end of them in order to usher in the New Age.

The principal parallels to our Canaanite myth in the literature of the ancient Near East are the following:

1. the Sumerian myth of the battle of Ninurta against the monster Asag;

2. the Accadian myths of the combat of Marduk against Tiamat and of the discomfiture of the dragon Labbu;

3. the Indian myth of the combat of Indra against Vritra;

4. the Greek myth of the fight between Zeus and the monster Typhon or Typhoeus;

5. the Hittite myth of the struggle between the weather god and the dragon Illuyankas;

6. the Iranian myth of the discomfiture of the serpent Azi Dahak;

7. the Egyptian myth of the battle between Horus and Set;

8. the Phoenician myth of the combat of Kronos (El) against the dragon Ophion or Ophinoeus (= virtually, Leviathan);

9. the Old Testament myth of Yahweh's fight against a dragon variously named Rahab ("Rager"), Leviathan ("Coiled One"), Tannin ("Dragon"), "the Evasive Serpent," and "the Tortuous Serpent."

To these parallels may be added that of the Teutonic myth of the conflict between Thor and the cosmic serpent Midhgardsormr; while certain late Jewish and Arabic legends may also be adduced as supplying one or another trait or detail.

These parallels would be interesting rather than illuminating were it not for the fact that by comparing them carefully it is possible to recover a series of characteristic traits which recur in our Canaanite text and the detection of which helps to clarify many details otherwise obscure. These are pointed out in due order in the commentary which accompanies our translation. Here we shall confine ourselves, for purposes of general reference, to a brief summary of the several versions enumerated.

THE SUMERIAN VERSION is preserved in the poem *Lugal-e u -me-lam-bi-nir-gal.* The hero is the god Ninurta, and the adversary is the monster Asag, who has allowed the subterranean waters to rise and threaten the land. When he is vanquished, the land is hemmed in by a protective wall of mountains, and the unruly waters are channeled between the banks of the river Tigris. The weapons with which the god achieves victory, after initially fleeing in terror, are two bludgeons called respectively SHAR.ÚR, "World-Crasher," and SHAR.GAZ, "World-Smasher."[1]

An alternative version credits the victory to the goddess Inanna, counterpart of the Babylonian Ishtar and the Canaanite Ashtareth.[2]

THE ACCADIAN VERSION exists in several forms. The most familiar is that embodied in the Epic of Creation (*Enuma elish*).[3] This describes how, when all the other gods failed, Marduk defeated the marine monster Tiamat and all her allies, using as his weapons a lance, a net, a thunderbolt (*abubu*), the stormwind and the hurricane. The vanquished monster was split in two, to make earth and the firmament. Another version identified the adversary as a dragon-like creature called Labbu ("The Raging One"). The weapons are there a rain cloud (*urpu*) and the stormwind (*mekhu*).[4] Yet a third version, known only from a passing allusion, features a six-headed dragon,[5] while a fourth refers to a similar monster with *seven* heads.[6]

The myth is also represented on cylinder seals of the first millennium B.C., and it is significant that in several such seals the victorious god is *accompanied by a goddess,* as in our Canaanite text.[7]

THE INDIAN VERSION occurs in a classic passage of the Rig Veda,[8] dating about 1000 B.C.:

> Indra slew the Serpent; he released the waters; he slit open the bellies of the mountains. Tvashtri (the divine smith) fashioned his whizzing thunderbolt . . . His missile the Bountiful One (Indra) grasped, and smote that first-born of serpents . . . Indra slew Vritra . . . with his thunderbolt, that great weapon of death . . . Indra, the lightning-armed, is the king of him that goes and him that rests and of the tame cattle; yea, he rules over busy men.

This account is amplified in several later sources, notably in the Satapatha Brahmana, a ritualistic compendium compiled (probably) in the fifth century B.C.[9] There we are told that Indra was at first frightened of his opponent and fled "to farthermost distances." Subsequently, however, he regained his courage and came to grips with the monster. Eventually he subdued him and thereby forced back the overflowing waters of the western and eastern oceans. Vritra thereupon besought the victorious god to cut him in twain, but not to annihilate him; and this request was granted.

THE GREEK VERSION, narrated principally by Hesiod[10] and

Aeschylus,[11] describes how Zeus slew a fire-breathing, hundred-headed dragon called Typhon, or Typhoeus.[12] This monster lived in the sea, which he continually embroiled, causing sudden squalls and threatening the lives of mariners. He had the temerity to challenge the sovereignty of Zeus, and would have succeeded in making himself king of gods and men, had not the supreme deity smitten him with a thunderbolt and lashed him with a flail of lightning. Finally, he was imprisoned beneath Mount Etna, the volcanic fires of which are caused by his snortings.

Another version[13] says that the other gods fled in terror to Egypt at the sight of the monster. Zeus, however, gave chase and pursued him to Mount Casius, in Syria. But Typhon managed to wrest the god's adamantine sickle out of his hand and therewith to cut off the sinews of his hands and feet. He then carried him off to the Corycian cave in Cilicia. Hermes and Aegipan, however, recovered the sinews and fitted them to Zeus, who thereafter accomplished the final defeat of his adversary, imprisoning him under Mount Etna. This extended version, a form of which occurs already in earlier Hittite sources,[13a] is of particular interest to us because it connects the legend with Mount Casius, in the immediate neighborhood of Ras Shamra.[13b]

THE HITTITE VERSION need not long detain us, since it is discussed in detail in a subsequent chapter.[14] Overladen with other motifs (some of which have familiar folkloristic parallels), it is concerned basically with a fight between the storm and weather god and a dragon called Illuyankas. Of especial interest, however, for reasons which will appear later, is the fact that the story was the cult myth of the annual Puruli Festival and that it was recited in order to bring increase and prosperity to the country.[14a]

A representation of the myth, showing a god about to attack a coiling dragon, is to be found among the rock sculptures at Malatya;[15] while a relief at Karatepe, in which a man is depicted assailing a snake with a sword, has been interpreted in the same sense.[15a]

THE IRANIAN VERSION[16] tells of a rebellious serpent named Azhi (Serpent) Dahaka, a monster with three heads, who was slain by the hero Thraetaona. A later version, comparable with the Sumerian and Greek accounts, maintains, however, that he was not slain but imprisoned beneath the volcanic mountain of Demawend, and that he will be finally annihilated only at the millennium by the hero Sama Keresaspa. This version, it may be added, is also preserved in Armenian sources.[17]

THE EGYPTIAN VERSION[18] relates how the sun-god Ra defeated a dragon called 'Apep, transpiercing him with a flinty sword[19] and with the aid of fire. According to the version preserved in inscriptions at Dendereh, however, the god did not immediately annihilate him, but drove him back into his cavern,[20] and placed over him a stone forty cubits long.[21] This, of course, parallels the Sumerian, Indian, and Greek accounts. Moreover, as in those versions, it is said distinctly that Ra', as well as all the other gods, were at first "in a flutter" about the monster.[22]

The Egyptian version has taken on the complexion of a solar myth, 'Apep having come to be identified with the familiar folkloristic dragon who is believed to attempt daily to swallow up the sun and to succeed in so doing at eclipses. As we shall see presently, there is likewise an allusion to this in Canaanite mythology.[23] Nevertheless, the characteristics of the original myth are still clearly discernible.

Another Egyptian version may be recognized in the dramatic myth of Horus at Edfu. This, as Blackman and Fairman have shown,[24] was enacted at the annual festival in that city. Its central theme was the triumph of Horus of Behdet over his enemies, his consequent enthronement as king of Upper and Lower Egypt, and his sacred marriage with the goddess Hathor of Dendereh. The principal enemy, called "the Caitiff,"[25] is represented as a hippopotamus, i.e., a marine creature directly comparable with Yam, Tannin, and Leviathan of the Canaanite-Hebrew version. The weapon used is a harpoon,[26] and Horus is assisted by Isis, just as is Baal by 'Anat. Significantly, too, the harpoon is said to have been made in copper by Ptah,[27] just as Baal's bludgeons were made by Ptah's Canaanite counterpart Koshar, the thunderbolt of Indra by Tvashtri, and the weapons of Zeus by Hephaistos. Indeed, the fact that they are said specifically to have been made of copper adds to the force of the parallel, for Koshar, like Hephaistos, was primarily a worker in metals.

Noteworthy also is the fact that Horus is armed not only with a harpoon but also with a rope, and that he not only smites his adversary on the head but also, apparently, binds him.[28] Here again we have a striking parallel with our

Canaanite myth; for while in this text Baal is said to smite Yam on the brow and back, in II AB, col. iii, Koshar is instructed to furnish a large net wherein to imprison the monster.

THE PHOENICIAN VERSION is known to us as such only from stray references by Maximus Tyrius[29] and Celsus;[30] but it is mentioned also, without reference to its source, by such late Greek poets as Apollonius Rhodius,[31] Lycophron,[32] and Nonnus.[33] According to this version, necessarily Hellenized, before Zeus could bring the world into being, Kronos had first to fight the dragon Ophion (or Ophioneus) for lordship over nature. Once vanquished, the dragon was cast into the sea. Despite the obvious confusion between El (i.e., Kronos) and Baal, it is clear that this is substantially the same story as is related in our Canaanite poem, Ophion Ophioneus (from *ophis,* "serpent") being a manifest translation of some such Phoenician name as B-sh-n, Leviathan, or Tannin — appellations of the dragon in the Ugaritic and Old Testament texts.[34]

Last, but by no means least, we come to THE HEBREW VERSION of our myth. This has to be pieced together from scattered allusions in the later books of the Old Testament; and the fact that there is a noticeable variation in details makes it uncertain that they all reflect the same tradition. Without exception, the passages in question are of exilic or post-exilic date — the product of a general archaeological revival which swept the whole of the Near East in the sixth–fifth centuries B.C. and, more specifically, of an attempt to recapture the allegiance of the returning and assimilated Jewish exiles by representing their ancestral religion in terms of the "heathen" mythologies with which they had become acquainted. The conquering hero is, of course, Yahweh, in accordance with the propagandistic tendency of attributing the exploits of pagan deities to Israel's own god.

The principal passages which allude to the myth are as follows:[d]

(1) *Isaiah 51:9–10:*

Awake, awake, put on strength
  O arm of Yahweh!
Awake as in ancient days,
  as in olden times!

[d] Emended passages are enclosed between asterisks.

Was it not thou that hewed Rahab,
  transfixed the Dragon (Tannin)?
Was it not thou that dried up the Sea,
  the waters of the great deep?

(2) *Nahum 1:3b–4, 8b–9, 12:*

In the gale and the flail is His way,
  and a cloud is the dust at his feet.
He rebuketh the Sea and drieth it up,
  and all the streams he rendereth dry.
. . .
He maketh an end *of them that rise up against him,*
  and his foemen he chaseth into darkness.
How would ye plot against him?
  He maketh a full end;
Hostility shall rise not twice!
. . .
Thus saith Yahweh:

*What though great waters gushed,
  yet have they ebbed and passed o'er;*
Though I afflicted thee,
  I will afflict thee no more.

These verses occur in an alphabetic hymn which forms a kind of prologue to the oracle of Nahum against Nineveh. From the fact that wherever the name Yahweh occurs (e.g., vv. 2, 3, 7, 9, 11) it is hypermetrical, or else (as in v. 3) the result of manifest interpolation, it is probable that the hymn was originally addressed to some other, Canaanite god, such as Baal, lord of the storm. In it, allusion was made not only to his prowess and might in general, but also to his conquest of the Dragon in particular, since this provided an excellent "object lesson" against Nineveh.

The reference to "plotting" against the god is admirably illustrated from the Babylonian version, which states expressly that the rebel coterie of Tiamat "plotted" against the supreme deity (EE. i, 110).

The reference to the gushing of the great waters (i.e., the streams of the ocean) has added point when it is remembered that, according to Diodorus (II, 27, I) and Xenophon (*Anab.* iii 4, 7–12), Nineveh was destroyed through an exceptional rising of the Tigris!

(3) *Habakkuk 3:8:*

Is it against the rivers, O Lord,
Is it against the rivers
That now thine anger is kindled,
Or thy rage against the sea,
That Thou ridest upon thy horses,
Upon Thy chariots in triumph?

The verse occurs in a poem describing the warlike exploits of Yahweh. The picture of Israel's god riding forth to combat conjures up that of his primeval conflict with the Dragon.

(4) *Psalm 74:13–14:*

Thou didst break up the Sea by thy strength,
shattered the heads of the Dragon (Tannin).

Thou didst crush the heads of Leviathan,
didst give him as food to *fowl and jackals.*

(5) *Psalm 89:9–10:*

Thou rulest the pride of the sea,
When the waves thereof storm Thou stillest them.

Thou didst crush Rahab like one transfixed,
With thy mighty arm didst scatter Thy foes.

(6) *Psalm 93:*

Yahweh is become king;
In majesty is He robed;
Yahweh is girded with might.

. . .

The streams lifted up, O Yahweh,
The streams lifted up their voice;
The sea lifted up . . . .

Mightier than the voices of great waters,
More majestic than the breakers of the sea
Is Yahweh majestic in the height!

Thine ordinances are very sure,
Verily, an abode of holiness is Thy house,

. . .

The psalm clearly alludes to the combat of Yahweh (i.e., Baal) against the Sea and River in order to ensure his sovereignty. The reference to His "ordinances" becomes readily intelligible when it is remembered that Marduk, in token of his victory over Tiamat, received the tablets of fate by which the destinies of mankind were ordained. Similarly, the reference to Yahweh's "house" links up at once with the fact that Marduk had a special fane built for himself when he had vanquished the Monster.

(7) *Job 7:12:*

Am I Sea or Dragon (Tannin),
That Thou shouldst set watch over me?

The passage is explained from the Babylonian version of our myth which says distinctly that after vanquishing Tiamat, Marduk set a watch over him (EE. iv, 139). The reference is particularly significant since it shows that, at least in one version, the Dragon was not slain, but imprisoned. This recurs, as we have seen, in the Sumerian, Indian, Iranian, and Greek accounts.

(8) *Job 26:12–13:*

With his strength He quelled the Sea,
and with His skill He smote Rahab.

• • •

His hand pierced the slant Serpent (*Bari^ah*).

Closely related to these passages are others describing the victory of Yahweh over various other monsters styled Rahab ("Rager" or "Proud One"), Leviathan ("Coiled One"), and Tannin ("Dragon"), the last two of which are mentioned also in the Ras Shamra texts. According to some scholars, all of these are but alternative names of Yam ("Sir Sea"). It would appear, however, from the inclusion of them side by side in the list of monsters enumerated in a passage of *The Poem of Baal* (below, *The Reinstatement of Baal*, §V) that they must be clearly distinguished.

These subsidiary allusions are as follows:

(1) *Isaiah 27:1:*

In that day Yahweh will punish with his sore and great and strong sword Leviathan the slant serpent (*Bari^ah*) and Leviathan the tortuous serpent (*ʿaqallaton*), and he will slay the Dragon (*Tannin*) which is in the sea.

(2) *Isaiah 30:7* ("Oracle against the Beasts of the South"):

And Egypt gives vain and useless help
So I have called her *the stilled Rahab.*

The point here is that Rahab, a common name for the Dragon, means properly "Rager, Stormer." The prophet says, therefore, that the weak and ineffective Egypt will be like the turbulent Dragon after it had been subdued!

There is also a mythological allusion to the ineffective "helpers" of the Dragon in the old myth. They are mentioned again in Job 9:13 where they are said to "sink" before Yahweh (see below). Similarly, the Babylonian version states expressly that at the approach of Marduk, the "helpers" of Tiamat, "quivered, feared, turned tail" (EE iv. 107–108).

(3) *Ezekiel 29:3–5:*

Lo, I am against thee, O Pharaoh,
  king of Egypt,
That art as the great Dragon (Tannin)
  crouching in the midst of his river,
Who said, "The river is mine,
  and I it was who made it."
I will put hooks in thy jaws,

. . .

  and haul thee up from the midst of thy river;
And all the fish of thy river[d]
  shall stick to thy scales.
And I will cast thee into the desert,
  thee and all the fish of thy river.
Out on the fields shalt thou be flung,
  ungathered and unburied shalt thou lie;
To the beasts of the earth and the fowl of the air
  I have given thee as food.

To appreciate the full force of this oracle it is necessary to bear in mind that, according to Egyptian ideas, the Pharaoh caused the annual inundation of the Nile. It is this that gives the prophet the opportunity of likening him to the mythological Lord of the River who was in the end subdued!

(4) *Ezekiel 32:2–6:*

But thou art as the Dragon (Tannin) in the seas,
  and thou belchest with thy snortings,

And muddiest the waters with thy feet,
    and foulest their streams.

Thus saith Yahweh:

I will spread my net over thee,

. . .

    and haul thee up in my mesh,
And I will cast thee upon the land;
    out on the fields will I fling thee.
And I will make all the fowl of the air to settle on thee,
    and sate all the beasts of the earth on thee.
And I will place thy flesh upon the hills,
    and fill the dales with *thy rot;*
And I will water the earth with what exudes (?) from thee,

. . .

    and the wadies shall be replenished with *thy blood.*

(5) *Job 9:13:*

God turns not back His anger;
    (Even) the helpers of Rahab sank under Him.

For this reference to the "helpers" of the Dragon, see above (2).

(6) *Job 41:17–26* [EV. 25–34]. Description of Leviathan:

At his *raging* gods are affrighted,
At his destruction, stalwarts take to hiding.

If a sword *come near him,* it avails not,
Nor a spear, a dart, or a shaft.

He regards iron as chaff,
Brass as rotting timber.

No arrow can put him to flight,
Slingstones are turned with him to stubble.

The club is regarded by him like stubble,
And he laughs at the whizz of the lance.

. . .

He causes the deep to seethe like a pot;
He makes of the sea a stew-pan.

He makes a path to gleam behind him;
One would think the deep to be hoary.

There is none upon earth *that can rule him;*
He is made to cower at naught.

Him do all high things fear;
He is king over all proud things.[35]

THE TEUTONIC VERSION[36] relates how Thor, the thunder god, vanquished the cosmic serpent Midgardsormr with the aid of a hammer called Miölnir, or "Crusher," generally identified by modern scholars with the thunderbolt. Some accounts say that the weapon was fashioned by the subterranean dwarfs, the Teutonic counterpart of the Classical Cyclopes. This detail is of importance because, as is well known, the Cyclopean forge was managed by Hephaistos, and Hephaistos is the equivalent of the Vedic Tvashtri and the Canaanite Koshar, both of whom feature in the respective sister versions as the fabricators of the conqueror's club.

Another version is the slaying of the Lintrache by Siegfried.

It will be seen at once that there are certain motifs which are common to all these versions and which likewise occur in our Canaanite text.

1. In all of them the combat involves a question of sovereignty, the antagonist flinging a challenge at the victor. So too in our Canaanite version, Baal is assured that if he conquers Prince Sea he will acquire undisputed kingship forever; and when he does so, the vanquished adversary indeed exclaims, "Let Baal be king!"

2. In most of the sister versions a special point is made of the fact that the warrior god, or some other gods before him, turned tail at the sight of the Dragon. So in our Canaanite version, the initial speaker — probably the goddess Ashtareth — exclaims that "(even) warriors there grow faint!"

3. In the Indian and Greek versions, the victor's weapons are supplied by the artisan gods — Tvashtri and Hephaistos; while in the Teutonic version they are made by the subterranean dwarfs who fill the same role. So too in our Canaanite version, they are handed to Baal by Koshar, elsewhere described as the divine smith.

4. In many of the sister versions, the weapons are identified with thunderbolt and lightning. In the Indian and Greek versions, this is explicit; also, apparently, in the Teutonic version, where Mjolnir, the maul wielded by Thor, is regarded by most modern scholars as the thunderbolt. In the

Accadian versions there seems likewise to have been a tendency to identify the weapons of Marduk with the cyclone or storm wind. This suggests the true significance of the twin bludgeons in our Canaanite version.

5. In some of the versions, the Dragon is not slain, but imprisoned. So, too, in our Canaanite version, Ashtareth restrains Baal from killing him, preferring to have him held captive.

An over-all conspectus of these parallels, with references to the original sources, is presented in the table on page 150.

NOTES

1. Hrozný, *Ninrag*, iii; Pinches, PSBA 28 (1906), 203–18, 270–83; Witzel, *Ninib;* Deimel, *Orientalia* 5 (1922), 26–42; Langdon, *Sem. Mythol.*, 119 ff. See especially Jacobsen, in JNES 5 (1946), 146–47, which corrects Kramer's account in *Sum. Mythol.*, 80 ff.

2. Kramer, *op. cit.*, 82 ff.

3. EE, tab. iv.

4. CT XIII 33, ii; Heidel, *Bab. Genesis*, 119 ff.

5. Hommel, *Babyloniaca* 2 (1908), 60–61.

6. Smith-Sayce, *Chaldean Genesis*, 87. The seven-headed dragon appears on a seal from Tell Asmar. Pinches, *JRAS Centenary Supplement* (1924), 65, sees an allusion to the dragon combat in a hymn to Ninurta.

7. Frankfort, *Cylinder Seals*, Pl. xxii, a, d; Jeremias, *Handbuch*, 431; Ward, in AJSL, 1898. 94 ff.

8. i. 32; cf. Macdonell, *Vedic Mythology*, 56–60, 158 f.

9. I Khanda, 6 Adhyaya, Brahmana 3–17 = Eggeling, SBE, xiii, 164 ff.

10. *Theog.*, 820 ff.

11. *Prometheus Vinctus*, 351 ff.

12. So too Pindar, *Ol.*, iv.8; *Pyth.*, viii.16; *fr.* xciii.4 Donaldson.

13. Apollodorus, *Bibl.*, I, vi.3; cf. Ovid, *Met.*, v. 319 ff.; Hyginus, *fab.*, 152.

13a. Cf. Porzig, in KIF 1 (1930), 379–86.

13b. Similarly, Strabo (xvi, 2.7) and Malalas (ii, p. 38 Dindorf) locate the battle in the region of the River Orontes (cf. Baudissin, *Studien*, ii, 163), while the latter also records a tradition that it took place at Apameia (xii, 8.19; xiii, 4.11). In the legend of St. George, the dragon was first pinned down at Ascalon, then bound with the maiden's girdle, and finally slain at Beirut. One

CONSPECTUS OF MOTIFS

	CANAANITE	SUMERIAN	ACCADIAN	INDIAN
I	Goddess participates in combat, "brings out weapons," etc.	Innana brings out weapons: Kramer, *Sumerian Mythology*, 83	Ishtar shown on seals standing on dragon; Ward, 135, 415, 420; Legrain 392	
II	Gods/warriors quail at presence of Dragon	Ninurta at first flees: Kramer, 80	Anu flees: EE ii 81–2	Indra flees: SB., I Khanda, 6 Adh. 4 Br.
III	Dispute concerns Dragon's attempt to secure dominion			
IV	Weapons furnished by divine smith(s)			Furnished by Tvashtri
V	Victor equipped with thunderbolt and flail of lightning	Ninurta equipped with SHAR.ÚR and SHAR.GAZ "Crasher" and "Smasher"	(a) Marduk equipped with lance (*mulmullu*^{m}) and *abubu*. Latter also means "cyclone." (b) Equipped with storm (*mekhû*) and rain cloud (*urpu*)	Indra equipped with "whizzing club" = thunderbolt: Rig Veda 1, 32
VI	Dragon vanquished but not slain	Asag held under heap of stones	Seals show dragon yoked to divine chariot; EBi. s.v. Dragon	Vritra cut in twain, but not annihilated; SB., *loc. cit.*

CONSPECTUS OF MOTIFS

EGYPTIAN	GREEK	O.T.	TEUTONIC	OTHERS
Isis aids Horus				
	Gods flee: Apollodorus I vi. 3	Gods flee: Job 41:17		
Set challenges Horus on issue of dominion				
Ptah furnishes weapons of Horus	Furnished by Cyclopes, whose forge is managed by Hephaestus		Furnished by dwarfs, who are the divine smiths	
	Zeus equipped with thunderbolt and flail of lightning: Hesiod, *Th.* 853 ff. Nonnus, *Dionys.* ii 478; Apollodorus, lvi 3		Thor equipped with thunder-hammer called Mjolnir, "Crusher, maul"	In Iranian version, Azhi Dahaka held under Mount Demawend, but not slain
Set eventually reconciled to Horus	Typhon held under Mount Etna	Dragon imprisoned, but not slain: Job 7:17; 40:26 (v. Gunkel, *Schöpfung und Chaos,* 86)		In Jewish version, Leviathan unmanned, but not slain

wonders, therefore, whether Iliad ii 783 does not refer, after all, to Syria (Aram) when it locates the discomfiture of Typhon *ein Arimois.* (On Arimoi = Arameans, see Strabo, xvi, 4.27.)

14. See page 246.

14a. It has been suggested that there is an allusion to the Combat in the Hittite text, KUB XXXIII 108, where the personified Mount Pisaisa says to the goddess Ishtar (lines 16–17): "Behold, with what [vehemence] the weather god subdues the sea"; see Güterbock, *Kumarbi,* 112; Friedrich, *Jahrb. f. kleinas. Forschung* 2 (1952), 147–50. More probably, however, the words possess a purely general reference and allude only to the constant action of the winds upon the ocean.

15. Garstang, *Hittite Empire,* fig. 17, pp. 206–07; Goetze *Kleinasien*[1], fig. 13.

15a. H. Bossert and U.B. Alkim, *Karatepe, Kadirli ve Dlaylari Ikinci ön-rapor* (Istanbul Universitesi Yayinklari, No. 340 [1947]), 26, fig. 137.

16. Yasht 19, 38–44; Bundahish xxix.9; Datistani Denig xxvii, 1.9; Dinkart vii, 1.26, ix.21.

17. Moses of Chorene: Azhi Dahak is imprisoned by Hruden in the mountain of Demawend.

18. The principal sources are BD, ch. xxix and the quasi-magical papyrus of Nesi-Amsu (311–10 B.C.), edited by Budge in *Archaeologia* 52 (1890), 502 ff., and translated in Gressmann, AOTB, 181 ff. Cf. also Budge, *Gods,* 324–28; Roeder, *Urkunden,* 98–115.

19. Eg., *d-s.*

20. Eg., *kh-b.t.*

21. Cf. Le Page Renouf, in TSBA 8 (1883), 217. Although mainly antiquated, this article contains several useful observations.

22. BD, ch. xxix.

23. See Comm. on Baal, §LXXII.

24. Blackman-Fairman, in JEA 21 (1937), 26 ff.; 28 (1942), 32 ff.; 29 (1943), 3 ff.

25. 63, 6.

26. 61, 8; 62, 4; 64, 11; 76, 4, etc.

27. 67, 1–5.

28. 73, 5.

29. *Dissert.* xxix, p. 304 Davis.

30. *Apud* Origen, *c. Cels.*, vi, 42 et al.

31. *Argonautica* i, 503 ff. (where the tale is put into the mouth of Orpheus!).

34. Milton, *Paradise Lost,* X, 570 f.

35. The myth survives also in later Jewish legends, where the dragons are identified as Rahab and Leviathan; cf. Ginzberg, *Legends,* v. 26, where sources are quoted.

36. Cf. Dumezil, *Festin;* Brunnhofer, *Die schweizerische Held-*

ensage, 196, 207; Deutschbein, in *Germ. Montasschrift*, 1 (1909), 109; Bechstein, *Thüringer Sagenbuch*, ii. 64 f., No. 190. (For these references the writer is indebted to his friend, the late A. Haggerty Krappe.)

The Dragon of the Waters is Subdued

BAAL CHALLENGES THE AUTHORITY OF YAM, PRINCE OF THE SEA AND RULER OF THE STREAMS

III AB, B Gordon: 137

VI

Yam, god of sea and stream, has been granted dominion over the earth. Baal, genius of rainfall and fertility, challenges his authority. The two indulge in mutual threats.

(*The text begins at the end of Yam's speech*)

* *
*

Thou hast risen up overweening, O Ba[al] * * !"

[Then answered] Baal Puissant:
"[I will drive thee from the throne] of thy [do]minion;
* * the Hammer of Heaven [will smite] thee on the head,
[the Mallet of Heaven on the skull!]

O Ruler of the Streams,
"May [the Lord of Hell] split op[en]

VI. This passage reflects a standard element of the Ritual Combat. What it mythologizes is that exchange of curses or taunts which was the regular preliminary of *all* combats in the ancient Near East. Thus, in the Mesopotamian *Epic of Gilgamesh* (V, 1), when Enkidu declares his intention of challenging that hero, he says that he will "speak boldly" to him (see Oppenheim, *Orientalia* 17 [1948], 28, n. 1). Similarly, in I Samuel 17:25, David says of Goliath: "Surely to taunt Israel is he come up," and asks (v.26), "Who is this uncircumcised Philistine that he should have taunted the ranks of the living God?" The actual taunts exchanged between the Philistine and Israelite champions are fully described (vv.43–46), and it is significant that each boasts the prowess of his god (v.43; "And the Philistine cursed David by his god[s]"; vv. 45 f.: "Then said David: . . . 'YHWH will deliver thee this day into

[may the Lord of Hell split open] thy head,
'Ashtart, [the "Name of Baal," thy skull]!
[Even no]w mayest [thou] fall down,
[headlong] over a cl[iff],
(and find, when you reach the bottom,
that) your teeth [have been knocked out into your fist!]
May (your) twain wives also * * * * !"

---

my hand' "), just as do the two antagonists in our present Canaanite text. Cf. also Isaiah 42:13; Job 15:25.

For a modern survival of these taunts in Oriental warfare, cf. the description of a conflict between the Shafat and Lifta tribes of Palestine given by Mrs. Finn in her *Palestine Peasantry,* 26.

The taunts are a regular feature of modern folk plays which revolve around the Ritual Combat. Indeed, E. K. Chambers (*The English Folk-Play,* 13) lists them as one of the essential ingredients. Thus, in the Minchinhampton play (Tod, FL 46 [1935], 361 ff.), Black Knight informs his adversary Gallantyne that "I'll cut thee up in slices / in less than half an hour." In the Cornwall play, St. George says of the Dragon: "I'll clip his wings, he shall not fly; / I'll cut him down, or else I die." And in the Frodsham "Soul-Caking" play (Myers, FL 43 [1932], 97 ff.), King George boasts: "Is there a man before me will stand, / I'll cut him down with my iron hand." To which Turkish Knight retorts: "I'll cut thee, I will slash thee, and after that, I'll send thee over to Turkey land to be made mince pies of."

The taunts (*aischrologiai*) which characterized primitive seasonal performances (e.g., in the cult of Apollo at Anaphe; Apoll. Rhod., *Argonautica* iv, 1726), seem also to have been incorporated into later Greek drama; for Cornford (*Origins of Attic Comedy,* 119 ff.) and others would thence derive the epirrhematic structure of the Parabasis in Aristophanic comedy, holding that it originated in the exchange of taunts and curses between the participants in fertility rites.

The *hija* poetry of the Arabs is likewise but a literary expression of the taunts and curses exchanged before combat; and many scholars would recognize even earlier specimens of this genre in such Old Testament compositions as the Song of Lamech (Genesis 4:23–24), the Oracles of Balaam (Numbers 23–24) and the Song of Deborah (Judges 5); see Goldziher, *Abhandlungen zur arabischen Philologie,* i, 1–121; Gray, *A Critical and Exegetical Commentary to Numbers,* 327–28; Montgomery, *Arabia and the Bible,* 6, 15. Cf. also Jacob, *Das Leben der vorislamischen Beduinen,* 144 ff.; Margoliouth, *The Poetics of Aristotle,* 142.

VII

Yam sends messengers to the divine assembly demanding that Baal and his henchman be handed over.

Thereupon Sir Sea sends [m]essengers,
[and raises his voice and cries;]
"At the very height of their triumph,
let us shatter [their] * * * *,

Analogous to the Arabic *hija* was the Irish *glam dichen,* or formal exchange of curses in which champions indulged before combat. This was "no mere expression of opinion, but a most potent weapon of war, which might blister an adversary's face or even cost him his life. Like the Arabic *hija,* too, it was at one time accompanied with ritual action; it was uttered 'on one foot, one hand, one eye' "; cf. E. Welsford, *The Fool* (London, 1935), 80, 89; Raglan, *The Hero* (Thinker's Library ed., London, 1949), 217 ff.

Word-duel songs, called *nith* songs (cf. Norwegian *nith,* "contention") are sung in Greenland, Baffinland, and among Eskimo groups elsewhere as a means of publicly settling disputes; specimens are translated in Goldenweiser, *Anthropology,* 97 ff.

Lastly, it should be observed that the ritualistic exchange of taunts also gave rise to the medieval literary genre of the *débat,* e.g., dialogues in verse between Summer and Winter, Life and Death, etc., wherein each heaped abuse upon the other (see Dieterich, quoted in Cornford, *Origins of Attic Comedy,* 119).

The "Hammer of Heaven" and the "Mallet of Heaven" are the two divine weapons (called in the original Aymr and Ygrsh) with which Baal is indeed subsequently equipped and with which he subdues Yam. On their significance and mythological parallels, see Commentary on §XV.

The curse pronounced by Yam recurs in the Ugaritic *Poem of Krt,* C iv 55–56, and the text is restored from that passage. The "Lord of Hell" is, in the original, the god Horon (cf. Arabic *haur,* "pit"). He is mentioned occasionally in Egyptian texts of the New Empire, notably in the Harris papyrus (i 7), where he is associated with the goddess 'Anat, just as is his equivalent Rashap in the RS texts (i 7; iii 16; Krt B ii 6) and in an Egyptian altar list (TSBA 3 [1874] 427, no. 11; 429, No. 69). The Syrians around Gizeh seem to have given this name to the great sphinx. Horon survives also in the Biblical place name Beth-Horon (Joshua 16:5); while on a third-century Greek inscription from Delos (Picard,

* * * * * * break their * * * * !
Ye servitors, speed away, [stay not;]
[straightway turn ye your faces]
toward the assembly of the Parliament (divine);
in the midst of [Mount L-l];
at the feet of El do ye fall,
make obeisance to the assembly of the Parliament,
and impart your intelligence,
and say unto [El], the Bull-god [his] father,
[declare to the assembly of] the Parliament:
"This is the command of Sir Sea, your lord,
of your master, the Rul[er of the Stream(s)]:
Hand over, O gods, him to whom they would be paying respect,
him to whom the multitudes would be paying respect,
hand over Baal [and his henchman]
even the scion of Dagan! Let me possess me of his gold!"

VIII

At the approach of the messengers, the gods grow frightened, but Baal boastfully reassures them.

Syria 17 [1936], 315 f.) "Horon of Jabneh" figures beside Hercules. The "wife of Horon" is invoked, like her equivalent Ereshkigal in Mesopotamia and even in late Greek charms, in a Canaanite magical inscription from Arslan Tash, dating from the eight century B.C. (Gaster, *Orientalia* 11 [1942], 61 f.). See in general: Albright, AJSL 53 (1936), 1 ff.; id., BASOR 84:7–12; Posener, JNES 4 (1945), 240–42; Sauneren, *Rev. d'Égyptol.* 7 (1950), 121–26.

Ashtart is here introduced as the goddess of warfare and bellicosity – equivalent of the Mesopotamian Ishtar (Tallquist, *Götterepitheta*, 161 f.; Dhorme, *Rel. bab. et assyr.*, 90). On a fragmentary stele from Memphis, for example, dating from the time of Merneptah (1232–1224 B.C.), she is represented holding shield and spear. The epithet "Name-of-Baal" recurs on the fifth century B.C. inscription of Eshmun'azar of Sidon, but its meaning is disputed (Cooke, NSI, 37). Most probably, it denotes a hypostatized manifestation of Baal, the phrase "Name-of-Yahweh" being similarly employed in Isaiah 30:27 ("Behold, the Name-of-Yahweh cometh from afar, burning with His wrath," etc.). On the theological implications of the phrase, see the excellent remarks of Ernst Mueller, *A History of Jewish Mysticism*, 17.

VIII. The Mountain of Assembly is mentioned in Isaiah 14:13: "But thou hast said in thine heart, I will go up unto heaven, above

So away speed the messengers; they do not stay;
[straightway] they turn [their faces]
toward Mount L-l,
the assembly of the Parliament (divine).

Now, the gods are . . . ing,
the Holy Ones are sitting at their meal,
and there is Baal standing beside El.

As soon as the gods catch sight,
catch sight of the messengers of Sir Sea,
the delegation of the Ruler of the Stream(s),
the gods on their princely thrones
bow their heads upon their knees.

But Baal upbraids them, saying:
"Wherefore, O gods on your princely thrones,
have ye bowed your heads upon your knees?
Do I see gods being cowed with terror
before the messengers of Sir Sea,
the delegation of the Ruler of the Stream(s)?
O gods on your princely thrones,
raise your heads from your knees,
Verily, *I* will cow those messengers of Sir Sea,
that delegation of the Ruler of the Stream(s)!"

So the gods on their princely thrones
raised their heads from their knees.

IX

The messengers relay the demands of Yam.

Then, when they had reached their destination,
the messengers of Sir Sea,
the delegation of the Ruler of the Stream(s)

---

the loftiest stars will I set my throne, I will dwell in the Mountain of Assembly, in the farthermost recesses of the North." Cf. also Ezekiel 28:14, 16. On its location and on parallels in other mythologies, see below on §XXVIII. The precise meaning of L-l, however, is yet unknown.

IX. For the messengers (i.e., "angels") with swords in their hands, cp. Joshua 5:13. For the idea that messengers come in pairs, cf. *UH*, 63, n. 1. This probably corresponded to actual practice. Note that in the Egyptian "Poem of Pentaur"

fell at the feet of El,
made obeisance to the assembly of the Parliament (divine).
Then, standing upright, they * * * ed,
imparted their intelligence.
They twain flashed looks of fire;
[in their e]yes was a burnished sword.

Said they unto El, the Bull-god, his father:
"This is the command of Sir Sea, your lord,
of your master, the Ruler of the Stream(s):
'Hand over, O gods, him to whom they would be paying respect,
him to whom the mul[titudes]would be paying respect,
hand over Baal and his henchman,
even the scion of Dagan. Let me possess me of his gold!' "

X

El replies complacently that Baal is not really hostile and that Yam has no real reason to be afraid of him.

(= Breasted, *AR* iii, 144–45, §§319, 321, 322) *two* Shasu come from the Shabtuna district to speak with Ramses II, and *two* scouts are dispatched by the vanquished Hittite king. Cf. also *Iliad* i. 320–21. Similarly, in the Persian Ayatkar-i-Zareran (fifth century A.D.), *two* messengers, Vidraish and Namkhyast, come from Arzasp, king of Hyonan, to the court of King Vishtasp to urge him, under risk of war, to give up Mazdaeism; cf. Pagliaro, *Epica e Romanzo nel medievo persiano* (Florence, 1927), 4. One messenger alone might meet with an accident.

Noteworthy also in this connection is the fact that Semitic gods are often provided with *two* escorts. In Gilgamesh xi. 98, Shullat and Hanish precede Adad when he brings the flood; cf. Gelb, AOr., 18 (1950), 189–98. In Habakkuk 3.5, Deber and Resheph escort Yahweh. With this may be compared the fact that in *Iliad* iv. 440 and xv. 119 Deimos (Terror) and Phobos (Fear) escort Phoebus and Ares – resembling somewhat the Old Bohemian Tras (Tremor) and Strakh (Terror) who leap on foes: Grimm, *Teutonic Mythology*, 208.

Sometimes the idea survives in poetic metaphor. Thus, in Psalm 88:15 "Lovingkindness" and "Truth" attend upon Yahweh (Hebrew *y*[e]*qadd*[e]*mu panaw*, with which cp. Akkadian *manzaz pani*, in the sense of "courtier").

X. A "perpetual slave" is one who enjoys no manumission; the

But El the Bull-god, his father, [replied]:
"Baal is your servant, Sir Sea,
Baal is your [perpetu]al slave,
the son of Dagan is your bondman!
He will surely pay tribute to you;
for, see, the gods pay you tribute,
and (all) the Holy Beings bear presents unto thee!
Indeed, Baal is friendly!
[What if] he were to grasp a knife in his hand,
or a weapon in his right hand?
* * * * servitors * * * * * !
And [what if 'An]at herself were to hold his right hand,
and 'Ashtart his left?
How could he ever [assail] the messengers of Sir Sea,
the delegation of the Ruler of the Streams?
Why, the one messenger would * * * *,
while the other [would smite him] between the shoulders!
Indeed, Baal is friendly!
"
. . . .

XI

Nevertheless, the messengers rebuke Baal for his insulting attitude toward Yam

Howbeit, the messengers of Sir Sea,
the delegation of the Ruler of the Streams,
. . . ; [lifted their voices and cried:]

---

term recurs in Krt A 127 and in Exodus 21:6; Leviticus 25:46; I Samuel 27:12.

The term rendered "tribute" properly means "purple," since the purple dye yielded by the murex was the principal product of the Syro-Phoenician coastal cities. In Hittite, this term came, indeed, to mean "tribute" in a general sense; Goetze, *Madduwatas*, 130; id., *Mélanges Pedersen,* 491, n. 2.

'Anat and 'Ashtart are here introduced as goddesses of combat. In illustration of this, cf. the inscription of Ramses III (1198–1166 B.C.) at Medinet Habu: "'Anat and 'Ashtart are as a shield unto him"; Breasted-Nelson, *Medinet Habu,* 80; Pritchard, *Figurines,* 79.

For the two assistants holding either hand of a combatant in battle, in order to confer extra strength on him, cp. Exodus 17:12, where Aaron and Hur hold up the hands of Moses during the battle against Amalek.

"Naughtiness have you uttered against your lord, Sir Sea,
ag[ainst your] mas[ter, the Ruler of the Streams!]

* * * * * * * * * *

(There is now a gap in the text. The narrative is resumed on the reverse of the tablet.)

III AB, A Gordon: 68

XII

Baal is in no mood to surrender to Yam, but decides to offer combat. He bids some female helper (probably 'Anat) engage the monster, but this helper reports that she cannot secure victory.

* * * * * * * * * *

My hand has proved weak; I am as good as dead!
[Though I fling] my [spe]ars [and javelins],
yet can I not make him to depart,
and though I furb[ish my weapons],
yet has Sir Sea not lost his composure!
From Sir Sea [do all turn] tail (?),
* * * * [the Rul]er of the Streams!
Why, warriors there grow scared!
I am forced to beat a retreat,
. . . . !
The force of us twain will (but) fall to the ground,
and the might of us twain to the dust!"

XII. The beginning of this passage being lost, the identity of the speaker is uncertain. However, from the fact that later (V AB, D 36) the goddess 'Anat boasts expressly of having "crushed Sir Sea . . . made an end of Lord Stream," it would appear that it is she – the goddess of war and constant partner of Baal in his battles – who here addresses him. Her role would then correspond to that of Inanna in the Sumerian version of the myth; for that goddess similarly endeavors to defeat the monster Asag before his final subjugation by Ninurta; Kramer, *Sumerian Mythology*, 82–83.

The statement that "warriors there grow faint" finds excellent parallels in the sister versions of the myth. In the Sumerian version, Ninurta, on first encountering Asag, "flees like a bird"; *ibid.*, 80. In the Babylonian version, Anu first "turns back" upon approaching Tiamat (EE ii 81–82). In the Vedic version, Indra "retreats to farthermost distances" at the onset of Vritra (Satapatha

XIII

Thereupon Baal takes up position beside the throne of Sir Sea.

So goes forth the word from [her] mouth,
her utterance from her lips,
and she gives forth her voice,
but (Baal) keeps lying in wait (?)
beside the throne of Sir Sea.

XIV

Direct combat proving hazardous, the divine smith Sir Adroit-and-Cunning (Koshar-wa-Khasis) supplies Baal with two magic bludgeons which can dart from his hand automatically and fell the monster without danger of hand-to-hand encounter. The first bludgeon, however, proves ineffective.

Thereupon says Sir Adroit-and-Cunning:
"See, I have been telling thee, Lord Baal,
apprising thee, thou Rider on the Clouds,
if this foeman of thine, O Baal,

Brahmana I Khanda 6 Adhyaya 4 Brahmana = SBE XII 164 f.). In the Greek version, the gods flee to Egypt before the assaults of Typhon (Apollodorus I vi 3). In the Old Testament, "the gods are affrighted" at the presence of Leviathan (Job 41:17 [EV. 25]).

XIV. The god Koshar who is here introduced as the forger of Baal's weapons, is elsewhere called more fully Koshar-wa-Khasis, a name which means properly "Adroit-and-Cunning" and refers to his manual and mental skills. He is the Phoenician Chusor mentioned by Sanchuniathon (Eusebius, *PE* I, 10.11 f.) and by Mochos of Sidon (quoted by Damascius, *De prim. principiis* §125 *ter* = i, 323 Ruelle) and expressly identified by the former with the Greek Hephaistos. He seems to be mentioned also in Egyptian texts: Leibovitch, ASAE 48 (1948), 435–44. According to Albright (*Archaeology and Rel. of Israel,* 82), he is also the Kautar said by Melito to have been the father of Tammuz. His name survives in the Ugaritic personal name Kshr-mlk (314, r. 5) and in such late Punic names as 'bd-Kshr, "servant of Koshar" (JA 1916 ii 494; 1917 ii 49) and Auchusor (CIL viii 5306). He figures in the Ugaritic myths as the divine artisan and

if this foeman of thine thou slay,
if thou but destroy this thy rival,
then shalt thou get thee kingship for all time,
dominion for all generations!"

---

smith, who equips sanctuaries for the gods (II AB i 24 ff.), supervises the building of Baal's palace (II AB v 43 ff.), and makes bows for the gods (II Aq: v). All of this is consistent with Sanchuniathon's statement that Chusor first discovered the use of iron. Moreover, his role accords with that of Hephaistos in Greek myth. Hephaistos builds the divine abodes (*Iliad* i 607), fashions the mansions of Zeus (Il. xiv 338), Hera (*ibid.*, 166), Helios (Ovid, *Met.* ii 5) and Aphrodite (Ap. Rhod. *Argonautica* iii 37 ff.). He is also the designer and forger of the divine insignia, e.g., the scepter and aegis of Zeus (Il. ii 101; xv 309), the sickle of Demeter (Schol. Ap. Rhod. iv 984), the weapons of Apollo and Artemis (Hyginus, *fab.* 140), the arms of Achilles (Hesiod, *Shield* 123, 319, etc.) and the magic spear of Peleus (Hesiod *frag.* 38). In addition, he supervises the Cyclopean forge (Callimachus iii 48; Orphica, *fr.* 92, 135; cf. Gruppe, *Griech. Mythol.*, 1307, n. 3).

Koshar also performs another function: under the name of "Sir Fisherman" (Dg-y), he is responsible for imprisoning the defeated Yam in a net (§XXII; II AB ii 30), and it is he too who is said to toss him into the sea when he would rise to encroach upon the earth (§LXXII; I AB vi 50 f.). Here again, his role corresponds closely to that of the Phoenician Chusor; for Sanchuniathon states explicitly (*loc. cit.*) that the latter was the discoverer of fishing tackle.

Lastly, the god appears to have had some interest in music and song. Sanch. says of Chusor that he invented the art of "tricking out words" and of composing incantations and spells. Nowhere in the Ugaritic texts does he explicitly fill this role; but the association comes out clearly in the fact that professional songstresses are called *k-sh-r-t*. The connection is readily explicable when we bear in mind the similar relation of our own words "artisan" and "artist" or of the Arabic *q-y-n*, "to forge, be a smith" and the Hebrew, Syriac, and Ethiopic words for "to sing, chant a dirge" (cf. Ginsberg, BASOR 72: 13–15). Similar, too, is the derivation of "poet" from the Greek *poietes*, "maker," while the Old Norse *loða-smiðr*, "song-smith" and the modern Rhenish *reimschmied*, "poetaster," provide an even more illuminating parallel; Grimm, *Teutonic Mythol.*, 900. In Sanskrit, *taksh-*, "to fabricate," is used of composing the songs of the Rig Veda (RV i 62.13; v 2.11). Moreover, in further illustration of Sanchuniathon's statement, it

Therewith Sir Adroit fashions a bludgeon out of stone,
and pronounces its name, saying:
"Thou, thy name is EXPELLER (*Ygrsh*);
Expeller, expel (*grsh*) Sir Sea,
expel Sir Sea from his throne,

---

should be observed that throughout the Near East, magical healing and similar occult practices involving incantations are especially associated with smiths and itinerant tinkers; Eisler, *Messiah Jesus*, 327.

Two of the standard epithets of Koshar are: (*a*) "deft" or "expert" (*hyn*) and (*b*) "handyman." Both claim a word of comment. The former is related to a noun *hauna* used in the Aramaic Targum (e.g., Proverbs 28:16) to render the Hebrew *tebunah*, and *tebunah* is specifically mentioned in Exodus 31:3 as one of the requisite qualities of Bezalel, designer of furniture for the Israelite sanctuary! The latter connects with the fact that from the time of the Middle Kingdom onward, Ptah, the Egyptian counterpart of Koshar, was indeed regarded as a master craftsman; Homberg-Sandman, *Ptah*, 47 ff. It should be observed also that both the name Koshar ("Skilled, Adroit"') and the epithets Khasis ("Cunning"), Hayin ("Deft"), and "Handyman" find excellent parallels in the adjectives *klytometis*, "renowned for mind," and *klytotechnes*, "renowned for skill," applied to Hephaistos in Homeric Hymns xx 1, 5.

In 'Anat F, 13–16, the seat of Koshar is located at KPTR. This is the cuneiform Kaptara (first mentioned in a text dated ca. 2200 B.C.; cf. JAOS 45 [1925], 236), the Hebrew Kaphtor (Genesis 10:14; Deuteronomy 2:23; Jeremiah 47:4; Amos 9:7) and – in all probability – the Egyptian Keftiu. A vase, a weapon, and a certain type of garment are described in the Mari texts (ca. 1775 B.C.) as "Kaptarian" (Dossin, *Syria* 20 [1939], 111). The location is disputed. The Ancient Versions identify Hebrew Kaphtor with Cappadocia – an identification based on similarity of sound. In modern times, the favored localization has been Crete (Calmet, *Dissert.*, ii. 441; Macalister, *Philistines*, 13 ff.; Dussaud, RHR 118 [1938], 156; Dossin, *loc. cit.*). It has also been suggested however, that Kaphtor may be the island of Carpathos (modern Scarpanto), between Crete and Rhodes (cf. Albright, BASOR 77:31, n. 46); while E. F. Weidner (AJA [1940],) has even proposed an identification with Kyphtheira, i.e., the isle of Cythaera. The location of Koshar's seat on an Aegean island would be readily explicable from the fact that, during the second millennium B.C., a great deal of the ceramic- and metalware in use on the

the Ruler of the Streams from the seat of his dominion!
Spring from the hand of Baal,
like a vulture with its talons smite Sir Sea on the shoulder,
the ruler of the streams on the back!"[e]

[e] Lit., "between the hands."

Syrian mainland was indeed imported from the Aegean or fashioned locally after Aegean models (Picard, *Rel. préhelleniques*, 98 ff.; Wooley, JHS 56 [1936], 125–32; *idem.*, *Antiquaries Journal* 28 [1948], 1–19). On the other hand, it should be observed that, according to Marian Welker (TAPS, N.S. 38 [1948], 221–22), the affinities of "Keftian" ceramics and costume point to a location in northern Syria (though Wainwright's well-known identification of Kaphtor with Cilicia is seemingly excluded).

In II Aq v 20 f. Koshar is associated with a place named ḤKPT. This is the Egyptian Het ka Ptah, "sanctuary of Ptah," the regular name of Memphis, seat of the Egyptian potter god Ptah (and, incidentally, the origin of the word Egypt). It is thus apparent that in the days of Egyptian domination and influence the Canaanite god was understood to be the equivalent of the corresponding figure in the pantheon of Canaan's overlords; and this squares with the statement of Mochos of Sidon that Chusor was "the first *opener*," since that curious designation is nothing but a bizarre attempt to explain the Egyptian name Ptah from the Semitic root *p-t-kh*, "to open" (cf. Hoffman, ZA 11 [1896], 254). The identification is the more interesting when it is observed that the resultant figure of a divine "Egyptian" smith distinguished not only for his craftsmanship but also for his proficiency in magical arts (incantations) corresponds, to the last detail, to the later conception of the *gypsy*, the itinerant "Egyptian" likewise renowned not only for his ability as a tinker but no less for his proficiency in music, healing, and mantic arts!

On the figure of the divine smith in mythology, cf. Fox, *Greek and Rom. Mythol.*, 206; Hermann, *Nordische Mythol.*, 115; Gray, *Baltic Mythol.*, 330; Keith, *Indian Mythol.*, 50; McCulloch, *Celtic Mythol.*, 28.

The role here played by Koshar is paralleled in other versions of our myth. The weapons, as we shall see presently, are symbolizations of thunderbolt and lightning. It is therefore pertinent to note that in the Indian version, the thunderbolts with which Indra vanquishes Vritra are forged for him by the divine smith Tvashtri (RV i, 32; Satapatha Brahmana I Khanda 6 Adhyaya 3 Brahmana

So the bludgeon springs from the hand of Baal;
like a vulture with its t[a]lons it smites Sir Sea on the shoulder
the Ruler of the Streams on the back.[f]

[f] Lit., "between the hands."

= SBE XII, 164 ff.). Similarly, in Greek myth, lightning – the weapon used to subdue Typhon – is said to have been made in the Cyclopean forge, which was controlled by Hephaistos, the equivalent of Koshar; Gruppe, *op. cit.*, 413, n. 7. In the Egyptian version, as preserved in the Edfu Drama, the weapons wherewith Horus defeats Set are furnished by Ptah (cf. Blackman-Fairman, JEA 29 [1943], 10). In the Teutonic version, Thor subdues the serpent Midhgardhsormr by means of the hammer Mjölnir, and the latter is identical with the thunderbolt or lightning, fabled to have been made by the dwarfs, who are the counterparts of the classical Cyclopes; Grimm, *op. cit.*, 40.

The weapons constitute a pair. Here, too, we have a trait which recurs in other versions of the myth. In the Sumerian version, preserved in the poem *Lugal-e* u_4*-me-lám-bi-nir-gál* (Kramer, *Sum. Mythol.*, 80; Deimel, *Orientalia* 5 [1922], 26–42; DVI; Hrozný, MVAG 1903.3; Langdon, *Semitic Mythol.*, 119 ff.), the victorious Ninurta is armed with two bludgeons called respectively SHAR.UR, "world-crusher, razer," and SHAR.GAZ, "world-pounder" (cf. Jacobsen, *Orientalia* 16 [1947], 392; Jensen, *Kosmologie*, 504). In the later versions, these weapons are identified with such meteorological phenomena as the thunderbolt, lightning or storm wind. Thus, in the Babylonian myth of the defeat of the dragon Labbu, the weapons used are the rain cloud (*urpu*) and the tempest (*mekhû*) (CT XIII 33 ii 2–5). Similarly, in the so-called *Epic of Creation*, Marduk attacks Tiamat with two weapons called *mulmullu*[m], "lance" and *abubu*, and the latter word means "avalanche, cyclone" (iv 36, 49; Albright, AJSL 34 [1918], 222, connects *abubu* with Arabic *abab*, "avalanche"). Moreover, the meteorological interpretation is there emphasized by the express statement (iv 39–40) that the god also armed himself with "the evil wind, the tempest, the hurricane." In the Vedic version, Indra vanquishes Vritra (identified with the serpent Ahi) with the thunderbolt, called "the whizzing club" (RV i, 32). In the Greek version, as related by Hesiod (*Theogony* 853 ff.; cf. Aeschylus, *PV* 351 ff.; Apollodorus I vi 3; Nonnus, *Dionys.* ii 478), Zeus attacks Typhoeus with thunder, levin bolt, and lightning, expressly described as his "weapons." Moreover, when the Greek poet speaks, like Homer before him (Il. ii 780 f.), of Zeus' *lashing* the monster, the use of

Howbeit Sir Sea prevails; he does not collapse;
his crest does not sag;
his countenance does not droop.

---

lightning is again indicated; for it is a commonplace of folklore that lightning is regarded as a whip or lash (Harris, *Picus,* 57 ff.; Cook, *Zeus,* ii. 824; Grimm, *op. cit.,* 178, quotes a Prussian tale in which lightning is likened to a *blue whip*). Lastly, in the Teutonic version, as observed above, Thor uses a hammer (*mjölnir*) which, according to Grimm, is "obviously the crashing thunderbolt," since its blows are preceded by thunder and lightning; *op. cit.,* 180. Grimm (*op. cit.,* 1221) also compares the name Mjölnir with Slavic *molnija,* "lightning."

In the light of these parallels, it would appear that the bludgeons wielded by Baal similarly represent *thunderbolts.* This explanation is the more plausible when it is remembered that the maritime squalls which are attributed in most of the sister versions to the action of the Dragon are usually accompanied by thunder and lightning. The idea would therefore easily arise that the thunder god was using those weapons to tame the monster. (Note that in later Jewish lore, the Dragon is said to fear thunder and lightning; Trachtenberg, *Jewish Magic,* 40.)

The precise significance of the weapons seems, however, later to have been forgotten; for Isaiah 27:1 speaks of Yahweh's using "his sore and great and strong *sword*" to punish Leviathan. Similarly, Psalm 74:13 employs the noncommittal term "broken in pieces" (*p-r-r*). More decisively, both Isaiah 51:9 and Job 26:13 speak of the Dragon's being "pierced" or "riddled" (*kh-l-l*) – a term clearly inapplicable to the use of a club or bludgeon. This development is paralleled by the gradual elimination of the thunderbolt in the iconography of the Greek Zeus; Gruppe, *op. cit.,* 119 ff.; Cook, *op. cit.,* 722 f.

It is impossible to determine whether the names here given to the bludgeons were invented by our Canaanite poet or inherited by him from tradition and merely given an *ad hoc* interpretation. In support of the latter view is the fact that the connection of the name AYMR ("Driver") with the root *m-r-y,* "drive," here assumed by the poet, looks uncommonly like folk etymology, for Aymr would more properly derive from a root *y-m-r* (whatever its meaning may have been). If this hypothesis be accepted, it is in turn possible that YGRSH ("Expeller") had originally nothing to do with the root *g-r-sh,* "expel," as again assumed by the poet, but that it was connected rather with *g-r-sh,* "crush, pound," on

XV

Thereupon the divine smith hands Baal another bludgeon. This proves effective, and Yam is subdued.

Then (again) Sir Adroit fashions a bludgeon out of stone,
and pronounces its name, saying:
"Thou, thy name is DRIVER (*Aymr*);
Driver, drive (*mr*) Sir Sea,

---

the analogy of the Sumerian SHAR.ÚR and SHAR.GAZ and of the Teutonic Mjölnir (from **mal-*, "crush, maul").[a]

The bludgeons are said to *spring* from the hand of Baal. In this statement lies the whole point of the episode, though that point has been strangely overlooked. None of the gods has been able to approach Yam in hand-to-hand encounter, and Baal has been warned that he himself will scarcely fare better. Accordingly, Koshar supplies him with magical weapons *which can be flung from a distance.* Note that in the analogous Greek myth of Zeus' fight with Typhon, as related by Apollodorus (I, vi, 3), it is stated expressly that, after all the gods had fled the monster in terror, "Zeus pelted him *from a distance* (*porrō*) with thunderbolts" and then engaged him at close quarters. It may be suggested that in the primitive form of the story, the weapon employed was an *automatic club* – that is, a club which can automatically beat an enemy until called off by its owner. On this idea in folk tales, cf. *MI*, D 1094; 1401.1. Noteworthy in this respect is the fact that in Teutonic mythology, Thor's hammer possesses the magical quality that "when thrown, it returns to his hand of its own accord" (Bullfinch, Thomas, *Age of Fable,* ch. xxxviii). It is therefore a miraculous weapon.

The bludgeons are said to smite Yam "like a vulture with its talons." The simile, implying sudden and vicious assault, is, of course, perfectly natural, especially when it is borne in mind that the Semitic word for "vulture" derives from a root meaning primarily "rend, raven." The notions of swiftness and savagery are thus combined. As a matter of fact, the simile is quite common in both Semitic and Classical literature; cf. Habakkuk 1:8; Job 9:26; Assurnasirpal, *Annals* ii 107; *Iliad* xxi 251–53; Sophocles, *Antigone* 112–13.

[a] To the IE cognates of *mjölnir,* we may now add Hittite *malla-*, "crush," on which cf. Sommer, ZA 33 (1921), 98, n. 2; Friedrich, ZDMG 76 (1922), 159.

drive Sir Sea from his throne,
the Ruler of the Streams from the seat of his dominion!
Spring from the hand of Baal,
like a vulture with its talons smite Sir Sea on the skull,
the Ruler of the Streams between the eyes,
so that Sir Stream may fall and sink to the ground!"

So the bludgeon springs from the hand of Baal;
[like] a vulture with its talons it smites Sir [Sea] on the skull,
the Ruler of the Streams between the eyes.

Sir Sea falls and sinks to the ground;
his crest sags;
and his countenance droops.

From the point of view of comparative mythology, however, there is far more to the employment of this simile than meets the eye. The eagle, by reason of its swift descent, is commonly regarded as the storm bird, the bearer of lightning and thunderbolt. Thus, in Sumerian mythology, the storm wind is symbolized by an eagle called Im-Dugud, "Flashing Wind" (the Semitic Zu), while another eagle (or perhaps only an earlier form) bears the name Im-Gig, "Dark Wind"; Langdon, *op. cit.*, 115 ff. Classical sources likewise attest this association of the bird with wind or tempest – Cook, *op. cit.*, 751 f. – or with Zeus as god of the sky (Mylonas, CJ 41 [1945], 203–07). According to Aeschylus, for example, when Zeus threatened to strike the house of Amphion with lightning, he declared that he would burn it up "by means of eagles bearing fire" (*Niobe*, quoted in Aristophanes, *Birds* 1247 f.; cf. Usener, *Rhein. Mus.* 60 [1905], 26). Similarly, Horace (*Odes* iv 4, 1) describes the eagle as "wing'd agent of the levin bolt" (*ministrum fulminis alitem*). What underlies the association is eloquently expressed in a passage of Apuleius (*Flor.* 2) wherein the swoop of an eagle is likened to the fall of a thunderbolt – a comparison which recurs, as A. B. Cook points out, in Tennyson's fragment, *The Eagle*: "The wrinkled sea beneath him crawls: He watches from his mountain walls, And *like a thunderbolt he falls.*"

In several mythologies, winds and thunder are said to be caused by the flapping of the wings of a giant eagle; cf. *MI*, A 284.2. In India, it is the eagle Garuda (Samaveda 2:102), and in the Eddas it is Hraesvelgr (Grimm, *op. cit.*, 633); while the belief is also attested among the Chinese (Smith-Sayce, *Chaldaean Genesis*, 123), the Burmese (Scott, *Indo-Chinese Mythol.*, 323), the Finns

XVI

Baal proceeds to give the coup de grâce *to Yam, but the goddess 'Ashtareth objects that he ought not to claim this moment of triumph for himself, seeing that the monster has been the common enemy of all the gods.*

Thereupon Baal drags Sir Sea along.
He is about to hack him into pieces(?),
to make a full end of that Ruler of the Stream(s),
when 'Ashtart [calls him] by name
and utters a rebuke:

---

and Shetland Islanders (Grimm, *op. cit.*, 633, 635), the Thlingits, the Aztecs, and the Vancouver Islanders (Spence, *Introd. to Mythology*, 123). Here we have in formulated myth an alternative expression of the basic mythopoeic concept which is also articulated in metaphor.

In describing the collapse of Sir Sea, the poet uses terms which are applicable at the same time to the abatement of embroiled waters. There is thus a kind of *double-entendre*, whereby the real character of Yam is brought home more forcibly to the audience. Thus, the term rendered "collapse" (*ymk*) means properly "sink," and suggests the subsidence of the towering billows. Similarly, the phrase here translated "his crest sags," while used elsewhere (II AB ii 19; V AB, D 31) to describe bodily agitation, means properly "its points oscillate" and at once suggests the undulation of the waves. Lastly, the words here reproduced as "his countenance droops" (*ydlp tmnh*) suggest at the same time an homophonous word (Arabic *d-l-f*, etc.) meaning "move gently, trickle," and therefore conjure up the picture of the angry sea's sinking to a mere ripple. We shall see later that the poet again employs this device in describing how Baal mistreats his fallen enemy.

XVI. The "dragging" or hauling up of the Dragon from the sea is admirably illustrated by Job 40:25 (EV. 41:1): "Canst thou *draw out* Leviathan with a fishhook?" The audience, however, would at once have associated this act with the common practice of *dragging* captives before their victors or their victors' gods; cf. Mesha Inscription, lines 12, 18: "I fought against the city and took it . . . and I captured . . . and dragged him/them before Chemosh." (In reading these texts we must be sensitive to such *double-entendre*, for it is of the essence of popular drama.)

"Shame, O [Baal] Puissant!
Shame, thou Rider on the Clouds!
For Sir [Sea] is now our (common) captive,
the Ruler of the Stream(s) is our (common) captive,
and [it was against us all that] he went forth!"
Then Baal (indeed) feels ashamed, and . . .

XVII

Yam acknowledges the sovereignty of Baal.

[Then up speaks] Sir Sea:
"Lo, I am as good as dead!
Surely, Baal now is kin[g]!
* * * * * * * * * * * * * * *"

In sister versions of the myth, the Dragon is often represented as *bound* or *imprisoned*, rather than slain. Thus, in the Sumerian version, he is held down by a heap of stones (Kramer, *Sum. Mythol.*, 80). In the Egyptian version, as related in inscriptions at Dendereh, the dragon 'Apep is forced back by Ra into his cavern (*khb.t*), and a stone "of forty cubits" is placed over him (cf. Le Page Renouf, TSBA 8 [1883], 217 – antiquated but still useful). In the Indic version, Vritra asks expressly to be divided in half, but not slain, and the request is granted (see above, page 140). In the Iranian version, Azhi Dahaka is imprisoned beneath Mount Demawend, but not killed (Bundahish xxix 9; Datistāni Denig 37 i 9; Dinkart ii 1, 26; ix 21); while in the Greek version, Typhon is incarcerated beneath Mount Etna, but not slain. Furthermore, as Gunkel has pointed out (*Schöpfung und Chaos*, 86), there are several references to the Dragon in OT (e.g., Job 7:12; 40:26) which imply that he was not killed but imprisoned (cf. also *EBi.*, s.v. Dragon, at end).

XVII. This incident complements the assurance given to Baal by Koshar (lines 9–10): "If now thy foeman, O Baal, if now thy foeman thou slay, if now thou destroy thy rival, then shalt thou secure thy kingdom for all time, thy dominion for all generations!" In the Indic version the victory of Indra over Vritra is associated with an acknowledgment of the former's sovereignty. So, too, in the Greek version, what Zeus defends against Typhon is expressly his title as king of gods and men. Moreover, in Psalm 93, which recounts the combat of Yahweh against the rivers (cf. Gaster, *Iraq* 4 [1937], 24–25), the poem opens with the declaration that, in consequence of his victory, "Yahweh is become king."

Then Baal (indeed) feels ashamed,
while Sir Sea keeps saying:
"Lo, I am as good as dead!
[Surely, Baal is king!]
. . . ."

XVIII

A female speaker — this time, evidently, 'Anat — now intervenes and suggests to Baal that he ought to make a real end to his foe.

(The text is fragmentary, so that the complete sense cannot be made out.)

Thereupon * * * takes up wo[rd]:
* * * * *
O Baal, these (?) * * * *
* . . . .
on his head * * * * *
his hand(s) * * * * *
[be]tween his eyes * * * *

XVIII. These lines are altogether obscure. Significant, however, is the occurrence side by side of the words: *on his head, his hand(s)*, and *between his eyes;* for this suggests, on the strength of analogies in the sister versions (EE iv 130; Psalm 74:14; Hesiod, *Theog.* 856), that 'Anat here advises Baal, contrary to the suggestion of 'Ashtart, to *bludgeon his vanquished rival to death* — advice which he appears eventually to adopt (§XXXIX; II AB vii 1–4).

If this interpretation be correct, an interesting possibility arises. The expressions *head, hand,* and *eye* are applied in Semitic speech to the *parts of a river.* As in English, the source of a river is known in Hebrew, Arabic, and Accadian as its *head* (cf. Genesis 2:10; Accadian *resh eni;* Arabic *ras al ain;* so too in Greek, *Tearou potamou kephalai* [Herodotus iv 91], and in Latin, *caput unde altus primum se erumpit Enipeus* [Vergil, *Georgica* iv 368]). Again, both in Hebrew (Exodus 2:5; Deuteronomy 2.37), Accadian, Arabic, Syriac and Ethiopic, the *bank* of a river is called its *hand,* just as in English we speak of the right and left *hands* of a stream. Lastly, the *spring* from which a stream flows is called *eye* in all of the Semitic languages (cp. also Hittite *sakwis,*

The Victor is Installed as King

BAAL ACQUIRES A PALACE

II AB Gordon: 51

XIX

Baal points out to 'Anat that although he has achieved sovereignty by vanquishing Yam, he has no palace upon earth and is therefore exposed to the ridicule and contempt of the gods. Indeed, even his wives and his children have to be accommodated in the palaces of El and Asherat. He begs 'Anat to present his case to Asherat, so that the latter may in turn relay it to El.

* * *

[Convey this word to El:]
"H[earken], O Bull-god, [his father],
O King [who appointed him],

"spring," which may be related to *sakwa*, "eyes"; Forrer, *Klio* 26 [1938], 182 f.). Hence, it is reasonable to suppose that here again the poet chose his words carefully in order to convey at one and the same time both a concrete and a figurative sense. By saying that Sir Sea was smitten on head, hand, and eyes, what he conveyed was that the turbulent waters were held in check—the real meaning of the myth.

XIX. It is to be observed that whenever the supreme god El is petitioned for favors, he is addressed as "Bull-god," "King," and "Father" (e.g., V AB, E 7, 43; II Aq i 24; Krt A 59, 76–77, 169). The title "Bull(-god)" may be compared with Th-w-r-a, "bull" and Th-r -B'l, "Bull-Baal," in South Arabian inscriptions. According to many scholars, the expression "Mighty One (*abir*) of Jacob" applied to God in Genesis 49:24 is a dogmatic alteration of an original "Steer (*abbir*) of Jacob."

On the identity and titles of Baal's three brides, P-d-r-aya, T-l-aya, and A-r-s-aya, see Introduction, §10.

Lines 20–44 describe the advisability of approaching Asherat rather than going direct to El. To bring home this point, the speaker (Baal) bids 'Anat consider what invariably happens when this technique is used and when efforts are first made to get into the good graces of the Queen Consort: in no time, the divine

[hearken what they are say]ing,
What Ashe[rat and her sons are saying,]
the Goddess [and the company]of her [kinsmen]:
'See, Baal has no house like the gods,
no abode like the (other) sons of Asherat!
The abode of El has to serve as the covert of his sons,
the abode of Queen Asherat of the Sea as that of his bewitching brides,
yes, even as the abode of P-d-r-aya, the Lady of Light,
as the covert of the Dew-nymph (T-l-aya), Lady of Rain,
as the abode of the Earth-nymph (A-r-s-aya), Lady of *y-'b-d-r!*'

---

architect and smith is commissioned to fashion gorgeous furniture for the desired abodes. The point is well illustrated when it is remembered that the divine artisan was regarded as the equivalent of the Greek Hephaistos, one of whose functions was indeed to construct abodes for the gods (see above, Commentary on §XIV).

The various objects mentioned constitute the typical furnishings of an ancient Near Eastern temple or palace. Herodotus tells us (i 181) that on the topmost story of the great tower at Babylon "there was a large shrine, and in the shrine was placed a *couch* sumptuously spread, and beside it a *golden table.*" Similarly, Assurbanipal, in describing the furnishings of the temple of Marduk, specifies the *couch* of that god (K 1794: x 35, 72; = Smith, *Keilschr. Asshurbanipals,* i. 18 ff.); while the tribute of the Hittite king Sangara to Assurnasirpal included *beds, thrones, and tables* (*Ann.* iii 67). The *golden table* was likewise a feature of the Israelitic sanctuary and temple (Exodus 25.23 f.; I Kings 7:48), and is mentioned also in Assyro-Babylonian literature (DT 15 + 109 + 114 + MNB 1848:386–410,412), while the *golden throne* recurs in Babylonian New Year rituals (Thureau-Dangin, *Rituels accadiens,* 90).

The poet then alludes to the theriomorphic dishes (rhytons, etc.) and to the colossi which were so common a feature of the equipment of Near Eastern temples. Specimens of the former have indeed been found at Ras Shamra (Schaeffer, *Cuneiform Texts from Ras Shamra-Ugarit,* 47, 88, n. 117; Pl. xxviii, figs. 2–3). Assurbanipal speaks similarly (RM 3 x 68–71; Streck ii 150) of setting up "wild oxen of silver to gore my foes . . . also two monsters to assure the safety of my royal path" and likewise (III R 28–29, 22; Streck ii 172) of erecting statues of "two lusty oxen equally shaped"; while Sargon in his so-called *Prunkinschrift*

'Anat is advised, in presenting this case, first to entreat the good offices of Asherat, consort of El. She is reminded that whenever a god enjoys the favor of that goddess, he is straightway provided with a sumptuous and gorgeous dwelling.

And here's something more I would tell thee:
Just consider them
who ingratiate Queen Asherat of the Sea,
who curry favor with the Mistress of the Gods:
(for them) Sir Expert goes up to the forge,
in the hand of Sir Cunning are the tongs,
to smelt silver, hammer out gold;
why, he smelts silver by the thousandfold,
why, he hammers out gold by the myriadfold;
he smelts, he . . . s and . . . (?):
a dais fit for a god,
weighing twice ten thousand shekels;
a dais cast in silver, coated with a film of gold;
a throne fit for a god, resting on top;
a footstool fit for a god,
spread with a spotless mat;
a couch fit for a god, with gold poured over its . . . ;
a table fit for a god, filled with all manner of game;
dishes fit for a god,
(made of metals dug) from the foundations of the earth,
(shaped like) the small cattle of Amurru;
steles (shaped) like the wild beasts of Yam'an,
wherein are wild oxen by the myriads!"

(Saal xiv 37 = Weissbach, ZDMG 72 [1918], 182) states that "in front of their gates, eight twin lions . . . mountain-sheep . . . towering colossi" were set up; and Tiglath Pileser I erected "three dolphines, four . . .(?), four lions made of basalt, two bull-colossi of marble, two white . . .(?) of gypsum" in the portals of the temple. Finally, we may recall the statement in I Kings 7:29, 31 that part of the furniture of Solomon's temple in Jerusalem consisted of "lions, cattle, and colossi [cherubim]" and that the steps to the divine throne were flanked by images of "colossi [cherubim] and lions."

Amurru corresponds approximately to North Syria. "Amurrian sheep" are mentioned specifically in the thirteenth tablet of the famous *KHAR.ra: khubullu* vocabulary, line 69 (Oppenheim-

XX

'Anat first disposes of the monster Yam by chasing him back into the sea.

* * *

Then, grasping her spindle [in her hand],
brandishing the spindle in [her] right ha[nd],
she proceeds to drive him forth.
She tears off her robe, the covering of her flesh,
and goes chasing him ever farther into the sea, into the streams.

Hartman, JNES 4 [1945], 161). The identity of Yman (mentioned also in RS 2:19) is uncertain.

XX. Not until later (§XXXIX; II AB vii 2–4) is Sir Sea finally discomfited. 'Anat first thrusts him back into the ocean to prevent his encroachment upon the earth. This is in accordance with the advice which 'Ashtart has given to Baal (§XVI; III AB,A 31–35). To facilitate her movements, she rips off her clothing.

In many of the seasonal mummeries representing the rout of the Dragon, or the expulsion of Death, Blight, or Winter, he is *flung into the water*. Thus, at Nuremberg, the traditional song specified that "we bear Death into the water" (Grimm, *Teutonic Mythology*, 767). At Tabor, Bohemia, it was said that "Death floats down the stream" (*ibid.*, 771); and at Bielsk, Podlachia, the effigy was drowned in a marsh or pond (*ibid.*). The same procedure is recorded also among the Sorbs in Upper Lausitz (*ibid.*); and in some parts of Poland, Marzana, the goddess of Death (cp. Polish *marznać*) was flung into a marsh (*ibid.*). Again, on March 13, the Roman vestals used to throw puppets into the Tiber (Ovid, *Fasti* v 621); and in early March, the Indian Kali similarly flung them into the Ganges (Frazer *ad* Ovid, *loc. cit.*). In Chrudim, Bohemia, Death was flung into the water on "Black Sunday," to be subsequently retrieved and burned (Vernalken, *Mythen und Bräuche . . . in Osterreich*, 294 ff.). In Silesia, children used to throw the effigy of Death into the river (Drechsler, *Sitte . . . in Schlesien*, i. 70.); while at Leipzig this was done by the local prostitutes and bastards (Sartori, *Sitte und Brauch*, iii. 131, n. 2.). At Dobschwitz, near Gera, Death was drowned annually on March 1 (Frazer, GB, one-vol. ed., 308); and in Thüringen, in the early part of the eighteenth century, he was cast into the streams (*ibid.*). A similar custom obtained at Gross-Strehlitz, where the image was called Goik (*ibid.*, 309). In villages

XXI

'Anat then prepares gifts for El and flies to him.

Then, having placed a *khupatar*-pot over the fire,
a *khubrush*-vessel over the coals,

---

near Erlangen, peasants used to throw puppets representing Death into the river Regnitz on the fourth Sunday in Lent (*ibid.*, 308).

There are indications that this custom was observed also in ancient Mesopotamia; for it is a curious fact that in some of the Babylonian chants of the Tammuz cult, that god is said to have been *submerged beneath the ocean* (e.g., CT XVI 10b; IV R 30.2); and, according to most scholars, the month of Tebeth (January) took its name from such immersion (Hebrew *t-b-'*).

Lastly, it is perhaps possible to detect a dim reminiscence of the mythological submersion of the Dragon in the metaphorical language of Micah 7:19: "He will again have mercy on us, tread our iniquities underfoot, and all our sins will be cast into the depths of the sea." This possibility is enhanced by the fact that the word rendered "tread underfoot" (viz., *k-b-sh*) is the same as that employed in the Babylonian version (EE iv 129) to describe the subjugation of Tiamat by Marduk (cf. Gaster, JRAS 1944, 33).

In the light of these parallels and of the general consideration that our poem harks back to a ritual pantomime, it would seem likely that *this incident of the myth corresponds to a feature of the original ritual in which the image of the Dragon was thrown into the water.*

The spindle here brandished by 'Anat was woman's standard weapon — like the rolling pin in modern times! Similarly, in the miracle play performed at the Council of Constance, in 1417, the 'good women of Bethlehem' attacked the villain *with their distaffs;* Hone, *Ancient Mysteries,* 170. On the spindle as a symbol of Near Eastern goddesses, see Poulsen, *Der Orient und die fruhgriech. Kunst,* 101. As a symbol of women, see Grimm, *Deutsche Mythol.,* ed. 2, p. 390; as the weapon of witches, see Bolte-Polivka, i. 440.

XXI. The words *khupatar* and *khubrush* are borrowed from Hurrian (Horite). The former is mentioned as a temple vessel in the great Temple Inventory from Qatna (Mishrife) in Syria, line 4. The latter is mentioned frequently in Hittite texts. C. G. von

she wings her way to the Bull-god,
to El of the gentle heart,
to entreat the Creator of all creatures.

XXII

Asherat is at first alarmed at the approach of 'Anat and Baal, fearing that their intentions are hostile. Eventually, however, she is placated by the sight of the presents which they have brought, and she orders her henchman, the Fisher-god Koshar, to imprison Yam in a net.

When Asherat lifts her eyes and espies,
when she sees the approach of Baal,
the approach of the Virgin 'Anat,
the advent of Y-b-m-t L-i-m-m,
her feet [start to tap],
she twists her hips,
as if her backbone were breaking,
over her face runs sweat,
her [hips] start to shake,
[her] spine quivers.
Then lifts she her voice and cries:
"What brings hither Baal Puissant?

Brandenstein (ZA, N.F. 12 [1940], 89) derives it from Hurrian *khubr-*, "earth," when the meaning will be "earthenware." The placing of the pots over the fire may here refer to *firing* them.

XXII. The broken state of the text prevents our knowing precisely what golden objects 'Anat brought to Asherat. Only the first letter of the crucial word, viz., *n*[ ], remains. However, if this be restored to read *n* [*z m*], the reference would be to the *earrings* which the latter goddess often wears in Palestinian figurines: see Sellin, *Taanek*, 80, 106; Vincent, *Canaan*, 165; Moorgat, ZA 41 (1933), 209 ff.; S. R. Driver, *Modern Research as Illustrating the Bible*, 57; Pritchard, *Figurines*, 52 ff. Golden earrings are mentioned in Exodus 32:2; 35:22.

That Koshar should here figure as a divine fisherman accords with Sanchuniathon's statement that Chusor was the inventor of fishing tackle! Note that in the Babylonian version, Tiamat is first imprisoned in a net and only later decapitated. Similarly, in later Jewish echoes of the myth, the angel Gabriel is ordered to haul Leviathan out of the sea (T.B., Baba Bathra 75a).

What brings hither the Vi[rg]in 'Anat?
Them that would smite me I surely sm[i]te!
Have my sons, perchance, [raised a rebellion],
[or the famil]y of my kinsmen [a revolt]?"

But as soon as Asherat catches sight of the silver,
the silver handiwork and the golden * * *,
Queen A[sherat]-of-the-Sea rejoices,
loudly to her servitor [she calls]:
"Attend now, Sir Adroit, I . . .,
thou fisherman of the Queen Asherat-of-the-Sea,
take a net in thy hand,
a large [mesh] in thy hands [do thou raise],
* * * * * * * * * * against Yam, the beloved of El,
* * * * * * * * * * against Yam will El * * *
[against the Ruler of the Str]eams will El * * *
* * * Baal Puissant * * Virgin 'Anat * * *
* * * * * * * * *

XXIII

Asherat then assures Baal that the Dragon will give him no further trouble and that his sovereignty is therefore assured.

* * *

Let him not escape!
* * * * thy foundation * * * * * * for all generations!
* * * * * thee/thy and * * * *
who hath (now) become king of the gods (?).

XXIII. The words "Let him not escape" obviously refer to the captured Sir Sea; while the words "Thy foundation . . . for all generations" just as clearly refer to the triumphant Baal. The latter phrase should be restored to read: "Be thy foundation established for all generations!" They may then be taken as reproducing a standard formula recited at the installation of kings; cf. Clay, *Morgan*, 38 ii 35–36: "May the foundation of his throne stand firm forever!" Similar phrases occur frequently in the reports of Assyrian and Babylonian astrologers (e.g., Thompson, *Reports*, No. 176; Jastrow, *Rel. Bab. und Assyr.*, ii. 662). Cf. also Psalm 45:6: "Thy throne be as God is – everlasting"; Psalm 72:5 (LXX text): "Mayest thou be long-lived like the sun, and like the moon for all generations!" (addressed to a king).

XXIV

Baal points out, however, that, being without a palace, he is subject to constant insult at the hands of the gods.

But up speaks Baal Puissant,
up starts the Rider on the Clouds:
"Here they go insulting me,
there they go reviling me,
amid the assembly of the gods.
Muck is placed on my table,
filth am I made to drink from my cup.
Behold, there be two kinds of feast which Baal abhors,
three He Who Rides upon the Clouds —
one marked by shamefulness,
one marked by lechery,
one marked by low-bred bawdry.[g]
Yet here is glaring shamefulness,
and here is low-bred bawdry!"

XXV

Asherat replies by inquiring why Baal and 'Anat have chosen to approach her rather than go direct to El.

After Baal Puissant has reached his destination,
after the Virgin 'Anat has reached her destination,
they start to entreat Queen Asherat-of-the-Sea,
to sue for the grace of the Mistress of the Gods.

Thereupon Queen Asherat-of-the-Sea replies:
"How come ye entreat Queen Asherat-of-the-Sea,
sue for the grace of the Mistress of the Gods?
Have ye entreated the Bull-god, El of the gentle heart?
Have ye sued for the grace of the Creator of all Creatures?"

[g] Lit., "lewdness of handmaids."

XXIV. Baal's objection to loud and ribald feasts finds an interesting counterpart in the Egyptian Maxims of Ani, §xi: "Noise is an abomination in the sanctuary of God." (Petrie, *Religion and Conscience in Ancient Egypt*, 160, actually renders: "Detestable in the sanctuary of God are noisy *feasts*," but there seems to be no authority for this.)

XXVI

To this ʿAnat replies that they prefer first to seek the intercession of the Mother of the Gods, and only then to approach the Father.

But the Virgin ʿAnat replies:
"We would first entreat the [Mot]her,
even Queen Asherat-of-the-Sea,
[sue for the gr]ace of the Mistress of the Gods.
[Thereafter] will we entreat *him*,
[sue for the grace of the Father of] Baal Puissant!"

XXVII

Thereupon Asherat accords a warm welcome to the suppliants, bidding them regale themselves with food and drink.

[Then answers] Queen Asherat-of-the-Sea:
"Hearken, O Virgin ʿAnat,
* * * * * eat [and] drink
[along with all of the gods] who suck [at my breast]!
[With a sh]arp blade cut up a [fatling];
[drink] wine by the [gob]letful,
[the 'blood] of trees' [from a golden cup!]"

* * * * * * * * * *

XXVII. The "blood of trees" evidently denotes a manna-like gum or resin. Analogous is the Accadian expression "blood of the cedar" (KARI 13 iv 22; 51 iii 18; KARI 56.10; CT XXIII 35.41; Johns, *Deeds* 43b, r. 7–8; cf. Thureau-Dangin, *Rituels accadiens,* 50, n. 19). Parallel expressions in primitive speech are cited by Frazer, GB ii 20, 248. Note also that in Accadian "blood" is sometimes used for wine (e.g., PSBA 23 [1901], 204) and that Dioscorides (i 172) similarly employs the Greek term *ichor* to denote "the juice of trees." In Genesis 49:11; Deuteronomy 32:14, wine is called more specifically "the blood of the grapes" – an expression comparable with *haima botruon* in Achilles Tatius ii 2. Cf. also, in Latin, Statius, *Theb.,* i, 329: *Baccheo sanguine,* and Nemesianus, Ecl. ii 50: *Pallas amat turgentes sanguine baccas.* For Arabic parallels, cf. Jacob, *Studien,* iv 6 ff.

XXVIII

The meal over, Asherat accompanies her guests to El.

Then [Queen] Asherat-of-the-Sea [commands]:
"Harness an ass, hitch a foal;
[place on it silver halters], golden [reins],
put halters on (my) she-ass!"

Sir Holy-and-Blessed obeys;
he harnesses an ass, hitches a foal,
He places on it silver halters, golden reins,

XXVIII. "Sir Holy-and-Blessed" is an approximate rendering of the original *Qdsh-w-Amrr.* The first word is the common Semitic term for "holy, sacred"; the second is evidently derived from the verb *m-r-r,* which occurs in the Ugaritic texts (I Aq 195; II Aq i 25, etc.) in parallelism with *b-r-k,* "bless." The god is a purely mythological figure, and does not appear in the ritualistic documents.

We are here introduced for the first time to the Canaanite conception of the heavenly abode. It lies in the north, on the top of a mountain, at the place where the upper and lower oceans meet. All of this can be illustrated from other mythologies.

First, as to the belief that the gods dwell in the *north.* The existence of this idea among the Hebrews is attested by such Scriptural passages as Isaiah 14:13: "I will ascend unto heaven . . . dwell in the Mount of Assembly, *in the recesses of the north";* Job 37:22: "Out of *the north* cometh a splendor (MT: gold), round about God is a wondrous sheen"; while in Psalm 48:2 Mount Zion is apostrophized as "Towering superb, joy of all the earth . . . *the Recesses of the North,"* i.e., the equivalent of the divine hill. (Cf. Alfrink, *Biblica* 14 [1933], 60–61; Virolleaud, CRAIBL 1937: 67–8; Morgenstern, HUCA 16 [1941], 65.)

In later Jewish thought, Paradise was likewise located in *the north* (Enoch 24:3 ff.; 25.1 ff.; Midrash Shir ha-Shirim Zutta §4.16 Buber; cf. Scheftelowitz, *Altpers. Rel. u. Judenthum,* 161).

The Mesopotamians likewise believed that the high god Anu dwelt in the extreme north, on the summit of a mountain (Jensen, *Kosmologie,* 23; Jeremias, *OT in light of Ancient Near East,* tr. Johns, i. 20; Delitzsch, *Wo lag das Paradies,* 117; Karppe, JA, 1897, 86 ff.). In Egyptian belief, the gods dwelt on a northern mountain (Maspero, RHL 15 [1887], 275–79). In Indic belief, they dwelt on the mythical mountain of Uttarakuru in the extreme north

he puts halters on her she-ass.
Then Sir Holy-and-Blessed claps her round the waist,
he places Asherat on the back of the ass,
on the gaily-trapped back of the foal.

Sir Holy blazes the trail;
Sir Blessed goes ahead like a (lode) star.

(Lassen, ZKM 2 [1839], 62 ff.); and in Avestan mythology, the mountain of Hara-berezaiti was located in the north (Meinhold, *Baudissin Festschrift,* 382). In the north, too, were located the mythical Himavata of the Tibetans, the Sumeru of the Buddhists, the Meru of the Aryans, the Kailasa of the Hindus, the Kwan-lun of the Chinese, the Asaheim of the Norsemen, and the mountain Myemnoh Toung of the Burmese, on the summit of which lived the seven *devas* (Smythe-Palmer, *Jacob at Bethel,* 17 ff.). A similar idea obtained also in ancient Finnish mythology (Schwenk, *Mythol. der Slawen,* 386). The Masai believe in a northern heaven (Merker, *Masai,* 197, 199); while the Dakotas of North America say that Heyoka, the god of the seasons, dwells on a mountain near the North Star (Brinton, *Myths of the New World,*[3] 95). The Khevsurs of the Caucasus locate their storm god on a high mountain in the north (ERE xii 485b, n. 3). The Parsis say that the gods live on the Elburz Mountains, and a similar idea is found in Hungarian folklore (Sklarek, *Ungarische Volksmärchen,* 50, 209). In the Syriac Alexander legend, that hero sees Paradise from a place in the north (Ps.-Cal. ii 32); and in the Scandinavian Flatey-book (fourteenth century), the hero Helge Thoreson goes to the north in order to join the blessed.

The numinous quality of the north also inspires the belief that it is the seat of demons. This idea obtained among the Iranians (Scheftelowitz, *op. cit.,* 59), the Mandaeans (Brandt, *Mandäische Rel.,* 67 ff.), the Manicheans (Flügel, *Mani,* 101), in Vedic belief (Satapatha Brahmana i 2, 4, 10; xii 5, 1, 11, etc.), among the Jews (Ziyyuni, 48d; Jerahmeel i 17 [= p. 6, ed. M. Gaster]; Lauterbach, HUCA 2 [1925], 369, n. 31), the Greeks (Gruppe, *Gr. Mythol.,* 815 ff.), and the Mexicans (Spence, *Mythol. of Mexico and Peru,* 24). In late Greek magical literature, demons are conjured from the north (Pap. Bibl. Nat. 269; Pap. Leyden W, col. 18.27); and Plutarch (*De Is. et Os.* 21) there locates Typhon (cf. Eitrem, *Papyri Osloenses* I, 34). Milton, in his *Paradise Lost,* makes the rebel angels assemble *in the north;* and in Shakespeare's *I Henry VI* v 3 La Pucelle invokes the aid of spirits "under the lordly monarch of the north."

The Virgin 'Anat and Baal go on foot,
proceed to the Height of the North.

Straightway she turns her face toward El,
at the place where the Two Streams converge,

Next, as to the *mountain*. The examples already adduced show that in most cases the belief that the gods live in the north is combined with the notion that they dwell on the summit of a mountain (e.g., Olympus). The latter was commonly regarded as a pillar stretching from the center or "navel" of the earth to the center of the heavens, identified as the Pole Star. The Lapps therefore know that star as *tjuöld,* "the Stake," the Turks as *deymir qaziq,* "the Iron Peg," and the Chinese as "the Pivot" (Smythe-Palmer, *op. cit.,* 38 ff.). Most cult centers were regarded as being at the foot of this cosmic mountain and therefore as marking the "navel" of the earth. In Greece, this idea was entertained about Delos (Pausanias x 13.7), Paphos (Hesychius, s.v. *omphalos*), Pythoi (Plutarch, *Moralia* 409 E), and other shrines (Roscher, *Omphalos,* 20 ff.; Cook, *Zeus,* ii. 166–68). Similar ideas obtained among the Semites (Wensinck, *Navel;* Burrows, in Hooke's *Labyrinth,* 45–70). Palestine itself was regarded in Jewish midrash as the "navel" of the earth (Grünbaum, ZDMG 31 [1887], 199), more precise localizations being Zion (Jellinek, *Beth ha-Midrash,* V. 63) and, among the Samaritans, Gerizim (M. Gaster, ZAW 17 [1911], 448). It is probable that the inhabitants of Ugarit (Ras Shamra) so regarded the neighboring Mons Casius (modern Jebel el-Akra) which is, in fact, the highest mountain in Syria; and it is, perhaps, not without significance that Casius is described in the Stadiasmos (ch. 143) as "the Throne," sc. of the divine king(?).

On the sacred mountain in general, see also: Dunbar, *Antiquity* 3 (1929), 408–13; Canney, JMEOS 20 (1936), 25–40.

Lastly, as to the idea that the heavenly abode marks the spot where the upper and lower oceans meet. For this it will suffice to refer to the treatment of the theme by Albright in AJSL 35 (1919–20), 161–95, and to recall that in the Babylonian *Epic of Gilgamesh,* the hero of the flood is transported, as a reward for his piety, to the "mouth of the streams." Not impossibly, as Albright has suggested (JPOS 12 [1932], 12, n. 35), this is the meaning of the curious Arabic expression *majma' al-bahrain,* "junction of the two oceans" in Koran, Sura 18. 59 ff. (cf. Lidzbarski, ZA 7 [1892], 104 ff.; 8 [1893], 263 ff.; Krappe, PQ 20 [1941], 125 f.; 21 [1942], 345 f.).

hard by the watershed of the Two Oceans,
she leaves the vast fields,
and comes to the pleasance of the King . . . . ;
at the feet of El she bows and falls,
prostrates herself and pays homage to him.

XXIX

El receives her kindly.

When El catches sight of her,
he parts his jaws (?) and laughs;
he places his feet on the footstool,
and twiddl[es] his fingers.
Then lifts he his voice and cries:
"What brings hither Queen Ashe[rat-of-the-Sea]?
What moves the Mistress of the Gods to come?
Thou art surely very hungry and foresp[ent];
Why, thou art surely very thirsty, and . . . .
Come, then, eat and drink!
Ea[t] food from the tables, drink w[ine] from the goblets,
the 'blood of trees' from a golden cup!
Why, the love of El will take care of thee,
the affection of the Bull-god protect thee!"

XXX

Thus encouraged, Asherat presents the case of Baal.

Then up speaks Queen Asherat-of-the-Sea:
"He sends thee word, O El,
thou who art ever so wise
(mayest thou thrive and prosper forever!),
Baal Puissant sends thee word,
even he who is now our king,
our ruler with none above him,
our . . . to whom we bring . . . in tribute,
our . . . to whom we bring . . . in tribute:
Hearken, thou Bull-god, his father,
O sovereign El who didst call him into being,
hearken what they are saying,
what Asherat and her sons are saying,
the Goddess and the company of her [kins]men:
'See, Baal has no house like the gods,

no abode like the (other) sons of Asherat!
The abode of El has to serve as the covert of his sons,
the abode of Queen Asherat-of-the-Sea as that of his bewitching brides,
yes, even as the abode of P-d-r-aya, the Lady of Light,
as the covert of the Dew-nymph (T-l-aya), Lady of Rain,
as the abode of the Earth-nymph (A-r-ṣ-aya), Lady of *y-ʿ-b-d-r*.' "

XXXI

El replies that he has no objection to the building of a palace for Baal, but asks whether that god really expects him and Asherat to do the manual labor.

Then answers the gentle-hearted El:
"Yes, but am I a slave, some henchman of Asherat?
Am I, then, a slave that I should . . . . . ?
Or is Asherat a handmaid
that she should go laying the bricks?
(By all means) let a house be built for Baal
as have all the other gods,
and a precinct as have all the sons of Asherat!"

XXXII

Asherat thanks El and conveys the glad tidings to Baal and ʿAnat, who have waited at a distance.

And Queen Asherat-of-the-Sea replies:
"Very wise hast thou shown thyself, O El;
truly, thy hoary old age lends sound judgment to thee,[h]
. . . . in thy breasts!
Why, see, Baal will thus be able to furnish his rains in due season,
in the seasons of . . . .,
and he will give forth his voice from the clouds,
his gleam darting earthward as lightning!
As a house of cedars let them perfect it,
as a house of brick — let them carry them hither!
Let the word be conveyed unto Baal Puissant:
'Summon a crew to thy mansion,

[h] Lit., "instructs thee."

a gang into the midst of thy palace!
Let the mountains yield thee abundance of silver,
the hills choice gold;
let the tall trees(??) yield thee logs(??),
and build thou a house of silver and gold,
a mansion of gems and lapis.' "

XXXIII

'Anat, hearing the news, repeats it exultantly to Baal, who has waited at a distance.

The Virgin 'Anat rejoices;
her feet tap vehemently on the ground.
Straightaway she turns her face toward Baal
on the Height of the North,
across a thousand acres, ten thousand tracts.

The Virgin 'Anat laughs;
she lifts her voice and cries:
"Baal, be of good cheer;
tidings of cheer have I brought thee!
There shall be built for thee
a house like thy brethren's
and a precinct like thy kinsmen's!
Summon a crew to thy mansion,
a gang to the midst of thy palace!
The mountains will yield thee abundance of silver,
the hills choice gold,
and build thou a mansion of silver and gold,
a mansion of gems and lapis!"

XXXIV

Thereupon Baal issues instructions for the building of the palace.

Baal Puissant rejoices.
He summons a crew to his mansion,
a gang to the midst of his palace.
The mountains yield him abundance of silver,
the hills choice gold;
the tall trees(??) yield logs(??).

XXXV

Sir Adroit-and-Cunning (Koshar-wa-Khasis), the divine architect and smith, is summoned to a banquet, where plans for the new building are discussed.

Sir Adroit-and-Cunning eats[1]

After Sir Adroit-and-Cunning has arrived,
an ox is set before him
and a fatling in front of him.
A seat is placed in position,
and he sits at the right hand of Baal Puissant.

Then, while [the gods] are eating and drink[ing],
[Baal Puis]sant exclaims:

[1] *Before these words the scribe had accidentally omitted a passage describing how the divine architect was summoned to the banquet. Realizing the omission, he inserts a note reading:*

> Go back to the passage: "When the two servitors bring the message . . ."

Unfortunately, however, he does not furnish the text of that passage.

XXXV. Sitting at a person's right hand was a sign of favor; cf. Psalm 110:1 (addressed to a king): "Saith YHWH unto my lord, Sit thou at my right hand"; Josephus, *Ant.* vi, 11.9: "On the following day, which was the new moon, the king came . . . to the banquet . . . and his son Jonathan sat beside him at his right hand"; I Esdras 4:29: "The concubine Apame was sitting at the right hand of the king"; Psalm 45:10 (EV. 9): "At thy right hand standeth a concubine [EV, wrongly, the queen]." In Semitic folklore, the right side was the lucky side; cf. Genesis 35:18 and Wellhausen, *Reste,*[2] 202.

Note also that in the medieval legend of Astolpho's visit to King Senapus of Abyssinia, it is stated expressly that at the feast of welcome he occupied the place of dignity at the king's right hand (*Bulfinch's Mythology,* Modern Library ed., 695).

On left and right in Classical lore cf. A. S. Pease on Cicero, *De Divinatione* ii 82 (UISLL, viii 3, 482–83); Pottier, in *Mel. Pedersen,* 405–13; Eitrem, *Opferritus,* 29 ff.; Weinreich, in GGA 1912, vii-ix, 135 ff.; Boll, *Sphaera,* 563 ff.; Dölger, *Sonne d. Gerechtigkeit,* 9 ff., 37 ff.; Eitrem, *Papyri Osloenses* I, 96 ff. For Egyptian ideas, see Roeder, *Urkunden* 107, 109, 112.

* * *

* * *

"[Has]ten, [build] the mansion . . .
hasten, uprear the pala[ce]!
Hasten, let a mansion be builded,
hasten, let a palace be upreared,
in the midst of the Height of the North!
Let the mansion occupy a thousand acres,
the palace ten thousand tracts!"

XXXVI

A discussion arises concerning the advisability of installing windows. The divine architect is in favor of them, but Baal objects that his maiden daughters may abscond or be abducted through them and thus provide cause for Yam to hold him up to ridicule.

Then says Sir Adroit-and-Cunning:
"Hearken, Baal Puissant,
mark thou, O Rider on the Clouds:
Let us put a casement in the mansion,
a window in the middle of the palace!"

But, "No," answers Baal,
"Put thou no casement in the [mans]ion,
[no window] in the middle of the pala[ce]!"

XXXVI. According to Cassuto (followed by Albright and Ginsberg), the reason why Baal objects to the installation of windows is that he fears lest Mot, genius of death and sickness, might climb in through them. This interpretation is based on the words of Jeremiah 9:20: "Death [Mot] is come up through our windows."

If the text is read more attentively, however, it will be seen that Mot does not come into the picture. There is explicit mention of "the lady of Ar" and the "lady of R-b" — standard epithets of Baal's two brides, P-d-r-aya and T-l-aya (cf. II AB i 17–18), and the former, at least, seems to be preceded by a verb with feminine prefix (*al td*). Moreover, the references to these two ladies is followed by one to "Sir Sea, the beloved of El" and to someone's eventually treating Baal with contumely. Surely, then, it is pretty obvious that what Baal fears is that his enemy, Sir Sea, bludgeoned but not yet slain, may revive, creep through the windows, and abduct his brides! It is, indeed, for this very reason

"Baal," rejoins Sir Adroit-and-Cunning,
"Thou wilt yet be converted to my word!"
Yea, again and again Sir Adroit-and-Cunning keeps saying:
"Baal, I implore thee, hearken;
let me put a case[ment] in the mansion,
a window in the mid[dle of the pala]ce!"

But, "No," Baal keeps replying,
"Put thou no case[ment] in the mansion,
no window in the middle of the palace,
lest [P-d-r-aya, the Lady of] Light depart,
lest the [Dew-nymph, the Lady of] Rain [be abducted?],
whereupon Sir Sea, the beloved of El, [will make sport of me],
will * * *, will revile me with contumely!"

But Sir Adroit-and-Cunning (merely) replies:
"Baal, thou wilt yet be converted to my word!"

XXXVII

The construction is put in hand. Fire is kindled to melt the silver and gold into ingots.

So the building of the mansion proceeds,
the uprearing of the palace.

---

that he first insists on dispatching that monster (§XXXIX; II AB vii 2–4, 14 ff.) before he consents to have the windows installed.

What we have here, therefore, is the very familiar idea that the *sea god or dragon claims boys and girls in tribute* (*MI*, B 11.10). The best example is, of course, the Cretan myth of the Minotaur, but there are also numerous tales revolving around the theme that water spirits kidnap mortals and confine them beneath the waves (*MI*, F 420.5.2.2). In all probability, such stories hark back to a primitive practice of periodic human sacrifice to the genius of the waters – a method of forfending inundation; cf. Frazer, GB, one-vol. ed., 146; *idem., Pausanias,* v. 145; Freytag, *Am Urquell* 1 (1890), 179 ff., 197. Such a rite would have formed part of the primitive seasonal pattern and thus have found place in myths which reflect it.

XXXVII. Siryon is the ancient name of the Anti-Lebanon range; cp. Psalm 29:6. The name occurs also, in association with Lablani-Lebanon, in Hittite texts, e.g., KBo IV iv 28–29 (cf. Luckenbill, AJSL 39 [1923], 64) and likewise in the Hurrian text, KUB

They go to Lebanon for its timber,
to Siryon for its choicest cedars;
* * Lebanon for its timber,
Siryon for its choicest cedars.

Fire is placed in the mansion,
flame in the palace.
Behold, for one day and a second,
fire devours in the mansion,
flame in the palace;
for a third day and a fourth,
fire devours in the mansion,
flame in the palace;
for a fifth day and a sixth,
fire devours in the mansion,
flame in the palace.
At last, on the seventh day,
the fire departs from the mansion,
the flame from the palace.
The silver is turned to ingots,
the gold is turned to bricks.

The Theoxenia

THE BANQUET OF THE GODS

XXXVIII

Baal regales the gods.

Baal Puissant rejoices:
"My mansion have I builded of silver, my palace of gold!"

Baal installs the installations of his mansion,
Haddu installs the [installa]tions of his palace.

XXXVII 14 iii 7 (cf. von Brandenstein, ZA, N.F. 12 [1940], 92). For the importation of cedars of Lebanon in the building of the temple, cf. I Kings 5:20, 23–24, 28; 7:2.

XXXVIII. This episode mythologizes the *theoxenia*, or regalement of the gods, which is a standard element of the Ritual Pattern; see fully, Chapter Two, §36. The *theoxenia* is similarly incorporated into most of the sister versions of our myth. Thus, the Egyptian Ramesseum Drama ends with the installation of the revived god and the celebration of a banquet attended, on the

He has oxen and sheep slaughtered,
has bulls [and a fat]ling felled,
rams also and yearling calves,
goats and kids.
He invites his brethren into his mansion,
his kinsmen into his palace;
he invites the seventy sons of Asherat.

He regales the lamb-gods with wine;
reglaes the ewe-goddesses [with wine].
He regales the ox-gods with wi[ne];
regales the cow-goddesses [with wine].
He regales the tribune-gods with wine;

---

durative level, by the gods and, on the punctual level, by the princes of the several nomes of Upper and Lower Egypt (Ramesseum Drama, §XXX, 89–90; §XXXIII, 97–100). In the Hittite Puruli myth, the weather god is installed at Nerik, with the gods around him (§VI); while in the Telipinu myth, that god's return is celebrated at a banquet (§IX). In the Babylonian New Year (Akitu) myth, Marduk, duly installed, presides at a banquet of the gods (EE iii 133–38; iv 54). Finally, as Cornford points out (*Origins of Attic Comedy*, 94 ff.), Old Attic comedy preserved this element of the primitive ritual pattern usually by inserting a banqueting scene between the Parabasis and the Exodos (cf. also Plutarch, *Lucullus* 39).

Within the framework of our poem, this ancient element also serves a further purpose: it conveys the idea that Baal, now ensconced in his palace, holds a constitutional assembly (as does Marduk in the Babylonian version) at which he determines the cosmic order and—specifically—relegates Mot to his proper domain. For the fact is that in ancient times such gatherings usually concluded with a *banquet*. This was certainly the case among the Mesopotamians (Jacobsen, JNES 2 [1943], 167, n. 49), the Homeric Greeks (Glotz, *Greek City*, 37), the Persians (Herodotus i 133), and the Teutons (Tacitus, *Germania* 22; Schrader, RIA², ii 30).

The gods who are entertained at the banquet are described generically as "the seventy sons of Asherat" or as the "nurslings" of that goddess, and specifically as "gods of rams, goddesses of ewes; gods of oxen, goddesses of cows; gods of tribunes, goddesses of thrones; gods of ewers, goddesses of beakers(?)." Seventy is, of course, merely a round number; cf. Genesis 4.24; 50.3; Isaiah

regales the throne-goddesses [with wine].
He regales the ewer-gods with wine,
regales the beaker-goddesses [with wine].

Continuously the gods eat and drink,
the nurslings (of Asherat) regale themselves;
a fatling is flayed with a sharp blade.
They drink wine by the gobletful,
[the "blood of trees" out of a golden cup.]

THE FINAL DISCOMFITURE OF SIR SEA

XXXIX

Baal now administers the coup de grâce *to the vanquished*

23.15; Jeremiah 25.12; *KAT* 634. It is interesting to observe that in the Hittite *Myth of Ullikummi* (IIIb, ii, 13 = Güterbock, *Kumarbi,* 24, 24) mention is likewise made of "seventy gods." For the rest, the styles are extremely significant for they define the guests as *the deities who preside over the livestock, the civil authority, and the vintage* – the three aspects of topocosmic life and activity upon which attention is especially concentrated at the autumn festival, when the god of the rains (Baal) resumes dominion over the earth.

Most – if not all – of the gods were, in theory, suckled by the mother goddess Asherat; so, too, according to the ancient conception, were kings. For Mesopotamia, cf. the conversation of Assurbanipal and the god Nabu, KB VI/2, 140–41.8 (= Streck, ii 348–49); Boissier, OLZ 1908: 234 f.; Zimmern, ZA 36 (1924–25), 85, n. 1; Labat, *Royauté,* 64–66. For Egypt, cf. the portrait, at Abydos, of Seti I being suckled by a goddess; Gressmann, *ATB,* No. 88; I, Pl. xxii, fig. 125; IV, Pl. 104–05; Maspero, PSBA 14 (1892), 308 ff.; Jocoby, ARW 13 (1906), 547 ff.; Sethe, *Pyramidentexte,* ii. §§910–13; Eisler, *Orphisch-Dionysische Mysteriengedanken,* 360 ff. For Greece, cp. Eratosthenes, *Katasterismos* 44: "The sons of Zeus were not permitted to partake of heavenly honor unless they had sucked the breast of Hera."

It is probable that in the ritual counterpart of the myth, the divine guests were represented by local princelings, as again in the case of the Ramesseum drama in Egypt.

XXXIX. The text is here extremely fragmentary, but the correctness of our interpretation is surely established by (*a*) the

Yam, in order to remove a potential threat to his daughters and to ensure his own sovereignty.

* * *

* * * Baal Puissant
* * * [smi]tes(?) Sir Sea, the beloved of El,
* * *s [him] on his skull.

The Tour of the Dominions

BAAL CONSOLIDATES HIS KINGDOM

XL

Leaving his guests at their revels, Baal embarks upon a one-man expedition in order to annex an "empire."

[While the] god[s are mak]ing merry on the Mountain,
while the gods are [regaling themselves] in the North,
[Baal] travels from city to city,
turns from town to town,
assumes possession of sixty-six cities,

---

analogy of the sister versions; (*b*) the fact that in V AB,D 36 the definite annihilation of the Dragon is mentioned; and (*c*) the consideration that something must here take place to justify Baal's otherwise inexplicable change of mind concerning the installation of the windows.

XL. This episode mythologizes the very common practice of acquiring territory by ceremonially walking round it. An excellent illustration of this in modern times comes from the enthronement ceremonies current in Malaya. R. O. Winstedt reports (JRAS 1945, 139–40) that at Perak, when the new sultan was installed, he had to circumambulate his royal demesne seven times, and that "to circumambulate his Meru, whether hill or palace, was for the new sovereign . . . to take possession of his kingdom in little." Similarly, in the annual Egyptian ceremonies, the king had to sail down the Nile and tour his realm; and this tour forms the background of the Ramesseum and Edfu dramas. So, too, in Hittite practice, the king had to make a tour of his dominion in connection with the winter festival of Nuntariyashas (KUB II

of seventy-seven towns,
yea, of eighty does Baal * *,
of ninety does Baal * * *.

9; IX 16; X 48; XX 70, 80; XXV 12–14; Goetze, *Kleinasien,*[1] 154). This prescription of the bounds of the realm forms a constant elemental of seasonal festivals. Warde Fowler has suggested (*Roman Festivals,* 319) that it provides the true explanation of the circumambulatory procession at the Lupercalia in Rome (cf. Frazer, *Fasti of Ovid,* ii. 336); and it is well attested in British and German calendar customs (Brand, *Observations,* i. 197 f.; Thistleton Dyer, *British Popular Customs,* 204 ff.; Leather, *Folklore of Herefordshire,* 149–51; Hull, *Folklore of the British Isles,* 77–80; Wright, *English Folklore* (Benn's Sixpenny Series), 44–45; Sartori, *Sitte und Brauch,* iii. 168, 216, 268).

This practice is especially common in African coronation ceremonies and is listed by Tor Irstam (*King of Ganda,* 26) among the standard elements of such rituals. Patai (HUCA 20 [1947], 176 ff.) would detect a reminiscence of it in the account given in I Samuel 10:2–5 of Saul's progressive journey to the grave of Rachel, the terebinth of Tabor and the Gibeah (hill) of God. In primitive societies circumambulation is a recognized method of taking possession; see Radermacher, in *Sitzb. Wien. Akad.,* 187 iii (1918), 127 ff.

Within the strict framework of our story, however, the episode may also possess another significance: it may be intended to suggest that Baal, like any earthly monarch, undertook the regular razzia or marauding expedition at the beginning of the autumn. The custom is well attested in ancient Near Eastern sources. In II Samuel 11:1 we are told distinctly that the "turn of the year" was the season for such royal campaigns — the time of "the going forth of the kings" (so read, with Versions, for MT's "messengers"); while the records of the kings of Assyria show that the same was true in that area (Meissner, *Babylonien und Assyrien,* i. 106–07). Similarly, the Hittite king Mursilis II relates that his military expeditions took place in the season of *hameshas,* which is identified by most scholars with late summer or early fall (cf. Ehelolf, SPAW 21 [1925], 267, n. 2; Goetze, KIF 1 [1929], 179). That the same usage was known to the Canaanites is seemingly indicated by the fact — hitherto unnoticed — that in the so-called *Poem of Nikkal* (77:2–3, Gordon), the word "razzia-makings" (*t-gh-z-y-t*) stands parallel to "late summer" (*q-tz*) as a designation of that season.

The Assurance of Rainfall

INSTALLATION OF THE WINDOWS

XLI

Having now disposed of Yam and consolidated his kingdom, Baal returns to his palace and announces that he has changed his mind and will permit the installation of windows. Whenever these are opened, the "windows of heaven" will correspondingly be opened by remote control, and thus the earth will be assured of rainfall in due season.

Th[en] Baal [retu]rns within his palace,
and [thus] speaks Baal Puissant:
Very well, Sir Adroit, I will have them installed.
On the very day, Sir Adroit,
yea, at the very moment
when the window is opened in the mansion,

Baal, having now obtained sovereignty, has to behave like a typical mortal monarch. He is therefore represented as conducting the typical seasonal razzia; and by thus providing it with a divine precedent, our myth at the same time endows the traditional institution with the appropriate degree of sanctity and authority.

XLI. This episode mythologizes a rain-making ceremony which formed part of the ritual of the autumn festival. The ceremony was obviously based on what has come to be known (perhaps inaccurately) as "sympathetic magic," windows being opened in the temple or chapel to simulate the opening of the "windows of heaven" through which the rain was released. The latter are mentioned expressly in OT; cf. Genesis 7:11: "All the fountains of the great deep were broken up, and the windows of heaven were opened"; Genesis 8:2; II Kings 7:2, 19; Isaiah 24:18; Malachi 3:10. Gesenius, *Thesaurus*, 145b., cites an analogous Persian expression. On the conception of the sky window in the folklore of other peoples, see *MI*, F 56. Note also that in a Wallachian folk song chanted by children in time of drought, the spirit Papaluga is invoked to "ascend to heaven, open its *doors* and pour rain from on high" (Schwenk, *Mythol. der Slawen*, 43. See also G. D. Teodorescu, *Poesil Populare Romane* [Bucharest, 1885], 208–12).

the casement within the palace,
a rift shall (likewise) be opened in the clouds,
according to [thy] counsel, Sir Adroit-and-Cunning!"

Acclamation of the New King

THE PRAISE OF BAAL

XLII

Sir Adroit-and-Cunning commends the decision of Baal and recites his praises as lord of the storm.

Sir Adroit-and-Cunning rejoices.
He lifts his voice and cries:
"See, I told thee, Baal Puissant,
thou wouldst yet be converted to my word!

XLII. Koshar's commendation of Baal incorporates several clichés familiar from Mesopotamian and Hebrew hymns addressed to the storm god. Compare, for example, the description of Hadad in W.A.I., iv 28.2 f.(= Strong, PSBA 20 [1898], 161): "When Baal (*belum*) rages, heaven is commoved; when Hadad waxes furious, earth shakes; the great mountains are cleft before him"; EA 147. 14–15: "Who gives forth his voice in heaven like Haddu (Hadad), and all the mountains quake at his voice"; King, *Babylonian Magic and Sorcery*, 21.83: "Hadad gives forth thunders . . . the mountains are [sha]ken." Transferred to Yahweh, cf. Psalm 29.5–6: "The voice of Yahweh breaks the cedars, Yahweh shivers the cedars of Lebanon. Why, he makes Lebanon to skip like a calf, and Siryon like a young wild ox"; Nahum 1:3 ff.: "In the gale and the flail is His way, and the clouds are the dust of his feet. He rebukes the sea (Yam!) and dries it up, and all the streams he renders dry. Bashan and Carmel droop, and the flowers of Lebanon wilt. The mountains quake before him, and the hills are commoved. The earth is made desolate (MT: lifts itself?) before him, . . . His fury who can abide? Who endure the heat of his rage? He makes a full end of His foemen (LXX text), and chases His enemies into darkness . . . What! Ye would plot against Him? Why, he makes a full end; trouble rises not twice!" It is therefore probable that *this speech by Koshar merely works into the fabric of the poem the text of a standard hymn to the rain god (Baal) recited as part of the liturgy of the autumn festival.*

Now, when the window is opened in the mansion,
the casement within the palace,
do thou, O Baal, open a rift in the clouds!

When Ba[al g]ives forth his holy voice,
when Baal keeps dis[charging the utterance of] his [li]ps,
his ho[ly] voice [sha]kes the earth,
* * * the mountains quake,
a-quiver are the * * * east and west,
the high places of the ea[rth] rock.
The enemies of Baal take to the woods,
the foes of Hadd[j] to the sides of the mountain(s)!"

The Ousting of Drought

THE BANISHMENT OF MOT

XLIII

Echoing the words of Sir Adroit-and-Cunning, Baal announces that he will brook no opposition to his kingship, particularly from Mot, the genius of drought and aridity.

"Yes, indeed," replies Baal Puissant,
"how the enemies of Baal quake,
oh, how they quake!
Stricken with terror are all who would ever challenge me!
Baal first marks down, then his hand strikes.[k]

[j] Another name of Baal.
[k] Lit. "Baal's eyes anticipate his hands."

XLIII (b). This passage is sufficiently explained by the fact that in Arabic desert and sterile soil is indeed called "dead land," i.e., land of Death (Mot); see fully Introduction, §4.

(c) The names Targhuzizza and Sharrumagi (vocalization tentative) contain those of two well-known Asianic deities, viz., Tarhu and Sharruma. This implies that they were thought to lie in a region *to the north* of the Canaanites and links up at once with the widespread notion that the *underworld lies in the north, beyond the mountains which enclose the earth.*

Thus, in the Babylonian Gilgamesh Epic (Tab. IX), that hero journeys thither over the "twin mount" Mashu, usually identified

Why, even cedars wilt(??) at the touch of his right hand!
Now that Baal has returned to his palace,
nor king nor commoner on earth shall install himself on my throne!
No! I will send a message to that godling Mot,
a dispatch to that youngster, the beloved of El.
Mot, maybe, is proclaiming in his soul,
saying seditiously in his mind:
' 'Tis I alone that shall reign o'er the gods,
give fatness to gods and men,
sate the multitudes of the earth!' "

---

with Masis, a hill in the province of Ararat (Aghri-Dag) and the tallest peak in that range (cf. Pseudo-Jacob of Serug in Knos, *Chrestom. Syriaca,* 72; Budge, *Alexander;* Anderson, *Gog and Magog;* Krappe, PQ 20 [1941], 126–27; 21 [1942], 341). A similar belief obtained among the Greeks, the region of the underworld being popularly located among the Cimmerians of Asia Minor (Nonnus, *Dionys.* xv 268 f.; Cicero, *Acad. Prior* ii 61 c. 19; PW xi 425–34; Ausman, *Babyloniaca* 6 [1912]; Berger, *Kosmogr. d. Griechen,* 15) or among the Hyperboreans (Körte, ARW 10 [1907], 153; cf. Pindar, *Pyth.* x 30 f.; Bacchylides iii 58 f.), or in other *northern* regions (Gruppe, *Gr. Mythol.,* 390, n. 4). In later Christian belief, the Lycian Olympus was regarded as the entrance to Hades (Brinkmann, *Rhein. Mus.* 69 [1914], 224). In the Alexander legend, that hero goes to the north to the land of the departed (Pseudo-Callisthenes ii 32). The Talmud (Hagiga 32b) records a statement by Rabbi Eliyahu that Gehenna lies "behind the mountains of darkness"; while Ephraim Syrus (*Op.* i, 121) quotes Jacob of Edessa as speaking of two mountains, called "Breasts of the North," the stones whereof were crystal and beyond which there was nothing but the cosmic ocean (cf. Wensincke, *The Ocean in the Literature of the Western Semites,* 34). This statement may be elucidated in the light of the fact the Caucasian word *m-kh-r* means both "breast" and "mound" (Tagliavini, *Caucasica,* fasc. iii, 1 ff.), so that what would be implied would be two mountains in Asia Minor, as in our present text. According to Wilamowitz-Moellendorf (*Ilias und Homer,*[2] 494), Odyssey xi supposes that the entrance to the netherworld lay in the north, viz., in the steppes of southern Russia.

The idea that the world is hemmed in by mountains is especially familiar from the Arabic conception of the *Qâf,* or "encircling range" (Wensinck, *Navel,* 6). But the notion is found also in

Baal sends his two couriers, Sir Vine (G-p-n) and Sir Field (U-g-r), to Mot to tell him that henceforth his permanent abode is to be the netherworld and that when he visits the earth he is to confine himself to the deserts and barren places.

Then loudly calls Baal to his two servants:
"Attend, Sir Vine and Sir Field!
'Mid the darkness, where daylight is obscured,
'mid the tall shaggy ostriches
[shall his po]rtion be;
the sun-scorched places [shall be his] province,
* * where rain clouds are wi[thheld?] * *

* * *

So now turn ye your faces
toward Mount Targhu/izziza
toward Mount Sharrumagi,
toward those twin mounds which hem in the earth.
Raise the mountain on your hands,
the holt upon your palms,
and go down into the corruption of the netherworld,
be counted among them that go down into the earth.

Zoroastrian thought (*ibid.*), and recurs in Teutonic belief (Meyer, *Altgerm. Religionsgesch.*, 468). See fully Gressmann-Ungnad, *Gilgames Epos*, 160 ff.; *MI*, F 145.

The reference to Mot's subterranean domain as his "city" (*qrt*) accords with the fact that "City" (*ganzir, irkallu*) was a recognized name for the netherworld in Sumero-Accadian mythology (Tallquist, *Namen d. Totenwelt*, 15 f., 36; Langdon, *Sem. Mythol.*, 161; Albright, AJSL 53 (1936), 11; idem, *Archaeology and Rel. of Israel*, 81). In the Sumerian story of Inanna's descent to the netherworld, the gate of Ganzir is described as the "face" of the underworld (Kramer, *Sumerian Mythology*, 91). Not impossibly, this is the real meaning of *polis* in Aeschylus, *Septem contra Thebas* 613: *ten makran polin molein*, as the Scholiast of the Medicean Codex indeed explains it. (Modern editors read *palin*, which seems banal.) The same usage may be recognized also in Dante's *Per me si va nella città dolente, Per me si va nell' eterno dolore* (*Inferno* iii, 1–2). Cf. also Shakespeare, *King Lear* III, ii. 186, where the quartos read "Childe Rowland to the dark *town* came," in place of the folios' *tower*. Both Byron and Edith Sitwell (*Atlantic Monthly*, May, 1950, p. 52): think this referred originally to the realm of death.

Then turn ye your faces
toward his . . . city,
to the pit where is the seat of his abiding,
to the filth of the earth, which is his estate.
But be on your guard, look you, ye gods,
approach not nigh to the godling Mot,
lest he put you like a lamb in his mouth,
lest like a goat ye be crushed to pieces in the . . . of his . . .!
(Why, 'tis at the whim of Mot, the beloved of El,
that the sun, that torch of the gods, scorches,
that the heavens flash!)
From a distance of a thousand acres, of ten thousand tracts,
bow and fall at the feet of Mot,
prostrate yourselves and pay homage to him.
Then say to the godling Mot,
repeat unto that youngster, the beloved of El:
'This is the message of Baal Puissant,
[the wo]rd of Him Who is Puissant among War[riors]:
My mansion have I builded [of silver], my [palace of gold].
* * * * * * * * my brethren,
* * * * * * * * my brethren,
* * * * * * * * my * * *
* * * * * * * * * * * * *
* * * * * * [with a sh]arp [blade] * *
* * * * * * * * gods
* * * * * * * * * * * * * * *
* * * * * * * * * * * * * * *

I* AB Gordon: 67

XLIV

The two messengers convey the words of Baal to Mot.

[Then away speed Sir Vine] and Sir Field;

* * *

B. THE SUMMER CYCLE

Ousting of the Spirit of Fertility: Deposition of the King

BAAL IS LURED INTO THE NETHERWORLD

I* AB Gordon: 67

XLV

Baal is bent on further conquests. Mot, anxious to lure him into the netherworld, tries to deter him, warning him that such exploits might spell his doom. In illustration, he points to his own fate as the result of challenging Baal.

* *
*

"If now thou go fighting Leviathan, that dragon evasive,
if now thou wouldst try to destroy the Slant Serpent,
that seven-headed monster of might,
thou wouldst (but) wear thyself out;
the girdle of thy robe — (that robe which is) the sky —
would (thereby) become loosed!

XLV. This passage is one of the most difficult in the entire poem, and our interpretation is therefore tentative. Presumably, Baal, flushed with triumph, is now bent on the elimination of other potential opponents – in particular, Leviathan, the monstrous dragon long known to us from allusions in Old Testament poetry (Isa. 27:1; Psalm 74:14; 104:26; Job 3:8). Mot, however, tries to lure him into the netherworld. To this end, he tells him that a tussle with the monster will merely exhaust him,. whereas, as things are, he is now "sitting pretty" and has turned the tables effectively on Mot.

To symbolize the fact that Baal would lose his strength if he were to tussle with Leviathan, Mot warns him that the girdle of his robe would thereby become loosened. The expression is readily explicable from Job 12:21, "He pours contempt on princes, and *looses the belt of the strong*"; cf. also Isa. 45:1, "Cyrus, whose right hand I have grasped, to subdue nations before him and *ungird the loins of kings.*"

Baal's enveloping robe is in turn identified with the sky. For

(As things are,) *I* am the one that has been swallowed up;
a stopper, as it were, has been placed upon me;
drained of strength (?) as I am, *I* am the one that is dying,
(whereas) *thou* hast escaped descent into the throat of divine
Mot (Death),
into the gorge of that brave who was indeed the favorite of
El!"

---

this idea, cp. Psalm 104:2: "Who coverest Thyself with light as with a garment, Who stretchest out the heavens like a curtain." Similarly, in Yasht xiii 3, "Mazda takes heaven to himself as a garment, star-embroidered, god-woven." In Teutonic mythology, Odin wears a blue or azure mantle representing the sky (Hermann, *Nord. Mythol.*, 259; Meyer, *Mythol. d. Germanen*, 370); while among the Ewe-speaking Negroes of Africa, the azure sky is the veil with which Maiou, the supreme god, covers his face, and the clouds are his garments and ornaments (Blanc, *Il sacro presso i primitivi*, 71). In the Phoenician cosmogony of Pherekydes (Clem. Alex., *Strom.* 621 A), Zas, after conquering the Dragon, makes a great garment and embroiders thereon the earth and the sea. Cf. also Nonnus, *Dionys.* xi. 367–577, where Heracles (i.e., Baal) of Tyre is described as "wearing a jerkin of stars" and as being wrapped in a garment which lights up the sky at night. In Rig Veda I, 173.6, Indra is said to wear heaven as a crown. In Sumerian hymns (SRT iii. 17, 37), the goddess Inanna is addressed as "she who dons the garment of heaven"; and the expression "garment of heaven" indeed occurs as a title of Ishtar (Langdon, JRAS 1925, 717 f.). Moreover, Meissner (AJSL 47 [1931], 202) reports a word-list in which "garment of heaven" is equated with "clouds." However, Weidner says (AfO 7 [1931], 115 f.) that all references to this garment allude to some kind of veiling of the moon, the only exception being Thompson, *Reports*, No. 151, rev. 4–9, where it denotes a star-spangled robe worn by kings on special occasions. These various usages are by no means irreconcilable; the detail cited by Pherekydes would be based on the customary type of regal vestment, while for the idea that the moon is so attired, cf. Orphica, *Argon.* 314 and Pap. Paris, Suppl. Gr. 574. 2559 (in R. Wuensch, *Aus einem griech. Zauberpaprus*, Kleine Texte 84), where the moon is styled "star-jerkined" [*astrochiton*].

LEVIATHAN means properly "the Coiled One" (rt. *l-w-y*). The epithets here applied to him accord with those in Isaiah 27:1, "In that day Yahweh with his sore and great and strong

XLVI

The two couriers return to Baal and relay the words of Mot. The latter has invited him to a banquet, pointing out that, though his food is now the mud of the netherworld, he nevertheless retains his erstwhile insatiable appetite and is therefore spreading lavish feasts for his companions in that murky realm.

Away speed the twain gods and do not stay.
Straightway they turn their face toward Baal in the Height of the North.

---

sword will punish Leviathan, the Serpent Evasive, and Leviathan, the Serpent Tortuous;" cf. also Job 26:13, "His hand pierced the Serpent Evasive." It should be observed, however, that the rendering "evasive" is not altogether certain; for other interpretations, see: Albright, BASOR 83 (1941), 39, n. 5; Gaster, JRAS 1944, p. 47, n. 49; Rabin, JTS 47 (1946), 38–41.

Môt's description of his sorry state is studded with subtle irony. Himself proverbially all-devouring, he now finds that it is he who is in fact being "eaten up" – a turn of expression reminiscent of Isaiah's reference (25:8) to Yahweh's eventually "swallowing up Death (Môt) for ever." Himself the lord of death, it is *he* who is now as good as dead! Moreover, although he is a full-fledged god, and no mere monster like Leviathan, and although his role in the scheme of things has been duly accredited by El (see above, Introduction, §5), Baal has been able to elude his gaping jaws!

XLVI. In this fuller version of Môt's message to Baal, the irony is even more apparent. Môt (Death) was proverbially credited with a voracious appetite: cf. Habakkuk 2:5, "His greed is as wide as the netherworld; like Death (Môt) he has never enough;" cf. also Proverbs 30:15–16; Isaiah 5:14. That appetite, Môt avers, is now being satisfied in the netherworld by lavish feasts of mud! If, therefore, Baal will not admit him to the banquet which he is spreading for the gods (above, §XXXVIII), Môt is quite prepared to play host rather than guest, and accordingly invites his adversary to join *him*.

This description of life in the netherworld, where the food is mud and dirt and where there is constant thirst and languor, has several interesting parallels. In the Mesopotamian myth of Ishtar's Descent to Hades, special mention is made (obv. 8) of the fact

Then say Sir Vine and Sir Field:
"This is the message of divine Mot,
the word of that brave who was the favorite of El:
'The appetites of lions by nature crave for sheep;
the desire of the whale is for the sea;
wild oxen hie (by nature) to the pool,
and hinds to the brake;
and (since) when, (since) when has my appetite failed?
Why, here I go eating mud in lavish portions,[1]

[1] Lit., "with both my hands."

---

that those who dwell there have "dust as their sustenance, mud as their food." So, too, in Egyptian thought, the denizens of the netherworld ate dirt and drank urine, and analogous ideas may be found in the Greek and Roman world (Eitrem, *Papyri Osloenses* I, 62; PW, s.v. *Katabasis,* coll. 2405 ff.) as well as in Avestan literature (Yasna xxxi, 20). Hades is a place of mud and slime; Aristophanes describes it (*Frogs,* 145) as a place of "deep, deep mire and everlasting filth" and as a region of "darkness and mud" (*ibid.,* 273); while Plato (*Rep.* ii 363 D) says that the wicked and impious are plunged into "a kind of mud" in Hades (cf. also *Phaedo* 69c). Seneca (*Hercules Furens* 686) mentions "the filthy marsh of stagnant Cocytus"; and Jewish folklore preserves much the same picture in Talmud, 'Erubin 19a. In medieval German, *pech,* "dirt," is a common name for Hell, and in modern Greek, the cognate *pissa* has the same meaning. Lettish *pekle,* "hell, cavern," Czech *peklo,* and Slavonic *Pikollos,* "god of Hell," have been derived by some from this same root (Schwenk, *Mythol. d. Slawen,* 79 n.).

The *thirst* of the dead is mentioned specifically in Isaiah 5:13, which speaks of man's glory being eventually "parched with thirst." The netherworld was known among the Babylonians as "the field of thirst" [*e-qi-il zu-ma-mi-ti*] (Tallquist, *Namen d. Totenwelt,* 37, n. 1.), and the Arabs believe that the dead experience excessive thirst (Wellhausen, *Reste,*[2] 182; Goldziher, ARW 13 [1915], 45 f.); while in Egyptian funerary texts, the soul of the dead is often represented as praying for water (Robertson Smith-Cook, *Rel. Sem.,*[3] 580). In modern Palestinian belief, the soul of the departed revisits his tomb on Friday night in quest of water (JPOS 4 [1924], 27). In the Orphic tablets, the soul parched with thirst requests cool water (Kaibel, CIGIS 638.8; Cretan tablets ed. Murray, in Jane Harrison's *Prolegomena,* 660–61). Late Greek belief held that libations to the dead were really designed

yea, in sevenfold portions is it served unto me,
and they mix me drinks of it by the cup and by the barrel!
(Come,) Baal, make merry along with my companions,
and tarry awhile, O Hadd, with my comrades!
Let us have a banquet here, O Baal, ...
If now thou go fighting [Leviathan, that dragon evas]ive,
if now thou wouldst try to destroy [the Slant Serpent],
that [seven-headed] monster of might,
thou wouldst (but) wear thyself out," etc.

---

to slake their thirst (Stengel, *Opferbrauche d. Griechen,* 129 f., 183 ff.); while already in *Odyssey* xi the dead greedily devour the blood poured out for them. Seneca (*Hercules Furens,* 691) speaks of the grievous hunger (*fames maesta*) which attends the dead; and in the light of the parallels adduced above, it seems not impossible that when he refers (*ibid.,* 702) to the filthy soil lying "forever parched" (*foeda tellus torpet aeterno situ*), we should introduce a slight emendation (viz., *aeterna siti*) and obtain an allusion to *everlasting thirst.* See also Jevons, CR 9 (1895), 247 f.; Déonna, RHR 119 (1939), 53–81.

The *languor* of the dead is likewise mentioned in other sources. Job 3:17 describes the inhabitants of Sheol (the netherworld) as being "weary of strength"; and in Psalm 88:5 the poet complains that he is "reckoned with them that go down to the Pit, become as *a man without vigor.*" The Egyptians called their dead "the weary of heart" (*wrd ib*; Erman-Grapow, *HWb* 38), and the Greeks *hoi kamontes* of the same general sense; cf. *Odyssey* xi 474 f.: "There dwell the dead without sense or feeling, phantoms of mortals whose weary days are done" (trs. W. H. D. Rouse). According to some, the Hebrew word *rephaim,* employed in OT and in certain Phoenician inscriptions for the denizens of the netherworld, really derives from the root *r-ph-y,* "be flaccid," and therefore expresses the same idea. This, however, is doubtful.

For the initial allusion to the appetite of lions for sheep, cf. Jeremiah 50:17; Amos 3:12. For the reference to the natural desire of hinds for the brake, cf. Psalm 42:1.

The invitation to Baal to "make merry" (reading *ts-h-q*) at Mot's banquet catches up the allusion in §XL to the gods' "making merry" on the mountain at that tendered by Baal.

XLVII

There ensues a gap of some 50 lines. Where the text resumes, Baal is revealed in a state of terror at the prospect of having to accept Mot's challenge. He sends him a message of appeasement or of abject surrender.

(*The passage begins in the middle of a speech addressed by Baal to his couriers for transmission to Mot.*)

* *
*

Its one lip (is stretched) upward to the sky
its other (downward) to the netherworld;
Baal will descend into its maw,
go down into its mouth,

XLVII. The subject of the opening lines is the netherworld, personified as a greedy monster with gaping jaws. The picture recurs in Isaiah 5:14: "Therefore Hell (Sheol) hath extended its gullet, and its mouth is agape without limit; and their glory and their multitude and their pomp descend into it"; Habakkuk 2:5: "Who extendeth his gullet as Hell (Sheol) and is insatiable as Death"; Proverbs 1:12: "Let us swallow them up alive as Sheol, and whole, as those that go down into the Pit." Cf. also Psalm 141:7: "Our bones are scattered at the mouth of Sheol." Similar is Tennyson's "Into the jaws of Death, Into the mouth of Hell Rode the six hundred." In Peruvian mythology, Supay, the god of the underworld, is "usually portrayed as an open-mouth monster of voracious appetite, into whose maw are thrown the souls of the departed" (Spence, *Mythol. of Mexico and Peru,* 57). Pictures in the manuscript of Caedmon represent Hell simply by a wide-open mouth (Grimm, *Teutonic Mythology,* 314). Cf. also Lampr. Alex. 6672–75: *der was der Hellen gelich Diu daz abgrunde Begenit mit ir munde Abe dem himel zuo der erden* ("He was like the Hell who the chasm be-yawneth with her mouth from heaven down to earth").

An engraving of "Christ's Descent to Hell" made (from an old drawing) by Michael Burghers for the antiquary Hearne and reproduced in William Hone's *Ancient Mysteries* (London, 1832), opposite p. 138, shows Hell as a huge monster with jaws agape, and the gaping Mouth of Hell is portrayed in an old English woodcut illustrating the Christmas carol *Dives and Lazarus.* In the east window of York Cathedral, Hell is likewise depicted as a gaping mouth, and so also on an ancient bas relief in the west

like a canape of olive,
like an herb or a piece of fruit!
Verily, Baal Puissant is frightened,
terror-stricken is the Rider on the Clouds.
Depart, then, bring word to the godling Mot,
relay (it) to that youngster, the beloved of El:
"This is the message of Baal Puissant,
the word of Him Who is Puissant among Warriors:
'Deign to show grace, O godling Mot;
thy slave am I and one of thy perpetual bondmen!'"

XLVIII

The couriers relay the message, but Mot merely taunts Baal for his lack of courage.

Away speed the gods and do not stay.
Straightway they turn their face toward the godling Mot
in his . . . city,
in the depth, where is the seat of his abiding,
the filth of the earth, which is his estate.

---

front of Lincoln Cathedral (Hone, *op. cit.,* 173 n.). A manuscript note in the Bibliothèque Nationale's copy of *Le mystère de la passion de Jésus Christ* (Paris, 1490) relates that in a passion play performed, on July 3, 1437, in the plain of Veximiel, the Mouth of Hell was shown opening and shutting whenever the devils required to go in or come out. Lastly, Sackville's introduction to the *Mirror of Magistrates* thus quotes an old writer on Hell: "An hideous hole all vast, withouten shape,/ Of endless depth, o'erwhelm'd with raggèd (jaggèd?) stone,/ With ugly mouth and grisly jaws doth gape,/ And to our sight confounds itself in one"; see Hone, *op. cit.,* 217 f. The Greeks also employed this image; cf. Pindar, *Pyth.* iv 44: "the subterranean *mouth* of Hades," and it is likewise known to Latin American mythology (H. B. Alexander, *Latin American Mythology,* 54).

But this is also the conventional description of an ogre. "The 'Arab' or black Negro ogre of Greek stories has an upper lip which stretches to the heavens while his lower lip touches the earth. This is a Persian literary commonplace for negro ugliness" (Halliday, *Indo-European Folk-tales and Greek Legend,* 37). The Prose Edda relates similarly that when Fenrir opened her mouth, the upper jaw reached to heaven, and the lower to the earth.

Then lift they their voices and cry:
"This is the message of Baal Puissant,
the word of him Who is Puissant among Warriors:
'Deign to show grace, O godling Mot;
thy slave am I and one of thy perpetual bondmen!' "

Thereupon the godling Mot rejoices.
[He lifts] his [voice] and cries:
"How shall he go on insulting me?
Why, the Thunderer (Hadd) is scared out of his wits!
Those that fight with me are [always la]id low (in the end);
[as with] a butcher's [kni]fe
[I smite them that] would smite me(?)!"

* *
*

XLIX

Nothing remains of the next column except the beginnings of the lines. Translation is therefore impossible, and interpretation hazardous. However, in view of the fact that there is a thrice-repeated phrase (lines 9, 18, 25), "Be still, O Mot, I speak [*or* invite (thee)]," *as well as a reference (lines 22,*

XLIX–L. If we are right in the assumption that Mot spreads a feast for Baal in the netherworld, then the entire incident receives its true interpretation from the ancient and primitive belief that *he who eats the food of the dead or of fairyland cannot return to earth.*

The idea is well attested in antiquity. It appears already in the Mesopotamian *Myth of Adapa* (ii obv. 29 f.); while the Egyptians believed that on its way to the land of spirits the soul was met by a goddess who offered it food and drink to prevent its escape (Maspero, *Hist. anc. des peuples de l'orient classique,* 184). Greek and Roman mythology preserves the same notion in the story of how Persephone was induced, while in Hades, to eat the seeds of a pomegranate, and was therefore unable to return to earth (Homeric *Hymn to Demeter* 371–74; Ovid, *Met.* v 530–32). In the Finnish *Kalevala* (xvi, fr. 293), the hero Wainamoinen refuses for this reason to partake of drink in Manala. In Shinto myth, the primeval goddess Izanami eats of the food of the "Land of Yomi" after her death, and this prevents her husband, Izanagi, from bringing her back (Aston, *Shinto,* 23). Among the Zulus of South Africa, it is held that

23) *to* great quantities of sheep, *and that certain* gods (*presumably Sir Vine and Sir Field*) *are bidden* go (*lines 14, 20*) *and* relay the word (*line 21*), *it would seem probable that Baal tries to appease Mot by offering him lavish and decent food in the netherworld.*

L

Here, too, the text is fragmentary. There is reference (line 5) to someone's lifting his voice *and making some allusion to* Baal's exalted (*or* overweening) state (*line 8*), *and this is followed by a verbatim repetition of the banqueting scene described in §XXXVIII. It is therefore probable that this passage relates how the couriers convey Mot's reply to Baal and repeat it to him while he is still in the midst of his revels.*

The nature of this reply can be inferred from the sequel: as we shall see, Baal is compelled to make the descent into the netherworld. Hence, it is apparent that Mot refuses to be bought off, but presses his challenge.

LI

Baal being thus compelled to go down into the netherworld, he is advised by some unnamed speaker ('Anat?) to take with

---

if the spirit of the dead touch food in the netherworld, it will never return to earth (Leslie, *Among the Zulus and Amatongas*, 121); while the natives of New Caledonia, as well as the Melanesians and Kiwai Papuans of British New Guinea tell how the departed are tempted to eat the food of the netherworld in order to insure their permanent incarceration in those regions (Gagnière, in *Ann. de la Propag. de la Foi*, 1860, pp. 439 ff.; Codrington, *Melanesians*, 277, 386; Landtmann, *Kiwai Papuans*, 289; Frazer, *Fasti of Ovid*, iii. 302 f.; *idem, Apollodorus*, i. 39, n. 4). The idea is transferred in folk tales to the world of fairyland; return thence is impossible, once its food has been tasted (Hartland, *Science of Fairy-Tales*, ch. iii; D. Grant, *A Feughside Fairy Tale* (Aberdeen 1937), p. vi).

These parallels suggest that Mot's second thought is to adopt the ruse tried by Hades (Pluto) on Persephone: he plans to get Baal into his clutches by inducing him to visit the netherworld and then persuading him to partake of its food and drink.

LI. Baal is instructed to take down with him into the netherworld his clouds, winds, *mdl*-s, and rains. The meaning of the

him all his equipment and appurtenances of office, as well as his brides and his staff. In addition, he is advised to copulate with a calf in order to provide himself with bull-like strength and at the same time to leave issue upon earth, should he fail to return.

* * * * [Baal] Puissant
* * * *. [Take in thy hand] thy torches(?),
* * * * [in] thy [ri]ght hand red ochre(?);

---

third term is uncertain. If it be rendered "buckets" (by comparison with the Akkadian *madlû* and the Hebrew *d^e^li*), the reference will be to the familiar idea that rain is poured from buckets, skins, or pitchers. Thus, in Rig Veda V, 83.7–8, the rain-god Parjanya is invoked: "Thine opened waterskin draw with thee downward. . . . Lift up the mighty vessel, pour down water" (tr. R. T. H. Griffith). Cp. also Job 38:37: "Who can number (but perhaps read *y^e^sappe^a^h*, "pour out," for *y^e^sapper*, "number") the clouds in wisdom, or *tilt the bottles of heaven?*" The Peruvians believed in a rain-goddess who sat in the clouds and sent rain by emptying a pitcher (Garcilasso de la Vega, *Commentarios reales*, tr. Markham, ii. 27). A similar conception obtained also in Teutonic mythology: rain was supposed to be discharged by the gods out of heavenly bowls (Grimm, *Teutonic Mythology*, 593). The Turks say likewise, "The bottles are emptied," when they mean, "It rains" (Jacob, *Altarab. Parallelen zum AT*, 20). See further, Schultens, *Job.* 1104 f.

On the other hand, the word *mdl* occurs elsewhere in the Ugaritic texts (Gordon, 51 iv. 4, 9; I Aq. 52, 57) in the sense of "hitch a beast to a chariot," and it is therefore possible that the reference here is to Baal's *chariot.* This would square with the fact that he is regularly styled "Rider on the Clouds." Similarly, in the Hurro-Hittite Kumarbi myth (KUB XXXIII 113 iii 14 ff.), reference is made specifically to the "massive chariot" of the storm-god (cf. Güterbock, *Kumarbi,* 76 f.). For parallels, see Grimm, *op. cit.,* 166 f.

Baal is instructed also to equip himself with red ochre (*sh-sh-r*) before descending to the netherworld. The reason is that red forfends demons (*MI,* D 1381. 15). In the same way, in the Babylonian *Epic of Creation* (iv. 61), Marduk smears red paste on his lips before engaging the monster Tiamat. So, too, in Israelite practice, the ashes of a *red* heifer removed impurity (Numbers 19:2). Ashanti mourners bedaub themselves with red

* * * * * the life essence of a heifer.
* * * * I will place in the holes of the numinous dead, even in the earth.

And thou, take thou thy clouds, thy winds, thy buckets,
thy rains:
[take] with thee thy sevenfold servitors,
thine eightfold serving maids;
[take] with thee P-d-r-aya, the Lady of Light,
[take] with thee the Dew-nymph, the Lady of Rain.
Straightway turn thy face toward the cavernous mountain,
Raise the mountain on thy hands,
the holt upon thy palms,
and go down into the corruption of the netherworld,
be counted among them that go down into the earth,
and thou wilt experience nothingness,
for thou wilt have become as one who has died!"

LII

Baal copulates with a heifer. The latter bears male offspring, which Baal acknowledges as his own.

Baal Puissant obeys;
he makes love to a heifer in the pasture,

---

ochre as a protective measure (G. Parrinder, *La religion en Afrique occidentale,* 134). Among the Tartars of the Crimea and in South China, and likewise in Greece and Albania, brides wear a red veil for apotropaic purposes (Seligmann, *Böser Blick,* 232, 254, 257), and this was also the custom in ancient Rome (Festus, s.v. *flammeum*). In Babylon, priestly sorcerers wore a red cloak (Furlani, *Rel. bab. e ass.,* ii. 351), and eyes were daubed with red paste to relieve sickness (Ebeling, *Tod und Leben,* No. 30, A 25). The Talmud states that red skeins were tied on the necks of children to avert disease (TB Shabbat 66b). See fully: Wunderlich, *Die Bedeutung der roten Farbe im Kultus der Griechen und Römer* (1925); R. von Duhn, "Rot und Tot," in ARW 9 (1906), 1–24; Samter, *Geburt, Hochzeit und Tod* 190 f.; Scheftelowitz, ZAW 1921. 117 f.; G. B. Laquet, *L'art et la religion des hommes fossiles* (1926), 185.

LII. The concluding lines of this passage are imperfectly preserved, so that the sense can be made out only provisionally. The reference in the words "to his breast" may be to a formal gesture

to a young cow in the . . . field.
He lies with it seven and seventy times,
it is mounted eight and eighty times,
and [it con]ceives and bears male offspring.
[Baal Puissant] . . . . clothe[s that offspring];
* * * * favored(?);
he * * *s [it, clasps it] to his breast.

* *
*

[Lacuna of about 30 lines]

LIII

Baal goes down to the netherworld. His couriers report his disappearance to El.

* *
*

"We reached the pleasant places of the pastureland,
the lovely places of the . . . field,
we reached [the place where] Baal [should have been];
he had sunk into the earth.
Dead is Baal Puissant,
perished is His Highness, the Lord (*Baal*) of the earth!"

The Ululation

BAAL IS BEWAILED

LIV

El mourns for Baal.

Thereupon the gentle-hearted El
comes down from his throne and sits upon the footstool,

---

of adoption or acknowledgment of paternity. For this gesture, cf. Grimm, *Deutsche Rechtsaltertümer*,[4] 1, 219, 638; Liebrecht, *Zur Volkskunde*, 432. Torczyner (Tur-Sinai) has suggested that an allusion to such a custom among the Hebrews may be seen in Psalm 2:7 by emending the corrupt text to read: " 'I will gather thee unto My bosom,' hath Yahweh said unto me, 'This day have I declared Myself thy parent, thou art My son.' "

LIV. The loincloth (*mizrt*) which El dons as a garment of mourning is the equivalent of the Hebrew "sackcloth" (*saq*)

and down from the footstool and sits upon the ground.
Ashes (?) of mourning he strews upon his head,
dust wherein mourners wallow on his pate;
for raiment he dons a loincloth.

Then he wanders in mourning o'er the upland,
in the manner of a . . . . through the woods.
Cheek and chin he gashes;
he scores the forepart of his arm;
he furrows his chest as 'twere a garden,
scores his back as 'twere a valley.
He lifts his voice and cries:
"Baal is dead!
What will now become of the clan of Dagan's son?
What will now become of the multitudes of Baal's posterity?
I will go down into the earth!"

The Funeral of the Spirit of Fertility

BAAL IS INTERRED

I, AB Gordon 67, obv. + 49 + 62 rev.

LV

'Anat too discovers the disappearance of Baal and mourns for

---

which was likewise *girt about the loins* (Genesis 37:34; I Kings 20:31, etc.) and in connection with which precisely the same verb (*k-s-y/h*) is employed (II Kings 19:1; Isaiah 37:1; Jonah 3:6, 8; cf. Isaiah 50:3). Note also that the Egyptian loan word *sag* (Coptic *sok*) denotes a garment *girt about the loins.* On mourning garb among the Semites, see Wensinck, *Mourning,* 56–72.

On the custom of sprinkling dust and ashes on the head as a sign of mourning, see Jastrow in JAOS 20 (1899), 133–50; Westermarck, *Ritual and Belief in Morocco,* ii., 439–41.

The word rendered "scores" (*y-th-l-th*) means literally "plows three times over." Threefold plowing was a general practice in antiquity; cp. II R 14, 20a: *shalashu* || *kharashu* (as here); Hammurapi, 71.20; RA 17 (1920), 13a: *eqla i-sha-la-ash.* Cf. also PW ii, 1215 ff.; Gruppe, *Gr. Mythol.,* 49; Usener, *Götternamen,* 141. Hence the term was a natural synonym for "plow, furrow."

LV. 'Anat's mourning for Baal (parallel to that of El) corresponds almost verbally to that of Aphrodite and Demeter in

him, resolving to go down into the netherworld in order to retrieve him.

'Anat, too, is strolling and walking abroad
o'er every mountain to the very heart of the earth,
o'er every hill to the innermost part of the fields.
She reaches the pleasant places of the pastureland,
the lovely places of the . . . field,
she reaches (the place where) Baal (ought to be);
he has sun[k into the] ear[th].
So for raiment she dons a loin[cloth];
she wanders in mourning o'er the upland, Gordon, 62, obv.
in the manner of a . . . through the woods;
cheek and chin she gashes;
she scores the forepart of her arm;
she furrows her chest as 'twere a garden,
scores her back as 'twere a valley.
She lifts her voice and cries:
"Baal is dead!
What will now become of the clan of Dagan's son?
What will now become of the multitudes of Baal's posterity?
I will go down into the earth!"

---

the cognate myths of Adonis and Persephone. Cf. Bion, *Lament for Adonis* 19 ff.: "And Aphrodite unbinds her locks and goes wandering through the woodlands, distraught, unkempt, and barefoot. The thorns tear her as she goes, and gather her holy blood, but she sweeps through the long glades, shrieking aloud and calling on the lad, her Assyrian lord"; Homeric *Hymn to Demeter* 40–42: "Sharp was the pain which beset her heart, and with her dear hands she kept rending the veil about her ambrosial locks, and over her shoulders she hung a dark blue cloth." Euripides, *Helen* 1301 ff.: "Whilom, with feet racing amain, the Mother of the Gods rushed o'er the hills, sweeping thro' the woodland glens . . . moved by longing for her vanished child." (The "dark blue" raiment to which allusion is made in the Homeric hymn is the equivalent of the blue veil worn by Arab mourning women; cf. Wensinck, *Some Semitic Rites of Mourning and Religion,* 60 ff.; Lane, *Lex.* i 86.) Similar, too, is the description in a Romanian Christmas carol of the Virgin Mary's mourning for Jesus: "And she went Wailing and crying, Wringing her hands, Scratching her white face, Weeping out of her dark eyes, Sighing from her heart, Going along the road, Searching for her Son" (M. Gaster, FL 34 [1923], 73).

LVI

The sun-goddess (who in any case descends nightly into the netherworld) goes down with her, retrieves the body of Baal, and loads it upon her shoulders. The two of them then ascend to the Heights of the North.

With her goes down the sun,[m] that torch of the gods.
The while she is sated with weeping,
drinking in tears like wine,[m]
loudly calls she to the sun[m] that torch of the gods:
"Load upon me Baal Puissant!"

The sun,[m] that torch of the gods, obeys.
She lifts up Baal Puissant.
When she has placed him upon the shoulders of 'Anat,
the two of them bring him up to the Recesses of the North.

LVII

Baal is buried and a hecatomb is offered in his honor.

They bewail him and bury him,
place him in the holes of the numinous dead, even in the earth.
Then ('Anat) slaughters seventy wild oxen
as a funeral offering to Baal Puissant.
She slaughters seventy bulls
as a funeral offering to Baal Puissant.
She slaughters seventy sheep
as a funeral offering to Baal Puissant.
She slaughters seventy harts
as a funeral offering to Baal Puissant.

[m] Shapash.

LVI. It is likewise to the sun-god (Helios) that Demeter addresses herself in her search for Persephone; while in the cognate Hittite *Myth of Telipinu*, it is that deity who is first summoned to discover the whereabouts of the missing god.

The point is, of course, that the sun not only traverses the whole earth but also descends nightly into the netherworld. The sun-goddess would therefore be in a special position to retrieve Baal. Moreover, the re-emergence of the sun at the solstice is usually the sign for the restoration of fertility.

She slaughters seventy wild goats
as a funeral offering to Baal Puissant.
[She slaughters seventy roe]bucks
[as a funeral offering] to Ba[al] Puissant.

The Interrex

A SUCCESSOR TO BAAL IS NAMED

Gordon 49

LVIII

'Anat then proceeds to El and announces ruefully that Baal is dead, adding that this will doubtless prove a source of satisfaction to Asherat, as well as to all the gods who have resisted his sovereignty.

Then turns she her face toward El,
at the place where the Two Streams converge,
hard by the watershed of the Two Oceans;
she leaves the vast fields,
and comes to the pleasance of the King . . . ;
at the feet of El she bows and falls,
prostrates herself, and pays homage to him.

Then lifts she her voice and cries:
"Let Asherat and her sons rejoice at this,
the Goddess and the band of her kinsmen,
that Baal Puissant is dead,
that His Highness, the lord of the earth is perished!"

LIX

El proposes that a successor to Baal be now appointed. Asherat nominates 'Ashtar.

LIX. On the mythological significance of this episode – 'Ashtar being the genius of artificial irrigation who seeks to dominate the earth during the time of year when the rains (Baal) are absent – see Introduction, §7.

But the episode has also another point: it mythologizes the institution of the interrex – the temporary king who is appointed to reign during the epagomenal days or during that brief period which elapses between the end of one life lease (year) and the

Then loudly calls El to Queen Asherat-of-the-Sea:
"Hearken, Queen A[sherat-of-the-]Sea,
Let me appoint as king one of thy sons!"

"Yes," replies Queen Asherat-of-the-Sea,
"But let us not choose as king one who, 'tis certain, will but insult us!"

"But," answers gentle-hearted El,
"One of meager strength will not be able to do battle like Baal,
one of scant fitness will not be able to poise a spear like that son of Dagan!"

"Very well then," Queen Asherat-of-the-Sea keeps retorting,
"Let us appoint as king none other than 'Ashtar the formidable!
Let 'Ashtar the formidable be king!"

---

beginning of the next, when the real king – the personification of topocosmic life – is thought to be "in eclipse," dead or ousted.

This institution is recorded in many parts of the ancient and modern worlds. Thus, Berossus informs us, on the authority of Ctesias (quoted by Athenaeus xi. 44; cf. Ctesias, ed. Baehr, 449 f.) that it was customary at the Persian festival of Sacaea, held on the sixteen day of Loos (July), to install one of the royal domestics as temporary king, under the name of *zoganes* (cf. Langdon, JRAS 1924, 65–72). Furthermore, Frazer has suggested (*Fasti of Ovid*, ii. 60.) that the annual "flight of the kings" (*regifugium*) at Rome on February 24 was a dim reminiscence of the earlier expulsion of the temporary king at the end of his reign, just before the New Year on March 1. The same scholar has also adduced modern examples of the interrex from Lhasa (Tibet), the Kwottos of Northern Nigeria, the Bakitara of the Uganda Protectorate and the Bastar of the Central Provinces of India (*ibid.*, 49–58). Moreover, in a classic chapter of *The Golden Bough* (one-vol. ed., 383–89), he has collected several extremely illuminating instances of the custom. Thus, in Cambodia, the king used annually to abdicate for three days in February, during which time his place was filled by a substitute. Similarly, in Siam, a temporary king is appointed at the end of April, or the beginning of May, while the real king remains confined to his palace (on this cf. also Cabaton, ERE xi 485a). So, too, in the kingdom of Jambi in Sumatra, each reign is inaugurated by the preliminary installation of a temporary king; while in Samarcand such a monarch reigns for three days in September during the time when the Nile reaches its highest

LX

Thereupon 'Ashtar goes up to the Mountain of the North in order to occupy the vacant throne of Baal. But he proves

---

point (*GB*³, iii, 148 f.). A more familiar modern example of the custom may be seen in the European usage of appointing a temporary "King of Fools" or "Abbot of Misrule" in connection with harvest celebrations. Lastly, it should be observed that Winckler attempted (*Altorientalische Forschungen,* ii, 351–58) to find mention of the interrex in a Sabaean inscription (CIS iv 83). On the other hand, the Babylonian *shar pukhi,* or "substitute king," who has sometimes been compared, is of quite a different order (cf. Labat, *Royauté,* 103 f.).

Of especial interest are the conditions here imposed for the selection of a king: he must not be a weakling or "one of scant beauty." This accords with the standard requirements of kingship among primitive peoples – requirements dictated by the fact that the king epitomizes the corporate health and welfare of the community. Thus, before his installation, the king of Konde is kept under surveillance, "lest, being a weakling, he should be a menace to the land" (Mackenzie, *The Spirit-Ridden Konde,* 72 f.); while among the Varozwe (a Shona tribe), "absence of bodily blemishes was considered absolutely necessary in the occupant of the throne" (Doran, SAJC 15 [1918], 397). As Patai has pointed out (HUCA 20 [1947], 155 f.), the same idea obtained among the Hebrews: Saul was chosen king by reason of his "countenance and tallness of stature" (I Samuel 16:7) and is described as "ruddy withal and of comely appearance" (*ibid.,* 12); while Absalom the pretender was the most beautiful man in Israel and "without blemish from head to toe" (II Samuel 14:25). When the king grew sick he was deposed or killed, as in the case of Uzziah-Azariah, smitten with leprosy (II Kings 15:5). This, in fact, is one of the central motifs of the Ugaritic *Epic of Keret,* where that monarch's son Yassib seeks to replace him when he grows ill. Deposition or death was likewise the fate of an ailing monarch among primitive peoples, e.g., the Fazoql tribes of Africa, the Shilluk of the White Nile, the inhabitants of Bunyoro in Central Africa, the Kibanga of the Upper Congo, the Hausa of Northern Nigeria, the Zulus, etc. (Frazer, GB, one-vol. ed., 265 ff.).

LX. The reason why 'Ashtar's claim is rejected is that he is physically too small to occupy the vacant throne of Baal. There is

physically too small and therefore descends to the earth to exercise there a more limited degree of sovereignty.

So 'Ashtar the formidable goes up to the Recesses of the North.
He takes his seat on the throne of Baal Puissant.
But his feet do not reach to the footstool;
his head does not reach to the top.[n]
Then says 'Ashtar the formidable:
"I cannot reign as king in the Recesses of the North!"

So down goes 'Ashtar the formidable,
down from the throne of Baal Puissant,
and proceeds to exercise sway o'er the whole wide earth.

[Lacuna of about 30 lines]

[n] Lit., "edge."

---

a special point in this: *primitive usage required that the king be not only physically flawless but also above average height.* Thus, of Saul it is said explicitly that "he was taller than any of the people from his shoulders and upwards," and Samuel is represented as therefore saying to the people: "See ye him whom Yahweh has chosen, how that there is none like him among all the people" (I Samuel 10:23–24). Similarly, the prophet at first considered Eliab to be the divinely chosen king on account of his "countenance and tallness of stature"; see Patai, *loc. cit.* It is likewise recorded of Xerxes that he was the tallest of all his people (Herodotus, vii 187).

Note that when, at a preceding stage of the story (§V), 'Ashtar aspires to the sovereignty granted to Sir Sea, he is rejected because *he has no wife.* This means simply that he is still a minor. The objection is thus the same as in the present instance. This is, of course, merely a mythological way of saying that the genius of artificial irrigation is no equal of the natural force of the rain (Baal)!

C. END OF THE SUMMER SEASON

The Ousting of Infertility

ʿANAT'S VENGEANCE UPON MOT

LXI

ʿAnat goes roaming the earth in search of Baal who, though his corpse has been duly buried, has not yet returned to life. She encounters Mot and demands the restoration of the ousted god. Mot rejects her request.

* * * * *

* * * * *

* * * * *

* * * * *

[Days] pass [into months].

ʿAnat goes searching for him.
Like the heart of a cow for her calf,
like the heart of a ewe for her lamb,
so is the heart of ʿAnat on account of Baal.

She grasps Mo[t] by the hem of his robe,

LXI. It is of interest to observe that Ovid (*Fasti* iv 495 f.) uses the same imagery in describing Demeter's search for Persephone: *Ut vitulo mugit sua mater ab ubere rapto Et quaerit fetus per nemus omne suos, Sic dea nec retinet gemitus et concita cursu Fertur*. For the simile, cf. also the Babylonian magical text, *Maqlu* vii 25: "Like a ewe loves its lamb, a gazelle its young, a she-ass its foal . . . so do I love thee, mine own body." So, too, in the Hittite text, KUB XXX 70 iii(?), 14 ff.: "As the ewe loves the lamb, the cow its calf, parents their child, so, O Sun-God, do thou also . . ., etc." (Otten, *Telipinu*, 10, n. 1). It occurs also in Egyptian (Spiegelberg, *Sonnenauge* 7.31) and in Sumerian (SRT, No. 5, 34–36). Cf. also Lucretius, ii. 355–63.

For the grasping of the hem in supplication, cf. the Mesopotamian texts: JRAS 1929, 2.73; OECT vi 25 r. 18; KARI 223, r. 4.

The "flashing" of the heavens refers to electric storms – a common feature of the dry season in Palestine (Dalman, *Arbeit u. Sitte*, i. 114).

holds [him] tight by the edge of his cloak;
then lifts she her voice and [cr]ies:
"Thou Mot, surrender my brother!"

But the godling Mot keeps retorting:
"What is it that thou art asking of me, O Virgin 'Anat?
See, an I stroll or walk abroad
o'er any hill to the very heart of the earth,
o'er any hillock to the innermost part of the fields,
life-breath quits mankind,
life-breath quits the multitudes of the earth!
An I come to earth's pleasant places,
to the lovely places of the . . . field,
an I encounter Baal Puissant,
I place him like a lamb in my mouth,
like a kid in the . . . . of my . . . is he crushed!
Why, 'tis at the whim of the godling Mot
that the sun, that torch of the gods, scorches,
that the heavens flash!"

LXII

'Anat bides her time. Then, encountering Mot again, she attacks him savagely and slays him.

Day follows day;
from days they pass into months.
Still the Virgin 'Anat goes searching for him;
Like the heart of a cow for her calf,
like the heart of a ewe for her lamb,
so in the heart of 'Anat on account of Baal.

(At length) she seizes the godling Mot;
with a sword she rips him up;
in a sieve she scatters him;
in a fire she burns him;
in a mill she grinds him;
over the fields she strews him,
so that the birds may devour his remains,
the sparrows consume the morsels of him,
go screaming from one remnant to the next!"

[Lacuna of about 40 lines]

The Spirit of Fertility Returns: The King is Reinstated

THE RESTORATION OF BAAL

LXIII

'Anat reports to El a dream which she has had portending the revival and imminent return of Baal.

* * *

"Surely he perished!
Is Baal Puissant, then, indeed alive?
And does His Highness, the lord of the earth still exist?
  In my dream, O gentle-hearted El,
in my vision, O Creator of all Creatures,
the skies were raining fatness,
the wadies were running with honey.
So I know that Baal Puissant is alive,
that His Highness, the lord of the earth still exists!"

LXIII. The idea that rivers and wadies will flow with honey features prominently in ancient conceptions of the Golden Age; and it is, in effect, such a golden age that is inaugurated year by year when Baal returns to the earth. For this picture, cf. Amos 9:13; Joel 4:18; Oracula Sibyllina iii 774–77; Slavonic Enoch viii, §5; see especially, Jeremias, *Babylonisches im NT*, 45, n. 1; Eitrem, *Opferritus,* 101, 457. It is this conception that underlies the Biblical description of the Promised Land as "a land flowing with milk and honey" (Usener, *Rhein, Mus.* 57 [1902], 177–92; Guidi, RB 12 [1903], 241 f.). Similarly, in Celtic legend, the chief Irish god, Manannan, praises the Isle of Man, the island paradise, as a place where "rivers pour forth a stream of honey" (Beck, *Honey and Health,* 169); while Euripides says (*Bacchae,* 143) that the rivers ran with honey when Dionysus first revealed himself. Honey features also in rites of regeneration (Keith, *Indian Mythology,* 158, *MI,* D 1338.9), especially in the Mithraic mystery cult (Headlam-Knox, *Herodas,* 271). It was employed in Mesopotamian cultus at the dedication of new images and in the New Year (Akitu) ritual (KB VI/2, 48.21), and is still eaten by Jews at New Year. In popular lore, honey expels evil spirits (Fallaize, ERE vi 770).

LXIV

El, jubilant at the glad tidings, bids 'Anat inquire of the sun-goddess° as to the exact whereabouts of Baal, of whose ministrations the earth stands in direct need.

El, the gentle-hearted, rejoices.
He places his feet on the footstool,
banishes all sorrow and laughs.
Then lifts he his voice and cries:
"Once more I shall know repose,
and my spirit lie calm in my breast,
for that Baal Puissant is indeed alive,
for that His Highness, the lord of the earth still exists!"

Then loudly calls El to the Virgin 'Anat:
"Hearken, O Virgin 'Anat,
carry this word to the sun, that torch of the gods:
'The furrows of the fields have gone dry, O sun,
the furrows of (all) the vast fields have gone dry!
Baal is neglecting the furrows of the plowlands!
Where now is Baal Puissant?
Where is His Highness, the lord (*baal*) of the earth?'"

LXV

'Anat carries out these instructions, and the sun-goddess promises to search for Baal.

So away speeds the Virgin 'Anat.
Straightway she turns her face toward the sun, that torch of the gods.
She lifts her voice and cries:
"This is the message of El, the Bull-god, thy sire,
the word of the Gentle-hearted One, thy progenitor:
'The furrows of the fields have gone dry, O sun,
the furrows of (all) the vast fields have gone dry!
Baal is [neglecting] the furrows of his plowland!
Where now is Baal Puissant?
Where is His Highness, the lord (*baal*) of the earth?'"

And the sun, that torch of the gods, replies: * * *
". . . . .

° Shapash.

. . . . thy kinsman/kinsmen * * *
and I will go seek Baal Puissant!"

Then answers the Virgin 'Anat:
"Wheresoever[p] thou goest, O sun,
wheresoever[q] thou goest, may El attend [thee],
may [protective spirits?] guard thee!
* * * * * *
[thy] pa[th??] * * * * * *

[Lacuna of about 40 lines]

The Ritual Combat

BAAL DISCOMFITS MOT

LXVI

Baal, now fully revived, does battle with those of his brethren who have countenanced the usurpation of his sovereignty.

Baal seizes the sons of Asherat.
Great though they be, he smites them on the shoulder;
resplendent though they be, he smites them with a bludgeon;
effulgent(?) though they be, he fells them to the ground.

[Then Ba]al [ascends] the throne of his kingship,
[tak]es [his seat] on the tribune of his domi[ni]on.

LXVII

After a time, Mot also revives and proceeds once more to challenge the sovereignty of Baal.

[Days pas]s into months,
months into years.

[p] Lit., "hence (and) thither."
[q] Lit., "hence (and) thither."

LXVII. Mot's words refer, of course, to the treatment previously meted out to him by 'Anat (§LXII). It should be noted, however, that this form of commination is also purely general, for cf. the Accadian text in Abel-Winckler, *Keilschrifttexte* 50 (end): "May he kill thee like Death, and grind thee in a mill!"

[At length,] in the seventh year,
the godling Mot is roused from his fall,
and (thus) addresses Baal:
"'Twas through thee, O Baal,
I experienced[r] disgrace;
'twas through thee I experienced
being scattered in a sieve;
'twas through thee I experienced
being ripped up with a sword;
'twas through thee I experienced
being burned in fire;
'twas through thee [I experienced]
[being gr]ound in a mill;
'twas through (thee) I experi[enced]
* * * * * ;

'twas through thee I experienced
that my remains were strewn o'er the fields;
'twas through thee I experienced
that my morsels were cast upon the sea!
Hereafter I will feed and * * * * *
* * * * * * *

'tis I alone [who shall rule] o'er the ea[rth];
behold, I shall enjoy good fortune; * * * *;
* * * * I will make an end of * * *
* [them that] would make an end of me, the multit[udes?]
of * * *
* * * * * * * * *
* * * * * * * * *
* * * * * * * * *

[Lacuna of about 35 lines]

LXVIII

Mot is driven forth by Baal, who uses the defeated gods as his allies. Mot complains to him.

* * * [dri]ves him forth;
* * * * * [exp]els him;
* * * * * * * * *
* * * * * * * * *
* * * * * * * * Mot

[r] Lit., "beheld."

* * * * * * * * * *
* * * * * * the god[ling] Mot
* * * * * * his sevenfold servitors.

Then the godling Mot [cries out]:
"Look you, mine own brethren hath Baal turned into my destroyers!
Why, the very sons of my mother are become my annihilators!"

Yea, again and again he lifts up his voice,
and cries to Baal in the Recesses of the North:
"Why, mine own brethren, O Baal, hast thou turned into my destroyers!
Why, the very sons of my mother are become my annihilators!"

LXIX

Baal engages Mot in a furious fight.

They go prancing like antelopes;[s]
now triumphs Mot, now Baal.
They go goring like wild oxen;
now triumphs Mot, now Baal.
They go stinging like asps;
now triumphs Mot, now Baal.
They go butting like charging beasts,
now falls Mot, now Baal.

LXX

The sun-goddess, viewing the combat from on high, urges Mot to surrender.

On high the sun-goddess cries unto Mot:
"Hearken, I beseech thee, O godling Mot!

[s] Reading *kzmrm* for the *kgmrm* of most editors.

LXX. The words "He will surely pluck up," etc., constitute a cliché. They are likewise employed in §III (III AB,B 15–18^{b}) when 'Ashtar is urged to give up his claims against Sir Sea. Moreover, the greater part of the sentence occurs in the commination which Ahiram, king of Byblus (early tenth cent. B.C.) invokes

How wouldst thou contend with Baal Puissant?
Beware lest thy father El, the Bull-god, hear thee;
he will surely pluck up the mainstays of thy dwelling,
overturn the throne of thy kingship,
break the scepter of thy dominion!"

LXXI

Frightened by this warning, Mot surrenders.

Then the godling Mot goes frightened;
terror-stricken is that youngster, the belo[ved] of El.

Mot rises from his prostration [and cries]:
" * * * * * * * * * *
Let Baal then install himself [on the throne of] his kingship!
[Let him take his seat on the tribune of] his dominion!

Celebration of the Equinox

COMMENDATION OF THE SUN-GODDESS

LXXII

The sun-goddess is commended and rewarded for her solicitude toward Baal.

* * *

---

against the violators of his tomb in the well-known sarcophagus inscription (Albright, JAOS 67[1947], 155).

LXXII. These lines describe the reward which Baal grants to the sun-goddess for her sympathy and aid.

The beginning of the passage is imperfectly preserved; but if our restoration is correct, the sun is promised the privilege of feeding upon Baal's rains by drinking them up. She is then told that she will have sway not only over the upper region but also, when she descends nightly, over the netherworld. The latter idea recurs in both Hittite and Mesopotamian texts. Thus, in the Hittite document KUB XVII 14 iv 21, the sun-god of the earth (*taknas* ᵈ*Istanus*) is associated with the nether gods (*katterus* DINGIR.MESH), and in KBo V 3 i 53 with Allatum, queen of the netherworld. Similarly, a Babylonian hymn to Shamash (Gray, *Shamash Texts*,

[Inasmuch as] thou hast been kind,
[whenas thou com]est forth, my [r]ains will depart (before thee)![t]

[t] This rendering depends upon a conjectural restoration of the damaged text.

---

9 ff.) thus addresses him: "Thou art the shepherd of all both above and below, The realms above Thou disposest as a dwelling for all; Thou overseest also the realms below, even those which belong to Ea, to the water-spirits and to the Anunnaki!"; while in IV R[2] 19, No. 2 it is said of him: "The great gods wait upon thy light; all of the Anunnaki [the underworld gods] look on thy face!"[b]

Finally, the sun-goddess is promised the friendship and protection of the god Koshar-wa-Khasis, Sir Adroit-and-Cunning, whose participation in the defeat of Sir Sea has been described in preceding portions of the poem (§XIV: III AB,A 8–18[a]; §XXII: II AB ii 12–48). What is of especial interest here is that, in assuring her of the friendly companionship of that god, Baal feels it necessary to point out particularly that her protector will be he who formerly distinguished himself by casting the dragon into the sea. This is more than an assurance that she will be in good hands. As is well known, the belief obtains in many parts of the world that *solar eclipses are caused by a dragon or monster who assails and swallows up the sun.* Thus, in Indic belief, it is the dragon Rahu (who in this capacity bears the name of Svarbhanu) who periodically swallows up the sun and moon (Rig Veda v 40); and this piece of mythology was adopted also by the Buddhists (Buddhaghosa i 9; Samyutta i 50; trs. C. A. F. Rhys Davids, *Kindred Sayings,* i 71). In Chinese belief, eclipses were likewise

[b] It must be admitted, however, that our rendering, "shades" and "upper gods," is not entirely certain. The first word represents the *rpim* of the original, which we have combined with the *Rephaim,* or Shades, of OT and of certain Phoenician inscriptions. However, it is to be noted that in the Ugaritic text 124 Gordon, the word *rpum* occurs as denoting the coterie of Baal, while, on the other hand, the term *ilnym,* here rendered "upper gods(?)," is employed in ʿnt IV 79 of beings (divine?) who live "two layers beneath the springs of the earth, three spans . . ." It is therefore equally possible that the translations should be reversed, and that the *rpum* are the upper and the *ilnym* the lower gods. Together, they will correspond to the Igigi and Anunnaki of Babylonian, and to the "upper" and "lower" gods of Hittite mythology (Goetze, *Kleinasien,* 136).

Moreover, thou shalt eat the bread of aggrandizement,
drink the wine of favor!
O sun-goddess, o'er the shades(?) shalt thou bear sway;
O sun-goddess, thou shalt bear sway o'er the upper gods(?)!
The gods shall be thy witnesses,
and mortals too!

---

attributed to the devouring of the sun or moon by a monstrous beast; and in the Confucian classic *Tsun Tsiu* ("Springs and Autumns"), the word "eat" is employed to describe the eclipse of April 20, 610 B.C. (Fu, ERE xii 77). Similarly, in Scandinavian lore, the sun is believed to be pursued constantly by a wolf called Skoll (Welsford, ERE xii 102a). The Tatar tribe of Chuwashes use the phrase "a demon has eaten it" (*vubur siat*) to denote an eclipse (Schott, *De lingua Tschuwaschorum,* 5). The Esthonians have a similar expression; while the Lithuanians assert that the demon Tiknis (or Tiklis) attacks the chariot of the sun. A Mongolian myth says that semi-serpentine creatures called *Trachen* lie in wait for sun and moon; and south of Lake Baikal, it is the king of hell that tries to swallow the moon (Grimm, *Teutonic Mythology,* 707). In Jewish folklore, the sun was said to be swallowed by a great fish (Saadya, Introduction to *Emunoth we-De*ᶜ*oth*; Ginzberg, *Legends of the Jews,* V, 108, 116); and the same notion was entertained by spectators of a lunar eclipse at Hastaya, west of Hermon, in 1891 (G. A. Smith, *Twelve Prophets,* ii, 524). Cf. also Tacitus, *Ann.* i. 28; Maximus of Turin *apud* Migne, vii. 337; Hrabanus Maurus, *op.* v. 606, Colyr. Lastly, the Negritos of Borneo say that eclipses are caused by a python who tries to swallow up the sun or moon (Blagden, *Pagan Races of the Malay Penninsula,* ii, 203–04); and the idea is also attested in Greek mythology (Lasch, ARW 3 [1900], 136). On the subject in general, cf. Tylor, *Primitive Culture,* i. 325 f.; Gunkel, *Schöpfung und Chaos,* 41–69. It is from such a fate that Baal promises to deliver the sun-goddess, and it is for this reason that he mentions especially the dragon-slaying prowess of the god of whose protection he assures her. (This does not mean, of course, that the sun will never be eclipsed, but that whenever the dragon seizes her, she will eventually be rescued!)

Thus, the passage emerges as a kind of solar myth, relating all the main features of the sun's course through the heavens to the good services which she performed (or, in fact, performs each year) in helping to restore to the earth the ousted lord of fertility. It is as a reward for those services that she drinks up the rain and

Sir Adroit shall be thy companion,[u]
yea, Sir Cunning thy comrade-in-arms[u]
— even that same Sir Adroit-and-Cunning
who can hurl both Monster and Dragon into the sea,
even that same Sir Adroit-and-Cunning
who can toss them (therein)!

[u] Lit., "thine acquaintance."

dew; that when she sets, she does so only to exercise further dominion in the netherworld; and that though at times momentarily eclipsed, she is never wholly swallowed up, but always emerges in the end in her full radiance and strength.

It is not improbable that this speech – like that of Koshar in §XLII (II AB vii 21–37) – really incorporates into the fabric of the myth the text of a hymn to the sun recited as part of the seasonal ceremonies. Those ceremonies, as we have seen, usually coincided with solstice or equinox, so that the adoration of the solar deity came to figure as a cardinal element of the proceedings.

THE REINSTATEMENT OF BAAL

V AB Gordon, ʿnt: i–iii

§1. A tablet discovered in 1931 and known conventionally as V AB rounds out the story of Baal. This describes his ultimate restoration to power, the feast which celebrated that event, the annihilation of his enemies and opponents, and the eventual inauguration of an era of peace and goodwill.

§2. The action commences with a lavish banquet in celebration of Baal's reinstatement. Colossal flagons "such as no housewife has ever seen" and goblets "such as (even) Asherat has ne'er beheld" are set before the guest of honor, while a "sweet-voiced stripling" sings and plays before him and his brides wait attendance.

The guests, however, are not all of them friends or partisans of Baal; they include also many of the gods who had originally opposed his dominion and held him in contumely. This inspires his loyal sister Anat to use the opportunity in order to exact vengeance upon them. While the festivities are in full swing, therefore, she suddenly shuts the gates of the palace, thereby preventing anyone from getting out. Then she falls to a savage slaughter, overturning chairs and tables and wallowing in blood. This done, she calmly washes herself in dew and rain water, adorns herself with cosmetics, and prepares to resume the celebration.

But Baal himself is far more gently disposed. Thrilled at the reunion with his brides and feeling, no doubt, that all opposition has now been quelled, he sends his two couriers (i.e., Gpn and Ugr) to bid the goddess relinquish her ugly mood, let bygones be bygones, and help usher in an era of peace and goodwill. Instead of bending her energies to the weaving of traps and the contriving of plots, she is now to weave upon earth a mesh of love and banish warfare forevermore. Moreover, says Baal, as a token of his power and authority, he will create lightning to flame from his holy hill and he will also reveal himself in all the sounds of nature, in the whisper of stones, the rustling of trees, the roar of the deep, and the music of the spheres. The heavens shall declare the glory of God and the firmament shew forth his handiwork.

When the messengers arrive, ʿAnat is at first apprehensive

that some further enemy may have risen up against Baal. She therefore assures them that, if such be the case, she will again take up the cudgels for her brother, and to illustrate the extent of her power, she recites the list of her former triumphs, even claiming a share in the defeat of Yam! The couriers reassure her, however, that her fears are unfounded and repeat to her the message of Baal. 'Anat then expresses her compliance and proceeds to Baal on the "Height of the North." Baal greets her and regales her.

§3. From the standpoint of the Seasonal Pattern, this text mythologizes the RITUAL COMBAT, the REINSTATEMENT OF THE KING, the FEAST OF COMMUNION, and the subsequent inauguration of an era of bliss and fertility. But what lends it added interest is that it recovers to us the mythological prototype of a picture painted by several of the Old Testament prophets in describing the Last Day. Projecting into eschatology the circumstances which were thought to attend the *annual* renewal of life, these prophets speak of Yahweh's holding a banquet of his holy mountain and of his then annihilating his enemies and opponents, revealing himself as the savior for whom the faithful have been waiting, and ushering in an era of bliss and prosperity.[1] Naturally, they adapt the traditional picture to the circumstances and events of their own day, identifying the routed foemen with the specific enemies of Israel; but beneath this later political veneer the old contours are still discernible. Hear, for example, the words of Isaiah 25:6–10:

Then on this hill of Zion for all nations
  Yahweh Sebaoth will spread
a banquet of rich food and of rare wines,
of marrowy dainties and of choice old wines;
and on this mountain shall he strip away
  the mourning shroud from all mankind,
the veil of sorrow from all nations.
Death (Mot!) shall he destroy forevermore
and wipe away the tears from every face,
  and free his own folk from taunts everywhere
  ('tis Yahweh's own decree).

And on that day it shall be said:
  " 'Here is our God for whom we were a-waiting
  that he might bring salvation unto us;

This is Yahweh whom we were a-waiting;
 let us be glad and joy in his salvation!' "

The last words, it may be added, find an echo in the ritual cry which greeted the reappearance of Attis in the Asianic mysteries. The votaries rejoiced and bade one another "be strong" because their own salvation had been assured in that of the god himself.[2]

Similar is the description of the Last Day as given by the prophet Zephaniah, I:8–9:

Hush at the presence of Yahweh God!
for nigh is Yahweh's day;

Yahweh hath prepared a meal,[3]
hath invited his guests.
And it shall be on the day of Yahweh's meal
that I will punish the princes and the sons of the king
and all who don exotic garb;
and I will punish all who leap o'er the threshold,
who fill the house of their lord with violence and deceit.

Although adapted to a commination upon idolators, it is not difficult to recognize in this utterance a trace of the old myth relating how the god saw the upstart rebels annihilated at a feast held in his honor.[4]

Joel too makes use of the traditional picture; for he states explicitly (4:18–21) that the era in which "the mountains shall drop sweet wine and the hills flow with milk" — an expression analogous to that which describes the imminent return of Baal in the Canaanite poem (I AB iii 6) — will be marked by the fact that Yahweh will again take up residence on his holy mountain and that all foreign intruders will be ousted from it.

Ye shall know that I, Yahweh, am your God,
dwelling on Zion, my sacred hill;
Jerusalem shall be inviolate then,
never shall aliens invade her again.

Then thus shall it be:
the mountains shall drip wine,
the hills be aflow with milk,
and all the brooks of Judah run with water.
From Yahweh's house shall pour a stream

to water the Wady of Acacias.
Egypt shall be turned to desolation,
And Edom be a desert waste,
for their outrage on the men of Judah,
for innocent blood shed within their land.
But Judah shall be inhabited forever
and Jerusalem for all generations.
And I will avenge that bloodshed
which aforetime I did not avenge;
and Yahweh shall dwell in Zion.

Moreover, just as the return of Baal will be heralded, according to our myth, by the visible display of his presence and power in the lightning, so too, says the Hebrew prophet, will Yahweh, prior to his return, "set signs in the heavens, fire and blood and columns of smoke, the sun being turned to darkness and the moon to blood" (3:2–3; cf. 15). True, the nature and motivation of the display is different, but — given the close parallelism which otherwise obtains between the prophet's eschatological picture and the description of Baal's return, and given also the fact that, in preceding passages, Joel consciously plays on the Seasonal Pattern (see Chapter Three, Excursus) — it can surely not be doubted that in the introduction of this motif Joel was drawing, with appropriate adaptation and elaboration, on traditional mythological lore.

NOTES

1. The banquet at the end of days is a motif which recurs in apocalyptic and rabbinic literature, e.g., Syr. Apoc. Baruch xxix 3–8; IV Ezra vi 52; Baba Bathra 74a–75a; Targ. Ps.-Jon., Numbers 9:26 ff.; cf. Oesterley, *Last Things,* 60–61; 122 ff.; 142 ff.; 187 ff. The meat is to consist of the flesh of the defeated monsters Leviathan and Behemoth. Alternatively, it is to be supplied by a gigantic ox. For this last Bousset, *Religion des Judentums,* 271, cites an Iranian parallel which relates that the marrow of the slain ox Hadhayos is to provide the food of immortality for the righteous.

2. Firmicus Maternus, *De Errore Profanarum Religionum,* XXII, 1.

3. Hebrew *zebah* means properly "the slaughtering of an animal," and does not necessarily denote a *sacrifice.* Moffatt's "The Eternal has ready a victim for sacrifice" therefore obscures the point.

4. In support of the view that Zephaniah is here harking back to the old mythological tradition, it may be observed that, like Joel, he too casts his prophecy in the form of a sustained satire upon typical seasonal rites. Thus, he begins (1:2 ff.) with a reference to the impending desolation of man and beast – a picture drawn from that of the preliminary Mortification in the seasonal myths. He then refers pointedly (1: 4–5) to idolatrous worship, such as the adoration of heavenly bodies, and specifies the "remnant of Baal" and the eunuch-priests (*kemarim*). Then, when he speaks of the Banquet, he introduces an allusion to "them that don exotic raiment" (1:8), which may be interpreted to refer to the common seasonal practice of the *masquerade* or to the custom whereby, in the mysteries, the *galli* donned female attire (cf. Lucian, *De Dea Syria* §6; Herodian, 1.10, §§5–7; GB vi 253 ff.; Gaster, JBL 60 [1941], 302). Lastly, the reference to the "wailing" (*yelalah*) in Jerusalem and Makktesh (I, 10–11) may have been suggested by the seasonal Ululation; while the statement that Yahweh will search out Jerusalem with lights (1: 12) may in the same way have been suggested by the seasonal torchlight processions.

I

The restoration of Baal is celebrated.

* * * * *

They do service to Baal Puissant,
extol His Highness, the lord (*baal*) of the earth.

They proceed to fete him and dine him;
with a sharp sword they cut up a fatling;
they go about feasting him and wining him.
A cup is placed in his hand,
a goblet in his two hands,
a large beaker, great to see,
a jar such as sky folk use(?),
a holy cup such as never housewife beheld,
a goblet such as never goddess espied;
it holds a thousand barrels,
wine enough to be mixed in ten thousand portions.
While he is mixing it,
a sweet-voiced youngster proceeds to chant and sing
a pleasant chant to the accompaniment of cymbals,
over Baal in the Recesses in the North.

When Baal catches sight of his brides,

sees P-d-r-aya, the Lady of Light;
thereupon the Dew-nymph (T-l-aya), Lady of Rain,
* * * * * * * * *
* * * * * * * * *
* * * * * * * * *
* * * * * * * * *

[Lacuna of about 20 lines]

II

Meanwhile, however, 'Anat indulges in a rampage of vengeance on the henchmen of Baal's rival. Locking the gates of the temple to prevent their taking refuge in it, she confronts them in hill and dale, east and west, and massacres them.

[There comes she, bathed in the scent]
of seven maidens' henna
in a fragrance of coriander and perfumes.
Then, after locking the gates of the mansion,
'Anat confronts (Mot's) henchmen in the . . . . . of the hill(s);
yea, in the valley(s) 'Anat falls to the slaughter;
in the open ground between the cities[a]
she falls to the massacre.
She slaughters the people of the coast lands,[b]
annihilates the population of the east.

[a] Lit., "between two cities," i.e., in the neutral ground between any two settlements.

[b] I.e., the west.

II. The words "henna as of seven maidens" allude to the wonderful aroma which attended the presence of the goddess 'Anat. The belief that divine beings are accompanied by a special scent recurs in the Egyptian Ramesseum drama, line 39 (§XI). There are also frequent references to it in Classical literature, e.g., Homeric *Hymns,* III. 231; v. 277; Aeschylus, *Prometheus Bound,* 115; Euripides, *Hippolytus* 1391 (see Monk *in loc.*); Aristophanes, *Birds,* 1715–16; Vergil, *Aen.*, i. 403. Cf. Schwenk, *Philologus* 17 (1861), 451; Lohnmeyer, "Der göttliche Wohlgeruch," in *Sitzb. d. Heidelberg. Akad.*, 1919.

Henna, or camphor, was used in antiquity not only as a cosmetic but also as a perfume; cf. Song of Songs, 1:13–14; 4:13–14; Theophrastus, *Odor.*, 26 f.; Pliny, *HN*, xiii 9, 18.

At her feet (roll) heads like balls;
above her (fly) limbs like locusts;
the limbs of the henchmen . . . . like . . . . .
She ties the heads around her bosom,
dangles the limbs from her girdle;
up to the knees she wades in the blood of the soldiers,
up to her hips in the gore of the troops.
She drives them staggering along (?)
. . . .

Then on to the house (temple) ʿAnat proceeds,
the goddess repairs to the palace.
Unslaked by the slaughtering in the valley(s),
by her massacring in the open ground between the cities,
she (now) imagines that the chairs are soldiers,
imagines that the tables are troops.
Mightily falls she to the slaughter,
and when she beholds the massacre,
her inwards swell with glee,
her heart is full of joy,
yea, the inwards of ʿAnat . . . . . .
while she wades in the blood of the soldiers,
to the hips in the gore of the troops.
She slaughters her fill in the house,
massacres amid the tables.
The house (?) is drenched in the blood of the soldiers
— (that is,) the oil is poured forth in streams from (every) bowl.

III

ʿAnat cleanses herself.

Then the Virgin ʿAnat washes her hands,
Y-b-m-t L-i-m-m her fingers;[c]
she washes her hands of the blood of the soldiers,
her fingers of the gore of the troops.

[c] An alternative name of ʿAnat, of uncertain meaning.

III. The words "the shower which *the stars* pour forth" allude to a common belief that rain is an effluvium from the stars. The belief is well attested in Classical literature, e.g., Aeschylus, *fr.* 812; Ovid, *Fasti,* v. 166; *Pervigilium Veneris,* 20. Cf. Gruppe, *Gr. Mythol.,* 823–24. It obtained also among the early Arabs; Wellhausen, *Reste,* 210.

The chairs turn back (?) into chairs,
the tables into tables,
the footstools turn back (?) into footstools.
Then she draws water and washes
[in the d]ew of heaven, the oil of earth,
in the shower which the clouds rain down,
[the shower] which the stars pour forth.
She adorns herself with cosmetics,
[with the ambergris] which a thousand demons excrete upon
the sea.

IV

Baal sends messengers to 'Anat intimating that he wishes to inaugurate an era of peace and bliss.

[Lacuna of about 15 lines]

"A feeling of tenderness is implanted into his breast,
there hath been conveyed unto the bosom of Baal Puissant
a feeling of affection for P-d-r-aya, the Lady of Light
of love for T-l-aya, the Lady of Rain,
of endearment for A-r-s-aya, the Lady of *y-'-b-d-r*.

Forthwith, O servitors, enter,
at the feet of 'Anat bow and fall,
prostrate yourselves, do homage unto her,
and bring the word unto the Virgin 'Anat,
repeat unto Y-b-m-t L-i-m-m:
"This is the message of Baal Puissant,
the word of Him Who is Puissant among Warriors:
Now do thou banish warfare from the earth,
and love do thou emplant within the land!

IV. Baal's promise of a majestic display of lightning probably mythologizes the fact that in Syria and Palestine, the return of the rainy season is actually preceded by electric storms. Indeed, the Arabs of Palestine have a proverb: "The lightning is a sign of rain" (Dalman, *Arbeit und Sitte*, iii/1, 114). Cf. Jeremiah 10:13; 51:16; Psalm 135:7: "He maketh lightnings for the rain."

The mountain of the North, whence the display is to come, was probably localized by the people of Ugarit (Ras Shamra) as Mons Casius (modern Jebel el-Akra). It here ranks as a typical "thunder mountain," like the Greek Etna and like those common in Teutonic folklore (cf. Grimm, *Teutonic Mythology*, 185 ff.).

Now do thou weave no longer on the earth
Tissues of lies, but rather threads of peace;
I bid thee, twine no longer in the land
a mesh of guile, but rather skeins of love!

Now haste, now hurry, now bestir thyself,
and let thy feet come speeding unto me,
yea, let thy steps now haste to where I am.
For there's a rede that I would rede to thee,
a word that I would fain relate to thee;

That word it is which wind-swept trees repeat,
which pebbles in the whisp'ring brooks receive,
which, like the murmur of a threnody,
heaven repeats to earth, and deeps to stars.

Yea, I, install'd as godhead of the North,
will fashion now upon that hill of mine,
a lightning such as heaven doth not know,
a voice the like of which men do not know,
greater than all mankind yet understand.

Come thou, and I, even I, will light a flame (?)
Upon that holy place which evermore
shall be the hill of mine inheritance,
upon that lovely place which evermore
shall be the mount where my puissance rests!

V

'Anat receives the messengers.

When 'Anat espies the two gods,
her feet start to tap,
it seems as if her backbone were about to break;
sweat runs down her face,

V. We cannot yet identify the mythological monsters whom 'Anat here enumerates. Conceivably, the "mighty bitch" was some Semitic counterpart of Cerberus. Note that in Mesopotamian mythology, the infernal goddess Ninkarrak is attended by a hound (or hounds), and with this Gelb (AJSL 55 [1938], 200–03) identifies the Hittite "hounds of Nikarawas." The hellhound also appears in Teutonic folklore: Grimm, *Teutonic Mythology,* 996–97. See also Casartelli, JMEOS 12 (1926), 55–59; Chambers, *Book of Days,* ii. 433–36.

her back shakes,
her spine shivers.

Then lifts she her voice and cries:
"What brings hither Sir Vine and Sir Field?
Has some foe ris(en up) against Baal,
some enemy against the Rider o'er the Clouds?
Why, did I not crush Sir Sea, favorite of El though he was?
Make an end of Sir Stream, mighty god though he was?
Did I not bridle the Dragon — bridle him, I say?
Did I not crush the Serpent Tortuous,
that benighted villain(?) with the seven heads?
Did I not annihilate *'-t-k*, the mighty calf?
Did I not crush *H-sh-t*, the mighty bitch?
Did I not make an end of *Zh-b-b*, that mighty maid(?)?
Well, then, I will again do battle and possess me of the gold
of him that would thrust Baal from the Height of the North,
that raises uproar and withholds obedience,[d]
that would drive him from his royal throne,
from the seat, the tribune of his dominion!
Has, then, some foe risen up against Baal,
some enemy against the Rider o'er the Clouds?"

VI

The messengers convey the words of Baal.

(Thereupon) the servitors reply:
"Nay, no foe has risen up against Baal,
no enemy against the Rider o'er the Clouds,
(But here) is the message of Baal Puissant,
the word of him Who is Puissant among Warriors:
'Now do thou banish warfare from the earth,
and love do thou emplant within the land!
Now do thou weave no longer on the earth
tissues of hate, but rather threads of peace;
I bid thee, twine no longer in the land,
a mesh of guile, but rather skeins of love!
Now haste, now hurry, now bestir thyself,
and let thy feet come speeding unto me,
yea, let thy steps now haste to where I am.
For there's a rede which I would rede to thee,
a word which I would fain relate to thee;

[d] Lit., "stops his ears."

That word it is which wind-swept trees repeat,
which pebbles in the whisp'ring brooks receive,
which, like the murmur of a threnody,
heaven repeats to earth, and deeps to stars.

Yea, I, install'd as godhead of the North,
will fashion now upon that hill of mine,
a lightning such as heaven doth not know,
a voice the like of which men do not know,
greater than all mankind yet understand.

Come thou, and I, even I, will light a flame (?),
upon that holy place which evermore
shall be the hill of mine inheritance,
upon that lovely place which evermore
shall be the mount where my puissance rests!'"

VII

'Anat signifies compliance.

Then ans[wers] the Virgin ['Anat]:
[Y-b-m-t]-L-i-m-m replies:
"Warfare will I banish [from the earth],
and lo[ve will I empla]nt within the land!
Let Baal . . . . . . his buckets,
let him cause his . . . . to shine forth!
Warfare will I banish from the earth,
and love will I emplant within the land!
No longer will I weave upon the earth
tissues of hate, but rather threads of peace;
no longer will I twine within the land
a mesh of guile, but rather skeins of love!

Yet there's a further word that I would say:
Be off, be off, ye twain gods;
laggard ye are, while I am keen!
Rouse yourselves! Off to H-n-b-b,
where dwell the distant gods!
Off to the distant netherworld gods,
two layers beneath the springs of the earth,
three spans under ground (??)!
Thereupon she sets her face toward Baal

on the Height of the North,
across a thousand acres, ten thousand tracts.

Baal espies the coming of his sister,
the advent of his father's . . . .
he sends out a woman afar to meet her.
He sets an ox before her,
and a fatling in front of her.
Water is poured for her and she washes
(in) the dew of heaven, the oil of earth,
in the dew which the heavens pour forth,
the showers which the stars pour forth.
She adorns herself with cosmetics,
with the [ambergis which] a thousand [demons excrete upon the sea],

* * * * * * * * * *

[The rest is lost]

The remainder of V AB (on the reverse of the tablet) needs but be presented in summary. *Columns iv–v* are largely a variant of §§XIX and XXX of the main version. They describe how Asherat cajoles El into permitting a palace to be built for Baal. The present account, however, adds a few interesting details. El at first bellows something — evidently, a preliminary refusal — through the courts of heaven, while the gods, on the whole hostile to Baal (cf. §XXIV of the main version), are warned not to rejoice prematurely. Subsequently, Asherat presses her case, and El accedes to her.

Column vi, again fragmentary, describes how Sir Holy-and-Blessed (Qdsh-w-Amrr), the lackey of Asherat, is commissioned to go to Memphis (Hk[q]pt) or to the island of Carpathos (or Crete, Kptr) and fetch Koshar, the divine architect and smith (cf. §XXXV of the main version).

APPENDIX

UNPLACED FRAGMENTS

The excavations at Ras Shamra have also brought to light a number of other poetic texts which appear to belong to the myth of Baal but which, being fragmentary and incomplete, cannot yet be fitted into the main narrative nor even interpreted with certainty. Some may eventually turn out to represent variant versions of the story.

The texts in question are those known as IV AB and as VI AB, the latter having also been published as ʿnt, Plates ix, ix and x. For the sake of completeness, we here present a brief summary of them.

IV AB — Gordon 76

Column i. Only the ends of lines remain. However, there is mention of "Baal [Pu]issant" (1.6), "the Rider on the Clouds" (1.7) and of Anat (1.14). There is also a reference to some male character's "returning to the earth" (1.9), indicating that the passage deals with the departure of Baal. It is probably part of a speech by Anat, since it is followed by a "reply" addressed to that goddess.

Column ii: The servitors of Baal "reply" to some previous speaker saying:

Baal is not in his mansion,
the god Hadd in his palace.
Why, he took a bow in his hand,
yea, his arc in his right hand,
and behold, he headed for the region of Samach
which abounds in wild oxen.

(It should be noted that, according to BH, it was while hunting in this very region that Baal was lured to his doom. The two texts may therefore belong to the same version of the myth.)

On hearing this report, Anat flies to Samach. Baal welcomes her and boasts his prowess.

Column iii: The first part is fragmentary. Apparently, Baal expresses his reluctance to return. The second part (lines 26 ff.) indicates that Anat pleads with him "in dulcet tones" to reoccupy his throne on the sacred mountain. There is an obscure reference to breeding oxen and cows.

VI AB — ʿnt: Pl. ix–x

Obverse:

This consists of two columns. The first column is a variant of V AB, §IV. Sir Holy-and-Blessed is instructed to repeat to Koshar the message of Baal concerning his intention to inaugurate an era of bliss and peace. The second column describes how the lackey indeed conveys that message, and how Koshar thereupon speeds hotfoot to the court of El.

Reverse:

Column i describes a banquet spread (apparently) by El, at which the authority and divine appointment of Yam are proclaimed. This episode clearly precedes that related in III AB, C, where the appointment of Yam is assumed and the subsequent rebellion of Baal described.

Column ii is fragmentary, only the ends of the lines remaining.

* * *

A text (No. 3) published in *Ugaritica V* (Paris 1966), 557 ff., describes the enthronement of Baal on the Mount of the North (Ṣapân, i.e. Casius). He sits upon the mountain as upon a flood (*mdb*) – a motif discussed below, Part III, §4. On the mountain he stores his lightnings and thunders (*rᶜt*; cf. Job 36.33) – an idea which recurs later in Sirach 39.17; 43.14; Enoch 17.3; 60. 13-15; TB Ḥagigah 12ᵇ. His bodily beauty and majesty are described, and ᶜAnat is said to take harp in hand and sing of her love for him. The text clearly complements that which we have translated under the name of *The Reinstatement of Baal.*

B. THE COMBAT TYPE

1. THE HITTITE MYTH OF THE SNARING OF THE DRAGON

§1. EVERY autumn, at the beginning of the agricultural year, when the earth stood in imminent need of water,[1] the ancient Hittites held a festival which they called Puruli.[2] The festival went back to remote antiquity; it had been inherited along with many other religious usages and traditions, from those earlier inhabitants of Asia Minor whom modern scholars term the Hattians.[3] The name itself was of Hattic origin; its earlier form was Vuruli,[4] and in the Hattic language the word *vur* meant "earth."[5] The P/Vuruli, therefore was "the Festival of the Earth," a seasonal celebration designed to regulate the subterranean waters and to insure due meed of rainfall for the crops.

The ritual of the festival and its attendant myth are preserved to us on six mutually complementary tablets unearthed at Bogazköy, site of ancient Hattusas, the capital of the Hittites during the heyday of their empire.[6] Composed, about 1350 B.C., by a priest named Killas,[7] they present the "order of service" as observed at the important cultic center of Nerik.[8]

A. SYNOPSIS

§2. The text may be divided, for convenience, into four parts.

(I) First, there is a brief *preamble*, specifically relating what follows to the Festival of Puruli, and giving the words of a doggerel petition (ROGATION) for the increase and prosperity of the land, customarily recited at that season.

(II) This is followed by a brief *myth* relating how the weather god, with the aid of the goddess Inaras and of a mortal named Hupasiyas, once succeeded in subduing a contumacious dragon (Illuyankas),[9] who had been attacking him. The fight is said to have taken place in the city of Kiskilussa.

> The traditional tale is embellished with several subsidiary traits, of purely literary or artistic origin. The dragon and his allies, we are told, were lured to a banquet, where they gorged themselves so full that they could not re-enter their lairs and were therefore easily dispatched. The mortal hero acquired the necessary supernatural strength by first embracing the goddess, but to prevent his transmitting this divine power to his human progeny, he was translated, immediately after the victory, to a house especially built on a remote and inaccessible cliff. One day, however, while the goddess was temporarily absent, he chanced, against her express command, to look out of the window, and caught sight of his wife and children. When the goddess returned, he betrayed his offense by importuning her to let him go home to them. Thereupon she became furious and apparently — the text is here incomplete — burned down the house with him inside it.

Once the dragon had been subdued, the goddess committed her palace (i.e., temple) in the city of Kiskilussa, together with the outlet of the subterranean waters (i.e., those which the dragon had previously controlled), into the charge of the king. So long, adds the writer, as the archetypal ritual of the Puruli is regularly performed, these will remain safely in the royal hands.

Next come a few badly mutilated lines in which reference is made to the falling of rain upon the city of Nerik, and to the neighboring Mount Zaliyanu.[11] The details are uncertain, but what appears to be stated is that needed rainfall was once furnished to the city by that mountain, in response to someone's request. This, too, is related to the ritual of the festival by the observation that, from that time forth, whenever rain water begins to course down from the mountain, the deity of the latter receives gifts of offertory bread brought by a sacred person.

(III) There follows a *second version of the myth*. This is of more literary character and takes up more specifically a passing allusion in the first to the fact that, in their initial encounter, the dragon succeeded in maiming the weather god. This, we are now informed, consisted in plucking out his heart and eyes; and our story is concerned mainly with the way in which they were recovered. The weather god—so the tale runs—took to wife the daughter of a pauper, and begat a son. When the lad grew up, with whom should he fall in love but the daughter of his father's inveterate enemy, the dragon? The weather god resolved, however, to exploit the situation to his own advantage. He therefore instructed his son to demand the stolen heart and eyes as part of the marriage settlement. This the lad did; but no sooner had his father recovered the precious organs and thus regained his former powers, than down he went to the sea, engaged the dragon, and defeated him. It so happened, however, that his own son was, at the time, in his father-in-law's house. Outraged at the thought that he had been led unwittingly to betray hospitality—the deadliest of sins in all Oriental countries—he begged his father to allow him to expiate his offense by sharing the fate of the dragon. Thereupon the dragon and the lad were slain together.

(IV) Finally, the text deals with the program of the Puruli Festival at Nerik. The gods, we are told, were conducted thither in procession, the general order of which is described. Special honors were paid to Zashapunas, god of the city of Kastama, and to his consort, Zalinuis. The former ranked on this occasion as superior to the weather god of Nerik himself, while the latter was provided with lavish cereal offerings. Furthermore, special protocol was observed regarding the seating of the deities, once they reached their destination; while all the others had to compete (or draw lots?)[12] for places, the deity of Mount Zaliyanu was accorded an uncontested throne "over the well." In addition, Zashapunas, together with his consort Zalinuis and his concubine Tazuwassi, was (subsequently) accommodated in special quarters provided for them by the king in the city of Tanipiya.

B. INTERPRETATION

§3. It is apparent that this text, with its sequence of ROGATION, DRAGON COMBAT, REGULATION OF THE WATERS, and REUNION OF THE GODS, reflects the Seasonal Pattern which we have discussed in detail in the preceding chapters of this book, and which is represented pre-eminently in ancient Near Eastern ritual by the Mesopotamian Festival of Akitu, and in ancient Near Eastern myth by the Babylonian *Epic of Crea-*

tion (*Enuma Elish*), the Canaanite *Poem of Baal,* and the Egyptian Edfu ceremonies, all of which involve combat against a dragon (or similar monster) and a foregathering of the gods.

§4. A striking modern parallel may also be adduced. The basic structure of the Puruli Festival, with its combination of the prayers for fertility and the mimetic conquest of the dragon, finds its almost exact analogue in ceremonies associated in Europe with Rogationtide, which is celebrated in April, at a season regarded in the popular calendars of that continent as likewise marking the beginning of the year.[13] (These ceremonies, it may be added, are often in fact duplicated on such other "crucial" dates as St. George's Day [April 23] and the solstitial festival of Midsummer [June 24.])

As currently observed, the rites of Rogationtide divide into (*a*) those performed under the auspices of the Church, and (*b*) those — deemed more "pagan" — which retain their primitive popular character and survive only as folk usages. For comparative purposes, however, the two must be regarded as constituting a single complex.

§5. The "ecclesiastical" part of the ceremony takes the form of a perambulation round the fields or towns, led by the clergy or sacristans carrying crosses and sacred emblems. A number of stations are made, and at each of them rogations, or supplicatory prayers, are offered for the fertility of the earth and the aversion of noxious influences.[14] Typical is the following description by Naogeorgus:[15]

> Now comes the day wherein they gad abroad, with cross in hand,
> To bounds of every field, and round about their neighbor's land;
> And as they go, they sing and pray to every saint above,
> But to our Lady specially, whom most of all they love.
> Whenas they to the town are come, the church they enter in,
> And look what saint that church doth guide, they humbly pray to him,
> That he preserve both corn and fruit from storm and tempest great,
> And them defend from harm, and send them store of drink and meat.

The procedure thus described is but a Christianized version of ceremonies which, in fact, form standard and characteristic elements of spring and summer festivals in many parts of the world, and which are attested not only in modern but also in ancient civilizations. A few examples must suffice. In the Canaanite *Poem of the Gracious Gods,* which is really the cult text of a spring festival, the ritual drama is preceded by a rogation for prosperity and well-being [*shlm*] and by an appeal to the sun as fructifier of vines.[16] Similarly, at the Roman Ambarvalia, in April, the fields were circumambulated and Mars, as god of crops and of the yield of the earth, was entreated to "grant that crops and must and vine thrive and turn out well."[17] So, too, in the daily liturgy of the Jews, during the period between Passover (in April) and early December — that is, between the cessation and resumption of the heavy "latter rains" — a special prayer is inserted in the statutory Eighteenth Blessings begging God to "bless our year with beneficial dews . . . that it may issue in life, plenty, and well-being, like those (previous) years which proved a blessing."[18] Lastly, it is still customary at this season for the peasants around Jerusalem to repair to the Well of the Virgin and chant this jingle:

O Lady, O Moon,
water our crops with moisture!
O Lady, O Spring of Siloam,
water our shriveled seeds![19]

while at Bethlehem a similar doggerel is chanted.

Water our blighted crops!
Make green our parched seed![20]

Here, clearly, we have the ROGATION element of our Puruli Festival; and the parallel becomes even more striking when it is observed that, just as in the Christianized and popular Palestinian versions the petition is often addressed to the Lady Mary or the Lady Moon (Bedr), so in our text the heroine of the myth is the goddess Inaras, elsewhere expressly associated (if not actually identified) with an earlier Hattic Tahatenuit, described as "Lady of Wells"![21]

§6. Equally arresting is the similarity between the theme of the Puruli myth and the more popular part of the Rogationtide ceremonies. For the fact is that in many places, Rogationtide and the analogous "crucial" calendar dates are marked in folk custom by the enactment in pantomine of a BATTLE AGAINST A DRAGON, whose grisly effigy is also paraded in the procession. Although the fact is not always explicitly brought out — sometimes, indeed, he is transmogrified as Satan! —[22] the dragon really represents the nether waters, supposed source of rivers as well as springs, which have annually to be "tamed" or subdued lest they flood the earth instead of fructifying it,[23] or — according to a variant notion — lest they be malevolently impounded instead of beneficially released.[24] A few examples must suffice. As late as 1903, it was customary at Ufford (Suffolk), in England, to parade such a dragon through the streets during Rogationtide;[25] while at Ragusa, in Sicily, an enormous effigy of a dragon, complete with movable tail and eyes, was likewise borne in procession on St. George's Day (April 23).[26] The latter custom obtained also, at an earlier period, in the city of Leicester, a local chronicle recording an annual disbursement, during the years 1536–41, "for dryssing the dragon."[27] Similarly, as comparatively late as 1823, a dragon called Snap used to be carried round Norwich, county town of Norfolk, on the same day;[28] while in several parts of England — notably in Kent and Derbyshire — the Feast of St. George is still characterized by the performance of a mummers' play dealing with the defeat of the monster.[29] Again, in the local folklore of Rouen it is asserted that St. Romanus anciently delivered the city from a dragon called Gargouille on Ascension Day;[30] while a writer of 1638 records that it was customary in his day for the inhabitants of Kennoul Hill, England, to foregather on May 1 for special exercises at a neighboring rock called Dragon's Hole.[31] Further, at Fuerth, in Bavaria, the slaying of the dragon was enacted annually on the Sunday following Midsummer (Corpus Christi);[32] and at Burford, in Oxfordshire, the dragon was paraded on Midsummer Eve.[33] Similar ceremonies take place also, on analogous dates, at Tarascon,[34] and in other French towns and villages.[35] So prominent, in fact, is the discomfiture of the dragon in these seasonal rites that Frazer has characterized it as one of the essential ingredients of the myth and ritual associated with such occasions.[36]

§7. But it is not only in general structure that the myth and ritual of the Puruli Festival conform to the standard Seasonal Pattern. The similarity extends to details.

(*a*) A natural sequel to the subjugation of the dragon is that the control of the subterranean waters should be transferred forthwith to someone who might be trusted to wield it beneficently — viz., in ritual, to the king; in myth, to the victorious deity. In ritual, the idea finds expression in the practice of requiring kings, at major seasonal festivals, to perform rites designed to ensure water and rainfall for the ensuing year.[37] In myth, it is represented, for example, by the insistence, in the Babylonian version, that Marduk, after conquering Tiamat, produces fertility (*khegallu*),[38] and, in the Canaanite version, by the elaborate procedure whereby Baal, after vanquishing Yam, is induced thenceforth to regulate the discharge of the rains, so that they may fall in due season.[39]

Now, it is precisely this that is implied by the otherwise inconsequential passage of our text which states that, after subduing the dragon, the goddess Inaras promptly committed "the house of the nether upsurge"[40] into the charge of the king. Moreover, in order thereby to validate existent ritual practice, it is affirmed that so long as the traditional rites are observed regularly, that control will remain in the king's hands — a statement which is further illustrated by sundry references in Hittite texts to the important role played by the king in the Puruli ceremonies.[41]

(*b*) The subterranean waters are, after all, only one source of the earth's fertility. Apart from rainfall, another source is provided by the streams which gush from the mountains when the snow melts. Accordingly, our text passes immediately to a reference to this alternative source, for it mentions how the neighboring Mount Zaliyanu once furnished this boon to the inhabitants of Nerik, when someone besought it. And here, too, the incident serves as the mythological validation of a punctual ceremony in the Puruli rites, for we are told that whenever (nowadays) the mountain sends those welcome "rains," it is to receive thank offerings.

(*c*) In its mythic form, the conquest of the dragon often involves the intriguing detail that the victor subsequently installs himself on a throne, or in a palace, upreared directly over the outlet of the subjugated waters, thereby, as it were, "putting the lid" on them. As documented more fully in our Commentary, this idea obtains not only in the Babylonian *Epic of Creation*, but also in respect of several Mesopotamian temples, and it recurs in connection with the Syrian temple at Hierapolis and (in later Jewish legend) with that of Yahweh in Jerusalem. Indeed, it is not improbable that this is the true sense of Psalms 29:10, which speaks of Yahweh's being enthroned upon the floods; and a further allusion to it may perhaps be detected in Psalms 93:2–3. This notion finds expression in our text in the statement that at the Puruli Festival the goddess Zalinuis — evidently the deity of Mount Zaliyanu — is given a throne *over the well.*

§8. We have already observed that, in the course of its transmission, the basic material of the traditional ritual drama was embellished and transformed by the introduction of extraneous elements and of subsidiary traits and motifs, due partly to conscious literary creativity and partly to the irrepressible and playful inventiveness of the common people who acted it or participated in the attendant ceremonies. In both cases, there was a tendency to draw generously upon contemporary folklore, a vast conglomeration of unassorted ideas and impressions being grafted upon the time-honored nucleus, and the original material being overlaid with elements transplanted boldly from other current tales and legends. In this connection, it must be remembered that while the festival itself was of Hattic origin, and while the Hattic background was indeed retained in the more conservative ritual,[42] the accompanying myth has come down to us through a Hittite medium. Accordingly, we must allow for the possibility that the popular accretions which now appear in it may have been due to distinctive Hittite influences and have been gathered during the course of its transmission.

NOTES

1. Mursilis II refers specifically (KBo II 5 r, iii, 14 f.) to his celebration of "the great Puruli festival" in the season of *hameshas*, and this would appear to denote a time of year suitable for military campaigns (cf. Hrozný, HKT, 190, n. 4), i.e., one in which the ground is not yet rain-soaked. It is generally identified as late summer; see Goetze, in *Language* 27 (1951), 467 ff.

2. Cf. KUB VIII 69.5; XVI 35.3; XXII 25 i 21, 33; XXII 46.14. The ritual must have been elaborate, for the complete catalogue of it covered thirty-two tablets: KUB XXX 42 i, 5–7; cf. Laroche,

in AOr. 17 (1949) iii-iv, 16. A portion of it is preserved in KUB XXV.31. It is probable also that descriptions of the "New Year Festival" in KUB XXXVI 97 (cf. Otten, OLZ 1956: 101 ff.), and allusions to it in KUB XVII.24; XXVII 59; XXXIII.105, refer to the same occasion.

3. Cf. Friedrich, AfO 6 (1930), 115.

4. Cf. KUB XXII 25 i, 21, 33; 1 BoT II 17, 3.

5. Cf. KUB II, 2, 40, where Hattic *es-vu-ur* is equated with KUR.MESH, "lands"; cf. Forrer, ZDMG 76 (1922), 234; Sayce, JRAS 1924: 255. For the adjectival suffix-*u/ili*, see Forrer, op. cit., 231.

6. KBo III.7; KUB XII.66; XVII.5–6; XXXVI.54; Bo. 2020/f.

7. The name invites comparison with Killas, charioteer of Pelops (Pausanias V, 10.7); Killeus, father of Akrisios (Schol., Il. ii 173, 631); and Killa, sister of Hecuba (Schol., Lycophron 224, 315) and daughter of Laomedon (Appolodorus, Bib., iii, 12.2). It appears also in Asianic toponyms, e.g., Killa, in the Troad (Il. i 38; Herod. i 149) and "the Killanian Plain" in Phrygia (Strabo xiii. 4, 629).

8. For the location, see Cornelius, RHA 57 (1955), 51. Hrozný (AOr. 7 [1935], 173) would identify it with the classical Maroga (modern Maragos), N.E. of Goksun. Reference to Hattic festivals at Nerik are made in KUB XXVIII. 80–90, 92, 99; while the Puruli in that city is mentioned in KUB XII 31, obv. 2, 7, 12, 15.

9. This is not a proper name, as was at first supposed, for the word occurs as a common noun in other Hittite texts, e.g., in the Legend of Kessi, KUB XVII, I ii 13; XXIV 7, iii 70; XXXVI. 55, rev. 28; cf. Laroche, OLZ 1956: 422.

10. The operative word is *hwanhwar*. This is related to *hwanhwessar*, which is associated, in KBo III 21 ii 8, with Ea, god of subterranean waters; in KBo VIII 3 i 20, with rivers; and in KUB XVII 10 i 24 (the Telipinu myth) with "high mountains" and "deep valleys"; while in KBo VI 54 ii 5 f. a goddess throws some gravel into it. Some such meaning as "swell, upsurge" is therefore indicated, the reference in the third of these passages being, perhaps, to the springs which, in Syria and other Near Eastern countries, burst forth at the foot of the hills (cf. G. A. Smith, *Historical Geogr. of the Holy Land,* 77), and which were believed in antiquity to issue from the nether ocean (cf. A. J. Wensinck, *Ocean,* 17). The *hwanhwar* would be, in fact, the same as "the upwelling of the oceans" (*sh-r' t-h-m-t-m*) mentioned in the Canaanite *Poem of Aqhat* (I, 49; §XXVIII).

11. Mentioned beside the city of Kastama in KUB VI 45 v 46. It is identified by Cornelius (RHA 57 [1955], 51) with Ak-Dagh.

12. The Hittite word (*pultiya-*) does not occur elsewhere. The meaning "compete" is suggested by Goetze.

13. It is no valid objection to this comparison that Rogationtide, as a Christian institution, is no older than the sixth century; what

matters is not the date of its Christianization but the antiquity of the underlying pattern.

The usual view is that Rogationtide is a Christianization of the Roman Festival of Robigalia, held on April 25. But this could apply at best to the Major Rogationtide, ordained for that day by Gregory the Great (d. 604). It could certainly not apply to the Minor Rogationtide, introduced between 471 and 475 by Mamertus, bishop of Vienne (in the Dauphiné), for this was celebrated during the three days preceding Ascension, and the date of that festival is variable, being determined by that of Easter. Moreover, there is really very little to recommend a derivation of Rogationtide from the Robigalia, since not only the dates but also the rituals are totally distinct. The Robigalia was designed expressly to avert mildew (*robigo*) and – since this a kind of rust – it was characterized by the sacrifice of two rust-brown puppies to the deity Robiga. There is nothing of this in the ceremonies of Rogationtide. Conversely, the processions and the dragon slaying which mark the Christian festival have no counterpart in the ritual of the Robigalia. – On the institution of the Minor Rogationtide by Mammertus, cf. Sidonius Apoll., *Epist.* V, xiv, XVII; Avatus, in Migne, *PL*, LIX, 289–94. For its formal adoption at the Council of Clovesho, cf. Thorpe, *Ancient Laws and Institutes of England* (1840), 1. 64.

14. An excellent account may be found in J. Brand, *Observation on the Popular Antiquities of Great Britain* (1902), i.197 A. In England, the rogation days were popularly known as *gang-days*, from the custom of *ganging*, i.e., going in procession.

15. Barnaby Goodge's rendering, quoted in Brand, *op. cit.* i, 208.

16. Ritual, line 7 (§1); Drama, 11. 23–27 (§1).

17. The traditional formula is quoted by Cato, *De re rusticâ*, 141.

18. M. Gaster (ed.), *The Book of Prayer . . . acc. to the Custom of the Spanish and Portuguese Jews*, i (1901), 32.

19. PEFQS 1893, 218; 1925, 37; G. Dalman, *Arbeit u. Sitte*, I,i 139.

20. P. Kahle, *Paläst. Diwan* (1931), 56 f.

21. Hittite *wattarwas annas* SAL.LUGAL-*as;* KUB VIII 41, obv. 2; XXVIII 75, iii 5–6; V BoT 124, rev. 3–5; cf. Laroche, JCS I (1947), 209, 214 f.

22. Cf. Naogeorgus (tr. Goodge), in Brand, *op. cit.*, i, 209:

"Then out of hand the dreadful shape of Satan down they throw
Oftimes, with fire burning bright, and dash'd asunder tho';
The boys with greedy eyes do watch, and on him straight they fall,
And beat him sore with rods, and break him into pieces small."

23. See *Baal*, Introd., §3.

24. On this motif in folk literature, see *MI*, A 1111; V. I. Propp, *Radiche storiche*, 411. In Indic myth, when Indra defeats Vritra,

he releases impounded waters: Rig Veda I, 32, i,8; II. 12,3; IV. 24,4; V. 32,1; VII. 1,49. Similarly, the release of impounded waters was, *au fond,* the special feat of Perceval and Gawain in the Grail Legend; cf. J. L. Weston, *From Ritual to Romance,* ch. iii.

25. W. C. Hazlitt, *Dictionary of Faiths and Folklore* (1905), ii, 523.

26. G. Pitrè, *Feste patronali in Sicilia* (1900), 323 ff.

27. Thomas North, *A Chronicle of St. Martin in Leicester* (1866), 136: "1538–41. Item paid for dryssing the dragon . . . 4s."

28. *Edinburgh Review* 77 (1843), 143 f.

29. W. S. Walsh, *Curiosities of Popular Customs,* 462.

30. R. Chambers, *The Book of Days* (1886), i. 540.

31. H. Adamson, *Muses' Threnodie.*

32. Thomas Keightley, *Popular Tales and Fictions* (1824), ii, 107 f.; Frazer, *GB* ii, 163.

33. Frazer, *GB* XI (*Balder*), 37 f.

34. A. Nore, *Coutumes . . . des provinces de France* (1846), 245–50.

35. P. Sébillot, *Le folklore de France* (1904–07), i, 468–70.

36. Frazer, *GB* iv (*Dying God*), 105 ff.

37. For documentation, see Commentary *in loc.*

38. *Enuma Elish,* VII, 21.

39. See above, *Baal,* §XLI.

40. Hittite É *hwanhwanas;* see above, n. 10.

41. E.g., Mursilis II, in KBo III. 5, rev. iii, 14 f.

42. Thus, the deities Zashapunas and Zalinuis, there mentioned, are elsewhere attested as of distinctly Hattic character (see Commentary); while the city of Nerik (Hattic *Na-ra-ak,* KUB XXVIII. 73,5; cf. Guterbock, OLZ 1938, 24), in which the ceremonies took place, is known to have been one of the great Hattic culture centers (cf. Goetze, *Kleinasien,*[1] 50, 126), and it is frequently specified in Hittite ritual texts that its supreme god must be addressed "in the Hattic tongue" (cf. Forrer, ZDMG 76 [1922], 193, Nos. 9, 10,12, 14).

AN ACCOUNT OF THE PURULI FESTIVAL OF THE WEATHER GOD OF HEAVEN

by

Killas, Priest of the High God of Nerik

I

PREAMBLE: ROGATION

When men keep repeating the formula:

May the land thrive, increase!
May the land be blest with peace!

and it really does thrive and increase, they celebrate the Puruli Festival.

I. The rhymed jingle represents the customary rogation formula; cf. above, p. 249. Only when the prayer has been duly answered, and the earth indeed shows signs of renewed fertility, is the actual celebration of the festival appropriate.

That the reference is more particularly to *rainfall* is suggested by the precise parallelism of the phrases "the land thrives" (*utne mai*) and "rains occur" (*heyus kisanta*) in another Hittite text (KUB VIII. 27, 1-Friedrich, *Staatsverträge,* ii, 166).

Not impossibly, the prayer eventually became a mere stereotyped formula, like our own "Happy New Year," characteristic of the festival.

A different interpretation of these lines is suggested by Goetze. The Hittite words *nu man,* here rendered "when," might be read alternatively as a single word (*numan*), meaning "no longer." On this basis, Goetze translates the lines: "The following version of the Puruli myth is one which they no longer recite." The first version is thus the archaic and obsolete one; the second, that actually current. It should be observed, however, that a re-collation of the text confirms the writing *nu man,* in *two words* (cf. H. Otten, *apud* H. Güterbock, *Orientalia* 20:331, n. 1). Goetze's view is therefore tenable only on the supposition of a scribal error.

II

THE MYTH OF THE FESTIVAL

(First Version)

a. The Subjugation of the Dragon

When the weather god and the Dragon came to blows in the city of Kiskilussa, the Dragon succeeded in [over]coming the weather god.

Thereupon the weather god called to all the gods: "Gather together!"

II. FIRST VERSION OF THE PURULI MYTH. (*a*) The story here narrated incorporates two elements which demand special attention. The first is that when his aid is solicited by the goddess Inaras, the mortal hero Hupasiyas stipulates that he must first sleep with her — a condition readily granted. The second is that after he has assisted in vanquishing the Dragon, Hupasiyas is transported by the goddess to a special abode on an inaccessible cliff and ordered not to look out of the window, lest he see his wife and children. When he disobeys, he is destroyed.

The two incidents hang together. The intercourse with the goddess was designed not to satisfy passion but for the magical purpose of acquiring necessary superhuman strength. Among primitive peoples, the belief is pretty universal that personal characteristics can be transmitted and acquired through sexual intercourse (cf. E. Crawley, *The Mystic Rose,* passim). This is, of course, merely one specialized form of the notion that properties and qualities, both positive and negative, can be acquired by any form of contact or "absorption." It is this, for example, which inspires the Zulus, when going out to war, to eat the flesh of cattle in order to receive their strength (H. Calloway, *Amazulu,* 438). It also underlies the similar custom of the Amaxosa to drink the gall of an ox in order to become strong (J. Shooter, *Kaffirs,* 216), or that of the Bechuanas to do likewise (H. Lichtenstein, *Travels in S. Africa,* ii 290). Similar, too, is the Halmaherese usage (Riedel, *Zs. f. Ethn.* 17 [1885], 86); while in Central Australia, human blood is drunk before embarking on an avenging expedition (Spencer-Grillen, *Native Tribes of Central Australia,* 461). As Crawley points out (*op. cit.,* i 142), the notion is frequently entertained that the seat of strength is the seminal fluid,

The goddess Inaras spread a feast. She arranged everything on a lavish scale — wine by the barrel, fruit juice by the barrel, *walhi*-drink by the barrel; and she filled every barrel brim full.

Inaras then went to the city of Ziguratta, where she met a mortal (named) Hupasiyas.

"Look you, Hupasiyas", said Inaras, "I am about to do such and such. Come along and help me!"

---

and that the vigor and other properties which can be acquired by smelling, seeing, anointing, and the like can be acquired a fortiori by the more intimate contact of sexual intercourse. It is, indeed, this that underlies the Hebrew story in Genesis 6:1 ff. which relates how Yahweh was obliged to curtail the natural life of man after the minor gods had consorted with the daughters of men; he could not tolerate that his "spirit should continue in man forever." It is this and this alone that likewise underlies our present incident. *The mortal Hupasiyas is being asked to face a dragon which has already maimed so powerful a being as the weather god himself. He therefore stipulates that he will do so only if he be first equipped with superhuman, divine strength; and the most immediate method of acquiring such strength is by sexual relations with the deity who makes the request.*

Our second incident now provides the logical complement to this magical acquisition of superhuman strength. If contact with the strong confers strength, by the same token, contact with the weak confers weakness. It is, indeed, for this reason that in so many civilizations men avoid women – the weaker vessel – whenever they are about to embark on an enterprise requiring the full measure of their vigor. Odysseus, it will be remembered, feared to ascend the couch of Circe lest he lose his virility (*Od.* x 301, 339–41). Analogously, the Galela and Tobelorese avoid contact with women in wartime (Riedel, *loc cit.*). In the same way, too, the Zulus believe that if a newly married man falls in battle, his wife's "lap is unlucky" (Macdonald, JAI 20 [1891], 140); while "in South Africa, a man, when in bed, may not touch his wife with his right hand," for "if he did so, he would have no strength in war, and would surely be slain" (Calloway, *op. cit.*, 441–43). The same notion certainly obtained among the Arabs, sexual intercourse being taboo to warriors (Aghani XIV 67 [Tabari, ed. Kosegarten, i 144]; XV 161; Al-Ahtal, *Diwan* 120.2; Masudi VI 63–65; *Fr. Hist. Ar.* 247 ff.; Robertson Smith, *Rel. Sem.*,[3] 455); while from such Old Testament passages as Deuteronomy 33:10–11 and I

Said Hupasiyas to Inaras, "If I may lie with you, I will indeed come and do what you wish."

So she lay with him.

Inaras then brought Hupasiyas into (her) house and concealed him.

She put on her finery and invited the Dragon up from his hole. "Look you," (said she) "I am spreading a feast. Come to eat and drink!"

Samuel 21:5–6 [EV. 4–5], as well as from the use of the verb *q-d-sh,* "hallow, purify," in connection with warfare (Jeremiah 22:7; 51:27 f.; Joel 4:9), Robertson Smith (*loc. cit.*) and Schwally (*Semitische Kriegsaltertümer,* 46 f.) have deduced a similar usage in Israel. Nor is it only physical contact with a woman that can sap a man's strength; the very sight of her can produce the same effect; and this is, in fact, a common motif in folk tales of all peoples (*MI,* C. 312). That the idea obtained already in the Hittite world has been shown, in another connection, by Friedrich (*Staatsverträge,* ii, 159, 171). *The point of Hupasiyas' incarceration on an inaccessible cliff and the prohibition against seeing his wife is therefore designed to prevent impairment or transmission to mortals of the divine "essence" which he received through intercourse with the goddess Inaras.*

A further element of the narrative also claims our attention. Instead of the traditional account, in which the monster is defeated in straightforward combat, our narrative attributes his downfall – with obvious comic effect – to the result of a ruse: the Dragon and his aides are lured to a banquet, where they gorge themselves to such an extent that they cannot return to their holes and are thus easily dispatched. Now, this motif happens to recur in folk tales from many parts of the world dealing with the defeat of ogres and dragons (see *MI,* G. 521 and K. 871; Bolte-Polivka, iii. 106; De Vries, *Typen-register,* No. 32). It is therefore a reasonable inference that the introduction of it into our story was due not to the inventiveness of a particular author but to the characteristic injection into the traditional material of new elements derived from popular lore and transferred bodily from tales familiar in the home of the common folk.

In support of this view, it should be noted that, as here related, the story implies characteristics of the Dragon which are foreign to the more formal religious myths but exceedingly common in popular folk tales. The first of these is gullibility. In the religious myths, the Dragon is a formidable monster, like Tiamat, Leviathan,

So up came the Dragon along with [his crew]. They ate and drank. They drank up every barrel, and were so glutted that they could no more get back into their hole.

Thereupon Hupasiyas came and bound the Dragon with a rope. And the weather god came and slew the Dragon, and (all) the gods rallied around him.

Then Inaras built herself a house on a crag in the region of Tarugga, and she settled Hupasiyas in that house.

"When I go out," Inaras instructed him, "You are not to look out of the window, for if you do, you may see your wife and children."

---

or Typhon. But in folk tales – as Grimm pointed out (*Teutonic Mythology,* tr. Stallybrass, 528–29) – the analogous ogre or giant is frequently portrayed as a stupid and credulous creature. In Old Norse, for instance, the word *dumbr,* "dunderhead," actually occurs in the sense of "giant" (*ibid.*), and in later German folklore, giants are called *dumme Lutten* or *lubbe,* "lubbers" (66., 525 f.); while in Hebrew, the giant Orion bears the name *K*^{e}*sil,* "lumbering fool." Stories of the stupid ogre who is bested by trickery are common among many peoples, no less than two hundred variations on this theme being listed in Aarne and Thompson's standard index (I, Nos. 1000–1199).

The second characteristic of the Dragon in our tale is gluttony. This, too, does not appear in the formal religious myths, but is a common trait in folk tales of analogous ogres and giants. A classic example is that of the Cyclops who, in the Homeric account (*Od.* vii 288–89), spends much of his time in unrestrained eating and drinking. Similarly, according to Grimm (*op. cit.,* 522), the Old Norse giant Suttungr derives his name from a word *supt-sopi,* "sup" or "draught," while the common Teutonic designation *durs* (<Low German *duris/turs, drost;* Swiss *durst*) properly denotes one who is fond of wine, thirsty or drunken, just as the Old Norse *jotunn,* Anglo-Saxon *eoten,* Scottish *ettyn,* Swedish *jatte,* "giant," properly denotes "voracious," being connected with the Latin *edax,* etc.

The location of Tarugga is unknown. It is mentioned again in KUB XVII.21, ii 24 (= *ANET* 399b) beside Tapa[panu]wa and Ilaluha. Possibly, it is the same as Turukki, mentioned in the thirty-seventh-year formula of Hammurapi, beside Kakmu and Subartu, and by Adadnirari I (IV R 44, 16) beside Nigimti. It is located by Albright (JAOS 45 [1926], 235) in northern Zagros, and the Turukkû are mentioned in the texts from Mari (e.g.,

Well, when the twentieth day arrived, he did indeed push open the window, and indeed caught sight of his wife and children.

When Inaras returned from her excursion, he started whining, "Let me go home!"

"(Ah,)" said Inaras, "You have pushed open [the window]! . . .

Thereupon, in a burst of fury, she demolished the house, (and) the weather god [strewed weeds] over the ruins.

(Thus) he (i.e., Hupasiyas) came to a sor[ry end].

b. The Control of the Nether Waters

When Inaras [returned] to the city of Kiskilussa . . . she committed . . . her house and [the House] of the Nether Upsurge into the hand of the king. And now, so long as we keep performing the archetypal Puruli rite, the king's hand remains in control of the house of Inaras and of that of the Nether Upsurge.

ARM I, 16. 13–14) as a remote and outlandish people, somewhat like the Lullu, or the "Gothamites" of modern folklore (cf. Oppenheim, JNES ii [1952], 132).

(*b*) THE CONTROL OF THE NETHER WATERS. See above, Introduction, §7(*a*).

A "house of Inaras" in the capital city of Hattusas is mentioned in the ritual of the annual AN.TAH.SHUM festival: Güterbock, JNES 19 (1960), 83, 86, 87 [iii. 18; iv. 4]. The king and queen repair to it at one stage of the proceedings.

(*c*) THE SECURING OF RAIN. See above, Introduction, §7(*b*).

A rite in honor of the rain god was likewise performed by the king at the annual AN.TAH.SHUM festival: Güterbock, *op. cit.*, 84, 87 [iv. 19; KUB XXX. 39, 3′]. It is mentioned also as having been observed at Ankuwa: KUB XXX. 73.

The "he" of the second clause is probably the king. This is a modification of his familiar role as rain bringer; see on this Frazer, *GB*, one-vol. ed., 85–87; P. Hadfield, *Traces of Divine Kingship in Africa* (1949), 19 ff. In Pap. Anastasi, the Hittite King quite naturally regards Ramses II as a rain bringer!

c. The Securing of Rain

(Then) Mount Zaliyanu bes[towed] her boons upon everyone.

(So nowadays,) when once she has vouchsafed rains on the city of Nerik, an official (goes forth) from the city of Nerik (and) proffers offertory bread (to her).

(Then) he besought Mount Zaliyanu for rain. . . . it. . . . proffers, and he . . . proffers . . . it . . . proffers . . .

III

THE MYTH OF THE FESTIVAL

(Second Version)

The Subjugation of the Dragon

He (i.e., the weather god) took to wife the daughter of a pauper.

She bore a son.
When he was grown up,
he took as his bride the daughter of the Dragon.

III. SECOND VERSION OF THE PURULI MYTH. This story is a conflate of several elements; and the significant thing is that, while all of them are foreign to formal religious myth, each is well represented in popular lore and folk tale.

First, there is once again the implication of the Dragon's gullibility – a trait which we have already seen to be characteristic of folk conceptions. The whole point of the story depends – though no commentator has yet observed it – on the Dragon's being duped by the mortal character of his daughter's suitor and thus not connecting him with his enemy, the weather god. Only on this basis is his ready delivery of the heart and eyes at all intelligible; for he would obviously not have delivered them, had he realized for what purpose they were being demanded. In this respect, therefore, our story may be regarded as but another variation of the Tale of the Stupid Ogre.

Second, there is the theft of the vital organs and their ultimate restoration. That this was drawn from the common stock of popu-

Thereupon the weather god instructed his son, saying,
"When you enter the house of your bride (to arrange the marriage),
demand from them my heart and eyes!"
So (the lad) went and demanded from them the heart,

lar legend is shown by the fact that a virtually perfect parallel occurs, as Porzig has pointed out (KlF 1 [1930], 379–86), in the second account given by Apollodorus (I 6 iii 7 f.) of the battle between Zeus and the monster Typhon.

> Zeus pelted Typhon at a distance with thunderbolts, and at close quarters struck him with an adamantine sickle, and as he fled pursued him as far as Mount Casius, which overhangs Syria. There, seeing the monster sore wounded, he grappled with him. But Typhon twined about him and gripped him in his coils, and wresting the sickle from him, severed the sinews of his hands and feet, and lifting him on his shoulders carried him through the sea to Cilicia and deposited him, on arrival, in the Corycian cave. Likewise he put away the sinews there also, hidden in a bearskin. . . . But Hermes and Aigipan stole the sinews and fitted them unobserved to Zeus. And having recovered his strength, Zeus suddenly from heaven riding in a chariot of winged horses, pelted Typhon with thunderbolts and pursued him to the mountain called Nysa.
>
> (Trs. Frazer)

That this is merely a local variation on a more widespread theme is evident from the fact that there actually exists an alternative version of the story, preserved by the poet Nonnus (*Dionysiaca* i 481 f.), in which the place of Hermes and Aigipan — who happen, significantly, to have been among the deities especially associated in cultus with the Corycian cave — is taken by the Phoenician hero Cadmus! We are therefore surely entitled to regard it as one of the many popular tales which must have been "familiar in men's mouths as household words" and upon which our Hittite author — or the tradition which he reproduces — drew readily in embellishing and elaborating the ancient ritual myth.

Lastly, there is the specification of the severed organs. In the Greek version, these are the sinews of Zeus' hands and feet. In the Hittite version, however, they are the weather god's heart and eyes. Now, at first sight, it might appear perfectly natural to select the latter organs as indicative of the source of vitality. The

They gave it to him.
Next, he demanded from them the eyes.
These too they gave to him.
Then he brought them to his father, the weather god.
The latter took possession of the heart and eyes.
When his body had (thus) been restored to its former state,

---

fact is, however, that the selection of them is informed not so much by natural observation as by folk belief. In many cultures, the heart is believed to be the seat of the "soul" or vital essence, and not merely the physical motor of the body. Thus, to cite but a few examples, the Ahts maintain that the soul of a man resides in his heart and head (G. M. Sproat, *Savage Life*, 173 f.); while the Caribs and the natives of the Nisas, both of whom believe that the individual possesses several "souls," assert that the chief of these is in the heart (J. G. Müller, *Amer. Urreligion*, 207 f.; A. E. Crawley, *The Idea of the Soul*, 120 f.). Similarly, the Ba-Huana of Africa and the Mexicans both have but one word for both "heart" and "soul" (Jorday and Joyce, JAI 36 [1906], 291; E. J. Payne, *History of the New World*, i, 468); while in Norse folk tales the identity of the two may be recognized at once in the many stories relating how giants or similar personages secreted their hearts in external objects in order to render themselves deathless (cf. G. W. Dasent, *Popular Tales from the Norse*, 47). It should be observed also that in ancient Egypt the heart possessed a spiritual as well as material aspect. In Hebrew, the expression "steal the heart" is used for getting a man into one's power (Genesis 31:20, 26).

As for the eyes, it may be suggested that the specification of these organs – not similarly specified in the parallel Greek version! – was motivated not only by their obvious importance but also by the influence of popular tales dealing with the blinding of the ogre. The ubiquity of such tales is well known; we need but mention the instances of Polyphemus (cf. J. Grimm, "Die Sage von Polyphem," in *Kleine Schriften*, iv. 428–62; W. Merry, *Odyssey*, 546–50; O. Hackmann, *Polyphemsage;* A. van Gennep, *Religions, moeurs et légendes*, 155–64; Bolte-Polivka, iii. 374–78; Frazer, *Apollodorus*, ii. 404 f.), of the Basque giant Tartaro (W. Webster, *Basque Legends*, 4), of the Cornish ogre of St. Michael's Mount (M. Yearsley, *The Folklore of Fairy Tale*, 42), of the monster blinded by the Red Indian hero Glooskap (*ibid.*), of the one-eyed giant treated likewise by the Celtic hero Fionn (Camp-

he went straightwayto the sea to do battle.
Having done battle,
he succeeded eventually in overcoming the Drag[on].
Howbeit, the son of the weather god
happened at the time to be (lodging as a guest) in the Dragon's house;
so he cried to his father aloft in the heavens,
"Include me too!
Show no compassion for me!"
Thereupon the weather god slew both the Drag[on] and his own son.

BOTH THIS AND THE PRECEDING ARE (VERSIONS OF THE MYTH) OF THE WEATHER GOD [AND] THE DR[AGON].

IV

THE RITUAL PROGRAM

by

Killas, Priest of the High God of Nerik

Procession and Installation of the Gods

When the gods go in procession to the city of Nerik, this is the procedure.

---

bell, *The Fions,* 207), and of parallel figures in the folklore of the Russians, Lapps, Indians, Africans, and Melanesians (Yearsley, *op. cit., loc. cit.*). The blinding of the Biblical Samson (Judges 16:21) will spring readily to mind.

IV. The Foregathering of the Gods is, as we have seen (*Baal,* §XXXVIII), a common element of the Seasonal Pattern. The best parallel in antiquity is afforded by the program of the Mesopotamian Akitu Festival; see especially the text published by Pinches in PSBA 1908; 84 f., Col. D, and cf. Pallis, *Akitu,* 131 ff.; Frankema, *Tâkultu.* But this is attested even in Hittite sources, for a portion of a New Year ritual (KUB XXXVI. 97), published by Otten (OLZ 1956: 101 ff.), describes how the gods then convene in the house of the weather god of Nerik. The purpose of the gathering is to determine destinies for the ensuing year. This is

In relation to the marshal, they make the first gods the last, and the last the first.[a]

A large-scale cereal offering is provided for the goddess Zalinus; while her husband, Zashapunas, ranks superior (even) to the high god of Nerik (himself).

The gods say to the marshal. "When we get to Nerik, in what order will we be installed?"

"Any of you," replies the marshal, "might potentially occupy the seat of honor.[b] So the sacristans are going to . . . . .[c] However, the sacristan who holds (the image of) Zalinuis is (in any case) to take a seat on the throne of honor[b] over the well."

All of the gods are (eventually) brought in; whereupon they indeed. . . . Of all the gods, Zashapunas of the city of

[a] I.e., those who join the procession last, walk in front? But the meaning is uncertain.

[b] Lit., "the diorite throne."

[c] Possibly, "compete."

---

likewise a feature of the Mesopotamian *Epic of Creation* and of the Canaanite *Myth of Baal* (see above, Baal, § XXXVIII).

The god ZASHAPUNAS (miswritten Za-ha-pu-na-as!) is again associated, as here, with the weather god of Nerik, as well as with the city of Kastama and Mount Zaliyanu, in the Sacrificial Decree of King Muwatallis, KUB VI 46, obv. i 67 (= Böhl, TT 50 [1916], 309). His *Hattic* character is further attested by the text, Bo. 468, 9′ (= Forrer, ZDMG 76 [1922], 193, No. 25: [d]Za-ah-puna-an!), where it is expressly prescribed that he is to be supplicated *in the Hattic tongue* (*hattili*). According to Laroche (RA 41 [1947], 78), his name means properly "the God" *par excellence*, being compounded of the Hattic prefix *z/ta* + the word *asha*, "god" + the suffix *-puna*.

The deity ZALINUIS is mentioned again in Bo. 3249 (= Forrer, ZDMG 76 [1922], 193, No. 12: [d]Za-li-nu!) in association with the weather god of Nerik and the goddess NIN.É.GAL. It is prescribed that she must be addressed *in the Hattic tongue*.

KASTAMA, which is associated with Nerik in KUB VI 45 i 62 ff. and *ibid.*, 46 ii 27 ff., has been identified by Hrozný (AOr. 7 [1935], 159) with ancient Kastabala (Strabo xii, 1. 534), in Cappadocia, near modern Ekbez. This, however, is uncertain.

TANIPIYA is tentatively identified by Laroche (JCS 1 [1947], 213) with the city of Ta-a-an-pi mentioned in KUB VIII 41 iii 10. Its location is unknown.

Kastama ranks supreme. Moreover, since Zalinuis is his consort, and Tazuwassi his concubine, these three personages are accorded quarters in the city of Tanipiya, an estate being granted them by the king. It consists of six acres of meadowland, one acre of orchard, a house and a threshing floor (apiece in all) three houses.

SO IT STANDS ON THE TABLET. I HAVE RELATED THE SACRED MATTER AS IT IS FOUND THERE.

2. A HITTITE RITUAL COMBAT

§1. A cardinal element of the Ritual Pattern is, as we have seen (Chapter Two, §§20–25), the staging of a mimetic combat between principals or teams representing respectively Old Year and New, Rain and Drought, Summer and Winter, Life and Death, etc.

This element was also present in Hittite usage, a description of such a combat being found, incorporated in a ritual program, in KUB XVII 95, iii 9–17. The text reads as follows:

§2.

(9) Then the men divide into two companies. They give them names.

(10) The one company they call the men of the city of Hatti;

(11) the other company they call the men of the city of Masa.

(12) The men of Hatti have bronzen weapons, but the men of Masa

(13) have weapons made out of reeds. Then they fight.

(14) The men of Hatti win. They take booty,

(15) and dedicate it to the god. Then they lift up the (image of) the god

(16) and lead it forth into the temple. They set up an altar;

(17) they offer a handful of bread; they pour a libation of beer; they set up sun disks.

§3. It will be observed that in accordance with the common process of historicization (cf. Chapter Two, §§21–22), the Ritual Combat is here taken to commemorate a battle between the Hittites and their neighbors the Masa, who are probably to be identified with the Classical Maeonians of eastern Lydia.[1] This represents a tendency which can be illustrated from both ancient and modern sources.

§4. It is significant that the defeated men of Masa are said to carry weapons made of reeds (l. 13), as against the "bronzen" weapons of their opponents (l. 12). In the popular performance, of course, this would have suggested no more than the relative impotence of the former. Considering, however, that in other parts of the world the antagonists are very often dressed specifically (*e.g.*, in greenery and furs, ivy and straw, respectively) to indicate their seasonal characters,[2] it is at least possible that the equipment of the Masa teams with reeds was originally motivated by the same symbolism, and that the bronzen weapons of their antagonists were a later substitution for similar symbolic accoutrement.

On the other hand, it is worth observing that in the English mummers' plays, the adversary (Beelzebub) is usually furnished with a rude club, in contrast to the iron weapon, or sword, of "St. George." As Lady Gomme has pointed out (FL 40 [1929], 292 f.), in folk tales of the "Jack the Giant Killer" type the giant is usually armed with a wooden club, and is defeated by the "Man with the Sword." This is intended to portray his ruder and more savage character. Our Hittite text may thus provide the prototype of a convention which has survived to this day!

NOTES

1. Goetze, *Kleinasien zur Hethiterzeit*, 23. The identification is questioned by Bilabel, *Geschichte Vorderasiens*, i, 267; and in *Kleinasien*,[1] 169, Goetze is less committal, saying only that the land of the Masa must have been situated somewhere "in N.W. Asia Minor, in the uncharted gap between Arzawa and the Kaska-territories." For the location of the Maeonians, cf. Strabo, xii 572, 576; xiii 625. In the *Iliad* (ii, 864) they are mentioned beside the Mysians, Phrygians, and Carians; while Herodotus asserts (i, 7; vii, 74) that the Lydians were anciently called Maeonians. The Masa are perhaps identical with the Ms mentioned in the Egyptian lists

of the allies of the Hittites at the battle of Kadesh (Breasted, *AR*, iii, §§306, 309) and possibly also with the Asianic Mash, mentioned beside Lydia in Genesis 10:22–23 and usually identified with Mons Masius=Tur Abdin.

2. Cf. Gomme, *Children's Singing Games*, 764 ff. In Styria and in the neighboring mountains of Carinthia, two teams, one dressed in winter clothes and armed with snowballs, the other with green summer hats and armed with pitchforks and scythes, used to engage in combat on St. Mary's Candlemas; *ibid.*, 769 (quoting Sartori, *Neueste Reise durch Oesterreich*, ii, 348). Similarly, in Sweden, "Summer" and "Winter," dressed respectively in greenery and furs, stage a set-to on May Day; *GB* iv (*The Dying God*), 254.

C. THE DISAPPEARING GOD TYPE

1. A HITTITE YULETIDE MYTH

(The Yuzgat Tablet)

§1. Another ancient Near Eastern myth which would seem to reflect elements of the standard Seasonal Ritual and which is accompanied by a detailed "order of service" is furnished by a Hittite cuneiform tablet acquired, in 1905, by the late A. H. Sayce at Yuzgat (Yozgad), some one hundred miles east of Ankara. This tablet, now in the Louvre,[1] probably came from the main Boghazköy archive. Only a portion of it has been preserved, two entire columns (more than 100 lines) being missing in the middle. Nevertheless, sufficient remains to make out its general purport and character.

A. SYNOPSIS

§2. The myth deals with the ravages of a malevolent being called Hahhimas, who has been paralyzing the earth. A goddess,[2] whose name is broken away but who appears to be fearful especially of the fate which may lie in store for living creatures, appeals to the Supreme God to lend the aid of his sons in relieving the situation. The Supreme God replies, however, that neither his own nor the goddess' sons have yet given any indication that they will indeed revive any men or beasts that might be slain, seeing that the monster has already laid hands on the vegetation and dried up the waters without resistance. Nevertheless, the goddess importunes him in his capacity of genius of the wind to arrest Hahhimas' further depredations (2–11).

When, however, Hahhimas proceeds to assail not only the vegetation and the waters but also the livestock, the goddess' fears mount apace, and she again importunes the Supreme God to intervene. How, she asks pointedly, can the monster be expected to respect the lives of other people's children, when his parents are in fact so complacent about his nefarious conduct (12–20)?

At this, the Supreme God is indeed stirred to action and orders the sun to be summoned to put an end to the havoc. But the sun cannot be located. The Supreme God declares, however, that his body actually feels warm, so that the sun cannot have perished, but must be in the offing and simply have met with some mishap. He therefore orders the god ZABABA to go in search of him, evidently to rescue him from any possible assailant. But Zababa is seized by Hahhimas.

Thereupon the Supreme God orders the Genius of the Fields (LAMA) to go forth and rescue Zababa. But he too is seized.

The Supreme God then sends for TELIPINU, god of vegetation and fertility, to revive the earth by direct action. But he too falls prey to Hahhimas (21–31).

His sons having thus come to grief, the Supreme God now summons the Great Goddess (MAH), one of the Gulses — Hittite counterparts of the Fates or Norns — who presides over procreation and childbirth and determines destinies. As an escort he proposes to give her "the brothers of Hasamilis," a god who is mentioned in other Hittite texts as possessing the power of screening his protégés from sight in moments of peril. But Hahhimas, flushed with triumph, retorts by telling him that he is "losing his grip" and will eventually have to capitulate and cede the kingship of heaven. The proposed escorts, he adds, will prove unavailing. Nevertheless, the Supreme God summons those escorts and warns Hahhimas that, far from having "lost his grip," he (the Supreme God) is in fact firmly entrenched. Moreover, he adds, even if Hahhimas is able to immobilize the *hands and feet* of his victims, he will never succeed in impairing or eluding the (all-seeing) *eyes* of the Supreme God! (32–41).

Undismayed, Hahhimas rejoins that all the Supreme God will in fact see with those eyes is that his own and the goddess' sons [will perish], whereupon he (Hahhimas) intends to carry his attacks to heaven itself! The Supreme God, he adds — though the passage is incomplete and obscure — can then try by his own unaided efforts to save his protégés! (42–44).

It is evident that a combat ensued between Hahhimas and the Supreme God, and the former's mocking words may be read as the typical taunting challenge which preceded such encounters in the Ancient Near East (see Commentary on *Baal,* §v4).

The rest of the story has not been preserved, but from the fact that it was recited, as we shall see, at a ceremony in which thank offerings were presented to the sun and to Telipinu, it is apparent that those gods were eventually restored, and Hahhimas therefore discomfited.

§3. After a gap of two columns, the text continues (on the reverse of the tablet) with the description of a ritual ceremony in joint honor of the sun and Telipinu. The myth, we are informed, is duly rehearsed and the rogation recited, "when(ever) the sun and Telipinu press hard" — that is, whenever the situation described in the story happens to repeat itself and the absence of those two gods proves especially disastrous. On the other hand, it is added, whenever the sun bestows his benefits on anyone, he is to be rewarded with an offering of nine sheep, though in the case of a poor man, one alone will suffice (rev. 8–12).

A colophon (13) defines the myth as a "rogation to the sun and to Telipinu," and it is said (3) to have been composed (or rehearsed) by a woman named Annanas.[3]

A kind of appendix enumerates the implements required and the offerings presented at the ceremony, and also describes the manner of its performance. Two tables are set up, the one for the sun and the other for Telipinu (23–33). Telipinu receives, in addition to food and drink, various bronze utensils, including — appropriately enough — a hoe. A lamb and a goat are offered to the two gods jointly (25–33; 46–48).

The ceremonies commence at nightfall (1; 36), and continue, after a break, at dawn (40). They are attended by male and female magicians (2; 37), and are accompanied by the recital of spells (37–38; 41). At one point (19), water drawn from three wells is introduced; at another (36–37), fire is taken from a brazier and set (at nightfall) before the god.

B. INTERPRETATION

§4. The primary occasion of our text is easily determined. We note at once that the deities with whom it is mainly concerned are the god of vegetation (Telipinu) and the sun, and that they are joint recipients of a single act of thanksgiving.[4] From this we may infer initially that it was designed for a solar date associated in some crucial way with the agricultural year. Such a date would have been, most naturally, one of the solstices or equinoxes.

§5. The decisive clue is furnished by the identification of Hahhimas, the villain of the myth, whom the two gods must eventually have subdued. He is described as a being who (a) paralyzes the earth (obv. 8, 12, 20); (b) impedes the flow of the waters (obv. 8); (c) afflicts man and beast alike (obv. 5, 12); (d) seizes all the gods of fertility, i.e., brings agriculture to a standstill (obv. 26, 31); (e) lays hold on his victim's hands and feet (obv. 40); and (f) operates at a time when the sun cannot be readily located (obv. 11–14), but is eventually overcome by its heat. Moreover, his ravages seem to proceed in successive and intensifying stages: he first invades the waters (obv. 8); then assails plants and livestock (obv. 12); and finally poses a threat to man and to the grain sown in the earth (obv. 13). Obviously, then, *he is none other than Jack Frost;* and this is further indicated by the fact that his name actually means Stiffness,[5] and is formed on a pattern common especially in nouns denoting meteorological phenomena.[6] Hence, whatever other use may eventually have been made of it in private and domestic rites, our text was clearly designed in the first instance for the celebration of what is known as Yuletide, culminating at the winter solstice, when the sun was believed to head back from the nether regions, acquire new strength, and break the grip of cold and frost, and when the ousted or absent spirit of vegetation was thought to begin his journey back to the earth or be "reborn."[7]

§6. On this basis, everything falls immediately into place. The general theme of the myth, with its adoration of the sun and the genius of vegetation (Telipinu), accords at once with what elsewhere characterizes this season of the year. Thus, in Mesopotamia, it was at the winter solstice that Tammuz was thought to return from the netherworld;[8] while in Egypt that date was regarded as the birthday of Osiris;[9] in imperial Rome, as that of the Unconquered Sun (*Sol Invictus*),[10] in turn identified with Mithra;[11] and among the Nabataeans, of the Adonis-like god, Dusares.[12] In Hellenistic times, January 6 — the older calendar date of the solstice[13]

— was recognized as the birthday of Aion[14] and the Festival of the New Age,[15] while in Christianity, the winter solstice became the natal day of "the Light of the World."[16]

§7. The important role of the Great Goddess (Mah) likewise becomes clear. Elsewhere in Hittite literature, she is identified explicitly with the patroness of procreation (NIN. TUD).[17] What this character mythologizes, therefore, is the regeneration of nature by the awakening of sexual energies in springtime, or after the return of the sun — a concept represented on the ritual plane by the familiar rites of sexual license at seasonal festivals.[18] At the same time, she is the direct mythological counterpart not only of Ishtar, Isis, Aphrodite (Astarte), and Demeter in sister versions of the story of the ousted and restored spirit of fertility, but, even more significantly, of Eileithyia, goddess of birth, who is associated, in Greek myth, with the revival of that deity,[19] and the figure of whom was indeed recognized by later astronomers beside Capricorn, the zodiacal sign of the Yuletide season![20]

§8. The element of the search likewise acquires added significance when it is observed that this was a feature not only of the myths but also of the rituals of this season. It was, for instance, one of the leading ingredients of the corresponding Festival of Isis, celebrated at the winter solstice.[21]

§9. Scarcely less arresting, though admittedly more ambiguous, are certain indications in the ritual portion of the text.

(a) At one point in the proceedings, fire is taken from a brazier and placed before the image of the god (obv. 36). This is followed immediately by the chanting of spells (37–38). Hence it must possess some magical significance relevant to the purpose of the ceremony as a whole; and since that ceremony is in fact addressed to the sun and bound up with a myth relating to his "recovery," we are reminded at once of the ceremonial kindling of fire which is elsewhere associated with solstitial festivals.[22] The practice is most familiar to us, of course, from the midsummer and midwinter fires which are lit on hilltops[23] or carried across the fields[24] in European popular observances, and from its survival in the Christmas candles[25] and in the name "Holyday of Lights" by which Epiphany (i.e., the ancient festival of the winter solstice) is known in the Greek Church. Its remoter antiquity, however, is well attested and generally acknowledged. Classical authors tell us in several passages of the ritual lustration of the fields by fire at seasonal festivals,[26] and it has been recognized by most modern scholars that the well-known story of how Demeter and Hecate roamed the earth, with torches in their hands, in search of the lost Persephone, is simply the mythic counterpart of such a ritual usage.[27] Furthermore, we have references to the kindling of fires at such solstitial festivals as the ancient Indic Mahavrata[28] and the Isia of Hellenistic Egypt;[29] and it is perhaps not without significance that, according to the Assyriologist S. H. Langdon, as far back as the third millennium B.C., the Sumerians of Nippur called the pertinent month by a name, viz., *kan-kan-e,* which means properly "(Month of) the Festival of Lighting Braziers"![30]

(b) In the list of objects required for the ceremony, mention is made of three jars of water drawn from three wells (rev. 19–20). To be sure, they are enumerated alongside of other sacrificial and purely utilitarian material, but it is not improbable that they were designed for a special magical act, since water drawn from three wells (or springs) is indeed mentioned elsewhere in magical recipes.[31] In that case, we are reminded at once of the ceremonial drawing of water which figures prominently in solstitial rituals in many parts of the world. Epiphanius tells us, for instance, that such drawing of water from the Nile took place in Egypt at the festival on January 6;[32] and a myth of that festival, recorded by Plutarch, says that the birth of Osiris was then revealed by a miraculous voice to a certain Pamylês while he was in the act of drawing sacred water.[33] Similarly, Babylonian sources prescribe that water be poured out before the cattle on the new moon of the relevant month (Kislev), and before Ereshkigal, goddess of the netherworld on the sixth and fifteenth days of that month;[34] while the statement of Lucian[35] that sacred water was imported into the sanctuary at Hierapolis twice yearly (viz., at a summer and a winter festival?) may also be pertinent in this connection. The importance of water at solstitial festivals (e.g., at the ancient Indian Mahavrata) has been noted by many observers,[36] and a Christian transmutation of the time-honored practice may be seen in the rite of the Syriac, Coptic, Armenian, and Greek churches of consecrating waters for baptism at the

Feast of Epiphany.[37] Moreover, rites involving water (performed by women) still figure in the popular celebration of that festival in Serbia,[38] Palestine,[39] and other parts.[40]

(c) The ceremonies begin at dusk (rev. 1, 36) and culminate at dawn (40). This too accords with the practice at solstitial and equinoctial festivals. Thus, according to Epiphanius[41] and Macrobius,[42] the winter solstice was celebrated in Roman Egypt by a gathering of the faithful in an underground chamber during the night of December 24–25. In the gray of dawn they emerged carrying the image of a man child (prototype of the Holy Babe of Catholic ceremonies) and proclaiming, "The Virgin has given birth! Light will increase!" Similar rites in a cavern are mentioned by the prophet Ezekiel in connection with the annual weeping for Tammuz, and there too they are associated with an adoration of the rising sun.[43] Again, the birthday of Aion, as described by Lydus, began on January 5, and since that god was said to have been born only on the sixth, the celebration must have commenced at nightfall.[44] It was likewise at night that the "mysteries" of Attis[45] and Dionysus began;[46] while at Eleusis, an all-night vigil on Boedromion 19 was taken to represent the wandering of Demeter through the darkness in search of Persephone.

(d) The composer (or redactor) of our text is a woman (rev. 3). True, she is known also as the composer (or redactor) of other Hittite ritual texts. Here, however, she says explicitly — speaking in the first person — that she herself has performed the rite and cried on the god (rev. 3–10). Now, admittedly, the point cannot be pressed unduly, but it is perhaps worth pointing out that in ceremonies of the type we have been discussing a major role is in fact usually played by women. Thus, the rites of the Greek seasonal festival at Thesmophoria, as well as of several similar festivals, were confined exclusively to women, and at the Eleusinian Mysteries, the all-night vigil was kept by women only.[47] In the Attis cult, both in its earlier Phrygian form[48] and later, after it had been introduced into Greece,[49] the official personnel consisted primarily of women; while the mock burial and subsequent disinterment of Adonis was performed, says Plutarch, by women;[50] and in the fifteenth idyll of Theocritus, it is a woman who sings the dirge (albeit as the diva at a public "show"), and it is women that are said to rise at daybreak and commit the "corpse" of that god to the waters.[51] Similarly, it was women who wept for Osiris at the annual ceremonies in Egypt;[52] and its was likewise women that bewailed Ta'uz, i.e., Tammuz, in the medieval ceremonies at Harran.[53]

A modern parallel may also be cited. In Roumania, on the Monday before Assumption (August 15),[54] groups of girls go out from the villages, carrying under a pall a miniature coffin in which is deposited a clay image called the Kalojan. Strewn with mint, basil, and other aromatic herbs, the coffin is subsequently interred, and on that and the following day the girls sing over it such dirges as these:

Jan, Kalojan,
as our tears drop, so may the rain drop,
night and day,
to fill the ditches and water the grass.

Jan, Kalojan,
your mother has been seeking you,
broken-hearted,
through deep woods and glades.
Jan, Kalojan,
your mother is weeping for you
with searing tears.[55]

Kalojan — i.e., *kalos Ioannes* (beautiful John) — is here simply a Christian substitution for the more ancient *kalos Adonis* (beautiful Adonis),[56] so that the ceremony is a direct survival of the age-old seasonal wailings by women.

This feature of the seasonal ritual, it should be added, is likewise caught up in the mythological portion of our text in the role assigned to the Great Goddess; for in addition to personifying the regeneration of sexual energies (see above), that role also represents on the mythic plane the part played by women in the punctual ceremonies.[57]

§10. Our myth has all the earmarks of a liturgical "book of words" rather than of a purely literary composition. It is defined expressly in the colophon (rev. 13) as being itself the text of the ritual rogation (*mugawar*) of the sun-god and Telipinu, and such rogations (also called *mugessar*) constitute a distinct genre of Hittite liturgical literature.[58] Moreover, the style of the piece seems of itself to indicate that it was but the script for a performance. It is noteworthy, for instance, that the crucial words, "Then said the weather god," are omitted before the summons to the Genius of the Fields (obv. 27), to Telipinu (29), and to the Great Goddess (32). In a purely narrative text, these words would have been indispensable, but in the script of a drama, where the action was in any case presented visibly, they would naturally have been discarded.

Again, when Hahhimas threatens the Supreme God with imminent discomfiture, the words he uses mean literally, "You will no longer keep hold on the chalice" (obv. 35–36), and this turn of expression would have been far more readily understood and have produced a far greater effect upon the audience if the myth had been acted out, and the Supreme God portrayed, as he often is on cylinder seals, holding in his hands the chalice of tribute customarily proffered to kings.[59]

§11. The ultimate provenience of our myth cannot at present be determined. It is probable, however, that — like so much else in Hittite religion — it came originally from the Hattians, that element of the older population of Asia Minor whom the invading "Hittites" subdued, but whose culture they so largely absorbed. The names of the Supreme God, the sun-god, the Genius of the Fields, and the Great Goddess are all written ideographically (viz., ^{d}ISKUR, ^{d}LAMA, and ^{d}MAH), so that they might easily represent Hattic rather than Hittite deities; while Telipinu himself possesses a Hattic name, and Hahhimas is treated throughout as a common noun, i.e., a mere personification, never being preceded by the sign of deity. In the Commentary we have indicated what the original Hattic names may have been. In addition, it may be pointed out, in regard to the god called Zababa, that while in *Hittite* (and Sumerian) texts, he is usually a god of war, his *Hattic* equivalent was Wurunkatte, which means properly "King of the Land."[60] The appeal to him would therefore have been far more intelligible and apropos, if he had in fact been so designated in the original version of the text.

NOTES

1. AO 4703. According to E. Laroche's inventory (RHA 59 [1950], 105 ff. the texts KUB XXIII 121 and XXIV 44 are related in some way to our myth.

2. The identity of the gods and goddesses mentioned in the myth is discussed more fully in our Commentary.

3. She is mentioned again as a composer or redactor of ritual texts in KUB XXX 41 i.3, iv.6; 51 i 6, 22; 58.7.

4. Note that in the Canaanite *Poem of Baal*, appeal is likewise made to the sun to help locate the absent god of fertility (I AB iv, 1 ff.) and the sun is subsequently rewarded for her co-operation (I AB, col. vi). Similarly, in the Homeric *Hymn to Demeter*, it is the sun who reveals the rape and present whereabouts of Persephone (62 ff.; cp. Ovid, *Fasti*, iv. 683); while in the Canaanite *Poem of the Gracious Gods*, the sun receives "sacrifices in acknowledgment of favors" (25–27).

5. Cp. Hittite *hahh-*, "be stiff" (Goetze, *Tunnawi*, 84 f.). The name is thus semantically parallel to Frost (*frigus*), which likewise derives from a root meaning primarily "be stiff" (cf. Greek, Latin *rigeo*, etc.)

6. Cp. *ekun-imas*, "cold"; *want-emas*, "heat"; *lalukkimas*, "lightning"; *teth-imas;* "thunder"; etc.

7. The action of the story covers the season known to the Romans as *bruma*, viz., from November 24 until December 24; see E. Norden, *Geburt des Kindes*, 18, n. 4. Hahhimas is thus a personification of Vergil's *brumale frigus* (*Aen.* vi. 205).

8. ZA 6:244, lines 52–54. (The tablet dates from 138 B.C.).

9. Plutarch, *De Is. et Os.*, 12. 355 E; Epiphanius, *haer.*, Li, 22. 8 ff.

10. Wissowa, *Rel u. Kultus d. Römer*,[2] (1912), 367. F. Cumont, "Le *Natalis Invicti*" in CRAIBL, 1911. Cf. also Augustine, *Sermo* 190.

11. Relevant texts in CIL I, p. 410. Cf. also F. Cumont, *Textes et monuments figurés relatifs aux Mystères de Mithra* (1890), i. 342, n. 4.

12. Cf. K. Holl, in *Sitzb. d. Berl. Akad.*, 1917. 428; Weber, in ARW 18 (1919), 330 ff. In Waddington, *Inscr. de la Syrie*, 2312, Dusares is styled "Great Unconquered God," specifically identifying him with Sol Invictus; cf. Norden, *op. cit.*, 27, n. 2.

13. As Norden has pointed out (*op. cit.*, 39), the date of the winter solstice recedes by one day every 128 years. Hence, the celebration of it attested in the third century B.C. for Dec. 24–25 would have taken place in the second millennium B.C. around January 6. The festivals on the latter date are thus survivals of the older usage.

14. Lydus, *De mensibus* IV, i. p. 64.12 W; Epiphanius, *Panarion* 51; Macrobius, *Sat.*, I. 18, 9; Cosmas Indicopleustes, in *PG* 38. 464.

15. See fully O. S. Rankin, *The Origins of the Festivals of Hanukkah* (1930).

16. See L. Duchesne, *Christian Worship*,[3] tr. McClure (1920), 261 f. The winter solstice became Christmas by order of Pope

Julius I, between 354 and 360. The transmutation was adopted by the Greek Church in 378. Cf. also A. Tille, *Yule and Christmas* (1899). The Christian view is well epitomized in Philip le Grève's famous hymn, *In Nativitate Christi: Festa dies igitur*/ (*Mundo salus redditus*)/ *In qua sol exoritur* / *Qui mundum replet lumine* / . . . *Gaudeamus igitur*/ (*Mundo salus redditur*) / *In Sole qui dictur* / *Verus Deus in homine.*/ *Mundo salus redditur* / *Christo nato de Virgine* ("Salvation to the world returns! / Let then this day be festive bright / Whereon the sun doth rise again / to bathe the world entire in light! / . . . O let us in that Sun rejoice/ (Salvation comes again this morn!) True God in human form yclept,/ Messiah from a Virgin born!" [tr. T. Gaster.])

The winter festival marked, of course, the end of a crisis which had begun in summer, and in many cases the demise or withdrawal of the god of fertility was likewise marked by a festival. Apart from the familiar wailings for Tammuz in June–July, Plutarch informs us (*De Is. et Os.*, 69) that the Attis cult centered in the figure of a dying and reviving god of vegetation, recognized *two* sacred moments during the year: "the one when he fell asleep, and the other when he awoke"; and this testimony is corroborated by an inscription of the second century B.C. (CIA II, 1.622; cf. Hepding, *Attis,* 79 f.), in which mention is made expressly of "*both* the Attis festivals." Other writers mention only a single festival at the vernal equinox, at which the demise and mimetic burial of Attis were followed, after three days, by his "resurrection." The same thing (though with a different date) is reported also of the cult of Adonis. The testimony of Plutarch et al., however, as well as our own common sense, should show us that the single festival was but an economical telescoping of two occasions properly falling at different periods of the year, the celebration of the god's re-emergence being then introduced, for reasons of convenience, consolation, and dramatic effect, by a preliminary ululation.

17. See Commentary *in loc.*

18. See Chapter Two, §27. Note, too, that among the Southeastern Bantus, "sexual intercourse is part of certain magic rites which are performed in times of trouble in the life of the tribe or the clan." H. Gunod, *The Life of a South African Tribe* (Neufchâtel, 1913), i. 153, 292; cf. also Petersson, *Chiefs and Gods,* 220.

19. Cf. Boll, *Sphaera,* 212 ff.; Norden, *op. cit.,* 20; Allen-Sikes-Halliday, *Homeric Hymns,*[2] 215 f. Her Latin name was *Lucina;* cf. Vergil, *Ecl.* iv. 10; Horace, *Carm. Saec.,* 13 ff.

20. In Sumerian calendars, Capricorn is the regnant constellation of the first decan of Kislev: Langdon, *Menologies,* 8. Cf. also Pliny, *N. H.,* xviii. 220 . . . *bruma Capricorni a.d. viii Kal. Jan. fere;* Julian, *Or.,* 4.156 A.

21. Cf. Moret, *Mise à mort,* 18, n. 2. Insofar as the search for the sun is concerned, the basic idea is well illustrated by a story

in Procopius (*De bell. got*, ii. 15) that the inhabitants of Thule, deprived of sunlight for thirty-five days in succession, once sent messengers to the highest point in the area to ascertain if the sun would soon return. On being reassured, they held a festival.

22. See Grimm, *DM*, 509 ff.; Mannhardt, *WFK*, 477–566; Frazer, *GB*, X.246 ff.

23. The custom is fully documented in the works cited in the previous note; cf. also: F. C. de Khantz, *De ritu ignis in natali S. Ioannis Baptisti accensi* (Vienna, 1759); P. Sartori, *Sitte und Brauch*, iii. 226, n. 26; Wright-Lones, *Brit. Calendar Customs*, ii (1938), 57–60, 85; T. F. Dexter, *Fire Worship in Britain* (1931). It is by no means confined to Europe; cf. Westermarck, *Pagan Survivals in Mohammedanism*, 148, 169 ff.; F. Corjon, "Les rites du feu et de l'eau chez les Berbères du Maroc," in *Bull. Publ. Maroc.* 39 (1953), 199–208; Th. Bent, *Sacred City of the Ethiopians* (1893), 53, 83–84.

24. Frazer, *GB* x. 107 ff., 339 ff. For the practice in Germany, cf. U. Jahn, *Die deutschen Opfergebrauche bei Ackerbau und Viehzucht* (1884), 85 ff., 97 ff.

25. Probably also in the lights of the Jewish festival of Hanukkah, celebrated at the same time of year; cf. J. Morgenstern, in HUCA 20 (1947), 1 ff.

26. E.g., Tibullus, I, ii. 61 (*lustravit taedis*); Frazer, *Fasti of Ovid* iii, 374 ff.; Farnell, *Cults*, iii. 103. Such torchlight processions were a feature of the Attis cult (Hepding, *Attis*, 165) and of the Greek mysteries; cf. Vassits, *Die Fackel im Kultus. und Kunst der Griechen* (1900); Diels. *Sib. Blätter*, 47 f.

27. Homeric *Hymn to Demeter*, 48, 61; cf. Allen-Sikes-Halliday, *op. cit.*, 131 f.

28. A. Hillebrandt, in *Romanische Forschungen* 5 (1887), 229; O. Schrader, in ERE ii, 48 a.

29. A. Moret, *Gli Dei dell'Egitto* (1945), 83.

30. *Babylonian Menologies*, 135.

31. E.g., (a) Menander, *Inc.* 530 Koch, ex Clem. Alex., *Strom.*, iv. 27; (b) a late Hebrew charm from Mossul: R. C. Thompson, in PSBA 1906, 104, No. 12; (c) on June 24, in Germany: Hartlieb, *Anh. Abergl.*, c. 55–57, quoted by Grimm, *DM*,[4] 487; (d) in some parts of Germany, if a new mother has no milk, an old woman soaks a wheat cake in water drawn from three wells: *Zeitschr. f. Volkskunde*, 4. 146. Similarly, at Meshed, in Iran, malign influences are averted by filling a bottle with water drawn from *seven mills:* H. Massé, *Persian Beliefs and Customs* 91954, 314.

32. *Haer.* LI, 30. 3; Chabas, *Calendrier*, 69. Cf. also Servius on Vergil, *Aen.* 4. 512.

33. *De Is. et Os.*, xii, 355 E.

34. Langdon, *op. cit.*, 138.

35. De dea Syria, c. 13.

36. Cf. Hillebrandt, *op. cit.*, 299; Schrader, ERE ii, 48 a.

37. The rite is as old as Chrysostom, who mentions the special importation of the water at Epiphany: II 369 ed. Montfaucon. In Russia, it was customary until recent times to bless the waters of the Neva at St. Petersburg at a grandiose ceremony. Those of the Don and Volga were also blessed.

38. Frazer, *GB,* X. 261.

39. Dalman, *Arbeit u. Sitte in Palästina,* I/i, 278.

40. Grimm, *DM,*[4] 486; F. Nork, *Festkalender* (= Scheible's *Kloster,* vii [1847], 420 ff). On the custom in general, see H. Pfannenschmied, *Das Weihwasser im heidnischen und Christlichen Kultus* (1869), 79 f.; Holl, *op. cit.,* 435 ff.

41. *Loc. cit.*

42. *Sat.* I 18, 10; cf. Norden, *op. cit.,* 25.

43. Ezekiel 8:7–16. The prophet may, in fact, be satirizing the "heathen" procedure when he says (v. 12) that the rite was performed in darkness because the participants maintained that "Yahweh doth not see us; Yahweh hath forsaken the earth!"

44. *De mensibus,* iv. i, p. 64, 12 W; cf. Norden, *op. cit.,* 33 f.

45. Firmicus Maternus, *De errore profan. relig.,* XXII. 1–3.

46. Sophocles, *Antigone* 1146 f.; Euripides, *Bacchae* 485–86; 862 ff.; Aristophanes, *Frogs* 340; Vergil, *Georgica* IV. 521.

47. Allen-Sikes-Halliday, *op. cit.,* 120 f.

48. A. Furtwängler, *Die Sammlung Sabouroff,* ad Pl. 137.

49. CIA II, 1.610; Ropp in Roscher's *Lex.,* ii. 1656.

50. *Alcibiades,* c. 18.

51. Lines 132 f. The point of these lines lies in the fact that the effigy of the fertility spirit is usually consigned to the waters.

52. Cf. Faulkner, in JEA 22 (1936), 132; Davies-Gardiner, *Tomb of Amenemhet* (1915), 42.

53. En-Nedim, quoted in D. Chwolson, *Die Ssabier* (1856), ii. 27.

54. The mourning for the absent lord of fertility persists, of course, throughout the summer, so this early date need cause no surprise. Plutarch says distinctly (*De E apud Delph.,* ix, 289 A–C) that Dionysus was bewailed for a full three months.

55. M. Beza, *Paganism in Roumanian Folklore* (1928), 27 ff.

56. Such, at least, is Beza's explanation, and it may be supported by the fact that the idol is addressed not only as Kalojan, but also specifically as Jan. Moreover, precisely the same substitution is made at the Maltese spring festival; see R. Wuensch, *Das Frühlingsfest der Insel Malta* (1902), 49–57. It should be observed, however, that the name of the puppet is given by other authorities as Scalojan, and this would be a good Romanian word meaning "drought, dearth"; see E. Fischer, "Paporuda and Scalojan," in *Globus* 93 (1908), 13–16.

57. The reason why women play so prominent a role in these ceremonies is twofold. First, the ceremonies are mock funerals, and at funerals the "keening" was led by women; see the Commen-

tary on *Aqhat* §XXXIII. Note that in modern Anatolia, rites of mourning take place in the courtyard of the deceased's house and are attended by professional wailing women and relatives; the public exercises, which take place at the actual interment, are quite distinct: W. M. Ramsay, *Asianic Elements in Greek Civilization*[3] (1928), 93 ff. Second, these ceremonies are at the same time agricultural, and in ancient and primitive cultures, women play a dominant role in agriculture: Frazer, *GB* vii. 113; *idem., Aftermath,* 379–84; Jane Harrison, *Prolegomena,*[3] 272; Allen-Sikes-Halliday, *op. cit.*, 165.

58. Cf. O. R. Gurney, in AAA 27. 45 ff.; *idem., The Hittites* (1952), 189. A *mugessar* to Telipinu is mentioned specifically in KUB XXIV, 2 i 5 f.: "Go, invoke (*mugai*) our lord Telipinu."

59. See Commentary *in loc.*

60. Cf. Laroche, *Dieux,* 37 f.

A. MYTH

Mortification

Obverse

2–11: The earth is in the grip of Jack Frost (Hahhimas). A goddess, who is interested especially in saving human and animal life, entreats the Supreme God to lend the aid of his sons in arresting the disaster.

2–11: The beginning of our text is missing, so that we are plunged *in medias res.* A goddess is speaking to the supreme god. She refers to "*your* sons," and the god replies by referring in turn to "my sons . . . and your sons," and by observing that both seem thus far to have been quite indifferent to the ravages of Jack Frost (Hahhimas). From this it is clear that what the goddess has been requesting is that the supreme god's sons join her own in a combined *démarche* against the monster; and this interpretation is supported by the fact that later on (line 42), when Jack Frost refers to the discomfiture of those divine beings who have opposed him, he implies that the sons of more than one person are involved, for in calling them "your sons" he uses the plural form of the possessive pronoun.

The name of the goddess is imperfectly preserved. It is written ideographically, and begins with the element NIN, "Lady." From the dramatic point of view, she represents the quality of motherly compassion, since she is apparently concerned first and foremost with the resuscitation of man and beast and refers (line 13) to

The Supreme God replies that neither his own nor the goddess' sons have yet shown any sign that they would indeed revive man or beast, should these be slain by Jack Frost. On the contrary, the monster has thus far assailed vegetation and water supply without resistance.

The goddess begs him, however, in his capacity of genius of the wind, to prevent Jack Frost from extending his attacks to the "grassy alps" (yaylas), *the one potential place of refuge for man and beast during the hot summer which is yet to come.*

* * *

[Says the goddess . . . : "Lend me the aid of] your sons . .

---

the potential victims of Jack Frost's further assaults as "children of the heart" (Hittite DUMU MESH *kar-ta-as;* cf. Akkad. *mar libbi*), i.e., "dearly beloved children."

The name of the supreme god is likewise written ideographically, viz., ^{d}ISHKUR, which means properly "weather god." In Hattic, he was called TARU. Eight sons of this god are mentioned in another Hittite text (KUB XXXIII. 66 iii 7), but in an obscure context.

The wind and the supreme weather god are usually one and the same, what appears as the former (Hittite *huwant-*) in some texts (e.g., KUB VI 46 iii 49; XXIV 2 ii 17) appearing as the latter in duplicate copies (e.g., KUB VI 45 iii 10; XXIV 1 iv 16). Hence the most natural interpretation of our passage would be that, the god having proved lukewarm to the proposal that he should dispatch his sons to bring relief, the goddess importunes him to do so by his own direct efforts. What she invites him to do is highly significant: he is to let his "soothing words" (Hittite *wa-ar-su-la-as* INIM.MESH) go forth and thereby deter Jack Frost from paralyzing "the waters of the mountains, woodlands (and) leas." Now, "word (voice) of the weather god" (KA. ^{d}ISHKUR) is a common expression for thunder, and the early spring thunders are regarded as a presage of returning rainfall and fertility (cp. *Aqhat,* §xxvii). It is these thunders, therefore, that he is begged to send. Moreover, the "woodlands and leas of the mountains" denote, in all likelihood, the slopes of the Taurus, which are in fact covered with forests of oak and fir, and also the numerous *yaylas* or " 'grassy alps' with abundant water, to which the villagers and nomads move with their flocks during the summer months" (*Enc. Brit.,*[11] ii. 537a). The thought is, therefore, that if Jack Frost be permitted to extend his ravages to these, he will imperil life not only during the winter but also during the

[Say]s the Supreme God to the goddess . . . : "Tell me this: suppose a human being were to be killed, suppose an ox or a sheep were to be killed; what indication are either your or my sons giving that they would (indeed) bring it back to life? Why, Jack Frost has (already) paralyzed the entire land and dried up the waters! Jack Frost is the boss!"

(Nevertheless), she kept repeating to her brother, the wind: "(Yes, but) the waters of the mountains, the woodlands, the leas — go forth (with) thy soothing words, let him not (also) paralyze those!"

12–20: But Jack Frost continues his attacks and now indeed assails the livestock, posing a threat to the children of

---

ensuing summer! The wind is besought to prevent this from happening.

An alternative interpretation is, however, also possible. Since the person who addresses the wind is not specified, it may be that this sentence is a continuation of the supreme god's reply to the goddess and that what he tells her is that Hahhimas, flushed with triumph, is now flinging challenges at the wind to arrest his progress!

Concerning "Jack Frost" (Hahhimas), see Introduction.

12–20: The translation of this passage is tentative, but it is in any case clear that Jack Frost is represented as stepping up his attacks and now assailing living creatures. Thereby he poses a threat to men's own "dear children" (lit., "children of the heart") as well as to the prospective harvests. This interpretation likewise lends added point to what immediately follows; for the reference to the indifference of the monster's own father and mother implies that they, as parents, show so little concern for other people's children that their wayward "juvenile delinquent" of a son can scarcely be blamed for following suit!

21–31: The name of the sun(-god) is written ideographically, viz., ^{d}UTU. In Hattic, he was called ESTAN.

The fact that he cannot be readily located indicates that the action of the story takes place *in winter*, when the sun was believed to be in the netherworld.

ZABABA is an ideographic writing for the name of a warrior god, frequently mentioned in Hittite texts (cf. Laroche, *Dieux*, 16). Such a god might readily be expected to deliver the sun from any malevolent power that might be halting its return. In Hattic, however, he was known specifically as WURUNKATTE, "King

men and to the yet unripened grain. Thereupon the goddess pointedly reminds the Supreme God that thus far Jack Frost has been given no indication that his own divine parents are other than indifferent to what he is doing to other people's offspring!

He had (now) paralyzed plants, oxen, sheep, hounds, and pigs. But would he [not] also paralyze the dear children (of men and) the grain? If once he entrenched himself within their bodies, would he not also paralyze them? . . .

So (again) she went to the Supreme God and said: "In regard to what has been happening here, Jack Frost might

---

of the Land" (cf. Laroche, in JCS 1 [1947], 196, 215), and he might therefore have been presumed also to have a special interest in protecting the terrain from devastation.

"PROTECTIVE SPIRIT" renders the ideogram ^{d}LAMA, used in Hittite texts to designate an assorted range of spiritual beings, or "providences," who protect houses, guide men's paths, and shelter them in moments of hazard (cf. Laroche, *Dieux,* 100 f.). A particular form of such being is "the LAMA of the fields" (Hittite ^{d}LAMA *gimras*), and it is obviously that special spirit (a virtual equivalent of the Canaanite GPN-W-UGR, "Spirit of Vine and Field"; see Introduction to *Baal,* § 9) whose services are here recruited and who is specifically designated "a child of the outdoors [lit. field]." What is meant by the capture of this god is, of course, that the "benefits of nature" are withheld from the fields by frost.

ZABABA and LAMA (THE PROTECTIVE SPIRIT) are likewise associated, in other Hittite texts, with the Sun-god, Telipinu, and the Gulses. As to the former, cf. the Hattic text, KUB XXXVIII 15, obv. 4*a*; as to the latter, cf. KUB VV 12 i 15; XVII 10 (the Telipinu myth), iii, 30 ff.

TELIPINU is the genius of vegetation. His name is of Hattic origin (cf. Laroche, *op. cit.,* 34 f.). His function here is not to rescue ZABABA and THE PROTECTIVE SPIRIT but to insure the fecundity of the earth by direct action. The capture of him signifies that frost has brought agricultural operations to a standstill.

32–37: The GREAT GODDESSES (written ideographically ^{d}MAH.MESH or ^{d}MAH.HI.A) are a group of female deities always associated with the GULSES, or Fates (see below), and apparently representing the forces of fecundity and procreation (cf. Laroche, *Dieux,* 101). In the singular, "GREAT GODDESS"

(well) say to his father and mother: 'Here you go guzzling and swilling. You have cared not a whit!' "

(Yes), shepherd and oxherd [were now in sorry plight.] Not only had Jack Frost paralyzed the entire country, but the Supreme God was taking no notice!

21–31: The Supreme God is now stirred to action. He orders the sun to be summoned to put an end to the havoc. But the sun cannot be located. He then orders the god ZABABA *to go in search for him. But Zababa is seized by Jack Frost. Thereupon the Protective Spirit of the Fields* (LAMA) *is summoned to rescue Zababa. But he too is seized.*

(^{d}MAH) often alternates in Hittite texts with the goddess of birth (^{d}NIN.TU; cf. Laroche, *loc. cit.;* Otten, *Telipinu,* 9, n. 1; Forrer, in RHA 1 [1932], 145, 155). It is therefore in the capacity of one who might restore fertility by direct action that her services are here enlisted. She is, so to speak, the personification of "spring in the blood." At the same time, however, she is also the counterpart, on the mythic plane, of the women who play so important a role in seasonal rituals; see Introduction.

The GULSES (or GUL-*asses*) are a group of female deities who preside over births and prescribe the destinies of the newborn. In KUB XXIV 53, ii 14 f., they are invoked to grant that a prospective child be born of a good mother, and are asked to "prescribe blessing for him." In KUB XXXIII 118, 17–21 (ed. Friedrich, JKF 2 [1952], 150–52), it is said of Mount Wasitta, which has miraculously become pregnant, that "from childhood on you have never known what it means to be pregnant. This is something that the GULSES never prescribed for you." And in KUB XXII 85, rev. 5 ff., the premature death of a young bride is ascribed to the harsh fate decreed by the GULSES for her husband. The GULSES thus correspond to the Roman Parcae (Fates) and the Teutonic Norns.

The idea of "Weird Sisters" who determine the destinies of individuals is common to many cultures. In addition to the Teutonic Nornir and Udhir, and to the analogous Anglo-Saxon *Mettena* ("Meters-out") and the Middle German *Geschaepfer* ("Shapers"), we may cite the seven Hathors of Egyptian belief (Maspero, *Contes populaires de l'Égypte ancienne,* 51), the *deiwes walditoyes* of Lithuanian folklore (Schwenk, *Mythol. d. Slawen,* 121), and analogous figures in Lapp mythology (Holmberg, *Finno-Ugric Mythology,* 256 ff.). See especially Wehran, *Die Sage,* 81; *MI,* A 463. i.

Finally, the Supreme God sends for TELIPINU, *god of fertility, to restore the earth by direct action. But he too falls prey to Jack Frost.*

(But then) the Supreme God sent for the sun, (saying): "Go, fetch the sun!" They went and searched for the sun, but could not find him.

Then said the Supreme God: "Although, to be sure [you have] not found him, my body feels warm; so he can but somewhere have met with mishap!" Whereupon he sent for Zababa, (saying): "Go, fetch the sun!" But Jack Frost seized Zababa.

(Then said the Supreme God:) "Go, summon the Pro-

The name GULSES appears to be connected with the verb GUL-, "write, inscribe" (cf. Friedrich, in JCS 1 [1947], 283 f.). It should be observed therefore that both the Parcae and the Norns are said expressly to keep a written record. Concerning the former, cf. Klausen, in *Zeitschr. f. deutsch. Alt.*, 1840. 226; and concerning the latter – who are sometimes called *Die Schreiberinnen* – cf. Grimm, *Teutonic Mythology*, tr. Stallybrass, 406. Similarly, Tertullian, *De anima*, c. 39, says that at the conclusion of a child's first week of life, prayers are offered to Fata Scribunda.

The basic conception of the heavenly tablets or book of fate meets us also on Semitic soil. The Babylonians believed that Nabu, the divine scribe, possessed such tablets. Assurbanipal, for example, addresses to him the words, "My life is inscribed before thee" (K. 1285), and similar expressions occur in other texts (cf. Jeremias, *Babylonisches im Neuen Testament*, 69–73; KAT,[3] 401). On New Year's Day, the gods assembled in the "chamber of fates" and determined the destinies of men as well as the vicissitudes of nature (Jeremias, *loc. cit.;* Meissner, *Babylonien und Assyrien*, ii, 125) – an idea which survives in the "Book of Life" of Jewish belief. In the Old Testament, the idea occurs especially in Psalm 139:15 f.: "My frame was not hidden from Thee, and when I was being fashioned in secret, knit together (as if) in the depths of the earth, Thine eyes beheld mine unformed substance. In Thy book are all of them written – the days when such are to be created, and among them one was (assigned) thereto." A further allusion to it has been recognized in a Punic inscription of the third to second centuries B.C. which has been interpreted to read: "Moreover, the gods have . . . my name; my mark . . . along with their names have they inscribed, and the glory and [splend]or of my

tective Spirit (of the Fields), that he may rescue him! Is he not a child of the (great) outdoors?" But him too Jack Frost seized.

(Then said the Supreme God:) "Go, summon Telipinu! That son of mine is a doughty wight! He can hoe, he can plow, he can irrigate, he can sow! What is more, he is as hardy as rock(?)!" But him too Jack Frost seized.

32–33: His sons having thus come to grief, the Supreme God now decides to relieve the situation by sending out the Great Goddess (MAH), *one of the Weird Sisters* (GULSES) *or Norns, who determine destinies and preside over procreation and birth.*

---

name did they record from the beginni[ng] forever" (cf. Lidzbarski, *Ephemeris* i, 164 ff.).[a]

The words, "You are losing your grip (lit., will no longer keep hold) on the (royal) chalice" may be explained as a reference to the chalice of tribute normally proffered to kings. In the Hittite *Myth of Kumarbi* (KUB XXXIII 120, 10–11, 17; tr. Güterbock, *Kumarbi,* 6; Goetze, *ANET*, 120), a sign of kingship in heaven is that the god who wields it is constantly handed chalices by his minister; while in the Canaanite *Poem of Baal* (II AB iv, 43–45), that god is described as "our king, our ruler . . . to whom we bring the cup, to whom we bring the chalice." On ancient Near Eastern cylinder seals, gods are often portrayed holding goblets, while their votaries stand before them (e.g., Ward, *Seal Cylinders of Western Asia,* No. 917 [Syrian, c. 1900–1200 B.C.]; E. Porada, *Mesop. Art in Cylinder Seals,* fig. 44 [IIIrd Dyn. Ur]; cf. O. Weber, *Altorient. Siegelbilder,* 111).

HASAMILI is mentioned elsewhere in Hittite literature (KBo. IV 4 iii 34; KUB XIX 37 iii 16) as a god who possesses the power of screening his protégés in moments of peril. In the Akkadian treaty of Suppiluliuma with Mattiwaza of Mitanni (KBo 1.1; tr. Goetze, *ANET*, 206), he is included among warrior gods. His Hattic equivalent is at present unknown, but it has been suggested that his name is itself of Hattic origin, being derived from a root *hasm-*, of yet undetermined meaning, which indeed appears in that language (cf. Laroche, *Dieux*, 23). The "brothers of Hasamili" are evidently a group of minor gods — not unlike the Kabeiroi of Graeco-Asianic belief — who sheltered men when they were exposed

[a] Distinct from the Book of Fate, but often confused therewith, is the heavenly ledger or scroll in which the deeds and misdeeds of men are recorded; cf. Psalm 69: 29, etc.; KAT,[3] 402.

(Then said the Supreme God:) "Summon the Great Goddess of Birth, the Weird Sister! If those (others) have perished, if indeed those (others) have perished, yet (will) Jack Frost . . . her . . . !"

Ritual Combat

34–37: Jack Frost, flushed with triumph, retorts by taunting him that he is "losing his grip" and will eventually have to yield the dominion of heaven. Moreover, he adds, the escorts which the Supreme God proposes to provide for the goddess will prove quite ineffectual(?).

But Jack Frost says to the Supreme God: "You are headed for a fall! You will have to surrender! All her brothers have (indeed) perished! You are losing your grip on the (royal) chalice! As for (those) brothers of HASAMILI, they are mere weaklings (?). Will not Jack Frost seize them?"

38–41: Nevertheless, the Supreme God summons those escorts and warns Jack Frost that, far from "losing his grip," he is in fact firmly entrenched. Moreover, he adds, even if Jack Frost can immobilize the hands and feet *of his victims,*

---

to peril or attack. Jack Frost, however, contemptuously discounts them.

38–41: Supreme gods are necessarily all-seeing. Similarly, in another Hittite text (KUB XIII 3 ii 7 ff.; tr. Goetze, *ANET*, 207) it is said that if a palace servant is guilty of uncleanliness or otherwise offends the king, the latter's gods will certainly espy him; while in the Canaanite *Poem of Baal* (II AB vii 40; above, §XLIII) we are told that "Baal's eyes (always) anticipate (the actions of) his hands." On the concept in general, see R. Pettazzoni, *The All-Knowing God* (1956), *passim,* where it is pointed out that the omniscience of gods is essentially visual, being really *omni-surveillance.*

(The immediate point of the supreme god's words is, of course, that while frost may immobilize hands and feet, it still does not affect the eyes!)

42–44: In the original Hittite, Jack Frost's reply reads simply, "You will see," etc., but there is a special point in his words, for they hark back immediately to the supreme god's reference to his *eyes.* I have tried to bring this out by the turn of phrase employed in the translation.

he cannot impair or elude the (all-seeing) eyes *of the lord of heaven!*

(Nevertheless), the Supreme God summons them, and to Jack Frost he [say]s: "My hands are (in fact) glued — yes, glued — to the chalice! What is more, even if [you can paralyze] these hands and feet, you (still) cannot take my eyes!"

42–44: The Supreme God's reference to his (all-seeing) eyes prompts Jack Frost to retort that all he will see with them is that his own sons and those of the goddess [will alike perish,] for he (Jack Frost) is minded to carry his attack to heaven itself! Then, he adds as a parting shot, the Supreme God can look to his own unaided efforts to rescue or revive his protégés!

[But Jack Frost] keeps saying to the Supreme God: "Then all you will see is that the children of both of you [will perish(?)]! I am coming up to heaven! [Then you yourself, go] save (*or* revive) the . . . !"

* * *

[An ensuing combat between Jack Frost and the Supreme God was evidently related in the missing portion of the text.]

B. RITUAL

Reverse

1–13: What follows obviously concludes the description of a ritual. We learn only that when the moon becomes visible, an official

slides back the [bolt] of the gate, and the male and female magicians [depa]rt.

The writer then declares:

I am the woman Annanas,

and professes her piety, saying that she has [paid due heed to] the words of the gods, has ritually sprinkled her mouth [with . . .], and has made various installations for the ceremony. She continues:

The words of the gods have I in no wise set at naught, but

whenso . . . , and Telipinu presses hard on anyone, I (duly) recite the word of the gods (i.e., the myth) and make rogation unto him.

She then affirms that the ritual has been ordained by the sun-god himself, and concludes:

(Moreover,) the Great Goddess has spoken thus: "O sun, whenever thou doest good to anyone, let him give thee nine sheep. If, however, he be a poor man, let him give thee (but) one!"

A colophon adds:

ENDED IS THE ROGATION OF [THE SUN] AND OF TELIPINU.

EXCURSUS

The ritual portion of our text has here been presented only in summary. A few notes on particular features of it may, however, perhaps prove useful.

a. Among the ritual procedures which the composer professes punctiliously to have observed is that of sprinkling her mouth with a substance the name of which is no longer preserved on the tablet (line 6). Similarly, Firmicus Maternus informs us (*De errore prof. relig.*, XXII. 1–3) that in the rites of the Attis cult, votaries had their throats anointed by the officiating priest prior to the great moment when the resurrection of the gods was proclaimed; while in the Egyptian ceremonies for Osiris, the two wailing women had likewise to cleanse their mouths and chew natron (cf. Blackman-Fairman, in JEA 29 [1945], 12, note *c;* Pleyte-Rossi, *Papyrus de Turin,* Pl. LVII. 9 ff.).

b. The ritual, we are told (9–10), is repeated every time similar conditions of crisis occur; for what proved efficacious *in illo tempore* will, it is assumed, prove equally efficacious again. In the same way, the Telipinu myth was recited whenever the presence or favor of the god was thought to be withdrawn (cf. Otten, *Telipinu,* 66). This is one of the essential uses of myth, and it is illustrated especially by the employment of myths as "narrative spells" in magic (see W. R. Halliday, *Folklore Studies,* 89; G. Kittredge, *Witchcraft in Old and New England,* 32, 40, and notes). In our view, however, it is a mistake to regard such use as mere repetition of a primordial archetype; what is involved is far more the fundamental parallelism between ideal and real, punctual and durative situations; see Chapter One, §3. Nor, it may be added, does such secondary and extended use invalidate the assumption that several of the myths *originated* on a *seasonal* basis.

c. The sun-god, we are informed (11–12) is to receive nine sheep for every act of beneficence. In the case of a poor man, however, one alone will suffice.

Similar concessions to the poor are made also in other Ancient Near Eastern sacrificial systems. Thus, according to the code set forth in the Biblical Book of Leviticus, a poor person might substitute two turtledoves for the statutory one sheep of a sin offering, and if he could not afford even that, he might bring one tenth of an ephah of fine flour (5:11, 16). So too, a poor woman might substitute two turtledoves for the sheep required in clearance from impurity after childbirth (*ibid.*, 12:8); and similar modifications were permitted in the case of a poor man released from the contagion of vitiligo (*ibid.*, 14:21). A Babylonian ritual tariff from Sippar prescribes that where a "nobleman" (*rubu*) has to offer a dove, one of lower estate (*mushkenu*) need bring only the intestines (?) of a sheep (Zimmern, *Ritualtafeln,* No. 60. 30 f.; cf. *KAT,*[3] 598–99). Again, in Phoenician sacrificial tariffs from Marseilles and Carthage (*NSI,* Nos. 42–43; *ANET,*[2] 502 f.), in the case of offerings brought by the poor, the priests must forego their usual share.

d. On the bringing of water from three wells (19), see Introduction, § 9(*b*).

e. The setting of fire before the enthroned god (35–36) recalls the widespread practice of carrying it ceremonially before kings (cf. Frazer, *GB* ii, 363 ff.). Ammianus Marcellinus tells us, for instance (XXVI. 6, 34), that part of a sacred fire, said to have fallen from heaven, was always carried before Oriental monarchs, and his statement is illustrated by a Hittite text (Bo. 2089; cf. Hrozný, *BoSt.,* v/3, 27–28) which speaks of a marshal's bearing it before the king. The custom obtained also in Sparta (cf. Cook, *Zeus* ii, 34, n. 1), and was continued in the court protocol of Hellenistic kings and Roman emperors (Q. Curtius, iii. 3, 9; Clem. Rom. *hom.* 9.6 [= ii. 245 Migne]; cf. A. C. Eschenbach, *Diss. Academicae,* 519 ff; W. Otto, "Zum Hofzeremoniell des Hellenismus," in *Epitymbion Swoboda* [Reichenberg, 1927], 194 ff.). Moreover, in African coronation and installation ceremonies, the extinguishing and subsequent rekindling of fire on the communal hearth is a frequent element of the ritual – e.g., among the Zulu (cf. H. Brincker, "Pyrolatrie in Südafrika," in *Globus* 67 [1895], 96 f.; Petersson, *Chiefs and Gods* [1953], 333 f.; A. T. Bryant, *The Zulu People* [Pietermaritzburg, 1949], 469); among the Cwana (Petersson, *op. cit.,* 337), and among the Tonga, Sotho, and Venda (*ibid.,* 214–15). Among the Loveda, fires are extinguished throughout the country at the death of the reigning queen (E. J. and J. D. Krige, *The Realm of a Rain Queen* [1947], 168); and among the Hungwe, a Shona tribe, a chief's first act on accession is to light new fires (L. Frobenius, *Erythräa* [1931], 117). On the symbolism of such fires, see the Commentary on *Aqhat*, §§II-V, 2; Petersson, *op. cit.*, 215. They exemplify the corporate vitality of the community, which is respectively eclipsed and regenerated at the death of the old king and the installation of the new. On the face of it, then, the rite described in our text might be simply a gesture of recognition of the god's reasserted sovereignty. In a larger sense, however, what it symbolizes is the rebirth of life at the winter solstice, and thus links up with the universal practice of kindling fires at solstices and equinoxes. The latter is not a sun charm, but a token of the fact that the "home fires" are now rekindled.

2. THE HITTITE MYTH OF TELIPINU

§1. Related to the Yuzgat Tablet, and representing a variation on the same theme, is the *Myth of Telipinu,* which deals with the desolation on earth through the angry withdrawal of that god of fertility, and with the measures adopted to appease him and procure his return. Preserved in at least three versions and in a number of mutually complementary recensions,[1] this myth came later to be used as a "narrative spell" for the aversion of more private and domestic disasters. In its original form, however, it must clearly have been designed for a more public and general occasion, for the result of the magical procedure is said to be the return of prosperity and increase to the king and queen, implying a state ritual.

A. SYNOPSIS

§2. The text falls into four main sections.

It opens with a description of the disaster which attends the withdrawal of Telipinu, of various abortive searches that are made for him, and of his eventual recovery.

The effect of his disappearance is related in terms which leave no doubt that what is being described is the dreary winter season. Houses are said to be filled with soot and smoke, the embers (or logs) of continuous fires accumulating on the hearth. In the barns, the cattle huddle together. On hillside and pasture everything is bleak and bare. The trees are denuded of leaves, and the springs are frozen over (*lit.,* dried up). Men and gods are faced with starvation.

It is in this situation that the sun-god intervenes by inviting all the gods to a banquet at which the deity of the weather points out that the current disaster is due to the angry withdrawal of his son Telipinu. Thereupon the gods "great and small" conduct an extensive search for him; and when this proves abortive, the sun-god sends out an eagle to explore the mountains and valleys to the same end. The eagle, however, sends back word that no trace of the missing god can be found.

At this stage, feminine influence comes into play. The great Mother Goddess, alive to the emergency and seemingly impatient of the measures thus far adopted, resolves to employ her own devices. She therefore dispatches a bee, instructing it to find Telipinu, sting him, cleanse him with its wax, and bring him to her. The weather god protests that the tiny bee can scarcely be expected to accomplish what the mighty gods themselves have failed to achieve. But the Mother Goddess rejoins that such will indeed be the case. The bee flies forth and eventually locates Telipinu asleep in a forest. The god is angry at being roused, and appears to fly into a further fit of rage, thereby threatening mankind with even greater calamity. The suggestion is therefore made (by some deity whose name is broken away) that the services of man should also be enlisted and the use of special water from a spring on Mount Amuna and of an eagle's wing are recommended as effective means of stirring the angry god into movement.

§3. There is now a gap in the text. At the point where it resumes, we hear of a series of magical rites designed to convert the anger of Telipinu to the mild and gentle qualities of various objects displayed before him. The phrasing is uniform. As the fig is sweet, so is the anger of Telipinu to be turned to sweetness. As the olive has its oil and the grape its wine within it, so is Telipinu to have grace within his soul. As honey is sweet, and as oil is soft, so is the fury of Telipinu to be sweetened and softened. As his path is ritually besprinkled with fine oil, so is Telipinu to take to smooth ways; and as saplings and new shoots are tender, so is the spirit of Telipinu to be.

It is not stated explicitly who performs this magical ceremony, but the probability is that it is the goddess Kamrusepas. There are two reasons for this assumption. First, in the very next episode, it is this goddess who suddenly appears — without appropriate introduction — as the performer of magical rites designed to appease the anger of Telipinu, and she there speaks expressly (in the past tense) of having already done certain other things calculated toward the same end. Second, Kamrusepas was pre-eminently the goddess of magic cures and spells, so that any divine performance of magical rites would naturally have devolved upon her. (She was first introduced, no doubt, in a preceding passage, now lost.)

At the conclusion of the magical ceremony, Kamrusepas lifts her eyes and beholds that her magic has been partially effective. Telipinu has been roused, but he is still in an angry and ugly mood.

§4. The third portion of our text describes how the continuing anger of Telipinu is finally exorcised by rites performed severally by gods and men.

First, Kamrusepas bids the gods slay twelve male sheep out of a number which Hapantali, the divine steward, is tending for the sun-god. As is shown fully in our Commentary, twelvefold sacrifices and oblations are not uncommon in Hittite magical rituals. The presentation of the twelve sheep may therefore be construed as a necessary preliminary to the subsequent procedure. Moreover, as we shall see presently, the fleeces of sheep are later dedicated to Telipinu; and these may well have been obtained from the present sacrifice.

Next, Kamrusepas announces that she is about to perform a certain ceremony directed toward Telipinu. To this announcement she adds that she has already carried out various preliminary procedures whereby the actual return of the god has been achieved and the noxious contagion which possessed him removed.

Further details of the magical practice are now described. The goddess declares that she has "removed from his (i.e., Telipinu's) body its evil" and that she has "torn that evil to shreds." Thereby, she adds, she has succeeded in removing his wrath, fury, and rage. The magical formulas were evidently recited while sacrificial animals were being roasted, drawn, and quartered, the removal of their "evil parts" — as the entrails were indeed called by the Hittites (NIG GIG)[2] — being taken to symbolize the removal of the "evil" from the body of Telipinu.

While the fires are being banked, and while subsequently they burst into blaze and then burn out, Kamrusepas recites a series of formulas in which she prays that the anger and fury of Telipinu may behave in similar fashion. The formulas follow a standard pattern: "Firewood is banked. As this firewood burns out, so too may the anger and fury of Telipinu."

The succession of similes is now interrupted by a direct invocation: "O Telipinu, abandon thine anger, abandon thy wrath, abandon thy fury, abandon thy rage!" This, we suggest, was recited when the fires had died down and no further simile could be drawn from them.

Finally, Kamrusepas pronounces a further "comparative" formula: "As water which issues from a pipe can never be reunited therewith, so may the anger, wrath, fury, and rage of Telipinu, once vented, never return to him!" The significant point here is that while in all of the incantatory similes which precede this invocation, the comparison is with *fire*, in this one, which follows it, it is with *water*. The inference is obvious: these words were recited as the dying embers of the fires were being doused.

The ceremony being concluded, the gods foregather to welcome Telipinu and further entreat his grace. They include: the Gulses and MAH goddesses (corresponding, more or less, to the Roman Parcae [Fates] and the Teutonic Nornir); Halkis, god of grain; Miyatanzipas, god of growth and vegetation; the "providence" (^{d}LAMA) of the fields; Hapantali, the divine steward; and others whose names are no longer preserved. In their midst sits the newly arrived Telipinu himself.

§5. This is followed by an account of the corresponding rites of placation, performed by men.

Following various symbolic acts, accompanied by appropriate magical spells, an incantation is recited, banishing the said anger and fury from the house and its interior, the windows, the forecourt, the gate and porch, and likewise from the stalls(?). (Note especially the sevenfold specification, which must be interpreted in connection with the widespread prevalence of the number seven in magic!) The anger and fury of the god are solemnly exorcized from "verdant meadow, garden, and orchard" and consigned to "the path of the sun-god of the netherworld"—*i.e.*, to those gloomy subterranean regions whither the sun was thought to betake himself at night and during the "dark" period of the year.

The incantation is followed by a further piece of magical "business." The seven gates of the temple (again the magical seven!) are unbolted and flung open. Then pots are placed on the ground while an accompanying formula is recited: "As that which goes into these pots nevermore comes forth, but remains confined therein, so too, O Telipinu, may thine anger nevermore come forth, but go to perdition!"

The magical procedure proves effective. The wrath of Telipinu is assuaged, and he proceeds to bestow his grace. The concluding portion of the text describes the consequent restoration of prosperity. The calamities specified in the opening portion are now enumerated in reverse. Soot leaves the windows, and smoke the house. The pedestals of the gods, previously neglected, are now tended. The embers (or logs) no longer accumulate on the hearth. Flocks and herds breed. Telipinu bestows his grace upon the king and queen, granting them life and strength and length of days.

In return for his favor, the god receives honors. An evergreen (*eyan*)[3] is set up in the temple, and from it are suspended the fleeces of lambs, while sheep's tallow, grain, an ox, and a sheep are offered to him.

B. INTERPRETATION

§6. The very fact that our text consists of a ritual as well as a myth shows that it is more than a mere literary *tour de force*, but belongs rather to the category of liturgy. Now, since all the parallel versions of this myth (e.g., those of Tammuz, Osiris, Baal Puissant, Attis, Adonis, etc.) were, as we have seen, actually enacted at appropriate seasonal festivals, there is an initial presumption that, so, too, was our present version; and this presumption is strengthened by the fact that the action of the piece moves progressively through the standard stages of the Seasonal Pattern, viz., (a) Mortification; (b) Purgation; (c) Invigoration; and (d) Jubilation. The first is represented by the description of the blight on earth and the infecundity of man and beast; the second by the elaborate ritual designed to remove the "evil" which possesses the body of Telipinu; the third by the ceremonies which accomplish his revival; and the fourth by the concluding account of how he was indeed appeased, and bestowed his beneficence on the earth.

§7. Even more significant, however, than such general considerations is the fact that almost everything which now appears as a purely circumstantial detail of the myth or as an integral element of the magical procedure can be shown to reflect or project a typical feature of seasonal festivals.

Take, for instance, the concluding rite involving the erection of an evergreen standard (*eyan*) in the temple of Telipinu and the suspension therefrom of fleeces. In KUB XXV 31 these two objects are specified among the paraphernalia used in the cult of Telipinu *at the annual Puruli Festival*, the former being expressly dedicated to him on that occasion. Accordingly, it is not unreasonable to suppose that the seasonal rite has been worked into the plot of our myth under the influence of a standard magical usage at the ceremony for which it was designed. Moreover, as shown fully in our Commentary, the use of such evergreens and fleeces was a characteristic of the seasonal "mysteries" in many other ancient cults, the former even surviving in the modern "maypole."

§8. Scarcely less transparent a reflection of seasonal ritual is the central ceremony whereby the "evil" is exorcized from the body of Telipinu and its noxious contagion averted. Although this incident has been integrated perfectly within the dramatic framework of the myth, the fact is that such purgation is one of the most common and constant features of seasonal festivals. Here again, therefore, we may recognize a mythic projection of standard seasonal ritual.

§9. Or take the passage which describes how, after the forced return of Telipinu, the gods foregather at a sort of collation, with him in their midst, and finally persuade him — not without the aid of further magical devices — to abandon his anger. In this incident we may recognize a reflection of the Theoxenia or regalement of the gods which, as we have seen (Chapter Two, §36), formed a cardinal element of the ancient seasonal mysteries. Moreover, it should be observed that in one version of the myth reference is actually made to the "couch" of Telipinu; for in this we may see a counterpart of the festive couches customarily spread for the gods in connection with that entertainment, *i.e.*, the so-called *lectisternium.*

§10. So, too, when it is said, toward the end of the text, that Telipinu "took thought for the king and queen and blessed them with life and strength for the future," it is not difficult to see a reflection of the ceremonial reconfirmation of the king which formed so cardinal a feature of the analogous Babylonian Akitu Festival and which recurs so often in seasonal celebrations elsewhere. In KBo III 7 the re-confirmation of the king as the agent of fertility is expressly associated with the Puruli Festival, while according to Tertullian, a sacrifice for the health and welfare of the emperor (*pro salute imperatoris*) was one of the features of the Attis mysteries on March 24.

§11. The position occupied by the sun-god in the mythological portions of our text may likewise be construed as an indication of its ritual basis, though the point should perhaps not be pressed unduly. It is the sun-god who first convenes the gods when the absence of Telipinu begins to create alarm, and it is worth remembering that seasonal festivals were often celebrated at solstice and equinox (see Chapter Two, §37), and that their relevant myths therefore attach special importance to the part played by the sun. Moreover, we have learned explicitly from the Yuzgat Tablet that in Hittite cultus the "mysteries" of Telipinu were indeed associated with adoration of the solar deity, the two gods jointly receiving offerings and that document being entitled specifically "Rogation to Telipinu and the sun-god." Accordingly, it is permissible at least to suggest that the fairly prominent role assigned to the sun-god in our myth may be a token of the story's seasonal basis.

§12. Finally, it is worth observing that the text actually incorporates certain of the standard clichés of the seasonal myth. To be specific, the initial description of the infertility caused by the absence of Telipinu corresponds almost verbatim to that in the Yuzgat Tablet, the Canaanite *Poem of Baal,* the Homeric *Hymn to Demeter,* and the "harvest litany" embodied in the first chapter of the biblical Book of Joel; and there is here the same particular emphasis as in the last two of these sources on the possible starvation of the gods.

§13. Like its counterpart, the Puruli myth, our text evidently derives from a Hattic original, its present form representing a modified and freely adapted version of that primitive source. The Hattic provenience is shown by the fact that the very name Telipinu belongs to that language; for although its full significance still eludes us, we know that the element *pinu* was the Hattic word for "son." Similarly, the goddess Kamrusepas bears a name the second part of which (viz., *-sepas*) is characteristically Hattic, while the deity of growth and vegetation here appears as Miyatan*zipas,* where an alternative form of the same element may be recognized.

RECENSIONS OF THE TELIPINU MYTH

A: KUB XVII 10
XXXIII 1, 2, 3

B: Chantre, *Mission en Cappadoce*, 58 f.
KUB XXXIII 5
KUB XXXIII 4, 8

C: KUB XXXIII 9, 12, 13, 14, 33, 41, 42

D: KUB XXXIII 15, 16, 19, 20, 21

Subsidiary Texts: KUB XXXIII 67 iv; 32 obv.

See: Otten, Heinrich, *Die Ueberlieferungen des Telipinu-Mythus* (MVAG 46.1), Leipzig, 1942.

NOTES

1. For details, see the table above. Our text is composite.
2. See Sommer, *Hattusilis*, 78 ff.
3. See Eheloff, KUB XXIX, Vorwort, iii; von Brandenstein, in *Orientalia* 8 (1939), 75 f.
4. *Apologet.*, 25; cf. Hepding, *Attis*, 33.

TRANSLATION

I

Mortification

DISAPPEARANCE OF THE GOD

A i, 3–20

The god of fertility departs in anger, and all life languishes.

(*The beginning is lost*)

In such haste was he to run off that he put his right boot on his left foot, and his left boot on his right.

Thereupon soot beset the windows; smoke beset the house.

The ashes lay crammed on the hearth. The gods lay crammed [in their shrines]; the sheep lay crammed in the fold; the oxen lay crammed in the stall. The ewe paid no attention to her lamb; the cow paid no attention to her calf.

Off stalked Telipinu. Grain and . . . and increase and abundance he took away from field and meadow. Off to the copses stalked Telipinu, and in a copse he buried himself. Fatigue(?) overcame him. . . .

Forthwith the seed ceased to yield produce; forthwith oxen, sheep, and men ceased to breed, while even those that had conceived did not bear.

Hillsides were bare; trees were bare and put forth no new branches; pastures were bare; springs ran dry.

A famine arose in the land; men and gods alike were about to perish of hunger.

So the great sun-god arranged a repast and invited the thousand gods. But though they ate, they could not be satisfied; though they drank, they could not slake their thirst.

THE SEARCH

A i, 21–29[a]

Thereupon the weather god called to mind his son Telipinu. "The fact is" (cried he) "that my [son] Telipinu is not here! He has flown into a temper and carried off all good things!"

Then the gods great and small proceeded to search for Telipinu, and the sun-god dispatched an eagle at full speed (saying), "Go, search the steep mountains, search the deep valleys, search the darkling swirl of the nether waters!"

Away went the eagle, but it could not find him. It brought back a report to the sun-god: "I have not been able to find him, even Telipinu, that mighty god!"

A i, 29[b]–34

Then said the weather god to the queen goddess: "We must act at once! We shall perish of hunger!"

Said the queen goddess to the weather god: "Do something! Thyself, O Weather God, go seek Telipinu!"

So the weather god proceeded to search for Telipinu. Going to[b] the latter's city, he [knock]ed on the gate, but could get no one to open. So he smashed its bolt and lock. When he got inside, however, he . . . and then sat down in despair.

A i, 34–39
B i, 17–29

Thereupon the queen goddess [dispat]ched a bee. "Go" (said she), "seek Telipinu! When thou findest him, put a sting in his hands and feet, and let it bring him to his feet! Then apply wax, smear him, purify him, cleanse him, and bring him to me!"

But the weather god said to the queen goddess: "Why, the

[b] Lit., in.

Two ideas are here combined. The first is that the sting of a bee or ant can cure paralysis of the limbs. On this, see: Beck, *Honey and Health,* 96, 101; Jühling, *Tiere* 88 f.; Rohde, *Psyche,*[2] 45–51; Frazer, *GB* v, 35. The second is that honey or wax is a purifying agent, capable of expelling evil spirits and of accomplishing rejuvenation. On this, see: Beck, *op. cit.,* 209 ff.; Keith, *Indian Mythology,* 158 (= *MI,* D 1338.9); Rohde, *op. cit.,* 51 ff.; Fallaize, in ERE vi, 770. An excellent illustration of the latter belief occurs in the pseudepigraphic Story of Joseph and Asenath, where the archangel Michael miraculously provides the Egyptian princess with a honeycomb by the use of which she achieves both purification and immortality.

There is a remarkable parallel to this incident in the Finnish *Kalevala.*

Lemminkainen, the handsome young hero, woos the daughter of the king of Pohjola, the "North country." He is subjected to various tests. While performing one of them, he is bitten by a serpent. His enemies thereupon cut up his body and throw the parts into deep water. His mother is informed that blood is oozing from his hairbrush, and thereby knows that things have gone ill with him. She goes in search of him, questioning trees, rivers, the moon, etc. They tell nothing. She then goes to the sun, who tells all. Eventually, she retrieves and reassembles the parts of her son, but cannot revive him. She therefore summons Mehilainen, "Little Bee" (cp. Finnish *meh,* "bee"), ordering him to gather nectar. He returns with it; but it proves ineffective. She then bids him gather

gods great and small have searched for him, but have not been able to find him! Will, then, this bee be able to go [and find him]? Why, it is tiny, and its wings are tiny! Will they stand up any better to the effort?"

Said the queen goddess to the weather god: "Have done! It will surely be able to [go and] find him!"

C ii, 7–25

So away [flew] the bee. It searched the steep mountains, it searched the [deep valle]ys, it searched [the darkling] swirl of the nether waters. When its honey was [well nigh] exhausted within it, when [its wax] was (well nigh) exhausted, [it came upon him] in a grove, in a meadow beside [the city of Lih]zina. It put its sting into his hands and feet, and he was brought [to his feet].

Howbeit Telipinu [cried]: "I am furious! . . . Why, when I am sleeping and nursing a temper, do you force me to make conversation?"

And therewith he [made] the springs spurt forth so violently that they threatened a flood; he made the rivers flow madly; he sought to make them overflow their banks(?). He swept away the . . . he swept away houses. He ravaged humankind; he ravaged the oxen and the sheep. He . . .

The gods were [stricken with panic.] "Now" (they cried), "see[ing that] Telipinu has [become even more enraged,] what shall we do? . . [What] shall we do?" . . .

[Then said . . . : "Why go and summon] man! Let him fetch (water from) the spring of Hattara (which is) on Mount Ammuna. . . . Let him (take measures to) make

---

nectar from a special island beyond the seven seas. He finds the island, full of jars containing the precious substance, and brings back seven jars on his shoulders and seven in his lap. This, too, proves ineffective. Lemminkainen's mother then tells the bee to fly to the ninth heaven and gather special honey blessed by the Lord for the purpose of "resuscitating his children." The bee flies to the castle of Jumala, the supreme god. There he finds urns containing various kinds of magic honey. He brings some of it back, and when it is rubbed on Lemminkainen, the latter revives.

It is not difficult to recognize in this tale an elaboration of the typical seasonal myth, with its characteristic motifs of the dismembered god, the search conducted by his mother, the appeal to the sun (cf. Demeter and Hēlios), etc. The eventual revival

him move! With the aid of a (magical) eagle's wing [let him be made to move!]" . . .

* * *

II
Purgation

A ii, 12–32

Thereupon a magical ceremony is performed to remove the disastrous anger of Telipinu, so that his return may indeed produce a return of prosperity.

* * *

Here is malt, O Telipinu . . . sweet and soothing. . . . [Even as this malt] . . . [so] may that which is now stifled (within thee) [be eventually . . . .]!

---

through the dispatch of a bee and the action of honey thus provides a perfect parallel to our Hittite version.

The episode follows the standard mythological pattern. Osiris is found in the marshes and fenland. Indra is found in a forest. Baal is found beside "Lake Samach," *i.e.*, in the marshes of the Huleh district.

LIHZINA is known from other Hittite texts. It is mentioned beside the cities of Hurma, Halab (Aleppo), Sarissa, and Sabinuwa, but its precise location is uncertain.

II. The goddess KAMRUSEPAS, who here performs the magical ceremony, is elsewhere described as a goddess of spells, cures, and incantations (cf. KBo III 8 ii 6, iii 16; KUB IX 3 i 19; XII 26 ii 1). A myth relating how she was translated to heaven and there given authority over crops and over blight is preserved in KUB XVII 8. She is described also as a goddess of health and of medicinal cures (KUB XVII 15 iii 12; 34 i 5). See fully: Furlani, *Rel. d. hittiti,* 86 f.; Goetze, *Kleinasien,*[1] 136; Laroche, *Noms des dieux,* 67. In KUB XXVIII 3:5 she is equated with the Hattic deity Katahzipuri, the first element of whose name means "Queen."

It should be observed that, as preserved in Recension A, the magical ceremony falls into *twelve* parts. This may be related to the fact that in the immediately succeeding episode the gods are instructed to flay twelve rams in connection with some further ritual procedure. Moreover, it is to be observed that twelvefold offerings are a not uncommon feature of Hittite rituals. Thus, for example, in the funerary ritual preserved in KUB XXX 15,

Here is pounding(?) water. Even as this water . . . so may . . . thy heart and spirit, O Telipinu . . . . May it(?) . . . toward the king in favor!

Here is a sop for appeasement(?) * * * So may thy spirit, O Telipinu, be appeased!

Here is wheat(?) [Even as wheat is husked from the ear] so may (his) heart husk [its grace from its present wrapping of evil]!

Here is sesame. Even as sesame . . . so, O Telipinu, may thy spirit *cease imme*diately from its rage![c]

[c] The rendering is a mere approximation. In the original, the point depends on a pun, viz. "Here is sesame (*samama*). Let the spirit of Telipinu be '*sauma-ted*,'" but we do not know what the verb means.

---

it is expressly prescribed (i 11) that "twelve ordinary loaves" be placed beside the cremated corpse, and at a subsequent stage of the proceedings (i 23–24) the fleeces of twelve unblemished sheep are dedicated to the gods as part of an apotropaic and propitiatory offering. Similarly, in a ritual designed to expel pestilence (KUB IX 32 = Friedrich, *AHS* ii 12), provision is made for the presentation of twelve large vessels and twelve loaves of bread (i 34); while in another (KBo IV 2 = Friedrich, *op. cit.*, 14) for the removal of evil spirits from a palace, twelve loaves of *huri*-bread and twelve of some other kind are likewise presented. We may suppose, therefore, that the division of the incantation into twelve formulae corresponds to the accompanying performance of some twelvefold act or the presentation of some twelvefold offering, characteristic of purgatory rituals.

Nor was this twelvefold offering confined to the Hittites. In the Homeric *Hymn to Hermes* 128, the sacrifice is divided into twelve parts. Twelvefold sacrifices are also mentioned specifically by Eustathius on *Iliad* vi 93 (p. 1386.48); cf. also Sophocles, *Trachiniae* 760 f. Twelve also played a prominent role in Israelitic ritual (cf. Numbers 29:17; I Kings 7:44; II Chronicles 4:4).

An alternative possibility, however, should not escape us. In the subsequent episode, Kamrusepas asserts that by means of her magical practices she has succeeded in removing "the evil" from the body of Telepinu. The magical ceremony may therefore be regarded as having been designed toward this end. Now, it was a belief of the Hittites that the body consisted of twelve essential

Here is a fig. Even as [this fig] is sweet, so may thy spirit, O Telipinu, become sweet!

As the olive has its oil within it, and [as the grape] has wine within it, so mayest thou, O Telipinu, have grace within thee, in (thy) spirit!

Here is pine oil. Even so, may [grace] anoint [the spirit of] Telipinu!

As malt and wort are inextricably fused in the making of a malt cake, so, O Telipinu, may thy spirit be inextricably fused with the concerns of mankind!

[Here is spelt. Even as spelt] is clean, so may the spirit of Telipinu become cleansed!

As honey is sweet and as oil is soft, so may the spirit of Telipinu become sweet, and so may it become soft!

Behold, O Telipinu, I have besprinkled thy paths with fine oil. Now, therefore, O Telipinu, come upon paths besprinkled with fine oil.

Let moss(?) and fern(?) be at hand! Even as each of these, though pleasant by nature, is brought into even better condition by being tended, so may Telipinu (by nature gentle), be brought into even better state (by means of this rite)![d]

[d] The passage is obscure, and the translation therefore tentative. But it gives the general sense.

---

parts. This is stated explicitly in KUB IX 4 i 3 ff., 22 ff., iii 33 ff.; IX 34 ii 23 ff., 38 ff.; while in KUB IX 4 and 34 (duplicates), the twelve limbs of the suppliant are healed by treatment of the twelve limbs of a sacrificial beast; see Goetze, *Tunnawi,* 42 ff. (For analogous magical practices based on the assumed number of the bodily parts, see Boll, *Sphaera,* 471 ff.; Eitrem, *Papyri Osloenses I.* 41 ff.) Accordingly, it is at least possible that the twelvefold division of the incantation was motivated by the fact that it accompanied a series of rites in which the noxious anger of Telipinu was exorcized from the twelve essential parts of his body.

The scene as a whole finds a striking parallel in Indic myth. When Indra depart from mankind, after slaying the son of Tvashtri, the earth languishes. In order to restore him and to cure him of the taint of bloodshed, the gods perform magical ceremonies under the leadership of the magician-god Brahmisapti.

A ii, 33–36

The god indeed returns, but is still angry.

Then came Telipinu at full speed. Lightning was seen; there was thunder. Below, the dark earth was in turmoil.

The goddess Kamrusepas espied him. (Surely enough,) the eagle's wing had made him move . . . !

III

DIVINE RITES OF PLACATION

A iii, 1–34

Thereupon she proceeded to remove from him his anger, to remove from him his wrath, to remove from him his rage.

Kamrusepas then said to the gods: "Come, ye gods, Behold, Hapantalis is tending the sun-god's sheep. Pick out a

---

III. HAPANTALI appears to have been the divine steward. In the Alaksandus treaty IV 10–11, in the treaty of Suppiluliuma and Hukkanas of Hayasa (Friedrich, *Staatsverträge,* ii, 110–12) and in that of the same monarch and Mattiwaza of Mitanni (Weidner, *Dokumente,* 28–30), he is equated with ^{d}LAMA, the protective spirit, and it is to be noted that it is the latter who acts as master of ceremonies at the divine banquet described in the Puruli myth. See fully, Laroche, *Recherches,* 22–23.

As part of the magical paraphernalia, Kamrusepas takes a feather and a thousand "eyes." The former is readily explicable; for in the Tunnawi ritual, the wing of an eagle is expressly mentioned (i 46; ii 4; iii 12) as part of the equipment used to remove "evil uncleanness" (*idalu papratar*) and "divine anger" (DINGIR. MESH-*as karpis*) from a person (ii 36–37; 58–59; iii 4–5, 9; 40–41; 50–51). It is therefore probable that it was used for a similar purpose in the present case. As for the eyes, it is noteworthy that in KUB XII 44 iii 8, failure of the vines is attributed to the evil eye, as is general sterility in KUB XVII 28, ii 44 ff. The eye might therefore well have been used in homoeopathic rites for exorcizing infertility.

Unfortunately, the text is mutilated and the crucial verb, which would have revealed the *tertium quid* of the comparison between Telipinu's wrath and the water of a pitcher, is missing. We believe, however, that the sense can be restored with confidence in the light of a remarkably parallel expression in an Accadian incantation.

dozen of them. I am going to perform a rite [to bring calm to the spirit of] Telipinu. I have provided myself with a platter. . . . .

Over Telipinu, up and down and back and forth, this way and that way, have I made the due waving motions, and have removed from the body of Telipinu its evil and its mischief. I have removed the anger, I have removed the wrath, I have removed the mischief, I have removed the rage.

When Telipinu was angry, his spirit and heart were choked as (by) logs (that choke a fire). But just as those logs burn down, so shall the anger, the wrath, the mischief, and the rage of Telipinu burn down!

Just as [wort] is a sterile thing, which no one takes into the field to use as seed, of which no one makes bread, and which no one lays away in the barn, so may the anger, the wrath, the mischief, and the rage of Telipinu be turned into a sterile thing!

When Telipinu was angry, his spirit and heart burned like a fire. But just as this fire [dies down], so shall the anger, the wrath, and the rage [of Telipinu] die [down]!

O Telipinu, abandon thine anger! [Abandon] thy wrath! Abandon thy rage!

Even as [the water] of a pitcher (once poured) can no more be gathered together, so may the [anger, the wrath

---

In Ebeling, *Quellen*, 15.6, there occurs the phrase, "as waters once poured from a pitcher do not return, so . . . etc. (*kima me pishani ana arkishu*[*nu*]*la itaru*)," which accords perfectly with what remains of our Hittite text. The same simile recurs also in Maqlu I, 118: "As waters of a bottle, so may they be exhausted by being poured out! (*kima mê nadi ina tiqi liqtû*)," and again in Zimmern, *Hymnen* 22 (in a prayer to Ishtar): "As waters which gush forth in streams, so may thy passion be dispelled!" Cf. also Psalm 58:8, compared by Tallquist, *Hakedem* 1 (1907), 9. Moreover, the same locution is also found in II Samuel 14:14: "For we needs must die, and are as water spilt on the ground which cannot be gathered up again."

Recension B gives another version of the simile:

As the water of a pitcher cannot flow backward,
so may the anger, wrath, fury, and rage of Telipinu never
return back (to him)!

and] the rage of Telipinu be gathered back (unto him) no more!

The gods shall yet foregather (once more) beneath a blossoming tree, for (by this rite) I have secured the continuance of that blossoming tree. All the gods will be there—the . . . gods, and the Ladies of Fortune and the Great Goddesses, and the Spirit of the Grain and the Spirit of Increase and Telipinu and the Spirit of Providence, and Hapantalis. For by this rite I have secured continuance for the gods, (in that) I have purged him (of his evil temper)!"

HUMAN RITES OF PLACATION

A iv, 1–19

Not only the gods but also men perform rites to remove the disastrous anger of Telipinu. This is in accordance with the divine command (at the end of §IV) that man be summoned. (The beginning is lost. The human priest is speaking.)

"O Telipinu, ever since thou departedst from the blossom-

This episode mythologizes the ritual *lectisternium* or *theoxenia.* On the deities here mentioned, see on Yuzgat Tablet, Commentary, §IV.

As we have seen (Chapter Two, §36), the theoxenia, or regalement of the gods, was an essential feature of the Hittite Puruli Festival, being expressly described in the cult myth of that occasion (KBo III 7). Similarly, in the Canaanite *Poem of the Gods Gracious,* which is really the "book of words" for a spring festival, the erection of "cathedrae" (*mthbt*) for the accommodation of the gods is expressly described (lines 19–20). Inscriptional evidence attests the same usage for the Attis cult, wherein it was the duty of the priestess to "spread the couch" for the gods at the annual panegyries (CIA II i 624, 662; IV ii 624b; cf. Livy xxix 14.13; Hepding, *Attis,* 136–37).

So prominent, indeed, was the *lectisternium* as a feature of the seasonal festivals that it almost invariably found place as an episode of the relevant cult myth or drama. Thus, in the Babylonian poem *Enuma Elish,* which served as the cult myth of the New Year (Akitu) Festival, the return of the triumphant Marduk after defeating the monster Tiamat is made the occasion of a banquet (*kirêtu*) in which all the gods participate (vi 53–54). So too, in the Canaanite *Poem of Baal* (II AB vi 44–57), the return of that god to earth, after defeating the monster Yam, and the dedication to him of a special palace, are likewise made the

ing trees, all vegetation has turned brown, even in midsummer! Ever since thou didst drag away the ox after thee, ever since thou didst drag away the sheep after thee, thou hast reduced (men's) frames and bodies to leanness!

So now, O Telipinu, put a stop to thine anger, thy wrath, thy mischief, and thy rage!

When the wind is about to come at full speed, the true devotee of the wind god is able to ensure that it be stayed. When a pot is about to boil over, a spoon can stay it. Even so may my words, mere mortal though I be, now stay the anger, wrath, and rage of Telipinu!

May the anger, the wrath, the mischief, and the rage of Telipinu be gone! Let the house say good-by to it! Let the interior and the . . . say good-by to it! Let the window say good-by to it! Let the . . . say good-by to it! Let the forecourt say good-by to it! Let the gate say good-by to it! Let the porch say good-by to it! Let the highway say good-by to it! (But) let it not hie to fertile field or garden or orchard! Let it (rather) take the path of the sun of the netherworld!

The turnkey has opened the seven gates, drawn back the seven bolts!

On the ground bronze jars have been placed, the lids of which are made of . . . and the handles of iron. Whatever goes into them, comes out no more, but remains there to rot. Even so may it receive the anger, the wrath, the mischief, and the rage of Telipinu, that it issue forth no more!"

IV

Jubilation

THE RESTORATION OF FERTILITY

A iv, 20–34

So Telipinu returned to his house. He took thought for his land. The window said good-by to soot; the house said

---

occasion of a banquet attended by all the gods. Lastly, as F. M. Cornford has pointed out (*Origins of Attic Comedy*, 99), Greek classical comedies, which evolved out of the primitive seasonal drama, usually end in a scene of banqueting, in which we may see, albeit through a glass darkly, a lingering trace of the original ritual *lectisternium.*

IV. This episode reflects standard rites of the Puruli Festival.

good-by to smoke. The shrines of the gods were restored to good state. The hearth said good-by to the ashes (that were piled upon it). He released the sheep which were in the

---

The erection of the evergreen and the suspension therefrom of fleeces are specifically mentioned in connection with that occasion in KUB XXV 31. Not improbably, the rite was part of the annual purgation ceremonies; a Babylonian magical text (Meissner, *Bab. u. Ass.*, ii. 209) specifies the erection of such a standard, coupled with the display of a fleece, as part of a ritual for expelling disease.

The rite in question can be shown to have formed part of the seasonal "mysteries" in many other ancient cults and even to have survived into modern times. According to both Johannes Lydus (*De Mensibus* iv 59) and the Emperor Julian (*Orat.* V, p. 186 C), a prominent feature of the Asianic "mysteries" of Attis celebrated at the spring equinox was the introduction of a pine log into the sacred precincts. March 22, says the Calendar of Philocalus, was therefore known as Arbor Intrat, "Day when the Log comes in" (Hepding, *op. cit.*, 151). From other sources we learn that the priests charged with this office were called specifically "carriers of the tree" (*dendroforoi; op. cit.*, 152 ff.). Analogous rites were performed also, according to Firmicus Maternus (c. 27, 1–2; Hepding, *op. cit.*, 51), in the parallel "mysteries" of Isis, Adonis, and Persephone; while Lucian (*De Dea Syria*, ch. 49), describing the festival of the Syrian Goddess at Hierapolis (Membij) at the beginning of spring, furnishes the interesting information that "they cut down tall trees and set them up in the courtyard; then they bring goats and sheep and cattle and hang them living to the trees." In modern times, the rite survives in the erection of the maypole at the beginning of summer; while a further survival, in what is, significantly enough, an "Asianic" part of the world, may be recognized in C. F. Lehmann's report (*Die Zeit* 2 [1902], 468), at the close of the nineteenth century, that it was customary at Banga, in Georgia, to bring a felled oak into church during the last days of April.

What we have in all these ceremonies is, of course, a symbolic representation of the death and resurrection of the year spirit or genius of fertility, the erection or adoration of the sacred tree going closely together with the antecedent felling of it. This comes out especially in the more explicit symbolism of earlier examples from Egypt and Mesopotamia. A feature of the great Egyptian festival in the month of Khoiakh, immediately preceding the first day of spring, was the ceremonial raising of the djed column, repre-

fold; he released the oxen which were in the stall. Mother (once again) nursed child; ewe nursed lamb; cow nursed calf.

---

senting the resurrection of Osiris (Blackman in S. H. Hooke's *Myth and Ritual*); while Mesopotamian seals, dating to the latter half of the third millennium B.C., sometimes figure a god felling a tree which stands on a mountain in which another god is imprisoned (cf. Frankfort, H., in *Iraq* 1 [1934], Pl. iv f. v a; Hooke, *Origins of Early Semitic Ritual*, 14). Since, in the literary version of the myth (VAT 9555 [= Langdon, *Epic of Creation*, 34 ff.], i, 6, 23, 29, 38), the year spirit is described as having been shut up in the mountain (i.e., the underworld), it is obvious that the felling of the tree is intended to symbolize his discomfiture.

The ritual text KUB XXV 31, to which we have already drawn attention, specifically associates the dedication of the evergreen to Telipinu with an antecedent burning and replacement of the old and evidently worn-out equipment of the temples (lines 5–7). This lends further support to our identification of it, in the present context, with the poles of Attis and cognate cults; for Firmicus Maternus tells us explicitly (c. 27.2) that these were burned from year to year, while Lucian relates (*loc. cit.*) that at the end of the festival of the Syrian Goddess the sacred trees were set ablaze. Similarly, at the Scottish Beltane festival, at the beginning of summer, it was customary in many parts to fell a tree and cast it upon the sacred fire, while an analogous disposition of the maypole is recorded from Prague, Wurtemberg, and other European centers (Frazer, *GB*, one-vol. ed., 125).

It is possible also — though the point cannot be pressed — that the mention of the fleeces is likewise an indication of seasonal ritual; for while it is true that these were a standard appurtenance of Hittite temples (Sommer, *Ahijava-Urkunden*, 181–82), we should not overlook the evidence that more was involved in the present instance than a mere replenishment of stock. The fact is that the fleeces here in question were not merely brought into the temple and deposited there, but were suspended from the sacred evergreen. Now, when we compare this with the statement of Lucian that at the summer festival at Hierapolis live sheep and goats were similarly suspended from sacred poles, and when we recall that (according to KUB XXV 31) the evergreen was set up at the Puruli Festival, which fell at virtually the same time of year, we can scarcely fail to conclude that our text implies a specific seasonal usage. Consonant with this is the well-known fact that

Telipinu (likewise) took thought for the king and queen; he took thought for them to grant them life and vigor and continuance. Yea, Telipinu took thought for the king.

In the presence of Telipinu an evergreen (?) was set up, and from it was hung the fleece of a sheep. Enwrapped in that fleece were the fat of sheep, grains of corn, fruit of the vine, (symbolizing) increase of oxen and sheep, continuance in life and (assurance of) posterity.

(*The last three lines are obscure*)

---

fleeces of sacrificial animals were believed in antiquity to possess certain magical properties (cf. Pley, F., "De lanae in antiquorum ritibus usu," in *Rel. Vers. und Vorarbeiten* X/ii [Giessen 1911], 1 ff.; Riess in PW, s.v. "Aberglaube"; 73, 79, 82; ARW 12 [1910], 491 f.; Kroll, *Antiker Aberglaube,* 27; Fehrie, *Alemannia,* 3rd ser. IV, 16, 19; Deubner, L., in ERE s.v. "Fleeces") and that for this reason they were indeed employed in Greek cults in the apotropaic and similar rites connected with seasonal festivals. Thus, at the Festival of the Diasia, which was celebrated at Ilissos (cf. Cook, *Zeus,* ii. 1140) in honor of the chthonic deity Meilichios, and which appear to have fallen – like the Hittite Puruli – at the summer solstice (Eustathius on Od. xxii 481, p. 1935; Harrison, *Prolegomena,* 27 ff.; Nilsson, M., in *Athen. Mitt.* 33 [1908], 285), a "divine fleece was ceremonially paraded, being apparently carried around the tilled land so as to protect the seed within the charmed circle" (Deubner, in ERE vi 52a; Preller, *Polmonis frag.* [Leipzig, 1831]; 141). A similar custom obtained at the Festival of Skirophoria, held in June–July (Suidas, s.v. *dion kodion*); while, according to Dicaearchus (FHG ii 262), worshipers of Zeus Akraios used to make a pilgrimage up Mount Pelion, in the height of summer, clad in sheepskins. So great, indeed, were the apotropaic properties attributed to the fleece that anyone in need of purification could obtain it by merely placing his left foot on that object (Hesychius, s.v. *Dios kodion;* Amelung, *Atti della Pontif. Acad.* 1905; 128 ff.; Phryn., *Praep. soph.* p. 19, 14 f., ed. Borries).

3. THE CANAANITE MYTH OF AQHAT

or

THE STORY OF THE DIVINE BOW

We now move from the phase of primitive sacred drama to that of developed literary composition. This development is perhaps best exemplified in the literature of the ancient Near East by the Canaanite *Poem of Aqhat,* discovered at Ras Shamra. No one who reads this text will doubt that in the form in which it has come down to us it was never formally acted and probably not even formally recited as a liturgical chant. It is a piece of literature pure and simple. Nevertheless, its roots lie in the ancient Ritual Pattern, and the very reason why it became part of the sacred repertoire of Ugarit (in the temple library of which city it was found) is that it was, *au fond,* nothing but an artistic transformation of the time-honored seasonal drama.

A. SYNOPSIS

§1. The essential portion of the story is preserved on three clay tablets and runs to approximately four hundred and fifty lines. Although it seems reasonably certain that the tablets which we possess follow one another consecutively, they preserve but a fraction of the original text, and even what has survived is frequently preserved in poor condition, full of breaks and of passages which are now illegible, now unintelligible. Nevertheless, sufficient remains to make out the general drift of the tale, and this may be summarized as follows.

§2. Once upon a time there was a chieftain named Daniel, who had no son and badly desired one. He therefore repaired to the temple of the god Baal and performed the rite of *incubation,* serving as an acolyte for seven days and sleeping at night in the sacred precincts. His devotion was rewarded. Upon the intercession of Baal, the supreme deity El promised him issue. Thereupon he returned home and summoned professional songstresses to celebrate the impending birth of his heir. In due course the child was born and was named Aqhat.

One day, while Daniel was sitting at the city gate, exercising his judicial functions ("judging the cause of the widow, dispensing justice to the orphan"), he chanced to espy Koshar-wa-Khasis ("Sir Adroit and Cunning"), the divine smith and artisan, passing by on the way from his forge in Egypt, carrying a consignment of bows and arrows destined for the gods and goddesses. With true Oriental hospitality, Daniel invited him into his house and regaled him with food and drink, at the same time "toasting" or sacrificing to the gods of his guest's native country. In acknowledgment of this hospitality, Koshar presented to him one of the bows. Upon the god's departure, Daniel in turn presented this to his son, instructing him how to use it and reminding him only that whenever he went out hunting he was to be mindful to offer the first "bag" as a gift to the gods.

Aqhat grew up into a handsome and sturdy youth. One day while he was out hunting, the virgin goddess 'Anat, queen of the chase, suddenly confronted him and, after partaking of food and drink with him, demanded the surrender of the bow. In order to persuade him, she revealed her charms to him and at the same time promised him wealth and immortality if he would comply with her demand. Aqhat, however, brusquely rejected these offers, remarking that the materials out of which a bow might be made lay readily to hand and that if the goddess were so anxious to possess one, all she had to do was to collect them and present them to Koshar-wa-Khasis, who would surely be willing to make one for her. Moreover, he added, promises of wealth and immortality were fairy tales which adults could scarcely be expected to believe. And anyway, he fired as a parting shot, what business had women with bows and arrows?

'Anat, though amused at this retort, was not prepared to take the rebuff lying down nor to tolerate a motal's retention of the bow which had really been designed for her. Warning him that persistence in his arrogant attitude would bring dire consequences, she therefore sped hotfoot to her father El and indulged in a wild tirade against Aqhat. That aged and gentle deity was at first disposed to treat the matter lightly, but under force of his daughter's threats and cajolings finally pronounced the decision that insults against goddesses could not be tolerated and that anyone who defrauded 'Anat of her rightful property "must assuredly be crushed."

Armed with this expression of divine approval, 'Anat immediately set about preparing the downfall of Aqhat. First, she lured him to the city of A-b-l-m, pretending that she wished to make her peace with him, asserting that she had absconded from her father's house and desired to elope with him, and offering to teach him the art of hunting. Aqhat fell for the bait. Thereupon, Anat proceeded to enlist the services of her henchman Yatpan. Yatpan suggested that she should invite Aqhat to a banquet, whereat he (Yatpan) would spring upon him unawares. Anat, however, proposed a more elaborate plan of attack. Aqhat would indeed be invited to a banquet, but the sight and savor of the food would at the same time attract the attention of eagles and similar birds of prey. Concealing Yatpan in a sack, 'Anat herself would fly in the midst of those eagles and, when they were directly above the head of Aqhat, she would release her henchman — history's first paratrooper! — who would then proceed to attack him. At the same time, she made it plain that she had no desire to kill the youth, but only to render him unconscious, so that the bow might be more easily removed from him. Yatpan, however, proved faithful more to the letter than to the spirit of these instructions, with the result that Aqhat was actually put to death. Chagrined at this unexpected turn of events, the goddess hastened to declare that, having now recovered the bow, she was certainly prepared straightway to restore him to life.

But a contretemps ensued. Flying away from the scene of the murder, Yatpan clumsily dropped the bow into the sea, and it broke. 'Anat, now desperate, turned fiercely upon him, pointing out in no uncertain terms that not only had his bungling ineptitude now deprived her altogether of the bow but it had also resulted in the unnecessary slaying of Aqhat — a circumstance which would have the most serious consequences inasmuch as the "uncovered" blood of the youth would pollute the earth and render it infertile.

Meanwhile, Daniel was sitting, as usual, at the city gate. Suddenly, his daughter Paghat came running toward him, observing that a flight of eagles was wheeling ominously overhead and that, at the same time, a mysterious drought had set in. Putting two and two together, she deduced that a murder must have been committed nearby, for this would account not only for the presence of those birds of prey but also — according to primitive Semitic ideas — for the infertility of the soil. Thereupon, his garment rent in token of grief, Daniel pronounced a curse upon the polluted soil, and immediately thereafter set out on a personal tour of inspection around the fields. Surely enough, no trace of vegetation remained save a stray blade here and a stray ear of corn there. Eventually, messengers came running from the fields, their breath coming in gasps, their hair flowing in the wind, and copious tears streaming down their cheeks. They reported to Daniel that it was his son Aqhat who had been slain.

Daniel, wishing to accord his son honorable burial and thus to "cover" the blood and restore fertility to the soil, at once made efforts to retrieve the remains of Aqhat from the gizzards of the eagles. After two unsuccessful attempts, he finally detected traces of fat and bone, which he duly interred. Then, in accordance with established practice in the case of homicide by an unknown hand, he journeyed to three cities nearest the scene of the crime and pronounced a collective curse upon each of them. As it turned out, the third of these cities happened indeed to be none other than A-b-l-m, where the murder had been committed, though this fact was, of course, unknown to Daniel.

These preliminaries concluded, Daniel next instituted rites of mourning for his slain son. For seven years, professional male and female mourners performed a ritual "keening" in his house, while he himself offered sacrifices. Funeral dances were also performed.

Finally, Paghat approached her father with the proposition that she should embark on an expedition of vengeance for her brother. Daniel approved the enterprise. Thereupon Paghat proceeded to the deed. First, she beautified herself. Next, she donned the garb of a soldier, complete with sword and scimitar, but over it she wore the raiment of a woman. Then, at sundown, she set out to raise the posse. And to whom should her steps lead her if not to Yatpan himself — that same "thug" whom Anat had approached in similar circumstances? Yatpan received her cordially, plying her with wine and pledging support. Moreover, in accordance with established custom — the same custom as Daniel had observed in entertaining Koshar — he suggested that "toasts" be drunk to the gods of his own and his guest's countries. Then, under the influence of the liquor, his tongue was loosed and he started to brag of his prowess. "Why," said he, by way of assuring Paghat of the weight of his assistance, "the hand that slew doughty Aqhat can slay foes by the thousands!" And thereby, of course, he betrayed himself as the murderer of that youth. Paghat was quick to seize her opportunity. Plying him with more and more drink, she resorted to the tactics of Jael with Sisera, and sought to bemuse him so that she might slay him. But at this dramatic point our text unfortunately breaks off.

B. INTERPRETATION

§3. If our basic approach is correct, this story will go back to a primitive seasonal myth relating how a mortal huntsman challenged the supremacy of the goddess of the chase and how his subsequent execution for this impiety caused infertility upon earth. The primary purpose of the myth would have been to acount for the summer drought, and its essential elements, viz., the huntsman and the bow, would therefore reflect natural phenomena associated with that season. Moreover, since the drought eventually breaks and fertility eventually returns, the myth would have had to end with the resurrection of the discomfited hero, or at least with a promise of that event. In other words, his character would have had to be assimilated, more or less, to that of such "dying and reviving" gods as Tammuz, Osiris, Adonis, and the like.

§4. Now, as it happens, these conditions are fulfilled by one of the most famous myths of antiquity — namely, that of Orion.[1] Consequently, by applying to *The Poem of Aqhat* the same interpretation as scholars have long since established for the myth of Orion, we shall be able to discover its basic character and the reason for its inclusion in the sacred repertoire.

The myth of Orion is preserved in a bewildering variety of versions. Moreover, as Otto Gruppe has pointed out,[2] its basic elements are often to be detected in less familiar and more severely localized tales, such as that of Leimon of Tegea or of the giants Otos and Ephialtes, in which even the central character takes a different name. All these multifarious versions, however, ascend to the single basic story of how a mighty huntsman, distinguished alike for his strength as for his beauty, somehow offends the goddess of the chase and is therefore put to death at her hands or at her instigation. The nature of the offense is variously given: according to some, he challenged her supremacy in the chase;[3] according to others, he attempted to rape her[4] or otherwise affronted her feminine pride.[5] Everywhere, however, it is represented as an act of *presumption.*

From the earliest times this story was invested with astral traits; and it is in this form that it has come down to us. The insolent huntsman was recognized in a group of stars which disappear from the evening sky towards the end of April,[6] and on the basis of this identification his discomfiture came naturally to be associated with attendant celestial phenomena. Thus, because the constellation in fact approaches nearer and nearer the sun until ultimately rendered invisible by its glare, one version asserted that he was blinded by Helios, the sun-god.[7] Similarly, because it sets beneath the western horizon at the time when Scorpius is ascendant on the eastern, another version attributed the rout of Orion to the pursuit of a scorpion;[8] while a third, with obvious allusion to the neighboring figure of Canis Major, had him torn to pieces by hounds.[9] In other words, by the time it entered formal classical mythology, the story of Orion had developed into a myth designed expressly to account for the celestial phenomena of the summer months.

§5. Now turn to *The Poem of Aqhat*, and the following arresting similarities at once present themselves:

(*a*) Aqhat, like Orion, is portrayed as a huntsman. Indeed, when Anat finally lures him to his doom, one of the main inducements is that she is inviting him to a hunting expedition (§XIX).

(*b*) Like Orion, Aqhat offends the goddess by an act of presumption. It is of this that she specifically accuses him when he refuses to surrender the bow (§XV), and it is as one "of insolent (or irreverent) heart" that he is characterized by El (§XVIII). Moreover, if we follow the version of Ovid[10] and of a scholiast on the *Theriaca* of Nicander,[11] the offense is in both cases of the same order; for it is obvious that Aqhat's retention of the divine bow implies the same sort of insolent challenge to the goddess' supremacy as those writers attribute to Orion in the arrogant boast that there was no wild beast which he could not tame.

(*c*) Both meet their death through the machinations of the goddess.

§6. With all these points of similarity, however, there is also one significant difference: in the myth of Orion, no particular importance is attached to the bow, whereas in *The Poem of Aqhat* it is the principal element of the plot. Yet this divergence can be very simply explained and, far from militating against a comparison of the two myths, actually supports it. The fact is that in ancient Near Eastern astronomy — as represented by that of the Babylonians — the figure of Canis Major was not recognized; instead, the stars ϵ, σ, δ, and τ of that constellation together with κ and λ of the neighboring constellation of Puppis were grouped together *as a bow.*[12] Moreover, this bow was regarded as the regent constellation of the first decan of the month of Tammuz (or, in a later period, of Ab),[13] and it was mythologically identified as the standard perquisite of the war goddess and goddess of the chase,[14] corresponding to that of Artemis in classical lore. Accordingly, the bow had perforce to occupy a prominent role in any myth relating to Orion and the neighboring astral bodies; it had to take the place of the Huntsman's Dog in corresponding classical and other versions![15]

§7. On general grounds, then, there is ample reason for identifying the basic myth of Aqhat with that of Orion. To clinch the argument, however, it would be as well to show that the latter was indeed known in the ancient Near East. This can be done on the basis of the following evidence.

(*a*) In Mesopotamian texts the constellation Orion sometimes bears the added epithet "he that was smitten by the weapon,"[16] showing knowledge of a myth analogous to that related in classical sources to the effect that Orion was slain by the arrows of Artemis.

(*b*) In Sumerian mythology, the constellation of Orion was identified with the stalwart warrior god Ninurta,[17] who is described as carrying the typical equipment of a *huntsman,* viz., bows and nets.[18]

(*c*) In Job 38:31 there is a specific allusion to the "binding" of Orion ("Canst thou bind the Pleiades °with chains,°[19] or loosen the bonds of Orion [*K^esil*]?"), consistent with the classical myth that, after his resuscitation, Orion was chained to the heavens in the form of a constellation.

(*d*) If the Hebrew name of Orion, viz., *K^{e}sil,* really means "lumbering fool" (the normal sense of the word),[20] it will constitute further evidence that the myth of the Gigantic Huntsman was indeed known; for that name will be most readily explicable from the fact that giants are usually represented in mythology as *gawkish dunderheads.*[21]

§8. It should be observed also in this connection that the figure of the Heavenly Huntsman is not, in fact, confined to clasical and ancient Near Eastern astronomy. In recognizing it, the Canaanites would have been in line with a tendency well represented among primitive peoples. Thus — to cite but a few examples — the Tuaregs identify the constellation as a huntsman followed by a dog;[22] while the Buriats of Eastern Mongolia see in it the picture of three marals being chased by a huntsman and three hounds.[23] The Zuni call it "The Celestial Hunter,"[24] and it is likewise, in all probability, Orion who is intended by the Mexican mythological figure of Citli, "The Bowman."[25]

Among the Chukchee of North America, it is delineated as an archer with a crooked back who shoots a copper arrow (Aldebaran) at a group of maidens (the Pleiades);[26] and in Peru the constellation is symbolized by crossed arrows, indicating huntsmen or hunting.[27] A Peruvian myth represents him as a Promethean criminal raised aloft by two condors.[28] Among the Hottentots, the Belt of Orion is identified as the line whereby a huntsman leads his dog;[29] and this picture is seen also by the Loango.[30] Lastly, both the Bakongo[31] and Wagogo[32] of Africa give the name of "Chief Hunter" to one of the stars of the Belt.

§9. If, then, we may regard the story of Aqhat — in its original and basic form — as a version of the myth of Orion, the reason for its inclusion in the sacred repertoire at once becomes clear. The constellation of Orion sets late at the end of April[33] and rises early at the beginning of July.[34] Its absence from the evening sky thus coincides with the onset and first part of the dry season. The point of the story is now obvious: *it mythologizes in astral terms the climatic and agricultural conditions prevalent during this time of year. The drought and desiccation on earth are correlated with and explained by the discomfiture and disappearance of the Great Huntsman; but his eventual "resurrection" or re-emergence is already foreshadowed.*[35]

§10. The inclusion of our poem in the sacred repertoire was thus due to the same process as obtained in the case of *The Poem of The Gracious Gods.* Just as the latter, relating the birth of the Heavenly Twins, was, as we shall see, the astral myth of June, in which month they are a regent constellation, so *The Poem of Aqhat,* relating the death of the impious huntsman, was the astral myth of the early summer during which period he in fact disappears from the evening sky.

§11. The season covered by the celestial disappearance of the Great Huntsman corresponds, on earth, to those dry and torrid months wherein the lord of fertility (Tammuz, Osiris, Adonis, Dionysus, etc.) was believed to be suffering a similar "eclipse" or discomfiture. June through July, as is well known, was the month of Tammuz, when he was said variously to have been "bound" or "thrust beneath the waters," and when ritual lamentations were performed for him. What more natural, then, than to assimilate to each other the two parallel astronomical and agricultural myths of one and the same season, to see in "Orion" a heavenly "Tammuz" and in "Tammuz" an earthly "Orion"? Were not both associated with comparable goddesses, and was not the death of each followed inevitably by his resurrection? And this is, in fact, what took place; the "Orion" and "Tammuz" myths were blended and fused. Mesopotamian texts, for example, specifically equate the two heroes;[36] while the "binding" of Tammuz, of which so much is made in Babylonian myth, is transferred in the Book of Job (38:31) to the figure of Orion![37] So, too, the Egyptians commonly assimilated both Osiris[38] and Horus[39] to Orion; while among the Greeks, typical features of the Orion myth are to be found associated with such "dying and reviving" gods of fertility as, for instance, Zagreus-Dionysis[40] and Hyas-Adonis.[41]

The Canaanite mythographers followed suit. What we have, therefore, in *The Poem of Aqhat* is no longer the unvarnished tale of Orion but a conflate myth in which that basic nucleus has been blended with the traits and motifs of the Tammuz cycle. Not only is Aqhat invested with several of the characteristic marks of the "dying and reviving god," but the story is told in such a way as to incorporate salient features of the Tammuz and cognate mysteries.

§12. Special importance is attached, for instance, to the fact that Aqhat was not only slain but also *dismembered* and that, prior to his resuscitation, the several portions of his body — "the fat and bone," as they are called — had to be recovered and interred (§XXXI). Now, from the point of view of the story, this is an utterly unnecessary and extraneous detail; it does not appear in the classical versions of the myth of Orion. Once it is recognized, however, that Aqhat is not only "Orion" but also "Tammuz," the reason for its introduction becomes clear: the dismemberment and reassemblage of the slain lord of fertility is an essential part of his myth. Osiris is dismembered and reassembled; so is Zagreus; so is Adonis; so too, apparently, is Mot. Indeed, as Gilbert Murray has pointed out,[42] the dismemberment [*sparagmos*] is one of the essential elements of the pattern underlying Greek tragedy; and Cornford would even see a survival of it in the characteristic distribution of sweetmeats (i.e., originally, the parts of the dismembered body) at the conclusion of a Greek comedy.[43] Similarly, the punctilious reassemblage of Aqhat's remains and their interment in a jar (§XXXI) is but the mythic counterpart of ceremonies performed in many parts of the world as part of the mysteries of "dying and reviving gods." The Egyptian Osiris and the Syrian Attis, for example, were similarly "collected" and buried; while mock funerals of a comparable character were a common feature of seasonal rituals.[44] Daniel, the father of Aqhat, does in fact precisely what the goddesses Isis and Nephthys are represented as doing in the Egyptian rites of Osiris.[45]

§13. In the same way, it is not difficult to recognize in the weeping for Aqhat (§XXXIII) a mythological counterpart of the seasonal ululation,[46] corresponding to the ritual wailing for Tammuz, Osiris, Telipinu, Attis, Adonis, Persephone, and the like which, as we know, usually took place at the very season of year covered by the absence of the celestial huntsman.

§14. So, too, it is by no means improbable that the passage in our poem (III, 28^b–37) which describes how Daniel and his daughter Paghat made the rounds of the fields and how the former clasped and kissed an ear of corn and a blade of grass(?) reflects a magical ceremony connected with the reaping of the corn. Such ceremonies, as we shall see (below, §XXIX), do indeed obtain in several parts of the world.

§15. Assuming, then, that our story goes back to a seasonal myth, the analogy of similar texts discussed in this volume would suggest that, *in its original form,* it was acted or recited at a specific festival. The quesion then arises: When did that festival take place?

The theme of the myth is, as we have seen, not only the death and (apparent) resurrection of the huntsman but also the loss and (apparent) recovery of the bow. Hence, the underlying festival must have taken place between the late setting and early rising not only of Orion but also and more specifically of the bow star i.e. (virtually), Sirius. Moreover, since the story evidently concluded with the recovery of the bow, it could not very well have been acted or recited before the corresponding astral event had actually occurred. Accordingly, we are led to the conclusion that *the most probable date of the festival here mythologized was that of the early rising of Sirius toward the end of July or the beginning of August*[47] — a conclusion strongly supported by the fact that in many calendars (e.g., the ancient Egyptian) the rising of Sirius is indeed regarded as the beginning of the year and is therefore celebrated as a festival.[48]

§16. It is true, of course, that in the form in which it has come down to us the original motivation of the story has been entirely forgotten, its primitive ritual elements being thoroughly integrated into a purely literary composition. The reader may consequently be inclined to suspect that perhaps, after all, we are going beyond the evidence. It is therefore pertinent to point out, in concluding our inquiry, that the method here adopted is, in fact, that pursued by folklorists everywhere in the analysis of tales and legends. The process which we imply in the evolution of our story is, in other words, no whit different from that which has been revealed by Bolte and Polivka in their classic analysis of Grimm's Marchen,[49] or by Lady Gomme[50] and Lewis Spence[51] in their examination of children's games and nursery rhymes, or by the late Jessie L. Weston in her famous demonstration of ritual elements in the Grail legend.[52]

NOTES

1. On the Orion myth in general, see: K. O. Müller, *Kl. Schriften,* ii. 113 ff.; Suchier, *Orion der Jäger* (1859); Allen, *Star Names,* 303 ff.; Drews, *Sternhimmel,* 53 ff.; Basset, *Rev. d. trad. pop.* 4 (1899), 616 f.; Kuenztle, in Roscher's *Lexicon.*

2. Gruppe, *Gr. Mythol.,* 69–70.

3. Ovid, *Fasti* v 539–40; Schol. in Nicander, *Ther.,* 15.

4. Horace, *Odes* iii, 4.72; Aratus, *Phaen.,* 636–46; Eratosthenes, *Katastr.,* 32; Nicander, *Ther.,* 13–16; Euphorion, *fr.* 108, Meineke; Nigid. Figul., *fr.* 86, Swob.

5. For the various traditions, see Apollodorus, ed. Frazer, i. 33, n. 2; Gruppe, *op. cit.,* 953, nn. 5–7.

6. Eudoxus, *apud* Gem. 11, p. 230, Mar., puts the date at April 23, but Pliny, *HN* xviii 248 assigns it to April 28. The *Geoponica* (i. 9) says that the late setting occurs on April 29. According to Dalman, *Arbeit u. Sitte,* 1/ii, 493–94, Orion β sets in the Palestinian sky on April 20, and Orion α on May 6.

7. Gruppe, *op. cit.,* 952.

8. Lucan, *Phars.* ix 836; Ovid, *Fasti* v 541; Eratosthenes, *Katasterismos* 32; Nicander, *Ther.* 15 ff.; Aratus, *Phaenomena* 634 ff.; Schol. in Il. xviii 486; Schol. in Od. v 121; Lactantius Placidus on Statius, *Theb.* iii 27.

9. This version survives only in the cognate myth of Otos and Ephialtes: Apollodorus i 55; Eustathius on Od. xi 316. On the ultimate identity of these giants with "Orion," see Gruppe, *op. cit.,* 67–70.

10. *Fasti* iv 539–40.

11. In *Ther.* 15.

12. Sum. [mul]BAN; Semitic [kakkab]Qashtu; cf. Kügler, *Ergänzungen,* 201.

13. Astrolabe Pinches = JRAS 1900. 573–75; Kügler, *Ergänzungen,* loc. cit.; Weidner, *Handbuch,* 65–66. For the shift to Ab in the Aries period (after 1100 B.C.), see KAVI, pp. 123–5; CT XXXIII, 2. 7; Streck, *Assurbanipal,* 72, ix. 9; Langdon, *Menologies,* 21, n. 1. According to CT XXXIII, 7. 22–23, it rises on Ab 15, but *ibid.,* 4. 14 gives the date as Ab 5.

14. Cf. V. Rawl. 46 A 23; CT xxiii 2 ii 7; Virolleaud, *Ishtar,* Suppl.², No. 67.15; KAVI, p. 121:15. The association appears already on the sculptures of Mari. Note also that in Callimachus, *Hymn to Artemis* 9–10, the goddess says expressly that the Cyclopes (i.e., the workmen of Hephaistos = Koshar!) will make arrows for her.

15. It may be tentatively suggested that another ancient Semitic myth concerning the constellation of the Bow really underlies

Genesis 9:13–14. We have been wont to assume that the bow which God set in the clouds after the Flood was the rainbow, and very probably, the author of the Biblical version of the tale himself thought so (note his reference to "the cloud" rather than "the sky"). But the fact remains that, in ancient times, people do not seem to have recognized the figure of a bow in that celestial phenomenon. In Lithuanian mythology, for example, it is Laima's girdle, and in Estonian superstition, it is the thunder god's sickle (Grimm, *Teut. Mythology*, 733). So, too, in the Armenian version of Philo's *Quaestiones et solutiones in Genesin et Exodum*, ii 54 (148, Aucher), it is the girdle of Aramazd (cf. Marcus, JNES 7 [1948], 113); while in ancient Mesopotamian literature, it is "the ornament of heaven" or "the ring" (*marratu;* cf. Jeremias, *Handbuch*, 139 f.). Accordingly, it may be suggested that what God did (in the original version of the tale) was to set in the sky the victorious weapon wherewith he had subdued the dragon or demon who (in that more primitive version) was the causer of the flood. He did, in fact, precisely what Qozahi is said in Arab legend to have done with his bow (Wellhausen, *Prol.*,[6] 311) and what, in the Mesopotamian poem *Enuma Elish*, Marduk does with his after vanquishing Tiamat. This element of the story then survived vestigially even when the Flood itself was given a different motivation – a process familiar to every student of folklore.

16. Cf. K.250 iv 2–3; II R 49 iii 20: ^{mul}SIB.ZI.AN.NA | *sha ina kakki makhtsu*. See Ungnad, ZDMG 73 (1919), 159 ff.; but note also the objections of Bezold, ZA 32 (1916–17), 210, to some of Ungnad's deductions.

17. Cf. Dhorme, *Hilprecht Volume*, 365 f.

18. Cf. Hrozný, MVAG 1903, No. 3, col. iii, obv. 34, rev. 4, 6, 8, 10 (mentioning *allukhapu, suskallu, ariktu, qashtu,* and *tilpanu*). The arrows of Ninurta are mentioned in Assurb., *Annals* ix 84 f. Cf. Frank, *Bilder und Symbole*, 27–28.

19. This is the correct rendering. The word *ma'adanot* of MT must be emended to *ma'anadot*, as most modern scholars have seen.

20. The general view of Biblical scholars is that the word must have the connotation of "impious rogue"; but, as Cheyne rightly pointed out, it nowhere else carries this sense, which is reserved to the term *nabal*. (Note that in Psalm 14:1 [53:2] it is the *nabal*, not the *kesil*, who says in his heart, "There is no God.") *Kesil*, connected with *kesel*, "loin," means rather a lumbering fellow, a *gawk*.

21. See Commentary on *The Snaring of the Dragon*, II.

22. Duveyrier, *Les touaregs du nord*, 424.

23. Klemenz, ERE iii, 11 a.

24. Hagar, ERE xii, 71 a.

25. *Ibidem.*

26. Bogoras, *Chuckchee*, ii. 307 f.

27. Hagar, loc. cit.

28. *Ibidem.*
29. Schulze, *Aus Namaland u. Kalahari,* 367 ff.
30. *Loango Expedition,* ii/2, 135 ff.
31. Weekes, *Among the Primitive Bakongo,* 293 ff.
32. Claus, *Wagogo,* 39.
33. See above, n. 6.
34. Hesiod, *Works and Days,* 597. The date usually given is July 9; cf. Nilsson, *Primitive Time-Reckoning,* 112 *Geoponica* i 9 puts the early rising between June 23 and July 10. In the Taurus period (ca. 3000–1100 B.C.), Orion was regarded as the regent constellation of the first decan of Sivan; KAVI, p. 123.8; CT xxxiii 2 ii 2; 9 r 10; Virolleaud, *Ishtar* xxvi 7. In V R 43 a 11 and Langdon, *Drehem,* 9, Sivan is characterized as the month of the god NE.GUN, who is in turn identified with Ninurta-Orion in CT XXV, 12.33. A festival of "Shemal and the Bowman" was celebrated by the Mandaeans on the twenty-seventh of Haziran (Sivan); cf. Chwolson, *Ssabier,* ii. 26; Langdon, *Menologies,* 119.
35. That Aqhat was eventually resurrected is obvious from the fact that 'Anat repeatedly states that she will revive him. This has been recognized by almost all scholars who have dealt with the text; cf. Aistleitner, *Mahler Festschrift,* 37; T. H. Gaster, SMSR 12 (1937), 127; Spiegel, JBL 59 (1940), p. viii; *idem., Louis Ginzberg Jubilee Volume,* 316, nn. 13–14; Gordon, *The Living Past,* 155; Engnell, *Kingship,* 135; Albright, BASOR 94 (1944), 34; Ginsberg, *ibid.,* 97 (1945), 7.
36. SIB.ZI.AN.NA (Orion) is given as a name of Tammuz in CT XXIV 9, XXV 7, etc.; cf. Zimmern, *Tammuz,* 7, n. 1; Weidner, *Handbuch,* 50; Dhorme, *Les rel. de Bab. et Ass.* (1945), 81, 119; Jeremias, *Geisteskultur,* 129.
37. For the "binding" (*kamûtum*) of Tammuz, cf. V R 48 iv 23; Reisner, *Sum.-bab. Hymnen,* ii 213.
38. Boll, *Sphaera,* 164–68; Brugsch, ZDMG 10 (1865), 665; Lefebvre, *Mythe osirien,* ii 213.
39. Plutarch, *De Is. et Os.,* 21.
40. Cf. Gruppe, *op. cit.,* 948, 962 f.
41. *Ibid.,* 950, n. 1.
42. In Harrison, *Themis,* 341 ff.
43. Cornford, *Origins of Attic Comedy,* 101.
44. See *Hittite Yuletide Myth,* Introd., §11.
45. Moret, *Mystères égypt.,* 29–31.
46. See Chapter Two, §§8–13.
47. See above, n. 13.
48. Cf. Censorinus, *De die natali,* xxi. 13; Nilsson, *Primitive Time-Reckoning,* 279.
49. *Anmerkungen zu . . . Grimm.*
50. *Children's Singing Games* (1894).
51. *Myth and Ritual in Dance, Games and Rhyme* (1947).
52. *From Ritual to Romance* (1930).

DANIEL ACQUIRES A SON

I

I i, 3–16ᵃ: Daniel, seeking the divine gift of a son, serves in the sanctuary of Baal for seven days, passing the nights in the sacred precincts.

Clothed in the (ritual) loincloth, he gives food to the gods;
Clothed in the (ritual) loincloth, he gives drink to the holy beings,

---

I. (I i, 3–16ᵃ). What is here described is the well-known rite of *incubation.* The suppliant lodges for a few days in the precincts of the sanctuary in order to entreat the god and obtain the divine oracle in a dream or by some other manner.

Daniel is described as giving food and drink to the gods [*ilm*] and holy beings [*bn qdsh*] for seven days. He performs this pious task in the capacity of "one clothed in a loincloth [*uzr*]."

The significance of the term becomes clear when we study the religious customs of the Semites: *the ritual garb of a suppliant or pilgrim was the loincloth.*

Thus, in Arab usage, the standard costume of a *muhrim,* or pilgrim, was the *izar* (Wensinck, *Mourning,* 63 f.). Similarly, worshipers at the Kaaba in Mecca wore a *raht* or *hauf* – that is, "a girdle or short kilt slashed with thongs" (Robertson Smith-Cook, *Rel. Sem.,*[3] 437, n. 2).

In ancient Israel, the typical raiment of an ascetic or anchorite was the *ezor,* or loincloth, as we learn from the description of Elijah in II Kings 1:8. Analogous, as most scholars have recognized, was the linen *ephod* (Old Assyr. *epadatum,* "wrap"), which was not only the official uniform of the priests (Exodus 25:7; I Samuel 14:3; 22:18, etc.) but which is said expressly in I Samuel 2:18 to have been worn by the young Samuel *when he served as an acolyte in the sanctuary at Shiloh.* Note, too, that David is said in II Samuel 6:14 to have worn the linen *ephod* while performing religious exercises.

So great, indeed, was the importance attached to the special raiment of votaries that, according to II Kings 10:22, the clothes of the worshipers of Baal of Tyre in Samaria were provided out of a special wardrobe. Similarly, both Silus Italicus (iii, 23 f.) and Herodian (v, 5.10) state explicitly that worshipers at Phoenician shrines were required to wear special dress (cf. Lods, *Israel,* 312);

Proceeds (duly) [to his cell] and lies down,
Proceeds duly [to his cell] and passes the night.

Behold, one day and a second,
[Clothed in the (ritual) loincloth],
[Clothed in the (ritual) loincloth], Daniel gives food to the gods,
Clothed in the (ritual) loincloth, he gives drink to the holy beings.

---

while a similar rule applied to persons consulting the oracles of Trophonios at Delphi, in Greece (Pausanias ix, 39; Livy xxiii, 11). Moreover, Yakut II, 108.7 ff. (= Goldziher, WZKM 16 [1902], 138, n. 8) relates the following:

> A man of the tribe of Kinda lost some camels which had strayed. So he went to the god Jalsad and asked for two pieces of clothing from the garments of the keepers of the sanctuary. These he rented and put on. This was the regular usage of the pagan Arabs.

The term "clothed in a loincloth" is thus seen to have special point: it indicates the precise capacity in which Daniel served in the sacred precincts for seven days.

The custom of *incubation* was widespread in the religious life of the ancient Near East. The basic idea that the will of a god was revealed especially in dreams dreamed in sacred places is well illustrated by I Samuel 3 – the story of the infant Samuel at the sanctuary of Shiloh. Cf. also Jacob's dream at Bethel (Genesis 28:10–22) and Numbers 22:8, where Balaam, the Syrian seer, tells the envoys of King Balak to "*lodge here this night,* and I shall report to you as YHWH shall speak unto me." This might suggest that he practiced the rite of incubation. (Jirku, ZAW 33 [1913], 151–53, finds many other instances in the Old Testament, but most of them scarcely carry conviction.)

For Babylonian examples, see Furlani, *La religione babilonese e assira,* ii, 254.

For Hittite evidence, cf. KUB VII 5 iv, 1 ff. Note also that Mursilis II refers to the rite of "incubation in a state of purity [*suppaya seskiskanzi*]" as a means of seeking divine aid in removing a plague (II xi 5 = Goetze, KlF 1 [1929], 161–251; Furlani, *Rel. d. hittiti,* 152–53; Goetze, *Kleinasien,*[1] 139–40).

It has also been suggested that the verb *t-l-l,* lit., "to shelter, bivouac," so frequent in the Safaitic inscriptions, really refers to

For a third day and a fourth,
[Clothed in the (ritual) loincloth],
Clothed in the (ritual) loincloth, Daniel gives food to the gods,
Clothed in the (ritual) loincloth, he gives drink to the holy beings.

For a [fi]fth day, a sixth and a seventh,
Clothed in the (ritual) loincloth, Daniel gives good to the gods,
Clothed in the (ritual) loincloth, he gives drink to the holy beings.
(Nightly) [Dani]el proceeds to his cell,
Ascends (his couch) and lies down,
[Doffs] the (ritual) loincloth and passes the night.

II

I, i, 16ᵇ–34: Baal intercedes with the supreme god El to grant Daniel a son and heir.

Then, on the seventh day,
Baal accedes to his supplication, (saying):
"[Dani]el the Rapheite is filled with grief,

---

incubation (Dussaud-Macler, *Safa,* 165, 179, 210, etc.); while Grimme has sought (ZDMG, N.F. 12 [1934], 194) to read this sense into the word *n-m,* "he slumbered," which he would recognize in the enigmatic proto-Hebrew inscriptions from Serabit al Hadim in Sinai. This last, however, is very doubtful.

The custom was also common in the Graeco-Roman world: see Melibomius, *De incubatione in fanis deorum medicinae causa olim facta* (Helmst., 1659); von Rittersheim, G., *Der medizinische Wunderglaube und die Inkubation im Altertum* (Berlin, 1878); Deubner, L., *De incubatione* (Leipzig, 1909). On incubation at Delphi, cf. Rohde, *Psyche,*[3] ii. 58, n. 1. On the same custom in the temple of Asklepios at Lebena, Crete, see Kaibel, EG, No. 839. See also Gruppe, *Gr. Mythol.,* 928 ff. On modern survivals in Greece, cf. Schmidt, *D. Volksleben d. Neugriechen,* 77.

II–V (I i, 16ᵇ–ii, 23). The sanctuary in which Daniel performed his service was evidently that of Baal. It is for this reason that Baal is represented as conveying his suppliant's request to El. Indeed, it is to be observed that throughout the Ugaritic texts El occupies the position of what anthropologists have called "the

The H-r-n-m-ite hero with sighs,
For that he hath no son like his brethren,
Neither scion like his kinsmen.
No son hath he like his brethren,
Neither scion like his kin.

Clothed in the (ritual) loincloth, he keeps giving food to the gods.
Clothed in the (ritual) loincloth, keeps giving drink to the holy beings.

So bless him, O El, thou Bull-god, my sire,
Be gracious unto him, O Creator of all creatures,
That there be a son of his in (his) house,
A scion within his palace;
One who may set up the statues of his departed ancestors,
Who may . . . his (departed) kinsfolk in the sanctuary,
Who may make his smoke to go forth from the ground,

---

remote high god," whereas Baal is the demiurge, who actually rules over gods and men and who ranks as the more prominent figure in cult and myth.

Many of the filial duties here enumerated can be illustrated from other sources.

1. The duty of erecting steles or statues to departed ancestors – which would include the father himself – is well illustrated by II Samuel 18:18, where Absalom is said to have erected a monument to himself during his lifetime "because, said he, I have no son to commemorate my name." Similarly, in the inscription of Bar-Rekub of Sama'l (745–727 B.C.; Cooke, *North Sem. Inscriptions,* 62. 16–20) we are told expressly: "I set up this pillar to my father . . . in front of my father Panamuwa's tomb, and it is a memorial of him." Illuminating also in this connection is the statement of the Phoenician mythographer Sanchuniathon (ed. Orelli, p. 18) that when the demigods Ousoos and Hypsouranios died, "their survivors . . . adored the stelae and celebrated annual festivals in their honor."

Typical examples of such commemorative steles may be found in CIS I 58 and 60 (from Kition, Cyprus); while on the subject in general, see Cook, *Rel. Ancient Palestine* (1930), 19–20.

Of particular interest is the word used in the original to denote "ancestral spirit, departed ancestor," viz., *ilib.* The first part of this word is the familiar *il,* "god, numen"; the second has been

Who may guard his place upon earth,
Who may quash(?) all slander leveled against him,
Who may drive away any that would assail his guests,
Who may hold his hand when he is drunken,
Support him when he is full with wine,
Who may eat (for him) his slice in the house of Baal,
[Consume] (for him) his portion in the house of El,
Who may plaster his roof when it rains,
Who may wash his clothes when they are soiled."

III

I, i, 35–48: El accedes to the request.

Thereupon El grasps his servant [by the hand],
Blesses [Danie]l the Rapheite,
Shows grace to the [Ḣ-r-]n-m-ite [hero], (saying):

---

brilliantly connected by Albright (*Archaeology and the Rel. of Israel*, 203, n. 31) with the obscure Hebrew *ob*, which means properly "ghost, *revenant*" (cp. Arabic *'aba*, "return," and cp. the Old Norse term *aptrganga* and the Danish *gienfard, gienganger*, "returner" in the sense of "specter, ghost"; Grimm, *Teutonic Mythology*, tr. Stallybrass, 915). If this identification is correct, it is interesting to note that in the story of the Witch of Endor (I Samuel 28) that sorceress is described as a *ba'alath ob*, i.e., "one in control of a revenant (*ob*)" and the spirits which she evokes as *elohim*, i.e., "gods, numina" (vv. 7, 13).

The precise significance of the parallel expression in this first couplet is obscure, because the meaning of the crucial verb (*ztr*) is unknown. Obviously, it refers to something done *in the sanctuary* and necessarily in connection with the cult of ancestors. A clue may perhaps be found by reference to commemorative usages in other parts of the Semitic world. The Babylonian text CT xvi, pl. 10, v. 10–14 prescribes three duties toward the dead, viz., (i) "pronouncing the name" (*zakar shumi*); (ii) "offering food" (*kasap kispi*); and (iii) "pouring water" (*naq mê*). Similarly, in the Hadad inscription from Zenjirli (Cooke, *op. cit.*, 61. 14–18), the erection of a statue, the proffering of food and drink, and the pronouncing of the name are mentioned as three collateral duties which a son owes to his deceased father. Now, from II Samuel 18:18 (the incident of Absalom's pillar) we know that the erection

"Let Daniel the Rapheite be revived in spirit,
The H-r-n-m-ite hero in soul,
. . . . he . . . .
Let [Daniel] ascend his couch;
By reason of his kiss, let his wife [be brought to labor];
By reason of his ardent embrace, let her [con]ceive and bear.
. . . .
So shall there be a son of his [in (his) house],
[A scion] within his palace;
[Who may set up the statues of his de]parted ancestors,
[Who may . . . . his (departed) kinsfolk] in the sanctuary,
Who may make [his smoke] to go forth [from the grou]nd,
[Who may gua]rd his place [upon earth],
[Who may quash(?) all slander leveled against him],
[Who may drive] away any that would assail [his guests]."

* * *

of the statue and the pronouncing (*z-k-r*) of the name were considered as virtually one ceremony. The latter, therefore, would be covered in our text by the single phrase "one who may set up the statues of his deceased ancestors." Accordingly, the supplementary clause, "who may . . . his (departed) kinsfolk in the sanctuary" may reasonably refer to *the proffering of food and drink.*

2. The second item in the catalogue of filial duties is that of guarding the home and maintaining its security.

The first clause defines the dutiful son as "one who makes his (father's) smoke to issue from the earth." This has been generally explained as referring to the burning of incense in funerary rites. The structure of the passage, however, demands that the words be parallel in sense to the immediately succeeding clause, "one who guards his place upon earth." We therefore suggest that they are nothing but the equivalent of our own "keep the home fires burning." In support of this is the fact that the *extinguishing* of household fires (or lamps) is a common metaphor in Hebrew for domestic or personal misfortune; compare, for example, Job 18:5–6: "The light of the wicked is put out, and the spark of his fire doth not shine; the light in his tent is darkened, and his lamp above him is put out"; *ibid.*, 21:17: "Dimmed is the light of the wicked"; Proverbs 13:9; 24:20: "The lamp of the wicked is put out"; *ibid.*, 31:18: the virtuous woman's "lamp is not extinguished at night"; *ibid.*, 20:20: "Whoso curseth his father or his mother, his lamp shall be put out"; II Samuel 21:17: "Then

IV

I, ii 1–8ᵃ: Baal transmits El's decision to Daniel.

* * *

"[There shall be a son of thine in (thy) house],
[A scion of thine within thy palace],
[One who may set up the statues of thy departed ancestors],
Who may . . [. . thy (departed) kinsfolk in the sanctuary],
[Who may make thy smoke to go forth from the ground],

David's men sware unto him, saying, Thou shalt go no more out with us to battle, that thou quench not the lamp of Israel." Similarly, in Arabic idiom, the *extinction of a light* is a synonym for disaster (Schultens, *Job,* 440 f.). Conversely, then, the maintenance of the household fires implies the preservation of the home. On this usage, see further II Kings 8:19; Psalm 132:17; KB vi/2, 132 ii 86–87; Haupt, JBL 33 (1914), 166; 35 (1:91:6), 319; Landsberger, OLZ 19 (1916), 33–39; Cook, *op. cit.,* 87; Smith, *Isaiah XL–LV,* 164. Somewhat similar is Othello's "Put out the light, and then put out the light" (Shakespeare, *Othello,* Act V, sc. ii, 7). For classical parallels, see Fustel de Coulanges, *The Ancient City* (Anchor Books ed.), 25, n. 2.

3. The third couplet refers to the duty of defending one's father's reputation and honor. The first hemistich is philologically difficult, and a variety of interpretations have been proposed. It is evident, however, that it must provide a parallel to the second, wherein is prescribed the duty of "expelling him who steals up under cover of darkness against him who lodges with him [i.e., the father] overnight." As is well known, such violation of hospitality is regarded in the East as the supreme dishonor. Hence, what is here indicated is not so much the protection of the guest as the defense of the host from such shame and obloquy. (After all, it is the duty of the son to his father, not to his father's guests, that is the theme of this passage.) Accordingly, the obscure first hemistich must likewise refer to the obligation of championing one's father's reputation.

4. The fourth couplet is plain sailing: another of the son's duties is to bring his father home when he is in his cups – the familiar task of all dutiful offspring everywhere!

Cassuto and Ginsberg have found an excellent illustration of this in the words addressed to Jerusalem in Isaiah 51:17–18:

Who may [gu]ard [thy place] upon earth,
Who may quash(?) all slander leveled against thee,
Who may drive away [any that would assail thy guests],
Who may eat (for thee) thy slice in the house of [Baal],
[Who may consume (for thee) thy portion] in the house of El,
Who may hold thy hand when [thou art drunken],
Support thee when thou art full with wine,
Who may [plaster] thy roof when it rains,
Who may wash thy clothes when they are soiled."

V

I, ii 8b–23: Daniel rejoices at the news.

Daniel's mien is cheered,
His countenance is all aglow.
He puts away all grief and laughs,
Places his feet on the footstool,
Lifts his voice and cries:

Thou hast drunken from YHWH's hand
the cup of his wrath;
The goblet of reeling
hast thou drunken, yea, drained.
There is none to lead her (home)
of all the sons she hath born,
And none to grasp her hand
of all the sons she hath reared!

5. The fifth of the filial duties enumerated is that of serving as proxy for one's father in religious ceremonies. A son may substitute for him at sacrificial feasts. The relevant words, meaning literally "Eat his slice in the house of Baal, consume his portion in the house of El," refer, of course, to participation in communal sacrifices or sacraments. The words are to be explained in the light of the ancient and primitive belief that partaking of the sacrificial meal symbolized and insured relationship with the god and at the same time cemented the ties of the kindred. He who failed to do so was automatically "cut off from his people" (as in the case of the Israelitic paschal meal). Accordingly, it was of advantage to a man to have a son who could deputize for him in his old age or in the event of unavoidable absence and thus "represent the family." See the classic discussion of Semitic commensality by Robertson Smith, in *Rel. Sem.*, 217, 236 ff.

"I shall now have rest again,
And repose shall lie in my breast,
For that a son is to be born unto me as unto my brethren,
A scion as unto my kinsmen;
One who may set up the statues of my departed ancestors,
Who may . . . my (departed) kinsfolk in the sanctuary,
<Who may make my smoke to go forth from the ground,>

Who may guard [my] place upon earth,
Who may quash(?) all slander leveled against me,
Who may drive away any who would assail my guests,
Who may hold my hand when I am drunken,
Support me when I am full with wi[ne],
Who may eat (for me) my slice in the house of Baal,
Who may [consume] (for me) my [portion] in the house of El,
Who may plaster my roof when it rains,
Who may wash my clothes when they are soiled."

VI

I, ii 24–38: Daniel goes home and celebrates.

Daniel repairs to his house,
Daniel betakes himself to his palace.
Artistes now enter his house,

These lines are well illustrated by I Samuel 1:3–4, which describes how Elkanah, the father of Samuel, "used to go up annually from his city to worship and celebrate a sacrificial meal unto YHWH Sebaot in Shiloh," and how, on such occasions, he used to distribute "portions," sc. of the sacrifice, among the members of his family. (The same term – *mnt* – is used in the original as in our text.)

6. Lastly, it is the duty of a son to attend to such menial chores as may promote his father's personal comfort. He must "plaster the roof when it rains" and "launder his clothes when they are soiled." This requires no comment.

VI (I ii, 24–46). This scene is illustrated completely by modern Arab usage, where the birth of a child is marked by a seven-day celebration at which the guests are entertained by female singers

Daughters of melody, swallows.
    Then Daniel the Rapheite,
Thereupon the H-r-n-m-ite hero,
Slaughters an ox for the artistes;
Gives the artistes to eat,
And the daughters of melody, the swallows, to drink.

    Behold, for one day and a second
He [gives] the artistes to eat,
And the daughters of melody, the swallows, to dr[i]nk.

---

and musicians (*awalim* or *gaziyalis*); cf. Lane, *Modern Egyptians*, ch. xxvii.

The songstresses are called *k-th-r-t,* a name which properly combines the twin notions of "artisan" and "artist." It is from the same root that Kosh/thar, the divine smith and handyman, derives his name, and it is significant that, according to Sanchuniathon, that god was the discoverer not only of iron and smelting but also of literary composition and song.[a]

It is noteworthy also that the ancient Hebrew tradition embodied in Genesis 4:21 represents "the father of all such as handle the harp and pipe" to have been a certain JUBAL, whose name connects with the root *w-b-l/b-l-l* (cf. Accadian *bullulu*), "to found, smelt," and who was the half brother of TUBAL-QAIN, "the forger of every cutting instrument of brass and iron" (cp. *w-b-l/b-l-l* and Arabic *qayin,* "smith"!).

The *k-th-r-t* are described as "swallows" (*snnt*) and as "daughters of the loud cry" (*bnt hll*). The former expression is directly comparable with the English use of "nightingale" or "thrush" to denote a prima donna. The latter, it may be suggested, was not just an epithet for a sweet singer, but likewise properly denoted "songbirds," on the analogy of the Hebrew expression, "daughters of song" = "birds," in Ecclesiastes 12:4. This is supported by the fact that in Arabic, the word *muhelhel* from the same root is the popular name for the Roller (Coracias garrulus, Linn.), with which in turn Campbell Thompson (JRAS 1924, 258 f.) would identify the *allallu* of the Gilgamesh Epic, who keeps crying *kappi.*

The suggestion is further supported by the fact that in the Canaanite *Poem of Keret* (C i 5) women who sing joyful songs are termed *ts-r-r-t,* a name which may be connected, similarly, with the Accadian *zirzirru,* "cricket, katydid," and with Hebrew and Arabic *ts-r-ts-r,* "to chirrup." So, too, the two priestesses

[a] See Commentary, *Baal,* §XIV.

Behold, for a third day and a fo[urth]
He gives the artistes to eat,
And the daughters of melody, the swallows, to drink.

For a fifth day and a sixth
He gives the artistes to eat,
And the daughters of melody, the swallows, to drink.

Then, on the seventh day,
The artistes depart from his house,
The daughters of melody, the swallows.

I, ii 39–46: Daniel's son Aqhat is begotten and born.

[Spread is] the lovely [royal] couch,
The beautiful, princely marriage bed.

Then Daniel goes counting his months:
One month [goes by and a second],
A third and a fourth . . .
. . . . months
. . . . departs . . . . .

* * *

AQHAT ACQUIRES THE DIVINE BOW

VII

I v, 2–13ᵃ: Koshar ("Sir Adroit"), the divine artisan, comes from his forge in Egypt, bearing a consignment of bows destined for the use of the gods and goddesses.

---

who impersonate Isis and Nephthys and mourn for Osiris in the annual mysteries in Egypt are termed "the two kites" (Faulkner, JEA 22 [1936], 132; Davies-Gardiner, *Tomb of Amenemhet*, 42).

VII (I v, 2–13ᵃ). From the concluding words of the preceding passage ("Daniel goes counting his months . . .") it is clear that a period of time has elapsed. Aqhat is now a grown youth, old enough to handle a bow. This scene describes how he received one. Since it is, in a sense, the crucial scene of the poem, and since the entire plot hinges upon it, it is especially important that it be understood correctly.

The bow which Aqhat acquires is no ordinary bow, as the

(*Loquitur Koshar.*)

* * *

Then, behold, on the sev[enth] day,
There is Daniel the Rapheite,
There is the H-r-n-m-ite hero,
Sitting high enthroned at the gate,

---

majority of commentators have assumed. The whole point is that *it is a divine bow* withdrawn from a stock which the artisan god Koshar was carrying to the gods.

Only on this interpretation does the sequence of events make sense, and only thus does the present episode fall into place as an integral element of the story. For, in the first place, if the bow had been such as any youth or huntsman might have possessed, there would have been no point in introducing Koshar as the presenter of it; Aqhat could just as well have acquired such a bow through less exalted channels. As it is, however, the very presence of Koshar shows that the bow was divine; for Koshar was the Canaanite Hephaistos (see Commentary, *Baal,* §XIV) and, like his Greek counterpart, one of his functions was to forge weapons for the gods (cf. I vi, 24–25). Secondly, it is only on this basis that 'Anat's subsequent eagerness to recover the bow becomes at all intelligible. If it had been an ordinary one, and her motive had been merely to forestall a potential rival in the chase, this would have been quite absurd, since – a point strangely overlooked by previous commentators – even if Aqhat had been forced to surrender it, he could readily have acquired another. The same would hold true also if her motive had been mere covetousness; why should she covet a plebeian bow when she presumably possessed a divine one? Besides, there would have been thousands of other mortals who also owned such bows. Once we realize, however, that *the bow was of divine character and that by retaining it Aqhat was in fact depriving 'Anat of it,* all becomes clear: the goddess is naturally indignant at the manner in which a mere mortal dares to rob her of what is, in fact, the characteristic perquisite of her office, she being the Canaanite Artemis.

The scene opens with what are evidently the last words of a speech delivered by Koshar. He declares that he is "carrying bows by the dozen." It may be supposed that in the large gap which separates this passage from the preceding, the scene shifted from the earthly affairs of Daniel to events in the abode of the gods. It was, we may assume, in response to some divine order that Koshar

Next to the threshing floors which are beside the granary,
Judging the cause of widows,
Dispensing justice to orphans,
When, lifting his eyes, he espies
Sir Adroit coming along
From a journey of a thousand acres,
Ten thousand tracts.
He catches sight, yea, he catches sight
Of Sir Cunning speeding nigh.
There he is carrying bows,
Bearing arcs by the dozen.

---

now came speeding from his forge in Egypt, laden with bows destined for the gods.

It was a long journey, described – by a formula regularly employed in such cases – as covering "a thousand tracts, ten thousand acres." Koshar traveled for a whole week, for our text says expressly that it was on the seventh day that he fell in with Daniel.

Meanwhile Daniel was sitting "at the gate, beside the threshing floors which are next to the granary," exercising the functions of a judge or cadi. In terms reminiscent of the Old Testament (cf. Deuteronomy 10:18; Isaiah 1:17; Psalm 68:6), he is said to have been "judging the cause of the widow, administering justice to the orphan."

All this follows common Semitic usage. From numerous references in the Old Testament (e.g., Deuteronomy 21:19; 22:24; I Kings 23:8; Isaiah 29:21; Amos 5:12; Zechariah 8:16; Proverbs 22:22; Job 31:21) we know that the gate of the city, a natural place of concourse, was the spot where magistrates dispensed justice (cf. Smith, PEQ 78 [1946], 5–14). So too in ancient Babylon, judicial decisions were rendered at the gates of Shamash, Nin-Gal, and other deities (Meissner, *Beitr. zum altbab. Privatrecht*, Nos. 43, 78, 100, etc.). In rural communities, the same role was played by the threshing floor. Situated "in a low-lying, treeless place, just outside the village," it served – and still serves – as a kind of plaza, the scene not only of weddings and funerals but also of many other communal ceremonies (cf. Wetzstein, ZE 5 [1873], 273 ff.; Wensinck, *Mourning*, 1–11). Hence, it too became a natural place for the settling of legal disputes (cf. Hirschfeld, JRAS 1919, 254). Pertinent and illuminating in this connection is the statement in I Kings 22:10: "Then the king of Israel and Jehosaphat, the king of Judah, sate each on his throne, robed in

VIII

I v, 13b–31a: Daniel and his wife entertain Koshar and, as a customary mark of respect to their guest, present offerings to the gods of his country.

Then Daniel the Rapheite,
Thereupon the H-r-n-m-ite hero
Calls loudly to his wife:

"Hearken, Mistress Danatiya,
Set a lamb from the flock
Before Sir Adroit-and-Cunning for refreshment,
Before Sir Expert, the artisan, for regalement.

(Moreover,) give food and drink to the gods,

(regal) vestments, at the threshing floor, at the entrance of the gate of Samaria."

VIII (I v, 13b–3a). This, too, is in conformity with established Semitic practice, and is best illustrated by a passage in Robertson Smith's informative "Journey to the Hedjaz" in which that scholar observes that "among the Bedouins the slaughter of a sheep takes place only on festive occasions or *on the arrival of a guest.*" (*Lectures and Essays,* 527; Jacob, G.,*Das Leben der vorislamischen Beduinen* [Berlin, 1893], 86.)

Daniel's wife is also instructed to prepare food and drink for the gods and thereby to pay respects to "the lords (*ba'alim*) of great Memphis." Memphis in Egypt was the seat of the artisan god Ptah, with whom Koshar is here equated. Hence, the meaning is that not only the guest himself but also his native deities are to be regaled. This is to be explained from the fact that, in ancient Semitic usage, all meals involved sacrifice, the gods being thought to join the human company as members of the clan (Robertson Smith, *Rel. Sem.,* 241; Wellhausen, *Reste,*[2] 117). Hence, when persons of different clans or groups sat down to a repast together, it was necessary that the host provide fare not only for his own deities but also for those of his guest. We shall see later (§XXXV) that when Yatpan, the hatchet man employed by 'Anat, entertains Paghat, the sister of Aqhat, he punctiliously observes the same custom; for in proffering drink he remarks expressly, "Let our gods also drink of the wine, even the god of . . . (and) the god who owns the territory."

Pay honor and make your respects unto them,
The lords of the whole of great Memphis!"[e]

Mistress Danatiya obeys,
She sets a lamb from the flock
For the refreshment of Sir Adroit-and-Cunning,
For the regalement of Sir Expert, the artisan.

Then, after Sir Adroit-and-Cunning has (duly) arrived,
He places one of the bows in the hand of Daniel,
Places one of the arcs on the latter's lap.
Then Mistress Danatiya
Proceeds to give food and drink to the gods,
To pay honor and make her respects unto them,
The lords of the whole of great Memphis.

IX

I v, 31^b–39: Aqhat comes into possession of the bow.

(Eventually) Sir Adroit departs for his tent,
Sir Expert departs for his dwelling.
Then Daniel the Rapheite,
Thereupon the H-r-n-m-ite hero,
Flexes the bow [and ben]ds (it).
As he bends it, aiming it at Aqhat, [he cries:]
"The first fruits of thy hunting, my son,
. . . . the first fruits of thy hunting,
Behold, ... the game
[Do thou remember always to set] in his temple!"

'ANAT TRIES TO RECOVER THE BOW

X

I vi, 2–15: Aqhat is now a grown youth. One day the goddess 'Anat encounters him. They eat and drink together, and 'Anat seeks to recover the bow.

The opening lines of this passage are too fragmentary to be translated with confidence. They contain a description of

[e] In the original *Hqpt*, which is a distortion of the Egyptian *het ka Ptah*, "sanctuary [soul house] of Ptah," the regular name for Memphis, from which derives the word "Egypt."

X (I vi, 2–15). There is a gap of about 20 lines between the last preserved words of the preceding passage and the beginning

eating and drinking and a statement that 'Anat eyed the burnished bow which "gleamed like lightning" and became desperately anxious to recover it. With "serpent heart hid with a flowering face," she endeavored to tempt Aqhat into giving it up.

---

of this one. Aqhat is now in full possession of the bow, and the present scene describes how the goddess 'Anat seeks to retrieve it.

We have already discussed the general reason for the attitude and action of the goddess: the bow was of divine character and had evidently been designed for her specifically. She was therefore anxious to recover the property of which she had been so cavalierly deprived. It is not improbable, however, that the motive of jealousy also came into play. 'Anat was, after all, the goddess of the chase, and it will be recalled that one of the gifts which her classical counterpart Artemis requested of Zeus was, specifically, a silver bow (Callimachus, *Hymn* iii), subsequently fashioned—according to tradition—by the artisan Hephaistos (Hyginus, *fab.* 140), counterpart of Koshar in our poem. Accordingly, Aqhat's possession of the divine weapon would have made him virtually her equal and thus have threatened her status and supremacy. Moreover, it is noteworthy that when, later in the story (§XVIII), El characterizes the offense of Aqhat, he describes him expressly as the would-be "supplanter" (*m'qb*) of 'Anat; while it should also be borne in mind that the offense for which the huntsman Orion was punished by Artemis in the analogous classical myth was—according to Ovid and other writers—that of boasting that he was her equal in the chase (see Introduction, §4).

In order to accomplish her purpose, 'Anat resorts to typical feminine wiles; she endeavors to bribe the youth.

The scene opens with some badly mutilated lines (2–10) which may be restored from parallel passages elsewhere (notably I*AB, iv 11 ff.) as a description of feasting and carousal. There is mention of "cutting up [or flaying] a fatling" and of drinking wine and "the blood of trees" out of gold and silver cups.

> The vestige of the first two lines seem to accord with a formula of invitation ("Ho, eat of the viands, and ho, drink of the foaming wine. Greetings!") at the beginning of the *Poem of the Gracious Gods.*

It is therefore apparent that 'Anat's overtures are made after she and Aqhat have been wining and dining, i.e., at a time when he might be supposed to be peculiarly susceptible to such approaches.

14 Her [mi]nd is twisted like a serpent;

. . . .

15 She lifts her skirt from the ground.

XI

I vi, 16–19: The goddess offers wealth in exchange for the bow.

[Then lifts she her voice and] cries:
"Hearken, pray, [O valiant Aqhat],
[Ch]oose silver, and I will give (it) thee,
[Gold, and I will best]ow (it) on thee,
But let ['Anat possess thy] bow,
Y-b-m-t L-i-m-m thine [ar]c!"

The next lines (11–15) are likewise poorly preserved. Hence, any detailed interpretation is necessarily tentative. The general drift, however, is reasonably clear: the goddess eyes the bodily beauty of the youth and conceives the design of accomplishing her purpose by means of seduction. The attempted seduction of the virile hero and his rebuff of the goddess who would entice him is a common theme of ancient Near Eastern mythology (cf. the stories of Bitis in Egypt, Gilgamesh in Babylonia, Kombabos in Syria, etc.; see Albright, JBL 37 [1918], 116 ff.). Moreover, a scene in which a goddess is shown lifting her skirts before a male onlooker is common on Syrian seals ca. 1700–1200 B.C. (Ward, *Seal Cylinders of W. Asia,* ch. 50; Frankfort, *Cylinder Seals,* 270 ff.; Pritchard, *Figurines,* 36–37).

XI (I, vi, 16–19). This incident strongly recalls the scene in the Babylonian *Epic of Gilgamesh* (VI i 6 ff.) wherein the goddess Ishtar attempts similarly to seduce the hero.

When thou enterest our house,
threshold and stoop shall kiss thy feet.
Beneath thee shall kings, lords and princes fall.
Thy she-goats shall bring forth abundantly,
thy ewes bear twins;
thine asses shall be each as big as a mule;
thy chariot-horses shall be renowned for speed;
thy yoked mules shall have no equal.

XII

I vi, 20–25[a]: But Aqhat spurns the offer.

But the valiant Aqhat replies:

"Strong are the birches(?) from Lebanon,
Strong are the tendons from wild bulls,
Strong are the horns from mountain goats,
The sinews from the hocks of bulls;
Strong, too, are the reeds in the vast marshes;
Give (of them, then,) to Sir Adroit-and-Cunning,
That he may make a bow for thee,
Yea, an arc for Y-b-m-t L-i-m-m!"

XIII

I vi, 25[b]–33[a]: 'Anat presses her demand and offers immortality.

Howbeit, the Virgin 'Anat replies:

"Choose life, O valiant Aqhat,
Choose life, and I will give (it) thee,
Immortality, and I will bestow (it) on thee;
I will make thee to count years like Baal;

XIII (I vi 25[b]–33[b]). These lines are best illustrated by the parallel passage in the *Poem of Baal* (V AB, A 4 ff.) which describes the festive scene at the installation of that god and the language of which corresponds closely to that of our text.

Here they go . . . ing and offering him viands,
there they go feting him and plying him with drink;
goblets in both hands,
jars by the thousand he receives
wine in ten thousand portions he mixes.
While he is mixing it,
a sweet-voiced stripling stands chanting and singing
a pleasant strain to the tune of the cymbals,
singing over Baal in the Height of the North!

This picture of paradisal bliss is echoed in Psalm 36:8–9:

YHWH, how precious is Thy grace!
Gods and men alike
take refuge in the shadow of Thy wings!
They are sated with the richness of Thy house,

Thou shalt number months like the gods.
Behold how Baal lives:
He is feted and plied with drink;
They make music and sing sweet strains over him,
And they indite him!
Even such a life will I straightway grant (thee), O valiant Aqhat!"

XIV

I vi, 33b–40: But again Aqhat spurns the offer.

But Aqhat the valiant replies:

"Young lady, spin me no fancy tales,
Seeing that unto an adult
Thy fancy tales are but rubbish!
What is it that a mortal acquires as (his) future?
What is it that a mortal acquires as (his) hereafter?
The glaze (of old age) will be poured o'er my head,
The fine powder over my pate;
I shall die the death of all men;
Surely, I too shall die!

Moreover, this I would add:
A bow is a thing for warriors.
Are women, then, taking up hunting?"

XV

I vi, 41–45: 'Anat, though amused at the lad's retort, nevertheless warns him of the dire consequences which will attend his insolence and disobedience.

---

and of the stream of Thy luxuries Thou givest them to drink;
For with Thee is the wellspring of life . . .[b]

[b] Unfortunately, the Masoretic text, followed by most commentators, obscures the mythological background of the passage by faulty interpunction. The initial "YHWH" has been thrown to the end of the preceding verse ("Man and beast Thou savest, *O YHWH*"), while "gods" has been separated from the following "and men" and treated as a vocative ("How precious is Thy grace, *O God, and men* take refuge," etc.). Metrical considerations alone show that this is wrong, while it should be noted that our rearrangement gives point to the expression "and men," now in contrast to "gods." The reference to God's possessing the "wellspring of life" is explained by the juxtaposition of "life" and paradisal bliss in our Canaanite text.

[There]upon 'Anat laughs,
But already within her heart
She is busily framing [a plan].
"Be reconciled unto me," (she says,)
"Be reconciled, O valiant Aqhat,
And thou shalt have [pea]ce!

I am not prepared to encounter thee
On the path of disobedience,
[I am not prepared to meet thee]
On the path of arrogance;
I shall make thee to fall at [my feet],
I shall . . . . . thee,
My doughty Prince Charming![a]

THE PUNISHMENT AND DISCOMFITURE OF AQHAT

XVI

I vi, 46–55: 'Anat complains to El of Aqhat's disobedience and presumption.

She taps wildly with [her fee]t upon the ground.
Then [turns she her fa]ce toward El,
At the source of the Two Streams,
[Hard by the fountains of] the Two Oceans.
She leaves the wide fields
[And comes to the pleas]ance of the King, the Father . . . ;
[At the feet of El she] bows and falls,
Prostrat[es herself and pays homage to him].

Then she gives tongue against valiant Aqhat,
[Rails against the son of] Daniel, the Rapheite;
And she takes up word, [lifts her voice] and cries:
"Him [do thou . . . .],
Even Aqhat [do thou . . . . . .]!"

* * *

[a] Lit., "Thou most handsome, strongest of men!"

XVII

II i, 6^b–14: El replies, but the words of his reply are almost entirely lost. Evidently he does not take 'Anat's complaint any too seriously, for she now proceeds to cajole him with threats.

* * *

Then answers [the Virgin 'Anat]:

"[Behold, I counsel] thee, O El,
[I warn thee, thou Bull-god, my sire],
Do not make [fun of this!]

[Take care lest I] grasp them [with my hands],
[Lest with my mi]ghty strength(?)
[I pluck out the hairs of thy he]ad,
Lest I make [thy gray locks] to run [with blood],
[Thy gray beard] with gore!
Then [go cry to] Aqhat, and let *him* rescue thee,
To the son of [Daniel], and let *him* deliver thee
Out of the hand of the Virgin ['Anat]!"

XVIII

II i, 15–19^a: El, bullied into compliance, now assures 'Anat that Aqhat must certainly be punished for his arrogance and for defrauding her of the bow.

Then answers El, the kind, the warmhear[ted]:

"My daughter, I know that thou art gentle,
And [against goddesses] must there be no insult.
Now one has risen up, my daughter, of insolent heart.
Grasp inwardly things as they are,
Set (them) in thy breast;
He that has defrauded thee must surely be crushed!"

XIX

II i, 19^b–34: 'Anat thereupon prepares the downfall of Aqhat. She first lures him to the city of A-b-l-m.

XVIII (II i, 15–19). There is now a large gap in the text. The story continues on another tablet, but how much came between this and the preceding section we have as yet no means of knowing.

[Then away speeds the Vir]gin ʻAnat.
Straightway she turns her [face] toward valiant Aqhat,
Across a thousand ac[res, ten thousand tra]cts.

Then, laughing (inwardly),
The Virgin ʻAnat [lifts] her [voice] and cries:

"Hearken, pray, [O valiant Aqhat],
[I have a word to tell] thee:
Thou art my brother, and I am [thy sister];[b]
. . The fullness of thy flesh will I [enjoy];
. . . . [from the house?] of my father have I absconded;
[Come, live with me in ease and pe]ace(?);
Thou shalt go on the hunt
. . . .
. . . . mortal . . . happiness(?);
I will teach thee . . . . . .

So [go thou to] the city of A-b-l-m . . . .,
[The city of his highness the Mo]on-god,
Whose tower[s] . . . .
. . . . . . the cloud[s]

* * * *

XX

II obv., 5–11[a]: In order to accomplish her purpose, ʻAnat enlists the services of Yatpan, henchman of the queen goddess Asherath.

* *
*

[b] "Brother" and "sister" were common expressions for lovers in the ancient Near East.

XX (II, ii 5–11[a]). ʻAnat advises Yatpan to take care "lest the new moon rise." There is a twofold point in these words, but it has strangely eluded the commentators.

First, it should be observed that the city of A-b-l-m is expressly described, elsewhere in the poem, as "the city of His Highness the Moon-god [*qrt zbl Yrkh*]." Hence, a reference to that deity would be calculated to make a special impression on one destined or requested to undertake a task there.

[Away spe]eds the Virgin ʿAnat,
and [sets her] face toward Yatpan, the . . . henchman.
[She lifts her voice] and cries:
"He is now dwelling, O Yatpan, . . .
in the city of A-b-l-m
Look out that the new moon rise not,
[for] in its last quarter [it is auspicious for thine emprise],
whereas, at its beginning, it is kindly (to men)!"

XXI

II obv., 11ᵇ–15: Yatpan suggests a surprise attack.

Then answers Yatpan, [the henchman of Our Lady]:
"Hearken, O Virgin ʿAnat;
Come . . . .
Thou shalt [wrest?] from him his arc,
And him thou shalt . . . . .
Now, when that doughty Prince Charming has prepared (his) meal,

---

Second, there is here an obvious allusion to the widespread belief that the best time to work mischief is in "the dark of the moon," the period of its waxing, and especially the new moon, being considered one of good rather than bad omen. What ʿAnat implies, therefore, is that Yatpan had better not wait till new moon before undertaking the enterprise, because the new moon will be favorable for Aqhat.

For this belief in India, cf. Kath. xi, 3; Maitr. II 2, 7; Taith. II 3, 5; and for its prevalence in Jewish superstition, cf. Scheftlelowitz, *Altpal. Bauerngl.*, 137 ff.; Trachtenberg, *Jewish Magic,* 255–56.

For Teutonic beliefs of the same nature, cf. Tacitus, *Germania* 11; Caesar, *Bell. Gall.* i 50 (a belief allegedly revived by Hitler when he contemplated invasion of Britain!); and cf. Grimm, *Teutonic Mythology,* 713 ff.

In Morocco, the waxing moon is propitious, the waning moon baleful; cf. Westermarck, *Pagan Survivals,* 114.

Above all, note the explicit statement appended to a curse in the London Magical Papyrus, xlvi 344: "But you do better if the moon is waning." Cf. also Pap. Leyd. V ii 28, and Eitrem, *Papyri Osloenses, I,* 128.

[By the glare of his fire?] will I be lighted through the fields,
And I will draw near (?) . . . ."

XXII

II obv., 16–27[a]: But 'Anat suggests a more strategic plan.

But the Virgin 'Anat replies:

"Sit down, Yatp<an> and [I will instruct] thee:
I will place thee like a griffon in my sack,

XXII (I, ii 16–27[a]). This entire passage has hitherto been gravely misunderstood, most scholars assuming that the goddess really plans the death of Aqhat. This, however, is scarcely reconcilable with the fact that when the youth is actually slain, she is said to weep (line 39). Nor is it consistent with her explicit statement (line 27) that she desires to revive him, being interested only in retrieving the bow (cf. III, 14–17). The real point is that in giving her instructions she unfortunately uses ambiguous terms, and these mislead her henchman in precisely the same way that they have misled modern commentators. Thus, when she orders him to strike Aqhat "twice on the head, three times about the ears," this does not mean, as Yatpan and the commentators take it, that he is to smite the youth *many* times but, on the contrary, *just a couple of times;* for this is the way in which the gradation "two . . . three" is used constantly in the Bible (Isaiah 17:6; Amos 4:8; cf. II Kings 9:32). Similarly, the words which Yatpan and the modern commentators understand as an order to "shed Aqhat's blood to his knees, like one who is slain" really mean, "Spill (a little) blood, as when a man has a scratch on the knee"; for while the word rendered "slain," viz., *sh-kh-t,* indeed has that meaning in Hebrew, in Arabic and Ethiopic it also means merely "injure." The sense is, therefore, that Aqhat is not to be mauled and lacerated but merely beaten unconscious, only sufficient blood being shed as will be necessary to lend an air of reality to the attack. Lastly, when the goddess states that Aqhat's breath "will go forth like smoke," she does not mean that he will expire, but merely that his breath will come heavily.

The ambiguity of the instructions, however, has fatal results; for Yatpan interprets them to mean that Aqhat is to be belabored to death. He therefore proceeds to "annihilate" the youth. 'Anat, seeing this, bursts into tears, assuring her victim that she will indeed restore him (lit., "build" him up). At the same time she

Like a hawk in my sheath.
Then, when Aqhat [sits down] to the meal,
And the son of Daniel to the repast,
Griffons will come hovering [above him],
[A flight of h]awks will swoop down.
Among those griffons I [myself] will hover;
I will poise thee (directly) [ab]ove Aqhat.
Then strike him a couple of times on the head,
Three times about the ear(s);
Spill blood like . . . .,
As when a man has a scratch on his knee.
His breath will start going forth like a wind,
His spirit like a gust(?),
Like smoke out of his nostrils.
(Howbeit) I will (thereafter) quickly (??) revive him!"

XXIII

II obv., 27ᵇ–37ᵃ: The plan is executed.

Then takes she Yatpan, the . . . henchman,
Places him like a griffon in her sack,
Like a hawk in her sheath.

When Aqhat sits down to the re[past],
[And] the son of Daniel to the meal.

---

again formally demands the surrender of the bow which, however, Yatpan has in any case already retrieved.

If, as we have suggested, the present story evolves out of an astral myth of Orion, it is possible that the bizarre manner of his death in this literary version is but a dim reminiscence of an original astronomical motif. Just as Orion was said to have been attacked by a scorpion or by hounds because the constellations of Scorpius and Canis Major happen to be near him at the time of his late setting, so the discomfiture of Aqhat by eagles – more specifically, by the mother eagle Sml (see §XXXI) – may reflect the fact that the constellation of Aquila, the Eagle, appears in the month of June–July (Tammuz) on the opposite side of the heavens; see the Mesopotamian texts, K.2894 obv. 20; III R i, rev. 21; K.2310, 8; cf. Bezold, PSBA 11 (1887), pt. 5, pl. iii; R. Brown Jr., *ibid.,* 14 (1892), 283. The original myth would have attributed the rout of the Huntsman to an attack by the Eagle, and this detail would have persisted, albeit in distorted and forgotten form, in the literary development of the story.

Griffons come hovering above him,
A flight of hawk[s] swoops down.
[Among] those griffons hovers ʻAnat.
She poises him (directly) above [Aqhat].
He strikes him a couple of times on the [head],
Three times about the ear(s),
Sp[ills] his blood like . . .,
As when a man has a sc[ratch on the knee].
His breath starts coming forth like a wind,
His spirit [like a gust],
Like smoke [out of his nostrils].

XXIV

II obv., 37[b]–42: On seeing that Aqhat has been slain (which was more than she really intended), ʻAnat weeps and breaks out into expressions of grief, assuring him that she will yet revive him and that her only interest is in the recovery of the bow.[c]

When ʻAnat [perceives] that her henchman has destroyed,
Yea, [destroyed] Aqhat,
She starts to weep (crying):

"[O Aqhat], I will yet restore . . . .
But [thy bow] must thou [surrender unto me],
Thine arc must thou [give over unto me]!"

Then they twain[d] depart on the wing.

* * * *

XXV

III, 2–5[a]: On the flight homeward, Yatpan accidentally drops the bow, which falls into the sea and breaks.

* * *

[c] The passage is imperfectly preserved. Restoration and rendering are therefore tentative.
[d] i.e., ʻAnat and Yatpan.

XXV (III, 2–5[a]). This passage is very imperfectly preserved, and for that reason most commentators have skipped over it. In so doing, however, they have missed one of the essential elements

Into the midst of the waters it falls.
    * * * ; the bow is broken.

* * *

XXVI

III, 5^b–19^a: This infuriates 'Anat, who now realizes that all her plans have gone amiss: not only has she not *recovered the bow but also Aqhat has been slain unnecessarily and in consequence of this murder the earth has been polluted and rendered infertile. She therefore turns roundly upon the bungling Yatpan.*[e]

[e] The passage is poorly preserved, and it is among the most obscure in the entire poem. The interpretation is therefore tentative.

    (Thereupon) the Virgin 'Anat
Raises [her spindle] and beats (him) again and again.
* * her hands like a flash,
Her fingers like a flame,
Her molars like a threshing sledge;
Her teeth seize and devour**;
She whets her tongue like a hound**
* * * * * * * (crying):

---

of the story. Even though much else must remain irrecoverable or obscure, there are two phrases which are crucial. The first reads "into the waters it falls," and the second, "broken is the bow." And these phrases are followed by the words "The Virgin 'Anat raises . . . and beats (him)." Moreover, in a subsequent speech (§XXVI) the goddess, evidently addressing Yatpan, declares explicitly: " 'Twas only on account of his bow that I was thus attacking him [sc. Aqhat], 'twas only on account of his arc that I was attacking him. Yet him dost thou not spare to life, nor even hand over his bow unto me." It is apparent, therefore, that what fell into the waters and was broken was, indeed, the precious bow itself. Yatpan, blundering as usual, not only killed Aqhat when he was really supposed only to knock him unconscious, but also fumbled in conveying the bow to 'Anat, and let it drop into the waters!

Not impossibly, this incident has an ultimately astral significance, referring to the disappearance of the Bow constellation beneath the horizon.

"Here am I bleating like a ram in the sheepfolds,
Like a whipped cur,[f]
Because Aqhat has been so roundly felled;
Verily, 'twas (only) on account of his bow
That I was thus attacking him,
'Twas (only) on account of his arc that I was attacking him!
Yet him art thou not sparing alive
Neither is his bow handed over to me,
Whereas, on account of [his] death,
* * * the first fruits of the summer now will [fail],
The ear of corn in its sheath!"

XXVII

III, 19[b]–28[a]: The scene now reverts to Daniel.

Meanwhile, there is Daniel the Rapheite,
There is the [H-r-n-m]-ite he[r]o,
Sitting in state at the gat[e],
[Be]side the [threshing floors which are near the granary],
[Jud]ging the [cause of widows],
[Dis]pensing justice to [orphan(s)],
[When, lifting] his [eyes, he espies]
* * * * * * [Paghat] com[ing along].

[f] Lit., "(Like) a hound before (or from) its stick."

XXVII (III, 28[b]–37). The point of this passage lies very largely in the ancient Semitic idea that the shedding of innocent blood pollutes the land and renders it infertile. Thus, when Cain slays Abel, YHWH curses him with the words: "Cursed art thou off the soil which opened its mouth to receive thy brother's blood at thy hand. When thou tillest that soil, it will no longer yield its strength unto thee" (Genesis 4:11–12). Cf. also Numbers 35:33: "And ye shall not pollute the land wherein ye are, for blood pollutes the land, and bloodshed cannot be wiped away except by the blood of him who sheds it"; II Samuel 1:21: "Be there no dew upon you, O hills in Gilboa, neither rain, O ye death-stained fields (LXX)!" Ezekiel 36:17–18, 30. Agadath Shir Hashirim, ed. Schechter, JQR 7 (1895), 160, says that the spot where Cain killed Abel was barren forever. On the whole subject, cf. Patai, JQR, N.S. 30 (1939), 59–69; Frazer, *Folk-Lore in the O. T.*, i. 82 ff.; Patai, *Man and Temple*, 151–52. Cf. also Sophocles, *Oedipus Rex* 25 ff.; Livy, xlv 5; Pettazzoni, *La confessione dei peccati*, iii (Bologna, 1936), 167.

III, 28[b]–37: Paghat, the daughter of Daniel, perceives that a drought has set in and notices griffons and hawks hovering overhead. She therefore deduces that a murder has been committed nearby, since, according to ancient Semitic ideas, "uncovered" blood renders the earth polluted and barren.

[Lif]ting her eyes, she espies
* * * * *
The . . . in the granary is dried up;
Blighted, blasted are the green shoots . . .;
While over her father's house griffons are hovering,
A flight of hawks is sweeping down.

Paghat weeps in her heart,
Inwardly sheds tears.

Rent was the garment of Daniel the Rapheite,
The mantle of the H-r-n-m-ite hero.

XXVIII

III, 38–48: Daniel, realizing that the land has been polluted by bloodshed, pronounces a solemn curse upon it.

Thereupon Daniel the Rapheite
Utters a prayer:

"May the rain clouds . . . . in heat!
The early rain which the clouds pour down in the fall,
The light shower which distills upon the grapes,
For seven years may Baal withhold,
Yea, for eight He Who Rides upon the Clouds!
No light rain, no shower may there be,
No upwelling from the Two Oceans,[g]
Neither welcome thunder,[h]
See, the garment of Daniel the Rapheite is rent,
The mantle of the H-r-n-m-[ite] hero!"

XXIX

III, 49–74: Daniel, exercising his judicial functions, makes the

[g] i.e. the celestial and subterranean oceans.
[h] Lit., "Neither the goodly voice of Baal."

XXIX (III, 49–74). This passage is illustrated by I Samuel 7:15–17.

rounds of the neighboring territory, but finds that the crops are indeed blighted.

[*Col. ii*] Then loudly [calls Daniel] to [his] daughter:

"Hearken, O Paghat,
Thou that carriest the water on thy shoulders,
That brushest the dew from the barley,
That knowest the courses of the stars,[1]

[1] These words mean simply that Paghat works assiduously from dawn to dusk, not, as some scholars have supposed, that she is proficient in astronomy!

And Samuel judged Israel all the days of his life. And he went from year to year in circuit to Beth-el and Gilgal and Mizpah; and he judged Israel in all those places. And his return was to Ramah, for there was his house; and there he judged Israel.

(It is worthy of note that in the original Hebrew the same technical term, viz., *s-b-b,* "go in circuit," is used as in our Canaanite text.)

While on his rounds, Daniel has occasion to verify his daughter's report; he now sees with his own eyes that everything has indeed dried up. Thereupon he performs a curious act. Catching sight of a solitary ear of corn left over in the harvested field, he clasps it and kisses it, expressing over it the hope that it may betoken an eventual abundance of crops which Aqhat (whose death is still unknown to him) may yet reap.

It may be suggested that this somewhat bizarre episode really mythologizes rites connected with the reaping of the last sheath. As Mannhardt (WFK, 30 f.) and Frazer (GB, one-vol. ed., 408) have shown, such rites are an exceedingly common feature of harvest ceremonies all over the world and frequently involve the participation of the king or ruling authority. Now, the last sheaf is very commonly represented as a *young bride* (Banks, Brit. *Calendar Customs,* 73–79; Sartori, *Sitte u. Brauch,* ii, 97, 117, n. 64), and sometimes it is actually personified by a maiden swathed in straw who is ceremonially "wedded" to a bridegroom similarly attired (GB one-vol. ed., *loc. cit.*). Moret has made it clear (*La mise à mort du dieu en Égypte,* 29) that this usage was known already to the ancient Egyptians, for in texts of the New Empire there is mention of a female image, directly comparable to the "corn-maiden," which is used in harvest rituals and which bears the

Saddle an ass, hitch a foal;
Set upon it my silver reins,
My golden bridles!"
  Paghat obeys,
Even she who carries the water on her shoulders,
Who brushes the dew from the barley,
Who knows the courses of the stars.
Straightway she saddles an ass,
Straightway she hitches a foal,
Straightway she lifts up her father,
Seats him on the back of the ass,
On the gaily trapped back of the foal.

Then <Dani>el proceeds to perform his duties as judge,
But finds himself making the rounds of fields becoming arid.
He espies a blade of grass(?) in the arid fields,
Espies a blade of grass(?) in the blighted meads.
He clasps and kisses the blade;
"Ah, would," (says he,) "that this blade of grass(?)
May yet grow tall 'mid the arid fields,
That this blade(?) may yet grow tall 'mid the blighted meads!
* * May the hand of young Aqhat yet gather thee,
To place thee in the midst of the storehouses!"

He proceeds to perform therein his duties as judge,
But finds himself making the rounds of fields consumed by drought.

---

name of "the beloved (*mer.t*)," i.e., the bride. If, then, we assume that this strange episode of our poem is really but a literary and half-forgotten reminiscence of such a custom, Daniel's bizarre clasping and kissing of the ear of corn will be at once explained. In other words, this episode will be seen to preserve, in attenuated and somewhat grotesque fashion, one of the cardinal elements of the underlying Ritual Pattern.

The harvesting of grain takes place in Syria and Palestine during the month of April. It is at the close of that month, therefore, that the events here narrated must be presumed to have taken place, for the text says distinctly that the stray ear of corn was found "amid the *harvested* field." This is important in connection with our thesis that the entire poem mythologizes the climatic and agricultural situation during the period between the late setting of Orion (at the end of April) and the early rising of Sirius (or of the "Bow") in the second half of July.

He espies an ear of corn amid the fields consumed by drought,
Espies an ear of corn amid the swathe.
He cl[asps] and kisses the ear of corn;
"Ah, would," (says he,) "that this ear [of corn]
May yet grow tall amid the fields consumed by drought,
That this ear of corn may yet grow tall [amid the swathe]!
* * May the hand of yo[ung] Aqhat yet gather thee,
To place thee in the midst of the storehouse!"

XXX

III, 75–93: Daniel is informed that Aqhat is dead.

[*Much of this passage is illegible and the whole of it poorly preserved. The identity of the persons involved is therefore uncertain, and the following rendering must be regarded only as giving the general sense.*]

Scarce has the word gone forth from his mouth,
[The utterance] from his lips,
When, lifting her eyes,
(Paghat) espies two slaves approaching.
[Their breath] comes from their breasts in intermittent gasps;[j]
They are beating themselves twice upon the head,
Thrice about the ears;
Their locks are all [un]bound,
Their tresses [flowing wild],
Heavy fall their tears
Like quarter-shekel weights.
And their tears are streaming down.

* * *

"We bring thee tidings, O Daniel," (they cry);

* * *

They approach, lift up [their] voice[s and cry:]
"Hearken, O Daniel,
Dead is [thy son],

[j] Lit., "Now it comes forth, now it does not come forth."

Dead is the valiant Aqhat!
The Virgin 'Anat [has made his breath to go forth] like [a wind],
His spirit like a gust!"

III, 94–104: A few fragmentary lines express Daniel's agitation at this news.

THE BURIAL OF AQHAT

XXXI

III, 105–151[a]: Daniel, wishing to accord his son proper burial, endeavors to retrieve his remains from the gizzards of the griffons. After two unsuccessful attempts, he eventually detects traces of fat and bone.

Lift[ing his eyes he espies]
[Griffons veering straight toward him] from the clouds.
[*Col. iii*] [Then lifts he his voice] and cries:

"May Baal break [the griffons' wings],
May Ba[a]l br[eak the pinions of yon birds],
So that they may fall at my feet!
Then will I rip ope[n their gizzards and] inspect;
If there [be] fat, if there [be] bone,
I will duly bewail and inter it,
Place it in the holes of the numinous dead, in the earth!"

Scarce has the word gone forth from his mouth,
The utterance from his lips,

XXXI (III 105–151[a]). The recovery and interment of Aqhat's remains is a necessary preliminary to his ultimate resurrection. Analogous scenes were a cardinal element of the Osiris and Adonis mysteries. This episode therefore goes back to the usages of that seasonal festival for which the underlying myth was originally designed; see Introduction, §11.

XXXI. The father and mother griffon (or eagle) are called respectively HRGB and SML. These are concocted names, of mutually antithetical meaning. The former derives from the root *r-g-b*, "be gentle," which in most of the Semitic languages yields the word for "dove." The latter connects with an Arabic word meaning "be fierce."

Than Baal breaks the griffons' wings,
Baal breaks the pinions of those birds,
So that they fall at his feet.
He rips open their gizzards and [inspects];
There is no fat, there is no bone.
So he lifts his voice and cries:
"May Baal repair these griffons' wings,
May he repair the pinions of these birds!
Griffons, fly off and soar aloft!"

Then, lifting his eyes he [espies]
"Softie," the father of the griffons,
Veering straight toward him.
So he lifts his voice and cries:
"May Baal break yon 'Softie's' wings,
May Baal break the pinions of [yon bird],
So that he falls at my feet!

Then will I rip open [his] giz[zard] and inspect;
If there be fat, if there be [bone],
I will duly bewail and inter (it),
Place it in the holes of the numinous dead, in the earth!"

[Scarce has the word gone forth from his mouth,]
His utterance [from] his [li]ps,
Than Baal breaks "Softie's" wings,
Baal breaks the pinions of that bird,

So that it falls at his feet.
He rips open its gizzard and inspects;
There is [no] fat, there is no bone.
So he lifts [his] voice and cries:
"May Baal repair 'Softie's' wings,
May [Ba]al repair the pinions of that bird!
'Softie,' fly off [and] soar aloft!"

Then, lifting his eyes, he espies
"Toughie," the mother of the griffons,
Veering straight toward him.
So he lifts his voice and cries:
"May Baal break yon 'Toughie's' wings,
May Baal break the pinions of yon bird,
So that she may fall at my feet!
Then will I rip open her gizzard and inspect;
If there be fat, if there be bone,

I will duly bewail and inter it,
Place it in the holes of the numinous dead, in the earth!"

Scarce has the word [gone forth] from his mouth,
His utterance from his lips,
Than [Ba]al [breaks] "Toughie's" wings,
Baal breaks the pinions of that bird,
So that it fa[lls at] his feet.
He rips open its gizzard and inspects;
Fat there is, bone there is!
So he takes them and pieces Aqhat together.
He performs wailing, performs burial;
He buries him in a dark place(?), in a jar.

Then lifts he his voice and cries:
"May Baal break the griffons' wings,
May Baal break the pinions of yon birds,

If they fly o'er the grave of my son,
Swoop down on him while he sleeps!"

THE CURSING OF THE UNKNOWN ASSASSIN

XXXII

III, 151ᵇ–169: In accordance with established practice in cases of homicide by an unknown hand, the local king (perhaps Daniel himself) pronounces collective curses on three cities nearest to the scene of the murder. As it happens — though the fact is, of course, unknown to him — the third of these, A-b-l-m, is indeed the place where the crime was committed.

XXXII (III, 151ᵇ–169). What is here described is best illustrated from the analogous procedure set forth in the Israelitic legislation of Deuteronomy 21:1–9. In cases of homicide by an unknown hand, the city nearest to the scene of the crime is to be held collectively responsible and is to expiate the pollution of the land by breaking the neck of a heifer (a substitute for the undiscovered culprit) on a plot of uncultivated soil at the side of a perpetual stream (which will bear away the contaminating blood). Although the full details of the procedure are not here recorded, or even necessarily implied, the basic idea is the same; and it is significant that while in the Israelitic practice the rite is performed by the

Then the king curses Q-r M-y-m:[k]
Next he repairs to M-r-r-t T-gh-l-l B-n-r.[l]
"Woe unto thee, Q-r M-y-m,
Upon whom lies the murder of valiant Aqhat!
Always as a refugee, seeking sanctuary at shrines,

[k] The name means "Well of Water."

[l] The meaning of this name is uncertain. It is tempting to connect T-gh-l-l with the Semitic verb *gh-l-l*, "bind beneath the yoke," and B-n-r with the noun *nr*, "yoke," but what the whole phrase denotes as a place-name eludes us.

"elders and judges," here it is said expressly to be performed by "the king" (line 152), who is, of course, none other than Daniel himself. Moreover, just as in the Israelitic system the procedure has to be carried out beside running water (on the significance of which see Patai, R., "The 'Egla 'Arufa or the Expiation of the Polluted Land," in JQR, N.S. 30 [1939], 59–69), so here the first place to which Daniel repairs is called Qr-Mym, or Water-Spring.

The practice thus indicated was also current in early Arabian society. Kitab al-Aghani ix 178: 25 ff. says expressly that in cases of homicide by an unknown hand, responsibility developed upon the nearest *dar* or settlement, and similar testimony is borne also by Khalil, art. 1835–37 (see: Dareste, *Journal des Savants* 1902, 521, n. 4; Robertson Smith, *Kinship*, 64, n. 2; Wellhausen, *Reste*,[2] 188 f.; Driver, S. R., *Deuteronomy*, 241). The basis of the custom is, of course, the familiar idea that "no expiation can be made for a land in respect of blood shed within it except by the blood of him who has shed it" (Numbers 35:33). Accordingly, when that individual cannot be traced, the desired end has perforce to be accomplished by the performance of a symbolic ceremony.

Of interest also is the form of commination employed in the rite. In each case, Daniel first curses the city, then identifies it with the unknown murderer, invoking upon it as a collective unit the penalty which would normally be visited upon that individual malefactor. The cities are to "flee like a perpetual refugee," to have neither root below nor blossom above, and to be rendered blind by Baal "henceforth and forever."

The first curse (152–55), invoked against the city or village of Qr-Mym, is that, in the capacity of a collective murderer, it is to "flee continually like a client of the sanctuary." The words are to be explained from the common ancient usage whereby, after a hue and cry had been raised for him, a criminal might find at least temporary shelter within the precincts of a sanctuary, abiding

Even now and forever do thou flee,
Even now and for all ge[ne]rations,
Thou stabber-in-the-back!"

---

there as a "guest of the god." The meaning is, therefore, that the city, personified as an individual, is to be, like Cain, a perpetual exile, an eternal refugee, ever seeking sanctuary from the violence of those who would visit retribution upon him. A specific allusion to such refugees is made in the Ras Shamra text 2. 27–28, where they are called "guests of the sacred enclosures" (*gr khmyt;* cp. Arabic *hima*), just as in Arabic usage one who seeks shelter beside the Ka'aba at Mecca is styled a "guest of God" (*jar Allah*). The institution is mentioned also in the Old Testament; in Exodus 21:14 the privilege of protection at the altar of Yahweh is withdrawn in the case of intentional homicide; in I Kings 1:50, Adonijah, fleeing the wrath of Solomon, "rises and goes and grasps the horns of the altar," and *ibid.*, 2:28, his ally Joab does likewise. On the institution in general, see Robertson Smith, *Rel. Sem.*,[3] 148, n. 2.

Seeing that Daniel is, in fact, the king of the land, the execration has the force of an edict of expulsion. The words *"continually flee . . . now and forever, now and for all generations,"* with their significant threefold iteration, may therefore be regarded as a legal formula. Comparable is the phrase *καὶ αὐτὸς φευγέτω Ἀμφίπολιν ἀειφυγίην* in the decree issued by Philip of Macedon ordering the banishment of Philon and Stratocles of Amphipolis (Dittenberger, *Syll.* 113:21).

The second curse (157–62), invoked against the city or village of Mrrt-tghll-bnr, is that its "root may not rise from the earth, (its) top drooping into the hand of an uprooter." This is a standard comminatory formula. In the Hittite text, KUB XXIX 1, which includes the "book of words" for a rite of public purgation, the king pronounces against his enemies the curse that they may have "neither root below nor fruit above"; while in the Phoenician inscription of Eshmum'azar of Sidon (CIS I 3:11) a similar execration is invoked against the violators of that monarch's tomb. Similarly, too, in Amos 2:9 Yahweh declares that he "has destroyed the Amorite . . . destroying his fruit above and his roots below." In Malachi 3:19, he declares that "every man that doeth wickedness shall be as stubble, and the Day that cometh shall burn him up, that there be not left unto them [sic!] root or branch"; and in Job 18:16 the statement is made concerning the wicked that "below his roots wither, and above his bough is cut off."

Here too the curse may be regarded as amounting almost to a

He lifts his voice and cries:

"Woe unto thee, M-r-r-t T-gh-l-l B-n-r,
Upon whom lies the murder of valiant Aqhat!
May thy root not rise from the ground,
Thy top droop into the hand of one who plucks thee!

---

legal formula. It may be compared with the Greek expression ἐκριζωσθήσεται πανγένει in CIG 916:8.

The third curse (165–69), invoked against the city of A-b-l-m is that "Baal may render it blind, henceforth and forever, now and for all generations." Here again we have a common formula of execration. The Babylonian text III R 41 ii 19–20 invokes Shamash, the sun-god, to strike a man blind; while North Arabian inscriptions sometimes contain the formula: "May he who alters this become blind" (Lidzbarski, *Ephemeris*, ii. 14, 347). Similarly, one of the curses invoked on the disobedient in the Great Commination of Deuteronomy 28 is that Yahweh may visit them with blindness (v. 28); and this is indeed the penalty inflicted by that god on the lustful men of Sodom in Genesis 19:11 and on the people of Aram in II Kings 6:18. Illuminating also is a passage in the Hittite ritual KBo VI 34 dealing with the punishment of disloyal citizens: not only are they to be symbolically "unmanned" by being dressed in female clothing and handed a distaff and mirror but they are also to be *blinded:*

> Then they shall lead forth a [blind woman] and a deaf man. Thereupon thou shalt say as follows: "See, here is a blind woman and a deaf man. Whoever contrives evil against the king and queen, let the oaths of the gods seize him! Let them make him blind! Let them [ma]ke him deaf! Let them [blind] him like a blind man, [make him deaf] like a deaf man . . .," etc.

In Classical antiquity, blinding was regarded as the usual retribution for blasphemy and infamy; see Frazer on Pausanias iii 19, 13 and Mayor on Juvenal viii 93. Apuleius, *Met.* viii 25 preserves a form of commination not unlike that in our text: *at te omnipotens et omniparens Dea Syria et sanctus Sabadius (Sabazius) et Bellona et Mater Idaea et cum suo Adonide Venus domina caecum reddant*, "May the Syrian Goddess, mistress and mother of all things, and holy Sabazius and Bellona and the Idaean Mother and Queen Venus with her Adonis render thee blind!" On blinding as a punishment for *hybris*, see also J. Wurtheim, *Versk. en Meded.*, V/2 (1916), 409 ff., Pettazzoni, *Confessione*, iii 99; *MI*, Q 451.7.

Now and forever do thou flee,
Now and for all generations,
Thou stabber-in-the-back!"

[*Col. iv*] Next he repairs to the city of A-b-l-m,[m]
Even A-b-l-m, the city of his highness the moon-god.
He lifts his voice and cries:

"Woe unto thee, city of A-b-l-m,
Upon whom lies the murder of valiant Aqhat!
May Baal render thee blind henceforth and forever,
Now and for all generations,
Thou stabber-in-the-back!"

THE MOURNING FOR AQHAT

XXXIII

III, 170–188: Daniel institutes rites of mourning for his slain son, engaging the services of professional wailers and performing sacrifices.

[m] The name A-b-l-m probably connects with such Hebrew toponyms as Abel-beth-Maacah, Abel ha-Shittim, Abel Mizraim, etc. According to Albright (*The Vocalization of the Egyptian Syllabic Orthography* [New Haven, 1934], 39), the basic meaning is "brook, running steam." Not improbably, our author here plays on the name and connects it with the word *'-b-l*, "mourner."

It is to be observed that this episode works up artistically to a dramatic climax. Only after two "false starts" does Daniel hit upon the true culprit, the city of A-b-l-m, from which, as we have seen, the murderer Yatpan really hailed. The fact is, of course, still unknown to him, though it is apparent to the hearers or readers of the tale. This device, by which storytellers everywhere strive to increase the dramatic tension, is the same as the poet has already employed so effectively in the preceding scene, where only after two abortive attempts does Daniel come upon the particular griffon in whose gizzard the remains of Aqhat are concealed.

XXXIII (III, 170–188). In these rites of mourning we may recognize three elements:

(1) introduction of professional wailers;
(2) sacrifice;

Daniel repairs to his house,
Daniel betakes him to his palace.

Into his palace come weeping women,
Into his courts they that beat the breast,

---

(3) performance of ritual dances.
These elements may be considered *seriatim*.

1. *Professional Wailers*

The professional mourners are described as "women who weep" (*bkyt*), "women who mourn" (*mshspdt*), and "men who tear their skin" (*p-ts-gh-m gh-r*). Female mourners are, of course, familiar enough (cf. Scheftelowitz, ARW 19 1916–19, 221, n. 1), especially from modern Arab usage (Lane, *Modern Egyptians*, 478), but it is noteworthy that they occur already not only in ancient Egypt (cf. Werbrouck, M., *Les pleurueses dans l'Égypte ancienne* [Paris, 1939]), but also among the Hittites (KUB XXX 15.27), while Homer mentions them specifically in his account of the obsequies of Hector (*Iliad* xxiv 746). They are the later Roman *praeficae*, who lead the dirge (Festus, 223 M; Ovid, *Met.*, ii 340–43; Mayor on Juvenal x 261). In modern Armenia they are known as "dirge mothers" (Ananikian, M., *Armenian Mythology* [Boston, 1920], 95). On the survival of them in legends of the Holy Grail, cf. Jesse L. Weston, *From Ritual to Romance*, 46.

It is of especial interest to observe that the name *mshspdt* by which such women are here called corresponds exactly to the Arabic *terminus technicus lattamat*, both words meaning properly "women who beat their breasts" (cp. Syriac *s-p-d*, "beat," and Arabic *l-t-m*, of the same meaning).

Daniel's summons to these women to enter his "house" and "court" is well illustrated by modern Anatolian usage, as reported by Ramsay, *Asianic Elements in Greek Civilization*,[2] 93 ff.: "Mourning takes place in the court of the house. Only the professional mourning women and the relatives of the deceased attend there. More public mourning takes place at the actual funeral."

2. *Sacrifice*

Besides presenting something called *d-gh-sh* to the deities of sky and stars, Daniel also offers a "sacrifice to the numina [called *ilm*]." The *ilm* or numina in question are probably the same as those in whose "hollows" Aqhat is interred (above, lines 112, 127, 141), i.e., the numinous dead or the deities of the netherworld. Significantly enough, in the Hittite funeral ritual, KUB XXX 27,

They also that gash(?) the skin(?),
To weep for young Aqhat,
To shed tears for the child of Daniel the Rapheite.

For days and months on end,
For months and years on end,
Continually for seven years,
They keep weeping for valiant Aqhat,
Shedding tears for the child of Daniel the Rapheite.

---

offerings are presented to "the Sun-god [^{d}UTU-i], the gods of heaven; Allani, queen of the earth; the gods of the earth; and Aras."[e] The custom survives in the Arab sacrifice of a lamb or goat at the conclusion of mourning ceremonies (Lane, *op. cit.*, 488).

3. *The Funeral Dance*

Another feature of the mourning ceremonies here described is the performance of dances [*mrqdm*], but once again the true meaning of the text has hitherto escaped recognition.

The term used in the original, viz., *mrqdm* is of especial interest. In Biblical Hebrew, the verb *r-q-d* means "to skip, leap" (e.g., Psalm 29:6), and this is also the normal meaning of Accadian *raqadu* and of Arabic *r-q-ts* and *r-q-z.* But an Accadian syllabary (B.M. 83–1–18, 1846, rev. i, 6–7 = Pinches, PSBA 18 [1896], 253) lists *ru-qu-ud-du* as a term meaning "professional mourner" (equivalent of Sumerian LU.TU.IGI.GUGU(?), "one who weeps with troubled eye"), while in Arabic and Syriac, the corresponding nouns *raqtsath* and *marqodeta* denote *a special kind of hopping or limping dance performed at funerals* (cf. Jahnow, *D. hebräische Leichenlied,* 75, n. 6; *Ridgeway Presentation* Vol., 379 ff.; Wensinck, *Mourning,* 43). An excellent description is given by Roger, *La terre saincte* (1664), 265, while Lane (*op. cit.*, 488) informs us that

> it is customary among the peasants of Upper Egypt for the female relations and friends of a person deceased to meet together by his house on the first three days after the funeral, and there to perform a lamentation and a strange kind of dance. They daub their faces and bosoms and part of their dress with mud; and tie a rope girdle . . . round the waist. Each flourishes in her hand a palm-stick or a *nebroot* (a long staff), or a drawn sword [sc. to forefend demons], and dances with a slow move-

[e] For the deity Aras, I call attention to KUB XVII 20 ii 7 ff.

Then, in the seventh year,
[Daniel the] Rapheite utters a word [in response],
Yea, the [H-r-n-m-ite] hero utters a word in reply;
He lifts his voice and cries:
"De[part], ye weeping women, from [my] palace,
Ye that beat the breast from my courts,
Ye also that gash(?) your skin(?)!"

Then presents(?) he a sacrifice unto the gods,
Offers up a *d-gh-sh*[n] offering unto heaven,
Even the (customary) H-r-n-m-ite *d-gh-sh*[n]-offering to the stars.

THE AVENGING OF AQHAT

XXXIV

III, 189–202: Paghat resolves to avenge her murdered brother, and sets forth to execute her purpose.

[n] Meaning unknown (it is possible that the word is to be recognized also in *Gracious Gods,* 15).

ment and in an irregular manner; generally pacing about and raising and depressing the body.

Wetzstein also has given an account of this curious ceremony, adding that among the Syrian peasantry it is known as *ma'id,* or "limping" (ZE 5 [1873], 296 ff.).

This last detail is of peculiar interest since it explains the famous passage in I Samuel 15:32 where Agag, king of the Amalekites, is said to have "walked delicately [Hebrew *ma'adanot*]," exclaiming, "Surely the bitterness of death is past," when summoned before Samuel to receive retribution for his barbarity. What really happened was that Agag, like an arch-hypocrite, approached the prophet *with the traditional limping gait of mourners* (Hebrew *me'odanit!* cf. LXX *tremon;* Vulg. *tremens*), uttering a typical dirge: "Truly, death is bitter." The passage thus provides early evidence of the limping dance as a *ceremony* of mourning; and our present Canaanite text pushes it back to an even higher antiquity!

XXXIV (III, 189–202). There is a special point in the expression "my kinsman" (lit., "male member of my mother group"; cf.

At the end of the mourning rites which * *,
Up speaks Paghat,
Even she who carries water on her shoulders:

"(Since) my father has (duly) presented(?) a sacrifice to the gods,
(Duly) offered up a *d-gh-sh*ⁿ offering unto heaven,
Even the (customary) H-r-n-m-ite *d-gh-sh*ⁿ offering to the stars,
May they[o] bless me, that I may go in blessing,
Favor me, that I may go in favor
To smite him who smote my brother,
To make [an end of] him who [made] an end of my ki[n]sman!"

Thereupon [Dani]el the Ra[phe]ite replies:
"May Paghat be revived in spirit,
Even she who carries water on her shoulders,
Who brushes the dewfall from the barley,
Who knows the courses of the stars!
I . . . . ;
Go smite him who smote [thy brother],
Make an end of him who made an end of [thy] kinsman!"

III, 203–224[a]: Rendering herself as attractive as possible, but concealing beneath her garments the accoutrements of a warrior, Paghat sets out at nightfall to recruit mercenaries to assist in hunting down the murderer of Aqhat.

[o] I.e., the divine recipients of the offerings. What is probably meant more specifically is that Paghat may now safely trust to embarking under a "lucky star."

I AB iv 43), for what Paghat envisages by employing it is the institution of an intertribal vendetta. On blood revenge in Semitic life, cf. Jacobson, *Social Background of the OT*, ch. viii; Kennet, *Bedouin Justice;* Proksch, *Blutrache.*

XXXV (III, 203–224[b]).The precise nature of the cosmetic used by Paghat is uncertain. Possibly it is *ambergris.* But it could also be *sepia,* which would be especially appropriate for the rouging which is specifically mentioned.

What is here described is admirably illustrated from several ancient sources. Taking his visitor under his protection, Yatpan is said to proffer food and drink, pouring a libation also to a certain god described as "he who owns the fields." What we have here

So she [fet]ches up a fish from the sea,
Washes and rouges herself
With the red dye of that cosmetic of the sea
Which a thousand demons have excreted into the sea.

Then she [takes] and puts on the garb of a warrior,
Places the kn[ife in] its sheath,
Places the sword in [its] scabbard;
And above she dons the garb of a woman,
But beneath, [that] of a soldier.

Then, when the sun, the torch of the gods, go[e]s [do[w]n,
* * * the fields.
At the going [down] of the sun, the torch of the gods,
Paghat reaches the tents.

---

is the common Semitic practice of concluding covenants by means of *commensality*, i.e., eating and drinking together. The best example of this is afforded by Genesis 14:18–20 which records the conclusion of a pact between Abram and Melchizedek, the king-priest of Salem:

> And Melchizedek, king of Salem, brought forth food and wine – he was a priest unto El Elyon – and he said: "Be Abram hereby endowed with *berakah* [numinous mana; cf. Plassmann, *The Significance of Beraka* (1913); Westermarck, *Morocco*, i, 35–261] from El Elyon, owner [*qoneh*] of heaven and earth, and be El Elyon recognized as possessing such *berakah* by delivering thy foemen into thy hands!"

Similar, too, is Genesis 26:30, which describes an analogous pact between Isaac and Abimelech.

> And they said: . . . Be thou hereby [*'attah*] endowed with the *berakah* of YHWH. And he prepared a feast for them, and they ate and drank.

Note especially that in both cases the ceremony is accompanied by a sacrificial rite and that an essential element of it is to embrace the guest within the sphere of influence covered by the numinous protection [*berakah*] of his host's local or tribal deity. The latter, in fact, is the real meaning of the formulas lamely rendered in EV as "Blessed be Abram" and "Thou art now blessed of the LORD."

Again, in Joshua 9:14 the Israelites conclude a treaty with the Gibeonites by partaking of their victuals; while in Obadiah 7,

Word is then brought to Yat[pan]:
"She that hired us is come into thy territory,
[She that engaged us] cometh hither!"

III, 214^b–224: The person whom Paghat first approaches is, naturally enough, none other than Yatpan, chief of the professional mercenaries. Yatpan welcomes her and proffers wine. Eventually, however, under the influence of liquor, he is led to betray himself as the murderer of Aqhat.

Then up speaks Yatpan, the [henchman] . . . .

"Come, take and drink wine!
[Receive] the cup from my hand,
The goblet from my right hand!"

"men who ate thy food" and "men in compact with thee," occur side by side as variant readings.[a]

The same usage likewise obtains among the Arabs; cf. Burckhardt, *Bedouins and Wahabys*, i. 329; Doughty, *Arabia Deserta*, i. 228; Robertson Smith, *Rel. Sem.*, 271 ff.; Wellhausen, *Reste*,[2] 124; Westermarck, *Survivals*, 17.85.

An especially effective illustration of our text, wherein Yatpan invites Paghat to drink wine "from the cup in my hand, the goblet in my right hand," is provided by Herodotus' description (IV, 172) of covenant ceremonies among the Nasamoneans: "They conclude covenants in this manner: one party gives the other to drink out of his hand, and vice versa."

As a concomitant of the ceremonies, Yatpan invites his god to partake of the wine. That deity is described as "our god, the god (of?) sh . . . the [g]od who owns the fields [*iln il sh* . . . [*i*]*l dqny zh-d-m*]." Here we have a remarkable but hitherto unnoticed parallel to Genesis 14:18–20 where, as we have seen, Melchizedeq, in concluding a treaty with Abram, invokes El Elyon (EV. "the Most High God"), *owner of heaven and earth.* The same Hebrew word (*q-n-h/y*) is used in both cases.

The formula "the god who owns the land [*d-yqny shdm*]" also finds a parallel in the words "Unto the Lord, unto the god, owner of the land" [*l'adn l'il qn ars*] in a neo-Punic inscription from

[a] That the latter is but a gloss on the former is shown by the fact that it is hypermetrical. The expression "men who ate thy bread" is the exact semantic equivalent of our *companion.*

[So] Paghat takes and drinks it,
[Receives] the cup from his hand,
The goblet from his right hand.

Then says Yatpan, [hench]man: . . . .
"Let our god (also) be given to drink of the wine,
Even the god * *, * the god who owns the land![p]

Why, the hand that smote valiant Aqhat
Can smite foes by the thousands!
Verily, thou workest a magic o'er (our) tents!"

But her [heart] . . . . like a . . .,
Her mind moves nimbly like a serpent;

[p] The traces in the original would also permit the translation: "Let our god (*or* gods) also be given to drink of the wine, the god of hea[ven] and (*or* who is also) the god who owns the earth." Cf. Genesis 14:18–20, and see the Commentary.

Leptis Magna in Tripolitania,[e] and again in the phrase "God, owner of the land [*Il qn (a)r('a)*]" in a bilingual Palmyrene inscription dated 39 A.D.[f]

The custom of proffering drink to the supreme god is admirably paralleled – though from an admittedly late source – Vergil, *Aeneid* i 728–40, where the following scene occurs at Dido's banquet to Aeneas in the Semitic city of Carthage.

> Then filled she with unmixed wine the bowl which Belus and all his descendants had been wont to use and, when silence had been imposed throughout the halls, thus she prayed: "O Jupiter – for men say that thou presidest over covenants with guests – grant that this be a happy day both for the Tyrians and for them who set out from Troy. . . ." So saying, she poured a libation upon the table.

The words of Yatpan's effusive greeting are imperfectly preserved, but the sense is scarcely in doubt and restoration is not difficult.

The phrase "The hand that slew doughty Aqhat can slay foes by the thousands" finds its closest parallel in I Samuel 18:7: "Saul hath slain his thousands."

[e] *Libya* 3 (1927), 105–07.

[f] Cantineau, in *Syria* 19 (1938), 78–79, reading ELQWND. The correct reading is due to G. Levi della Vida, in JBL 63 (1944), 8.

[She contrives to render] him [wea]ry.
So again and again she proffers him the mixture to drink,
Proffers him the mixture to drink.

* * *

(The rest is lost)

D. THE CORONATION TYPE

1. THE EGYPTIAN RAMESSEUM DRAMA

The following presentation of the Egyptian Coronation Drama is based on the German rendering and interpretation of Kurt Sethe. The material has been rearranged, however, in order to bring out more clearly the interrelation of punctual ritual and mythological drama. Using as a guide the rubrics actually contained in the text, these have been expanded for the sake of clarity and sometimes grouped together to indicate more precisely the correspondence between ritual action and mythological representation. Rubrics printed in *italics* indicate the ritual actions; those printed in SMALL CAPITALS (with the sign ¶ prefixed), the mythological interpretation.

The rendering seeks to be faithful, but not pedantic. It must be borne in mind that the Egyptian text is of the nature of a scenario, its obscurities resulting largely from the fact that the modern reader is not, as was his Egyptian predecessor, a spectator at an actual performance. Accordingly, it is often necessary to be explicit where the Egyptian text is merely implicit; and I have therefore not hesitated at times to trick out the original wording with such explanatory matter as may make it more intelligible. It should also be borne in mind that the relationship of ritual to myth is often brought out by a play on words. I have tried, whenever possible, to reproduce this effect.

In reading the text, it must be remembered that the ritual and drama were performed at successive stations along a processional route. There is consequently a good deal of repetition and no regular sequence. Scenes previously enacted had to be performed over again for the benefit of a new audience. Moreover, some of the central rites were of such importance that they had to be performed, not merely once, but at every distinct shrine and center to which the procession came.

CAST

RITUAL	MYTH
The new king	*Horus*
Mummy representing the old king	*The corpse of Osiris*
Chief officiant	*Thoth*
Two wailing women	*Isis and Nephthys*
A precentor	*Geb*
Chief steward	*Sokar*
Staff of embalmers, morticians, etc.	*Followers of Horus*
Princes	*Followers of Horus*
Notables of Upper and Lower Egypt	*Gods*
Temple and sacral personnel	*The henchmen of Set*
	Set

1–4 SCENE I

¶ THE CEREMONIAL BARGE IS EQUIPPED.

Horus requests his Followers to equip him with the Eye of power.

¶ THE LAUNCHING OF THE BARGE MARKS THE OPENING UP OF THE NILE AND INAUGURATES THE CEREMONY OF INSTALLING OR RECONFIRMING THE KING.

HORUS (*to his Followers*):
Convey to me the Eye that by its power
This waterway may now be opened up!

Horus also instructs his Followers to bring upon the scene the god Thoth, who is to act as master of ceremonies, and the corpse of his father, Osiris.

¶ BEER IS PROFFERED.

SCENE I. This entire ritual is performed against the background of a royal cruise down the Nile, its several elements being performed at successive stations en route. The cruise is but the Egyptian form of the widespread practice, discussed above (Commentary *Baal*, §XL), whereby a newly appointed king has to take possession of his dominion by traveling around it.

The ritual takes place at the season of the year when the waters of the Nile subside and the river is again open to navigation. The launching of the royal barge marks that event. The ceremony is best illustrated by its modern counterpart, the festival of Cutting the Dam of the Nile, which takes place annually on June 17. There

5–7 SCENE II

¶ THE ROYAL PRINCES LOAD EIGHT *mnsh* JARS INTO THE BOW OF THE BARGE.

Thoth loads the corpse of Osiris upon the back of Set, so that it may be carried up to heaven.

THOTH (*to Set*):
Behold, thou canst endure and stand no more
Against this god who mightier is than thou!

(*to Osiris*):

Let not this villain chill thy heart again!

¶ THE ELDERS OF THE COURT ARE MUSTERED.

8–10 SCENE III

¶ A RAM IS SENT RUSHING FROM THE PEN, TO SERVE AS A SACRIFICE IN BEHALF OF THE KING. MEANWHILE — AS AT ALL SUCH SACRIFICES — THE EYE OF HORUS IS DISPLAYED TO THE ASSEMBLY.

Isis appears on the scene.

ISIS (*to Thoth*):
Out of thy lips may now the word rush forth,
Permitting Horus to possess the Eye!

¶ THE ANIMAL IS SLAUGHTERED. ITS MOUTH FALLS OPEN UNDER THE KNIFE.

ISIS (*to Thoth*):
Open thy mouth, and let the word go forth!

---

too the central element of the proceedings is the launching, under official auspices, of a gaily decorated ship, called *akabeh.* For a graphic description, see Lane, *Modern Egyptians,* ch. xxvi.

On the relationship of the Pharaoh to the regulation of the Nile, cf. A. Moret, *L'Egypte pharaonique* (1932), 81–82. The power was attributed also to *defunct* kings (Drioton, in *Egyptian Religion* 1 [1933], 39–51).

SCENE III. With this presentation of a ram by way of offering to the king we may perhaps compare the ram of consecration at the investiture of the Israelitic high priest: Exodus 29:22–25.

11–14 **SCENE IV**

¶ PRIESTS SLAUGHTER THE RAM. THE CHIEF OFFICIANT HANDS A PORTION TO THE KING AND FORMALLY PROCLAIMS HIS ACCESSION.

Thoth conveys the Eye to Horus.

THOTH (*to Horus*):
* * * * * * * * * * *
The son shall in his father's place arise!
The prince shall now succeed unto the lord!

¶ THE KING IS ACCLAIMED BY THE ASSEMBLY.

CHORUS:
Fish of the deep, fowl of the skies,
Go, seek Osiris, where he lies!

15–17 **SCENE V**

¶ GRAIN IS STREWN UPON THE THRESHING FLOOR.

Horus requests his Followers to convey to him the Eye which survived the combat with Set.

HORUS (*to his Followers*):
E'en as conservèd grain is to the barn
Convey'd, so now do ye convey to me
That Eye which was from Set's assault conserv'd!

SCENES V–VI. The scattering of grain, as well as of figs, raisins, and the like, was a regular feature of ancient sacrifices. In the primitive stage, where the commensal aspect of sacrifice was predominant, it was strewn among the participants in the ritual. Thus, in the Hittite installation ceremonies described in KUB XXIX 1, ii 14–16 (= Schwartz, *Orientalia* 16 [1947], 30), the king scatters (*suhhai*) figs, grapes, portions of meat and *hasikka* fruit among the palace staff before being anointed. Similarly, at the Delphic Festival of Charilia, in Greece, the king scattered grain and pulse among the assembled congregation (Plutarch, *Quaest. Graec.* XII); and a survival of this usage is to be recognized also in the custom of throwing grain, nuts, raisins, etc., among the audience at the performance of Greek comedies (Aristophanes, *Vespae* 58; *Plut.* 789 ff.; *Pax* 962 ff.; cf. Cornford, *Comedy,* 100–02). Analogous, too, is the scattering of grain or

18–20 SCENE VI

¶ THE CHIEF OFFICIANT HANDS TWO LOAVES TO THE KING.
The two loaves symbolize the two eyes of Horus, viz., the one retained by Set, and the one restored to Horus by Thoth.

THOTH (*to Horus*):
Behold, I do convey to thee that Eye
Which in the future thou shalt never lose!

¶ DANCERS ARE INTRODUCED.

HORUS (*to Thoth*):
Before thee now mine Eye doth dance for joy!

21–24 SCENE VII

¶ A FRAGRANT BOUGH IS HOISTED ABOARD THE BARGE.
The corpse of Osiris is hoisted onto the back of Set, his vanquished assailant.

THE GODS (*to Set*):
Henceforth, O Set, thou never shalt slip free
From him who is thy clear superior!

---

beans by the king at African installation rites (Irstam, *King of Ganda,* 56, 72); while Patai (HUCA 20 [1947], 202) ingeniously suggests that David's distribution of bread, raisin cakes, and *eshpar* (= ?), recorded in II Samuel 6:19 (= I Chronicles 16:3), reflects a parallel New Year installation rite among the Hebrews. Later, when sacrifice lost its commensal character and degenerated into mere offering to the gods, the grain was simply strewn upon the altar (cf. *Odyssey* iv 761; Euripides, *Electra* 804; Aristophanes, *Aves* 622; Eustathius, 132.3 [on *Iliad* i 499]; Fritze, H. von, in *Hermes* 32 [1897], 236).

SCENE VII. In illustration of what is here described, Sethe quotes Mariette, *Dendereh* iv 71, Naville, *Horus,* 16,4/5: "The forepart of the solar barque is made of *im,* the rear part of acacia-wood, and these two trees are therefore 'holy trees' unto this day."

The word here rendered "fragrant bough" is *imî,* which Gardiner (*Egyptian Grammar,* 468) tentatively identifies with the male date palm. What is evidently indicated is the introduction into the proceedings of something analogous to the maypole or evergreen which is so common a feature of seasonal rituals throughout the

HORUS (*gazing on the corpse of Osiris*):
How noble! Oh, how fair and beautiful!

¶ THE WORKMEN STAGGER UNDER THE WEIGHT OF THE BOUGH.

HORUS (*to Set*):
Bow'd under him, thou shalt connive no more!

25–28 SCENE VIII

¶ THE ROYAL INSIGNIA, VIZ., THE "SCEPTERS OF HORUS," THE FOOTSTOOL, THE CINCTURE, AND THE STAVE ARE BROUGHT FORWARD BY THE PRINCES.

¶ (a) THE CHIEF OFFICIANT PRESENTS THE TWO SCEPTERS TO THE KING IN THE NORTHERN CHAMBER, THE CUSTOMARY LOCALE OF STATE COUNCILS.

Thoth presents the Eye to Horus.

THOTH (*addressing the corpse of Osiris*):
See, [I bestow on] him [the Eye of power]!

---

world; cf. Sartori, *Sitte u. Brauch,* iii 173: "The blessing attendant upon the incoming spring is expressed in a variety of more material forms . . . pre-eminent among which are the young 'spring trees' and the 'may-boughs' now decked with their first leaves. Branches of birch and fir – sometimes even whole trees – are carried home from the woods to be used as festal decorations. . . . Originally, these 'may-boughs' symbolized the entire wealth of that fertility which Nature had now brought to birth, and they were believed to be endowed with specially beneficent properties by virtue of the power dwelling in them." On the presence of such maypoles in Hittite rituals, see *Telipinu,* §XII; and on the conception that the tree symbolizes the spirit of fertility, cf. Mowinckel, S., AcOr 15 (1936), 141 ff.; Engnell, *Divine Kingship,* 25 f.; Hooke, *Early Semitic Ritual,* 14.

It is not improbable, however, that the "fragrant bough" is also the counterpart of the "life tree" customarily planted by African kings at their installation – an institution believed to be of Near Eastern origin (Irstam, *op. cit.,* 22, 68, 193; Engnell, 25 f.; Patai, *op. cit.,* 177–78).

SCENE VIII. On the scepter as a standard element of the royal insignia, cf. Irstam, *op. cit.,* 56, Point 14; Patai, *op. cit.,* 190 ff.

The traversal of the mountains clearly refers to a standard instal-

¶ (b) THE CHIEF OFFICIANT PRESENTS THE CROWN OF LOWER EGYPT (?) IN THE HALL OF THE GODS.

THOTH (*again addressing the corpse of Osiris*):
Horus hath now attained to man's estate,
And so receives from me the Eye of power!

¶ (c) THE ROYAL STAVE IS PRESENTED.

Thoth presents the Eye to Horus.

THOTH (*addressing the corpse of Osiris*):
See, I have invested him with power
To stave off every violence from thee!

29–33 SCENE IX

¶ (a) GOATS AND ASSES TRAMPLE THE GRAIN ON THE THRESHING FLOOR, AND ARE SUBSEQUENTLY DRIVEN OFF WITH BLOWS.

This symbolizes how Osiris was at first discomfited by Set, but how the latter was subsequently driven off by Horus, who thus defended his father.
(The Egyptian word for "grain" is it, *and this sounds exactly like the word for "father.")*

HORUS (*to the henchmen of Set*):
Behold, [O ye confederates of Set],
[I strike you as ye erewhile struck my sire]!

---

lation rite. Sethe compares *Urkunden* I, 110–11, where King Merjenre is said to stand "on the back of the mountains" at Assuan. A similar expression is used of Amenemmes I in Pap. Millingen II, 10. The rite is best illustrated from the Hittite text, Bozkurt-Cig-Güterbock, *Istanbul Arkeoloji Müzelerinde Bulunan Bogazköy Tableterinden Secme Metinler* (Istanbul 1944), I, colophon, where the king is said to go to Mount Piskurunuwa on the occasion of the AN.TAH.SHUM festival. For full discussion of this common motif, see Commentary on *Baal,* §XL.

SCENE IX. On the identification of the grain with the spirit of fertility (i.e., Osiris, Attis, Adonis, etc.) cf. Frazer, GB, v 325 f.; Eisler, *Orphisch-Dionysiche Mysterien-gedanken* (1925), 235 ff. Cf. especially, Hippolytus, *Refut,* V, 8.162; 9.170; Eusebius, *PE* III 11–12 (from Porphyry); III 13–14; Augustine, *De Civ. Dei* VII, 25.

Lo, I command you: thrash my sire no more!
(*to Osiris*):
See, I beat them who were beating thee!

¶ (b) THE THRESHED GRAIN IS LADEN ON THE BACKS OF THE ANIMALS. IN THE PROCESS, SOME OF IT IS SPILLED ON THE GROUND.

Osiris is loaded upon the back of Set to be conveyed aloft to heaven.

HORUS (*to the corpse of Osiris*):
Set's poison shall no more be splash'd o'er thee!

34–36 SCENE X

¶ A FRAGRANT BOUGH IS BROUGHT FROM THE ROYAL STOREHOUSE (THE "WHITE HOUSE") AND PLACED ABOARD THE BARGE. [SEE ABOVE, SCENE VII].

THOTH (*to Horus*):
How sweet the fragrance issuing from thy sire!
(*to the corpse of Osiris*):
O thou my lord, come nigh to me again!

37–40 SCENE XI

¶ (a) THE BARGE IS DRESSED WITH RED PAINT. (RED IS THE COLOR OF SET.)

Horus gives Set a "dressing down."

HORUS (*to Set*):
Sooth, thou red devil, thou shalt ne'er slip free
From him who is thy clear superior!

¶ (b) THREE BOUGHS AND EIGHT *mnsh* JARS ARE PLACED ABOARD.

SCENE XI. On the idea that deities exude a special aroma, cf. Homeric *Hymns* III 231; V 277; Aeschylus, *Prometheus Vinctus* 115; Euripides, *Hippolytus* 1391 (v. Monk *in loc.*); Vergil, *Aeneid* i 403. Cf. also: Schwenk, K., in *Philologus* 17 (1861), 451; Lohnmeyer, "Der göttliche Wohlgeruch," in *Sitzb. d. Heidelb. Akad.* 1919; MacCulloch, ERE vii, 201b.

ISIS and NEPHTHYS (*to the corpse of Osiris*):
How sweet art thou, Osiris, to the scent,
More redolent than all things in the world!

¶ (c) FEMALE WAILERS UTTER A DIRGE.

HORUS (*to Thoth*):
Behold, how grievous is their sorrowing!

41–45 SCENE XII

¶ ALL ALONG THE ROUTE, TRIBUTE IS PAID TO LOCAL DEITIES.

Horus receives the Eye.

¶ A SPECIAL OFFERING OF A GOAT AND GOOSE IS PRESENTED IN EACH CASE. THESE ARE DECAPITATED.
(a) THE GOAT IS DECAPITATED.

Set is beheaded.

THOTH (*to the henchmen of Set*):
Confederates of Set, now bow his head!
(*to Horus*):
Behold, I bring his sever'd head to thee!

HORUS (*to Thoth*):
Present it rather unto yonder god![a]

¶ (b) WATER IS POURED OVER GOAT AND GOOSE. A BRAZIER IS PRODUCED, AND THE COOKING OF THE FORMER BEGINS.

HORUS (*to the local god*):
Behold, my mouth is watering at the smell!

¶ (c) THE GOOSE IS DISPATCHED.

Set's discomfiture is completed.

[a] I.e., the local god.

SCENE XII. The offering here specified is a libation made over the severed heads of a goose and an animal from the herd, especially at the foundation of temples. It accompanied the ceremony of "stretching the line" (ZÄS 37 [1899], 13; Brugsch, *Thes.* VI, 1264 ff.). The ceremony is portrayed in the Fifth Dynasty sun sanctuary at Abu Gorab (ZÄS 38 [1900], 94, Pl. V) (Sethe).

On Set as the headless demon, cf. K. Preisendanz, *Akephalos, der kopflosige Gott* (Leipzig, 1926); Eitrem, *Pap. Osloenses* I (1925), 47 ff.

HORUS (*to Set*):
Ah, what a consummation here is wrought!

46–47 SCENE XIII

Horus now reaches the zenith of his power and authority.

HORUS (*to Thoth*):
Be now the royal headgear brought to me!

¶ THE SEVERED HEADS OF THE GOAT AND GOOSE ARE DEPOSITED BESIDE THE *djed* PILLAR IN THE HOUSE OF GOLD.

GEB, god of the earth (*to Thoth*):
Not once alone, but twice, for emphasis,
Proffer to him the sever'd head of Set!

48–50 SCENE XIV

¶ THE PROCESSION REACHES HELIOPOLIS. PRINCES AND LOCAL PRIESTS RAISE THE *djed* PILLAR.

At the command of Horus, his Followers hoist the corpse of Osiris upon the back of Set.

HORUS (*to his Followers*):
Let Set be bow'd beneath Osiris' weight!

Two wailing women recite a dirge over the deceased king. Isis and Nephthys wait upon the corpse of Osiris.

ISIS and NEPHTHYS (*to the Followers of Horus*):
Load the corpse upon the back of Set!

51–52 SCENE XV

¶ A ROPE IS THROWN AROUND THE *djed* PILLAR, AND IT IS LOWERED.

Horus commands his Followers to bind and subdue Set.

HORUS (*to his Followers*):
Let him stand discomfited in bonds!

SCENE XIII. The "House of Gold" is the workshop of the guilders and goldsmiths (Sethe).

53–54 SCENE XVI

¶ THE PRINCES EMBARK UPON TWO BARGES.

Horus orders his faithful Followers to be led into his presence.

HORUS:
Let now my Followers, who raised my sire,
Be led into my presence!

54–55 SCENE XVII

¶ THE PROCESSION REACHES LETOPOLIS. A LOAF AND A JUG OF WINE (OR BEER) ARE PRESENTED BY THE CHIEF OFFICIANT.

Horus presents a pair of eyes to the Eyeless goddess of Letopolis.

HORUS (*to the goddess of Letopolis*):
Receive, I pray thee, these two Horus eyes;
Set them in thy face, that thou may'st see!

¶ HANDS ARE LIFTED.

56–58 SCENE XVIII

¶ A PUNCHING MATCH IS STAGED BETWEEN TWO CHAMPIONS.

Horus and Set engage in combat. Geb, god of the earth, eventually bids them desist.

GEB (*to Horus and Set*):
Ex*punge* the thought of *punch*ing one another!
HORUS (*to this Followers, who aid him*):
'Tis *you* he means! He tells you to desist!

SCENE XVIII. The word rendered "punching-match" is *mnʿ*, which is not found elsewhere in Egyptian literature. However, the hieroglyph, which portrays two men in hand-to-hand combat, shows clearly what is meant, and Sethe cleverly compares the term *ʿmn.t*, "ceremonial bout at the jubilee of kings" (Brugsch, *Thes.* V, 1193.35 f.).

What is implied is, of course, the Ritual Combat, fully discussed above, ch. II, §20.

By a grotesque pun, the word *mnʿ* suggests *ʿm w ib*, "expunge

59–63 SCENE XIX

¶ (a) A PAIR OF MILKMAIDS COME BRINGING MILK (WHICH IS EVIDENTLY POURED OUT).

Horus bids his Followers let the sweet influence of his Eye be diffused abroad.

HORUS (*to his Followers*):
Be the sweet influence of this mine Eye
Throughout my earthly mansion now poured forth!

¶ (b) A PAIR OF SLAUGHTERERS BRING SACRIFICIAL MEAT.

Horus bids Thoth bring his Eye into the palace.

HORUS (*to Thoth*):
Thoth, bring thou mine Eye into this palace!
(*to his Followers*):
Hereby is my protection shed o'er you!

* * * * * * * * * * * * * * * * *

64–65 SCENE XX

¶ A PAIR OF CARPENTERS SPLIT WOOD FOR THE FURNITURE OF THE NEW KING'S PALACE.

During the combat, Set splits one of the eyes of the Horus, and retains it in his possession. Horus warns his Followers of Set's baleful influence.

HORUS (*to his Followers, who act as his seconds*):
See, he has split mine eye and taken it!
I warn you, keep away from yonder Set!

---

from the mind, forget." We have tried to reproduce this pun by rendering "punch" and "ex-*punge*" respectively.

SCENE XIX. What we have here is a typical dairy-charm. Milk was likewise produced at the Babylonian Akîtu-festival, and was there taken to symbolize the nursing of the savior-god by Ishtar. For other parallels and full discussion, see Comm. on *Gracious Gods,* Ritual, §III(c). Comparable also is the Galaxia as an element of the corresponding Attis-rites (Hepding, *Attis,* 197 f.).

Milk is often regarded, in Egyptian literature, as typifying the beneficent influence of the Eye of Horus (Sethe).

66–68 SCENE XXI

¶ (a) PRIESTLY MORTICIANS BRING IN A TABLE OF SACRIFICIAL MEATS.

Horus' Eye is restored to him by his Followers.

HORUS (*to his Followers*):
Restore mine eye, I pray you, to my face!

¶ (b) THE SACRED CHOIRMASTERS BEAT TIME, AND THE CHORISTERS CHANT.

THE FOLLOWERS OF HORUS (*to Geb, imploringly*):
Yon Set is out of tune with us; alone
Disturbs the harmony of all our ways!

68–71 SCENE XXII

¶ THE PRINCES PROFFER JARS OF WINE FROM BUTO AND PELUSIUM.

Horus' Eye is restored to him by his Followers.

THE FOLLOWERS OF HORUS (*to Horus*):
See, we restore unto thy face the eye
Which erewhile was wine-red with flowing blood!

HORUS (*to his Followers*):
Never again shall it be ta'en from me!

72–75 SCENE XXIII

¶ IN THE TEMPLE OF THOTH, AT LETOPOLIS, A STRING OF CARNELIAN BEADS IS HANDED TO THE KING.

Horus recovers the eye wrested from him by Set.

SCENE XXI. On choir-leaders in Egyptian ritual, cf. Sethe, *Urkunden* IV, 978.12; Naville, *Osorkon,* ii, 6, Pl. I.6; Schiaparelli, *Funeri* i, 150, etc. According to Eerdmans, the term "Chief Musician" in the titles of Biblical Psalms really denotes such a metronome or conductor.

On choirs in Egyptian temples, cf. Blackman, A. M., in JEA 7 (1921) 8 ff., 22; id., ERE xii, 780a.

SCENE XXII. Buto was the capital of a large nome in the N. W. delta of the Nile. It is the modern Tell el-Fera'in.

HORUS (*to Set*):
Hand back mine eye which was incarnadined
When thou didst bite it, and suffus'd with blood!

The eye is handed over.

See, I have now retrieved mine eye from thee,
Which was blood-red, like a carnelian bead!
Turn thou thy back, for, lo, these eyes of mine
Now fix their fearsome gaze upon thy face!

76–79 SCENE XXIV

¶ THE PROCESSION REACHES HRY-THNW, A PLACE IN LIBYA. A CHAIN OF GREEN FAIENCE BEADS IS HANDED TO THE KING.

Horus bids his Followers[b] *bring him his other eye, i.e., the one Set did not wrest from him.*

HORUS (*to his Followers*):
Now bring to me my bright, translucent eye!
The one Set spared!
(*to the henchmen of Set*):
Behold, this eye of mine
The one Set spared,[c] will beautify my face!

80–81[a] SCENE XXV

¶ THE ROYAL OFFERING IS PROFFERED BY THE CHAMBERLAIN TO THE KING.

Thoth conveys the eye to Horus.

THOTH (*to Horus*):
I bring to thee thine eye. Delight in it!

¶ THE EYE OF HORUS IS ELEVATED BEFORE THE CONGREGATION.

THE FOLLOWERS OF HORUS (*to Horus*):
Now lift we up thine eye unto thy face!

[b] NOTE IN THE ORIGINAL TEXT: The Followers of Horus are here played by Libyan women.
[c] In the original, there is a pun: the word for "chain," viz., *sh.t.b.w*, suggests that for "spare," viz., *kh.t.b*.

81b–82 SCENE XXVI

¶ PRIESTLY EMBALMERS (CALLED "REVIVERS OF THE SPIRIT") CIRCULATE AROUND TWO FALCON STANDARDS. THE KING THEN COMMITS THE STANDARDS INTO THE CUSTODY OF THE CHIEF OFFICIANT.

Thoth receives the two eyes in order to convey them to Horus.

HORUS (*to Thoth*):
Receive these standards in thy custody,
For lo, they twain do represent mine eyes!

83–86 SCENE XXVII

¶ TWO MACES ARE PRESENTED TO THE KING. THE CEREMONY TAKES PLACE ON THE WAY(?) OF THE GODS, I.E., THE PROCESSIONAL HIGHWAY(?).

(*The Egyptian word for "mace," viz.,* b, *suggests that for "engraft," viz.,* i b.)
Horus engrafts upon himself the two testicles of Set which he had wrested from him in the combat.

THOTH (*to Horus*):
Engraft these testicles upon thyself!
Thereby increase still more thy potency!

¶ TWO PLUMES ARE PLACED ON THE KING'S HEAD. THIS TAKES PLACE ON THE GREAT BEACH.

Horus orders the Confederates of Set to place the eyes in his head.

HORUS (*to the Confederates of Set*):
I order you to place them in my head!

87–88 SCENE XXVIII

¶ A GOLDEN(?) CORONET IS PRESENTED TO THE KING.

The coronet symbolizes the Eye of Horus.

SCENE XXVIII. The word which we have rendered "coronet" is translated "ring" by Sethe; but, as Frankfort observes (*Kingship*, 377, n. 10), what is implied is a diadem rather than a finger-ring. The diadem was likewise an element of the Hebrew regalia; cf.

Horus officially informs Set that Geb has decided the issue between them in his (Horus') favor.

HORUS (*to Set*):
Geb has found thee guilty in the case
Of thy contention against my sire!

89[a] SCENE XXIX

¶ A LIBATION IS OFFERED ON BEHALF OF THE KING'S PROSPERITY BY REPRESENTATIVES OF THE TWO "DEMESNES"—EVIDENTLY, UPPER AND LOWER EGYPT (SETHE).

(*The text is damaged*)

89[b]–90 SCENE XXX

¶ DIGNITARIES OF UPPER AND LOWER EGYPT ARE INTRODUCED.

Geb orders the gods to wait upon Horus. Thoth summons them.

GEB (*to the Followers of both Horus and Set*):
Wait upon him!
(*turning to Horus*):
Thou, Horus, art their lord!

91–96 SCENE XXXI

¶ THE CHIEF OFFICIANT PRODUCES COSMETICS FOR THE ADORNMENT OF THE KING.

II Kings 11.12 (= II Chron. 23.11), and note especially that, according to Josephus (*B.J.* I.33,9), Herod had both a diadem and a crown. On the distinction, cf. Löw, I., "Kranz und Krone," in his *Ges. Schriften,* iii, 407–39. See also Patai, *op. cit.*, 194–95.

However, it is not impossible that what is intended is rather a royal bracelet, corresponding to the Hebrew *ets'adah* of II Samuel 1.10. Such bracelets likewise formed part of the insignia in Persia (ERE x 637a); cf. Patai, *loc. cit.*, Goodenough, E. R., in JBL 48 (1929), 190.

SCENE XXXI. On the aroma of the gods, see above, Scene XI.

The mythological interpretation of the ritual is reinforced by two verbal puns, the Egyptian word for "green pigment" suggests an

¶ (a) BRIGHT *green* EYE SALVE IS PRODUCED.

Thoth hands Horus his bright green *eye.*

THOTH (*to Horus*):
See, I set thy *bright* eye in thy face!

¶ (b) *Black* EYE SALVE IS PRODUCED.

Thoth hands Horus his dark (swart) *eye.*

THOTH (*to Horus*):
May this *swart* eye sit *sweetly* in thy face!

¶ (c) *Dull,* RAISIN-COLORED PIGMENT IS PRODUCED.

THOTH (*to Horus*):
Ne'er may the luster of thine eye be *dulled!*

¶ (d) FRANKINCENSE IS PRODUCED. THE WARDENS OF THE GREAT PLUMES PLACE THE ROYAL URAEUS ON THE KING'S HEAD.

Horus receives the eyes and is perfumed.

THOTH (*to Horus*):
I give to thee the fragrance of the gods!
Thine eye which was pluck'd out do I restore!
Now with this perfume do thou scent thy face
Till it be fragrant!

97–100 SCENE XXXII

¶ THE PROCESSION REACHES THE IBIS NOME. CRESCENT-SHAPED LOAVES ARE DISTRIBUTED AMONG THE DIGNITARIES OF UPPER AND LOWER EGYPT.

(*The crescent-shaped loaves symbolize the eyes of Horus.*) *Horus recovers his Eye and in turn restores their severed heads to the henchmen of Set* [*see above, Scene XII*].

HORUS (*to Thoth*):
I bid thee now restore to them their heads!

Thoth restores the heads.

---

homophonous term meaning "bright," and that for "black pigment" (the Greek *stimmi*) one meaning "be sweet."

SCENE XXXII. On the distribution of loaves, see above on Scene VI.

THOTH (*jointly to his own Followers and to the henchmen of Set, but referring only to the latter*):

Geb, the umpire of this cause, has shown
Clemency toward you and has ruled
That these your sever'd heads be now restored!

¶ THE KING RECEIVES A TRIBUTARY OFFERING.

Horus receives the Eye.

HORUS (*to his own Followers and to the henchmen of Set*):

Give me mine eye, that I may joy in it!

101–103 SCENE XXXIII

¶ THE PROCESSION REACHES BUTO.

¶ (a) THE CHIEF OFFICIANT PRESENTS THE ROYAL CORSELET TO THE KING.

(*The Egyptian word for "corselet" resembles that for "embrace."*)
Horus embraces the corpse of Osiris.

HORUS (*turning to Geb*):

See, I embrace my languid father here,
* * * * * * * * * * * * * * * * * *

¶ (b) THE EDGES OF THE ROYAL GARMENT ARE ADJUSTED.[d]

HORUS:

May he yet have the *edge* on all his foes!

104–106 SCENE XXXIV

¶ (a) A LOAF OF *akh* BREAD IS PRODUCED.

Another Egyptian word akh *means "spirit." The* akh *bread is therefore taken to symbolize the spirit of Osiris, which has been driven into the earth like grain whereof bread is made. Moreover, the Egyptian word for "father, sire"* (it) *is identical in sound with one meaning "grain."*

HORUS (*to Geb*):

See, they have driven my sire into the ground!

¶ (b) A MUG OF BEER IS PRESENTED. TWO PRIESTESSES RECITE A DIRGE.

[d] Text and translation are alike uncertain.

The beer symbolizes the tears shed for the dead Osiris.

HORUS (*to Geb*):

They make of him an object of lament!

107–111[a] SCENE XXXV

¶ VARIOUS TYPES OF MUMMY CLOTH ARE BROUGHT FROM THE ROYAL STOREHOUSE (THE "WHITE HOUSE") TO THE EMBALMMENT CHAMBER.

The corpse of Osiris is swathed.

¶ (a) MATERIAL CALLED *ifd* IS BROUGHT.

The word ifd *suggests* fdy, *"wrench, pluck out."*

HORUS (*to Osiris*):

Sooth, I *plucked* the thighbone from yon Set!

¶ (b) Material called *rs* is brought.

The word rs *suggests* rs, *"stir up, incite."*

HORUS:

That did I that his heart *be stirred* no more
To make assault upon my sovereignty!

¶ (c) MATERIAL CALLED *shsf* IS PRODUCED.

By a grotesque pun, shsf *suggests* *sfr, *a title of Nephthys as the panther-cat.*

HORUS:

E'en as this mummy cloth is bound on him,
So may my father now be bound to me
In close attachment! May the panther-cat,
Great Nephthys, reunite his limbs once more!

111[b]–113 SCENE XXXVI

¶ IN THE IBIS NOME.

THE PRIESTLY EMBALMERS RECEIVE THE BODY OF THE DEFUNCT KING.

Thoth and the Followers of Horus are ordered to minister to the corpse of Osiris. Moreover, because the words rendered "priestly embalmers" can be interpreted to mean "spirit seekers," this element of the punctual ritual is identified mythologically with the search for the lost Osiris.

HORUS (*to Thoth*):
Go, seek my father!
(*to his Followers*):
Seek my father too!

114–116 SCENE XXXVII

¶ THE PRIESTLY EMBALMERS, SOME MASKED AS MONKEYS AND OTHERS AS WOLVES, RAISE THE BODY OF THE DEFUNCT KING AND PERFORM OTHER CEREMONIAL ACTS.

HORUS (*to his Followers*):
Now raise ye up my father who lies here!
Stoop ye, and bow beneath the weight of him!

117–119 SCENE XXXVIII

¶ IN THE IBIS NOME, BUT REPEATED AT LETOPOLIS.
THE PRIESTLY EMBALMERS LIFT THE CORPSE IN THEIR ARMS.

Nut, the sky goddess and mother of Osiris, is bidden raise him on her back and convey him aloft to heaven.

HORUS (*to his Followers*):
Bestow your ministrations on[e] my sire!

THE FOLLOWERS OF HORUS (*to Nut*):
Now raise thy son to heaven, for thy back
A ladder is, its vertebrae the rungs!

120–122 SCENE XXXIX

¶ At Letopolis.
TWO PRIESTESSES ARE SELECTED TO CHANT A DIRGE.

Isis and Nephthys chant a dirge.

[e] Lit., "Seek;" see above, Scene XXXVI.

SCENE XXXVIII. On Egyptian conceptions concerning the ladder which leads to heaven, see Blok, H. P., in AcOr 6 (1928), 257–69. On the idea in general and with special reference to "Jacob's ladder" (Gen. 28.12), see Cook, *Zeus*, ii, 125 ff.; Frazer, FOT, one-vol. ed., 230. The idea survives in Dante, *Paradiso*, xxi. 25 ff.

ISIS and NEPHTHYS (*to Osiris*):
Lo, we are come to sing thy majesty!
Thou noble one, bestow on us thy grace!

123–125 SCENE XL

¶ (a) MUMMY CLOTHS ARE HANDED TO THE MASTER OF CEREMONIES, OR CHIEF STEWARD.[f]

Thoth orders mummy cloths applied to the corpse of Osiris.

THOTH (*to Horus*):
Be now these cloths applied unto thy sire!

¶ (b) THE THIGHBONE OF THE SACRIFICIAL ANIMAL IS LIKEWISE HANDED TO THE CHIEF STEWARD.

(The thighbone is taken to represent that wrested from Set in the combat, and therefore symbolizes him.)
Set is warned to accept the judgment passed upon him.

HORUS (*to Set*):
Justice has turned her face against thee; thou,
Accept what Justice hath decreed on thee!

126–129 SCENE XLI

¶ THE MATERIALS ARE IN TURN HANDED OVER TO THE PRIESTLY EMBALMERS.

Mummy cloths are handed to Horus.

THOTH (*to Horus*):
* * * * * * * * * * * * *[g]

¶ THE THIGHBONE OF THE SACRIFICIAL ANIMAL IS LIKEWISE HANDED OVER.

[HORUS (*to Osiris*):]
Behold, I plucked the thighbone from yon Set!
(*to Set*):
Begone, and let us meet with thee no more!

[f] NOTE IN THE ORIGINAL: The Chief Steward represents the god Sokar.

[g] There seems to be an error in the text, which here repeats the following line concerning the thighbone. What we require, however, is something relating to the mummy cloths, and appropriate in the mouth of Thoth rather than of Horus.

130–31 SCENE XLII

¶ FOOD IS PRODUCED FOR THE REGALEMENT OF THE PRIESTLY EMBALMERS, WHO NOW PROCEED TO THE DUAL SHRINES.

THERE IS GENERAL PROSTRATION AND KISSING OF THE GROUND.

Horus(?) addresses both his own Followers and the henchmen of Set, possibly inviting them to a banquet of reconciliation and jubilation.

(*The text is fragmentary*)

132–133[a] SCENE XLIII

¶ THE DIGNITARIES OF UPPER AND LOWER EGYPT ARE LIKEWISE REGALED.

Thoth and the followers of Horus are invited to enjoy the benevolence of the latter's protective Eye, and to commend it in hymns.

HORUS (*to Thoth*):
Oh, let them taste the goodness of mine Eye,
and let it be commended of their mouths!

133[b]–135 SCENE XLIV

¶ THE DIGNITARIES ARE ANOINTED.

(*The shining oil symbolizes the shining Eye of Horus.*) *Horus bestows on his Followers the radiant splendor of his Eye.*

HORUS (*to his Followers*):
Behold, there now is set upon your heads
That which once gleamed so brightly against Set!
Howbeit, Set shall have no part thereof!

136–138 SCENES XLX–XLVI

¶ THE SCENE NOW SHIFTS TO THE PALACE OF THE GODS.

NATRON AND WATER ARE PRODUCED FOR THE EMBALMMENT.

(*The Egyptian word for "natron" has the same sound as that for "dwelling place."*)

Horus observes that Osiris has now relinquished his earthly dwelling place and is about to be translated to heaven.

HORUS (*to Set*):
My father in the Fenland bides no more!
(*to Osiris*):
Greater than my divinity is thine!

(*The rest is lost*)

2. THE EGYPTIAN MEMPHITE DRAMA

What is known conventionally as the Memphite Creation Drama is inscribed on the so-called "Shabako Stone," now in the British Museum[1] — a basalt slab set up by King Shabaka (reigned 716–701 B.C.), founder of the Twenty-fifth or Ethiopian Dynasty, in the temple of Ptah, south of Memphis. The inscription was copied from an older, half-obliterated original,[2] dated by Sethe to the First Dynasty (ca. 3300 B.C.) but by Rusch[3] — with more probability — to the Fifth (ca. 2500 B.C.). It contains the "presenter" 's narrative and the accompanying libretto of a sacred drama dealing with the contest of Horus and Set, the accession of the former to kingship over Upper and Lower Egypt, and the death and resurrection of Osiris. To the main drama is appended a hymn to Ptah, prime god of Memphis.

The text was evidently designed for the annual festival which took place on the last days of the month of Khoiakh and on the first day of spring (Proyet). This festival, mentioned in the famous Calendar from Dendereh,[4] celebrated the periodic eclipse and revival of the topocosm. Special emphasis was placed on the death and resurrection of Osiris, *i.e.*, the topocosmic spirit, and on the coronation of the king (mythologically identified with Horus) as the symbol of the regenerated community. At Edfu, it was actually known as the "New Year of Horus"; while at Memphis, where it was associated with the god Sokar, it featured also a mimetic combat between two teams.

The program of the festival followed the standard Ritual Pattern. THE FIGHT BETWEEN HORUS AND SET is but the typical Ritual Combat between Old Year and New, Summer and Winter, Life and Death, Rain and Drought, etc., which we find in seasonal festivals everywhere and which is reproduced in ancient Near Eastern mythology in the battle of Baal and Yam (or Mot) in Canaan, of the storm god and the Dragon Illuyankas among the Hittites, of Marduk and Tiamat among the Babylonians, and of Yahweh and Leviathan (or Rahab) among the Hebrews. THE DEATH AND RESURRECTION OF OSIRIS is but the mythological counterpart of the eclipse and reinstatement of the king at the seasonal festival, and is paralleled in the myths of Tammuz, Baal, Telipinu, Attis, Adonis, etc. The INDUCTION OF HORUS is the familiar Coronation element; while the RESTORATION OF OSIRIS and his INSTALLATION IN A NEWLY BUILT CITY (*i.e.*, Memphis) is but a duplicate version of the same thing in more durative terms, Osiris representing the indesinent topocosmic spirit of which Horus is but the immediate avatar. Lastly, the BUILDING OF THE NEW CITY is likewise a standard element of the Ritual Pattern. The closest parallel is the erection of the special palace (Esagila) for Marduk in the Babylonian *Epic of Creation;* and we have already observed that this feature recurs in the Canaanite *Poem of Baal* and elsewhere.

Emanating as it does from Memphis, our text links these standard elements of the Ritual Pattern to the particular history of that city. Since it was there that King Menes (ca. 3400 B.C.) established the first capital of United Egypt, the building of Memphis, and the installation of Horus — prototype of the Pharaoh — as sovereign of the combined kingdom naturally appears as the crowning incident of the story. Exactly comparable is the importance attached to Babylon in *Enuma Elish,* to Saphon (Mons Casius) in the Ugaritic version, to Nerik in the Hittite version, and to Zion in the Hebrew version (*e.g.*, Psalm 76).

The concluding hymn to Ptah finds its closest parallel in the Hymn of the Fifty Names of Marduk appended to the Babylonian recension of *Enuma Elish.*

NOTES

1. "It is stated to have been presented to the Museum by Earl Spencer in 1805; we have been unable to trace its previous history." F. W. Read and A. C. Bryant, PSBA 23 (1901), 160.

2. Blanks are left where the original was illegible.

3. OLZ 32 (1939), 145–56; cf. Drioton, *Le théatre egptien*, 19, n. 1. The same date was assigned by Read and Bryant, *op. cit.*, p. 164.

4. Cf. Loret, V., in *Rec. Trav.* 3 (1882), 43 ff.; 4 (1883), 21 ff.; 5 (1884), 85 ff.; Brugsch, H., in ZÄS 19 (1881), 77 ff.

Long live Shabaka, beloved of Ptah, (the god) who has his dwelling to the south of his capital (and) who lives like Re forever!

His Majesty it was who had this text inscribed in the temple of his Father Ptah, (the god) who has his dwelling to the south of his capital. His Majesty found it as an old, worm-eaten document no longer completely legible from beginning to end. So His Majesty had it copied so that it might exist in better taste and so that his own name might be perpetuated, and so that there might be a memorial of him for all time in the temple of his Father Ptah (the god) who has his dwelling to the south of his capital, in the form of some object which he, the illustrious Shabaka, had caused to be made for his Father Ptah, and so that he might thus acquire perpetuity.

Act One

The struggle of Horus and Set and the subsequent division of Egypt into an Upper and Lower Kingdom.
This scene mythologizes the Ritual Combat. It is first rehearsed by a Presenter, then acted out.

PRESENTER:

This Memphis is the center of the realm
Known by the honor'd name of Tenen-land[a]
— Upper and Lower Egypt all in one.

The king is introduced.

The unity thereof is symbolized
In Pharaoh, called the Sovereign of Two Lands.

. . . .

The image of Ptah is displayed.

Here see you Ptah, the self-begotten he,
(So styl'd by Atum), who in turn begat
The Holy Family of the Nine Great Gods.

[a] On the meaning of this obscure term, see Holmberg, *Ptah*, 56–60.

Now, so to speak, the curtain rises.

And here — the Nine themselves a-clustering
Round Geb, the god of earth, the while he parts
The struggling Horus and his rival Set,
Enjoining them to strive again no more.

The Upper Land to Set doth he assign,
Setting him king in So, his native place;
O'er Lower Egypt Horus is made king,
There in the fenland, where his father drown'd.

And in Ayan, whereto their borders reach,
A covenant they make: his own to each.

THE STORY IS ENACTED

GEB (*addressing Set*):
Get thee to the place where thou wast born!
(*addressing Horus*):
Get thee thither where thy father drown'd!

(*addressing both together*):
Behold, I separate you each from each!

Act Two

Horus acquires dominion over both Upper and Lower Egypt, which become united. Geb, god of the earth, wishing to give preference to him, makes Horus his heir.
The scene mythologizes the Coronation or Periodic Reconfirmation of the king as ruler of the United Kingdom.

PRESENTER:
Howbeit Geb is saddened at the thought
That, though the son of his own favorite son,
Horus should receive no more than Set.
So he bestows on him his heritage.

THE STORY IS ENACTED

GEB (*addressing Horus*):
Thee alone do I appoint mine heir!

(*addressing the Nine Gods*):
He and he alone shall be mine heir
In Upper Egypt and in Lower too,
Mine own son's son, my sole inheritor!

PRESENTER:

So Horus shines as sovereign of both realms,
United in this single Tenen-land.
For all that southward lies of these great walls,
These mighty walls of everlasting Ptah,
Soon with the Northern Land is reconciled.
The symbol: these twin plumes on Pharaoh's head!

In this wall'd city is their union seal'd,
Which marks the spot at which their borders meet.
There Horus shrines effulgent as the sun,
Imperial Monarch of Two-Lands-in-One!

Reeds and rushes are placed side by side at both entrances of the temple of Ptah.[b]

PRESENTER:

These reeds and rushes here placed side by side
Symbolize Horus and his rival Set
As brothers now at one and reconciled.
Their struggle now is ended; peace is made
In Memphis, called the Balance of the Lands,
Because it stands athwart their boundaries
And holds the balance there between them both.

Act Three

The revival of Osiris.
The scene now shifts to the fenland, where Osiris lies on the point of death after the savage attack which Set made on him. His rescue and subsequent restoration at the hands of the goddesses Isis and Nephthys are rehearsed by the Presenter and then enacted.
This scene represents the death and resurrection of the topocosmic spirit, incarnate, in the corresponding ritual, in the person of the deposed and reinstated king.

PRESENTER:

This fenland in the realm which Sokar rules
Is where Osiris sank and nigh was drown'd.

See, Isis here and Nephthys hastening
Toward Osiris, who lies sinking fast.
Isis and Nephthys see it with dismay.

[b] This rubric is part of the original text.

Now, Horus bids them grasp him with their hands
And rescue him from drowning in the fen.

THE STORY IS ENACTED

HORUS (*to Isis and Nephthys*):
Grasp him!

ISIS and NEPHTHYS (*to Osiris*):
We come; we grasp thee by the hand!

PRESENTER:
And now, behold, they bring him to the shore,
[And presently restore him to] the land
And lead him to that royal citadel
Which northward lies of those abhorréd fens.

Act Four

The building of Memphis.
This act mythologizes the installation of the king in a newly constructed palace — a standard element of the Ritual Pattern. The scene is first rehearsed by the Presenter, then enacted.

PRESENTER:
And now a royal city is uprear'd

* *
*

THE STORY IS ENACTED

This portion of the text is fragmentary. Apparenlty, the gods Geb and Thoth take counsel (with other gods?) concerning the construction of the great White Wall of Memphis.

Act Five

Final pacification of the two lands and establishment of continued prosperity within them.
This scene mythologizes the final stage of the Ritual Pattern, whereby the topocosmic order is fixed for the next term.

PRESENTER:
(*The Presenter's speech is lost*)

THE STORY IS ENACTED

ISIS (*to Horus and Set*):

Hearken, [I pray you], make a covenant,
[Henceforth to banish enmity and strife],
For ne'er will life be pleasant unto you
Until that [ye make peace and ask the Lord]
To wipe away the tear [from every face]

* *
*

Act Six

Induction of the king in the royal city of Memphis(?). This was evidently mythologized as the induction of Horus.

PRESENTER:

This royal city is the place where erst

* *
*

(*The rest is lost*)

Epilogue

Hymn to Ptah

The performance ends with the chanting of a hymn to Ptah, prime god of Memphis, in which mention is made of his several hypostases. This hymn may be compared with the great Hymn to Marduk *appended to the Babylonian* Epic of Creation, *which was likewise the libretto of a seasonal pantomime.*

Great and mighty is the Lord who * * * *
[In whom the] * * * * * [are] combined
In one great whole * * * * * * * * * * * *

These godheads cosubstantial are with Ptah:
Ptah himself, upon the lofty throne;
Ptah-Nun, whom Father Atum * * * * *
Ptah-Naumet, the mighty mother she
Who Atum bore; and Ptah the Great who is
The heart and members of the Nine Great Gods;
And Ptah [the Potter], he who moldeth gods
[And men?] *

(*The rest is lost*)

E. THE BURLESQUE TYPE

THE CANAANITE POEM OF THE GRACIOUS GODS

§1. When once the ritual drama has lost its functional significance, it tends to survive only as popular entertainment, catering more and more to the ruder tastes of a holiday crowd. The basic plot is retained, but it comes to be treated in less serious vein, and elements of burlesque, farce, and ribaldry are freely introduced. What eventually results is the Carnival play of modern Greece or the mummers' play of English folk custom. An illuminating example of this development in the ancient world is afforded by a curious text from Ras Shamra-Ugarit known conventionally as the *Poem of the Gracious Gods.*

§2. Unfortunately incomplete, this text divides clearly into two parts. The first contains the rubrics and chants for a public ceremony in honor of two sets of gods named "the Gods Gracious" and "the Princes." The second contains a dramatic myth relating, in a markedly humorous tone, the conception and birth of those gods and describing how they came to be, respectively, tutelary patrons of the steppeland and translated to the stars. In this portion, the "Princes" are designated more specifically as Dawn and Sunset.

I

A. SYNOPSIS

§3. The first, or ritual, portion of the text opens with an invitation to the gods to partake of a ceremonial repast tendered to them in the presence of the king and queen. They are hailed respectively as dwelling on high and as operating in the bare tracts of the steppeland; and both the royal couple and other participants in the ceremony are formally welcomed (1–7).

This is followed by a chanty, repeated seven times to the accompaniment of the lute, celebrating a successful vintage and harvest. The normal procedure of pruning, binding, and grubbing up the vine are likened fancifully to the emasculation and discomfiture of Death and Dissolution; while (in an antiphone) the now fertile field is described as a veritable paradise (8–13).

Certain "young men" — evidently acolytes — are now said to perform seven times the act of seething a kid in milk, and another animal, called *annkh,* in curd. This is accompanied in turn by a sevenfold operation over a basin — probably some kind of libation or a rite involving the blood of the victim (14–15).

The two major goddesses of the Canaanite pantheon, viz., "the Virgin," i.e., Anat, and Asherat,[1] are next said to arrive on the scene. The text is here incomplete, but it would appear that they come gloriously attired, accompanied by a "handsome young man," and that the pilgrims who attend the ceremony (or the sacristans who minister at the shrine)[2] sing or dance in front of them as they march in procession (16–18).

The divine guests having reached their destination, seats are placed in position for them (19–20).

The precentor then recites two hymns. The first (of which the opening line alone is given) is addressed to "the Princes"; the second to "the Gods Gracious," coupled with the Sun, who is cited especially for her beneficence in bringing the vine to blossom. The participants in the ceremony, described as "coming with sacrifices (in acknowledgment) of (divine) favors," are again formally welcomed (21–27).

Thereupon the song of the vintage and harvest is repeated (28–29).

B. INTERPRETATION

§4. As shown fully in our Commentary, every element of this ritual can be amply paralleled elsewhere, the whole conforming to a more or less standard pattern of seasonal ceremonies.

(*a*) The *Opening Invocation* (1–7) is simply an invitation to the typical Theoxenia, or regalement of the gods, itself a development of the periodic Communal Banquet (see Chapter Two, §36; Chapter Four, §26, *Baal*, §XXXVIII), while the blessing on the king and queen finds its exact counterpart in Hittite rituals, and in the Attis mysteries as celebrated at Rome.

(*b*) The *Song of the Vintage and Harvest* resembles those which are still chanted in France at the season of pruning, and has analogies also in Palestinian Arab usage. Moreover, its basic reference to an indwelling spirit or demon who is thus unmanned and discomfited finds an exact parallel in ancient Greek vintage songs, when the successive viticultural operations were likewise represented as the emasculation of Dionysus.

(*c*) The *seething of kids in milk* is likewise mentioned in Exodus 23:19 (E) and 34:26 (J) in connection with the Feast of First Fruits, in June, and is illustrated also by the fact that goats were the only animals slaughtered for the ritual meal (*kopis*) at the comparable Festival of Hyakinthia in ancient Laconia. Furthermore, milk and dairy dishes are characteristic, in many parts of the world, of summer harvest festivals.

(*d*) The *arrival on the scene of the two major goddesses, one of whom is expressly characterized as "the Virgin"* recalls the joint celebration of Demeter and Kore (Persephone) at major Greek seasonal festivals, and likewise the prominence of the two goddesses Athene and Artemis at the Hyakinthia.

The *ceremonial clothing of the goddesses* (expressed by the word "they twain are begirt") recalls the common custom of providing new clothes for the deities — especially for female members of the pantheon — at seasonal festivals. Particularly illuminating in this respect is the ancient Greek rite of presenting a newly woven robe to the goddess at the Panathenaia and at the Hyakinthia; while an allusion to the weaving of such garments for the goddess Asherah may perhaps be recognized in II Kings 23:7.

(*e*) The *setting up of seats* [mthbt] *for the divine guests* reflects the *lectisternium* (Greek *strōnuein thronous*) characteristic of many seasonal festivals among the Greeks and Romans, and a feature especially of the Attis mysteries. The rite is well attested, at a late date, at Palmyra and in the Hauran.

(*f*) The *description of the participants as "coming with sacrifices in return for (divine) favors"* shows that what is involved is a festival of thanksgiving, like the Israelite Feast of First Fruits, at which everyone was obliged to bring of his produce as a gift to the god.

§5. A number of converging clues enable us to determine pretty definitely the occasion of this ceremony.

(*a*) The rite of *seething a kid in milk* is associated in the Bible (Exodus 23:19; 34:26) with the Festival of First Fruits, in June, and it will be recalled that our text speaks expressly of persons who come with sacrifices of thanksgiving.

(*b*) The use of *kids* in the aforementioned rite again implies a ceremony in June, since, as H. L. Ginsberg has pointed out, "goats normally yean in the winter in Palestine."

(*c*) The emphasis on the *vine* would be peculiarly appropriate to the month of June, since — according to an ancient Hebrew calendar found at Gezer — it was in that month that the trimming of the vine indeed took place. The special reference in this connection to the beneficent co-operation of the sun might indicate, in fact, a festival celebrated at the vernal solstice (June 21).

(*d*) The divine "Princes" who figure so prominently both in the ritual and the dramatic myth may be identified, as we shall see presently, with the Dioscuri or Heavenly Twins. Now, in ancient times these were in turn often identified with the constellation Gemini, and in the Mesopotamian and later Jewish caledars, Gemini was the regnant constellation of June. A myth relating the nativity and original "assumption" of those deities would therefore have been especially appropriate to a festival held in that month.

Accordingly, we may conclude that *our text is the "book of words" for the Cannanite Festival of First Fruits, prototype of the Israelitic Pentecost, held in June at the time of the vernal equinox.*

II

A. SYNOPSIS

§6. The second, or mythological, portion of the text opens with a scene in which the supreme god El is represented as going down to the seashore to fetch water for his domestic needs. This he does by the cumbrous method of scooping it up in his hands and then emptying it into a basin. His presence excites the admiration and passion of two female onlookers who "enthuse" over him in girlish glee and attempt to arouse his attention by making ribald remarks about his actions (30–36).

El then puts down his staff (or scepter) and proceeds to shoot an arrow into the air. His marksmanship proves unfailing and he at once brings down a bird which he prepares to dress and cook. Once again the spectacle excites the two female onlookers, and once again they attempt to arouse his attention by offering somewhat Rabelaisian comments upon it. Indeed, they even go so far as to offer themselves to him, though hesitating, either through coyness or in taunting provocation, whether to do so as wives or daughters (37–49[a]).

El chooses the former alternative, embraces the two women, and they conceive. Eventually they bear two sons, described as Dawn and Sunset.

The birth of the children is reported to El, who, on hearing them described as Dawn and Sunset, orders them translated to the stars (49[b]–54).

Once more El embraces the women, and once more they conceive. This time they bear a number of sons, described as "gracious [or handsome] gods," possessing an abnormally voracious appetite and sucking the breast from the very moment they enter the world.

Again the birth is reported to El, who, on hearing that the children cannot be satisfied with anything in the sky or in the sea, orders them consigned to the steppeland, there to fend for themselves as best they may (55–66[a]).

The children rove through the steppeland for several years, until at last they fall in with a man sowing grain. They beg him to supply them, but when he does so, they at once go on to demand bread and wine. Although he has but sufficient for his own modest needs, they greedily devour it, eating him out of house and home. But at this intriguing point the extant portion of our text unfortunately breaks off (66[b] ff.).

B. INTERPRETATION

§7. The functional purpose of this dramatic myth was, clearly, to explain to the participants in the ritual ceremony why the latter was addressed to the celestial princes Dawn and Sunset, and to the terrestrial Gods Gracious, and why bread and wine were especially proffered to them on that occasion.

§8. The divine pair Dawn (Shahru) and Sunset (Shalmu) are each known independently from other sources.

Shahru (Dawn) is mentioned as a mythological figure in Isaiah 14:12 (*Helal ben Shahar;* EV, "Lucifer, son of the morning"); while the South Arabian divine name Sh-h-r is so interpreted by Rhodokanakis.[3] More significantly, in a Mesopotamian text from Ashur, the old capital of Assyria, the god Shêru (i.e., Shahru) is listed behind such celestial figures as "the rainbow," (^{d}TIR.AN.NA) and the "ornament of heaven" (^{d}ME.TE.AN.NA);[4] while in the Hammurapi period, he appears in such personal names as Shêrum-ili, "Dawn is my god," and Sherum-nawir, "Dawn is bright."[5] In Phoenician and neo-Punic sources, his name occurs in, for example, ^{c}bd-*Sh-h-r,* "servant of Dawn,"[6] with which may in turn be compared the Assyrian Abd*isihar.*[7]

Shalmu (Sunset) is listed as a Canaanite deity in the Ras Shamra text, 17.12, and appears also in the Phoenician personal names Bt-Shlm, "daughter of Sunset,"[8] and Ykn-Shlm, "Sunset exists."[9] Some scholars[10] would also recognize him in the place name Jerusalem, but this is uncertain.

§9. As sons of the supreme El, born of mortal mothers, the divine pair Shahru and Shalmu thus constitute, at least in certain aspects, a Canaanite counterpart of the Classical Dioscuri, sons of Zeus, who are likewise frequently identified — as are also the analogous Vedic Asvins[11] — with the morning and evening star (Phosphoros and Hesperos),[12] and who are likewise known as "Princes."[13]

The astral character of the Dioscuri is well attested. Thus, Pindar (*Nem.* x, 49) associated them with Pamphaes — i.e., the Sun. Callimachus (*Lav. Pall.,* 24) speaks of them as "Lacadaemonian stars"; and Horace (*Odes* I, ii.3) as "brothers of Helen, shining stars." They are portrayed wearing conical hats adorned with stars (see A. B. Cook, *Zeus,* ii, 313, 574 f.), and on a Roman sarcophagus they are shown beside Sol and Luna (see Jahn, in *Arch. Beitr.,* 79 ff.).

§10. The Heavenly Twins are alternately identified with the constellation Gemini,[14] and this identification was certainly well known in the ancient Near East. They are frequently mentioned, under the name Mash-tab-ba (Semitic, *tuame*) in Babylonian texts, where they are sometimes associated with a divine heptad called "the Seven" (*Sibitti*).[15] They appear also, under the Indic name of Nasatya, in the Hittite treaty of Suppiluliuma, with Mattiwaza of Mitanni;[16] while the symbol of Gemini is included among the signs engraved on an ancient "calendarical" tablet unearthed at Gezer.[17] Now, in the Babylonian[18] and later Jewish calendars, Gemini is the regnant constellation of the month of Siwan (June), and this would at once provide the reason why the Heavenly Twins came to be regarded as the patrons of a festival celebrating viticultural and agricultural events performed, as we have seen, in that month!

Another Semitic myth about these gods seems to underlie the words of Psalm 82:6–7:

I said, *Gods* are ye,
and all of you *beings celestial;*
howbeit, like men shall ye die,
and like one of *the Princes* fall!

Here they appear to be identified with the rebellious members of the heavenly court, and in this respect it is significant that in later pseudepigraphic and apocalyptic literature, those rebels are indeed frequently represented as *stars* (e.g., I Enoch 86:1; 88; 90:20–21; Revelation 12:7–9; 20:1–7; cf. also II Corinthians 11:4, and see Morgenstern, HUCA 14 [1939], 100). Moreover, in rabbinic literature, the two ousted angels are called 'Azza and 'Azael — names which connect with the Palmyrene 'Azizu ("strong") as an epithet of Castor (see Grunwald, *Yalqut Sippurim u-Midrashim,* i, 36–37; Kohut, *Aruch Completum,* vi, 182).

§11. The dramatic myth is treated in burlesque fashion and is full of little touches designed to raise a laugh on the part of an audience in holiday mood. Thus, when El fetches water for his needs, he does so — almost in the manner of a Grock or a Chaplin — by the comically laborious method of scooping it up in his two cupped hands until his basin is filled to the very brim. When the two female onlookers "enthuse" over him, they start exclaiming "Oh, Mummy" and "Oh, Daddy" — exclamations far removed from the tone of a solemn ritual and suggestive rather of the squeals and giggles of pert minxes in a light comedy. Then, too, there are the typical *double-entendres* and off-color jokes of the folk play and the music hall. When the god drops his rod in order to free his hand for shooting the bird, the sexually excited women try to provoke his attention by remarking, as if with a sly wink, that his "rod" seems indeed to have dropped and to be out of use; and when he eventually roasts the bird, they tell him pointedly that what are really being burned up are — themselves. Again, when the birth of the children is announced to El, the reporter appears to speak of them as "*my* children," and of their mothers as "*my* wives," suggesting that he is none other than the cuckolded human husband of the women whom the god has seduced! If this interpretation is correct, we have yet another obviously humorous touch, not unlike the somewhat blasphemous characterization of the bewildered Joseph in the medieval English Nativity plays.[19] Finally, the voracious appetite of the newborn Gods Gracious cannot but have evoked guffaws, if the action of "putting things in their mouths right and left — fowl of the air and fish of the sea" were actually represented by stage "business"; while the subsequent scene in which they eat their chance acquaintance — the "man storing grain" — out of house and home, would likewise have lent itself readily to high — or low — comedy.

§12. Obviously, then, our text represents the same kind of degeneration from the original solemn *sacer ludus* as appears also in the English mummers' play and in the folk dramas still performed, at regular seasons of the year, in Thrace and Macedonia. Here, too, however, the contours of the original form are still discernible beneath the veneer of popular adaptation and almost Rabelaisian fun, for the successive episodes can be traced to well-attested elements of the Ritual Pattern.

Thus, the successive scenes of El's fetching water from the sea and shooting a bird, though now intelligibly integrated into the main action, may really go back to the disparate ritual practices of bringing water in this way for the performance of a rain charm and of shooting arrows into the air in order to drive away hovering demons. Both are well documented in the programs of seasonal festivals.

Similarly, the mating of the god with the two human women and the subsequent birth of divine offspring may well ascend to the familiar seasonal rites of the "sacred marriage" (*hieros gamos*) and sacred nativity.

§13. The "sacred marriage" is, indeed, well attested in the religions of the ancient Near East. It was a recognized element of the New Year festivities at Babylon, Lagash, and other Mesopotamian centers. Toward the end of the third millennium B.C., the inscription on a statue of Gudea, governor of Lagash, refers to "bringing wedding gifts on New Year's Day, the festival of the goddess Bau";[20] while a cylinder of the same ruler speaks of the ritual marriage of that divine bride and the god Ningirsu.[21] Similarly, a long Sumerian hymn describes the spreading of the nuptial couch for the "sacred marriage" of Idin-Dagan, third king of the Isin dynasty (ca. 1918–1897 B.C.), and the goddess Innini, equivalent of the Semitic Ishtar.[22] Further, a late mystagogical commentary on the New Year festivities in Babylon relates how, on the eleventh day of the month of Nisan, the god Marduk "speeds to the marriage";[23] while the same and other documents also describe the nuptials, at Borsippa and Calah, of the god Nabu and the goddess Tashmetu in the following month of Ayar.[24] Lastly, it should be observed that brick couches used in this ceremony have been discovered by Parrot in the ancient temple at Mari,[25] while the ceremony itself is reproduced on a seal from Tell Asmar.[26]

Egyptian texts give evidence of a similar "sacred marriage" between the god Horus and the goddess Hathor celebrated annually at Edfu on the first day of the month of Epiphi (May–June), and followed three days later by the conception of the younger Horus.[27] So too, a feature of the Theban Festival of Opet, held annually at Luxor in the autumn month of Paophi (December–January), was the sacred marriage of the god Amon and the goddess Mut;[28] while an inscription in the temple at Deir-el Bahri, accompanying reliefs which depict the event, describes the mating of god and goddess, impersonated (on the ritual level) by the Pharaoh and his consort.[29]

Unfortunately, there is as yet no definite evidence of the institution at an early date on Syro-Palestinian soil.[30] To be sure, S. A. Cook has argued[31] that the Phoenician and Punic female name Arsh-B'l,[32] which could conceivably be rendered "espoused of Baal," points to such a practice, but it is by no means certain that this interpretation is correct, for the name might mean only (born by) the wish of Baal." Similarly, the presence of sacred couches at Palmyra[33] and in the Hauran[34] does not necessarily imply the celebration of a sacred marriage, for they may have been designed solely for a *lectisternium*, or banquet, at which the gods were feted and regaled.[35]

The dearth of evidence from Syria and Palestine is compensated, however, by Greek sources, albeit of comparatively late date. No less an authority than Aristotle informs us, for instance, that the Boukolikon at Athens was primitively the scene of Dionysus' sacred marriage with the king's consort;[36] while Lucian describes a three-day festival, blasphemously travestied by the false prophet Alexander, at which the nuptials of Leto and the birth of Apollo, and those of Koronis and the birth of Asklepios, were celebrated.[37] That the "sacred marriage" was likewise part of the more exotic Asianic mystery cults is shown by the fact that *pastophoroi* and *thalamepoloi*, both meaning "bridesmen," were common titles of the priests of Attis and Cybele;[38] while the subterranean "bridal bower" of the latter is expressly mentioned by Nicander[39] and Hesychius.[40] Moreover, one of the ritual formulas recited by initiants into the cult was, "I have gone under the (bridal) canopy."[41]

§14. As for the sacred nativity, this is attested in Greek sources not only in the passage of Lucian already cited, but also by the statement of the anonymous author of the *Philosophoumena* that at one stage of the Eleusinian Mysteries the hierophant "shouted and exclaimed in a loud voice, 'Holy Brimo hath born a holy child, Brimos.'"[42] Moreover, we are told explicitly by Strabo that the birth of Zeus was ritually enacted in Crete.[43]

§15. It may be added that both marriage and nativity indeed survive, albeit in attenuated and garbled form, in the modern mumming plays performed in Thessaly, Macedonia, Thrace, Epirus, and the Northern Islands of Greece on such crucial seasonal dates as New Year, May Day, and the like; for the principal characters of those plays are often a bride and groom and the upshot of the dramatic action is the birth of a prodigious child who manifests the same insatiable appetite as characterizes the newborn gods in our text![44]

NOTES

1. To be sure, the name of the second goddess is lost through a gap in the text, but almost all editors agree that it must have been Asherat.

2. The Semitic *'rbm* is susceptible of either interpretation; see Commentary.

3. Lexicon, II, i. 8.
4. VAT 10173, v. 1–6 Schroeder, ZA 33 (1921), 133.
5. Ranke, *Early Bab. Personal Names,* 150–51.
6. RES 326, 1545.
7. Johns, *Deeds,* No. 254, r. 4.
8. CIS I, 93.3; 1495.
9. *Ibid.,* 10.3–4; 3547.
10. E.g., Dhorme, in RB 40 (1931), 36.
11. Oldenberg, *Rel. d. Veda,* 210.
12. See fully: Frazer, *Fasti,* iv. 116; Welcker, *Gr. Götterlehre,* i. 606; Gilbert, *Gr. Götterlehre,* 201; Mannhardt, in *Zeitschrift f. Ethnologie* 7 (1875), 309–14. Cf. Martianus Capella, 83: *alius lucis sidere, opacae noctis alius refulgebat.*
13. Greek *anakte:* Pausanias, ii, 36.7; Sophocles, *fr.* 871.2 Nauck; CIA iii 1015; *Archäol. Zeitung,* 1882, 383. Cp. Rig Veda vi, 59.3; Coomaraswamy, *Authority,* 33, n. 24.
14. On this identification, held to be original, see Gruppe, *Gr. Mythol.,* 164; Jensen, *Kosmologie,* 64, 82.
15. Zimmern, *Beiträge,* ii, No. 54. 12 ff.; Craig, *Shamash,* ii, Pl. 9–10.
16. *ANET,* 206.
17. Macalister, *Gezer,* ii. 347 f. As is well known, the cult of the Dioscuri was especially prominent in Syria and Palestine during the Hellenistic and Roman periods. On coins from Aelia Capitolina dating from the reign of Antoninus Pius (138–161 C.E.), they are shown with stars over their heads (*B.M. Cat.,* p. 86, Nos. 21–38), and they are similarly represented on coins from Ascalon dating from the same period and from the reign of Faustina Junior (*ibid.,* p. 132, No. 206.7; p. 135, No. 236.7). On the cult of the Castores Conservatores in Roman Syria, see Cumont, *Études syriennes,* 353; on the Dioscuri cult at Sebustiyeh in the third century C.E., see M. Narkiss, in PEFQS 1932, 210–12. At Edessa, the Twins appear in the form of Azizos, "the strong," and Monimos, "the beneficent" (cf. *Rev. d'archéol. orientale* 4, 165–67), and the former is actually identified in Latin inscriptions as *bonus puer phosphorus* (see fully: Cumont, *op. cit.,* 269, n. 2; Dussaud, *Notes de mythol.* syr., 9 ff.; Cook, *Zeus,* i. 706, n. 2), while a Palmyrene inscription speaks of them under the analogous names of 'Azizu, "the strong," and Arsu, "the gracious" (*Cooke,* NSI, 295 n.; Lidzbarski, *Ephemeris,* i. 20; Seyrig, in *Syria* 14 1933, 251, 279 ff.). As S. A. Cook hints (*Rel. Anc. Pal.,* 222), the Hellenic cult may have been grafted upon an ancient Oriental forerunner.
18. Thureau-Dangin, *Uruk,* 14.15, gives Gemini as the only regent of Sivan; *ibid.,* 12 r., sect. 10, gives both Gemini and Orion. See fully, Langdon, *Menologies,* 4.
19. E.g., in *Joseph's Jealousy,* Cotton MS., Pageant XII (Hone, *Ancient Mysteries,* 46 ff.); *The Trial of Mary and Joseph,* Cotton

MS., Pageant XIV (Hone, *op. cit.*, 59 ff.).

20. Statue E, 51–53.
21. Cylinder B, iv. 23–v. 19.
22. Langdon, PBS X, 1 (= JRAS 1926, 36 ff.).
23. VAT 633, obv. 1–10.
24. *Ibid.*, obv. 14–21; Reisner, *Sum.-bab. Hymnen*, ii. 12–32; Pfeiffer, *State Letters of Assyria*, No. 217 (reign of Esarhaddon, 681–668 B.C.).
25. *Syria* 19 (1938), 23.
26. Frankfort, OIC 17, p. 48, fig. 42.
27. Junker, *Onurislegende*, 116 ff.
28. Wolf, *Opet*, 72 ff.; Blackman, *Luxor*, 70.
29. Sethe, *Untersuchungen*, iv. 219 f.
30. To be sure, some scholars have seen in the Biblical Song of Songs "a thinly disguised survival of an Adonis-Tammuz liturgy," including cultic love poems and hymeneals. For a critique of this theory, see H. H. Rowley, in JRAS 1938, 251–76, and note that, at best, it might explain the *literary* antecedents of the Song, but would not necessarily testify to the actual existence of the *cult* on Palestinian soil. I may add that the theory seems to me highly farfetched.
31. In Robertson Smith, *Rel. Sem.*,[3] 515.
32. CIS I, 304, 1006 (Phoen.); RÉS, 502 (Pun.).
33. H. Seyrig, in *Syria* 14 (1933), 262 f.
34. Dussaud, *Mission*, 313, No. 19; Lidzbarski, *Ephemeris*, ii. 356: "This is the couch which Animu and Manullahi made . . ."
35. Rohde has shown (*Psyche*,[7] i, 129, n. 3) that the Greek expression, *stronuein thronous*, so common in the Attis cult, has this meaning; see Hepding, *Attis*, 136 f.
36. *De Rep. Ath.*, iii. 5.
37. *Alexander*, c. 38.
38. Hepding, *Attis*, 193 f.
39. *Alexipharmakon*, 7–8, and Scholiast *in loc.*
40. Lexicon, *s.v.* KYBE A.
41. Clement Alex., *Protrept.*, ii. 15; see Harrison, *Prolegomena*, 534–37, 548–51.
42. P. 170 Cruice.
43. X, 3.11.
44. See R. M. Dawkins, in JHS 26 (1906), 191.

A. THE RITUAL

I

EXORDIUM 1–7

I call on the GODS GRACIOUS AND FAIR
(and) on THE PRIN[CES who].
Let honor be paid to those that are on hi[gh, who],

I. EXORDIUM (1–7). This invocation to the gods to eat and drink is, in fact, an invitation to the *theoxenia,* or regalement of them, which as we have seen (*Baal,* §XXXVIII) was a characteristic element of the Seasonal Pattern. It was the natural concomitant of the commensal feast, whereby, at periodic intervals, the members of the community recemented their ties of kinship. By proffering food and drink to their gods, they likewise recemented ties with *them.*

Such invocation of the gods, itself the basic form of prayer (see Dussaud, *Les origines canaanéennes du sacrifice israélite,* 94, n. 2), became, indeed, the standard prelude to liturgical rites alike among the Egyptians (Blackman, ERE xi, 77b), the Hittites (e.g., HTBM I xxiii 34 = Schwartz, JAOS 58 [1934], 337 f.; KUB XXXVI. 97 = Otten, OLZ 1956: 102 f.); and the Greeks and Romans (Schwenn, *Gebet u. Opfer,* 1; Kretschmer, *Glotta 1* [1908], 28). The form in which it is here couched later became stereotyped in Semitic hymnody, and reappears, for instance, in the Biblical Psalms. Its leading features are: (*a*) introductory verb in first person singular jussive (cf. Gunkel, *Einleitung in die Psalme,* 26; Stummer, *Sumerisch-akkadische Parallelen,* 18 ff.); (*b*) the formula, "Honor/ glory be paid/ given" (cf. Psalms 29:1; 96:7; I Samuel 6:5; Jeremiah 13:16, and note the similar sequence, "I will call . . . give glory" in Deuteronomy 32:3); (*c*) a clause describing a trait of the god(s) invoked, i.e., "who . . . in the bare tracts of the steppeland" (cf. Gunkel, *op. cit.,* 49; Stummer, *op. cit.,* 14 ff. Similarly in the Greek *Orphic Hymns,* e.g., 25. 1–2; 39. 1–7; 53. 1–5).

The gods who are here addressed are characterized, on the one hand, as "those on high," i.e., celestial beings, and on the other as doing something in the steppeland. This accords with the

[and to those who] in the sand-swept tracts of the wilderness
[ ]!
[Let a cro]wn [be placed] on their heads
and se[t upon the]ir [brows]!
Ho, eat bread! And ho, drink of foaming wine!
Welcome, O king! Welcome, O queen,
pilgrims(?) and sacristans!

---

fact that in the ensuing dramatic myth, one pair of the divine children are raised to heaven, while the other offspring are consigned to the steppeland.

The blessing on the king and queen is again typical of the Seasonal Pattern. The most arresting parallel is afforded by a Hittite text for the "day of the year" (KUB XXXVI, 97), where not only are the gods summoned to eat and drink, but life and continuance is likewise invoked upon the royal couple. So too, at the end of the Telipinu text (above, p. 315), blessings are called down on king and queen; while in the Attis mysteries as celebrated at Rome, the *archigallus* offered a sacrifice and made vows for the well-being of the emperor (*pro salute imperatoris*) on the crucial "day of blood" (*dies sanguis*), i.e., March 24 (Tertullian, *Apologet.*, 25; cf. also an inscription published in *Korrespondenzblatt d. westdeutschen Zeitschrif*, 6 [1887], 179; Hepding, *Attis*, 165).

The rendering "pilgrims(?) and sacristans" for the *'rbm* and *shnnm* of the original is tentative, based on the fact that the former word is indeed used in Arabic in the sense of "come in procession" and that the *'rbm* are stated expressly, in lines 26–27 of our text, to come with sacrifices; while the latter are mentioned in other texts from Ras Shamra (80 ii, 11; 113, 70; 303, 1; cf. also *shanani*, RA 38 [1941], 8–9) beside officers of the temple. However, *'rbm* could also denote another type of sacristan, by comparison with the Akkadian *erib biti* (lit., "one who enters [i.e., has access to] the temple"), which bears that technical sense. Indeed, just as here the *'rbm* are first welcomed by the precentor (line 7) and then proceed to discharge their duties (line 12), so in the Babylonian New Year ritual, the *erib bitate* enter the sanctuary only after the chief officiant (*urigallu*) has duly pronounced a formula (*naqbit iqba*) and thrown open the doors; cf. Pallis, *Akitu*, 146. Moreover, just as it is the *'rbm* who here sing the antiphon (line 12), so in Babylonian ritual the *erib bitate* serve as a choir responding to the priest (*kalu*); cf. RA 8, 41 ff.

II

SONG OF VINTAGE AND HARVEST 8–11

Death-and-Rot may sit enthroned,
firm ensconced in regal sway,
in his either hand a rood —
Loss of Children, Widowhood;

II. SONG OF VINTAGE AND HARVEST (8–13). The first stanza of this song is really a chanty in which, as in many parts of the world, the operations of pruning and binding the vine, and of grubbing up the soil when planting it, are represented as the emasculation and discomfiture of an indwelling spirit.

The most arresting parallel comes from ancient Greece, where the "passion" of Dionysus was a common theme of vintage ritual. Diodorus, iii. 67 (from Dionysus Skythobracchion) mentions a "Linos-song" (i.e., threnody) in "Pelasgian script" which recorded it, while the Scholiast on Clement of Alexandria *Protrept.*, p. 297. 4 Stählin, speaks of a "rustic vintage song dealing with the dismemberment of Dionysus," and Plutarch, *Theseus* 22, refers to the practice of intoning an analogous dirge (*eleleu*) at the Attic vintage festival of Oschophoria, in June–July. Moreover, Kretschmer has suggested (*Glotta* 14 [1925], 13) that the mythological figure of Hylas was projected from such an *hylagmos*, or ritual lament.

The pruned vine was itself often personified as Dionysus (cf. Orphica, No. 214, Kern; Cornutus, c. 30, p. 185; Diodorus iii. 52, 3–8; Timaios in *Orphica*, No. 210b, Kern) and this idea was subsequently taken over into Christianity. Thus, Clement of Alexandria speaks of Christ as "the great grape-cluster, the Logos that was crushed for us" (*Paidag.* II, i. 11, 2); while a Middle German paternoster by Johann von Krolewitz (ed. Lisch, in Kirchner's *Bib d. deutsch. Nationalliteratur* 19 [1839], 26) refers to him as "gemen und gebunden als man ein Garben tut." See fully, Eisler, *Orphisch-Dionysische Mysteriengedanken*, 226 ff.

A modern illustration is afforded by the French song, quoted by Bucher, *Arbeit und Rhythmus*,[6] 124, sung at the pruning of vines: "*Vignon, vignette./ Vignon, vignette./ Qui te planta il fut preudon./ Tu fus taillée à la serpette!*" Similar, too, is Robert Burns' *John Barleycorn:* "They wasted o'er a scorching flame/ The marrow of his bones;/ But a miller used him worst of all,/ For he crushed him 'tween two stones."

The underlying symbolism is brought out by the fact that, alike

yet, when men do prune the vine,
'tis *he* they prune away;
when they come to bind the vine,
he it is that they entwine;
when they grub the soil all round,
beneath *his* feet they tear the ground!

This is recited seven times to the accompaniment of the lute, and the pilgrims (?) intone the response: 12

---

in the Semitic and in other languages, viticultural terms lend themselves readily to sexual imagery. There is thus a kind of sustained double-entendre.

(a) *Pruning suggests emasculating.* Cp. the Latin use of *castrare* in reference to the trimming of plants (Cato, *De Re Rustica,* 32.2; Vitruvius 2. 9; Pliny, HN xxii. 20, 33) and the somewhat analogous Greek expression, "to *circumcise* vines" (Hesiod, *Works and Days,* 570). Similarly, in the Egyptian Ramesseum Papyrus (31b), threshing is called "hacking the god."

(b) *The vinestalk suggests the membrum virile.* In Arabic, *zubr,* "vinestalk" is used colloquially in the sense of "penis" (Dozy, *Suppl.* I, 579 a), and in post-Biblical Hebrew, the cognate *zemorah* is employed with the same connotation (Lewy, *HW,* I, 544). Kohut, *Aruch Completum* III, 300, points out that in Ezekiel 8:17, *zemorah* is rendered *bahetha,* "pudendum," in Targ. Jon. and compares German *Ruthe* and Bactrian *fravaksh* similarly used. Noteworthy also is the fact that Greek *oschos, osche,* "grape cluster," comes also to denote "scrotum" (Hippocrates, 483:15).

J. Finkel has pointed out (*Joshua Starr Memorial Volume* [1952], 29 ff.) that the song is characterized by further wordplay of the type known to Arab rhetoricians as *tawriyya* or "*double-entendre.*" Thus, the word rendered "rood" (or "scepter") also means "twig, branch" (Isaiah 11:1); while that rendered "widowhood" at once suggests the usage (attested especially in Latin) whereby an unsupported vine or plant is said to be "widowed"; and the act of grubbing up the soil when the vine is planted (Latin *pastinatio*) conveys metaphorically the same idea as is conveyed in English when we speak of "tearing up the ground under somebody's feet." The idea is, in short, that the vine with its superfluous branches represents the spirit of infertility holding out two maces or scepters; and the lopping of those branches thus symbolizes his discomfiture.

It remains only to be added that the operation here called

Now, too, the field is like that field 13
wherein the gods do dwell,
where walk the Mother and the Maid,[a]
the Blessed Damozel!

III

PRESENTATION OF SACRIFICES 14–15

Divers young men then see[the a k]id in milk and an *annkh*

[a] Lit., "the field of Asherat and the Virgin, i.e., 'Anat."

"pruning" need not necessarily refer to the real pruning, which takes place in autumn, but rather to the preliminary trimming of superfluous branches (Greek *gyrosis*) earlier in the year. In Lebanon, this is indeed called *zabbar,* the very term used in our text (Dalman, *Arbeit und Sitte,* ix. 312), and it is also the *zmr* assigned to May–June in the agricultural calendar of the tenth century B.C. found at Gezer. Significantly enough, this was called by the Romans *amputatio* (Cicero, *De Senectute,* c. xv).

The antiphon has been variously translated and interpreted. In the original it reads: *sh-d sh-d i-l-m sh-d A-sh-r-t w-R-ḥ-m,* and the divergences hinge on the fact that the crucial *sh-d* can mean (a) "field," (b) "breast," (c) "spoil," and (d) "harrow, plow." But the expression *sh-d i-l-m,* "field of the gods," recurs frequently in the Ras Shamra texts as a designation of the terrain inhabited by the gods, and this provides an eminently suitable meaning here; the fields, now yielding their produce, are likened fancifully to the paradisal abode of the gods. In exactly the same way, the Akkadian text, CT XXV, Pl. 34, obv. 5 speaks of "soil of (the) god" (*qaqqaru sha ili*) in the sense of "fertile land"; while in Genesis 13:10 and again in Isaiah 51:3, the expression "garden of Yahweh" is employed in identical fashion. Analogous too, is the Greek use of the word *zatheos,* "very divine," in the same sense, e.g., in Euripides, *Hippolytus* 748–51; Pindar, *Ol.,* iii. 22; Bacchylides, xi. 24.

As for the complementary "field of Asherat and the Virgin," this finds a perfect parallel in Pindar's description of verdant Cyrene as "an orchard of Aphrodite" (*Aphrodites kapos; Pyth.* V. 31). Asherat and the Virgin are here, of course, Canaanite equivalents of the Classical Demeter and Kore.

III. PRESENTATION OF SACRIFICES (14–15). (1) Meat boiled or stewed in milk is a favorite dish among the Arabs; see Abraham ibn

in curd seven times. Furthermore, over a basin [they?] seven times.

Ezra, Comm. on Exod. 23.19; Burckhardt, *Bedouins and Wahabys,* 63; Mrs. Finn, *Palestine Peasantry* 71–72. It is especially significant, however, that in Exodus 23:19 (E) and 34:26 (J), seething a kid in its mother's milk is forbidden *in connection with the presentation of first fruits.* The medieval philosopher and commentator Maimonides deduced from this (*Guide of the Perplexed,* iii. 48) that the preparation of such a dish must have formed part of the "heathen" Canaanite first-fruits ritual, and his shrewd conjecture – endorsed by several modern scholars (see N. Schmidt, in JBL 45 [1926], 278 n.) – is now confirmed by our text. Not improbably, however, the Biblical prohibition was in fact aimed only against the cruel practice of cooking the animal *in the milk of its own dam.*

(2) The specification of *kids* as the victims of this sacrifice is strikingly illustrated by the fact, pointed out by Frazer (*GB,*[3] vii. 281 f.), that in many parts of the world *goats* feature prominently in harvest rites. An especially arresting parallel is afforded by the exclusive use of goats in the *kopis,* or ritual meal, of the ancient Laconian seasonal Festival of Hyakinthia (Athenaeus, 138 f., cf. Mellink, *Hyakinthos,* 9)

(3) In the present instance, the cooking in milk may have possessed a special added significance, for it is characteristic of harvest festivals in many parts of the world that dairy dishes are consumed and rites performed to promote the continued fecundity of the milch beasts and to avert damage to the milk produce. Thus, at the Babylonian Akitu Festival, held in the vernal month of Nisan, it was customary to milk an animal in the presence of the goddess Ishtar of Nineveh (VAT 9555, obv. 33). At the Roman Parilia, on April 21, milk and must were drunk, while the shepherds and the image of the god Pales were sprinkled with the former (Ovid, *Fasti* iv, 779–80; Tibullus I, i. 35–36). At the Scottish Beltane festival, on May 1, dairy dishes are consumed (Banks, *British Calendar Customs:* Scotland I, 234), and churning and cheese making are undertaken (*Household Words* 19 [1859], 515). In the Hebrides, a cheese made on May 1 is kept until next Beltane as a charm against the bewitching of the milk produce (Goodrich-Freer, in *Folk-Lore* 13 [1902], 41). At St. Briavel's, Gloucestershire, England, cheese is distributed among churchgoers at Easter. Cheese and dairy dishes are commonly consumed at Whitsun in Germany (Sartori, *Sitte*

IV

ARRIVAL OF THE GODDESSES 16–18

Now comes the Virgin (Goddess), and now [the goddess Asherat] proceeds (to the scene). They are begirt with

---

und Brauch, iii. 215, n. 102), and among Jews at Pentecost (Eisenstein, *Otsar Dinim u-Minhagim,* s.v. *Kreplach;* Schauss, *Jewish Festivals,* 94). In Macedonia, the Sunday before Lent is known as "Cheese Sunday" (Abbott, *Macedonian Folklore,* II 27 f.). It was common usage in Germany to pour milk over fields in order to render them fertile (Sartori, *op. cit.,* III 34, n. 46; 70, n. 74), and a Jewish (Karaite) writer, quoted in Spencer's *De Legibus Hebraeorum ritualibus,* I, 271, refers to a current custom whereby "when they had gathered all the crops, they used to boil a kid in its mother's milk and then, as a magical rite, sprinkle the milk on trees, fields, gardens and orchards in order to render them more fruitful next year." Similarly, at Florian, in the Steiermark, a bowl of milk used to be placed in the fields at Whitsun as a fertility charm (*Zeitschr. d. Vereins fur Volkskunde* 8 [1898], 455).

(4) The "young men" who are here described as performing the rite would have been acolytes (cp., for example, the *neaniskoi* ["youths"] at the Laconian Festival of Hyakinthia [Mellink, *op. cit.,* 15]); and it is significant that in two bilingual inscriptions from Tripolitania, the same Semitic word (*gh-z-r-m*) is indeed rendered *sacri* (Février, RA 42 [1948], 86).

IV. ARRIVAL OF THE GODDESSES (16–18). (1) The two goddesses are virtually a Canaanite counterpart of Demeter and Kore, likewise celebrated together at the Eleusinian Mysteries and other ancient Greek seasonal festivals. It is noteworthy too in this respect that the two goddesses, hellenized as Athene and the Virgin Artemis, likewise figured prominently at the Laconian Hyakinthia, being conjoined on votive inscriptions from Amyclae (*Ath. Mitt.* 52 [1927], 39) and in a relief on the Hyakinthos altar at that site (Pausanias iii. 19, 4)

(2) The ceremonial "begirding" of the goddesses recalls the Greek custom of robing deities at seasonal festivals (Frazer's *Pausanias,* II, 574 ff.). Thus, a newly woven robe (*peplos*) was presented to the goddess at the Panathenaia (Pausanias, V, 16.2; Diodorus XX. 26; Scholiast on Aristophanes, *Knights,* 569; cf. Preller-Robert, *Gr. Myth.,*[4] 211–13); and a similar usage obtained

[ ]. A hands[ome] young man [accompanies them?], and the people who make up the procession da[nce in front of them?].

V

INSTALLATION OF THE DIVINE GUESTS 19–20

Eight seats (are now set up) for the gods. [ ] seven times.

---

at the Hyakinthia (Athenaeus 139[b]); while at Amyclae, a robe was woven annually for Apollo in a chamber called Chiton (Pausanias, III. 16, 2). On Semitic soil, there appears to be a reference to the custom in II Kings 23:7, where we read of women who wove garments(?)[a] for the goddess Asherath.

(3) The text does not say definitely that the pilgrims (or sacristans) *danced.* The crucial verb is imperfectly preserved, only the initial letters *yr* now remaining. I have tentatively restored *yr*[*qdn*], "(they) dance," but *yr*[*nn*], "(they) sing," would be equally possible.

V. INSTALLATION OF THE DIVINE GUESTS (18–20). This rubric has a close parallel in a ritual text from Ras Shamra (3:50–51), where "four . . . and four seats [cathedrae]" are set up on a rooftop for the gods at a seven-day ceremony and where there is likewise mention, immediately afterward, of some action performed seven times or involving seven objects, exactly the same words (*shb' pamt*) being used as here. The setting up of such cathedrae [*mthbt*] is likewise mentioned in RS 33.6, while in RS 48 + 23, rev. 2 we read of the erection of "a throne for Elath." Similarly, too, the heathen "abominations" at Jerusalem envisioned by the prophet Ezekiel (8:3) included the erection of a cathedra [*moshab*] [*mosab*]; and such a seat for a god [*mêthbâ*] is mentioned also in a late inscription from Teima (CIS II. 114).

What is here implied is the LECTISTERNIUM, or spreading of couches (seats) for the divine guests at a theoxenia. This, as we have seen, was a common element of the Seasonal Pattern. It is specifically mentioned on inscriptions (e.g., CIA II, i. 622, 624; IV, ii, 624b) as a feature of the Attis mysteries, and Rhode

[a] The Hebrew word here rendered "garments" is *bathîm,* of doubtful meaning. LXX, however, reads *chettein,* and the Lucianic recension translates *stolas* (robes). This has led J. Plessis to the ingenious conjecture that the correct reading is **kittîm,* to be identified with the Akkadian *kitu,* a linen garment.

VI

HYMN OF PRAISE TO THE PRINCES 21–22

I am jealous for the names of THE PRINCES, etc.

VII

HYMN OF PRAISE TO THE GODS GRACIOUS AND TO THE SUN 23–27

I call on THE GODS GRACIOUS,
[those little gluttons] who went sucking straightway at the teats of Asherat!
Likewise I call on THE SUN,
who causes their tendrils[b] to blossom with [ ] and grapes!
Welcome, pilgrims(?) (and) sacristans,
ye who come with sacrifices in return for favors!

[b] I.e., those of the vines belonging to the pilgrims(?). (The possessive pronoun is proleptic.)

---

has shown (*Psyche* I,[1] 129–30, n. 3) that in Greek the expression "spread a couch/throne for (the) god [*klinên/thronon strôsai theô*]" has this technical meaning.

VII. HYMN OF PRAISE TO THE GODS GRACIOUS AND TO THE SUN (23–27). (1) All gods were regarded, at least formally, as nurslings of the Mother Goddess, and they are described expressly in the *Poem of Baal* (II AB, iii 41; vi 56) as "they that suck at the breast of Asherat." The theory is well illustrated by the statement of Eratosthenes (*Katast.* 44) that "no son of Zeus was permitted to partake of heavenly honors unless he had sucked at the breast of Hera." The present statement that they "went sucking straightway [*bn ym*] at the teats of Asherat" means, therefore, that they instantly revealed their divine character. But the words also carry a further implication: the children must likewise be potential kings, since it is not only gods but also kings who are thus suckled (see Commentary on *Baal*, XXXVIII). The phrase therefore explains and validates the invocation of them as "princes."

(2) The interpretation of the phrase here rendered, "Ye who come with sacrifices in return for favors" [*hlkm bdbkh nʿmt*] is supplied by a number of South Arabian votive inscriptions (e.g., CIS IV 28.5; 163.17; 180.8; 181.6; 197.12) where the similar expression "for past and future favors" (*ldt nʿmt wtnʿmn*) occurs

VIII

REPETITION OF THE SONG OF VINTAGE AND HARVEST

28–29

Oh, now the field is like that field
wherein the gods do dwell,
where walk the Mother and the Maid,
the Blessed Damozel!

[Death-and-Rot] may [sit] enthroned, etc.

B. THE MYTHOLOGICAL DRAMA

30–36

SCENE I: *El comes to the seashore to fetch water for his household needs. He excites the admiration and passion of two female onlookers, who try to arouse his interest by making ribald remarks about his actions.*

[El unto] the shore [has come];
see him striding to the beach.
[He fetches water for his needs],
scoop by scoop, in both his hands,
until the basin is brimful.
Down and up, there go his hands,

---

as a standard cliché. Similarly, a graffito from Serabit, in Sinai, bears the legend "in respect of (divine) favor" [*'l n'm*], and the Semitic term [*n'm*] is used in precisely the same sense in Psalm 90:17. *The phrase indicates clearly that our ritual was designed for a festival of thanksgiving, like the Israelitic Festival of First Fruits.*

For the reference to the SUN, implying a critical date in the solar year (i.e., the vernal equinox?), see Chapter Two, §37.

SCENE I (30–36). (1) As suggested in our Introduction to this text, the successive episodes of the dramatic myth may really hark back to successive elements of a traditional ritual, just as do those of the English mummers' play and of the Carnival plays of modern Greece. On this hypothesis, El's action in fetching water from the sea may be a transmogrification of an ancient practice

while, behold, one girl cries out:
"Oh, my daddy! Oh, my daddy!"
and, behold, another cries:
"Oh, my mummy! Oh, my mummy!
Look you, how long-limbed is El,
how far-reaching like the sea,
look you, how his limb extends
ever farther like the main!
El has shown himself long-limbed,
his limb extending like the sea,
ever farther like the main!"
  Scoop by scoop, in both his hands,
El keeps scooping up the water.
Then he puts it in his house.

---

of bringing water into the temple at seasonal festivals for the performance of a rain charm. Such a rite was in fact witnessed by Lucian, centuries later, at Hierapolis (Bambyke), in Syria. "Twice a year," he informs us (*De Dea Syria,* c. 13), "water is brought from the sea into the temple. Nor is it only the priests who bring it; the entire population of Syria and Arabia (!), and many from beyond the Euphrates, go down to the sea, and all bring its water, which they first pour out in the temple." In another passage (c. 48), he describes this as "the greatest of all sacred assemblies." What is indicated by his account is clearly a rain charm, and such a charm was performed also in Jerusalem, at the autumnal Festival of Ingathering (Mishnah, *Sukkah* iv. 9; cf. Feuchtwang, *Das Wasseropfer;* Patai, *Man and Temple,* 24–53; I. Levy, in RÉJ 43 [1901], 193; F. C. Burkitt, in JTS [1916], 141 f.). Moreover, rain-making ceremonies of this type are to this day a constant feature of African seasonal festivals (see O. Petersson, *Kings and Gods,* 264–75).

(2) The exclamation uttered by the two women contains a ribald *double-entendre,* such as would readily have amused a popular audience. In the primary sense, their allusion to El's extended hand refers to his far-reaching power; this is a regular Semitic idiom (cp. Arabic *t-w-l y-d,* and the antithetical Hebrew "short hand" [e.g., Numbers 11.23; Isaiah 59:1] in the sense of "powerlessness"), and in Oriental iconography, kings and emperors are often portrayed with outstretched arms in token of their power (see L'Orage, *Iconography,* 139 ff.). In a secondary sense, however, the word for "hand" also denotes "phallus" (Isaiah 57:8).

37–49[a]

SCENE II: *El shoots and cooks a bird. Again he excites the admiration and passion of the two female onlookers, and again they try to arouse his interest by making ribald remarks about his actions. Moreover, they offer themselves to him, but coyly hesitate whether to do so as wives or as daughters.*

Having let his baton drop,
having with his rod dispensed(?),
El now lifts his hands, shoots skyward,
shoots a bird from out the sky,
plucks it, sets it over coals.
How El thus intrigues those women!
See, those women call out loudly:
"You for husband! You for husband!
Is your 'baton' dropped for good?
Have you with your 'rod' dispensed?
Know you, while you're roasting fowl,
what are really being heated
o'er those coals are — human women,
yes, indeed, two human women
eager to become God's consorts,
mates of El's eternal being!"
Yes, those women cry out loudly:
"You for daddy! You for daddy!

SCENE II (37–49[a]). (1) This episode, too, may go back ultimately to an element of the pristine ritual, for the shooting of arrows is a common charm, in many parts of the world, either to forfend demons or to promote rainfall, and is frequently associated with seasonal ceremonies. The rite formed part of the service at the Babylonian Akitu Festival (K. 3476, obv. 4), and is (or was until recently) prevalent in Germany at New Year and Easter (Sartori, *Sitte und Brauch,* III, 68, n. 2; 153, 171). It was likewise an element of Egyptian coronation ceremonies (Seligman, *Egypt and North Africa,* 15–18, 59), and still obtains at the installation rites of the chief of the Kitara in Africa (J. Roscoe, *The Bakitara,* 184); while among the Lorango, the king shoots arrows in December to make rain (Frazer, GB *min.,* 99).

(2) Again the women indulge in ribald puns. (*a*) El is said to "put down his staff" and to discard (?) his rod, in order to free his hands for the shooting of the arrow. But the words "staff"

Is your 'baton' dropped for good?
Have you with your 'rod' dispensed?
Know you, while that fowl you're roasting,
what are really being heated
o'er the coals are — human women,
yes, indeed, two human women,
eager to become God's daughters,
serving El's eternal being!"

Again those women cry out loudly:
"You for husband! You for husband!
Is your 'baton' dropped for good?
Have you with your 'rod' dispensed?
Know you, while that fowl you're roasting,
what are really being heated
o'er those coals are — human women,
yes, indeed, two human women,
eager to become God's consorts,
mates of El's eternal being!"[c]

SCENE III: *El embraces the two women. They conceive and bear two children, Dawn and Sunset.*

[c] In order to bring out the somewhat Rabelaisian point of this passage, I have had to sacrifice the strict grammatical construction of the original and to translate some of the phrases *ad sensum* rather than literally.

---

and "rod" are here taken, as in many languages, to be vulgar terms for the phallus. Hence, the audience understands the women's remark to be a taunting imputation against El's virility — a challenge artfully designed to rouse him to practical refutation! Similarly (*b*) the roasting of the bird inspires the observation that what are really being heated and "burned up" are two human females, ready and eager to serve as El's eternal mates! Out of coyness or uncertainty, the women hesitate whether to offer themselves to him as brides or as daughters — a hesitation likewise calculated to rouse a laugh. The general spirit of their offer is admirably illustrated by the words which Helena addresses to Bertram in Shakespeare's *All's Well That Ends Well*, Act II, scene iii, 104–07: "I dare not say I take you; but I give/Me and my service, ever whilst I live,/Into your guiding power."

SCENE III (49^b–54). This scene goes back to the ritual "sacred marriage" and PROCLAMATION OF THE NEWBORN CHILD

49b–52a

Then El stoops, their lips he kisses;
sweet their lips, like full ripe grape[s].
[Through] the kissing and conceiving,
through the hot embrace the women
then in time are brought to labor
and give birth to — DAWN and SUNS[ET].

The birth is reported to El, evidently by the women's cuckolded human husband. On hearing the children described as Dawn and Sunset, El orders them translated to heaven.

52b–54

Now the word is brought to El:
"My wives, O El, have given birth,
and, oh, what babes have they produced!
My children — they are Dawn and Sunset!"
"Well then, pick them up" (says El),
"And beside the Lady Sun
and the fix'd stars set them down!"

("Unto us a child is born"); see Introduction (1) The description of the newborn children as "dawn and sunset" links up with a motif, which appears in several modern Greek folk tales, that maidens who mate with princes or kings are sometimes said to give birth to Sun, Moon, or Morning Star, or to offspring with starlight in their faces, etc. Examples of such stories are cited in full in A. B. Cook, *Zeus* ii, 1003 ff., where it is shown that the same motif may be traced in ancient Greek myths concerning the offspring of Zeus' amours with certain human women. This time-honored piece of folklore is here exploited to account for the birth of the gods Dawn and Sunset (Shr and Slm).

I have taken the suffix in the words *yld-y* (line 53) and *athty* (line 60) to be that of the first person singular possessive and not simply of the dual. In that case, the reporter must be the human husband of the women, who is surprised at their having given birth to such strange (i.e., divine) offspring. The amazement of the cuckold, and his naïve reporting of the fact to the very being who has cuckolded him, would obviously have raised a hearty guffaw on the part of a popular audience and may be compared with the portrayal of Joseph, betrothed of the Lady Mary, in medieval English miracle plays. In that case, too, the words "to what have they given birth [*mh ylt*]" will

SCENE IV: *El again embraces the women. This time they conceive and bear children named The Gods Gracious, immediately recognized as divine by the fact that they suck from the very moment of birth and possess superhuman appetites.*

55–59[a]

Again he stoops, their lips he kisses,
and behold, their lips are sweet.
Through the kissing and conceiving,
[Through] the hot embrace . . . .
both of them are brought to labor
and give birth — unto GODS GRACIOUS,
little gluttons who straightway
start imbibing from the teat!

The birth is reported to El, evidently again by the women's cuckolded human husband. On hearing that the children cannot be satisfied with the produce of sky and sea — i.e., birds and fishes — El orders them consigned to the desert (or steppeland), there to fend for themselves as best they may.

---

not be El's question, but an exclamation on the part of the reporter – i.e., "They have given birth – but to what!" It must be conceded, however, that the interpretation of the suffixes as pure duals is equally possible.

SCENE IV (55–66[a]). (1) On the expression, "One lip to the netherworld, the other up to heaven stretched," see Commentary on Baal, XLVII.

(2) The ravenous appetite of the newborn children recurs as a comic trait in the Thracian and Macedonian Carnival plays; these end with a scene in which the child born of the previously enacted marriage is shown eating his parents out of house and home (see Dawkins, in JHS 26. 191; Wace, *ibid.*, 16. 232 ff.; 19. 248 ff.).

(3) The wilderness of Kadesh is mentioned in Psalm 29:8. The name is here chosen, however, simply because Kadesh means "holy," so that "the Wilderness of Kadesh" appeals to the fancy of the writer as a suitable barren place to which the *divine* children should be expelled. It is, so to speak, as if a Christian folk tale were to say that the Virgin had been expelled to Maryland, or the Holy Child to Christchurch! Hence it is futile and undiscerning to discuss whether the southern Kadesh or a region beside the northern Kadesh-on-the-Orontes is intended!

59b–66a

Now the word is brought to El:
"My wives, O El, have given birth,
and oh, what babes have they produced
— gracious gods [who seem to bear
a strange resemblance to] thy[self],
little gluttons who, straightway
sucking, have drunk from the teat!
One lip to the netherworld,
the other up to heaven stretched,
yet nor fowl of heaven nor fish
from the sea has pleased their mouths.
From one gorging to the ne[xt]
have they sped, and, right and left,
things are put into their mouths,
yet they cannot e'er be sated!
Oh, what wives have I espoused!
Oh, what sons have I begot!"
"Pick them up" (says El), "and set them
in the wilderness of Kadesh,
there to seek from stock and stone
casual hospitality!"

SCENE V: *After wandering in the desert (or steppeland) for several years, the divine children eventually encounter a man storing grain. They beg him for some of it, but no sooner has he supplied them than they start demanding bread and wine. Although he has but sufficient of these to meet his own needs, he generously provides them.*

66b ff.

So for seven whole years, for eight
anniversaries they went.

SCENE V (66b ff.). The purpose of this episode is to explain how the Gods Gracious came to be patrons of the crops, and what is here related obviously connects with the description of them in the ritual portion of our text (line 4) as operating in some way in the barren tracts of the steppeland.

The passage has been much misunderstood by previous commentators, and we may therefore begin with a detailed analysis of it.

After wandering for several years in the steppeland, the Gods

Yea, those gracious gods went roaming
ever through the fields and wandered
through the outskirts of the desert.
Then at last a man they met
storing grain, and lo, they cried
to that man a-storing grain:
"You there storing, you there storing,
open up your store!" He opened,
doled a portion for their needs,
and it pleased them. Yet, [unsated,
they kept crying: "Have you] bread [there

Gracious at last fall in with a man storing seed (*n-ẓ-r m-d-r-'*; the verb *n-ẓ-r* is used in precisely the same sense in Akkadian, e.g. K 50, i. 29 ff.; see Meissner, ZA 9, 276–77). They importune him to open up his store (*p-t-h;* the verb is used in precisely the same sense in Hebrew, e.g. Genesis 41:56; Amos 8:5; so too in Akkadian: see Landsberger, MSL I, 170 ff.; Goetze, *Tunnawi,* 25), and he doles out portions for them (*w-p-r-ts b-'-d-h-m;* the verb is used in this sense in Arabic). Although it is pleasing to them (*w-'-r-b;* cf. Hebrew *'-r-b* II), they nevertheless go on to beg for bread and wine.

The rest of the text is admittedly very fragmentary, but there are a few valuable clues to the sense. In reply to the question, "Is there any wine?" the man storing seed answers, "There is wine for sipping in my . . .," and this is followed by a line in which the measures, ephah (*i-p-t*), hin (*h-n*) and log (*l-g*) are mentioned side by side, preceded by a verb meaning "departed." This is followed in turn by the statement, "And his jar (that was) full of wine" (*w-h-b-r-h m-l-a y-n*). Since ephah is a dry measure, and hin and log are liquid measures in descending scale, the sense would seem to be that what was once an *ephah* of bread dwindled to something considerably less (e.g., a *kab*), and what was once a *hin* of wine dwindled to a mere *log*. The phrase, "There is wine for sipping in (my) . . ." would then imply that the man storing grain had only enough wine for an occasional sip, and this must have been preceded by a similar statement about the bread. In other words, the general sense must have been that although he had only enough of each to meet his modest needs, the voracious gods ate and drank greedily until next to nothing was left.

But the passage could not have ended on this note, for that would not have explained why the gods should be recognized as patrons of a harvest festival, nor why "sacrifices in return

in your basket]? Let us eat it!
Have you [wine there in your bottle]?
Give it, then, and let us drink it!"
  But the man a-storing grain
gave them answer: "[In my basket
are but loaves to sate my hunger];
[in my] bot[tle] is but wine
for a casual sip or two."
[Yet they took them and devoured them].
[What had been a quartern loaf]
dwindled to an ounce; a quart
of wine diminished to a pint.
[The basket that was full of loaves
now held but crumbs]; his ewer, too,
that at first was full of wine
[soon showed nothing but the dregs].

[*The rest is lost*]

---

for favors" (line 26) should then be presented to them. It may therefore be suggested that the episode in fact turned on the familiar motif of "entertaining angels unawares" [Q 45]. The generous host was rewarded by a promise of increase and prosperity, as in the analogous stories in Genesis 18:1–10 and Gen. 19, and the tale of Hyrieus of Tanagra in Ovid, *Fasti,* V. 447–83 (see also similar tales in Grimm, No. 45; Bolte-Polivka, II. 210; Dähnhardt, *Natursagen,* II. 117). In this case, the reward would have been that the steppeland, seemingly barren, would yet yield produce annually – as in fact it does (see Montgomery, *Arabia and the Bible,* 79, 82 ff.). The annual fulfillment of this promise was the occasion of the festival and furnished the reason why the Gracious Gods were then especially honored!

In light of the foregoing, it is even possible – though the suggestion is made with reserve – that the incomplete phrase in the ritual exordium, which describes the activity of the Gods Gracious in the steppeland, should be restored to read "(Let honor be paid to those) who (even) in wind-swept(?) tracts of steppeland yet so[w seed]," i.e. *yd*[r^e].

EXCURSUS

AN ENGLISH MUMMERS' PLAY

The following specimen of the English mummers' play, acted in Stanford-in-the-Vale, Berkshire, is here reproduced in order to illustrate the persistence of the primitive Ritual Pattern in modern folk usages. The Invocation, it will be seen, has degenerated into a mere introduction of the players, though it is still put into the mouth of an extraneous "presenter" who does not otherwise figure in the action. The combat has become a mere exhibition of fisticuffs between two principals, and these have been crudely historicized as "King George" (himself a distortion of St. George) and "Turkish Knight," otherwise called "Bold Slasher." The resurrection of the hero has likewise lost all of its pristine solemnity, and now merely provides an excuse for the comic buffoonery of the "noble doctor." The Epilogue, in the form of an invocation, has given way to the *quête* – a barefaced appeal for cash.

The mummers' play represents the last stage in the evolution of the ritual drama, before it loses its theatrical structure altogether and becomes mere literary and poetic composition.

MUMMERS' PLAY

from

STANFORD-IN-THE-VALE, BERKSHIRE, ENGLAND

Source: Stuart Piggott, *Folk-Lore* 40 (1929), 262–64

§1. *Prologue*

Enter FATHER CHRISTMAS.

F.C. – "Here comes I, Father Christmas,
Welcome or welcome not,
I hope old Father Christmas
Will never be forgot.
A room, a room I do presume,
Pray give me room to rhyme,
For we have come to show activity
This merry Christmastime.

Acting youth or acting age
Was never seen before
Or acted on the stage.
If any man can do more than me,
Walk in King George and clear the way."

§2. *Ritual Combat*

Enter KING GEORGE.

K.G. – "Here comes I, King George, the valiant man,
With naked sword and spear in hand.
I fought the fiery dragon and brought him to slaughter,
And by these means I won the King of Egypt's daughter.
And what mortal man dare to stand
Before me with my sword in hand?
I'll slay him and cut him as small as flies,
And send him to Jamaica to make mince pies."

F.C. – "Come in, Bold Slasher."

Enter BOLD SLASHER.

B.S. – "In comes I, this Turkish Knight,
With thee, King George, I mean to fight.
I'll fight thee, thou man with courage bold,
If thy blood's hot, I'll make it cold."

K.G. – "Wo Ho, my little fellow, thou talk'st very bold!
Pull out thy sword and fight, or pull out thy purse and pay:
I'll have satisfaction with thee afore thou go'st away."

They fight, and King George falls.

§3. *Death and Resurrection* (*attenuated*)

F.C. – "Come in Doctor.
Doctor, doctor, where bist thee?
King George is wounded in the knee.
Five pound or ten pound I'll freely lay down
If there's a noble doctor to be found."

Enter DOCTOR. – "In walks the noble Doctor, – travels much in this country, more at home nor I do abroad. I ain't like these little quee-quack doctors, and goes about for the good of the country."

F.C. – "What diseases can'st thee cure, Doctor?"

DOCTOR. – "All diseases,
Just which my box of pills pleases.

Itch, Stitch, Palsy, and the Gout,
All pains within and pains without."

F.C. – "Do'st think thee can'st cure this man, Doctor?"

DOCTOR. – "What's the matter with your man?"

F.C. – "I think he's got toothache."

DOCTOR (To *Mary*). – "Bring me my spectacles and pliers and my box of pills and a little medicine."

MARY. – "Oh yes, sir."

Doctor draws tooth after much byplay.
"He's got him going rolling like a wheelbarrow, round and round like a grindstone."

DOCTOR. – "In my box I carry my pills
And in my bottle I carry my smills.
Hand by hand there's no restrain,
Rise up King George and fight again."

K.G. (*rising*). – "Here am I, King George, with shining armor bright,
Famous champion, also a worthy knight.
Seven long years in close cave I was kept,
Out of that into prison I leapt.
From out of that into a rock of stones,
There I laid down my grevious bones.
Many a giant did I subdue
When I ran the fiery dragon through.
I fought the man at Tollatree,[d]
And still I gained the victory.
First I fought in France,
Second I fought in Spain,
Third I came to Tetbury[e] to fight the Turk again."

§4. *Epilogue* (*Quête*)

F.C. – "Come in, Molly."

MOLLY TINKER. – "My name is not Molly Tinker,
My name is Mary Tinker,

[d] "You can say what you like, but we always said Tollatree." WILLIAM KITCHENER (rapporteur). I suspect that the line is corrupt and originally referred to *idolatry*, e.g. "and freed men from idolatry."

[e] In Gloucestershire. ? Original source of this version.

Small-beer drinker.
I told the landlord to his face
The chimbley corner was his place.
My head's so big, my wit's so small,
I've brought my fiddle to please 'ee all.
Ladies and gentlemen my story is ended,
The money box is well recommended.
Five or six shillings will do us no harm;
Silver or copper or a drop of beer if we can."

PART THREE

LITERARY SURVIVALS OF THE SEASONAL PATTERN

SURVIVALS IN BIBLICAL AND CLASSICAL POETRY

§1. The Seasonal Pattern survived also in the structure of hymns and similar liturgical compositions. Two factors especially conduced to this development. The first was that the Pattern was in any case inextricably associated with special liturgical ceremonies, and would therefore enter naturally into the established order of service. The second was that, even when it assumed the form of drama, the accompanying speeches were not originally delivered by the players themselves but rather by a "presenter" or "commentator" who recited the appropriate narrative and dialogue as each scene was enacted.[1] The distinction between this recitation and a liturgical poem of narrative content was thus, at all times, extremely narrow, and it is therefore by no means surprising that it should eventually have disappeared altogether.

I

§2. Nowhere is this development better exemplified than in certain of the Psalms of the Old Testament, a fact hitherto unobserved. The Psalms, it is now admitted, were, in general, more than mere lyric outpourings of individual piety. In many cases they possessed at the same time a distinctly *liturgical* function, being recited or chanted as the accompaniments of ritual ceremonies and procedures.[2] Those, for example, which begin with the words "The Lord is become king" (i.e., Psalms 93, 97, and 99) are now generally recognized to have been patterned after a traditional style of hymn composed for the annual enthronement of the deity at the New Year Festival. What has not been observed, however, is that there exists in the Psalter a whole group of compositions which exhibit a content and form in perfect accord with the theme and sequence of the Ritual Pattern. All of them present the same situation: the god is represented as acquiring kingship and as being installed in a special palace or city by virtue of having overthrown his enemies; and the latter — significantly enough — are usually identified with the rebellious *Sea* or *Dragon*. Moreover, once ensconced upon the seat of his dominion, the god is said to establish the cosmic order and to bring fertility either to the whole world or, more precisely, to his own peculiar city and people. Furthermore, there are occasional references to such subsidiary elements of the Seasonal Pattern as the ceremonial purgation of evil and sin, the presentation of offerings, and the promulgation of divine judgment upon men [see Table I]. In addition, there are frequent allusions to ritual practices characteristic of the seasonal festivals, and there are also constant echoes of the traditional vocabulary of the seasonal myths. We may therefore see in these Psalms a literary survival of the dramatic texts which were originally recited at the great calendar festivals.

§3. The most explicit example is PSALM 93.[3] The poem begins (1–2) with the statement that Yahweh has become king, that he is attired in the robes of majesty, and that he has established the cosmic order. After this exordium, however, it passes to the recitation of the particular triumph by virtue of which that sovereignty was secured: Yahweh subdued the rebellious streams (3–4). Finally (5) there is a reference to the fact that His decrees — that is, His dispensation of the world — is fixed and immutable, and that He has installed himself in an abode of befitting sanctity.

Now, it is obvious that in this hymnodic composition there are preserved all the standard elements of the Ritual Pattern. Yahweh becomes king by exactly the same process as does Marduk in the Babylonian New Year myth, Baal in its Canaanite counterpart, and the weather god in the cult text of the Hittite Puruli Festival: he subdues the rebellious power of the waters, the equivalent of the Babylonian Tiamat, the Canaanite Yam (alias Nahar), and the Hittite Illuyankas. Further, his assumption of power is marked by the establishment of the cosmic order and the promulgation of divine decrees and — above all — by occupancy of a newly constructed abode.

§4. Scarcely less arresting is PSALM 29, which begins (vv. 1–2) with an invocation to the *b^enê elim*, or lesser members of the pantheon, to pay homage to Yahweh and to render to Him "the glory of His name." The situation is thus identical with that of the Babylonian New Year myth (*Enuma Elish* VI, 47, 51, 117, 143–44) in which the minor gods are summoned to pay homage to Marduk, after his victory over Tiamat, and to recite his *names* and honorific titles. So, too, in the Canaanite *Poem of Baal*, that god, after conquering Yam (Sea), is said to go up to the sacred mountain of the North and there be feted and regaled by the gods (IV A B).

The initial invocation is followed (vv. 3–9b) by a vivid description of Yahweh's prowess in storm and tempest, this constituting the actual honorification which the gods are invited to recite. It takes place usually occupied, as we shall see, by a more precise reference to the god's defeat of the rebellious Sea or Dragon (cf. 65:8; 66:6; 74:13; 89:10–11; 93:3–4); but even in this more general form, it harks back to a standard element of the primitive Ritual Pattern. For in exactly the same way, the Canaanite myth of Baal introduces a laudation of that god as master of storm and tempest into the passage dealing with his installation (II AB vii 27b–41); and the language is very similar to that of our psalm:

When Baal opens a rift in the clouds,
When Baal gives forth his holy voice,
When Baal keeps discharging the utterances of his lips,
His hol[y] voice [convuls]es the earth;
. . . . the mountains quake;
A-tremble are the . . . .;
East and west the high places of the e[arth] reel.

* * * * * * * * * *

The eyes of Baal mark down, then his hand strikes;
Yea, very cedars quiver at the touch of his right hand!

Moreover, that this paean is based upon standard hymns to the storm god, such as would naturally have formed a part of the service at the seasonal festivals, is shown by the fact that parallel phrases are indeed quoted by Abimilki of Tyre in the Tell Amarna letter, 147 Kn., 14–15:

Who giveth forth his voice in heaven like Hadad,
And all the mountains quake at his voice.

Similarly, a hymn to Hadad printed in King's *Magic and Sorcery*, 21:83, contains the directly comparable expression:

Hadad giveth forth thunders;
The mountains are shaken.

At the end of the laudation (v. 9c) occur the obscure

words, "and in His palace all of it saith, Glory." The abruptness of this clause has been duly observed by most modern commentators, and the usual way of surmounting the difficulty is to assume an antecedent lacuna which would have contained the immediate subject to which the expression "all of *it*" referred.[4] What has not been observed, however, is that the clause is explicable only when read in the light of the Ritual Pattern. What is stated in these obscure words is precisely the same thing as is mentioned explicitly in *Enuma Elish* VI, 144: the entire company of the gods, duly assembled in the new-built palace of Esagila, sat in the fane, and "all of them recited the 'name' of Marduk." The words are a virtually exact equivalent of our Hebrew phrase, "all of them" answering precisely to "all of it" and thus showing that the missing subject is the divine assembly. Indeed, the immediately preceding verse in *Enuma Elish* (VI, 143) says explicitly: "in their convocation they celebrated his essence." Hence, it is apparent that we must restore something like:

[The assembly of the deities[5] acclaims Him,]
And in His palace all of it recites the Glory.

The Glory, of course, is the foregoing laudation.

"Yahweh," continues the Psalmist (v. 10), "sat enthroned at the storm flood, and Yahweh will sit enthroned forever." The abruptness of this statement is likewise perplexing, while scholars have also been exercised to determine whether the reference to the storm flood is to the specific Noachic Deluge or to *any* inundation caused by the display of Yahweh's powers.[6] Reference to comparative mythology will show, however, that this enigmatic expression is likewise drawn from the standard material of the Ritual Pattern. An essential element of the seasonal myth is that the weather god reins the turbulent Dragon or Spirit of the subterranean waters who threatens to flood the earth, and as a corollary to this he is often represented as holding down the floods by building his palace or erecting his throne over them. Thus, in the Babylonian *Enuma Elish,* it is said explicitly (I, 71) that after Ea had vanquished Apsu, "he established his dwelling place over the nether waters"; and Marduk does the same thing after the defeat of Tiamat (VI, 62–64). Similarly, the temple of E-ninu at Lagash was said to have been founded on the nether ocean,[7] while that at Eridu was termed "House of the nether sea (E-engura(k))."[8] In the sanctuary at Hierapolis, Lucian was shown a chasm into which the waters of the deluge were said to have collected,[9] and Jewish tradition asserted that the foundation stone of the temple of Yahweh at Jerusalem held down the flood.[10] An analogous myth was current also in the sanctuary of Olympian Zeus at Athens.[11] It is to this that our verse alludes. The interpretation is clinched by the words "and Yahweh will sit enthroned as king forever"; for here we have a reproduction of the cry "Marduk is king" uttered in exactly similar circumstances in *Enuma Elish* IV 28, and likewise of the cry "Let Baal be king" which bursts from the lips of the defeated Lord of the Sea in the Canaanite version of the story (III AB, A 32).

The psalm concludes (v. 11) with the words: "Yahweh giveth strength to His people, Yahweh blesseth His people with well-being [*shalom*]." This is usually regarded as an addition made when the poem was incorporated into or adapted for the public liturgy, and analogies to it may indeed be found in 28:8; 68:36, etc. It should be observed, however, that an exactly comparable expression occurs in *Enuma Elish* VI 113, where the minor gods hail their new king Marduk in the words, "Verily, Marduk is the help of his land and his people," acclaiming him also (*ibid.*, 114) as "the salvation of the people." This suggests that it was part of the original mythological hymn; in other words, vv. 10–11 are "in quotes," being a continuation of the "Glory" which the divine hosts are said (v. 9^c) to recite in the palace. In itself, of course, the phrase was no doubt a liturgical formula, probably used at ceremonies of inthronization and therefore readily adopted into the order of service whenever a god was hymned in the role of new-crowned king. This would account for its substantial recurrence in 28:8; 68:36, etc. The point is, however, that its presence in our psalm is not due to such adoption at a later date; on the contrary, it was adopted already in the original poem where the insertion of it was dictated by the requirements of the Ritual Pattern.

§5. PSALM 89 begins (2–3) with the statement that what is about to be recounted is to be construed as evidence of the grace [*hesed*] and trustworthiness of Yahweh, who faithfully maintains His pledges. The particular pledge which the psalmist has in mind is that whereby Yahweh anciently assured the perpetual survival of the royal Davidic line.

Yahweh's grace will I sing forever;
 to all ages proclaim His pledge with my mouth:
*(Such grace, I trow, is a structure eternal;
 like the skies unchanging Thou keepest Thy pledge):*
"I have made a pact with My chosen,
 have sworn unto David My servant:
Thy seed will I 'stablish forever,
 and build up thy throne for all time!"

Here is reproduced, clearly and unmistakably, the familiar coronation element of the Ritual Pattern. In this case, however, it is not the accession of the god that is represented but that of the king — a regular feature, as we have seen, of the seasonal festivals. Even the stereotyped terminology is preserved, for with the phrase "I will build up thy throne for all time" we may aptly compare the Babylonian coronation formula in Clay, *Miscellaneous Texts from the Morgan Collection*, No. 38, ii 35–36: "Verily, the foundation of his throne will stand firm forever," and we may recall also that similar expressions are to be found in the Canaanite *Poem of Baal* (III AB, A 10; II AB iii 6) in connection with the accession of that god to kingship.

The psalm next proceeds to a recitation of the triumphant exploits of Yahweh (vv. 6–11), and here again that triumph lies primarily in the subjection of the turbulent sea and the conquest of the Dragon (Rahab). Moreover, this action is taken to evince the supremacy of Yahweh over the *b^e^nê elim* and the *qedoshim* — two expressions which occur repeatedly in the Canaanite texts (and in similar juxtaposition) as indicating the members of the heavenly court.[12] We are reminded, therefore, of the scenes in the Canaanite *Poem of Baal* (V AB), the Babylonian New Year myth (EE VI, 72 ff.), and the Hittite Purulitext in which the gods foregather to acknowledge and pay homage to their new king.

Who in heaven to Yahweh compares,
 resembles him 'mid the Beings Divine [*b^e^ne elim*],
A god who is held in dread
 in the moot of the Holy Ones [*qedoshim*],
A chief is He, held in awe
 by all who surround Him!

* * * * *

* Emended passages are enclosed between asterisks.

Thou it is rulest the pride of the sea,
  stillest its waves when they roar;
Thou it is crushedst the Dragon Proud [*Rahab*],
  rendering him like a riddled corpse.
Yea, with Thy mighty arm Thou didst scatter Thy foes!

Then, just as in the Babylonian New Year myth (EE V) the triumph of Marduk over Tiamat issues in the establishment of the cosmic order, so here the psalm passes naturally to the celebration of Yahweh as lord and creator of the world (vv. 12–13).

Thine are the heavens, Thine too is the earth;
  the world and its fullness hast Thou confirmed!
North and south — Thou hast created them;
Tabor and Hermon ring to Thy name!

Finally (vv. 14–19), the psalm culminates in a laudation of the triumphant god as king of the world, ensconced upon his throne in righteousness and justice and affording protection to his people, who joyfully acknowledge him their lord.

Thine is an arm endued with might;
  strong is Thy hand, Thy right hand upraised!
Justice and Right are Thy throne's foundation,
  Grace and Truth do wait upon Thee!
Happy the people who mark the trumpet blast;
  these walk, O Yahweh, in the light of Thy face!
They rejoice all the day in what Thou art [lit., in Thy
  name],
  and through Thy righteousness are they uplifted!
For Thou art their glorious strength,
  and through Thy favor we flourish!

Verily, Yahweh is our shield,
  and the Holy One of Israel our king!

The phrasing of these last lines, it should be noted, echoes the profession of allegiance wherewith the gods acknowledge the sovereignty of Marduk in the Babylonian New Year myth (*Enuma Elish* VI, 113–14): "Truly, Marduk is the help of his land [and of] his [people] . . ."; "him do they verily extol, the salvation(?) of the people"; and it is reproduced also, in variant form, at the end of Psalm 29: "Yahweh gives strength to His people; Yahweh blesses His people with well-being."

§6. PSALM 74.12–17 reads as follows:

But from old has God been my king,
  performing in the midst of the earth deeds of salvation!

'TWAS THOU didst split Sir Sea by Thy strength,
  didst shatter the heads of the Dragons;

'TWAS THOU didst crush Leviathan's heads,
  to give him as food unto *fowl and* jackals.

'TWAS THOU didst cleave out spring and wady;
  'TWAS THOU didst dry up the perpetual streams.

Thine is the day, Thine too is the night;
  'TWAS THOU didst establish the light and the sun.

'TWAS THOU didst fix all the bounds of the earth;
  Summer and winter, 'TWAS THOU didst create them!

These verses are commonly cited by scholars as one of the parade passages witnessing to the currency among the Biblical Hebrews of the well-known myth of the Slaying of the Dragon. What has not been observed, however, is that, besides the combat, the passage also alludes to other equally significant elements of the Ritual Pattern and that these are arranged in the traditional order and sequence. Thus, the victory over the Dragon is cited only in illustration of the statement that "God is my King," implying — in accordance with the Pattern — that it confers sovereignty upon the divine hero. Similarly, the issue of the victory is here represented as the establishment of the cosmic order — a feature which recurs in Psalms 89:12–13; 93:2–5, and above all, in the Babylonian version preserved in *Enuma Elish*. Indeed, there is a marked parallelism between the phrasing of our passage and that of the Babylonian poem. For if the Psalmist declares that the triumphant gods appointed the luminaries of heaven, *Enuma Elish* likewise describes him (V, 1 ff.) as proceeding at once to determine the positions of the moon and stars. And if the Psalmist portrays him, somewhat allusively, as fixing "all the bounds of the earth," *Enuma Elish* clarifies the allusion by stating explicitly (VI, 56–57) that immediately after his triumph, "plans and designs were fixed, the stations of heaven and earth were disposed among all of the gods" — an interpretation which is in turn confirmed by a further reference to the same thing, and in the same terms, in

Deuteronomy 32:8 (LXX): "He fixed the bounds of nations in accordance with the number of the gods."[13] Again, if our text asserts that the victorious lord then "created" summer and winter, his words find a perfect parallel in *Enuma Elish* V, 3 where the triumphant Marduk is said to have "fixed the year and prescribed limitations [sc. of seasons]."

It is to be observed also that the language of the Psalmist is drawn largely from the traditional vocabulary of the seasonal myth. When, for example, he describes the god as shattering the *heads* of the Dragon, he is but echoing the words of the Canaanite *Poem of Baal* where that monster is portrayed as a kind of hydra possessing "sevenfold heads" (I* AB i 3; cf. V AB iii 39–40).

§7. We come next to PSALMS 96–98. It has long been recognized that these poems belong to the category of "Coronation songs" designed for the ceremony of divine inthronization at the New Year Festival. What has not been sufficiently observed, however, is that they preserve several significant echoes of the traditional language of the seasonal mysteries. In 96:4, for example, the expression "Great is Yahweh and highly to be praised" reproduces a cliché which actually recurs in 48:2, while the phrase (v. 10), "Say among the nations: Yahweh is become king" incorporates the traditional acclamation which is found also at the beginning of Psalms 93, 97, and 99. Again, both 96:13 and 98:9 allude, *in identical terms*, to the characteristic element of divine judgment, showing that both are drawing upon the same traditional model. Similarly, too, 97:2[b] is a duplicate of 89:15[a]; 97:8 recurs in 48:12; 98:4[a] in 66:1; and 96:7–9 is virtually identical with 29:1–2. These parallels show that all of the psalms enumerated belong to the same genre and hence that Psalms 96–98 are indeed attenuated forms of the Ritual Drama. The situation which they present is that of the god's being installed as king, but it is worthy of note that both in 96:13 and in 98:9 specific allusion is also made to the element of the divine judgment. Moreover, it should not escape notice that in 97:7 it is the *gods* who are bidden prostrate themselves before Yahweh, for this is in direct accord with the situation presented in the Babylonian New Year myth, the Canaanite myth of Baal, and the Hittite Puruli myth. This is the situation, it will be recalled, which is likewise echoed in Psalm 29:1–2.[14]

§8. The texts which we have thus far discussed preserve the original Ritual Pattern in more or less explicit form. There are others, however, where the survival is more attenuated. Take, for example, PSALM 47. Here, all reference to the Sea and Dragon has been eliminated, and all that remains is the bare picture of the god's assuming kingship as the result of a resounding defeat of His foes. Nevertheless, even in this attenuated form the poet cannot help incorporating reminiscences of the traditional vocabulary. He states, for example, that God "is gone up" (*'alah*) amid a fanfare of trumpets (v. 6). The term is usually explained as referring to his *ascent to the throne,* but it is significant that the expression "going up" (*tebû*) is used in the Babylonian New Year (Akitu) ritual as a *terminus technicus* to describe the festal procession of the god into his temple or palace,[15] and we may therefore safely assume that such is its meaning in our passage (cf. Psalm 68:25: "They have seen Thy processions, O God, the processions of My God, My *King,* into the sanctuary").

Similarly, in v. 10 we are told that

the princes of the peoples are gathered,
  the people of Abraham's God

wherein we may detect a very clear allusion to the parading of captive princes (evidently at the head of the troops) in the ritual procession.[16] The language is derived from military usage, the word rendered "are gathered" meaning strictly "bring up the rear" (cf. Numbers 10:25; Joshua 6:9, 13; Isaiah 52:12; 62:9) and that rendered "people" (viz., Hebrew *'am*) meaning strictly "host, crowd, retinue, entourage,"[17] i.e.:

the lordlings of the peoples bring up the rear,
  as the retinue of Abraham's God!

Finally, it should be observed that in concluding his poem (v. 10) with the motto, "Verily, Yahweh is our shield," the psalmist introduces a cliché which actually recurs in 89:19. It is thus apparent that he is drawing, albeit unconsciously, upon the traditional vocabulary of the Ritual Pattern.

§9. Of the same order is PSALM 48. Here, too, most of the mythological elements have been ironed out, yet at the same time echoes of the traditional phrasing have been perforce retained. The psalm was evidently composed to celebrate some historic deliverance of Jerusalem, but the event is recounted in terms of the traditional mythic combat and the subsequent installation of the victorious god in the palace of his sovereignty.

The poem opens (2–4) with the picture of Zion's god ensconced in his royal citadel[18] on the peak of the sacred mountain. The latter, however, is apostrophized as "the recesses of the north" — a reference to that mythological "recess of the North" whereon the gods are located in the Canaanite texts from Ras Shamra-Ugarit and to which both Baal and his would-be successor Ashtar are said to ascend in order to acquire kingship (I AB i 57; vi 12; vii 5; IV AB iii 31; V AB i 21, etc.). The Hebrew expression [*yarkᵉtê Safon*] is, in fact, employed again in exactly the same way in Isaiah 14:13–14:

> I will ascend to heaven,
> set my throne above the lofty stars,
> and dwell in the Mountain of Assembly
> in the recesses of the North [*yarkᵉtê Safon*];
> I will climb on the back of a cloud,
> be like a celestial being.[19]

TABLE I

THE RITUAL PATTERN IN THE PSALTER

	Psalm	29	47	48	74^{12-17}	89^{2-19}	93	98
A	1. The god assumes kingship	10	3, 6–10	2	12	8, 16	1	
	2. Summons to acknowledge the god as king	1–2	7	12–14				1, 4–8
B	God acquires kingship by victory in combat:							
	1. against Sea or Dragon				13–15	10–11	3–4	
	2. against human foes		4	5–8				1–3
C	God is installed in special habitation	9		2–4		8, 15–16(?)	5	
D	God ordains cosmic order				16–17	12–13		
	ATTENUATED FORM: God stabilizes his own city or people	11	5	9		18		

II

§10. Precisely the same development took place also on Greek soil. Scholars have long since observed that several of the so-called Homeric hymns, which look to all the world like mere mythological poems, were really liturgical chants de-

TABLE II

PHRASEOLOGICAL CORRESPONDENCES IN THE PSALMS

29. 1–2	96:7–9
47. 10	89:19; 97.9
48. 2	96:4 [cf. I Chronicles 16:25]
12	97:8
93. 1	96:10
96. 4	48:2
10	93:1
13	98:9
97. 2	89:15
8	48:12
9	47:10
98. 4	66:1
9	96:13

signed for one or other of the great seasonal festivals and embodying the cult myth peculiar to the occasion.[20]

Take, for example, the *Hymn to Demeter*. The central theme of this composition is the rape of Persephone and the consequent search for her on the part of her disconsolate mother. In its treatment of this theme, however, the hymn incorporates a number of singular and seemingly unimportant details which turn out, on examination, to reflect the ritual of the autumn Festival of Thesmophoria at which, as we know from other sources, it was customary to enact the story of the rape in the form of a sacred drama.[21]

It is said, for instance, that when she went in search of the abducted maiden, Demeter roamed the earth *carrying torches* (lines 47–48; 60–61). Now, we happen to know that a feature of the Thesmophoria and of the Eleusinian Mysteries was the *staging of a torchlight procession* by the female worshipers.[22] Such parades are, as we have seen, a common characteristic of seasonal festivals, where they serve as one of the methods by which blight and contagion are removed in preparation for the new lease of life. It is apparent, therefore, that when the poet introduces the picture of the goddess wandering hither and yon with her torches, he is but working into the durative myth an established element of the concomitant punctual ritual.

Similarly, when the poet makes a point of stating that the grief-stricken goddess wandered in this fashion *for nine days* and that for the entire length of that period "she tasted not of ambrosia neither of the sweet draught of nectar" (lines 46–50), it is again apparent that his words reflect a ritual usage. For the fact is, as we have seen, that the Thesmophoria was characterized by the observance of a fast and, in certain quarters (e.g., Cyprus) by a preliminary *nine-day lent.* Moreover, in order to underscore the allusion, the poet takes pains to observe that the goddess' abstention from food and drink was due to the fact that she was "*aching* with grief," in which expression his reader (or audience) would at once have recognized an oblique reference to Achaia, a traditional name of the festival popularly interpreted to mean "Festival of Aching Grief."[23]

Again, the poet asserts (lines 200–05) that when the goddess finally reached Eleusis and was welcomed hospitably by the female domestics of King Celeus, she at first proved inconsolable, sitting among them "without smiling and without tasting food or drink," and that her glum mood was resolved only when an old crone named Iambe started to crack jokes.[24] Here, too, we have a reflection of ritual practices at the Thesmophoria. The abstention from food and drink corresponds, as already observed, to the lenten fast. The avoidance of mirth and laughter finds its explanation in the statements of Plutarch and other writers[25] that the festival was observed in grim, lugubrious mood and that all expressions of merriment were forbidden. Lastly, the action of the old crone Iambe is explained by the fact that the chanting of ribald and obscene songs, *couched in iambic meter,* was a recognized procedure at the Thesmophoria and similar seasonal celebrations; such chanting was regarded as a means of stimulating fertility.[26] Here, too, the poet underscores the allusions by a dexterous choice of language. The terms which he employs to describe the actions of the old crone are not selected at random. They are technical terms specifically associated with the ritual of the festival. Aristophanes uses them to describe the lewd "mocking and clowning" in the Mysteries of Demeter. So, too, does Pausanias in speaking of similar practices at the seven-day festival of Demeter Mysia in Pellene; while Athenaeus calls the ritual jesters at Syracuse by the name iambists.[27] In this employment of a traditional ritual vocabulary we may recognize, as in the parallel case of the Hebrew Psalms, clear evidence that our hymn was indebted to, or ultimately derived from, the standard libretto of the seasonal drama.

The indebtedness is apparent also, as again in the case of the Hebrew Psalms, in the incorporation of clichés. A single example must suffice. When the poet wishes to describe the havoc wrought upon earth in consequence of the abduction of Persephone and the grief of her mother Demeter, he does so in the following terms (lines 302–13):

> So there she sate, the flaxen Demeter, apart from all the Blessed Ones, and there she remained racked with longing for her deep-girdled daughter. And she rendered the year most grievous and dire for men upon the teeming earth. No shoots did the earth put forth, for the fair-crowned Demeter kept the seed hidden in the ground. And many a crooked plow did the oxen drag in vain across the fields, and many a stalk of barley fell fruitless and unripened to the ground. She would, indeed, have destroyed the entire race of mortal men with sorry famine and have deprived of their offerings them that dwell in the Olympian mansions had not Zeus taken thought and reflected.

Now, this description follows a virtually stereotyped formula which recurs in all sister versions of the myth and which may be regarded as part and parcel of the primitive ritual *Urstoff*. Thus, in the Hittite *Myth of Telipinu* (KUB XVII 10) the effect of that god's disappearance is thus portrayed (i, 16–18):

> The hillsides were bare. The trees were bare. No branch came forth.
> The pasturelands were bare. The springs ran dry.
> Upon earth there was famine; men and gods were perishing from hunger.

Similarly, in the Canaanite *Poem of Baal* (I AB iii–iv, 25–27; 36–38) the departure of that lord of fertility results in the fact that

> The furrows of the fields are parched. . . . Parched are the furrows of the broad fields. Baal is neglecting the furrows of his plowland;

while in the harvest litany embodied in the first chapter of the Biblical Book of Joel, the devastation which follows the temporary withdrawal of Yahweh's favor is represented as involving desiccation of the earth, failure of crops and vines, and a threat of starvation to the gods (see Excursus to Chapter Three).

Thus it is apparent that the Homeric *Hymn to Demeter* is, like the Hebrew Psalms, an attenuated form of the primitive ritual drama, preserving in more stylized and literary form the essential traits and even the essential language of the original material and, like that material itself, projecting into durative myth all the cardinal features of the punctual Seasonal Pattern.

This conclusion is borne out by the actual *structure* of the hymn; and, it should be observed, what holds good for this particular example applies with equal force to the entire genre of similar compositions. The structure is one which we find also in Greek tragedy and comedy as well as in their more primitive Hittite and Canaanite forerunners. It consists in: (1) an Opening Invocation, naming the deities with which the poem or drama is concerned; (2) a Mythological Core, which forms the central "movement" of the composition; and (3) an Epilogue, in which the god or goddess is saluted and bidden good-by (*chaire*) before the poem ends or the curtain is rung down. Now, this structure reflects and is conditioned by the pattern of the earlier ritual performance. The Invocation represents the initial act of all public ceremonies — the *prorhesis* which in Sanskrit drama is significantly kept distinct from the dramatic prologue proper.[28] The Mythological Core, as it appears in hymns, is an attenuation of the dramatic performance itself, the degeneration from performance to mere recital being paralleled, as Hofer-Heilsberg has pointed out, in the treatment of the comedies of Terence and of Hroswitha of Gandersheim during the Middle Ages.[29] The Epilogue is, of course, nothing but the final Benediction — the element which survives in European mummers' plays in the form of the so-called *quête*.

§11. Another — and in some ways more striking — example of the development from drama to hymn is afforded by the first choral ode in the *Bacchae* of Euripides. As is well known, of all the ancient Greek tragedies that have come down to us, this is the one which preserves most closely the ancient ritual pattern. In the words of that prince of interpreters, Gilbert Murray:[30]

> A reader of the *Bacchae* . . . will be startled to find how close this drama, apparently so wild and imaginative, has kept to the ancient rite. The regular year-sequence is just clothed in sufficient myth to make it a story. The daemon must have his enemy who is like himself; then we must have the Contest, the Tearing Asunder, the Messenger, the Lamentation mixed with Joy-cries, the Discovery of the scattered members — and by a sort of doubling the Discovery of the true God — and the Epiphany of the Daemon in glory. All are there in the *Bacchae*. . . .
>
> But we can go further. We have enough fragments and quotations from the Aeschylean plays on this subject — especially the Lycurgus trilogy — to see that all kinds of small details which seemed like invention, and rather fantastic invention, on the part of Euripides, are taken straight from Aeschylus or the ritual or both. The timbrels, the fawnskin, the ivy, the sacred pine, the god taking the forms of Bull and Lion and Snake; the dances on the mountain at dawn; the Old Men who are by the power of the god made young again; the god represented as beardless and like a woman; the god imprisoned and escaping; the earthquake that wrecks Pentheus' palace; the victim Pentheus disguised as a woman; all these and more can be shown to be in the ritual, and nearly all are in the extant fragments of Aeschylus. . . . There never was a great play so steeped in tradition as the *Bacchae.*

This being so, it should not surprise us to discover that the initial choral ode (lines 64–169) is nothing but a stylized literary version of the traditional ritual chant; and such it in fact reveals itself to be in structure, content, and vocabulary alike.

The ode begins (lines 64–69; first strophe and antistrophe) with a declaration, couched in the first person singular, stating that the singer has come to adore "the Bacchic god" and is about to "recite the customary hymns to Dionysus." He enjoins silence upon the congregation and bids all the uninitiated depart. In these words we have nothing but the old ritual prologue recited by the high priest or precentor. The same type of prologue recurs in the Canaanite *Poem of the Gracious Gods,* where it likewise paves the way for the performance of the statutory ceremonies and the recital of the concomitant myth. It survives also in the opening speech of the European mummers' play, where the assembled multitude is similarly bidden "make way" for the sacred performers.[31]

The opening invocation is followed directly (lines 70–86; second strophe) by a summons to the Bacchic worshipers to perform the time-honored ritual and to escort the god "down from the Phrygian hills to the broad streets of Hellas." The inner blessedness of such worshipers is described and commended. This, too, is part of the traditional pattern. The Canaanite *Poem of the Gracious Gods* likewise couples the opening invocation with a summons to the assembled congregation to "let honor be rendered" to the gods, and it likewise calls down blessings of peace on the assembled votaries. Moreover, it is significant that in Psalm 89, which, as we have seen (above, §5), is based on the Seasonal Pattern, the opening invocation (vv. 2–9) and the recitation of the traditional myth (vv. 10–15) are followed immediately by a similar description and commendation of Yahweh's devotees.

Happy the people that know the trumpet blast;
  [YHWH,] they walk in the light of Thy face, etc.,

which read almost like a Hebrew equivalent of the phrases in our text. As in the case of the Psalms and of the Homeric *Hymn to Demeter,* so here the poet underscores the ritual derivation of his verses by introducing and playing upon terms derived from the technical vocabulary. The pious votary is described as one who "purifies his life," but the word rendered "purifies" (*hagisteuei*) has specific reference to *the observance of lenten austerity* (*hagisteia*), a characteristic element of the Seasonal Pattern. Similarly, he is described as one who "fills his soul with rapture," but the word rendered "fills with rapture" (*thiaseuetai*) is coined *ad hoc* from the technical term for *the ritual Bacchanalian revel* (*thiasos*). Lastly, he is said to perform his devotions "with holy purifications" in which words we may recognize a clear allusion to the ritual ablutions and *rites of purgation.*[32] Indeed, the sense and nuance of the passage may be best conveyed in a paraphrastic rendering.

Oh, happy he, by fortune blest,
  Who knows the rites by God ordained,
Whose life is one long sabbath rest,
  Who shriven, purgèd, and unstained,

His soul with holy rapture fills,
  A bacchanal upon the hills!

The second antistrophe (lines 87–105) contains the Mythological Core, describing the birth of the god Dionysus-Dithyrambos. Here, too, we may detect an underlying ritual basis; for the fact is that the seasonal rites of ancient Greece, as of many European communities in modern times, were frequently characterized by the introduction upon the scene of a young child thought to represent the personified New Year or, as the "Corn Baby," the nascent spirit of vegetation and fertility.[33] There is considerable evidence that this element appeared also in the traditional rites of Dionysus,[34] and the present passage of the choral ode would therefore be but a literary form of the accompanying chant.

The remainder of the ode (lines 106–169; third strophe and antistrophe and epode) is simply the revelers' song, punctuated with ritual cries of jubilation [*evoe*]. It is noteworthy, however, that here too the traditional pattern is markedly in evidence. There is a reference, for example, to the fact that when Dionysus appears on earth,

the plain flows with milk,
flows with wine,
flows with the nectar of bees.

In these words we have an almost literal counterpart of lines which occur in the Canaanite *Poem of Baal* [I AB iii 6–9] when the imminent return of Baal is being described:

The heavens rain down fatness,
the wadies flow with honey,
and so I know that Baal Puissant is alive,
that His Highness, the lord of the earth, still exists!

Moreover, it is to be observed that alike in prophetic and apocalyptic literature (Amos 9:13; Joel 4:18; Oracula Sibyllina III, 774–77; Slavonic Enoch, VIII §5) this picture forms a standard element in descriptions of the Messianic era; and since all such eschatological descriptions are ultimately based on ideas originally associated with the annual or periodic renewal of life, it is evident that the poet was here drawing once more upon the stock of the traditional Seasonal Pattern.[35]

§12. Our conclusions regarding this choral ode are confirmed by a discovery made in 1895 at the site of ancient Delphi. That discovery consists in a long ritualistic paean written by one Philodamus of Scarphe for the celebration of the Bacchic festival.[36] The paean reveals precisely the same structure as the Euripidean chorus, beginning with an invocation, proceeding to a description of the god's birth, commending the blessed state of his adorants, summoning them to his worship, and bidding them "welcome the Bacchic Dionysus in the streets." Moreover, it exhibits the same language, indicating that both poets were following a standard traditional model. Thus, if Euripides sings that

> at once will the whole earth start a-dancing
> when Bromios leads his bands unto the hills,
> where the womanish rout stand waiting,
> driven from loom and shuttle by the frenzy of Dionysus,
> (lines 114–119),

Philodamus, retrojecting the scene into the past, declares that

> the whole land of [Delphi], holy and blest,
> alive with the singing of hymns,
> started to dance,
> when thou didst reveal thy holy shape,
> standing, 'mid the maidens of Delphi,
> on the slopes of [Parn]assos!
> (lines 19–22).

Similarly, when Euripides bursts forth in praise of the votary with the words "Oh, happy he, etc." (lines 72 ff.), Philodamus uses exactly the same turn of expression (and likewise at the beginning of a stanza) to commend the Delphians for the worship of the god (lines 75 ff.). And when Euripides (line 108) employs the expression "yielding fair fruit" (*kallikarpos*) to describe the land of the god's birth, so too does Philodamus (line 17).

But Philodamus preserves one important element of the traditional pattern which Euripides omits. He commends the Delphians for having built a shrine for their god, and he describes how the god had himself ordained that it be constructed "with all dispatch" (lines 67 ff.). Here we have the familiar feature of shrine building with which we have already become familiar. The poet is, of course, celebrating the founding of the famous temple at Delphi, but the terms in which he does so are an echo of the traditional pattern which should not be overlooked.

III

§13. A final and more modern example of the way in which the seasonal drama degenerates into the liturgical chant may be found in the famous hymn composed by Adam of St. Victor (ca. 1130–1180) for the Feast of Michael and All the Angels (September 12).[37] Taking as a basis the description in the Book of Revelation (c. 12) of the archangel's triumph over Satan, the hymnographer nevertheless succeeds, albeit unconsciously, in preserving the structure, content, and even language of the more primitive material. He opens with the regular Invocation calling upon the devout to render praise and to partake of the bliss of that day whereon the ancient triumph of the angels is annually rehearsed.

Laus erumpat ex affectu
Psallat chorus in conspectu
  Supernorum civium!
Laus jucunda, laus decora
Quando laudi concanora
  Puritas est cordium!

Michaelem cuncti laudent
Nec ab hujus se defraudent
  Diei laetitia!
Felix dies, quā sanctorum
Recensetur angelorum
  Solemnis victoria!

Let the heartfelt praises ring,
Loudly let the chorus sing
In the sight of them that dwell
High in heaven's citadel!
  Comely is the strain and sweet
When in harmony there meet
Music of pure hearts and song,
  Praises ringing loud and long!

So let all men sound the praise
Of Michael, nor forego the day's
  Most blest felicity!

Oh, happy day whereon is told,
From year to year, that tale of old
— The angels' victory!

Then, immediately after the Invocation, he proceeds to the Mythological Core; and the language which he uses harks right back to the Babylonian, Hittite, Canaanite, and Egyptian prototypes. It is the "ancient Dragon" — Yam, Illuyankas, Tiamat, Set — who is "routed" along with his cohorts; and the reason for his discomfiture is that, like those rebels, he sought to promote confusion.

Draco vetus exturbatur
Et Draconis effugatur
Inimica legio.
Exturbatus est turbator
Et projectus Accusator[38]
A caeli fastigio!

Routed is the Dragon old
And his legion bad and bold
Rudely put to flight!
That Confounder is confounded
And from heaven's fastness hounded
— Satan from the height!

Moreover, through the defeat and banishment of that wily and venomous creature, an era of peace is ushered in both on earth and in heaven.

Sub tutela Michaelis
Pax in terra, pax in caelis,
Laus et jubilatio;
Cum fit potens hic virtute
Pro communi stans salute
Triumphat in proelio.

Suggestor sceleris
Pulsus a superis
Per hujus aëris
Oberrat spatia.

Dolis invigilat,
Virus insibilat,
Sed hunc adnihilat
Praesens custodia.

Michael our sentinel,
Peace now on earth shall dwell,
Peace now in heav'n as well,
  Loud jubilation!
Into the fray he goes,
Boldly he worsts his foes,
  All men's salvation!

Prompt ever to incite
Though driv'n from heav'n's height,
Satan still roams the night,
  Bent on seduction.
Guileful, he lies in wait,
Breathing his baleful hate;
Yet he who guards our state
  Wreaks his destruction!

Finally, after a homiletic interlude, the hymn concludes with the typical Epilogue — the final burst of prayer and salutation — all in accordance with the ancient, time-honored pattern.

De secretis reticentes
  Interim caelestibus,
Erigamus puras mentes
  In caelum cum manibus,
Ut superna nos dignetur
  Cohaeredes curia
Et divina colladetur
  Ab utrisque gratia.

Capiti sit gloria
Membrisque concordia!

Though heaven's hidden ways
Veil'd be from mortal gaze,
Heav'nward let each upraise
  Pure hand and mind;
That, like the angels there,
Each man be deemed an heir,
Worthy and fit to share
  God's high estate!
So may the chorus swell,
Angels and men as well,
Thanks from all hearts upwell,
  Early and late!

And may the Church's frame
Thrill with its Head's acclaim,
  Thrill with his praise!
And be the limbs thereof
Tied each to each in love
  All of their days!

It is the old pattern once more, the old refrain ringing down the ages; it is Baal defeating Yam and bringing in the new lease of life and the promise of peace on earth; it is Marduk vanquishing Tiamat and establishing the order of the world; it is Horus triumphing over Set, the Hittite weather god over the Dragon Illuyankas, and Yahweh over Leviathan, the evasive serpent. And when the music of this age-old anthem has swelled to its crescendo, it is the soul of man doing battle with evil.

NOTES

1. On such reciters at Babylonian festivals, see Ebeling, *Propagandagedicht,* 1; Smith, *Isaiah XL–LV,* 111, n. 138. For the "Chief Lector" at the Edfu play in Egypt, see Blackman-Fairman, JEA 28 (1942), 35 f.

2. Cf. the classic presentation in H. Gunkel, *Einleitung in die Psalme* (1917). Illuminating also is J. P. Peters, *The Psalms as Liturgies* (1922).

3. T. H. Gaster, JQR, N. S. 37 (1946), 55–65.

4. Cf. Briggs, ICC, *in loc.*

5. For this expression, cp. Psalm 89:6. Similar is *m-p-kh-r-t q-d-sh-m,* "assembly of the holy ones," in the tenth century B.C. inscription of Yehimilk of Byblos: Albright, JAOS 67 (1947), 156 f.

6. H. Chajes, *Sepher Tehillim* (1908), 62; H. Schmidt, *Die Psalmen,* 55.

7. Gudea Cylinder A, xii 11–13; cf. JNES 2 (1943), 118.

8. Cf. Jacobsen, JNES 5 (1946), 145, n. 28.

9. *De Dea Syria,* c. 13.

10. Cf. Targum Pseudo-Jonathan, Exodus 28:30; Midrash Tanhuma, Qedoshim §10.

11. Pausanias I. 18, 7.

12. Gaster, JQR, N.S. 37 (1946), 62, n. 27.

13. The LXX reading is supported by Vet. Lat. and Symmachus and by a fragment from Qumran. MT reads: "according to the number of the children of *Israel.*"

14. It may be suggested that Psalm 47:7 expresses the same idea in the words *zammeru ehohim zammeru, zammeru lemalkenu zammeru,* for the word *elohim* (pointedly without prefix, in contrast to *lemalkenu!*) may perhaps be parsed as a *vocative,* when the sense will be: "Sing praises, *O ye gods,* sing praises; sing praises to our King, sing praises!"

15. Cf. P. Jensen, *Assyro-bab. Mythen u. Epen,* 306.

16. Cf. Nabonidus Stele, ix 31–42; Pallis, *Akitu* 133.

17. Cf. Arabic *'amm* and the sense of Hebrew *'am* in, e.g., Numbers 20:20; 21:33; Joshua 8:3, 11; 11:7; Judges 5:13. So substantially Muilenburg, JBL 63 (1944), 242–43.

18. Hebrew *qiryath melek rab,* where *melek rab* (which recurs in the Ugaritic text 118:13, 26 Gordon) is the equivalent of Akkad. *sharru rabu,* "emperor."

19. Hebrew *'elyon* in this passage need not mean "the Most High," but merely "one of the upper gods," like *'ly*[*nm*] in the Ugaritic text, *Gracious Gods* 2.

20. Cf. Allen-Sikes-Halliday, *in loc.*

21. *Ibid.,* 120.

22. Cf. Ovid, *Fasti* iv. 493; *Met.* v. 441–43; Cicero, *In Verrem* II, iv. 48; Diod. Sic. v. 4, 3; Pausanias viii. 25, 7; Farnell, *Cults,* iii, pl. xii, xva, xxia, xxv, xxviib, and cp. with these literary and artistic treatments the ritualistic allusions in Statius, *Silv.* iv. 8, 50 f.; Clem. Alex., *Protrep.* ii. 12; Lactantius, *Div. Inst.,* i. 21; Pausanias ii. 22, 3.

23. Cf. Plutarch, *De Is. et Os.,* 69; Suidas, Hesychius Lexx., s.v. *Achaia;* Preller, *Gr. Mythol.,*[4] i. 752, n. 3; Gruppe, *Gr. Mythol.,* 1186, n. 4.

24. See also Apollodorus, *Bib.* i. 5, 1, and Frazer *in loc.*

25. *De Is. et Os.* 69; cf. Harrison, *Prolegomena* 128.

26. Cf. Cornford, *Origins of Attic Comedy,* 36 f., 42, 50 f.; Frazer, GB vii/1, 62 ff.

27. Aristophanes, *Frogs* 372 ff.; Pausanias vii. 279; Athenaeus v. 10, 181c; cf. Gruppe, *op. cit.,* 1175, n. 4.

28. Cf. Comm. on *Gracious Gods,* Ritual, §I.

29. "Ein Keilschrifttext ältester Mimus der Weltliteratur," reprint from *Theater der Welt* 1937, Nos. 3–4, p. 10, n. 24.

30. *Euripides and his Age,* 181–83.

31. E.g. in the Hope Benham version of the mummers' play (Piggott, FL 39 [1928], 274), where the Prologue ends: "Clear the way!"

32. See Chapter Two, §§14–18.

33. GB vii/i, 150 ff.

34. *Ibid.,* 5, 27.

35. Cf. especially Roscher, *Nektar u. Ambrosia,* 110.

36. Inscr. Delph., ed. H. Weil, BCH 19 (1895), 393 ff., 20 (1896), 237; 21 (1897), 510 ff.; Diels, SBAW 1896, 457 ff. Cf. Fairbanks, CSCP 12 (1900), 139 f.; Powell, CQ 9 (1915?), 288;

Deubner, *Neue Jahrb.* 22 (1919), 385 ff.; de Falco, Mouseion (Naples), I (1923), 3–13. Our translation follows the text of Diehl, *Anthol. Lyrica* ii. 252 ff., with minor variations.

37. The text is taken from J. G. Phillimore, *The Hundred Best Latin Hymns* (1926), No. 48.

38. The Latin *Accusator* is simply a literal rendering of the Hebrew *Satan.*

EXCURSUS

1. CHORUS FROM THE BACCHAE OF EURIPIDES

Bacchae, 64–169

[*First Strophe*

From Asia's land departing
and from holy Tmolus now I speed, on that sweet labor bent,
that toil which is no toil, the singing of the Bacchic god.

[*First Antistrophe*

Who walks upon the road? Who walks upon the road?
Who bides within his house? Let every such make way; let every mouth be hushed in hallowèd devotion;
for I will chant the old time-honored hymn of Dionysus!

[*Second Strophe*

O happy he, by fortune blest,
who knows the *mystic rites* divine,
who makes his life one long *austerity,*
who steeps his soul in *sacred revelry,*
who, amid the *sacred ceremonies of purgation,*
serves as a bacchanal on the hills
and as a votary in the revels of Cybele, that Great Mother,
who tosses high the thyrsus, his head with ivy crowned,
who ministers unto *Dionysus!*

Come, ye bacchanals! Come, ye bacchanals, down from the
[Phrygian hills
to Hellas' wideswept streets to lead
this Dionysus, god the son of god, – even this Bromios!

[*Second Antistrophe*

– this Bromios who filled his mother's womb
when, suddenly, Zeus' lightning struck,
and in forced labor she brought him to birth,
herself forsaking life thro' that fell stroke.

Then, in secret recesses of birth, Zeus the son of Kronos received him and, fastening him with golden clasps, kept him
[concealed within his thigh,

hidden from Hera.
And when the Fates determined, he bore that god, hornèd
like a bull, and garlanded him with wreaths of snakes
(wherefore the thyrsus-bearing revelers still twine their locks
with those most savage beasts).

[*Third Strophe*

O Thebes, thou nurse of Semele,
with ivy be thou garlanded;
burgeon, burgeon now with green, *fair-fruited* bryony!
Thou too now play the bacchanal,
decked with boughs of oak or pine,
clad in the dappled skins of fawns,
wreathed in fillets of white wool!
Toss thy wands most proudly in the air,
keep holy festival!
At once the entire land will break out dancing,
as soon as Bromios leads his revel bands
up to the hill, up to the hill,
where, leaving loom and shuttle, waits the throng
of women stung to frenzy by the goad
of *Dionysus!*

[*Third Antistrophe*

O chamber of the Kourētes,
most sacred cavern haunts of Crete
where Zeus whilom was born,
O caves wherein the triple-plumèd Korybantes erst
devised for me this tabret of stretched hide,
blending the cry of revel with the tone,
the sweet-voiced breath of Phrygian lutes,
and unto Mother Rhea handed it,
that it should thenceforth serve to mark the beat
of songs the bacchanals intone!
Then frenzied satyrs came and wrested it
out of the Mother Goddess' hands
and made it part and parcel of *the rites,*
those rites which in alternate years are held,
which are the rich delight of *Dionysus!*

[*Epode*

Ah, sweet upon the hills
when, weary from the racing bands
one falls upon the ground,
clad in the sacred fawnskin garb,
hunting the blood of the slain goat,
the delight of raw flesh devoured,
he reaches the Phrygian, Lydian hills

where the leader of the revels is none other
than *Bromios!* *Evoe!*
There flows the ground with milk, yea, flows with wine,
flows with the honey of bees,
and all the air is heavy with the scent
of Syrian incense.
And there the bacchanal races in his mad course,
tossing the flaming pinewood brands,
urging the chorus to rush to and fro,
shaking his torches while the cries resound,
his delicate locks streaming in the breeze.
And all the while the wild, wild songs ring out,
answered by thunderous antiphony:

"O come, ye bacchanals,
O come, ye bacchanals,
Delicate pride of Tmolus which flows with gold,
come, sing ye Dionysus
to the tune of deep-voiced drums!
Raise the cry Evoe to the god of all 'evoes'
with Phrygian cries and invocations,
what time the sacred flute melodious sounds
harmonious to the joyful shouts of those
who wander to the hill, yea, to the hill."

Joyful, like a foal beside the dam a-grazing,
so skips the bacchanal with tripping gait!

2. PAEAN TO DIONYSUS

By Philodamus of Scarphe

§1. INVOCATION

Hither, O Dithyrambos, Bacchus, come,
lord of the thyrsus and the revelers' cry;
come, O Bromios, O ivy-tress'd,

in springtime show thyself!
Evoe, Iobacchus! Paean, hail!*

§2. NATIVITY AND REVELATION OF THE GOD

Thou who of old in Thebes (where still ring out
the bacchic cries) Thyone bore to Zeus
– a child of beauty.
Lo, when thou wast born,

* I.e., Healer.

the Sons of God 'gan dance for very joy,
and all mankind.

Hail, O Paean! Savior, come!
Bless our city, of thy grace;
give us wealth and give us bliss!

Earth, too, into a bacchic rapture brake,
yea, Cadmus' far-famed land and yonder bay—
yon Minyan bay; and yon Augeia bloom'd,
bless'd with rich fruits.

Evoe, Iobacchus, etc.

And over Delphi's hallow'd, blessèd land
the air was fill'd with singing; and thyself,
while Delphian maidens circl'd thee around,
didst stand, a splendor on Parnassus' slopes,
for all to see.

Hail, O Paean, etc.

Tossing thy firebrands against the night,
with wild, ecstatic, frenzied steps didst come,
didst come unto Eleusis, there where bloom
the flower-fill'd groves.

Evoe, Iobacchus, etc.

'Tis there the people of the Grecian land,
that people dear to thee, still meet as one
and cry on thee, as every eighth year ends,
to see the glory of thy mysteries.
And there didst thou provide for all mankind
haven from toil.

Hail, O Paean, etc.

And, while the dancers danced the long night through,

* * *

Thence to the cities of fair The[ssaly]
didst come and to Olympus' sacred close
and fam'd Pieria.

Evoe, Iobacchus, etc.

The Muses there, their locks with ivy bound,
'gan circle thee and chant their sweet-voic'd songs,
calling thee deathless Healer; and that choir
Apollo led.

Hail, O Paean, etc.

§3. SHRINE-BUILDING AND THEOXENIA

Then did that god command th' Amphictyons
all things to speed, that, when the month came round,
th' appropriate month, he might have where to greet
his suppliants.

Evoe, Iobacchus, etc.

He bade them also in their yearly rites,
when they regal'd the gods at festive board,
this newborn kinsman with him to unite
in hymnal praises and in sacrifice,
and have the suppliants from Greece entire
call on them both:

Hail, O Paean, etc.

Oh, blest and happy was that race of men
which unto Phoebus reared the sanctuary,
to be an ageless, undefilèd shrine
for evermore!

Evoe, Iobacchus, etc.

New-gilt, with golden statues [was it decked],
* * * * * twain goddesses, their locks * * *,
with ivory and metals of the earth
all gleaming fair.

Hail, O Paean, etc.

He bade them also hail the newborn god,
e'en as they hailed himself, in song and dance
when, each fourth year, the sacred time came round
of Pythian festival.*

Evoe, Iobacchus, etc.

§4. PERVIGILIUM AND ERECTION OF IMAGE

And then he told them, when the morning light
first stole across the mountains, to set up
an image of this god like to his own,
wrought cunningly, and place it in the cave
where stood the golden lions, and prepare
a sacred grotto for him, as befits
a most high god.

Hail, O Paean, etc.

* The best comment on these lines is afforded by Cook, Zeus, ii, 233 ff.

§5. EPILOGUE

So come this Dionysus to receive,
this lord of revelry, and in the streets
whirl with the dancers ivy-tress'd and cry:

Evoe, Iobacchus! Paean, hail!

[Grant thou] to all the blessed land of Greece
* * * * * * * * * * * * * *
* * * * * * * * * * * * * *
* * * * * * * * * * * * * *

* * * * * * * [swe]et health!
Hail, O Paean! Savior, come!
Bless our city, of thy grace;
[*give us wealth and give us bliss!*]

* * *

ADDENDA

Text A (Baal), XLIII, Commentary (c).
Targhuzizza, there written *Sh*arghuzizza, recurs as the name of a mountain in a mythological text (*Ugaritica* V, 8.37) discovered in 1961.

Text E (Gracious Gods), 66[c] ff., Commentary.
The expression *n-ẓ-r m-d-r-*[c] has now appeared in an administrative document from Ugarit as the title of an official, i.e. "conserver of grain." It is such an official, then, that the two gods meet on "the outskirts of the desert."

BIBLIOGRAPHY

Aarne, A., *The Types of the Folk-tale*, tr. and enlarged by Stith Thompson. Helsinki 1928.

Abbott, G. F., *Macedonian Folklore*. Cambridge 1903.

Abu Yusuf Ya'cub, *Kitab al-Kharaj*. Cairo 1882–83.

Adair, J., *The History of the American Indians*. London 1775.

Adamson, H., *Muses' Threnodie*. London 1638.

Albright, W. F., *Archaeology and the Religion of Israel*. Baltimore 1942.

----, *From the Stone Age to Christianity*. Baltimore 1940.

Allen, R., *Star-Names and their Meanings*. New York 1899.

Allen, T. W., Halliday, W., and Sikes, E. E., *The Homeric Hymns*. Oxford 1936.

Anderson, A. R., *Gog and Magog and the Enclosed Nations*. Cambridge, Mass. 1932.

Angus, S., *The Mystery Religions and Christianity*. London 1925.

Apollodorus, *The Library*, ed. J. G. Frazer, Loeb Classics. 2 vols. London 1921.

Aristotle, *On the Art of Poetics*, tr. I. Bywater. Oxford 1920.

Aston, W. G., *Shinto*. London 1921.

Bacher, W., *Die Agada der Tannaiten*. 2 vols. Strassburg 1884–90.

Bancroft, H. H., *The Native Races of the Pacific States of North America*. New York, 1875–76.

Banks, M. M., *British Calendar Customs: Scotland I*. London 1937.

Barth, J., *Etymologische Studien*. Berlin 1893.

Barton, G. A., *A Sketch of Semitic Origins*. New York 1902.

Baudissin, W., *Adonis und Esmun*. Leipzig 1911.

----, *Studien zur semitischen Religionsgeschichte*. Leipzig 1876–78.

Baudissin Festschrift: *Abhandlugen zur semitischen Religionskunde und Sprachwissenschaft Wolf Wilhelm Grafen von Baudissin . . . überreicht, ed. W. Frankenberg and F. Küchler*. Giessen 1918.

Bauer, *Th., Die Ostkanaanäer*. Leipzig 1926.

Bechstein, L., *Thüringer Sagenbuch*. Leipzig 1885.

Beck, B. F., *Honey and Health*. New York 1938.

Behrens, E., *Assyrisch-babylonische Briefe aus der Sargonidenzeit*. Leipzig 1906.

Berger, E. H., *Kosmographie der Griechen*. Leipzig 1904.

Beza, M., *Paganism in Roumanian Folklore*. London 1928.

Bezold, C., *Oriental Diplomacy*. London 1893.

Bilabel, F., *Geschichte Vorderasiens und Aegyptens vom 16. Jahrhundert v. Chr. bis auf die Neuzeit*, Heidelberg 1927.

Blackman, A. M., *Luxor and its Temples*. London 1923.

Blackman, W. S., *The Fellahin of Upper Egypt*. London 1927.

Blagden, C. O., *Pagan Races of the Malay Peninsula*. London 1906.

Blinkenberg, C., *The Thunderweapon in Religion and Folklore*. Cambridge 1911.

Bochart, S., *Hierozoicon*. Third ed. Leyden 1692.

Bogoras, W., "The Chukchee," in *Memoir of the American Museum of Natural History, The Jessup North Pacific Expedition*, vol. vii. Leyden–New York 1904–09.

Böhl, F., *Nieuwjaarsfest en Koningsdag in Babylon en in Israel*. Groningen-Hague 1927.

Böttiger, K. A., *Ideen zu Kunstmythen*. 2 vols. Leipzig-Dresden 1826–36.

Boll, F., *Sphaera*. Leipzig 1903.

Bolte, J., and Polivka, G., *Anmerkungen zu den Kinder- und Hausmärchen der Brüder Grimm*. 5 vols. Leipzig 1913–18.

Bousset, W., *Religion des Judentums im neutestamentlichen Zeitalter*. Berlin 1903.

Brand, J., *Observations on Popular Antiquities of Great Britain* . . . London 1810.

----, *Observations on the Popular Antiquities of Great Britain*, ed. H. Ellis. 2 vols. London 1902.

Brandt, W. M., *Die mandäische Religion*. Leipzig 1889.

Breasted, J. H., and Nelson, H., *Medinet Habu*. Chicago 1933 ff.

Briggs, C. A. and E. G., *A Critical and Exegetical Commentary on the Book of Psalms* (ICC). 2 vols. New York 1914–17.

Brinton, D. G., *Myths of the New World*. Third ed. Philadelphia 1896.

British Museum, *Handbook to the Ethnographic Collections*. Second ed. London 1925.

Brock-Utne, A., *Der Gottesgarten*. Oslo 1936.

Brown, W., *New Zealand and its Aborigines*. London 1845.

Brugsch, H., *Die Adonisklage und das Linoslied*. Berlin 1852.

----, *Drei Festkalender des Tempels von Apollinopolis Magna*. Berlin 1877.

Brunnhofer, H., *Die schweizerische Heldensage*. Bern 1910.

Bucher, K., *Arbeit und Rhythmus*. Sixth ed. Leipzig 1924.

Budde, K., *Die biblische Urgeschichte*. Giessen 1883.

Budge, E. A. W., *The Book of Governors*. London 1893.

----, *Life and Exploits of Alexander the Great* . . . London 1896.

----, *Osiris and the Egyptian Resurrection*. 2 vols. London 1911.

----, *The Gods of the Egyptians*. London 1904.

Bullen, A. H. ed., *Lyrics from the Dramatists of the Elizabethan Age*. London 1891.

----, ed., *Lyrics from Elizabethan Songbooks*. London 1887.

Burckhardt, J. L., *Bedouins and Wahabys*. London 1831.

Burney, C. F., *Notes on the Hebrew Text of the Books of Kings.* Cambridge 1903.
Callaway, H., *The Religious System of the Amazulu.* Natal 1868–70.
Calmet, A., *Dissertations qui peuvent servir de prolégomenes de l'écriture sainte.* Paris 1720.
Campbell, J. G., *The Fions.* London 1891.
Canney, M., *Givers of Life.* London 1923.
Cassirer, E., *Language and Myth,* tr. S. Langer. New York 1946.
Chajes, H. P., *Sepher Tehillim,* in Kahana's *Pêrūsh Mādā'î.* Kiev 1908.
Chambers, E. K., *The Medieval Stage.* 2 vols. Oxford 1903.
Chambers, R., *The Book of Days,* 2 vols. London-Edinburgh 1886.
Charles, R. H. (ed.), *The Book of Enoch.* Oxford 1912.
Charlevoix, P. F. X., *Histoire et description de la nouvelle France.* Paris 1674.
Chateaubriand, *Voyage en Amérique.* Paris 1870.
Chwolson, D., *Die Ssabier.* 2 vols. St. Petersburg 1856.
Claus, H., *Die Wagogo.* Baessler-Archiv, Beiheft 2. Leipzig 1911.
Clayton, A. C., *The Rig-Veda and Vedic Religion.* London-Madras 1913.
Clement of Alexandria, *Opera Omnia,* ed. R. Klotz. 2 vols. Leipzig 1831.
Codrington, R. H., *The Melanesians.* Oxford 1891.
Cook, A. B., *Zeus,* ii. Cambridge 1925.
Cook, S. A., *The Religion of Ancient Palestine in the Light of Archaeology.* London 1930.
Cooke, G. A., ed., *A Text-book of North Semitic Inscriptions.* Oxford 1903.
Cornford, F. M., *The Origins of Attic Comedy.* Cambridge 1934.
Chauvin, V., *Bibliographie des ouvrages arabes.* 12 vols. Liège 1892–1922.
Crawley, A. E., *The Idea of the Soul.* London 1909.
----, *The Mystic Rose,* ed. Th. Besterman. 2 vols. London 1927.
Ctesiae Cnidii Operum Reliquiae, ed. F. Baehr. Frankfurt 1824.
Cumont, F., *Die Orientalischen Religionen im Römischen Heidentum.* Leipzig-Berlin 1931.
----, *Études syriennes.* Paris 1917.
----, *Les mystères de Mithras.* Third ed. Paris 1913.
----, *Mysteries of Mithra,* tr. G. Showerman. London 1903.
Curtin, J., *Hero-tales of Ireland.* London 1894.
Curtiss, S. I., *Ursemitische Religion im Volksleben des heutigen Orients,* tr. H. Stocks. Leipzig 1913.
Dähnhardt, O., *Natursagen.* 4 vols. Leipzig 1907–12.
Dale, Antonius van, *Dissertationes IX antiquitatibus quin et marmoribus cum Romanis tum notissimum Graecis illustrandis servientes.* Amsterdam 1702.

Dalman, G. H., *Arbeit und Sitte in Palästina.* 5 vols. Gütersloh 1928–37.
----, *Palästinischer Diwan.* Leipzig 1908.
Dasent, G. W., *Popular Tales from the Norse.* Edinburgh 1859.
David, M., *Die Adoption im altababylonischen Recht.* Leipzig 1927.
Davids, Rhys, C. A. F., *Kindred Sayings.* London 1918.
Davies, N. de Garis, and Gardiner, A. H., The Theban Tomb Series: First Memoir. *The Tomb of Amenemhet.* London 1915.
Deimel, A., *Pantheon babylonicum.* Rome 1914.
Delitzsch, Frd., *Wo lag das Paradies?* Leipzig 1881.
Dennys, N. B., *The Folklore of China.* London 1876.
Dexter, T. F., *Fire Worship in Britain.* London 1931.
Dhorme, E., *Les religions de Babylonie et d'Assyrie.* Paris 1945.
Diehl, E. (ed.), *Anthologia Lyrica.* Third ed. Bonn 1917.
Dieterich, A., *Eine Mithrasliturgie.* Second ed. (R. Wuensch). Paris-Berlin 1910.
Diringer, D., *Le Inscrizioni Antico-Ebraiche Palestinesi.* Florence 1934.
Dodds, E. R., *Euripides' Bacchae.* Oxford 1944.
Dölger, F., *Die Sonne der Gerechtigkeit.* Münster 1918.
Doolittle, J., *Social Life of the Chinese.* 2 vols. New York 1867.
Doughty, C. A., *Travels in Arabia Deserta.* 2 vols. Cambridge 1888.
Douglas, N., *Birds and Beasts of the Greek Anthology.* London 1928.
Drechsler, P., *Sitte, Brauch und Volksglaube in Schlesien.* 2 vols. Leipzig 1903–06.
Drews, A., *Der Sternhimmel in der Dichtung und Religion der alten Völker und des Christentums.* Jena 1923.
Drioton, E., and Vandier, J., *L'Égypte.* Paris 1946.
----, *Le théatre égyptien.* Cairo 1942.
Drower, E. S., *The Mandaeans of Iraq and Iran.* Oxford 1937.
Duhm, Hans, *Die bösen Geister des Alten Testaments.* Tübingen 1904.
Dukes, A., *Drama.* London [1926].
Dumézil, G., *Le festin d'immortalité.* Paris 1924.
Duncan, J. G., *Digging Up Biblical History.* 2 vols. London 1931.
Dürr, L., *Ursprung und Ausbau der israelit.-jüdischen Heilandserwartung.* Berlin 1925.
Dussaud, R., *Les découvertes de Ras Shamra et l'ancien testament.* Paris 1941.
----, *Les origines cananéennes du sacrifice israélite.* Paris 1921.
----, *Melanges syriens offerts à M. René Dussaud.* 2 vols. Paris 1939–40.
----, *Mission dans les regions désertiques de la Syrie moyenne.* Paris 1903.
----, *Notes de mythologie syrienne.* Paris 1905.

Dussaud, R., and Macler, F., *Voyage archéologique au Safa et dans le Djebel-ed-Druz.* Paris 1901.
Duveyrier, H., *Les touaregs du nord.* Paris 1864.
Ebeling, E., *Bruchstücke eines politischen Propagandagedichtes aus einer assyrischen Kanzlei.* Leipzig 1938.
----, *Quellen zur Kenntniss der babylonischen Religion.* Leipzig 1918–19.
----, *Tod und Leben nach den Vorstellungen der Babylonier.* Berlin 1931.
Eerdmans, B., *The Hebrew Book of Psalms.* Leyden 1947.
Eisenstein, J. D., *Osar Dînîm u-Minhagîm* (Hebrew). New York 1928.
Eisler, R., *Orphisch-Dionysische Mysterien-gedanken in der Christlichen Antike.* Leipzig 1925.
----, *The Messiah Jesus and John the Baptist.* London 1931.
----, *Weltenmantel und Himmelszelt.* Munich 1910.
Eissfeldt, O., *Baal Zaphon, Zeus Kasios und der Durchzug der Israeliten durchs Meer.* Halle 1932.
Eitrem, S., *Opferritus und Voropfer der Griechen und Römer.* Christiania 1915.
----, *Papyri Osloenses,* I. Oslo 1925.
Ellis, C. C., *A History of Fire and Flame.* London 1932.
Engnell, I., *Studies in Divine Kingship in the Ancient Near East.* Uppsala 1943.
Erman, A., *Handbook of Egyptian Religion,* tr. F. Griffith. London 1907.
Ewald, H., *History of Israel,* tr. R. Martineau. Fourth ed. 6 vols. London 1878–86.
----, *Commentary on the Prophets of the Old Testament,* tr. J. F. Smith. 5 vols. London 1875 ff.
Farnell, L. R., *Cults of the Greek States.* 6 vols. Oxford 1896–1909.
Fehlinger, H., *Sexual Life of Primitive People.* London 1921.
Feigin, S. I., *Missitrei Heavar (Hebrew).* New York 1943.
Finn, E. A. (Mrs.), *Palestine Peasantry.* London 1923.
Flügel, G., *Mani, seine Lehre und seine Schriften.* Leipzig 1862.
Fowler, W. Warde, *The Roman Festivals of the Period of the Republic.* London 1899.
Fox, W. S., *Greek and Roman Mythology.* Boston 1916.
Fraenkel, S., *De vocabulis . . . in Corano peregrinis.* Leyden 1886.
Frank, K., *Bilder und Symbole bab.-assyr. Götter.* Leipzig 1906.
----, *Studien zur babylonischen Religion, I–II.* Strassburg 1911.
Frankfort, H., *Cylinder Seals.* London 1939.
----, *Kingship and the Gods.* Chicago 1948.
Frazer, J. G., *Aftermath: A Supplement to the Golden Bough.* London 1936.
----, *Pausanias' Description of Greece,* tr. with comm. London 1898.

Frazer, J. G., *The Fasti of Ovid.* 5 vols. London 1929.

————, *Folk-Lore in the Old Testament.* 3 vols. London 1919.

————, one-vol. ed. New York 1923.

————, *The Golden Bough.* One-vol. ed. New York 1926.

Friedländer, M., *The Jewish Religion.* New York 1946.

Friedrich, J., *Hethitisches Elementarbuch,* I. Heidelberg 1940.

————, *Staatsverträge des Hatti-Reiches* (MVAG 34.1). Leipzig 1926–30.

Friedrich, Th., *Kabiren und Keilinschriften.* Leipzig 1894.

Froment, P. E., *Essai sur le role du feu en religion.* Montauban 1900.

Furlani, G., *La religione babilonese e assira.* 2 vols. Bologna 1928–29.

————, *La Religione degli Hittiti.* Bologna 1936.

Gagnière, *apud Annales de la Propagation de la Foi.* Lyons 1860.

Gallop, R., *Portugal: A Book of Folk-ways.* Cambridge 1936.

Garcilasso de la Vega, *Commentarios reales,* tr. C. R. Markham. London 1869–71.

Garstang, J., *The Hittite Empire.* London 1929.

Gaster, M., *The Asatir of Moses.* London 1927.

————, (ed.), *The Book of Prayer . . . according to the Custom of the Spanish and Portuguese Jews,* vol. i. London 1901.

————, *The Samaritans.* London 1925.

Gauthier, H., *Les fêtes du dieu Min.* Cairo 1931.

Gesenius, W., *Scripturae Linguaeque Phoeniciae Monumenta.* Leipzig 1837.

————, *Thesaurus . . . Linguae Hebraicae et Chaldeicae.* Leipzig 1829.

Gilbert, O., *Griechiche Götterlehre . . .* Leipzig 1898.

Ginsberg, H. L., *The Legend of King Keret.* (BASOR, Supp. 2). New Haven 1946.

Ginzberg, L., *The Legends of the Jews.* 7 vols. Philadelphia 1909 ff.

Louis Ginzberg Jubilee Volume. New York 1942.

Glotz, G., *The Greek City and its Institutions.* New York 1930.

Goetze, A., *Die Annalen des Mursilis* (MVAG 39). Leipzig 1933.

————, *Kleinasien.* Munich 1933.

————, *Kleinasien zur Hethiterzeit.* Heidelberg 1924.

————, *Madduwatas.* Leipzig 1928.

————, *The Hittite Ritual of Tunnawi.* New Haven 1933.

Gomme, Alice, B., *Children's Singing Games.* London 1894.

Gordon, C. H., *The Living Past.* New York 1941.

Graham, W. C., and May, H. G., *Culture and Conscience.* Chicago 1936.

Graillot, P., *Le culte de Cybèle.* Paris 1912.

Grant, D., *A Feughside Fairy Tale.* [Aberdeen 1937].

Gray, G. B., *Sacrifice in the Old Testament.* Oxford 1925.

Gray, C. D., *The Shamash Religious Texts,* Chicago, 1901.

Gray, L. H., *Baltic Mythology.* Boston 1918.

Gressmann, H., (ed.), *Altorientalische Texte und Bilder.* Second ed. Leipzig 1916.
----, and Ungnad, A., *Das Gilgames Epos.* Göttingen 1911.
Grimm, W., "Die Sage von Polyphem," in *Kleinere Schriften,* Gütersloh 1887, vol. iv, 428–62.
----, J., *Teutonic Mythology,* tr. F. Stallybrass. 4 vols. London 1880.
Grünbaum, M., *Gesammelte Aufsätze zur Sprach- und Sagenkunde.* Berlin 1901.
Grunwald, M., *Yalqūṭ Sippūrîm u-Midrašîm* (Hebrew). 2 vols. Warsaw 1923.
Gruppe, O., *Griechische Mythologie.* 2 vols. Munich 1906.
Gunkel, H., *Ausgewählte Psalme.* Göttingen 1917.
----, *Einleitung in die Psalme,* ed. J. Begrich. Leipzig 1925.
----, *Schöpfung und Chaos in Urzeit und Endzeit.* Göttingen 1895.
Güntert, H., *Von der Sprache der Götter und Geister.* Halle 1921.
Güterbock, H. G., *Kumarbi: Mythen vom churritischen Kronos.* (Istanbuler Schriften, No. 16.) Zurich–New York 1946.
Hackman, O., *Die Polyphemsage in der Volksüberlieferung.* Helsingfors 1904.
Hahn, J. G. von, *Griechische und albanesische Märchen,* 1–2. Leipzig 1864.
Haigh, A. H., *The Tragic Drama of the Greeks.* Oxford 1896.
Halliday, W. R., *Indo-European Folk-tales and Greek Legend.* Cambridge 1933.
Hampson, R. T., *Medii Aevi Kalendarium.* London 1841.
Harris, J. Rendell, *Picus who is also Zeus.* Cambridge 1916.
----, *The Cult of the Heavenly Twins.* Cambridge 1906.
Harris, Z., *Grammar of the Phoenician Language.* New Haven 1936.
Harrison, Jane, *Ancient Art and Ritual.* London [1913].
----, *Epilegomena to the Study of Greek Religion.* Cambridge 1921.
----, *Prolegomena to the Study of Greek Religion.* Third ed. Cambridge 1922.
----, *Themis.* Cambridge 1912.
Hartland, E. S., *The Science of Fairy Tales.* London 1891.
----, *The Legend of Perseus.* 3 vols. London 1894–96.
Hazlitt, W. C. (ed.), *Dictionary of Faiths and Folklore.* 2 vols. London 1905.
Hehn, J., *Hymnen und Gebete an Marduk.* Leipzig 1903.
Heidel, A., *The Babylonian Genesis.* Chicago 1940.
Hepding, H., *Attis.* Giessen 1903.
Hermann, K. F., *Lehrbuch der gottesdienstlichen Alterthümer der Griechen.* Second ed. Heidelberg 1858.
Hermann, P., *Nordische Mythologie.* Leipzig 1903.
Herodas, ed. Headlam-Knox. Cambridge 1922.

Herodoti Musae, ed. Schweighäuser. London 1830.
Hertel, J., *Die arische Feuerlehre.* IAQF, 6–7. Leipzig 1925–31.
Hilprecht Anniversary Volume: Studies in Assyriology and Archaeology. Leipzig 1909.
Hitti, K., *A Short History of the Arabs.* London 1940.
Hochmann, J., *Jerusalem Temple Festivities.* London 1908.
Hodson, T. C., *The Nága Tribes of Manipur.* London 1911.
Hodges, E. R. (ed.), *Cory's Ancient Fragments* . . . London 1876.
Höfler, M., *Volksmedizin und Aberglaube in Oberbayerns Gegenwart und Vergangenheit.* Second ed. Munich 1893.
Höfner, M., *Altsüdarabische Grammatik.* Leipzig 1943.
Höpfner, Th. (ed.), *Fontes historiae religionis aegyptiacae.* Bonn 1923–25.
Hole, Christina, *English Folklore.* London 1940.
Hollis, A. C., *The Nandi, their Language and Folklore.* Oxford 1909.
Holmberg, U., *Finno-Ugric Mythology.* Boston 1927.
Hone, W., *Ancient Mysteries Described, especially in English Miracle Plays* . . . London 1823.
————, *Every-Day Book.* London 1838.
Hooke, S. H. (ed.), *Myth and Ritual.* London 1933.
————, *The Labyrinth.* London 1935.
————, *The Origins of Early Semitic Ritual.* London 1938.
Horrack, J. de, *Les lamentations d'Isis et Nephthys.* Paris 1866.
Hose, C., and McDougall, W., *The Pagan Tribes of Borneo.* 2 vols. London 1912.
Hovorka, O. von, and Kronfeld, A., *Vergleichende Volksmedizin.* 2 vols. Stuttgart 1908–09.
Hrozný, F., *Sumerisch-babylonische Mythen von dem Gott Ninrag* (MVAG 8/5). Berlin 1903.
Hull, E. M., *Folklore of the British Isles.* London 1928.
Hurwitz, S., *The Responsa of Solomon Luria.* New York 1938.
Hutchinson, Wm., *A View of Northumberland.* 2 vols. Newcastle 1778.
Im Thurm, E. F., *Among the Indians of Guiana.* London 1883.
Inscriptiones Graecae Italiae et Siciliae, ed. G. Kaibel. Berlin 1890.
Irstam, Tor, *The King of Ganda: Studies in the Institutions of Sacral Kingship in Africa.* Stockholm 1944.
Jack, J. W., *The Ras Shamra Tablets.* Edinburgh 1935.
Jacobson, D., *The Social Background of the Old Testament.* Cincinnati 1942.
Jahnow, H., *Das hebräische Leichenlied im Rahmen der Völkerdichtung.* (Beih. ZAW, 36). Giessen 1923.
Jastrow. M., *Babylonian-Assyrian Birth-omens and their Cultural Significance.* Giessen 1914.
————, *Religion Babyloniens und Assyriens.* 2 vols. Giessen 1905–12.
Jaussen, J. A., *Coutumes des Arabes au pays de Moab.* Paris 1908.

Jean, C. F., *La religion sumérienne d'après les documents sumériens antérieurs à la dynastie d'Isin.* Paris 1931.
Jellinek, A., *Beth ha-Midrash.* 6 vols. Leipzig 1853–78.
Jensen, P., *Assyrisch-babylonische Mythen und Epen* (KB VI/i). Berlin 1900.
----, *Das Gilgamesch Epos in der Weltliteratur.* Strassburg-Leipzig 1906–24.
----, *Kosmologie der Babylonier.* Strasbourg 1890.
Jeremias, A., *Babylonisches im Neuen Testament.* Leipzig 1905.
----, *Handbuch der altorientalischen Geistesliteratur.* Leipzig 1936.
----, *The Old Testament in the Light of the Ancient East,* tr. C. L. Beaumont; ed. C. H. W. Johns. 2 vols. London 1911.
Johns, C. H. W., *Assyrian Deeds and Documents recording the transfer of property.* 3 vols. Cambridge 1890–1901.
Jühling, J., *Die Tiere in der deutschen Volksmedizin.* Mittweida [1900].
Junker, H., *Die Onurislegende.* Vienna 1917.
----, *Die Stundewachen in den Osirismysterien.* Vienna 1910.
Juvenalis Satirae, ed. J. E. B. Mayor. 2 vols. London 1872–78.
Kahle, P., *Palestinischer Diwan.* Leipzig 1901.
Keightley, T., *Tales and Popular Fictions.* London 1824.
Keith, A. B., *Indian Mythology.* Boston 1917.
Kennet, A., *Bedouin Justice: Laws and Customs among the Egyptian Bedouin.* Cambridge 1925.
Khunrath, H., *De igne magorum philosophorumque.* Strassburg 1608.
King, L. W., *Babylonian Magic and Sorcery.* London 1896.
----, *Chronicles concerning early Babylonian kings.* London 1907.
Kittel Festschrift: *Alttestamentliche Studien R. Kittel dargebracht. . . .* Leipzig 1913.
Klausen, R. H., *Aeneas und die Penaten.* 2 vols. Hamburg-Gotha 1839–40.
Knos, C., *Chrestomathia Syriaca.* Göttingen 1807.
Kramer, S. N., *Enki and Ninhursag* (BASOR Suppl. 1) New Haven 1945.
----, *Sumerian Mythology.* Philadelphia 1944.
Krappe, A. H., *Balor with the Evil Eye.* New York 1927.
Kroll, W., *Antiker Aberglaube.* Hamburg 1897.
Kügler, F. X., *Ergänzungen.* Münster 1935.
Kuper, Hilda, *Among the Swazi.* New York–London 1946.
Labat, R., *Le caractère religieux de la royauté assyro-babylonienne.* Paris 1939.
Lagarde, P. de, *Gesammelte Abhandlungen.* Leipzig 1866.
Landsberger, B., *Der kultische Kalender der Babylonier und Assyrer,* I. Leipzig 1915.
----, *Materialen zum sumerischen Lexicon.* Rome 1937.

Landtmann, G., *The Kiwai Papuans of British New Guinea.* London 1927.

Lane, E., *Manners and Customs of the Modern Egyptians.* Minerva Library ed. London 1890.

Langdon, S., *Babylonian Menologies and the Semitic Calendars.* London 1935.

----, *The Epic of Creation.* Oxford 1923.

----, *Semitic Mythology.* Boston 1931.

----, *Tablets from the Archives of Drehem . . .,* etc. Paris 1911.

----, *Tammuz and Ishtar.* Oxford 1914.

Langer, Susanne K., *Philosophy in a New Key.* New York (Pelican Books), 1948.

Langhe, R. de, *Les textes de Ras Shamra-Ugarit . . .,* etc. 2 vols. Paris 1945.

Larminie, W., *West Irish Folk-tales and Romances.* London 1893.

Laroche, E., *Recherches sur les noms des dieux hittites.* Paris 1947.

Lauha, A., *Zaphon: der Norden und die Nordvölker im AT.* Helsinki 1943.

Layard, A. H., *Monuments of Nineveh.* London 1853.

Leather, E. M., *The Folklore of Herefordshire.* Hereford 1912.

Lefébure, G., *Le mythe osirien, II: Osiris.* Paris 1875.

Lehmann-Haas, *Textbuch zur Religionsgeschichte.* Leipzig-Erlangen 1922.

Leslie, D., *Among the Zulus and Amatongas.* Edinburgh 1875.

Lewy, H., *Semitische Fremdwörter im Griechen.* Berlin 1895.

Lichtenstein, H., *Travels in Southern Africa.* London 1812–15.

Lidzbarski, M., *Ephemeris für Semitische Epigraphik.* 3 vols. Giessen 1902–15.

Littmann, E., *Publications of the Princeton Expedition to Abyssinia,* II. Leyden 1910.

Lobeck, C. A., *Aglaophanus.* 2 vols. Königsberg 1829.

Lods, A., *Israël.* Paris 1930.

Löw, L., *Gesammelte Schriften,* ed. I. Löw. 3 vols. Szegedin 1889–93.

Macalister, R. A. S., *The Philistines.* London 1914.

Macdonell, A. A., *Vedic Mythology.* Strassburg 1897.

Mackenzie, D. R., *The Spirit-Ridden Konde.* London 1925.

Macpherson, S. C., *Memorials of Service in India.* London 1865.

Mahler Festschrift. Budapest 1937.

Malinowski, B., *Magic, Science and Religion, and other essays,* ed. R. Redfield. Boston-Glencoe 1948.

----, *Myth in Primitive Psychology.* London 1926.

Mannhardt, W., *Wald- und Feldkulte.* Second ed. 2 vols. Berlin 1904–05.

Margold, C. W., *Sex Freedom and Social Control.* Chicago 1926.

Marquardt, K. J., *Römische Staatsverwaltung.* Leipzig ^{1}1873; ^{2}1881–83.

Maschke, E., *Sachsen-Märchen aus Siebenbürgen.* Potsdam 1925.

Maspero, G., *Contes populaires de l'Égypte ancienne.* Paris 1882.

----, *Histoire ancienne des peuples de l'orient classique.* 3 vols. Paris 1895–99.

McCulloch J., *Celtic Mythology.* Boston 1918.

Meier, G., *Die assyrische Beschwörungsammlung Maqlû* (AfO, Beiheft 2). Berlin 1937.

Meissner, B., *Altorientalische Texte und Untersuchungen.* Vol. I. Leiden 1916–17.

----, *Babylonien und Assyrien.* 2 vols. Heidelberg 1920–25.

----, *Beiträge zum altbab. Privatrecht.* Leipzig 1893.

Mélanges Boissier. Paris 1903.

Mélanges de linguistique offerts à M. Holger Pedersen . . . Copenhagen 1937.

Mellink, M. J., *Hyakinthos* (Diss.). Utrecht 1943.

Mémoires de la mission archéologique en Perse. 27 vols. Paris 1900–35.

Merker, M., *Die Masai.* Berlin 1904.

Merry, W. W. (ed.), *Odyssey.* Oxford 1876.

Meyer, E. H., *Mythologie der Germanen.* Strassburg 1903.

Meyer, G. F., *Tiermärchen.* Garding 1916.

Meyer, R. M., *Altgermanische Religionsgeschichte.* Leipzig 1910.

Midrash Rabbah, ed. I. Rubinstein. 5 vols. Warsaw 1924.

Montet, P., *Les scènes de la vie privée de l'ancien empire.* Paris 1925.

Moret, A., *Du caractère religieux de la royauté pharaonique.* Paris 1902.

----, *La mise à mort du dieu en Égypte.* Paris 1927.

----, *L'Égypte pharaonique.* Paris 1932.

----, *Mystères égyptiens.* Paris 1913.

----, *Rois et dieux d'Égypte.* Paris 1922.

Moulton, J. H., *Two Lectures on the Science of Language.* Cambridge 1903.

Movers, F. C., *Die Phönizier.* 3 vols. Bonn 1841–56.

Mowinckel, S., *Psalmenstudien,* II. Christiania 1922.

Mueller, E., *A History of Jewish Mysticism.* Oxford 1946.

Müller, J. G., *Amerikanische Urreligion.* Basel 1853.

Müller, K. O., *Kleine Schriften.* Berlin 1848.

Müller, R., *Die Zahl Drei in Sage, Dichtung und Kunst.* Teschen 1903.

Müller, W. Max, *Egyptian Mythology.* Boston 1918.

Mullo-Weir, C. J., *A Lexicon of Accadian Prayers in the Rituals of Expiation.* Oxford 1934.

Munch, P. A., *Norse Mythology.* New York 1926.

Murray, Gilbert, *Euripides and his Age.* London, n.d.

----, *The Rise of the Greek Epic.* Oxford 1907.

Musil, A., *Arabia Petraea.* Vienna 1908.

Myhrman, D. W., *Babylonian Hymns and Prayers.* Philadelphia 1911.

Naogeorgus, Th., *The Popish Kingdome,* tr. B. Goodge, ed. R. C. Hope. London 1880.
Naumann, H., *Grundzüge der deutschen Volkskunde.* Second ed. Leipzig 1929.
Naville, E., *Textes relatifs au Mythe d'Horus recueillis dans le Temple d'Edfou.* Geneva-Basle 1870.
————, *The Festival Hall of Osorkon.* London 1892 ff.
Nielsen, D., *Ras-Schamra Mythologie und Biblische Theologie.* Leipzig 1936.
Nilsson, M., *Griechische Feste von religiöser Bedeutung.* Leipzig 1906.
————, *Primitive Time-Reckoning.* Lund 1920.
Nöldeke, Th., *Neue Beiträge zur semitischen Sprachwissenschaft.* Strassburg 1910.
Nöldeke Festschrift: *Orientalische Studien Th. Nöldeke zum 70ten Geburtstag gewidmet,* ed. C. Bezold. 2 vols. Giessen 1906.
Norden, E., *Die Geburt des Kindes.* Leipzig-Berlin 1924.
Nore, A., *Coutumes, mythes et traditions des provinces de France.* Paris-Lyon 1846.
Oesterley, W. O. E., *The Doctrine of the Last Things.* London 1908.
————, *The Sacred Dance.* New York 1923.
Oldenberg, H., *Die Religion des Veda.* Berlin 1894.
Otten, H., *Die Überliefrungen des Telipinu-Mythus* (MVAG 46.1). Leipzig 1942.
Pallis, S. A., *The Babylonian Akîtu Festival.* Copenhagen 1926.
Panzer, F., *Bayerische Sagen und Bräuche.* Munich 1848 ff.
Pap, L. I., *Das israelitische Neujahrsfest.* Kampen 1933.
Patai, R., *Man and Temple in Ancient Jewish Myth and Ritual.* London 1947.
Patton, J., *Canaanite Parallels to the Book of Psalms.* Baltimore 1944.
Payne, E. J., *History of the New World called America.* Oxford 1892.
Pedersen, J., *Israel.* 2 vols. London-Copenhagen 1926–46.
Pennant, Thos., "A Tour in Scotland and the Hebrides in 1722," in Pinkerton, J., *General Collection of Voyages and Travels,* London 1808–14, vol. iii.
P^e^siqta d^e^ Rab Kahana, ed. S. Buber. Lyck 1868.
Peters, J. P., *The Psalms as Liturgies.* New York 1922.
Pfeiffer, R., *The State Letters of Assyria.* New Haven 1935.
Phillimore, J. G. (ed.), *The Hundred Best Latin Hymns.* London-Glasgow 1926.
Picard, Ch., *Les religions préhelleniques.* Paris 1948.
Pitré, G., *Feste patronali in Sicilia.* Turin-Palermo 1900.
Plassmann, Th., *The Significance of beraka.* Paris 1913.
Playfair, A., *The Garos.* London 1909.
Plessis, J., *Étude sur les textes concernant Ištar-Astarte.* Paris 1921.

Pleyte, W., and Rossi, F., *Les papyrus . . . de Turin*. Leyden 1869–76.

Preisendanz, K., *Akephalos, der kopflosige Gott*. Leipzig 1926.

Preller, L., *Griechische Mythologie*. Fourth ed. (ed. Robert). Berlin 1894.

----, *Römische Mythologie*. Third ed. Berlin 1881–83.

Prescott, W. H., *History of the Conquest of Peru*. 1890.

Pritchard, J., *Palestinian Figurines in relation to certain Goddesses known through Literature*. New Haven 1944.

Proksch, O., *Über die Blutrache bei den vorislamischen Arabern*. Leipzig 1899.

Ralston, W. R. S., *Songs of the Russian People*. London 1872.

Ramsay, W. M., *Asianic Elements in Greek Civilization*. Second ed. London 1928.

Ranke, H., Early *Babylonian Personal Names* . . . Philadelphia 1905.

Rankin, O. S., *The Origin of the Festival of Hanukkah*. Edinburgh 1930.

Redfield, R., *Tepoztlan*. Chicago 1930.

Reisner, G., *Sumerisch-babyl. Hymnen aus Tontafeln Griechischer Zeit*. Berlin 1896.

Renz, B., *Der orientalische Schlangendrache*. Augsburg 1930.

Rhodokanakis, N., *Katabanische Texte zur Bodenwirtschaft*. (SBWA, Phil.-hist. Kl., 194, 198). 2 vols. Vienna 1919–22.

Rhys, J., *Celtic Heathendom*. London-Edinburgh 1888.

Reidel, J. G. F., "Galela und Tobeloresen," in *Zeits. f. Ethnologie* 17 (1885). 58–87.

Richard, M., *Altgermanische Religionsgeschichte*. Leipzig 1910.

Richter, O., *Kypros, die Bibel und Homer*. 2 vols. Berlin 1893.

Ridgeway, Wm., *Essays and Studies presented to*, ed. E. C. Quiggin. Cambridge 1913.

Rodd, F. J. Rennel, *People of the Veil*. London 1926.

Roeder, G., *Urkunden zur Religion des alten Aegyptens*. Jena 1923.

Roger, E., *La terre saincte*. Paris 1664.

Rohde, E., *Psyche*. Second ed. Tübingen-Leipzig 1897.

Roscher, W., *Nektar und Ambrosia*. Leipzig 1883.

----, *Omphalos*. Leipzig 1913.

Ross, J., *History of Corea*. Paisley 1897.

Rossini, Conti, *Chrestomathia arabica meridionalis epigraphica*. Rome 1931.

Ruffini, E., *Il mito babilonese del dragone e la Sacra Scrittura*. Rome 1923.

Sahagun, B. de, *Histoire générale des choses de la Nouvelle Empire*, tr. D. Jourdanet et R. Simon. Paris 1880.

Saintyves, P., *Essais de folklore biblique*. Paris 1923.

Sanchoniathonis Beryti quae feruntur fragmenta, ed. J. G. Orelli. Leipzig 1826.

Sandman Halmberg, M., *The God Ptah.* Lund 1946.

Sartori, F., *Neueste Reise durch Oestreich.* Vienna 1841.

Sartori, P., *Sitte und Brauch.* 3 vols. Leipzig 1910–14.

Saussaye, de la, P. de Chantepie, *The Religion of the Teutons.* Boston 1902.

Schaeffer, C. F. A., *The Cuneiform Texts from Ras Shamra-Ugarit.* London 1936.

Schaeffer, H., *Die Mysterien des Osiris in Abydos.* Leipzig 1904.

Schauss, H., *The Jewish Festivals.* Cincinnati 1928.

Scheftelowitz, I., *Altpalästinensischer Bauernglaube.* Hannover 1925.

————, *Die altpersische Religion und das Judenthum.* Giessen 1920.

Schiaparelli, *Il libro dei funeri dei antichi Egiziani.* 2 vols. Turin 1882.

Schlobies, H., *Der akkadische Wettergott in Mesopotamien.* Leipzig 1925.

Schmidt, B., *Das Volksleben der Neugriechen.* Leipzig 1871.

Schmidt, H., *Die Psalmen.* Tübingen 1934.

————, *Die Thronfahrt Jahwes am Fest der Jahreswende im alten Israel.* Tübingen 1927.

Schott, W., *De lingua Tschuwaschorum.* Berlin [1841].

Schulze, L., *Aus Namaland und Kalahari.* Jena 1907.

Schultens, A., *Liber Jobi cum nova versione . . . et commentario perpetuo.* 2 vols. Leyden 1737.

Schwally, F., *Idioticon des christlichen palästinischen Aramäisch.* Giessen, 1903.

————, *Semitische Kriegsaltertümer,* I. Leipzig 1901.

Schwenk, K. *Die Mythologie der Slawen.* Frankfurt 1853.

Scott, J. G., *Indo-Chinese Mythology.* Boston 1918.

Sébillot, P., *Contes des provinces de France.* Paris 1884.

————, *Le folklore de France.* 4 vols. Paris 1904–07.

Seler, E. (ed.), *Sahagun, Historia generale de las cosas de Nueva España.* Stuttgart 1927.

Seligman, C. G., *The Melanesians of British New Guinea.* Cambridge 1910.

————, *Races of Africa.* London 1930.

Sethe, K., *Altaegyptische Pyramiden-texte,* II. Leipzig 1910.

————, *Dramatische Texte zu altaegyptischen Mysterienspielen I–II.* Leipzig 1928.

————, *Untersuchungen zur Geschichte und Altertumskunde Aegyptens,* III. Berlin 1905.

Shooter, J., *The Kaffirs of Natal and the Zulu Country.* London 1857.

Siecke, E., *Drachenkämpfe. Untersuchungen zur indogermanischen Sagenkunde.* Leipzig 1907.

Sklarek. E., *Ungarische Volksmärchen,* 1–2. Leipzig 1901 ff.

Smith, G., and Sayce, A. H., *The Chaldean Genesis.* London 1880.

Smith, G. A., *The Book of the Twelve Prophets.* 2 vols. New York 1944.
----, *The Historical Geography of the Holy Land.*
Smith, J. M. P., *The Origin and History of Hebrew Law.* Chicago 1931.
Smith, S. A., *Die Keilschrifttexte Asshurbanipals,* II. Leipzig 1887.
Smith, S., *Isaiah, Chapters XL–LV.* London 1944.
Smith, W. Robertson, *Kinship and Marriage in Early Arabia.* Second edition. London 1903.
----, *Lectures and Essays.* London 1912.
----, *Religion of the Semites.* Third ed. London 1927.
Smythe-Palmer, A., *Babylonian Influence in the Bible and Popular Beliefs: Hades and Satan.* London 1897.
----, *Jacob at Bethel.* London 1899.
Snaith, N. H., *The Jewish New Year Festival.* London 1947.
Snouck Hurgronje, C., *Mekka.* 2 vols. The Hague 1888–89.
Sommer, F., *Ahijava-Urkunden* (AAWB). Munich 1932.
----, *Die heth.-akkad. Bilingue des Hattusilis I.* Munich 1938.
Spanheim, E., *In Callimachi Hymnos Observationes.* Utrecht 1697.
Speiser, E. A., *Mesopotamian Origins.* London 1930.
Spence, L., *An Introduction to Mythology.* New York 1921.
----, *Myth and Ritual in Dance, Games and Rhyme.* London 1947.
----, *The Mythologies of Mexico and Peru.* London 1907.
Spencer, J., *De legibus Hebraeorum ritualibus et earum rationibus.* Hague-Comitum 1686.
Spencer, W. B., and Gillen, F. J., *The Native Tribes of Central Australia.* London 1899.
Sproat, G. M., *Scenes and Studies in Savage Life.* London 1868.
Stammer, *De Lino.* Bonn 1855.
Stengel, P., *Opferbräuche der Griechen.* Leipzig-Berlin 1910.
Strackerjan, L., *Aberglaube und Sagen aus dem Herzogtum Oldenburg.* Oldenburg [1]1867; [2]1909.
Streck, M., *Assurbanipal und die letzten assyrischen Könige bis zum Untergang Ninevehs.* 3 vols. Leipzig 1916.
Streitberg Festgabe. Leipzig 1924.
Strong, H. A., and Garstang, J., *The Syrian Goddess.* London 1913.
Stucken, E., *Astralmythen.* Leipzig 1907.
Stummer, F., *Sumerisch-akkadische Parallelen zum Aufbau alttestamentl. Psalme.* Paderborn 1922.
Suchier, *Orion der Jäger.* Hanau 1859.
Sundwall, J., *Die einheimischen Namen der Lykier.* (*Klio,* Beiheft 11). Berlin 1913.
Sykes, A. A., *Nature, Design and Origin of Sacrifices.* [London?] 1748.

Talbot, D. Amaury (Mrs.), *Women's Mysteries of a Primitive People*. London 1915.
Tallquist, K., *Akkadische Götterepitheta*. Helsingfors 1938.
———, *Namen der Totenwelt* . . . Helsingfors 1934.
Thackeray, H. St. John, *The Septuagint in Jewish Worship*. London 1921.
Thistleton-Dyer, T. F., *British Popular Customs*. London 1876.
Thompson, C. J. S., *The Hand of Destiny*. London 1932
Thompson, R. C., *The Chemistry of the Ancient Assyrians*. London 1925.
———, *The Devils and Evil Spirits of Babylonia*. 2 vols. London 1904.
———, *Reports of the Magicians and Astrologers of Nineveh and Babylon*. London 1900.
———, *Semitic Magic*. London 1908.
Thompson, J., *Through Masai Land*. London 1887.
Thorpe, B. (ed.), *Ancient Laws and Institutes of England*. London 1840.
Thureau-Dangin, F., *Rituels accadiens*. Paris 1921.
———, *Une relation de la huitième campagne de Sargon*. Paris 1912.
Thurston, E., *Omens and Superstitions of Southern India*. London 1912.
Tiddy, R. J. E., *The Mummers' Play*. Oxford 1923.
Toland, J., *History of the Druids*. London 1726.
Trachtenberg, J., *Jewish Magic and Superstition*. New York 1939.
Turner, G., *Samoa a Hundred Years ago and long before*. London 1884.
Tylor, E. B., *Primitive Culture*. Third ed. London 1891.
Urlin, Ethel, *Festivals, Holidays and Saints' Days*. London 1915.
Usener, H., *Götternamen*. Bonn 1929.
van Gennep, A., *Religions, moeurs et légendes*. 5 vols. Paris 1908–21.
Vernalken, Th., *Mythen und Bräuche des Volkes in Osterreich*. Vienna 1859.
Vogelstein, H., *Die Landwirtschaft in Palästina zur Zeit der Mišnah*. Berlin 1894.
Volz, P., *Das Neujahrsfest Jahwes* (*Laubhüttenfest*). Tübingen 1912.
Von Schroeder, L., *Mysterium und Mimus*. Leipzig 1908.
Vries, J. de, *Typen-register der Indonesische Fabels en Sprokjes*, No. 32 (Volkshalen vit Oostindie, ii 398 ff.). Zutphen 1926.
Walsh, W. S., *Curiosities of Popular Customs*. Philadelphia 1898.
Ward, W. Hayes, *Seal Cylinders of Western Asia*. Washington 1910.
Webster, W., *Basque Legends*. London 1859.
Weekes, J. H., *Among the Primitive Bakongo*. London 1914.
Wehrahn, K., *Die Sage*. Leipzig 1908.

Weidner, E. F., *Politische Dokumente aus Kleinasien. Die Staatsverträge in akkadischer Sprache aus dem Archiv von Boghazköi.* (BoSt. 8–9.) Leipzig 1923.
----, *Handbuch z. bab. Astronomie.* Leipzig 1915.
Weiss, I., *Dôr* (Hebrew). 5 vols. Vienna-Pressburg, 1871–91.
Welcker, F. G., *Griechische Götterlehre.* 3 vols. Göttingen 1857–62.
----, *Schriften.* Bonn 1844–47.
Wellhausen, J., *Reste des arabischen Heidentums.* Second ed. Berlin 1897.
Wensinck, A. J., *The Ideas of the Western Semites concerning the Navel of the Earth.* Amsterdam 1916.
----, *The Ocean in the Literature of the Western Semites.* Amsterdam 1918.
----, *Some Semitic Rites of Mourning and Religion.* Amsterdam 1917.
Westermarck, E., *A Short History of Marriage.* London 1926.
----, *Pagan Survivals in Mohammedan Civilization.* London 1933.
----, *The Goodness of Gods.* London 1926.
Weston, Jesse L., *From Ritual to Romance.* Cambridge 1930.
Widengren, G., *Psalm 110 och det sakrala Kungdaömet i Israel.* Uppsala 1941.
Wiedemann, A., *Herodots zweites Buch.* Leipzig 1890.
Wilamowitz-Moellendorf, U. von, *Ilias und Homer.* Second edition. Berlin 1920.
Williams, T., and Calvert, J., *Fiji and the Fijians.* 2 vols. London 1858.
Winckler, H., *Altorientalische Forschungen.* Ser. I–III. Leipzig 1893–1907.
Winnington-Ingram, R. P., *Euripides and Dionysus.* Cambridge 1948.
Winstedt, R. O., *Shama, Saiva and Sufi.* London 1925.
Wissowa, G., *Religion und Kultus der Römer.* Second ed. Munich 1912.
Witzel, M., *Der Drachenkämpfer Ninib.* Fulda 1920.
Wolf, W., *Das schöne Fest von Opet.* Leipzig 1931.
Wright, A. R., *English Folklore.* Benn's Sixpenny Library, No. 33. London 1928.
Wuensch, R., *Das Frühlingsfest der Insel Malta.* Leipzig 1902.
Yearsley, M., *The Folklore of Fairy Tale.* London 1924.
Zimmern, H., *Beiträge zur Kenntniss der babylonischen Religion.* II. Leipzig 1901.
----, *Christusmyth.* Berlin 1910.
----, *Das babylonische Neujahrsfest.* (AO 25.3). Leipzig 1926.
----, "Der babylonische Gott Tamuz," in ASGW 27. Leipzig 1909.
Zunz, L., *Gesammelte Schriften.* Berlin 1875.

ABBREVIATIONS

AAA	Annals of Archaeology and Anthropology
AB	The Ugaritic Poem of Baal, according to Virolleaud's numeration of the tablets
ABAW	Abhandlungen der Bayerischen Akademie der Wissenschaften
ABSA	Annual of the British School of Archaeology at Athens
AcOr	Acta Orientalia
AfO	Archiv für Orientforschung
AHS	Friedrich, J., Aus dem hethitischen Schrifttum. (Der Alte Orient 24/3, 25/2.) 2 parts. Leipzig 1925
AlM	Al-Machriq
AJA	American Journal of Archaeology
AJSL	American Journal of Semitic Languages and Literatures
AJV	[American Jewish Version.] The Holy Scriptures according to the Masoretic Text: A New Translation. Philadelphia 1917
AKRS	Bauer, Hans. Die alphabetischen Keilschrifttexte von Ras Schamra. (Kleine Texte für Vorlesungen und Übungen, No. 168.) Berlin 1936
ANET	Ancient Near Eastern Texts relating to the Old Testament, ed. James B. Pritchard. Princeton 1955.
AOr	Archiv Orientální
AP	Anthologia Palatina
APO	Ungnad, A., Aramäische Papyrus aus Elephantine. Leipzig 1911
Aq	The Ugaritic Poem of Aqhat
AR	Breasted, J. H., Ancient Records of Egypt. 5 vols. Chicago 1906
ARAB	Luckenbill, D. D., Ancient Records of Assyria and Babylonia. 2 vols. Chicago 1926–27
ARW	Archiv für Religionswissenschaft
ASGW	Abhandlungen der Sächsischen Gesellschaft der Wissenschaften, Phil.-hist. Klasse
BA	Beiträge zur Assyriologie
Baal	The Ugaritic Poem of Baal
BASOR	Bulletin of the American Schools of Oriental Research
BCH	Bulletin de correspondance hellénique

BD	The Egyptian Book of the Dead
BJPES	Bulletin of the Jewish Palestine Exploration Society
BM	British Museum
BO	Bibliotheca Orientalis
BoSt	Boghazköi-Studien. Leipzig 1917–24
BSGW	Berichte über die Verhandlungen der philologisch-historischen Klasse der königl. Sächsischen Gesellschaft der Wissenschaften
CGF	Fragmenta Comicorum Graecorum, ed. A. Meineke. 4 vols. Berlin 1839–41
CIA	Corpus Inscriptionum Atticarum
CIH	Corpus Inscriptionum Himjariticarum = CIS iv
CIL	Corpus Inscriptionum Latinarum
CIS	Corpus Inscriptionum Semiticarum
CJ	Classical Journal
CQ	Classical Quarterly
CR	Classical Review
CRAIBL	Comptes Rendus, Académie des Inscriptions et Belles Lettres, Paris
CSCP	Cornell Studies in Classical Philology
CT	Cuneiform Texts from Babylonian Tablets, etc. in the British Museum
DT	Tablets of the *Daily Telegraph* Collection in the British Museum
EA	Die El-Anarna Tafeln, ed. J. A. Knudzton. Leipzig 1915
EBi	Encyclopaedia Biblica. 4 vols. London 1889–1903
EE	*Enuma Elish*
EG	Epigrammata Graeca ex lapidibus collecta, ed. G. Kaibel. Berlin 1878
EJ	Nebuchadnezzar, East India House Inscription
EM	Etymologicon Magnum
ERE	Encyclopaedia of Religion and Ethics
ET	The Expository Times
EV	English Version (AV, RV) of the Bible
FHG	Fragmenta Historicorum Graecorum, ed. K. Müller. Paris 1868–83
FL	Folk-Lore
GB	Frazer, J. G., The Golden Bough. Third edition. 12 vols. New York 1935
GGA	Göttingische gelehrte Anzeigen
HTBM	Hittite Texts in the Cuneiform Character from Tablets in the British Museum. London 1920.
HTR	Harvard Theological Review
HUCA	Hebrew Union College Annual. Cincinnati
ICC	International Critical Commentary
ILN	The Illustrated London News
IQF	Indo-iranische Quellen und Forschungen

ISA	Thureau-Dangin, F., Die Sumerischen und Akkadischen Königsinschriften. (Vorderasiatische Bibliothek, I, 1). Leipzig 1907
JA	Journal asiatique
JAI	Journal of the [Royal] Anthropological Institute of Great Britain and Ireland
JAOS	Journal of the American Oriental Society
JBL	Journal of Biblical Literature and Exegesis
JCS	Journal of Cuneiform Studies
JEA	Journal of Egyptian Archaeology
JEOB	Journal of Egyptian and Oriental Bibliography
JEOL	Journal of Egyptian and Oriental Literature
JHS	Journal of Hellenic Studies
JMEOS	Journal of the Manchester Egyptian and Oriental Society
JNES	Journal of Near Eastern Studies
JPOS	Journal of the Palestine Oriental Society
JQR	The Jewish Quarterly Review
JRAS	Journal of the Royal Asiatic Society of Great Britain and Ireland
JSOR	Journal of the Society for Oriental Research
JTS	Journal of Theological Studies
JTVI	Journal of Transactions of the Victoria Institute [London]
KARI	Keilschrifttexte aus Assur religiösen Inhalts, ed. E. Ebeling. Leipzig 1919–
KAT	Die Keilinschriften und das Alte Testament. Third ed. Ed. H. Zimmern and H. Winckler. Berlin 1903
KAVI	Keilschrifttexte aus Assur verschiedenen Inhalts, ed. O. Schroeder. Leipzig 1920
KB	Keilinschriftliche Bibliothek, ed. E. Schrader. 6 vols. Berlin 1889–1915
KBo	Keilschrifttexte aus Boghazköi
KlF	Kleinasiatische Forschungen
KUB	Keilschrifturkunden aus Boghazköi
LXX	Septuagint (Greek) Version of the Old Testament
MDOG	Mitteilungen der Deutschen Orientalischen Gesellschaft
MGWJ	Monatsschrift für Geschichte und Wissenschaft des Judentums
MI	Thompson, Stith, Motif-Index to Folk Literature (FF Communications, 106–09, 116–17; Indiana University Studies, 106–12). 6 vols. Helsinki-Bloomington 1932–36.
MNB	Monuments de Ninive et de Babylone, Louvre
MR	Midrash Rabbâ
MT (or M)	Masoretic Text

MVAG	Mitteilungen der Vorderasiatisch-Aegyptischen Gesellschaft
NH	Neo-Hebrew
NTT	Nieuw Theologisch Tijdschrift
OECT	Oxford Editions of Cuneiform Texts, ed. S. Langdon
OIC	Oriental Institute Communications, Chicago
OLZ	Orientalistische Literaturzeitung
OT	Old Testament
PBS	Publications of the Babylonian Section of the University Museum, Philadelphia
PEFQS	Quarterly Statement of the Palestine Exploration Fund
PEQ	Palestine Exploration Quarterly
PQ	The Philological Quarterly
PRK	P^{e}siqtâ d^e Rab Kahana, ed. S. Buber. Lyck 1868
PS	Proto-Semitic
PSBA	Proceedings of the Society of Biblical Archaeology
PW	Pauly-Wissowa-Kroll, Realencyclopädie der klassischen Altertumswissenschaft
I, II, III, IV, V R	Rawlinson, H. C., The Cuneiform Inscriptions of Western Asia. London 1861–64
RA	Revue d'assyriologie et d'archéologie orientale
Ram.	The Ramesseum Dramatic Papyrus
RB	Revue biblique
RC	Revue celtique
RÉJ	Revue des études juives
RÉS	Répertoire d'épigraphie sémitique. Paris 1900–
RG	Revue des études grecques
RHA	Revue hittite et asianique
RHR	Revue de l'histoire des religions
RIA^2	Reallexicon der indogermanischen Altertumskunde. Second ed. Leipzig 1929
RR	Review of Religion
RŠ	Ras Shamra text
RSR	Revue des sciences religieuses
RV	Revised Version of the Bible
SAJC	South African Journal of Science
SBAW	Sitzungsberichte der Bayerischen Akademie der Wissenschaften, phil.-hist. Klasse
SBE	Sacred Books of the East
SMSR	Studi e materiali di storia delle religioni
SPAW	Sitzungsberichte der Preussischen Akademie der Wissenschaften, phil.-hist. Klasse
SRT	Sumerian Religious Texts, ed. E. Chiera. Crozer Theological Seminary, Upland, Pa., 1929
TAPS	Transactions of the American Philosophical Society
TB	Babylonian Talmud

TC	Textes cappadociennes. Musée du Louvre. 3 vols. Paris 1920–37
TJ	Jerusalemitan Talmud
TSBA	Transactions of the Society of Biblical Archaeology
TT	Theologisch Tijdschrift
UH	Gordon, C. H., Ugaritic Handbook. Rome 1947
UISLL	University of Illinois Studies in Language and Literature
UJE	The Universal Jewish Encyclopedia
UT	Ginsberg, H. L., Ugarit Texts. Jerusalem 1936 (Hebrew)
VAB	Vorderasiatische Bibliothek, ed. H. Winckler and A. Jeremias
VAT	Staatliche Museen zu Berlin, Vorderasiatische Abtheilung. Tontafeln
WZKM	Wiener Zeitschrift für die Kunde des Morgenlandes
ZA	Zeitschrift für Assyriologie und verwandte Gebiete
ZÄS	Zeitschrift für ägyptische Sprache
ZAW	Zeitschrift für die alttestamentliche Wissenschaft
ZE	Zeitschrift für Ethnologie
ZDMG	Zeitschrift der Deutschen Morgenländischen Gesellschaft
ZKM	Zeitschrift für Kunde des Morgenlandes
ZNTW	Zeitschrift für die neutestamentliche Wissenschaft

GENERAL INDEXES

INDEX OF MOTIFS *with Cross Index*

Numbers in brackets refer to the standard classification in Stith Thompson's *Motif-Index of Folk-Literature.*

Altar, as refuge [R 325], 366
Angels, entertained unawares, 435
Aquila, constellation, 354
Aroma of gods, 236, 384, 392

Banishment [Q 431], 365 f.
Banquet, foes lured to [K 811.1], 259
Bee, sting of, cures paralysis, 304
Blood renders soil infertile, 357

Cerberus [A 673], 239
Child born in answer to prayer [T 548.1], 330 f.
——— of supernatural birth exposed [S 313], 432
Cudgel, magic [D 1094], 166

Dawn, god of [A 270], 411
Dionysus, dismembered [V 63], 420
Dismemberment, rejuvenation after [D 1884], 325, 362
Dog with fiery eyes or body [B 15.4.2], 239
——— of netherworld [A 673], 239
Dragon [B 11], 137–71
———, fettered [A 1071], 170, 259
———, fight against [B 11.11], 137 f., 257 ff.
———, humans sacrificed to [B 11.10], 189
———, seven-headed [B 11.2.3.1], 450

Eclipse caused by monster [A 737.1], 228
Eagle, as thunder-bird [A 284.2], 168
———, constellation. *See* Aquila
Earth, goddess of [A 401], 134 n.49
———, rendered infertile by bloodshed. *See* Blood
Eyes torn out but replaced [E 781.2], 264 f.

Fate, book (tablets) of, 288
Fates, the [A 463.1], 288
Fettering of monster [A 1071], 260
Fisherman, divine, 162
Food of otherworld. *See* Taboo
Frost-spirit [A 289.1], 283 f.

Gargantuan appetite, 432
Giant with lower lip reaching earth [F 531.1.4.1], 207
Giants (rebels) imprisoned in netherworld [Q 433.2], 170
God, of dawn [A 270], 411
———, of lightning [A 285], 238
———, of moon [A 240], 351
———, of netherworld [A 300], 155
———, of rain [A 287], 124
———, of sea [A 421], 125
———, of sky [A 210], 124 f.
———, of water [A 420], 125
———, smith [A 451.1], 162
Goddess, of earth [A 401], 134 n.49
———, of sun [A 221], 47, 127, 227
———, of warfare [A 485.1], 156
Gods, aroma of. *See* Aroma
———, conflicts of [A 162], 116 ff., 126
———, garden of [A 151.2], 183
———, home of, on high mountain [A 151.1], 181 f.
——— intervene in battle [A 172], 289 f.
———, messengers of [A 165.1], 157

Hammer of thunder-god, 155

CROSS INDEX

INDEX OF SUBJECTS AND AUTHORS

This Index is not a concordance. It seeks to cover the principal themes and topics discussed in this volume, but it does *not* catalogue all of the references to ancient and modern literature given in the footnotes. Authors are listed only in cases where their views are expressly discussed or constitute the sole authority for a conclusion advanced.

Semitic words beginning with ʿ are listed as though they began with *d*.

BIBLICAL PASSAGES*

* According to the order and numeration of the *Hebrew* Bible.

70 71 72 73 12 11 10 9 8 7 6 5 4 3 2

Revised January, 1970

harper torchbooks

American Studies: General

CARL N. DEGLER: Out of Our Past: *The Forces that Shaped Modern America* CN/2
ROBERT L. HEILBRONER: The Limits of American Capitalism TB/1305
JOHN HIGHAM, Ed.: The Reconstruction of American History TB/1068
JOHN F. KENNEDY: A Nation of Immigrants. *Illus. Revised and Enlarged. Introduction by Robert F. Kennedy* TB/1118
GUNNAR MYDRAL: An American Dilemma: *The Negro Problem and Modern Democracy. Introduction by the Author.* Vol. I TB/1443; Vol. II TB/1444
GILBERT OSOFSKY, Ed.: The Burden of Race: *A Documentary History of Negro-White Relations in America* TB/1405
ARNOLD ROSE: The Negro in America: *The Condensed Version of Gunnar Mydral's* An American Dilemma TB/3048

American Studies: Colonial

BERNARD BAILYN: The New England Merchants in the Seventeenth Century TB/1149
ROBERT E. BROWN: Middle-Class Democracy and Revolution in Massachusetts, 1691–1780. *New Introduction by Author* TB/1413
JOSEPH CHARLES: The Origins of the American Party System TB/1049

American Studies: The Revolution to 1900

GEORGE M. FREDRICKSON: The Inner Civil War: *Northern Intellectuals and the Crisis of the Union* TB/1358
WILLIAM W. FREEHLING: Prelude to Civil War: *The Nullification Controversy in South Carolina, 1816-1836* TB/1359
HELEN HUNT JACKSON: A Century of Dishonor: *The Early Crusade for Indian Reform.* ‡ *Edited by Andrew F. Rolle* TB/3063
RICHARD B. MORRIS, Ed.: Alexander Hamilton and the Founding of the Nation. *New Introduction by the Editor* TB/1448
RICHARD B. MORRIS: The American Revolution Reconsidered TB/1363
GILBERT OSOFSKY, Ed.: Puttin' On Ole Massa: *The Slave Narratives of Henry Bibb, William Wells Brown, and Solomon Northup* ‡ TB/1432

American Studies: The Twentieth Century

WILLIAM E. LEUCHTENBURG: Franklin D. Roosevelt and the New Deal: 1932-1940. † *Illus.* TB/3025
WILLIAM E. LEUCHTENBURG, Ed.: The New Deal: *A Documentary History* ┼ HR/1354

Asian Studies

WOLFGANG FRANKE: China and the West: *The Cultural Encounter, 13th to 20th Centuries. Trans. by R. A. Wilson* TB/1326
L. CARRINGTON GOODRICH: A Short History of the Chinese People. *Illus.* TB/3015
BENJAMIN I. SCHWARTZ: Chinese Communism and the Rise of Mao TB/1308

Economics & Economic History

PETER F. DRUCKER: The New Society: *The Anatomy of Industrial Order* TB/1082
ROBERT L. HEILBRONER: The Great Ascent: *The Struggle for Economic Development in Our Time* TB/3030
W. ARTHUR LEWIS: The Principles of Economic Planning. *New Introduction by the Author*° TB/1436

Historiography and History of Ideas

J. BRONOWSKI & BRUCE MAZLISH: The Western Intellectual Tradition: *From Leonardo to Hegel* TB/3001
WILHELM DILTHEY: Pattern and Meaning in History: *Thoughts on History and Society.*° *Edited with an Intro. by H. P. Rickman* TB/1075
J. H. HEXTER: More's Utopia: *The Biography of an Idea. Epilogue by the Author* TB/1195
ARTHUR O. LOVEJOY: The Great Chain of Being: *A Study of the History of an Idea* TB/1009

History: Medieval

F. L. GANSHOF: Feudalism TB/1058
DENYS HAY: The Medieval Centuries ° TB/1192
HENRY CHARLES LEA: A History of the Inquisition of the Middle Ages. || *Introduction by Walter Ullmann* TB/1456

† The New American Nation Series, edited by Henry Steele Commager and Richard B. Morris.
‡ American Perspectives series, edited by Bernard Wishy and William E. Leuchtenburg.
a History of Europe series, edited by J. H. Plumb.
§ The Library of Religion and Culture, edited by Benjamin Nelson.
|| Researches in the Social, Cultural, and Behavioral Sciences, edited by Benjamin Nelson.
Σ Harper Modern Science Series, edited by James R. Newman.
° Not for sale in Canada.
┼ Documentary History of the United States series, edited by Richard B. Morris.
Documentary History of Western Civilization series, edited by Eugene C. Black and Leonard W. Levy.
^ The Economic History of the United States series, edited by Henry David et al.
¶ European Perspectives series, edited by Eugene C. Black.
** Contemporary Essays series, edited by Leonard W Levy.
* The Stratum Series, edited by John Hale.

History: Renaissance & Reformation

JACOB BURCKHARDT: The Civilization of the Renaissance in Italy. *Introduction by Benjamin Nelson and Charles Trinkaus. Illus.* Vol. I TB/40; Vol. II TB/41

JOEL HURSTFIELD: The Elizabethan Nation TB/1312

ALFRED VON MARTIN: Sociology of the Renaissance. ° *Introduction by W. K. Ferguson* TB/1099

J. H. PARRY: The Establishment of the European Hegemony: 1415-1715: *Trade and Exploration in the Age of the Renaissance* TB/1045

History: Modern European

MAX BELOFF: The Age of Absolutism, 1660-1815 TB/1062

ALAN BULLOCK: Hitler, A Study in Tyranny. ° *Revised Edition. Illus.* TB/1123

JOHANN GOTTLIEB FICHTE: Addresses to the German Nation. *Ed. with Intro. by George A. Kelly* ¶ TB/1366

H. STUART HUGHES: The Obstructed Path: *French Social Thought in the Years of Desperation* TB/1451

JOHAN HUIZINGA: Dutch Cviilization in the 17th Century and Other Essays TB/1453

JOHN MCMANNERS: European History, 1789-1914: *Men, Machines and Freedom* TB/1419

FRANZ NEUMANN: Behemoth: *The Structure and Practice of National Socialism, 1933-1944* TB/1289

A. J. P. TAYLOR: From Napoleon to Lenin: *Historical Essays* ° TB/1268

H. R. TREVOR-ROPER: Historical Essays TB/1269

Philosophy

HENRI BERGSON: Time and Free Will: *An Essay on the Immediate Data of Consciousness* ° TB/1021

G. W. F. HEGEL: Phenomenology of Mind. ° || *Introduction by George Lichtheim* TB/1303

H. J. PATON: The Categorical Imperative: *A Study in Kant's Moral Philosophy* TB/1325

MICHAEL POLANYI: Personal Knowledge: *Towards a Post-Critical Philosophy* TB/1158

LUDWIG WITTGENSTEIN: The Blue and Brown Books ° TB/1211

LUDWIG WITTGENSTEIN: Notebooks, 1914-1916 TB/1441

Political Science & Government

C. E. BLACK: The Dynamics of Modernization: *A Study in Comparative History* TB/1321

DENIS W. BROGAN: Politics in America. *New Introduction by the Author* TB/1469

KARL R. POPPER: The Open Society and Its Enemies *Vol. I: The Spell of Plato* TB/1101 *Vol: II: The High Tide of Prophecy: Hegel, Marx, and the Aftermath* TB/1102

CHARLES SCHOTTLAND, Ed.: The Welfare State ** TB/1323

JOSEPH A. SCHUMPETER: Capitalism, Socialism and Democracy TB/3008

PETER WOLL, Ed.: Public Administration and Policy: *Selected Essays* TB/1284

Psychology

LUDWIG BINSWANGER: Being-in-the-World: *Selected Papers. || Trans. with Intro. by Jacob Needleman* TB/1365

MIRCEA ELIADE: Cosmos and History: *The Myth of the Eternal Return* § TB/2050

SIGMUND FREUD: On Creativity and the Unconscious: *Papers on the Psychology of Art, Literature, Love, Religion. § Intro. by Benjamin Nelson* TB/45

J. GLENN GRAY: The Warriors: *Reflections on Men in Battle. Introduction by Hannah Arendt* TB/1294

WILLIAM JAMES: Psychology: *The Briefer Course. Edited with an Intro. by Gordon Allport* TB/1034

Religion

TOR ANDRAE: Mohammed: *The Man and his Faith* TB/62

KARL BARTH: Church Dogmatics: *A Selection. Intro. by H. Hollwitzer. Ed. by G. W. Bromiley* TB/95

NICOLAS BERDYAEV: The Destiny of Man TB/61

MARTIN BUBER: The Prophetic Faith TB/73

MARTIN BUBER: Two Types of Faith: *Interpenetration of Judaism and Christianity* TB/75

RUDOLF BULTMANN: History and Eschatalogy: *The Presence of Eternity* TB/91

EDWARD CONZE: Buddhism: *Its Essence and Development. Foreword by Arthur Waley* TB/58

H. G. CREEL: Confucius and the Chinese Way TB/63

FRANKLIN EDGERTON, Trans. & Ed.: The Bhagavad Gita TB/115

M. S. ENSLIN: Christian Beginnings TB/5

M. S. ENSLIN: The Literature of the Christian Movement TB/6

HENRI FRANKFORT: Ancient Egyptian Religion: *An Interpretation* TB/77

IMMANUEL KANT: Religion Within the Limits of Reason Alone. *Introduction by Theodore M. Greene and John Silber* TB/67

GABRIEL MARCEL: Homo Viator: *Introduction to a Metaphysic of Hope* TB/397

H. RICHARD NIEBUHR: Christ and Culture TB/3

H. RICHARD NIEBUHR: The Kingdom of God in America TB/49

SWAMI NIKHILANANDA, Trans. & Ed.: The Upanishads TB/114

F. SCHLEIERMACHER: The Christian Faith. *Introduction by Richard R. Niebuhr.* Vol. I TB/108 Vol. II TB/109

Sociology and Anthropology

KENNETH B. CLARK: Dark Ghetto: *Dilemmas of Social Power. Foreword by Gunnar Myrdal* TB/1317

KENNETH CLARK & JEANNETTE HOPKINS: A Relevant War Against Poverty: *A Study of Community Action Programs and Observable Social Change* TB/1480

GARY T. MARX: Protest and Prejudice: *A Study of Belief in the Black Community* TB/1435

ROBERT K. MERTON, LEONARD BROOM, LEONARD S. COTTRELL, JR., Editors: Sociology Today: *Problems and Prospects* || Vol. I TB/1173; Vol. II TB/1174

GILBERT OSOFSKY: Harlem: The Making of a Ghetto: *Negro New York, 1890-1930* TB/1381

PHILIP RIEFF: The Triumph of the Therapeutic: *Uses of Faith After Freud* TB/1360

GEORGE ROSEN: Madness in Society: *Chapters in the Historical Sociology of Mental Illness.* || *Preface by Benjamin Nelson* TB/1337